INTRODUCTION
to
FINANCIAL MANAGEMENT

INTRODUCTION
to
FINANCIAL MANAGEMENT

CHARLES P. JONES
North Carolina State University

IRWIN
Homewood, IL 60430
Boston, MA 02116

© RICHARD D. IRWIN, INC., 1992

Cover photograph © Bill Binzen/The Stock Market

Sponsoring editor: Michael W. Junior
Developmental editor: Thomas G. Sharpe
Project editor: Jean Lou Hess
Production manager: Irene H. Sotiroff
Interior designer: Tara L. Bazata
Cover designer: Ivy Snider
Compositor: Weimer Typesetting Co., Inc.
Typeface: 10/12 Bembo
Printer: Von Hoffmann Press, Inc.

Library of Congress Cataloging-in-Publication Data

Jones, Charles Parker, 1943-
    Introduction to financial management / Charles P. Jones.
       p.   cm.
    Includes index.
    ISBN 0-256-07311-2
    1. Corporations—Finance.   I. Title.
HG4026.J66   1992
658.15—dc20   91–2640

Printed in the United States of America
1 2 3 4 5 6 7 8 9 0 VH 8 7 6 5 4 3 2 1

To Helen
to the memory of Charles H. and Earl
and to Kay and Kathryn

ABOUT THE AUTHOR

Charles P. Jones is the Edwin Gill Professor of Finance in the Department of Business Management at North Carolina State University. He received his B.A., M.B.A., and Ph.D. all from the University of North Carolina at Chapel Hill. Professor Jones has written four textbooks and numerous articles on investments, financial institutions, and corporate finance. He also is an active consultant, most notably with candidates working toward the Chartered Financial Analysts designation.

P R E F A C E

The study of financial management is essential for anyone interested in the operation of a business firm. The subject itself is interesting and timely, with financial management issues and practices discussed daily in the popular press as firms continuously make financial decisions that have a major impact on both themselves and the economy. Financial management will continue to be as exciting a subject in the 1990s as it was in the 1980s, but with some different directions and with a renewed interest in maximizing the welfare of the owners of the firms, the stockholders.

PHILOSOPHY

This text will provide the reader with an understanding of the principles of financial management that are applicable to the current and future business environments. The emphasis of this text is on providing a clear, concise presentation of the analytical tools and background information needed to understand modern financial management. This streamlined approach is executed by covering, in the first 16 chapters, the essentials of financial management. Although the remaining chapters add significant details and cover significant topics, a thorough study of the first 16 chapters will provide the reader with a solid understanding of financial management and prepare him or her, from a financial management standpoint, for either entry into the business world or additional study in this area.

The approach described above distinguishes this text from others that either include some of the less essential material with the primary topics, or, perhaps worse, defer discussion of very important issues such as short-term financial management until the end of the text. (Short-term financial management is covered in Part III of this text.) Financial management in the 1990s will be different than it was in the 1980s and as such warrants an approach that is fresh while still manageable in a one-semester course. An additional aspect of the streamlined approach taken with this text is the introduction of material when and where it is actually applicable to the discussion and will be used. For example, the subject of taxes is not discussed in one of the early chapters because it is not used there, and it is largely forgotten by the time it is actually needed.

PERSPECTIVE

The text is written from a valuation perspective, which focuses on how the market value of a firm, and the wealth of its owners, is determined. As such, the emphasis is on markets, investors, and stockholder, and the time-honored valuation principles that underlie the entire subject matter of finance. Not only is this orientation consistent with the objective of financial management decision making as it applies to business firms, it is consistent with the general framework of finance and economics.

AUDIENCE

This text is intended for the first course in business or corporate finance and, as such, has been written without the assumption of prior knowledge of finance. A basic accounting background is expected, but these principles are reviewed early in the book. As a result, both majoring and nonmajoring students will find the text understandable.

ORGANIZATION

The text is divided into seven parts centered around the financial-management process.

Part I introduces the objectives of financial management, describes the scope of the field, and explains how financial management fits into the overall operations of the firm.

The aim of Part II is to provide you with all of the necessary information to understand valuation. It begins with a review of basic accounting information and an examination of cash flow, and then it turns to the time value of money and the various concepts of risk. Part II is capped off by a chapter devoted to valuation as it applies to financial management, which teaches the mechanics of stock valuation models and reviews the valuation of other securities.

Part III begins the study of financial-management decisions by examining short-term financial management. In the four chapters of Part III, the top half of the balance sheet is examined, combining investing and financing decisions. Although texts typically cover working-capital management in a later section, I have chosen to address this material earlier because of the importance of short-term financial management to the firm's success, particularly the small firm. In addition, managers beginning their careers most often find that short-term decision making occupies the majority of their time. The four chapters in this section cover working-capital management, cash and marketable securities, receivables and inventory, and short-term financing. The theme of value maximization has been carried throughout these four chapters.

The discussion of long-term investing and long-term financing is contained in Parts IV, V, and VI. Part IV investigates how a firm should make its capital budgeting decisions in regard to its goals and objectives. The three chapters in this part cover cash flow principles, capital budgeting techniques, discount rates, and risky projects. Part V concerns the planning and decisions pertaining to obtaining capital for the firm. The main topics in this section are cost of capital, leverage and capital structure, and dividend policy. Part VI is tied to the information covered in Part V in that it further explores long-term financing. The main focus is on deciding among a variety of financing vehicles, and the first chapter in Part VI provides an overall framework. The individual chapters of Part VI examine equity securities such as common and preferred stock, and debt securities such as bonds, convertibles, and warrants, as well as lease financing and term loans.

Part VII, the final part in the text, addresses those topics that are important to financial management but that are somehow special. The two main topics covered here are mergers and corporate restructuring, and international financial management.

PEDAGOGICAL FEATURES

In each chapter of this text, you will find a number of pedagogical devices that have been included to assist you in understanding the material.

1. *Learning Objectives*. Each chapter begins with an introductory paragraph followed by a numbered list of learning objectives for the chapter. These objectives provide you with perspective and help you in reading for the most significant content.
2. *Key Terms*. Key terms are boldfaced within the text at the point where they first appear and are defined. For easy reference and review, key term definitions are provided in the margin, and a list of key terms follows the chapter summary.
3. *Examples*. Within the text discussion are numerous examples that illustrate or apply concepts in real-world terms.
4. *Summaries*. At the end of each chapter, a summary outlines the significant concepts covered in the chapter.

In addition to the summary, each chapter concludes with a large series of questions and problems that test your comprehension of chapter material.

1. *Questions*. Each chapter contains questions that ask you to use the information obtained in the chapter either to explain a concept or to answer a question pertaining to a typical situation.
2. *Demonstration Problems*. In applicable chapters, self-test questions have been included, along with detailed explanations on how to solve the problems.
3. *Problems*. Finally, each chapter contains a set of problems that provide you with ample practice in working through financial calculations.

ILLUSTRATIVE FEATURES

Along with the basic pedagogy, special features appear in each chapter that assist in illustrating concepts being explained. These are as follows:

1. *Vignettes*. Each chapter in the text opens with a real-life vignette about a company; this introduces you to the concepts that will be covered in the chapter. Although the vignettes contain information that you may not be

familiar with, the example should provide a sense of context and a motivation for reading and understanding the chapter information.

2. *International Perspectives.* Whenever possible, I have attempted to include in the text discussion an example that considers how a situation would vary in an international setting or how international considerations would impact management decision making.

3. *Small Firm Considerations.* This feature discusses how a particular financial-management goal, strategy, or decision might be different for a small firm.

4. *Financial Management Insights.* Periodically throughout the text, you will find a boxed reading, derived from recent events or the popular press, that provides a living illustration of a concept being explained in the text discussion.

ACKNOWLEDGMENTS

A number of individuals have contributed to this project who deserve thanks and recognition.

I would first like to thank those who participated in our focus group meeting in Boston during the 1989 Financial Management Association meetings. They are: Ali Fatemi, Kansas State University; Richard Anderson, Stonehill College; Dan Vetter, Central Michigan University; Brian Maris, Northern Arizona University; and Henry Okleshen, Mankato State University.

Next, I would like to express my gratitude to Mike Alderson, Texas A&M University, for proofreading all of the math and problem material in the text.

Finally, and most importantly, I would like to thank those of my colleagues who reviewed various versions of the manuscript.

Thomas Bankston	Angelo State University
Thomas Berry	DePaul University
Ernest Bloch	New York University
Jay Brandi	University of Louisville
Claire Crutchley	Auburn University
Les Dlabay	Lake Forest College
John Dunkelberg	Wake Forest University
Ali Fatemi	Kansas State University
Stephen Ferris	Virginia Polytechnic Institute and State University
Steven Flint	University of Texas at Austin
Thomas Goho	Wake Forest University
Roger Hill	University of North Carolina at Wilmington
Val Hinton	Delta State University
Jarl Kallberg	New York University
Boyden Lee	New Mexico State University
Brian Maris	Northern Arizona University
William Nelson	Indiana University—Northwest
Henry Okleshen	Mankato State University
Robert Olsen	California State University at Chico

Barron Peake   Golden Gate University
Ralph Pope   California State University at Sacramento
Edward Pyatt   Hampton University
William Sartoris   Indiana University at Bloomington
Jan Squires   Southwest Missouri State University
Charlene Sullivan   Purdue University
Keith Taylor   Sonoma State University
Emery Trahan   Northeastern University
Daniel Vetter   Central Michigan University
Susan Visscher   University of Toledo
Herbert Weinraub   University of Toledo
Richard White   University of Northern Florida
Tony Wingler   University of North Carolina at Greensboro
John Zietlow   Ohio University
Terry Zivney   University of Tennessee at Chattanooga

A special acknowledgment is due O. Maurice Joy of the University of Kansas, who wrote *Introduction to Financial Management* a number of years ago. This book set the philosophical and organizational format for the current text, and contained a number of innovations that were both appreciated and retained. I have tried to preserve the best of this text while adapting it to the 1990s and making those changes that I felt would improve the overall product. Professor Joy's book was one of the few texts in a crowded field that offered a fresh approach and style, and that made a significant contribution to textbooks used in financial management. I hope that the current text will prove to be a worthy successor.

Charles P. Jones

NOTE TO STUDENTS

The study of financial management is both an exciting and rewarding experience. In the 1990s, as in the 1980s, the field of finance will undergo dynamic growth and changes in a variety of different directions. This will require that the managers of the future be fully prepared and capable to make sound management decisions in a constantly shifting environment.

Due to this dynamic quality, a study of financial management can prove to be a challenging endeavor. In order to assist you in your study of this field, a number of features have been included in this text along with the topical discussion. These features are designed to increase your understanding of the material and to focus your study and review on the most significant information being conveyed. These features and their benefits are outlined briefly below.

CHAPTER INTRODUCTIONS

Every chapter opens with a *vignette* about a real company that illustrates the key concepts being covered in that particular chapter. Within these vignettes, you will encounter terms and ideas that may be unfamiliar to you, but that's all right. You are not expected to understand immediately all of what's being said. The purpose of these vignettes is to provide you with a context for the discussion that lies ahead. We suggest you read them first and then reread them once you've completed the chapter.

Following each of the vignettes is a more formal introduction to the chapter that ends with the chapter's learning objectives. These objectives will assist you in focusing your study while reading the chapter.

CHAPTER LEARNING TOOLS

Within each chapter you will find a variety of tools intended to enhance your understanding of key concepts. Among these are:

1. *Key Terms*. All of the key terms in chapters are highlighted in **boldface** type and defined in the text when they first appear. Also, for easy referencing a *running glossary* is provided in the margin and *a list of the key terms* is provided following the chapter summary.

2. *Examples*. Interspersed with the discussion are numerous examples that support explanations. These examples may either be detailed demonstrations of mathematical calculations or they may be real-world illustrations of the concepts being discussed.

3. *Chapter Summaries*. Every chapter concludes with a bulleted summary highlighting the important points covered in the chapter.

4. *Selected References*. The final element of most chapters is a list of references that you may go to if you desire more information on a topic in financial management. Included in these lists are the most current books and articles available, as well as some of the classic works in the field.

QUESTIONS AND PROBLEMS

The ultimate goal of this text is for you, the student, to understand all important facets of financial management. To ensure that this aim is being achieved, we have included a series of question and problem sets at the end of every chapter that test your ability to apply the concepts explained in the text.

1. *Questions*. We have included review questions that check your level of comprehension by testing your ability to creatively apply the concepts covered in the chapter.

2. *Demonstration Problems*. These self-test questions enable you to check your understanding of formulas and equations introduced in the chapter before you begin working through a number of calculation problems. Accompanying these problems are detailed step-by-step solutions.

3. *Problems*. The practice problems are quantitative in nature, and provide you with plenty of practice in performing the calculations that are an integral part of financial-management techniques and decision making.

OTHER FEATURES

In addition to all of the tools built into the chapters in this text, you will also find other special features that have been included to enhance your study of financial management.

1. *Boxed Readings*. Periodically you will encounter boxed readings titled *Financial Management Insights*. These readings are taken from the popular business press. These readings, like the opening vignettes are meant to show you how financial-management decision making actually happens.

2. *International Perspectives*. In your reading, you will occasionally find a section called International Perspectives. This section is devoted to exploring aspects of financial management in an international context. The environment where firms of all sizes operate has broadened over the past few years, and this feature highlights this perspective.

3. *Small Firm Considerations*. Like the *International Perspectives,* these sections offer a different view of financial management. In this case, that view is of financial decision making in a small business environment. Both the international and small business sections demonstrate our recognition of the breadth and diversity of financial management and our desire to open up the scope of this field for our students.

CONTENTS

Brief

C O N T E N T S

Expanded

Introduction

Valuation: Components and Process

Short-Term Financial Management

Long-Term Investments

The Cost of Capital, Capital Structure, and Dividend Policy

Long-Term Financing Decisions: Needs and Sources

Special Topics

INTRODUCTION

to

FINANCIAL MANAGEMENT

Introduction

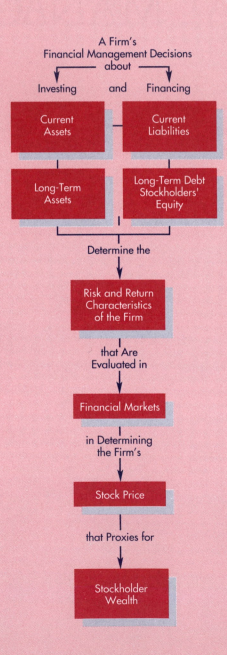

A Firm's
Financial Management Decisions
about

Investing   and   Financing

Current
Assets

Current
Liabilities

Long-Term
Assets

Long-Term Debt
Stockholders'
Equity

Determine the

Risk and Return
Characteristics
of the Firm

that Are
Evaluated in

Financial Markets

in Determining
the Firm's

Stock Price

that Proxies for

Stockholder
Wealth

Part I provides an overview of financial management. It examines the nature of the subject, considers the objectives of financial management, describes the scope of the field, and analyzes the way finance fits into the overall operations of the firm. Part I also considers the role of financial markets in the firm's decision making and in the achievement of the firm's financial objective.

Chapter 1 introduces the subject matter of financial management, showing what it is concerned with and the general range of activities normally associated with this field. In particular, Chapter 1 explains the framework for making financial decisions and illustrates the types of ongoing financial decisions that firms must make. The objective, or goal, of financial management is the central part of this discussion. It is crucial to understand at the outset of any study of financial management the principle to be used—shareholder wealth maximization—in making financial decisions. To understand this principle, it is necessary to understand the constraints that exist. It is also useful to examine some recent events in major corporations that revolved around the financial objective of the firm. Chapter 1 provides an in-depth analysis of such an episode.

Chapter 2 continues with the themes developed in Chapter 1 by examining the crucial—in fact, determining—role financial markets play in affecting financial decisions made by firms. Unless one is careful, one may fail to clearly understand the linkage between the firm's financial decisions and the achievement of its financial objective, shareholder wealth maximization. Investors trading in financial markets determine the stock price of a firm, and they use the results of the financial decisions made by the firm's managers in making their buy and sell decisions. It is thus absolutely crucial in understanding financial management to fully appreciate the pivotal role of financial markets.

Chapter 2 concludes with a detailed discussion of the valuation process. This discussion is important for two reasons: because the central theme used throughout is that of valuation, it sets the stage for the entire text. Throughout the discussion of financial management decisions, we ask, in effect, how a particular financial decision is related to the valuation of the firm. This allows us to tie each individual decision and concept to a central theme that is directly related to the objective of financial management.

The second reason for concluding Chapter 2 with a discussion of the valuation process is to prepare the reader for Part II, which discusses each of the components of valuation separately and then discusses the concept as a whole.

1

Financial Management Decision Making

Financial Management Decisions and Strategies

At the beginning of the 1990s several firms in the gold/silver mining industry offered an interesting contrast in their financial management strategies and decisions.[1] Pegasus Gold, selling at a price of $15, was pursuing a strategy of growth through acquisitions, financed by its own strong financial condition and cash flow. The firm had estimated earnings per share of common stock for one year of 70 cents. In contrast, Battle Mountain Gold Company, trading around $17 and with estimated earnings per share for the year of 60 cents, went to the debt markets in a major way to finance its ambitious acquisition program. Battle issued $100 million of international bonds, which could be converted into its common stock at some future date; lined up a bank line of credit of $150 million; and planned to sell 5 million shares of new common stock. Another firm in this industry, LAC Minerals, was trading around $13 and had estimated annual earnings per share of 55 cents. LAC was pursuing a policy of both acquisitions and additional explorations and development on its existing properties. In addition, to reduce the risk of declining metals prices, LAC engaged in a policy of hedging the price of its gold sales by contracting on a current basis at specified prices to deliver gold in the future.

---

[1]This information is based on *The Value Line Investment Survey*, Edition 8, *Ratings and Reports*, February 9, 1990, pp. 1220–28.

This book is concerned with the financial management decisions that business firms make. Such decisions are well illustrated by the various policies and strategies being pursued by these mining firms, all of which are in the same industry and had common stock prices that were relatively close at the time of this analysis. These companies were taking different approaches in building their asset base, in paying for these assets, and in dealing with the risks faced by firms in this industry. For example, Pegasus was financing its acquisitions of other companies through funds it generated itself, while Battle Mountain was borrowing funds to accomplish the same objective. Why? Why did Battle choose to sell international bonds rather than sell bonds in the United States, and why did it choose to sell more common stock? Why not borrow more from its banks? Why did LAC choose to sell gold for future delivery at current prices, given that this policy could reduce its potential earnings?

In order to understand financial management actions such as these, we must learn to identify financial management issues, to analyze financial problems, to judge financial decisions on the basis of the proper financial criteria, and to understand the expected implications of the financial decisions that are made by firms.

Primary *chapter learning objectives* are:

1. To explore the nature and scope of financial management.
2. To identify the fundamental financial management decisions that must be made.
3. To develop an appropriate framework for making financial decisions that can be used throughout the text.

WHAT IS FINANCIAL MANAGEMENT?

The wide array of topics under the title *finance* may be categorized under three broad subheadings: financial management, investments, and money and capital markets. Our primary purpose is to study financial management, but these three areas are so interrelated that we will necessarily become involved in the other two.

Business firms are primary production agents in the economy, organized for the purpose of making a profit for their owners. Because of economies of scale and specialization of labor, these firms can perform many economic production tasks much more efficiently than individuals. Given the vast array of industrial and consumer products that can be more efficiently produced by firms, their important role is apparent.

Economics is the study of how scarce resources should be allocated among competing uses, and *financial management* is, in effect, applied economics because it is concerned with the allocation of a company's scarce financial resources among competing choices.[2] Financial management has evolved over time since its emergence as a separate field of study in the early part of the 20th century. A brief sketch of its evolution follows:

- Pre–1930s—Descriptive emphasis on legal aspects of financial issues and the various types of bonds and stocks issued by a firm.

---

[2]Financial management is also referred to as *managerial finance, business financial management, business finance,* and *corporate finance.*

- 1930s—Descriptive emphasis on bankruptcy and reorganization (given what happened as a result of the Great Depression).
- 1940s—Descriptive emphasis on understanding the firm from an outsider's viewpoint (e.g., from the viewpoint of creditors).
- 1950s—Emerging emphasis on asset management (what the firm owns) rather than liability management (what the firm owes). Viewpoint began to shift to that of the financial manager of the firm. Important theoretical contributions emerged.
- 1960s—More theoretical developments in the major decision areas. Increased emphasis on the maximization of the stockholders' wealth because the stockholders are the owners of the firm.
- 1970s—Refinement of major financial theories and significant emphasis on research to support theories. Investment analysis (how to value and manage stocks and bonds as investments) increasingly integrated into financial management.
- 1980s—The use of computers in both financial decision making and financial research became widespread. Financial deregulation became important. New financing methods became popular.
- 1990s—?

As we will see, a firm's principal financial activities are investing in assets and raising funds to pay for those assets. A financial manager's job is to determine how those crucial activities may best be carried out. In doing this, the financial manager typically will use data prepared and presented by accountants. Whereas the accountant's focus is on the careful and correct preparation of financial data, the financial manager's focus is on using that data as an input in making decisions. Furthermore, accountants typically rely on an accounting method that recognizes revenues at time of sale and expenses when incurred, while financial managers emphasize the actual inflows and outflows of cash.[3]

Firms need to acquire funds to engage in production activities. Much of the money comes from cash flows the firms themselves generate, but other funds are provided by investors. To obtain funds from investors, firms issue financial securities such as stocks, bonds, and the like. The study of the analysis and management of financial securities is termed *investments*. This important area of finance is mainly concerned with the evaluation of securities from the perspective of investors and the construction and management of portfolios of securities.

Marketplaces where firms issue and investors buy and sell financial securities are very well developed in the United States and range from specialized businesses that assist corporations in selling their securities to large secondary markets, such as the New York Stock Exchange, where investors can buy and sell the stocks and other securities of major corporations. These markets, typically, involve a variety of financial intermediaries and middlemen such as investment bankers and stockbrokers. The study of these markets and financial intermediaries is the study of *money and capital markets*.

Relationships among these three areas are shown in Figure 1–1.[4] To make investments in physical, productive assets, firms must have capital. Much of this

---

[3]This is the accrual accounting method.
[4]We will expand this concept in Chapter 2.

■ *Figure 1–1*
Relationships among
Investments, Money and
Capital Markets, and
Financial Management

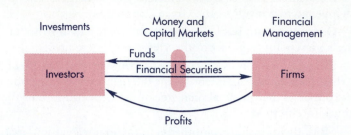

capital is obtained by issuing financial securities to investors through money and capital markets. Many firms also distribute part of their profits to investors. While this book is directed toward financial management, we will also be involved with both investments issues and money and capital markets issues. The ties between investors and financial management are particularly important because the goals of the firm are related to investor wants and desires. That is, since investors own the financial securities that control the physical assets constituting the firm, investment theory and the theory of financial management are merely two sides of the same coin.

FUNDAMENTAL FINANCIAL MANAGEMENT DECISIONS

What are the functions of a modern financial manager? Because today's approach to the study of financial management emphasizes a firm's decision-making process, we need to consider the types of financial management decisions that firms face. Although there are many specific kinds of such decisions, we can classify them into two major categories:

1. Investment decisions: What assets should the firm own?
2. Financing decisions: How should these assets be financed?

Investment Decisions

Although investment decisions cover a wide range of issues, the central focus is on the selection of assets to be held by the firm as it attempts to generate future cash flows. Firms continually search for new investment opportunities, trading current expenditures of cash for future receipts of cash. Assets can include both *financial assets* (a financial claim on an issuer) and *real assets* (tangible property, such as plant and equipment). In this text we are primarily concerned with the decision to acquire real assets.

At one extreme, the firm must decide in what industry (or industries) it wishes to operate. Once that is established, the firm will make investment decisions about individual assets. The size of these potential investments can vary considerably. For example, Atlantic Richfield, a major oil company, may consider drilling a new $100,000 developmental oil well, evaluate a multi-million-dollar project such as its Philadelphia refinery (which it sold), or consider acquiring another corporation (such as its decision to acquire Anaconda Company). Although the scale of these investments is quite different, each proposal requires an investment decision. Such decisions should be made on the basis of sound financial management practices, which we will analyze throughout the text.

Financing Decisions

Once the firm has committed itself to new investments, it must decide how to finance them. A large portion of these financing needs will be predictable as the firm replaces old assets with new ones and implements previously established investment plans. At other times, financing needs may be unexpectedly large—for example, the firm may decide to acquire another company. Consider the magnitude of Kohlberg Kravis Roberts & Company's buyout of RJR Nabisco, valued at roughly $25 billion. At the other extreme, the firm may be perilously close to failing and desperately need financing to stay alive. For example, Long Island Lighting was forced to agree to a cutback of $390 million in rate increases over a 10-year period and immediately announced plans to raise $375 million by selling debt issues.

Financing decisions comprise both the regular, ongoing need for funds as well as episodic needs. As we will see in Parts IV and V, such decisions address not only how best to finance new assets but also the best overall mix of financing for the firm. If the firm borrows, it generates *debt* claims; if it obtains funds from owners, it generates *equity* claims.

Setting policies regarding dividends also represents a kind of financing decision.[5] By paying out part of its earnings directly to its stockholders, a firm has less internal funds available for investment decisions, and it may have to raise funds externally in the capital markets (as discussed in Chapter 2). Dividend policy—deciding how much of the stockholders' earnings to pay out to them—is one of the most important issues in financial management.

A Schematic Representation

The notion that financial management falls into one of two categories, investment decisions or financing decisions, leads to an intuitive schematic representation of these two categories that utilizes the balance sheet. A very simplified balance sheet is shown in Figure 1–2.[6] Basically, it is a reporting of assets owned on one side and claims on assets on the other. Since assets are investments and claims are financing, the balance sheet is a reporting of the cumulative effects of investment and financing decisions. Notice that Figure 1–2 divides both investments and financing into short-term (usually less than one year) and long-term (one year and longer) periods. Thus the figure has four quadrants.

■ *Example*

Although our classification of major financial decisions into two principal types may seem an oversimplification, it really is all we need to study financial management. To demonstrate this, consider Utili Corp United, an electric and natural gas company operating in seven states (and in one Canadian province) through five divisions. Its stock is traded on the New York Stock Exchange. In one recent

---

[5]The dividend decision is sometimes identified as the third type of financial decision that firms must make.
[6]We will study the balance sheet in detail in Chapter 3.

■ *Figure 1–2*
A Schematic Balance
Sheet

	Investments (Assets)	Financing (Claims)
Short-Term	Current Assets	Current Liabilities
Long-Term	Fixed Assets	Long-Term Debt Stockholders' Equity

year Utili Corp reported earnings of $1.74 per share and paid cash dividends of 99 cents per share. The market price of the stock at that time was $15 per share, and its accounting value, or book value, was $15.06 per share.

In its annual report to shareholders, Utili Corp described the year as one of "continued growth and positioning within the utility business." During the year, Utili Corp made several important financial decisions, all of which can be classified into one of our two principal types of financial decisions:

1. Capital expenditures of $57 million, primarily to improve and replace operating facilities at all of its utilities. Furthermore, it planned a capital budget of $102 million for the subsequent year *(a basic investment decision involving the acquisition of real assets—Chapters 11 and 12).*

2. Purchased West Virginia Power for approximately $21 million *(an investment decision involving an acquisition—Chapter 21).*

3. Decided to become an international company by purchasing a Canadian subsidiary for about $62 million *(an investment decision involving an acquisition with international dimensions—Chapters 21 and 22).*

4. Executed a $60 million short-term bank loan *(a short-term financing decision—Chapter 10).*

5. Sold 2,000,000 new shares of common stock in a public offering at $17.375 per share, including the sale of a number of shares in Europe for the first time—thereby raising long-term financing internationally *(a long-term financing decision involving the sale of securities—Chapters 17, 18, and 19).*

6. Reduced its cost of capital by calling for redemption of all 320,000 outstanding shares of the $4.125 series of preference stock at $29.56, which carried a cost of 15.7 percent, and replacing it with short-term debt carrying an interest cost of 7.5 percent *(a long-term financing decision involving the replacement of one type of security with another (lower-cost) security—Chapters 14 and 15).*

7. Split the common stock 3-for-2 *(a type of financing decision involving the equity financing of the firm—Chapter 16).*

8. Paid two stock dividends during the year *(a type of financing decision involving the equity financing of the firm—Chapter 16).*

9. Increased the cash dividend by some 5 percent *(a form of financing decision involving how much to pay the stockholders directly versus how much earnings to retain—Chapters 14 and 16).* ■

A FRAMEWORK FOR MAKING FINANCIAL DECISIONS

We have now identified the two fundamental kinds of financial management decisions: investment and financing. The obvious question to ask now is, How should a firm actually make these decisions? In order to answer this question, we must develop an overall framework to give these decisions perspective. This framework is constructed to help the firm make good financial management decisions and has three parts:

1. A goal.
2. The identification of important variables.
3. Some decision rules.

The Goal of the Firm

It is impossible to work toward some goal until we define it. The identification of a goal will strongly influence how the firm addresses investment and financing decisions. We will consider first why a well-known objective often discussed in economics is not the proper goal of the firm from a finance standpoint, and then we will consider what is a proper goal.

Profit Maximization Is Not the Goal

In our introductory economics courses we learn that the goal of the firm is **profit maximization.** Is this the goal we should follow in making financial decisions? The answer to this question is no. There are three basic objections to profit maximization as a goal.

profit maximization
the maximization of a firm's net income

1. *The Concept of Profit Maximization Is Vague*   Does it refer to the dollar amount of profits or the rate of profitability? If the latter, how do we measure profitability? Does it refer to short-run profits or long-run profits? A firm may maximize profits in the short run to the detriment of long-run profitability—has it, therefore, maximized profits or not? This is one of the major criticisms of profit maximization as a goal, and the issue of focusing on the short run at the expense of the long run is receiving increasing attention in the United States.

2. *It Ignores the Time Dimension of Financial Decisions*   Profit maximization does not properly consider the timing of the cash flows to be received by the firm. The timing issue is of critical importance in financial decisions, and we will examine this issue in detail in Chapter 4.

3. *Profit Maximization Provides No Concrete Method of Dealing with the Risk Dimension of Financial Decisions*   As we shall see, return and risk are opposite sides of the same coin, and both must be dealt with simultaneously when making financial decisions; that is, intelligent financial decisions cannot be made without simultaneously talking about both of these determinants of value. A firm that maximizes profits may generate an excessive amount of risk to the detriment of the stockholder. That is, while profits are going up, the stock price is coming down because the increase in risk outweighs the increase in profits.

Stockholder Wealth Maximization Is the Goal

Financial theory envisions the firm as owing primary loyalty to its owners. Several other major groups of individuals are associated with the firm: employees (both labor and management), creditors, customers, and suppliers. While the firm is interested in the welfare of these other groups, it is a well-accepted doctrine that the financial goal of the firm should be owner-oriented—specifically, common stockholder–oriented because the common stock of the firm denotes the ownership interest.

Most businesses begin as small owner-entrepreneur operations where firm and owner interest coincide. As production in the United States has grown to the scale that is popularly called *big business,* large corporations have become the dominant form of business organization in terms of economic importance, but the concept of legal ownership is still clear. The common stockholder is the residual (last in line) claimant on the firm's income in normal times and on the firm's assets if the firm should fail. It is as if the original owner-entrepreneur had sold the business to several thousand investors, who are now the owners. In fact, this is exactly what has happened.

So, who owns the firm? The stockholders! Stockholders elect the board of directors, who, in turn, hire the firm's management. Thus, whose goal should be implied when we talk about the financial goal of the firm? The stockholders' goal! To equate the stockholders' and the firm's goals is to assert that the firm should act to enhance the stockholders' welfare. This means that we must next identify what is most important to stockholders and suitably phrase the stockholder-firm goal. Traditional economic theory maintains that the goal of any individual is to maximize personal utility (happiness or satisfaction). Individuals receive utility, or pleasure, from doing things that please them. Unfortunately, it is very difficult to quantify or operationalize utility maximization because an individual's utility is a function of many things.

Financial theory asserts that the closest single substitute for a stockholder's utility is *wealth*. If the firm acts to maximize stockholders' wealth, then individual stockholders can use this wealth to maximize their own utility. Therefore, a goal of **stockholder wealth maximization** is consistent with the principle of maximizing stockholder utility. We would like the goal to be both quantifiable and operational. To quantify means to express numerically. We want a goal that can be expressed in numbers so that we can measure how well the firm is achieving this goal. Also, we want a goal that is operational—that is, the goal should be explicitly tied to variables over which the firm has some control through its operations. Fortunately, the goal of stockholder wealth maximization can be made both quantifiable and operational by directly relating it to the price of the firm's common stock.

A stockholder's current wealth in the firm is the product of the number of shares owned times the current stock price per share.

$$\text{Stockholder's current wealth in firm} = \text{Number of shares owned} \times \text{Current stock price per share}$$

Given the number of shares any stockholder owns, the higher the stock price, the greater the stockholder's wealth. The firm may occasionally alter the number of shares held, through stock splits and stock dividends, but for any given number of shares, *stock price maximization is consistent with stockholder wealth maximization.*

stockholder wealth maximization
the appropriate goal for the financial decisions of the firm

In summary, we started with the standard economic premise of utility maximization and proceeded to substitute wealth for utility. Our position is simply that the firm should maximize stockholder wealth. This, in turn, implies that the firm should maximize its current stock price, given the number of shares outstanding. Our chain of events is thus:

In order to
Maximize utility → Maximize stockholders' wealth → By Maximizing current stock price

Constraints on Stockholder Wealth Maximization

Realistically, in order for the financial manager of a firm to maximize stockholder wealth by maximizing the current stock price, he or she must properly take into account constraints that exist in the business environment. These constraints include, but are not limited to, the following.

The Agency Problem   The modern large corporation is distinguished by the separation of ownership from management. Typically, managers own only a very small percentage of the common stock outstanding. Because of this separation of ownership and management, managers' interests may diverge from stockholders' interests. Managers may seek to achieve a level of performance that helps to protect their own positions, such as choosing a less risky project instead of a more risky project when the latter is clearly more profitable. They might prefer to earn a lesser, but still satisfactory return instead of risking an adverse outcome for which they could be criticized. In this situation, managers can be said to be satisficers rather than maximizers.

This situation is referred to as the **agency problem,** which occurs when stockholders (principals) employ other individuals (agents) to act on their behalf.[7] The costs shareholders incur to ensure that managers act in their best interests are called *monitoring costs* and are a subset of costs generally classified as *agency costs,* defined as the set of costs that arise when an agent is designated to act in the best interests of a principal and whose own interest may conflict with that of the principal.

Agency costs cover a wide range of issues, such as the use of debt, underinvestment, and so forth. Obviously, owners cannot closely monitor every management decision because of the costs and complexity involved. However, they usually choose to incur reasonable monitoring costs (such as reporting requirements and outside audits) in trying to ensure that managers are acting in their best interests. Stockholders want managers to maximize the total return they earn from their equity investment, while managers may be content to earn a satisfactory rate of return. The important point to remember is that if management interests differ substantially from the interests of the stockholders, the correct goal for the firm—stockholder wealth maximization—may not be realized.

Several factors keep managers working in the best interests of the stockholders. First, manager's compensation is often tied directly to the firm's performance, so the better the performance, the better the total compensation package for

agency problem
the potential conflict between principals (shareholders) and agents (managers)

---

[7]For a good discussion of the agency problem, see Amir Barnea, Robert Haugen, and Lemma Senbet, *Agency Problems and Financial Contracting* (Englewood Cliffs, N.J.: Prentice Hall, 1985).

managers. Lee Iacocca's performance at Chrysler is a good example—he was given stock options that would become very valuable if he turned Chrysler around, which he did. Therefore, managers have a strong personal incentive to act in the best interests of the stockholders. Alternatively, the threat of firing exists, perhaps more so now than in the past. Institutional investors, who often hold large blocks of stock, are more willing than ever to bring pressure on managers to perform. They may actively support attempts to force bad management out and replace it with a good management team. An important new precedent in the relations between institutional investors and corporate management is illustrated in the Texaco situation, discussed later in this chapter.

hostile takeover
a takeover where the management of the target company opposes the takeover

Hostile Takeovers   The threat of a **hostile takeover** (a situation where the management of the target company opposes the takeover) can represent a constraining force on managers' actions. If the firm is perceived to be performing poorly as a result of poor management, it could be viewed as undervalued by another firm, group of investors, or corporate raider. The assumption is that if the poor performer could be taken over and the top management fired, the rejuvenated firm would be more highly valued in the marketplace, thereby enhancing stockholder wealth. Even if the hostile takeover attempt fails, stockholder wealth may be improved, at least temporarily, as management is forced to respond. The Texaco case, discussed in the "Financial Management Insights" feature in this chapter, is a good example of this possibility.

Social Responsibility   Social responsibility deserves special consideration in our discussion of the goal of the firm. On the one hand, it can be viewed as a constraint on management's actions in maximizing the stockholders' wealth. Alternatively, it can be seen as a positive commitment that management either does make or should make, at least within reasonable limits.

Clearly, management has an ethical responsibility to sell products free of known defects and potentially harmful substances. Not only is this an ethical responsibility but also good business practice. A good example would be a pharmaceutical manufacturer's recall of a product that has been tampered with. Removing the product in an effort to prevent an accidental poisoning is the responsible thing to do. In addition, the potential loss of confidence in the company and its product as well as the possible lawsuits following a decision not to recall the suspected product make it a good business practice.

It is also obvious that a firm serves a variety of constituent groups in addition to its stockholders, including employees, suppliers, customers, and communities. What is the responsibility of the firm to these groups? There is no easy and definitive answer to this question, and in the final analysis, each firm must try to balance these claims with its primary objective of maximizing the stockholders' wealth. An individual firm cannot be everything to everybody, and alone it cannot solve the world's ills. Furthermore, if certain socially responsible actions would place the firm at a clear competitive disadvantage, who is to say that the firm should follow such a course? After all, a less-profitable firm presumably will have fewer resources to perform socially responsible acts. At the margin, a firm that goes bankrupt will be unable to help anyone except perhaps lawyers specializing in bankruptcies.

It is clear that one of the major issues of the 1990s will be the environment and the role of firms in helping to improve the environment. Each company will have to decide for itself how much of a role to take in contributing to a clean environment. Happily, it is possible to maximize the stockholders' wealth at the same time that environmental concerns are met, thereby providing the best of both worlds. Firms with the foresight to incorporate socially responsible issues into their own production processes may benefit greatly.

■ *Example*

Louisiana–Pacific, a forest products company, has developed a new wallboard that is stronger than conventional sheetrock, more fire- and moisture-resistant, and made from gypsum and wood fiber reclaimed from recycled paper.[8] Thus, no trees have to be cut to produce this product. The company had already developed a cheaper plywood substitute made from plentiful, fast-growing trees that are much less environmentally sensitive. Louisiana–Pacific has recently been one of the most profitable wood products companies, with a net profit margin that easily exceeds its two major competitors. ■

In the final analysis, a balance must be struck when the interests of the shareholders conflict with the interests of other constituent groups or with society at large. Management should strive for the stated objective of maximizing shareholder wealth, while recognizing and operating within reasonable and prudent constraints that include socially responsible actions.

Identification of Important Variables

The second part of our financial management decision framework involves identifying the most important variables in making financial decisions, and understanding the relationship among these variables. In fact, understanding these variables is essential to understanding finance itself.

Given the goal of stockholder wealth maximization, achieved by maximizing the stock price, we will find that two variables, risk and expected return, are important in making financial decisions because they are the variables used in the valuation of stocks. That is, investors in the marketplace estimate the expected return and risk for a stock in making their buy or sell decisions, which, in turn, determine the stock price. The concept of expected return refers to the cash flows the stockholder expects to receive from a firm, and the concept of risk refers to the quality or uncertainty of these cash flows.

The relationship between expected return and risk is very important and underlies all of finance. For rational investors, stockholders, and managers, there is always an upward-sloping trade-off between *expected* return and risk. This means that people involved in making financial decisions, being **risk averse,** *expect* the return to increase as the risk increases. Any attempt to earn returns in excess of those available from a safe asset, such as riskless Treasury bills, carries with it a certain amount of risk. The larger the expected return, the larger the risk. This upward-sloping trade-off between expected return and risk, shown in Figure 1–3, is the basis for all financial decisions.

Figure 1–3 illustrates the classic trade-off between expected return (vertical axis) and risk (horizontal axis) that underlies all of finance. As a general proposition,

risk averse
must expect to be adequately compensated in order to assume risk

---

[8] See Marc Beauchamp, "Friend of the Spotted Owl," *Forbes,* April 30, 1990, pp. 144, 148.

．．．

FINANCIAL MANAGEMENT INSIGHTS

Maximizing Stockholder Wealth—The Case of Texaco

In mid-1988, Carl Icahn, then probably the world's leading corporate raider, was involved in an intense proxy fight with the management of Texaco Inc. for control of the company. Icahn, owning about 15 percent of the stock, planned a $14 billion raid against Texaco. Texaco's management, having recently survived a $10.8 billion damage judgment in the Pennzoil case by agreeing to pay Pennzoil $3 billion in cash, fought to remain in control.

Icahn made a $60-per-share cash proposal to Texaco stockholders and promised to distribute $300 million, or $1.50 per share, to shareholders if they approved his proposal and he failed to secure the necessary financing. Texaco management refused to let stockholders vote on the Icahn proposal at a time when the stock was trading for around $50 per share. Icahn's solution was to replace management, which he could do only by placing five members on the Board of Directors at the annual stockholders' meeting in June 1988.

Both sides waged a very aggressive campaign to solicit stockholder votes. Although Texaco has more than 200,000 shareholders, institutional investors, such as pension funds and investment concerns, held about 40 percent of the common stock outstanding and were the key to the fight. Icahn counted heavily on the vote of one particular investment concern, which held about 5 percent of Texaco. But this group decided to support management, as did several other funds that often supported the dissident. However, several large pension funds supported Icahn, including the College Retirement Equities Fund-Teachers Insurance & Annuity Association, the Wisconsin Investment Board, and the California State Teachers Retirement System.[9]

On the day Icahn conceded defeat, Texaco was the most actively traded stock on the New York Stock Exchange, closing down below $47. Shareholders, of course, never received the chance to vote on the $60-per-share proposal. However, Texaco's management promised to work to improve the stockholders' position by selling off some assets and paying out one or more special dividends. Subsequently, Texaco noted that "the restructuring of Texaco flows from an overall plan designed to create *shareholder value* by reducing debt, increasing efficiency, and generating earnings growth."[10] Texaco also agreed to pay out a special dividend to stockholders of $8 per share as part of a package designed to prevent future takeover attempts by Mr. Icahn.

One result of the bitter proxy battle was that during the critical vote concerning Icahn, Texaco promised the pension funds holding large blocks of Texaco stock a voice on nominations to its board of directors. In January 1989, Texaco named as a director one of 14 people the pension funds had asked Texaco to consider. *The Wall Street Journal* referred to this as "an unprecedented step in corporate governance" by pension funds.[11] On the other hand, Texaco's stock price, having risen to over $55, fell at the time of this announcement presumably because Texaco's action reduced likely institutional support for a renewed proxy fight by Icahn, who had recently indicated that he might try again to unseat management.

---

[9]See Caleb Solomon and Carolyn Phillips, "Icahn Concedes Defeat in Fight for Texaco Seats," *The Wall Street Journal*, June 21, 1988, p. 22, *The Value Line Investment Survey*, various issues, and the *Annual Reports* of Texaco.
[10]Texaco Inc., "To the Stockholders," Third Quarter Report 1988, p. 1.
[11]See Allanna Sullivan and James A. White, "Texaco, Pressured by Pension Funds, Accepts Brademas as Nominee for Board," *The Wall Street Journal*, January 24, 1989, p. A2.

---

expected return cannot be expected to increase unless risk also increases. By assuming zero risk, one can earn the risk-free rate of return, designated *RF* in Figure 1–3, such as the rate of return available from Treasury securities. To have the opportunity to earn a larger return, more risk must be taken.

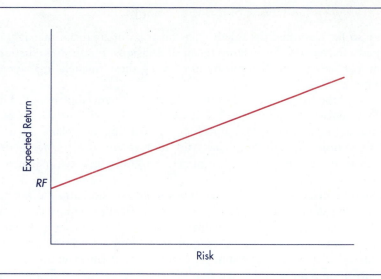

From the firm's standpoint, maximizing share price involves a trade-off between return and risk. A financial decision may increase expected return, but it may also increase risk to the point that it offsets the favorable impact from return, thus resulting in a lowering of share price. Conversely, a financial decision could lower risk proportionally more than expected return, leading to an increase in share price. The objective of financial decision making is to optimize the trade-off between expected return and risk, thereby maximizing the stock price.

Decision Rules

The last part of the decision framework is the development of rules that permit the important variables to be systematically analyzed so that the firm's decisions will be consistent with its goal. Decision rules are simply ways of using the relevant variables to make choices that are consistent with the goal. In the context of financial management, the firm should employ investment and financing decision rules that will help maximize stockholder wealth. For example, if the firm has several investment opportunities, all of which are profitable, but limited funds for investment, how should it decide which set of opportunities to accept? As another example, if several sources of funds are available for financing purposes, how should the firm decide which to use? In subsequent chapters we will formulate the rules and procedures for making sound financial decisions.

Good decision making necessarily entails careful attention to both planning and control. To make good financial management decisions, the firm should continually plan for future investment and financing and also have a control or monitoring system to evaluate how well these decisions are turning out. In normal times these functions ensure an orderly progression and integration of financial management decisions; in times of stress they prepare the firm for, and protect it against, adverse financial contingencies and emergencies that may arise.

An Overview of the Financial Management Process

We have so far identified the major decision areas of financial management and developed a framework for making financial decisions. Figure 1–4 illustrates what financial management is all about by integrating these financial management activities into a process.

We start at the top of Figure 1–4 with the firm's financial planning. The firm's planning activities are quite varied. For example, the principals must choose an organizational form and make long-range and contingency plans. Planning also includes providing specific guidelines for investment and financing decisions. The result of the planning is a set of policies to guide financial management decision making.

The two primary decisions are the investment decision and the financing decision. Making these financial decisions cause the firm to acquire certain risk and return characteristics, which are evaluated by investors as they buy and sell securities. Investors' actions, in turn, determine stock price and stockholder wealth. Notice also that there are feedback provisions. The firm monitors itself as part of its control function, and this activity includes supervision of financial management decisions and observation of the firm's risk and return characteristics and stock price.

 International Perspective

The international aspects of financial management continue to gain importance, and in today's world it is necessary to take an international perspective. There are many justifications for this position. For example, no one needs to be reminded of the profound influence of Japan on the economic system of the United States. In addition, Canada and the United States have concluded a treaty that will remove all tariffs on trade within a few years. Additionally, in 1992 many trade restrictions among the countries of the European Common Market will be lowered.

The implications of the move to a worldwide economy are already evident on the financing side. Recall from the opening vignette that Battle issued $100 million in convertible Eurobonds, thereby tapping the international financial markets for funds. As much as 25 percent of potential New York Stock Exchange volume is now being channeled through the International Stock Exchange, a computerized

■ *Figure 1–4*
Financial Management
Process

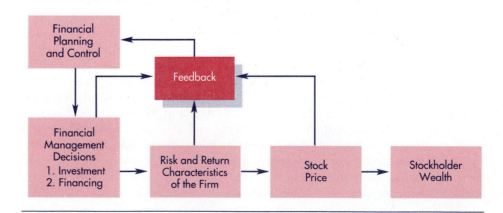

market in London. Japan's stock exchange has risen some 25,000 percent since 1949, and the value of Japanese companies now exceeds that of U.S. companies.

The bottom line of what has happened in the world is that firms must think globally rather than merely domestically. They must consider investment and financing opportunities abroad. They must respond to foreign competition in the United States. They must recognize and protect themselves against currency risk, the risk of an adverse change in currencies between two countries that lowers the value received by the firm.

We must recognize the international aspects of financial management at the outset. We will consider them in detail in Chapter 22. In addition, we will explore some of these issues as they arise in relation to other topics throughout the book.

ORGANIZATION OF THE TEXT

The balance sheet framework described earlier can also be used as an organizational guide to this book. For example, the discussion in each of the first six chapters of the text can be classified as either an investment decision or a financing decision, and therefore could be placed in one of the four quadrants of our balance sheet.

The first six chapters are preparatory ones, designed to provide an overview of the valuation approach to financial management. They will also present some necessary analytical tools for working on financial management problems. Given that this text takes a valuation approach as its central theme and basis for discussion, it is essential to establish the valuation framework at the outset.

The first two chapters explain the goal of the firm and how financial management decisions are evaluated within a market framework, thereby providing the framework for a valuation model. Chapters 3 to 6 discuss the basic elements of a valuation model by analyzing the nature (Chapter 3) and timing (Chapter 4) of cash flows, which are the basis of the firm's expected returns, and the risk involved (Chapter 5). Chapter 6 brings this material together by discussing the valuation of financial assets, primarily the stocks and bonds issued by corporations.

In Chapter 7, we begin systematically working our way through the four major quadrants of the balance sheet.

We start by analyzing current assets and current liabilities (Chapters 7 to 10), a topic often called working-capital management. Thus, the short-term investment and financing decisions are studied as a package, completing the top half of the balance sheet.

We next study long-term investments (Chapters 11 to 13), which for most firms are the backbone of profit generation. This is the process known as *capital budgeting;* its principles are well known and widely taught.

The last quadrant of the balance sheet involves the permanent financing of the firm. We will study both analytical issues and background information on the sources of long-term financing. This analysis will take us from Chapters 14 through 20. Chapters 14 to 16 analyze the key financial decisions in this area: cost of capital, capital structure, and dividend policy. Chapters 17 to 20 are more descriptive than analytical.

Finally, Chapters 21 and 22 address some topics that can be covered separately for expositional purposes. Mergers and acquisitions is a specialized topic that can be of major importance to a firm involved in such a transaction. International financial management, on the other hand, is an increasingly important topic that affects more and more firms as the world moves closer to a global economy. Although this topic is interspersed throughout our discussion of financial management issues, it also is covered separately at the end of the text in order to allow the reader to concentrate specifically on these issues.

Everything we discuss in this text revolves around the financial management process described in Figure 1–4. Because of the important role of financial markets in the firm's operations and the importance of the valuation concept to financial management decision making, we will continue our overview of financial management in Chapter 2 by considering in detail the role financial markets play in the financial management process and in the valuation process. We will learn the importance of the financial markets to the decisions made by the firm, and this will set the stage for a detailed study of the valuation concept in Part II.

SUMMARY

- Finance includes the subareas of financial management, investments, and money and capital markets.
- The two major types of financial management decisions are investment decisions (what assets the firm should own) and financing decisions (how these assets should be financed).
- Profit maximization is an inadequate goal for a firm because it is vague, it ignores the time dimension of financial decisions, and it provides no method for dealing with the risk dimension of financial decisions.
- The goal of the firm should be to maximize stockholder wealth, which is accomplished by maximizing the current stock price.
- The agency problem arises from stockholder attempts to ensure that managers act in their best interests.
- The two important variables in the financial decision process are expected return and risk.
- The financial management process involves all the firm's activities that link its financial decisions with the goal of the firm, maximization of stockholder wealth.

KEY TERMS

agency problem, p. 13

hostile takeover, p. 14

profit maximization, p 11

risk averse, p. 15

stockholder wealth maximization, p. 12

QUESTIONS

1–1. What is meant by the term *financial management*?

1–2. How is financial management related to the general area of finance?

1–3. How is financial management related to both accounting and economics?

1–4. What are the fundamental financial decisions that must be made? Where does a decision concerning how much to pay the stockholders fit into this framework?

1–5. With reference to the balance sheet, which side represents sources of funds and which side uses? Why?

1–6. Why is shareholder wealth maximization a proper goal for the firm? Is it a short-run goal or a long-run goal, and why?

1–7. Contrast shareholder wealth maximization with profit maximization.

1–8. State and explain three objections to profit maximization as the goal of the firm.

1–9. Why might management pursue goals other than shareholder wealth maximization?

1–10. How is the concept of utility maximization related to the goal of the firm?

1–11. What is meant by the term *agency costs*? Give three examples.

1–12. What effect does the threat of hostile takeovers have on the stockholders' position?

1–13. What are the important variables to consider in making financial decisions?

1–14. What is the shape of the trade-off between expected return and risk? Why is this true?

1–15. Your company is considering a major expansion of its Canadian smelting operations. During a planning meeting, two alternative investment plans are proposed. Each will allow the company to accomplish the needed expansion; however, the two plans have distinctly different financial consequences. Only one may be accepted. Indicate which plan you would prefer if the predicted impact on the firm is as shown, and justify your answer.

	Situation before Expansion	*Situation under Expansion Plan*	
		A	*B*
Sales	$100 million	$120 million	$115 million
Stock price	$20 per share	$21 per share	$22 per share
Earnings	$1.50 per share	$1.80 per share	$1.60 per share
Shares	10 million	10 million	10 million

What do you think could cause Plan B to have projected lower sales and earnings per share, but a higher stock price?

SELECTED REFERENCES

Agency problems and issues are discussed in:

Barnea, Amir; Robert A. Haugen; and Lemma W. Senbet. *Agency Problems and Financial Contracting*. Englewood Cliffs, N.J.: Prentice Hall, 1985.

A discussion of financial objectives for small firms can be found in:

Cooley, Philip L., and Charles E. Edwards. "Financial Objectives of Small Firms." *American Journal of Small Business,* July–September 1983, pp. 27–31.

A good review of the history of corporate finance can be found in:

Jensen, Michael C., and Clifford W. Smith, Jr. "The Theory of Corporate Finance: An Historical Overview." *The Modern Theory of Corporate Finance.* New York: McGraw-Hill, 1983.

Shareholder values and goals are discussed in:

Rappaport, Alfred. "Selecting Strategies That Create Shareholder Value." *Harvard Business Review,* May–June 1981, pp. 139–49.

Seitz, Neil. "Shareholder Goals, Firm Goals and Firm Financing Decisions." *Financial Management,* Autumn 1982, pp. 20–26.

2

The Role of Financial Markets

Maximizing Stockholder Wealth

Southdown, Inc., a cement company with oil and gas interests, made a cash offer to purchase all outstanding shares of Moore McCormack, another cement producer having oil and gas interests. The offer was $31 per share at a time when Moore McCormack's stock was trading for about $24 per share. The stock price jumped to approximately $34 per share on the day the offer was announced.

Southdown also filed a lawsuit to prevent McCormack from blocking the offer. McCormack previously had passed antitakeover measures; furthermore, the lawsuit alleged, McCormack officials previously had met to discuss a merger but failed to do anything because McCormack's chairman insisted he would have to be chairman and chief executive officer of the merged company.

One month later, McCormack escalated its fight against Southdown's subsequent offer of $35 per share by proposing to:

- Quickly pay a special cash dividend of approximately $25 per share.
- Burden itself with heavy debt; McCormack's new level of long-term debt would be almost five times its previous level.

At this point, McCormack's stock rose further and traded around $40 per share.

McCormack indicated it planned to follow through on these measures even if Southdown abandoned its takeover attempt (unless an acceptable bid was made). According to McCormack's chairman, "Our objective is to achieve the highest value for our shareholders."[1]

---

[1] See Jeffrey A. Tannenbaum, "Moore McCormack Debt-Dividend Plan Proposed as Firm Fights Southdown Bid," *The Wall Street Journal*, March 24, 1988, p. 8, and *Annual Report*, both companies.

We determined in the last chapter that the goal of financial management is to maximize the shareholders' wealth. The logical question to be answered now is, How is the value of the firm determined within our financial environment? Although Chapter 1 outlined the financial management process from an overall viewpoint, we did not examine sufficiently the process by which a firm's market value is determined, in particular, the important role of financial markets in that process. As we can see from the Southdown–Moore McCormack situation, *the determination of share price is a combination of firm actions and investor reactions in the financial markets.* In other words, it is insufficient in studying financial management to consider only the financial decisions made by firms—we must also consider the financial market reactions to those decisions.

Primary *chapter learning objectives* are:

1. To complete our overall discussion of financial management by integrating financial markets into the firm's decision-making process.
2. To obtain an overview of financial markets.
3. To develop the basis of the valuation process used in finance, thereby setting the stage for Part II.

FIRM VALUE AND ORGANIZATIONAL FORM

Given that our objective in this chapter is to analyze how the value of the firm is determined in the marketplace, we need to note at the outset the differences in organizational forms for a business. Specifically, business firms are organized as one of three major organizational forms: proprietorship, partnership, and corporation.

Of the more than 16 million firms in the United States, 80 percent are sole **proprietorships.** However, this number accounts only for about 8 percent of total business sales, although proprietorships do generate a very substantial portion of all new jobs created in our economy. **Partnerships** basically are proprietorships with more than one owner. **Corporations,** on the other hand, are few in number but large in terms of sales, profits, and employment. More than 80 percent of all sales in the United States are generated by corporations. The advantages and disadvantages of each of these three forms of business organization are discussed in Appendix 2–A, and are summarized in Table 2–1.

The principles of financial management that we will study are applicable to any form of business activity; therefore, both current and prospective owners and/or managers of small businesses and corporations can benefit from studying the principles and procedures of financial management. However, because of the importance of corporations in the economy, and because their stock price serves as a proxy for stockholder wealth, we will concentrate on companies with publicly traded stocks throughout this text. Thus, when we talk about a firm's market value, we are referring specifically to the value of the corporation's common stock as determined in financial markets.

ACHIEVING THE FINANCIAL MANAGEMENT GOAL

Investors who purchase the common stock of a company are interested in seeing the price of those shares rise to the highest possible level. Managers, who represent the owners, should have the same objective in mind when they make financial

proprietorship
a business owned by an individual

partnerships
proprietorships with more than one owner

corporation
a legal entity distinct from its owners and managers

	Main Advantages	*Main Disadvantages*
Proprietorships	Easily established	Unlimited liability
	Tight control	Limited access to outside financing
	Not doubly taxed	
Partnerships	Easily established	Unlimited liability
	Tight control	Limited access to outside financing
	Not doubly taxed	Interpersonal problems among
	Specialization of labor possible	partners possible
Corporations	Limited liability	Owners can lose control
	Unlimited life	Double taxation
	Good access to outside financing	More difficult to establish
S Corporation	Limited liability	Avoids double taxation

■ *Table 2–1*
The Primary
Advantages and
Disadvantages
of Business
Organization Forms

decisions. As noted in Chapter 1, the interests of managers and owners should be close most of the time. Clearly, when management's compensation is tied directly to enhancing the shareholders' interest, we can expect managers to maximize the value of the firm to existing shareholders. In some cases, the top management may resign if there is disagreement over how best to accomplish the goal of the firm. For example, in early 1989 the president and chief operating officer of SmithKline Beckman Corporation, a leading drug manufacturer, resigned over internal disagreements on how the company should respond to its financial problems. Finally, if management does not act in their interest, we should expect shareholders to eventually elect a new board of directors for the company, which in turn has the power to change managements.

In fairness to managers, we should note that they face a difficult task because they must work with imperfect information in an uncertain world. Measuring some returns and costs after they have occurred is difficult enough, but managers must *estimate* these variables in order to make decisions. Students of finance must remember a simple, but subtle, point about financial decision making. Finance is a forward-looking, not backward-looking, concept. Just as someone can tell you which stock you should have invested in last year, managers can see after the fact what they should have done. This does not, however, directly aid them in deciding what they should do now.

The firm's managers make decisions, and investors react to these decisions. The statement made by McCormack's chairman indicates that he believes that his company's objective is to maximize shareholder wealth and that the decisions being made by the management, although unusual, would accomplish that goal. Nevertheless, it remains for investors in the marketplace to interpret McCormack's actions as well as other information and determine the price they are willing to pay for the stock. In effect, McCormack made its investment and financing decisions—in this case, financing decisions—and investors reacted to these decisions as they bought and sold the stock.

One hopes that the managers of a firm will make optimal investment and financing decisions as they strive to meet the identified goal—maximizing stockholders' wealth. In the end, however, investors in the marketplace will determine the share price based on the two important variables identified in Chapter 1, the return expected to be generated by the firm and the estimated risk. The importance of this seemingly obvious point cannot be overemphasized.

▪ *Example*

For a dramatic example of the immediate impact of the financial markets on stockholder wealth, consider the case of General Motors in early 1989. After years of losing market share and facing a multitude of well-known problems competing in the auto industry, General Motors announced record earnings for 1988 of almost $5 billion. This news followed a widely publicized announcement a week earlier of a 2-for-1 stock split, the first for the company since 1955, and a sharp boost in the dividends paid on the stock. How did the stock market react? On the day of the earnings announcement, the stock price dropped more than $3 per share. In other words, despite GM's record earnings for the year, the first stock split in over 30 years, and a significant increase in the dividends to be paid to the stockholders, investors reacting to the news caused a significant drop in the price of the stock. ▪

Figure 2–1 illustrates the linkage between the financial decisions made by the firm and the actions of investors reacting to these decisions and other relevant information in estimating expected return and risk, the two factors of valuation that ultimately determine stock prices. *Figure 2–1 emphasizes the crucial role financial markets play in determining stock price.*

We learned in Chapter 1 that our primary concern is with the financial management decisions that business firms make. We now know that the firm does not directly determine the stock price—it is established by investors in the marketplace. Therefore, to fully understand the financial management process, we

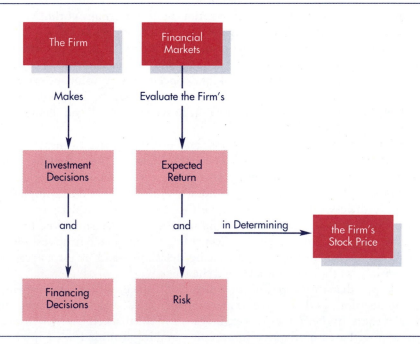

▪ *Figure 2–1*
The Role of Financial Markets in Determining Share Price

need to consider the firm in the context of the financial markets within which decisions made by the firm, as well as other relevant information, are evaluated by investors.[2]

AN OVERVIEW OF THE FINANCIAL SYSTEM

The purpose of the financial system is to channel funds from savers (lenders) to users (borrowers). Savers are sometimes referred to as *savings surplus units,* while users are referred to as *savings deficit units*. On an aggregate level, individuals (households) are the major surplus unit, while businesses are the major deficit unit. Of course, the federal government has also been a major deficit unit for years.

Individuals indirectly provide capital to corporations through **financial intermediaries.** These institutions provide funds directly to firms (e.g., loans) and purchase new securities both publicly and privately. In addition, they continually buy and sell securities already issued. The three types of financial intermediaries are (1) deposit institutions (banks, savings and loan associations, and credit unions); (2) investment companies (primarily, mutual funds); and (3) contractual institutions (such as insurance companies and pension funds).

financial intermediaries
financial firms that operate between savers and users of funds

Deposit institutions lend money to businesses, provide mortgage financing, and purchase securities. Investment companies collect capital from individuals by selling shares in themselves and then investing this capital in marketable securities. These companies invest in a variety of securities, but the majority of investment companies invest in stocks and bonds of corporations. Mutual funds are particularly important economic agents in the secondary securities markets, described below. Insurance companies collect insurance premiums and reinvest a portion of them. Insurance companies have been one of the more active groups in buying corporate securities—mainly debt—via private placements.

The financial markets, consisting of the institutions and mechanisms through which savings can be allocated, greatly enhance the flow of funds from surplus units to deficit units. As noted, financial intermediaries include commercial banks, savings and loans, credit unions, and other organizations that receive funds from savers and allocate them to borrowers. The mechanisms include financial markets such as the money market and the capital market, which make possible the borrowing and raising of funds.

Figure 2–2 illustrates the flow of funds through the financial system. The borrowers of funds seek to augment their current income in order to acquire assets, and they need financing to do so. Lenders have excess funds on which they wish to earn a return. The role of financial markets is to facilitate this transfer of funds in the quickest, most efficient manner. Figure 2–2 illustrates two ways by which funds can flow from savers to borrowers: directly and indirectly.

Funds can flow directly between lenders and borrowers, as illustrated at the bottom of Figure 2–2, with *primary securities* flowing back from borrowers to lenders as evidence of the funds lent. For example, Apple Computer could sell bonds or shares of stock directly to investors. However, this direct-flow process is typically not efficient because of the difficulty in matching the needs of

---

[2]In a broader sense, the external environment within which the value of a firm is determined consists of several aspects, including, but not limited to, the financial markets, general economic conditions, government policies and regulations, the tax structure, and competition, both domestic and foreign. In later chapters, we will consider several other aspects of the external environment such as the tax structure faced by business firms.

■ *Figure 2–2*   Flow of Funds from Lenders to Borrowers

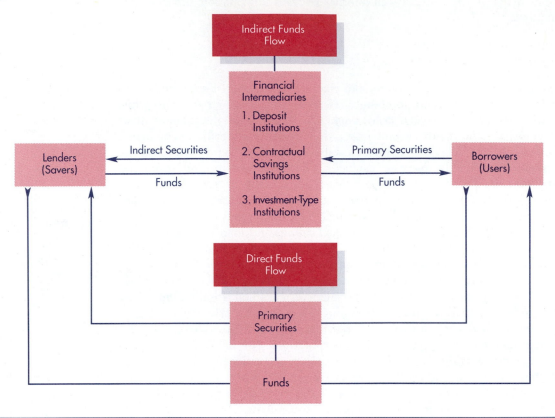

borrowers and lenders. Instead, what is needed are multiple institutions that stand between the ultimate lender and the ultimate borrower, providing services to both sides.

This process of accommodating both deficit and surplus sectors simultaneously is called *intermediation.* As Figure 2–2 illustrates, funds flow from lenders to the institutions, which, in turn, efficiently channel the funds to the borrower. For example, Chemical Bank of New York, having received the deposits of thousands of individuals, can efficiently lend large sums of money to a business firm. Chemical is in a position to service the needs and interests of both depositors and borrowers, to offer each what it desires in a cost-effective manner. The profit margin of the financial intermediary consists of the difference, or spread, between what it pays for funds it collects from savers and the rate at which it is able to invest or lend the funds.

Notice in Figure 2–2 that primary securities flow from the borrower to the institutions, and indirect assets from the institutions to the lenders. That is, the intermediaries effectively transform primary securities into *indirect securities,* which include the spectrum of financial assets institutions offer savers to attract their surplus funds, such as checking and time deposits, certificates of deposit, insurance policies, annuities, and so on.

FINANCIAL MARKETS

Financial markets play a key role in finance, and financial managers must understand that role to be effective. **Financial markets** are places where financial assets are traded. A **financial asset** represents a monetary claim on some issuer. We may broadly define financial assets as (1) money and (2) claims on issuers.

In the most common situation, a claim is issued by one party (A) in return for money provided by the other party (B) in the transaction. In finance jargon, A is acquiring money and B is investing money. As we will see, there are many kinds of financial claims. If A borrows money from bank B, the financial claim may be a note payable. If A sells common stock to investor B, the financial claim will be shares of common stock. The essential point about a financial claim is that it is a piece of paper (or electronic entry) evidencing a claim against an issuer, for whom it is a financial liability. For the holder, of course, it is a financial asset.

financial markets
markets where financial assets are traded
financial asset
a financial claim on an issuer

The Purpose of Financial Markets

Financial markets serve three basic purposes:

1. Facilitating the acquisition and investment of money.
2. Encouraging capital formation.
3. Establishing market prices.

1. Facilitating the Acquisition and Investment of Money   A firm with inadequate cash to accomplish all the business plans it has undertaken or to pay its current obligations needs to acquire money to meet the cash shortage. Financial markets facilitate this acquisition. The markets bring together the cash-needy firm and investors who are prepared to exchange money today for financial claims issued by the firm. For example, in a recent transaction American Savings & Loan Association of Florida sold $1 billion worth of mortgage-backed notes to raise funds. The more effective the market is in facilitating capital acquisition by borrowers, the less costly this acquisition will be.

Financial markets also provide investment opportunities for those who have surplus cash. The capital supply side of the market is populated by savers—individual investors and organizations, including business firms. Financial markets enable firms to invest surplus funds, thus creating financial assets. As in the acquisition-of-money side, firms prefer to operate in markets that are well functioning and inexpensive to the participants.

This discussion points out a simple fact: the financial markets are organized to satisfy both the capital needs of creditworthy firms and the preferences of investors who provide the capital. Transactions to accomplish these purposes occur every day in the financial markets. No example better illustrates the functioning of our financial markets than the financing of the acquisition of RJR Nabisco by Kohlberg Kravis Roberts & Company, outlined in the "Financial Management Insights" section of this chapter.

Figure 2–3 illustrates how the financial markets moved almost $19 billion in one day for one transaction. Although admittedly an unusually large transaction, the financing of the RJR Nabisco acquisition vividly illustrates how our financial markets facilitate the acquisition and investment of money.

■ *Figure 2–3*
How the Financial
Markets Financed the
RJR Deal

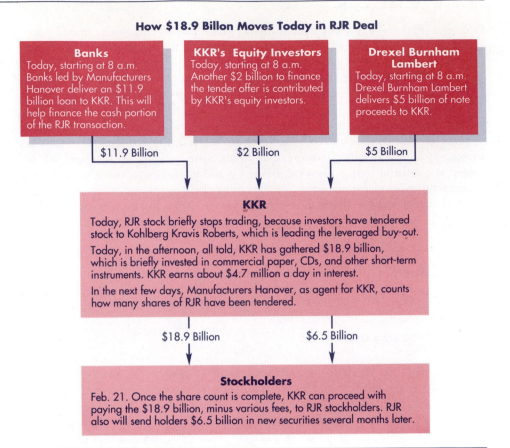

How $18.9 Billon Moves Today in RJR Deal

Banks
Today, starting at 8 a.m. Banks led by Manufacturers Hanover deliver an $11.9 billion loan to KKR. This will help finance the cash portion of the RJR transaction.

KKR's Equity Investors
Today, starting at 8 a.m. Another $2 billion to finance the tender offer is contributed by KKR's equity investors.

Drexel Burnham Lambert
Today, starting at 8 a.m. Drexel Burnham Lambert delivers $5 billion of note proceeds to KKR.

$11.9 Billion $2 Billion $5 Billion

KKR
Today, RJR stock briefly stops trading, because investors have tendered stock to Kohlberg Kravis Roberts, which is leading the leveraged buy-out.

Today, in the afternoon, all told, KKR has gathered $18.9 billion, which is briefly invested in commercial paper, CDs, and other short-term instruments. KKR earns about $4.7 million a day in interest.

In the next few days, Manufacturers Hanover, as agent for KKR, counts how many shares of RJR have been tendered.

$18.9 Billion $6.5 Billion

Stockholders
Feb. 21. Once the share count is complete, KKR can proceed with paying the $18.9 billion, minus various fees, to RJR stockholders. RJR also will send holders $6.5 billion in new securities several months later.

Source: Adapted from George Anders, "RJR Finale Will Send Money Coursing," *The Wall Street Journal*, February 9, 1989, p. C1. Reprinted by permission of *The Wall Street Journal*, © 1989 Dow Jones & Company, Inc. All Rights Reserved Worldwide.

〽Small Firm Considerations

Ease of access to capital markets is a good example of the commonsense nature of the finance field. Financial markets are organized to provide capital to all worthy candidates. Some firms, which prefer not to incorporate but to exist as proprietorships and partnerships, by their very nature have limited access to equity markets. Except to dispose of the business, a proprietorship cannot bring in other equity owners without changing into a partnership. Partnerships themselves have inherent difficulty in acquiring new outside equity capital because of an ownership illiquidity problem. Similarly, proprietorships and partnerships will not have access to the large end of the public long-term debt markets, like the public bond market, that operate for major corporations. Unincorporated businesses will rely on banks and other deposit institutions for most of their long-term debt needs.

Corporations also vary in their access to the financial markets. For several reasons, larger corporations generally will have access to more segments of these markets than smaller corporations. Smaller corporations often can tap local or regional debt and equity markets more cheaply than they can the larger national and international markets because there may be more interest within the smaller

• • •

FINANCIAL MANAGEMENT INSIGHTS

Financing a Major Acquisition—RJR Nabisco

In 1988 the management of RJR Nabisco proposed a buy-out of the company, thereby putting the company into play for other interested parties. In the highest-stakes takeover battle in U.S. corporate history, RJR's management team—and its well-known Wall Street partners, Shearson Lehman Hutton Inc. and Salomon Inc.—lost a dramatic battle despite making the highest bid for the company. RJR's board of directors awarded the company to Kohlberg Kravis Roberts & Company (KKR) for a price slightly in excess of $25 billion, or $109 per share. The board of directors apparently believed that KKR offered a better deal to all parties concerned, including employees and shareholders.

The financing deal itself was complex, consisting of some $81 a share in cash and the remaining $28 in preferred stock and convertible bonds. Regardless, the amount of cash needed to be raised and moved in the financial system for one transaction was staggering. Kohlberg Kravis Roberts & Company planned to collect $18.9 billion in cash from bankers, equity investors, and the sale of notes by Drexel Burnham Lambert, pool the bulk of it together, and complete the cash portion of the largest commercial financial transaction in history on one day, February 9, 1989.[3] Obviously, our economy must have well-functioning capital markets to be able to accommodate transactions of this magnitude.

[3]See George Anders, "RJR Finale Will Send Money Coursing," *The Wall Street Journal*, February 9, 1989, p. C1.

corporation's home region in servicing the firm's financing needs. There are, of course, exceptions. If a new concept captures the market's attention, financing from national sources can more easily be acquired. High-tech industries in the 1980s demonstrated that point. As firms get larger, they can tap the larger national and international equity and debt markets. These larger firms are also able to more easily issue some exotic forms of financial claims like convertible securities.

2. *Encouraging Capital Formation* By offering savers good investment opportunities through low-cost, convenient, and well-functioning capital markets, the financial markets are serving yet another function: encouraging capital formation. By encouraging capital formation, financial markets thus enhance the long-run economic well-being of the entire country. Without sufficient capital formation, economic growth will suffer, employment will be adversely affected, and the economic prosperity we all hope for will be frustrated. Well-functioning financial markets, where borrowers and savers can arrange mutually satisfactory financial contracts, benefit not only borrowers and savers but society as well because of the economic stimulation provided by the productive use of new capital.

3. *Establishing Market Prices and Rates of Return* This last function—establishing market prices and rates of return—is not always fully appreciated, but it is very important. Through the interaction of knowledgeable, wealth-motivated borrowers and savers transacting in well-functioning markets, prices of financial assets are established. Simultaneously, market rates of return are also established. When we say that financial markets establish returns, we really mean that the interaction of borrowers (demanding funds) and savers (supplying funds) determines returns in the marketplace.

Since there is a vast array of financial markets, there is also a vast array of market returns. As we will see later in the chapter, returns differ across financial assets because their perceived risk differs. On average, common stocks have earned much more over long periods than either government or corporate bonds. Also, corporate bonds earned a somewhat higher rate of return than government bonds.

Establishing market prices is beneficial for several reasons. At the most elementary level, price establishment affords a value verification of natural interest to parties not involved in the immediate transaction. If you bought 100 shares of Syntex stock last year for $40 per share, you would find the information that Syntex stock traded today for $65 per share of interest. Investors use such information in deciding whether to keep the shares, sell them, or possibly buy more. Having access to reliable, current prices is thus useful for investors interested in knowing their assets' market values.

Establishment of market values also provides a scorecard on managerial performance. If a company is performing well, the market value of the company's shares should do well also, other things being equal. Although other information regarding firm performance is available, the most important performance test from a finance standpoint is the market value test. Stock price behavior, as established in competitive financial markets, is the single best guide of aggregate investor opinion of the expected performance of the firm. And, as we know, the financial goal of the firm is the maximization of shareholders' wealth, which equals share price times number of shares.

✓ Small Firm Considerations

Knowledge of market-established values is also of benefit for use in situations where market values are not known. Suppose, for example, your family owns a small chain of restaurants and wants to sell them. Obviously, the family wants to receive a fair price for the assets. But if these restaurants are privately owned, then no shares are traded in the financial markets. As we shall see, the accounting value of the firm generally is not the same as the market value of the firm. Not having direct information about the value of these assets via market-established prices makes your problem of setting a price for them much more difficult. If, however, other small chains with reasonably similar characteristics have shares trading in the financial marketplace, you may be able to extrapolate from their values to an estimate of yours.

Having well-established financial markets for some assets thus helps financial market participants in estimating the value of other assets that are not traded and, therefore, do not have observable values as established in the marketplace. Comparative pricing can be of great value to analysts, managers, and investors. This technique is often relied upon by owners of small businesses when it becomes necessary to value the business for such reasons as estate purposes, divorce settlements, and lawsuits. Owners often hire consultants to make these types of calculations. In contested cases, where each side hires expert witnesses to testify about the value of the business, opinions can vary widely.

Interest Rates

As noted, financial markets facilitate the acquisition and investment of money and establish market prices and rates of return. A central part of financial market activities is the determination of market interest rates.

Capital is allocated on the basis of supply and demand. The price of debt capital is the interest rate. **Interest rates are determined in financial markets by the inter- actions of savers and borrowers. Interest is paid by the borrower and earned by the saver.**

The nominal (stated) interest rate on debt securities is composed of a risk-free rate of return plus a risk premium. The nominal risk-free rate of return is com- posed of a **real rate of interest** and compensation for expected inflation. The risk premium captures the effects of maturity, the risk of default, and any other risk factors. Stated as an equation,

$$NIR = RR + EI + RP \qquad (2\text{--}1)$$

where

$$
\begin{aligned}
NIR &= \text{nominal interest rate observed on debt securities} \\
RR &= \text{real rate of interest} \\
EI &= \text{expected rate of inflation} \\
RP &= \text{risk premium}
\end{aligned}
$$

RR is the opportunity cost of forgoing consumption. It is often referred to as the *real rate of interest* because it is unaffected by either price changes or risk factors. The real rate of interest is the equilibrium rate that equates the supply of loanable funds with the demand for loanable funds. This rate is not static over time but changes with economic conditions and people's preferences for current consump- tion rather than future consumption.

The expected rate of inflation, *EI,* must be added to the real rate of interest to obtain a nominal risk-free interest rate. Inflation, defined as a change in purchasing power as reflected by changes in the price level, lowers the real return on invest- ments. Investors, aware of this potential erosion, demand an inflation premium equal to the rate of inflation expected over the life of the security. Note that this is an expected rate for the future and cannot be known with complete certainty. The best that investors can do is to incorporate into interest rates the average rate of inflation expected over the life of the security.

Based on the above:

$$RF = RR + EI \qquad (2\text{--}2)$$

where *RF* is the nominal (stated) interest rate on riskless short-term U.S. gov- ernment securities. *RF* is the observed market-determined interest rate on short- term Treasury securities, and it is the vertical intercept of figures like 1–3.

The real rate of interest often is assumed to be in the range of 1 to 2 percent, although it can change. In general, if the nominal rate on short-term Treasury securities rises, it is because the rate of inflation expected by investors also rises. Likewise, if this nominal rate declines, it is generally because investors expect the rate of inflation to decline.

Nominal interest rates on risky debt securities must contain an additional term, a risk premium, to compensate investors for the assumed risks involved in various types of debt securities. The greater the assumed risks, the greater the risk pre- mium and, therefore, the greater the nominal interest rate. For example, an AAA- rated corporate bond, representing the highest rating, has a smaller risk of default than does a BBB-rated bond. Therefore, the risk premium on this bond is smaller, and the nominal interest rate for this bond would be smaller, other things equal. In a similar manner, a long-term debt security may be more risky than a short-term debt security, requiring a risk premium to compensate for the time element. This applies to Treasury securities as well as to corporate and municipal securities. This so-called maturity premium involves the term structure of interest rates, a subject considered in Chapter 7.

Interest rates are determined in financial markets based on supply and demand conditions. Investors react to their time preferences for consumption (RR), their estimates of inflation (EI), and the various risks anticipated from holding debt securities (RP). Other factors also affect the general level of interest rates, including the actions of the Federal Reserve, the general level of business activity, the budget deficit, and international considerations. For example, if the economy is undergoing a recession, interest rates typically decline. Also, in the modern global economy, interest rates in other countries bear a relationship to interest rates in the United States because money can be transmitted around the world to be invested in the highest yielding securities (net of costs).

The Structure of Financial Markets

From the business firm's perspective, financial markets provide a place to acquire funds when the firm needs some financing, and these same markets provide a place to invest money when the firm has surplus funds. The financial markets are worldwide with enormously complex interrelationships. This complexity need not bother us, however, because effectively all major parts of the financial market look alike: they are markets where financial assets are bought, sold, and traded.

Financial markets may be characterized in different ways. A distinction can be made on the basis of the maturity of the financial assets. From the firm's standpoint of issuing securities to obtain capital, there is a particularly important distinction between primary and secondary markets. We will consider each of these market classifications in turn.

Money Markets

money markets
markets where funds are borrowed and loaned for short periods

Short-term financial markets are called **money markets.** *Short-term* usually refers to situations where the financial claims involved will be outstanding less than one year.[4] Money market instruments are distinguished by short maturity, a high degree of safety, liquidity, and a competitive rate of return reflecting the relative risk of the asset and current money market conditions. In Chapter 8 we will analyze and discuss the features of money market instruments. For our current purpose of a general discussion, we can simply note here three major money market instruments:

- Treasury bills.
- Negotiable certificates of deposit.
- Commercial paper.

Each of these money market instruments is issued by a different issuer—the Treasury, thrift institutions, and corporations, respectively—and represents a

---

[4]This breakdown between short- and long-term is an arbitrary distinction based on the accounting distinction between current and long-lived assets and liabilities. It does not reflect a physical distinction between money and capital markets. This terminology has a long tradition of use and is one of those institutional facts with which you need to be familiar.

short-term IOU that will earn interest for the holder and can be sold to someone else if desired.

Capital Markets

Long-term financial markets, where financial claims with lives equal to or greater than a year are traded, are called **capital markets.** These markets make possible the long-term funds that firms need for long-term investment in plant and equipment and other physical assets that often last for many years. As with money markets the variety of instruments is large. Among the more common types of marketable securities, discussed in later chapters in detail,[5] are:

- Bonds.
- Preferred stock.
- Common stock.
- Convertible securities.

capital markets
markets where funds are borrowed and loaned for long periods

Each of these capital market instruments represents a claim on the issuer—a business or financial firm—and can be sold by the holder, if desired, for the current market price. The holder expects to earn a return by holding these securities.

Primary Markets

When the firm sells securities it does so in the **primary market,** which is also called the *new issues* market because the firm issues its new securities through this market. The primary market consists, on one side, of firms that wish to issue securities and, on the other side, of a collection of individual and institutional investors who will buy the newly issued securities. It is usually necessary to have middlemen (investment bankers and brokers) to bring the buyers and sellers together. In Chapter 18 we will examine in detail the alternative methods of issuing new securities and study the role of investment bankers in the primary markets.

primary markets
markets where new securities are purchased and sold for the first time

Secondary Markets

Once the firm has sold the securities, they may then be traded among investors. Original buyers of newly issued MCI Communications stock, for example, may decide after holding the stock for a few years that they need the money for other purposes or that the stock no longer suits their investment goals. Since the firm will only buy back securities under stipulated conditions that rarely match most individuals' selling decisions, the investor must find another investor to purchase the stock. When one investor sells a security to another, it is through the **secondary market.** The only effect on the firm is that ownership of a financial instrument the firm previously issued is changed. Stock ownership files of the firm will be changed, and future dividend checks and other stockholder mailings will be sent to the new owners.

secondary markets
markets where existing securities are traded

The secondary markets are essential to the operation of the primary markets. Without some means of bringing unacquainted sellers and buyers together there would be a very limited primary market. Each market participant would have to personally find a buyer or seller and negotiate a sale. In most instances this would

---

[5]See Chapters 18 to 20 for a full listing and discussion of capital market investments.

involve a costly and time-consuming search, and the result would be less invest-ment in corporate securities than now exists. As a result, companies would have more difficulty issuing securities in the primary market.

In effect, what the secondary markets offer is **liquidity,** or being able to realize the value of an asset in money. Secondary markets allow holders of financial assets to convert their claims into money easily and quickly (the time element aspect of liquidity) and at reasonable costs (the transaction cost aspect of liquidity). Another aspect of liquidity concerns the uncertainty of the price when selling an asset. Capital markets offer good liquidity in this respect, particularly the stock markets where securities sellers typically receive the price quoted to them at time of sale (or close to it).

liquidity
the ability to convert an asset into money

Secondary markets are characterized by their public accessibility. Anyone who possesses the necessary capital may purchase securities in secondary markets. These markets are of two general types: registered exchanges and over-the-counter (OTC) markets.

Registered *exchanges* are physical marketplaces established specifically for the trading (buying and selling) of securities. They are auction markets in that prices of securities are determined by competitive bids of buyers and sellers. The most prestigious U.S. exchange is the New York Stock Exchange (NYSE), and this is where the shares of IBM, General Electric, Exxon, General Motors, and so on, trade. The next most prestigious is the American Stock Exchange (Amex), where lesser-known firms such as Forest Labs, Echo Bay Mines, and Anglo Energy trade. Both exchanges have trading facilities for common and preferred stocks as well as other financial instruments issued by the major companies in the United States.[6]

For a company to have its securities traded on a registered exchange, it must be listed on the exchange. To be listed the firm must meet the listing requirements of the exchange. These are specified by each of the several exchanges, but generally they require that the firm keep the investing public apprised of its activities and meet certain standards of corporate size. Table 2–2 shows the listing requirements for the New York Stock Exchange.

Securities not traded on a registered exchange are, by definition, unlisted. Such securities are said to be traded *over the counter*. Unlike the exchanges, the over-the-counter market has no physical trading facility but is a far-flung collection of securities broker-dealers who participate in arranging transactions in unlisted se-curities. While the over-the-counter market does provide a secondary market for virtually all unlisted securities, only a few thousand unlisted securities have active secondary markets.

There are many thousands of companies in the over-the-counter market, but most are small and many are not actively traded. Some of these OTC firms, however, are quite large and well known, for example, Apple Computer and Intel. The NASDAQ market consists of the most actively traded OTC stocks. NASDAQ is an acronym for National Association of Securities Dealers Auto-mated Quotations and technically denotes "the worldwide electronic communi-cations network that receives, stores, and transmits price and volume data for more than 5,500 domestic and foreign securities, linking millions of individual

---

[6]There are also several regional exchanges, such as the Midwest Stock Exchange, the Pacific Coast Stock Ex-change, and the Boston Stock Exchange. These exchanges specialize in providing secondary markets for some of the more important regional companies.

While each case is decided on its own merits, the Exchange generally requires the following as a minimum:

1. Demonstrated earnings power under competitive conditions of either $2.5 million before Federal income taxes for the most recent year and $2 million pre-tax for each of the preceding two years, or an aggregate for the last three fiscal years of $6.5 million together with a minimum in the most recent fiscal year of $4.5 million. (All three years must be profitable.)

2. Net tangible assets of $18 million, but greater emphasis is placed on the aggregate market value of the common stock.

3. Market value of publicly held shares, subject to adjustment depending on market conditions, within the following limits:

Maximum	$18,000,000
Minimum	$ 9,000,000
Present (12/31/89)	$18,000,000

(The market value requirement is subject to adjustment, based on the NYSE Index of Common Stock Prices.)

4. A total of 1,100,000 common shares publicly held.

5. Either 2,000 holders of 100 shares or more, or 2,200 total stockholders together with average monthly trading volume (for the most recent six months) of 100,000 shares.

■ *Table 2–2*
Initial Listing Requirements for New York Stock Exchange Stocks

Source: Adapted from *Fact Book 1990* (New York: New York Stock Exchange Inc., March 1990), p. 28. Reprinted by permission.

and institutional investors and thousands of broker–dealers."[7] However, the term NASDAQ is used more broadly to denote the international stock market itself that includes these stocks.[8] Thus, one can discuss the NASDAQ market, NASDAQ's history, NASDAQ's strengths, and so forth.

In dollar value of shares traded, NASDAQ is the second largest stock market in the United States and the third largest in the world.

Figure 2–4 compares share volume for NASDAQ, the NYSE, and the Amex for the years 1979 and 1989. As we can see, the percentage of share volume accounted for by NASDAQ increased dramatically during that period, amounting to almost 43 percent of total volume at the end of 1989, with the NYSE's share decreasing to about 53 percent.

The figures at the bottom of Figure 2–4 indicate that by the end of 1989 there were almost 4,300 companies on NASDAQ, compared to 1,719 on the NYSE and 859 on the Amex. The total number of issues traded on NASDAQ has increased over time, although with ups and downs, while for the NYSE this figure has remained relatively constant. Amex growth is small, and the Amex is completely dwarfed by the other two markets in the volume of shares traded.

Government Regulation of the Securities Markets

After the collapse of the securities markets in 1929 it became evident that in too many instances, new securities issues had been misrepresented. Up to 1933,

[7]*Fact Book 1988—NASDAQ* (Washington, D.C.: National Association of Securities Dealers, Inc., 1988), p. 4.
[8]NASDAQ derives its name from NASD, the National Association of Securities Dealers, Inc., which is the self-regulatory organization for over-the-counter stocks.

Comparison of Share Volumes: NASDAQ, NYSE, and Amex

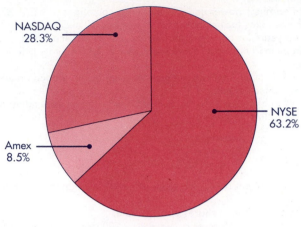

**1979
12.9 Billion Shares**

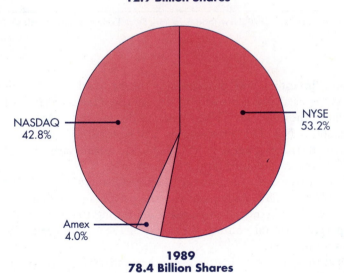

**1989
78.4 Billion Shares**

Five-Year Comparisons of NASDAQ, NYSE, and Amex

	Companies			Issue			Share Volume (in Millions)		
Year	NASDAQ	NYSE	Amex	NASDAQ	NYSE	Amex	NASDAQ	NYSE	Amex
1989	**4,293**	1,719	859	**4,963**	2,241	1,069	**33,530**	41,699	3,125
1988	**4,451**	1,681	896	**5,144**	2,234	1,101	**31,070**	40,850	2,515
1987	**4,706**	1,647	869	**5,537**	2,244	1,077	**37,890**	47,801	3,506
1986	**4,417**	1,573	796	**5,189**	2,257	957	**28,737**	35,680	2,979
1985	**4,136**	1,540	783	**4,784**	2,298	940	**20,699**	27,511	2,101

Source: *NASDAQ Fact Book 1990* (Washington, D.C.: National Association of Securities Dealers, 1990, p. 9). Reprinted by permission.

securities issues were regulated only by state agencies, but the quality of the regulation was judged to be spotty and ineffective. Today both the primary and secondary securities markets are regulated by state and federal agencies, but the more important regulation is at the federal level.

The Securities Act of 1933 regulates new securities issues. It requires issuers to provide prospective investors with full and truthful information about the company and the new securities being sold. The act is frequently referred to as the *Truth in Securities Act*. The reasoning behind the act is that a fully informed investor can make enlightened judgments about the risk and return of the new securities. The **Securities and Exchange Commission (SEC)**, established by the Securities Exchange Act of 1934 that extended disclosure requirements to secondary markets, enforces the Securities Act. While the SEC requires full and truthful information concerning new issues, it does not pass judgment on their investment quality. As long as there is full and truthful disclosure of the nature of the security and of the issuing company, the SEC is satisfied. Investors may then evaluate the new securities according to their own propensities for risk taking.

In enforcing the Securities Act, the SEC requires the firm to file a registration statement detailing all the particulars concerning the firm and the proposed new issue. The SEC then evaluates the registration statement. If the SEC does not object to the new issue, the firm is free to begin selling the securities. Final versions of the prospectus must be given each securities purchaser at or prior to sale. If the SEC does not approve the registration statement, the issuer is required to satisfy the SEC's objections, or else the issue cannot be sold.

Certain kinds of corporate securities issues are exempt from SEC regulation:

1. Nonpublic sales are exempted. Nonpublic sales are either privileged subscriptions or private placements.
2. Notes and bills whose maturity does not exceed nine months are exempted.
3. Small issues are exempted.
4. Intrastate offerings are exempted. Intrastate offerings are those in which all purchasers live in the same state where the firm is incorporated.
5. Securities of federally regulated companies are exempted from SEC regulation. Regulation of new securities of such companies is administered by the appropriate regulatory agency. For example, railroads are regulated by the Interstate Commerce Commission.

The SEC has the power to bring both civil and criminal charges against violators of the Securities Act. The SEC also regulates the secondary market for securities and has similar powers there.

Individual states regulate securities issued in their state through so-called *blue sky laws,* which are aimed at preventing fraudulent promotion and sales practices. Most states do not attempt to regulate new issues that are federally regulated, but there is considerable variability in other aspects of state regulation. Some states, for example, attempt to evaluate the investment quality of the new issue. Also, the regulatory zeal in different state agencies can vary considerably. The basic intent of the state regulatory statutes, however, is the same as the SEC's: to promote full and truthful disclosure of information to investors.

Securities and Exchange Commission (SEC) the federal regulatory agency that oversees the issuance and trading of securities

THE VALUATION PROCESS

As discussed, one of the functions of financial markets is the establishment of market prices and rates of return. The transactions of borrowers and savers in well-functioning markets establish the prices of financial assets. What remains is an overview of how stock prices—and thus the market value of the firm's stock—are actually determined. This will allow us to see how the financial management decisions made by the firm influence its value as determined in the marketplace, thereby linking these two important components.

Determination of Stock Price

The price of a share of stock is formally determined by the interaction of demand and supply, as illustrated in Figure 2–5. The initial price of the stock, P, and the number of shares, Q, are determined by the intersection of the demand and supply curves. If investors in the aggregate change their perceptions, the demand curve can shift to the left (downward) or to the right (upward). If investors increase their demand for a particular stock, its price will rise as the demand curve shifts to the right. Conversely, if they decrease their demand for the stock, its price will fall.

Figure 2–5 illustrates the case of an upward shift in the demand curve, with a resulting higher price and number of shares demanded. Such a shift could result from an increase in the expected return for the stock or a decrease in its perceived risk. A downward shift in the demand curve could result from opposite forces occurring.

■ *Figure 2–5*
Determination of Share Price

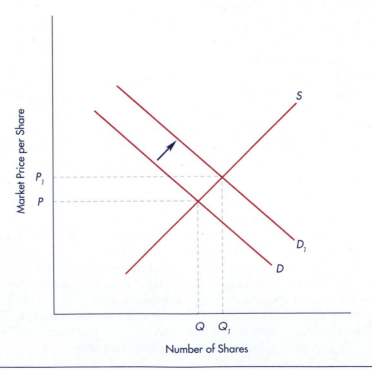

The Valuation Model Approach

Investors estimate the value of a stock by using a valuation model, which is simply a formal expression of the return/risk trade-off that underlies all financial decisions. As we shall see, valuation is always partly an art and not an exact science because the parameters of any valuation model involve estimates of the future, which is never known with certainty. However, certain basic valuation concepts are widely known and used, and it is important that we learn these concepts. This discussion is an overview of the valuation process; Chapters 3, 4, 5, and 6 will provide the detailed information and techniques needed.

Investors use a valuation model to determine the value of a stock according to its expected return and risk characteristics. Investors assess these factors:

1. The amount of the expected cash flows.
2. The timing of the expected cash flows.
3. The risks involved in realizing the cash flows.

The Expected Cash Flows

To maximize stockholders' wealth, the managers should, other things being equal, seek to maximize the value of the cash flows received by the stockholders. The owner of a common stock can expect to receive either or both of these cash flows:

1. Cash dividends paid directly by the company to its shareholders.
2. Capital gain or loss, representing the change in the value of the shares from the date of purchase to the date of sale.[9]

These expected cash flows are important because they are the basis for estimating the expected return to be earned from investing in common stocks. We have established previously that expected return is one of the two important variables determining stock price. Expected return will be discussed in Chapter 5. For our purposes here, consider the *rate of return* from an investment, calculated by converting the cash flows received by an investor into a **total return (TR),** to be defined as follows:

total return
the total percentage return on a financial asset, consisting of the income component and the capital change component

$$\text{Total return} = \frac{\text{Cash dividends}}{\text{Purchase price}} + \frac{\text{Sale price} - \text{Purchase price}}{\text{Purchase price}} \quad (2\text{--}3)$$

▪ *Example*

Assume an investor purchased UpJohn Company at year-end 1983 when the stock closed at $11.69 and sold it at year-end 1984 for the closing price of $22.22 (prices have been adjusted for stock splits). The dividend paid during the year 1984 was 44 cents. The total return (*TR*) for UpJohn for this one-year period was as follows:

$$\begin{aligned} TR &= \frac{\$.44}{\$11.69} + \frac{\$22.22 - \$11.69}{\$11.69} \\ &= .038 + .901 \\ &= .94, \text{ or } 94\% \end{aligned}$$

---

[9]A capital gain results when shares are sold for more than their purchase price; a capital loss occurs when shares are sold for less than their purchase price.

By contrast, if our investor had purchased UpJohn at the end of 1987 for $30 per share and sold at the end of 1988 for $28.75, collecting the 1988 annual dividend of 88 cents, the TR would have been:

$$TR = \frac{\$.88}{\$30} + \frac{\$28.75 - \$30}{\$30}$$
$$= .029 + (-.042)$$
$$= -.013, \text{ or } -1.3\%$$

Such is the nature of investing in common stocks! ▪

The total return is an all-inclusive concept that measures the total earned on any investment opportunity. This is because it converts the only two forms of cash flow that a security can provide, the *yield* component and the *capital change* component, into a rate of return. Some securities will offer no yield component (for example, a nondividend-paying stock), while others ultimately will have no capital change (for example, a bond purchased at par and held to maturity). Nevertheless, investors must receive their expected returns from one or more of these components. Of course, the capital change component can be negative, and if it is greater than the yield component, a loss on the investment will result.

If the managers make financial decisions that increase the stockholders' expected cash flows, holding risk constant, the share price should increase because the expected total returns will be larger. Alternatively, management can increase share price by increasing the stockholders' expected cash flows more than enough to offset any increase in risk. What is important to remember is that the expected cash flows generated by a firm are an important key to the determination of its value.

Timing of the Cash Flows

A basic concept of all finance involves the timing of the cash flows or benefits to be received in the future. *Timing* refers to when a cash flow is received or paid out and is important because of the time-value-of-money principle. This simple principle states that a dollar received today is more valuable than a dollar received sometime in the future because the dollar today can be reinvested to produce additional cash flows. Dollars received at distant times in the future may be worth very little today, and to make correct decisions, all dollars to be received in the future must be placed on a comparable basis with dollars available today (i.e., discounted back to present value). We will discuss present value concepts in Chapter 4.

Risk

Risk involves the uncertainty surrounding a future outcome. Specifically, we can think of **risk** as the probability that the actual outcome in the future will be unequal to the outcome that was expected. For example, if investors expect to earn a return of 20 percent in the coming year but actually earn only 5 percent, they have suffered the adverse effects of risk.

In Chapter 5 we will develop the idea of risk in detail. For the moment, simply acknowledging that risk differences exist across investments is sufficient. Smaller

risk
the probability that the actual outcome will differ from the expected outcome

common stocks have, on average, been riskier than the larger common stocks such as AT&T and General Electric; common stocks as a group have been much riskier investments than corporate bonds or government bonds; corporate bonds are riskier than government bonds; long-term Treasury bonds are riskier than short-term Treasury bills; and so on.

Differences in risk are associated with differences in return; that is, risk and return are closely related. More profitable investment opportunities, like investing in common stocks, will expose the investor to greater risk. Therefore, as investors or companies begin to seek more profitable investments, they are necessarily going to encounter greater risk. On the other hand, attempts to take less risky investment positions will necessarily bring lower rates of return. Why? Because just as high risk and high return go together, so do low risk and low return.

There exists well-documented evidence of the average historical relationships between risk and return for the major types of securities typically owned by investors. Ibbotson Associates compiles and publishes regular reports on the returns and risks of securities.[10] The starting point of the data is 1926, giving us 60-plus years of returns.

Figure 2–6 shows the mean returns and risk for the major categories of securities, including common stocks (separated into Standard & Poor's 500 Index of stocks as well as small stocks, defined as the smallest quintile of NYSE stocks based on market value); corporate bonds; government bonds; and Treasury bills. The rate of inflation is also shown for reference purposes.

Figure 2–6 shows both the geometric mean return—a measure of the compound return, or true average rate of return over time—as well as the more familiar arithmetic mean, both on an annual average basis. Risk is shown in the form of variability of return as measured by the standard deviation (which will be explained in Chapter 5). In this illustration, the larger the standard deviation, the larger the variability of return and, therefore, the larger the risk of the investment.

According to Figure 2–6, investors have earned a compound annual *average* rate of return of 10.3 percent on common stocks over this 60-plus years. In contrast, the corresponding figure for corporate bonds was only 5.2 percent. Notice, however, that investors assumed more than twice the risk of bonds by buying stocks (20.9 percent versus 8.5 percent). Corporate bonds returned more than government bonds, which, in turn, returned more than Treasury bills.

Finally, notice that small stocks earned more than the average stocks, with a compound average annual return on 12.2 percent, versus the 10.3 percent for all stocks. Once again, however, investors assumed far more risk (35.3 percent versus 20.9 percent) if they owned small stocks instead of average stocks.

This historical data clearly shows that over long periods of time, return and risk are positively associated. These return figures demonstrate with actual, realized results the concept of the return-risk trade-off illustrated in Chapter 1 (Figure 1–3). In other words, risk and return are opposite sides of the same coin. Investors in financial markets have had to assume larger risks in order to earn larger returns.

---

[10]This data is also available on computer disk from Ibbotson Associates, Chicago, Illinois.

■ *Figure 2–6*   Rates of Return and Risk Measures for Major Assets, 1926–1989

Series	Geometric Mean	Arithmetic Mean	Standard Deviation	
Common Stocks	10.3%	12.4%	20.9%	
Small Company Stocks	12.2	17.7	35.3	
Long-Term Corporate Bonds	5.2	5.5	8.5	
Long-Term Government Bonds	4.6	4.9	8.6	
Intermediate-Term Government Bonds	4.9	5.0	5.5	
U.S. Treasury Bills	3.6	3.7	3.4	
Inflation Rates	3.1	3.2	4.8	−90% 0% 90%

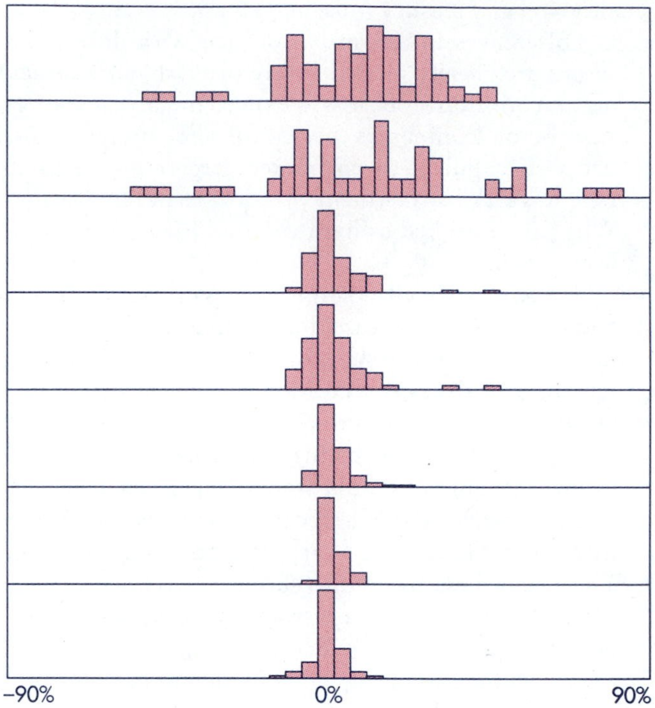

Organizing the Valuation Process

Our discussion throughout the book centers on the valuation process. The objective of financial management is to maximize the stockholders' wealth by maximizing the price of the common stock. The key to doing this is a valuation approach or model. *The valuation process is a combination of both the financial decisions made by the firm (and categorized by us as investment and financing decisions) and the actions of investors in financial markets as they estimate and react to the expected returns and risk of individual securities.* We cannot overemphasize the importance of the valuation process in general and this linkage between the firm and financial markets in particular.

Part II is devoted to the valuation process because of its importance. The following four chapters provide a detailed study of each of the points involved in the valuation process: Chapter 3 deals with the concept of cash flows; Chapter 4 deals with the time value of money; Chapter 5 concerns understanding and measuring risk because risk, as expressed in the required rate of return, is a central part of the valuation process; and Chapter 6 brings both of these parameters together in a valuation model in order to calculate the stock price.

SUMMARY

■ Business firms are organized under one of three organization forms: proprietorship, partnership, and corporation. More than 80 percent of all sales in the United States are generated by corporations.

■ Firm value, as proxied by the price of the common stock, is determined in the financial markets. The firm makes financial management decisions that affect the expected return and risk parameters of the firm, and investors react to these two parameters in determining the price of the stock.

■ Financial markets are where financial assets are traded.

■ Financial assets are claims on some issuer, and there are many types.

■ Financial markets serve three broad purposes: (1) facilitating the acquisition and investment of money, (2) encouraging capital formation, and (3) establishing market prices.

■ Short-term financial markets are called *money markets*, while long-term financial markets are called *capital markets*. A one-year maturity period is used to separate these two markets.

■ New securities are issued in the primary market and subsequently trade in the secondary markets, which consist of both organized exchanges, such as the New York Stock Exchange, and the over-the-counter market, a network of dealers who make markets in nonexchange-traded securities.

■ In practice, investors assess the expected return and risk of a firm by assessing the amount and timing of the expected cash flows and the risks involved in realizing those cash flows. These two key parameters are the basis of the valuation models used in finance.

KEY TERMS

capital markets, p. 35
corporation, p. 24
financial asset, p. 29
financial intermediaries, p. 27
financial markets, p. 29
liquidity, p. 36
money markets, p. 34
partnerships, p. 24

primary markets, p. 35
proprietorship, p. 24
risk, p. 42
secondary markets, p. 35
Securities and Exchange Commission (SEC), p. 39
total return, p. 41

QUESTIONS

2–1. Explain how the goal of financial management is achieved, integrating the actions of the firm with those of investors.

2–2. Assume that a firm's financial managers are correct in their assertion that they have made the best possible financial management decisions. Would you agree with their further assertion that the price of the stock has been maximized? Why or why not?

2–3. What are financial assets? Is a house mortgage, on which the homeowner must make monthly payments, a financial asset or a financial liability?

2–4. Would you expect the aggregate of all financial assets in the economy to equal the aggregate of all financial liabilities in the economy? Why or why not?

2–5. Distinguish between primary markets and secondary markets. If IBM were to sell a new issue of bonds, given that IBM already has bonds traded in the bond markets, would this involve the primary markets or the secondary markets?

2–6. Distinguish between money markets and capital markets, giving an example of a security in each market.

2–7. What factors determine a firm's access to the financial markets?

2–8. Why are proprietorships and partnerships limited in their access to equity markets?

2–9. Discuss the purpose of financial markets.

2–10. What benefits result from the establishment of market prices by financial markets?

2–11. Explain how a firm's value is determined, both formally and operationally.

2–12. What is meant by the term *total return*? Why is it correct to say that this is a total measure of return?

2–13. Why does the trade-off between expected return and risk slope upward?

2–14. Assume a corporation can provide for all its long-term financing needs by selling stocks and bonds in the capital markets? Is the money market of any importance to this firm?

2–15. What would you expect to happen to the demand for securities in the primary market if secondary markets did not exist?

2–16. What is the difference between an organized exchange and the over-the-counter market?

2–17. Why is the New York Stock Exchange referred to as an auction market?

2–18. Name the key variables involved in the listing requirements for New York Stock Exchange stocks.

2–19. What is NASDAQ?

2–20. As a secondary market, how important is the American Stock Exchange relative to the NYSE and to the over-the-counter market?

2–21. What is the definition of risk? Is there any risk to buying and holding a U.S. government security?

2–22. If we invest in common stocks in 1990 and the actual outcome for the year is greater than our expected outcome, did we assume any risk?

2–23. What is the time-value-of-money principle?

2–24. What are two primary disadvantages of operating a business as a proprietorship? A partnership?

2–25. What are two primary advantages of the corporate form of organization?

2–26. What corporate securities are exempt from federal securities laws?

2–27. Distinguish between the 1933 and 1934 federal securities laws.

2–28. How important is the role played by states in regulating securities?

SELECTED REFERENCES

Financial institutions are thoroughly discussed in:

Dougall, Herbert E., and Jack E. Gaumnitz. *Capital Markets and Institutions*. 6th ed. Englewood Cliffs, N.J.: Prentice Hall, 1989.

A detailed discussion of money and capital markets can be found in:

Rose, Peter S. *Money and Capital Markets*. 3rd ed. Plano, Texas: Business Publications, Inc., 1989. Chapter 2.

A good discussion of the flow of funds and related concepts is available in:

Van Horne, James C. *Financial Market Rates and Flows*. 3rd ed. Englewood Cliffs, N.J.: Prentice Hall, 1989.

APPENDIX 2–A   FORMS OF BUSINESS ORGANIZATION

One of the first decisions any new firm faces is the choice of organizational form. Although the principles of financial management we will study are applicable to any form, each presents certain advantages and disadvantages. There are three major organizational forms: proprietorship, partnership, and corporation.

Proprietorship

A proprietorship has only one owner, who receives all profits and suffers all losses, shares control with no one, and is personally liable for all debts incurred by the business. Business creditors can look to the proprietor's personal assets to satisfy business-related claims. The proprietor thus has unlimited liability. In essence, the law views the proprietor's personal and business assets as the same.

Despite this disadvantage, most U.S. businesses are proprietorships. Firms are often categorized into one of five industry types: (1) manufacturing; (2) agricultural, forestry, and fisheries; (3) transportation; (4) wholesale and retail trade; and (5) services. Except in manufacturing, there are many more proprietorships than partnerships and corporations. However, the typical proprietorship is small, and corporations are more important in the United States in terms of the amount of assets owned and income generated.

Advantages

One advantage of proprietorships is their ease and flexibility of organization. There are no articles of incorporation to secure and only minimal organization costs. Further, the proprietor is in complete control and is not required to make compromises with other owners. Another important aspect is that proprietorships, unlike corporations, pay no income tax. Instead, proprietorship profits are income to the owner and are taxed as personal income. This avoids the double taxation that corporate stockholders face— where the firm's profits are taxed before dividends are paid to stockholders, and then stockholders must pay taxes on dividends received.

Disadvantages

One of the foremost disadvantages of proprietorships is the unlimited liability feature. Another is that small businesses—typified by proprietorships—have difficulty raising external capital. They cannot sell stock or bonds. A disadvantageous tax feature is that certain fringe-benefit expenses that are tax deductible for the corporation—such as medical and other insurance expenses—are not tax deductible for the proprietorship. Also, it is frequently hard to sell a proprietorship because there is no organized marketplace for ownership transfers.

Partnerships

A partnership is basically a proprietorship with more than one owner. The partnership may be a general partnership, where all partners have unlimited liability, or it may be a limited partnership, where some partners' liability is limited to the capital contributed to the organization and they cannot participate in managing the enterprise.

Advantages

Because the primary difference between proprietorships and partnerships is the number of owners, most of the advantages noted in the proprietorship section also apply here. Recall that these pertain mainly to ease and flexibility of organization and the tightness of control. The same tax advantages apply; in addition, partnerships may provide a better opportunity for specialization of labor—for example, one partner may have primary marketing responsibilities, another primary financial management and accounting responsibilities, and so on.

Disadvantages

All the previously noted disadvantages of proprietorships also hold here: unlimited liability for some or all of the partners, difficulty in raising capital, inability to deduct from taxes certain expenses that are deductible for corporations, and the limited marketability of the ownership equity. There are other potential disadvantages. Partners may have difficulty agreeing, and many partnerships begun in harmony are dissolved with rancor. Furthermore, when a partner dies or withdraws, the organization is legally terminated, and it may be very difficult to arrange a settlement satisfactory to all parties.

Corporations

Corporations are regarded legally as entities separate from their owners. A corporation is like an artificial person, able to buy assets, raise funds, and perform all those other activities that proprietors and partners do. A corporation's assets are owned by itself, not by its owners, and a corporation's liabilities are obligations of the corporation, not of the owners. Thus, a principal feature of a corporation is the limited liability of the owners. The owners have claims on the firm through their ownership of the firm's stock. This also means, however, that stockholders who are not principal officers of the firm cannot establish policies.

Because corporations are the dominant form of U.S. business in terms of sales and assets, our orientation in this book is toward corporate finance. But this does not mean that the financial management principles we study are inappropriate for the other forms of business. However, it does mean that we will emphasize the concept of stockholder wealth maximization, which is most visibly applicable to corporations with widely held, publicly traded common stock.

Advantages

A primary advantage of a corporation is the limited liability of its owners. If the firm should fail, the stockholders will not be liable for the firm's debts. Another advantage is the ability of the corporation to raise new capital from sources other than the original owners. Small corporations may have as much difficulty raising money from the capital markets as proprietorships and partnerships, but medium-size and larger corporations will have good access to these markets. Ownership shares of corporations are also more easily traded, particularly if the firm's shares are traded on a major stock exchange.

Disadvantages

The main disadvantage of a corporation is that its owners face potential loss of control. Many corporations are effectively controlled by a few owners, but the hallmark of large

U.S. corporations is their diffuseness of ownership. Many U.S. corporations have thousands of stockholders. The control of any one owner in such a situation is usually nil, and not everyone's preferences can be satisfied; however, we assume that management will perform its duties so as to benefit stockholders collectively. The response of stockholders who do not approve of the firm's policies will be to sell the stock and invest the proceeds elsewhere. In some cases, stockholders with large enough positions may attempt to overthrow the management. But the fact remains that, for most large firms, ownership and control are effectively separated. Also, the owners face double taxation in the form of a corporate and a personal tax.

S Corporations

The IRS allows a corporation with 35 or fewer stockholders to have its income taxed as direct personal income to the stockholders (regardless of whether the income is distributed or not). Thus, the stockholders enjoy the advantages of the corporate form of organization, such as limited liability, while escaping the double taxation inherent in the ordinary corporate situation. It helps to think of the S corporation as a tax-reporting entity instead of as a tax-paying entity.

Valuation
Components and Process

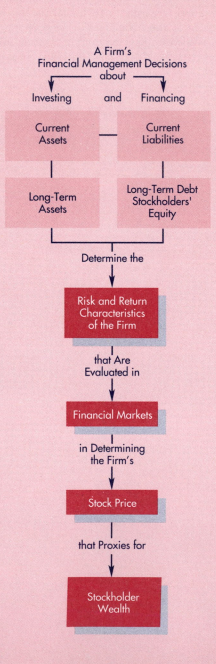

A Firm's
Financial Management Decisions
about
Investing   and   Financing

Current Assets — Current Liabilities

Long-Term Assets | Long-Term Debt Stockholders' Equity

Determine the

Risk and Return Characteristics of the Firm

that Are Evaluated in

Financial Markets

in Determining the Firm's

Stock Price

that Proxies for

Stockholder Wealth

Part II continues the discussion of valuation introduced at the end of Chapter 2. This is the critical component of the financial-management process, and it must be clearly understood. The emphasis throughout this text is on the valuation of the firm and the maximization of stockholder wealth. Financial decisions are properly made by asking what effect the decision will have on the value of the firm and the stockholders' wealth. While valuation will always be an art, not a science, there is a generally accepted framework within which the valuation process is conducted. Part II explains each of the components of this framework as well as the valuation process itself.

The two components of the valuation process are return and risk. Accordingly, Chapter 3 begins the discussion by focusing on the concepts of income and cash flows, which can be thought of as the return component of the valuation process. Chapter 3 focuses specifically on accounting income, which is an important concept for any discussion of financial management. Firms adhere to generally accepted accounting principles and report earnings to stockholders based on prevailing accounting practices. Stockholders and investors, in turn, rely on these reported income figures in determining how well the firm is doing and their own likely payoffs from owning the firm's stock. Since ratio analysis is an important part of the financial analysis related to accounting data, Chapter 3 examines the basics of ratio analysis, and Appendix 3–A provides a detailed examination of financial ratio analysis. Finally, Chapter 3 considers cash flow analysis because reported earnings from accounting statements are not necessarily the return variable of primary importance. As we shall see, the value of an asset is a function of the cash flows to be received from that asset. Accordingly, it is important that we consider the concept of cash flows.

Chapter 4 continues the analysis of the components of the valuation process by considering the time value of money. A basic premise of finance is that money has a time value—a dollar received today is worth more than a dollar received tomorrow. Cash flows must be adjusted for the time value of money in order to make them comparable. Having done the adjustment, we can then compare the benefits of an investment opportunity with its costs and determine if acceptance of the opportunity will benefit the firm's stockholders. Chapter 4 explains all the mechanics necessary for the application of time-value-of-money concepts to financial-management issues.

Chapter 5 continues the discussion of the components of the valuation process by analyzing the other side of the valuation equation, the risk involved. Valuation procedures must consider the risk involved as well as the expected returns. Accordingly, Chapter 5 considers the meaning of risk in some detail and then focuses on the part of risk that is most relevant for the stockholder, and doing so requires a basic understanding of portfolio concepts. Such an analysis allows us to understand the need for, and the derivation of, the concept of the required rate of return. This is the minimum expected rate of return necessary to induce an investor to purchase an asset, and it is a key concept in finance. In discussing this issue we will develop the capital asset pricing model (CAPM), a major cornerstone of finance over the last several years. The CAPM will be of use in later chapters when we need to estimate the required rate of return on a security.

Having analyzed the components of the valuation process in the preceding chapters, we are ready to bring them together in Chapter 6. This chapter explains the well-known and frequently used capitalization-of-income approach to valuation. Understanding this approach allows us to calculate the intrinsic value or estimated value of the major financial assets—common stocks, bonds, and preferred stocks. The mechanics are of primary importance and are used throughout the text whenever valuation concepts must be applied. Understanding the valuation process as explained in Chapter 6 is central to understanding finance in this text and generally. As part of the discussion, the concept of market efficiency is examined. It is useful for financial analysts to be aware of this concept and consider its implications for what is done in finance. Whether one agrees entirely with the efficient-market argument or not, there is considerable evidence to support the argument, and it has important implications that should be considered.

3

Accounting and Cash Flow Concepts

How Profitable Was General Electric?

General Electric (GE) recently reported annual net earnings of $2.9 billion, up from $2.5 billion the previous year. However, excluding various credits from accounting changes, GE showed a 15 percent drop in net income to $2.1 billion. Did GE really make more, or less?

As it turns out, GE recalculated its deferred-tax provision using the then-new corporate tax rate of 34 percent, creating a gain of $577 million. GE also changed its inventory accounting method for an ad-

ditional gain of $281 million. On the other hand, a $1 billion-plus debit to income was made for restructuring.

As a *Forbes* magazine article noted: "Add it all up and one can only conclude that General Electric did indeed probably make more money from continuing operations . . . than in the year before. The point here is, How is the average investor to make sense out of all these changes? The answers are anything but clear."[1]

---

[1]See Penelope Wang, "Solutions, Anyone?," *Forbes*, April 18, 1988, p. 72; General Electric's *Annual Report*, 1987; and *The Value Line Investment Survey*, various issues.

In the first two chapters, we established that the goal of financial management is to maximize the value of the stockholders' wealth as proxied by the price of the common stock. In Chapter 2, we learned a stock's price is determined within a valuation model based on its expected return and risk characteristics. To assess the expected return, investors must assess both the amount and the timing of the cash payments they expect to receive in the future. In particular, dividends, which will be used in Chapter 6 to value stocks, are the only cash payments received directly by the firm's stockholders.

The cash payments a firm pays to its stockholders are directly tied to the firm's cash flows, which, in turn, are related to the firm's accounting income—the earnings as reported by the firm to its shareholders. Therefore, shareholders, who ultimately are interested in the firm's cash flows, must also be concerned with accounting income. Accounting data and information are the starting point for analyzing and estimating a firm's cash flow. It is important to understand accounting income itself as well as its relationship to cash flow.

In this chapter, we concentrate on the firm's reported earnings and on its cash flows. We will discuss the timing issue in Chapter 4 and the *expected* nature of the cash flows in Chapter 5. As we can see from the GE example, understanding the profitability of a firm can be challenging without complicating the issue with other considerations.

Primary *chapter learning objectives* are:

1. To review basic accounting information and understand the reported financial statements of the firm.
2. To understand the process and procedures of financial analysis, particularly ratio analysis, that can be used to assess a firm's basic viability.
3. To consider the meaning and importance of cash flow as well as its calculation. While accounting income is important, the financial decision maker ultimately must think in terms of cash flows.

ACCOUNTING DATA AND ANALYSIS

The Financial Statements

Financial statements are a major source of information about a firm. The statements are accounting-derived compilations of the firm's activities as of a point in time or for a particular period of time. These accounting transactions are based on the accrual concept, reflect primarily historical costs, and are prepared according to generally accepted accounting principles (explained later).

annual report
a report prepared by management containing financial statements and other information, issued annually to stockholders

A firm's financial statements typically are part of the **annual report** that the firm sends its stockholders. The financial statements are presented along with any footnotes needed to explain or elaborate upon items in the statements themselves. These footnotes contain considerable detail and often cover several pages. By analyzing the firm's financial statements and the footnotes as necessary, one can obtain a useful assessment of the firm from an accounting standpoint, including its recent performance, its current financial position, and its general financial health.

It also is important for the analyst to read the prose part of the annual report wherein management describes what has happened to the firm and what it anticipates for the future. Typically this information will be contained in a letter from the president and/or chief executive officer, as well as in other qualitative statements about the company's activities. The reason that this information is important is that analysts, investors, and other interested parties seek to form expectations about the future performance of the company. To do this, one must do more than simply examine the firm's accounting numbers as reported in the financial statements because financial statements are designed to measure the past.

The Balance Sheet

A firm must have assets to operate, and it must finance these assets with capital. Every dollar of assets must be financed by some source of capital. Recall from Chapter 1 that financial management activities fall into one of two broad categories, investment decisions and financing decisions, and that a logical way to organize these activities is to place them within the context of a balance sheet, as shown below. This neatly organizes the firm's financial management activities.

Investment Decisions	*Financing Decisions*
Current assets	Current liabilities
Fixed assets	Long-term debt
	Stockholders' equity

The **balance sheet** provides an accounting picture of a firm's value at a particular point in time. The left side shows the assets, or how funds have been used, while the right side shows the liabilities, or how the funds have been raised, including stockholders' funds. In effect, the balance sheet shows the firm's investments and how it is financed. It is based on the following identity:

$$\text{Assets} = \text{Liabilities} + \text{Stockholders' equity}$$

balance sheet
an accounting statement of a firm's financial position at a specified point in time

The assets in a balance sheet are listed in approximate order of the time necessary to convert the assets into cash. Two broad distinctions are made, current assets and fixed assets; the dividing line between them is, by convention, one year:

- **Current assets** typically include four major components; in approximate order of liquidity they are cash, near-cash (marketable securities), accounts receivable, and inventory.
- Fixed assets include the firm's total property, plant, and equipment on both a gross basis and, by subtracting the accumulated depreciation, on a net basis.

current assets
the short-term assets held by a firm

The left side of the balance sheet reflects the nature of the business and the investment decisions made by management. For example, some firms hold a substantial amount of liquidity in the form of marketable securities. The relative proportions of accounts receivable and inventory generally reflect the particular industry the company operates in as well as prevailing business conditions.

The right side of the balance sheet reflects the firm's liabilities and owner's equity—the types and proportions of financing. Funds come from two broad sources: short-term and long-term (or permanent). Some long-term funds are provided by creditors and some by owners. Overall, exact sources and percentages reflect management's choice between debt and equity and between short-term and long-term financing.

stockholders' equity
total assets minus total
liabilities

Liabilities are obligations that require a cash payment at stipulated time periods. Most liabilities are contractual obligations to repay principal and interest; failure to pay as specified represents a default on the contract. But **stockholders' equity** is a residual item that is not fixed. It is, in fact, the difference between the assets and all other liabilities, as shown by the following identity:

$$\text{Assets} - \text{Liabilities} \equiv \text{Stockholders' equity}$$

book value
the accounting value of
the common stock

market value
the value of an asset
as determined in
the marketplace

It is important to note that stockholders' equity on the balance sheet shows the **book value** of the firm's equity—that is, the accounting value of the stockholders' interest in the firm. It reflects the initial issue of the common stock, any additional paid-in capital, and the retained earnings of the firm. It often differs from the **market value** of the equity, which reflects the price of the common stock as determined by investors in the market. Large adjustments to stockholders' equity can result from accounting changes.

- *Example*

In one recent year, IBM showed a $2.8 billion increase in stockholders' equity solely because of the strengthening of foreign currencies, whereas in the previous year the comparable change was an increase of only some $300 million. This change in the book value of the equity may have no effect on IBM's market value. ■

The best way to understand financial statements is to take an example set of statements and analyze them. Table 3–1 shows the consolidated balance sheets for Syntex Corporation and subsidiaries for 1989, 1988, and 1987. Syntex is an international health care company whose stock is traded on the New York Stock Exchange.

This is a relatively typical balance sheet for a large U.S. corporation. It is desirable to use the actual data of firms because that is what financial managers must work with daily. Although accounting is a complex subject requiring specialized study, we can learn the basics of financial statements relatively easily. We need not be intimidated by any complexities because we generally do not need to be involved to that degree. Furthermore, regardless of any complications, ambiguities, and controversies, accounting data is essential for an understanding of finance. We need to be comfortable with it, understand its usefulness, and recognize its limitations. Finally, we should remember that finance has its own complications, ambiguities, and controversies, and as we become comfortable with managerial finance and learn its usefulness, we also will see its limitations.

According to Table 3–1, at the end of 1989 Syntex had $766 million of total current assets, including $192 million of short-term investments (at cost). The first current asset listed, cash and cash items, is a very important variable that is discussed in detail later in this chapter. A firm's bills, as well as its payments to creditors and stockholders, must be paid from cash. A firm can show a profit and yet have little or no cash.

Fixed assets, identified as long-term bonds, property, plant and equipment, and other assets, amounted to $674 million. Notice that the property, plant and equipment is stated on a net basis, after accumulated depreciation and amortization have been subtracted, and represented $545 million of the $674 million total.

■ *Table 3–1*
Sample Balance Sheet

SYNTEX CORPORATION AND SUBSIDIARY COMPANIES
Consolidated Balance Sheet
July 31, 1989, 1988, and 1987
($ and shares in millions)

Assets	1989	1988	1987
Current assets			
Cash and cash equivalents	$ 189.7	$ 383.9	$ 160.3
Short-term investments	191.7	106.2	123.6
Trade receivables (less allowance for doubtful accounts:			
1989, $4.3; 1988, $4.1; 1987, $4.2)	163.3	166.3	151.8
Inventories	155.6	139.5	143.5
Other	66.1	58.9	40.1
Total current assets	766.4	854.8	619.3
Long-term bonds	100.0	100.0	100.0
Property, plant and equipment—net	545.4	457.7	391.4
Other assets	28.4	31.2	33.9
Total	$1,440.2	$1,443.7	$1,144.6
Liabilities and Shareholders' Equity			
Current liabilities			
Short-term debt	$ 158.7	$ 139.1	$ 42.5
Accounts payable and accrued expenses	136.6	114.1	92.0
Income and other taxes	123.4	122.0	107.3
Accrued compensation	69.8	62.8	57.4
Other	144.9	120.2	111.1
Total current liabilities	633.4	558.2	410.3
Long-term debt	219.6	131.7	129.5
Contingencies	—	—	—
Redeemable preferred stock	—	.3	.4
Shareholders' equity			
Common stock (shares issued—128.5)	128.5	128.5	128.5
Capital in excess of par value	12.1	18.8	21.1
Retained earnings	882.5	775.3	606.1
Cumulative translation adjustments	(18.7)	(18.2)	(21.5)
Common stock in treasury—at cost (shares in treasury			
1989—16.8; 1988—10.4; 1987—10.2)	(417.2)	(150.9)	(129.8)
Total shareholders' equity	587.2	753.5	604.4
Total	$1,440.2	$1,443.7	$1,144.6

Source: Syntex Corporation, *1989 Annual Report.*

Total **current liabilities,** representing short-term financing, amounted to $633 million. Long-term debt provided some $220 million of financing. Table 3–1 shows that although preferred stock as a source of financing has been authorized, no shares have been issued to date. Total shareholders' equity, consisting mostly of retained earnings, amounted to some $587 million. Syntex was holding a sizable amount of its own stock (common stock in treasury), and some 128.5 million shares had been issued and are carried on the books at a total value of $128.5 million.

current liabilities
liabilities of a firm with maturities less than one year

retained earnings
that part of a firm's after-tax earnings that is not paid out as dividends

It is important to recognize that the **retained earnings** figure shown on the balance sheet reflects historical decisions to retain part of the net income in the business. The aggregate amount of retained earnings is not available currently to be spent as cash.

par value
the nominal value of a security as established by the issuer

The common stock is carried on the books at $1 **par value**—since 128.5 million shares are outstanding, the balance sheet shows the common stock at $128.5 million. From a financial standpoint, par value is a meaningless concept. It is arbitrarily assigned to a common stock for accounting purposes but carries no economic significance (some stocks have no par value). As we will stress in this text, *what matters most to stockholders is the market value of the common stock*. The par value of the stock is unimportant, and the accounting (book) value of the stock, while not to be ignored, is not the variable of primary interest to the stockholders, whose wealth we are attempting to maximize.

The Income Statement

income statement
a financial statement showing a firm's revenues and expenses during a specified period

Whereas the balance sheet is a picture of the firm's accounting value on a particular date, the **income statement** measures performance over a particular time period, typically one year. Like the balance sheet, it is based on an identity:

$$\text{Revenue} - \text{Expenses} \equiv \text{Income}$$

depreciation
the allocation of an asset's cost to the life of the asset

A typical income statement can be divided into sections: the operating section shows the operations of the firm in terms of its sales and expenses, while the nonoperating section shows such items as interest expense. **Depreciation,** a noncash charge representing the use of capital assets, is an important item that is deducted along with the cost of goods sold and the selling and administrative expenses to obtain *operating income*. Subtracting interest expense (a tax-deductible item) and taxes from operating income results in **net income,** from which earnings per share (EPS) are calculated based on the number of shares of common stock outstanding.

net income
total after-tax earnings of a firm

Net income, the property of the common stockholder, can be divided into two parts:

> Dividends are paid directly to stockholders.
>
> Retained earnings are reinvested in the business.

If, as expected, retained earnings are reinvested profitably, the stock price should appreciate.

earnings per share (EPS)
total earnings available for common stockholders divided by the number of common shares outstanding

Earnings per share (EPS) and **dividends per share (DPS)** are basic variables of interest to stockholders and investors and are used in various valuation approaches to estimate the fair value of the common stock. We will use a dividend valuation model in Chapter 6.

dividends per share (DPS)
the total dollar amount of dividends paid divided by the number of shares outstanding

Revenue is recognized when an exchange has occurred and must be matched with expenses under the matching principle of accounting.[2] Income is reported when it is accrued (earned) rather than when cash is actually received. This important distinction will affect the remainder of our work in this text. Finance is primarily forward-looking, focusing on cash flows involving the actual receipt or expenditures of cash. Accounting, primarily concerned with the past, focuses on net income for some period as determined by a set of accounting principles.

---

[2]Unrealized appreciation (for example, from the ownership of property) is not recognized as income.

■ *Table 3–2*
Sample Income
Statement

SYNTEX CORPORATION AND SUBSIDIARY COMPANIES
Consolidated Statement of Income
For the Years Ended
July 31, 1989, 1988, and 1987
($ in millions except per-share amounts)

	1989	1988	1987
Net sales	$1,349.4	$1,271.5	$1,129.2
Costs and expenses			
Cost of goods sold	268.4	265.8	254.5
Selling, general and administrative	499.8	450.8	404.0
Research and development	245.2	217.9	175.1
Total	1,013.4	934.5	833.6
Operating income	336.0	337.0	295.6
Nonoperating income (expense)			
Interest income	45.0	36.0	26.7
Interest expense	(36.3)	(29.1)	(21.4)
Other—net	(7.8)	(3.0)	(10.0)
Total	.9	3.9	(4.7)
Income before taxes on income	336.9	340.9	290.9
Provision for taxes on income	33.7	44.3	42.1
Net income	$ 303.2	$ 296.6	$ 248.8
Net earnings per common share	$2.67	$2.51	$2.07

Source: Syntex Corporation, *1989 Annual Report.*

Table 3–2 shows the consolidated statement of earnings for Syntex for the years 1989, 1988, and 1987. In 1989, operating revenue (primarily sales) was approximately $1.35 billion. Subtraction of roughly $1 billion in operating costs and expenses resulted in an operating income of $336 million. Although not shown explicitly as a separate item, the depreciation expense in 1989 was $54 million.

Substantial adjustments to operating income basically offset each other, leaving earnings before taxes at the same level, $336 million. These nonoperating income (expense) items consisted of interest earned and interest expense and other items.

The provision for income taxes was $34 million. It is worthwhile to note in connection with this item that corporations keep at least two sets of books. The actual taxes paid to the IRS will typically differ from that reported to the shareholders in the income statement. One important reason is that corporations often use accelerated depreciation for tax purposes and straight-line depreciation for reporting purposes.

Net after-tax earnings amounted to some $303 million, with earnings per share—a result of dividing $303.2 million by the 113.7 million average shares outstanding—of $2.67.[3] Although not shown in Table 3–2, dividends of $154 million, or $1.35 per share, were paid in that year.[4]

[3]Average shares outstanding, which can be found in the *Annual Report,* is used to calculate EPS.
[4]All per-share data reflect a 3-for-1 stock split in April 1987.

Other Financial Statements

A complete set of financial statements consists of four parts: (1) the balance sheet; (2) the income statement; (3) a new statement required as of mid–1988, the statement of cash flows,[5] and (4) a statement of changes in stockholders' equity or a statement of retained earnings. The fourth statement is optional, but the other three must be reported.

The *statement of changes in stockholders' equity or the statement of retained earnings* shows how net earnings are allocated to dividends and retained earnings, how the capital in excess of the par value account changes, and any treasury stock transactions. In effect, it shows how the components making up the shareholders' equity changed from one year to the next. In the case of Syntex, which reports a statement of retained earnings, the 1989 statement shows how the retained earnings balance of $775 million at the beginning of 1989 (or the end of 1988) grew to the year–end figure of $883.[6]

statement of cash flows
a statement of a firm's cash receipts and cash payments during a period

The third statement, **the statement of cash flows,** shows a firm's cash receipts and payments, classified as to sources and uses. It is a new statement that reflects the changing needs of the users of financial statements. Its predecessor, the statement of changes in financial position, focused on the change in working capital. Because of the increasing emphasis on cash flows and the need to know more about cash movements in the firm, many people argued for the use of a cash basis, as opposed to a working-capital basis, in preparing the statement on financial position. This, in turn, evolved into a demand for a cash basis orientation, which ultimately led to the creation of the statement of cash flows. Since it fits in nicely with the discussion on cash flows, we will examine this statement in the cash flow section of this chapter.

Generally Accepted Accounting Principles

generally accepted accounting principles (GAAP)
accounting guidelines used to prepare financial statements

Guidelines called **generally accepted accounting principles (GAAP)** are used to prepare financial statements and deal with accounting issues. These principles are authorized by the rule-making body for the accounting profession, the *Financial Accounting Standards Board (FASB),* which is part of the *American Institute of Certified Public Accountants (AICPA).* The FASB has responsibility for periodically issuing authoritative standards called *Statements of Financial Accounting Standards* (SFAS); these are the official accounting procedures that firms use in preparing their financial statements.

The basic premise of accounting rules and procedures is that costs, which are recognized as incurred, should be matched with revenues, which are recognized at the point of sale. Unfortunately, it has proven very difficult, if not impossible, to produce GAAP rules that resolve problems in comparability and objective interpretation. Instead, wide differences exist in the reported income of similar (even identical) operations as a result of how and when the accounting standards are used.

---

[5]This statement was previously the statement of changes in financial position.
[6]For the sake of brevity, we do not show this statement in detail.

- *Example*

Firms were given the option to adopt SFAS 96, a recently issued accounting standard on treating income taxes, in 1987, 1988, or 1989, or follow one of two alternatives for dealing with the issue of taxes. This makes it difficult for the analyst to make comparisons among companies. As *Forbes* magazine recently noted in an article on changing accounting methods, "If as an investor you're not confused by corporate earnings statements, you ought to be."[7] ▪

Firms that are quite similar in terms of sales, costs, operations, and so on, can report widely varying profit figures. This can make comparisons among companies quite difficult. Some major reasons for differences in reported income include accounting for depreciation, inventories, pension costs, and subsidiaries. Depreciation and inventory treatments are particularly significant contributors.

Also, year-to-year comparisons of the same company's performance can be difficult, and misleading, for a variety of reasons. Write-offs resulting from restructuring and other events can cause a firm's reported earnings to fluctuate violently.

- *Example*

U.S. Steel absorbed a $1.4 billion write-off and loss in one year but showed an almost $1 billion operating profit in the following year. Investors must ask themselves if the company's true performance changed that drastically in a one year period. In other words, did U.S. Steel really do that much better *in its actual performance* between the two years, a turnaround of over $2 billion, or was that performance in large part a function of accounting practices? ▪

The potential effect of changes in accounting rules on the reported profits of companies can be staggering. Earnings can rise even though the true performance of the companies has barely changed.

- *Example*

According to *Forbes,* a pair of then-new FASB pension accounting rules made it easier than ever for publicly owned companies to add some $344 billion to their reported profits when aggregate pre-tax profits for U.S. companies the previous year amounted to about $227 billion. *Forbes* cited the case of Morrison-Knudsen Corporation, which by changing its pension cost accounting rules enjoyed a boost in per-share earnings of 63 percent, from $2.35 to $3.84.[8] Once again, stockholders and potential investors must ask themselves, what is the true earning power of this company? ▪

FINANCIAL ANALYSIS

Many diverse groups of people are interested in the information found in the firm's financial statements; they study the statements carefully, interpreting the information that relates to their particular interest in the company. For example,

---

[7]Wang, "Solutions, Anyone?" p. 72.
[8]See Laura Jereski, "Tapping the Golden Pool," *Forbes,* April 21, 1986, p. 35.

creditors (and potential creditors) analyze the financial statements with an eye toward the firm's creditworthiness. Short-term creditors are concerned primarily with the firm's liquidity, where liquidity refers to the firm's ability to pay bills as they arise. Similarly, long-term creditors are interested in the firm's ability to pay the scheduled interest and principal payments on the firm's long-term debt. Potential long-term debtholders' degree of confidence in the firm's ability to service the debt strongly influences the firm's ability to finance its investments with borrowed funds.

The firm's management also analyzes its financial statements. Although management, unlike creditors and stockholders, has internal reports at its disposal, the financial statements do add considerable information about the strengths and weaknesses of the firm. How efficiently the firm uses its assets, how it finances them, how risky the firm is, and how profitable the firm has been are all questions that can be at least partially assessed from the financial statements. Management can use this information to monitor the firm's activities, to ensure that its policy decisions are implemented by subordinate units within the firm, and, through projections based on financial statements, to plan for the future.

Finally—and importantly—stockholders (and potential stockholders) use the firm's financial statements to help assess what the future holds for the firm. In particular, they are interested in the stock's expected return and risk characteristics. (See Figure 2–1 for a review of share price determination.) In Chapter 6 we will present a stock valuation framework based on dividends. Shareholders analyze the net income of the firm as part of the process of forming expectations about the future dividends of the firm.

The object of all these analyses is an evaluation of the firm's performance.[9] Financial analysis can be used to analyze the determinants of a firm's reported earnings, thereby helping to identify the potential strengths and weaknesses of the firm's performance. Understanding a firm's profitability, in turn, can help in estimating the expected returns stockholders may receive in the future.

Ratio Analysis

ratio analysis
the calculation and analysis of a firm's financial ratios

Financial analysis typically is associated with **ratio analysis,** defined as the analysis of relationships among various financial statement items both at a point in time and over time. It uses the financial statements in a unique manner to provide a different perspective about the firm.

To carry out a ratio analysis, the financial statements are used to compute a *set* of ratios. Each ratio emphasizes a particular aspect of the balance sheet and/or income statement. The calculated set of ratios are then compared to industry averages (or historical standards) to assess the financial performance of the firm. The general rule is that ratios diverging extremely on either side from industry norms warrant further investigation.

Ratios for any one year can be misleading because they are high or low for some temporary reason. Therefore, it also is important to analyze trends in the

---

[9]In addition to the three groups discussed here, government agencies and labor unions will also be interested in the firm's performance. Many industries are regulated by government agencies, and the rate of return allowed companies in these industries is based on information in the financial statements. Similarly, unions frequently use financial statements to show that the firm's profits justify wage increases.

ratios to assess changes in the firm's performance over time. A *trend analysis* involves graphs of the various ratios, where each graph consists of a particular ratio plotted against time (typically, years). Trend analysis of the ratios adds depth to the study because it looks at several years and helps distinguish between isolated instances of suspicious ratios and the pervasive deterioration of ratios that indicates trouble.

Time trends in a company's ratios are informative, but it is often more informative to compare company trends with industry trends. This comparison illustrates how well the firm has been doing across time relative to its competitors and may help explain trends in the company's ratios. If the company's profit margin is declining over time, for example, analysts would like to know whether this decline is mainly because of declining industry profit margins or whether the firm is not competitive with other industry members.

Industry comparisons require a source of industry data. Probably the best known sets of ratios are provided by these sources:

1. Dun & Bradstreet (D&B), whose *Industry Norms and Key Business Ratios* reports 14 important ratios for some 800 lines of business based on the financial statements of over 400,000 companies. Three values are reported for each ratio: the median (the typical firm in the entire distribution), the upper quartile (the typical firm in the top half of the distribution), and the lower quartile (the typical firm in the lower half of the distribution).

2. Prentice Hall, whose *Almanac of Business and Industrial Financial Ratios* reports annually 22 ratios for over 160 industries. Firms in each industry are classified into 11 size groups.

3. Robert Morris Associates, whose *Statement Studies* reports 16 ratios for over 250 lines of business and four size groups. Like D&B, this publication contains the median, upper quartile, and lower quartile.

Traditionally, four groups of financial ratios have been used to assess a firm's performance: (1) liquidity, (2) activity, (3) leverage, and (4) profitability. A fifth category, market ratios, is also useful.

Consistent with our emphasis throughout the text on valuation, which is forward-looking, we will consider below only the basic nature of the ratios used in ratio analysis. Our concern will be with what they are, and how they are used. We will not concern ourselves with the actual application because a complete ratio analysis involves calculation of the ratios, comparison to one or more benchmarks, a trend analysis, and several other components. Appendix 3–A shows how these ratios are applied by illustrating a complete and detailed ratio analysis of one company, including all the interpretations, the trend analysis, and so on.

Liquidity Ratios

For the firm to continue in business, it must be able to pay its bills as they come due. *Liquidity ratios* measure the extent to which the firm can service its immediate obligations, in effect assessing the firm's ability to meet short-run financial contingencies. The two commonly used liquidity ratios are the current ratio and the quick ratio.

The **current ratio** relates current assets to current liabilities. Current assets include cash, bank balances, marketable securities, accounts receivable, and

current ratio
the ratio of current assets to current liabilities

inventory. Current liabilities include accounts payable, bank loans, that part of the long-term debt to be paid off during the coming year, taxes payable, and other accrued expenses.

$$\text{Current ratio} = \frac{\text{Current assets}}{\text{Current liabilities}} \qquad (3\text{--}1)$$

Relatively high current ratios are interpreted as an indication that the firm is liquid and in good position to meet its current obligations, and vice versa. The current ratio supposedly measures liquidity because it relates the firm's pending need for cash to the firm's present cash and *near-cash* position. Near-cash in this case is represented by marketable securities, accounts receivable, and inventory. One shortcoming of the current ratio as a measure of liquidity, however, is that it does not differentiate between the various liquidities of the near-cash assets. For example, the current ratio implicitly assumes that inventory is as liquid as marketable securities. The quick ratio attempts to correct for this.

quick ratio
current assets minus inventories divided by current liabilities

The **quick ratio** is the same as the current ratio except that the numerator does not include inventory. Inventory is typically the least-liquid component of current assets.

$$\text{Quick ratio} = \frac{\text{Current assets} - \text{Inventory}}{\text{Current liabilities}} \qquad (3\text{--}2)$$

Like the current ratio, the quick ratio, or *acid-test ratio,* is meant to reflect the firm's ability to pay its short-term obligations, and the higher the quick ratio, the more liquid the firm's position. There are two dangers in having too low a liquidity position; one is not being able to pay obligations as they come due. The second is that short-term lenders may perceive the firm as being unable to meet its obligations and refuse to advance new credit.

While such ratios provide an assessment of the firm's liquidity position, it is important to note that they do not assess the amount or timing of a firm's cash flows. Once again, this is a difference between accounting information and cash flows. To assess cash flows, additional information is necessary.

Activity Ratios

Activity ratios supposedly indicate how well the firm manages its assets by relating important asset accounts to operating results. These ratios are called *turnover ratios* because they show how rapidly assets are being converted (turned over) into sales. Although generalizations can be misleading, high turnover ratios are usually associated with good asset management and low turnover ratios with bad asset management. Activity ratios involve accounts receivable, inventory, fixed assets, and total assets.

inventory turnover
the ratio of sales to inventories

Inventory turnover shows how efficiently the firm's inventory is being managed. It is a rough measure of how many times per year the inventory level is replaced (turned over).[10]

$$\text{Inventory turnover} = \frac{\text{Sales}}{\text{Inventory}} \qquad (3\text{--}3)$$

---

[10]There are alternative ways to calculate inventory value—for example, *average inventory* and *ending* (end-of-period) *inventory*. Many analysts prefer the former since ending inventory is only a one-day snapshot. Also, since sales carry a markup over inventory costs, many analysts prefer to use cost of goods sold in the numerator rather than sales. However, cost of goods sold occasionally is not shown on the income statement, and industry averages are usually defined in terms of sales rather than cost of goods sold.

Generally, higher-than-average inventory turnovers are suggestive of good inventory management. Low turnovers may result from excessive inventory levels, the presence of damaged or obsolete inventory, or unexpectedly low sales levels. On the other hand, abnormally high inventory turnovers may indicate inventory levels so low that stockouts will occur and future sales will be impaired.

The **average collection period** indicates the efficiency of the firm's collection policy by showing how long it takes for accounts receivable to be cleared. Since

average collection period
the average time period between sales and receipt of payment for those sales

$$\text{Sales per day} = \frac{\text{Sales}}{365}$$

$$\text{Average collection period} = \frac{\text{Receivables}}{\text{Sales per day}} = \frac{(\text{Receivables})(365)}{\text{Sales}} \qquad \textbf{(3–4)}$$

The significance of the average collection period figure is this: Assuming all sales are made on credit, how many days worth of sales are tied up in receivables? The collection period supposedly measures the quality of the firm's receivables: the shorter the collection period, the better the quality of the receivables because a short collection period means that the firm's customers are prompt payers.[11]

Long collection periods may indicate the firm's receivables policy is not very effective. An important benchmark associated with the collection period is the terms stating within what period payment is due by the firm's customers. If the collection period is substantially longer than the stated credit terms, receivables are not being managed well in relation to the firm's credit policy.

Conversely, collection periods shorter than the industry average are usually viewed as an indication that the receivables policy is effective. However, a ratio may be too good. A collection period low in relation to the industry norm may mean that a company's credit policy is too restrictive. If the company were to relax its credit policy by extending credit to customers now on a cash basis, it might increase its sales and profits significantly.

The **fixed-asset turnover ratio** is a measure of how well the firm uses its long-term (fixed) assets and shows how many dollars of sales are supported by one dollar of fixed assets.

fixed-asset turnover ratio
the ratio of sales to net fixed assets

$$\text{Fixed-asset turnover} = \frac{\text{Sales}}{\text{Fixed assets}} \qquad \textbf{(3–5)}$$

Higher-than-average fixed-asset turnover ratios typically are associated with better-than-average fixed-asset management, and lower ratios with poorer management. However, since book value of fixed assets may be considerably different from the market value of these assets, the fixed-asset turnover may be deceptively low or high. For example, a firm with a relatively old but still serviceable plant that has been almost fully depreciated will have a lower book value than a competitor with a new plant, and for similar sales levels, the older plant will tend to have a higher fixed-asset turnover, even though both firms may be utilizing their fixed assets at about the same efficiency.

---

[11]A more refined definition of collection period would use credit sales in the denominator rather than sales, used in Equation 3–4. However, it is usually very difficult to ascertain credit sales from the income statement, and industry averages use sales rather than credit sales.

total-assets turnover ratio
the ratio of sales to total assets

The **total-assets turnover ratio** indicates how many dollars of sales are supported by one dollar of total tangible assets. It is a measure of the firm's total-assets management.

$$\text{Total-assets turnover} = \frac{\text{Sales}}{\text{Total assets}} \tag{3-6}$$

High total-assets turnover ratios are supposed to indicate successful asset management, and low ratios to indicate unsuccessful management. However, since total-assets turnover is a composite of all the firm's assets, both current and fixed, all the problems discussed in the other turnover ratio analyses are imbedded in the total-assets turnover. As with other ratios, the key point is to be wary of extremely high or low ratios. Extreme values should raise a red flag in the analyst's mind and lead to explorations beyond simple ratio analysis.

Leverage Ratios

Leverage ratios indicate to what extent the firm has financed its investments by borrowing. These ratios focus on the firm's financial structure. The issues are the amount of debt the firm is using and the firm's ability to service this debt. We will see in a later chapter that debt financing increases the bankruptcy risk, so the more extensive the use of debt, the larger the firm's leverage ratios and the more risk present in the firm.

debt-equity ratio
the ratio of total debt to stockholders' equity

The **debt-equity ratio** is the ratio of the total debt in the firm, both long-term and short-term, to equity, where equity is the sum of common and preferred stockholders' equity.

$$\text{Debt-equity ratio} = \frac{\text{Debt}}{\text{Equity}} \tag{3-7}$$

A high ratio means the firm has liberally used debt (has borrowed) to finance its assets, and a low ratio means the firm has paid for its assets mainly with equity money (preferred stock, common stock, and retained earnings). Any ratio over 1.0 means the firm has used more debt than equity to finance its investments. Debt-equity ratios may vary considerably within an industry, but many analysts feel that a radical departure from the industry norm is dangerous.[12]

debt-to-total-assets ratio (debt ratio)
the ratio of total debt to total assets

The **debt-to-total-assets ratio (debt ratio)** indicates the percentage of assets financed by debt of all types, whether short-term or long-term.

$$\text{Debt ratio} = \frac{\text{Total debt}}{\text{Total assets}} \tag{3-8}$$

The debt ratio reflects the *financial structure* of the firm by showing the firm's financial risk posture, of primary interest to investors. The higher the percentage of financing provided by creditors, the more financial risk in the firm.

times interest earned
the ratio of earnings before interest and taxes to interest charges

Times interest earned is supposed to measure how ably the firm can meet its interest obligations.

$$\text{Times interest earned} = \frac{\text{Net operating income}}{\text{Interest expense}} \tag{3-9}$$

[12]There are several variants of the debt-equity ratio. One is the *long-term debt-equity ratio,* which has only long-term debt in the numerator. Another version includes the preferred stock as debt rather than equity, thus viewing the debt-equity ratio squarely from the common stockholder's perspective.

Times interest earned is one of several *debt-service* ratios. These ratios describe how easily the firm can pay its interest obligations as they come due. Times interest earned is a kind of interest-coverage ratio that shows how many times the interest payments are covered by funds that are normally available to pay interest expenses. This does not include other financial resources that could be made available to meet interest expenses.[13]

Profitability Ratios

Profitability ratios measure the profits of the firm relative to sales, assets, or equity. It is important to emphasize that profitability ratios describe the firm's past profitability, especially because it is tempting to overemphasize these ratios when making an evaluation. Investors are continually bombarded with statements to the effect that a firm earned 10 percent on equity last year and therefore should earn 10 percent or higher this year. However, because there is little evidence that past profitability results foretell future profitability, we must be careful not to attach too much importance to these numbers. They tell a story about where the firm has been, not where it is going.

The **profit margin** shows what percentage of every sales dollar the firm was able to convert into net income.

$$\text{Profit margin} = \frac{\text{Net income after tax}}{\text{Sales}} \qquad \textbf{(3–10)}$$

profit margin
the ratio of net profit after taxes to sales

This is an important ratio because it describes how well a dollar of sales is squeezed into profit. The profit-margin numerator, net income, is sales less all expenses, including interest. For example, a company may use debt more aggressively than most of its competitors and have larger interest expenses; thus, except for interest expenses, the company may be performing satisfactorily.

Return on assets (ROA) relates net income to total assets; it measures how profitably the firm has used its assets.

$$\text{Return on assets (ROA)} = \frac{\text{Net income}}{\text{Total assets}} \qquad \textbf{(3–11)}$$

return on assets (ROA)
the ratio of net after-tax income to total assets

A low return on assets should be cause for some concern. However, while ROA does crudely reflect how well the firm uses its assets, there are some difficulties associated with it. Since a large part of many firms' total assets are fixed assets and since book and market values of fixed assets may be widely divergent, ROA differences can arise simply because of the degree to which the assets have been depreciated. Another problem is that net income is heavily influenced by capitalization and income tax changes.[14]

Return on equity (ROE) indicates the rate of return earned on the *book value* of the owner's equity.

$$\text{Return on equity (ROE)} = \frac{\text{Net income after taxes}}{\text{Common equity}} \qquad \textbf{(3–12)}$$

return on equity (ROE)
the ratio of net after-tax income to common equity

---

[13]Another debt-service ratio is the *fixed-charge-coverage ratio*. This ratio acknowledges that the firm may have fixed financial charges in addition to interest, such as repayment of debt principal, sinking-fund payments, lease payments, or rent.

[14]Some analysts prefer a definition of return on assets that uses net operating income instead of net income.

It is possible for a firm's return on equity to be better than the industry average although its profit margin and return on assets are both less than the industry average. This can result from the firm's aggressive use of debt. While debt financing causes net income to decline because of interest expenses, the cost of debt financing is fixed. The firm issues less equity, which gives Equation 3–12 a lower denominator. This results in a high return on equity.

Market Ratios

dividend yield
dividends per share divided by current market price

dividend payout
the ratio of dividends to earnings

Market ratios are of primary interest to participants in the financial markets. One important market measure, the **dividend yield,** measures the current return on the common stock by relating the firm's cash payments, or dividends, to its current market price. As we saw in Chapter 2, it is one of the two components of total return. The **dividend payout** measures the percentage of earnings paid out as dividends.

Focusing on the variable dividends shows why we consider both accounting and cash flow concepts in this chapter. Most investors think of dividends as being paid out of the accounting earnings that a firm reports, and in some sense they are. However, dividends, unlike accounting earnings reported on the books, must be paid out of cash. Therefore, the concept of cash flow, which is different from the concept of net income, is important. Whatever its reported earnings, a firm must have cash to pay dividends.

price-earnings ratio
the ratio of stock price to earnings per share

The **price-earnings ratio,** an important concept in valuation, indicates how much per dollar of earnings investors are willing to pay for a share of stock. It is reported for each company in the daily newspaper coverage of the financial markets along with the dividend yield. Typically, growth stocks and stocks currently in favor with investors sell at high price-earnings (P/E) ratios relative to the average for the market as a whole, while slow-growth companies and stocks currently out of favor with investors sell at low P/E ratios. P/E ratios can, and typically do, fluctuate sharply over time, making this variable very difficult to forecast.

Figures 3–1 and 3–2 show these three ratios for Syntex from mid-1970 through much of the 1980s. As would be expected, the P/E ratio in Figure 3–1 is very volatile, ranging from the low 20s to less than 10. This is because the P/E ratio reflects investor sentiment and expectations—their optimism and pessimism about stocks in general and Syntex in particular. The amount investors are willing to pay per dollar of earnings varies sharply over time. Although the financial decisions made by the firm's managers affect the P/E ratio, the P/E ratio is ultimately determined by investors in the market as part of their valuation process.

The dividend payout (D/E) ratio for Syntex, shown in Figure 3–2, has fluctuated around a rising trend. This is a fairly typical pattern for a successful, growing firm—as it begins to mature, the rapid growth slows down and the payout increases. Also, stockholders probably expect larger dividend payments. The dividend yield (D/P), also shown in Figure 3–2, has risen slowly over the years, from about 0.5 percent to 3.2 percent. At the time of this report, the average D/P for the drug industry was 3 percent and for the average stock in an index of 1,700 stocks it was 3.2 percent. Thus, the dividend yield on Syntex stock was directly in line with stocks as a whole.

Average Annual Price-Earnings (P/E) Ratio for Syntex, 1974–1989 ▪ *Figure 3–1*

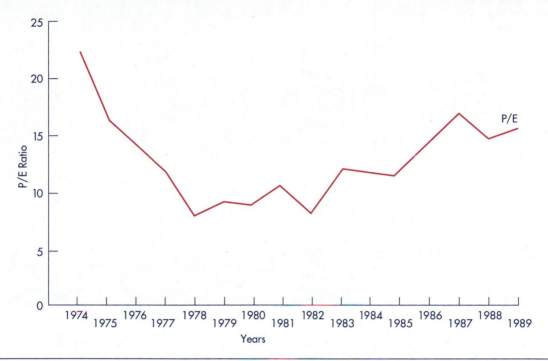

Source: *The Value Line Investment Survey*, Ratings and Reports, November 9, 1990, p. 1276. Copyright © 1990 by Value Line Publishing, Inc.; used by permission.

Table 3–3 summarizes the major ratios used in financial analysis, separated into the five categories just described. We will refer to these ratios throughout the text, integrating them into the discussion and showing how and where they are typically used.

The DuPont System of Analysis

Obviously many of these financial ratios are related to each other because the firm's activities, assets, and liabilities are interrelated. Thus, it has become commonplace to bring together balance sheet and income statement activities into a formal system for analyzing a firm's profitability. The **DuPont system of analysis** is widely used by financial managers to assess a firm's financial condition and examine the underlying determinants of its profitability.

We start with return on assets (ROA), which can be shown to be the product of the profit margin and the total assets turnover. Therefore, combining the equation for profit margin (3–10) with the equation for total assets turnover (3–6), we have:

DuPont system of analysis
systematic study of the financial ratios describing a firm's financial condition

$$\text{ROA} = \frac{\text{Net income}}{\text{Sales}} \times \frac{\text{Sales}}{\text{Total assets}} = \frac{\text{Net income}}{\text{Total assets}}$$

■ *Figure 3–2*
Dividend Payout (D/E)
and Dividend Yield (D/P)
Ratios for Syntex, 1974–
1989

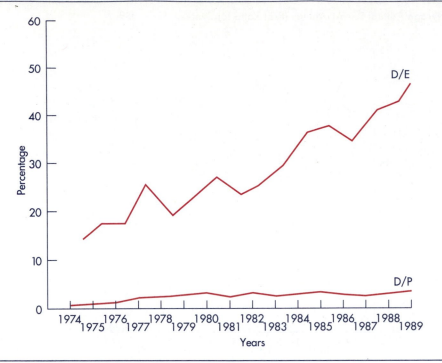

Source: *The Value Line Investment Survey*, Ratings and Reports, November 9, 1990, p. 1276.
Copyright © 1990 by Value Line Publishing, Inc.; used by permission.

For Syntex, based on Tables 3–1 and 3–2:

$$\text{ROA} = \frac{\$303.2}{\$1,349.4} \times \frac{\$1,349.4}{\$1,440.2} = .225 \times .937 = .211, \text{ or } 21.1\%$$

This produces the same result as directly dividing net income by total assets, of course, but this approach clearly shows the two determinants of ROA:

1. How much the firm earns per dollar of sales.
2. Asset utilization, or how many dollars of sales are generated by one dollar of assets (which has to be financed at a cost).

If ROA is judged inadequate, the source of the inadequacy can be analyzed. Is profit margin the problem? Or is asset utilization the problem? In the DuPont analysis, the determinants of each of these ratios can be examined. For example, we know that total assets can be decomposed into fixed assets and current assets, and there are ratios dealing with each of these items.

Although ROA is important—it is a measure of the return on assets—stockholders are more interested in the return on their equity since they have not put up all the funds to finance the firm; creditors have also put up funds. Under the DuPont analysis as typically employed, we examine the relationship that determines ROE, given ROA. In doing this it is convenient to use the **equity multiplier,** which is an alternative measure of leverage.

equity multiplier
a leverage measure defined as the ratio of sales to stockholders' equity

$$\text{Equity multiplier} = \frac{\text{Total assets}}{\text{Equity}} \qquad (3\text{–}13)$$

Key Financial Ratios by Category   ■ *Table 3–3*

Ratio	How Calculated	Purpose
Liquidity Ratios		
Current ratio	Current assets/Current liabilities	Shows short-term assets available to service short-term debt
Quick ratio	(Current assets − Inventory)/Current liabilities	Uses liquid current assets to measure ability to service short-term debt
Activity Ratios		
Inventory turnover	Sales/Inventory	Measures how well investment in inventory is being controlled
Average collection period	(Receivables) (365)/Sales	Measures success of firm in collecting receivables
Fixed-asset turnover	Sales/Fixed assets	Measures how well the firm uses its fixed assets
Total-assets turnover	Sales/Total assets	Measures how well the firm uses its total assets
Leverage Ratios		
Debt-equity ratio	Debt/Equity	Measures relative proportions of financing by creditors and owners
Debt-to-total-assets ratio	Total debt/Total assets	Measures the percentage of funds provided by creditors by including current liabilities
Times interest earned	Net operating income/Interest expense	Measures how well the firm can service its debt
Profitability Ratios		
Profit margin	Net income after tax/Sales	Measures the after-tax profit per dollar of sales
Return on assets	Net income after tax/Total assets	Measures the return on total assets after interest and taxes
Return on equity	Net income after tax/Equity	Measures rate of return on the stockholders' investment
Market Ratios		
Earnings per share	Net income after tax/Common shares outstanding	Places net income on per-share basis for investors
Dividends per share	Cash dividends to common/Common shares outstanding	Places dividends on per-share basis for investors
Dividend yield	Dividends per share/Market price of common	Measures current yield on a stock
Dividend payout	Dividends per share/Earnings per share	Measures percentage of earnings paid out as dividends
Price-earnings ratio	Market price of common/Earnings per share	A measure of what investors are willing to pay for a stock

The equity multiplier shows the dollar value of assets financed by one dollar of equity. If the ratio is 2.0, for example, creditors are financing one dollar of assets and stockholders are financing one dollar of assets. Since the cost of debt financing is fixed, the successful use of debt financing to finance part of the assets will magnify the accounting return to stockholders' equity, ROE. For Syntex, the equity multiplier is $1440.2/$587.2 = 2.45.

Using the equity multiplier, we can now see that

$$\text{ROE} = \text{ROA} \times \text{Equity multiplier} \tag{3-14}$$
$$= \frac{\text{Net income}}{\text{Total assets}} \times \frac{\text{Total assets}}{\text{Equity}}$$

For Syntex:

$$\text{ROE} = 21.1\% \times 2.45 = 51.7\%$$

This agrees with the basic ROE calculation for Syntex (ignoring the rounding error):

$$\text{ROE} = \frac{\text{Net income}}{\text{Stockholders' equity}} = \frac{\$303.2}{\$587.2} = 51.7\%$$

Figure 3–3 illustrates the DuPont analysis using the balance sheet and income statement numbers for Syntex. We can immediately see the income statement factors that determine the firm's profit margin (the left side of Figure 3–3), and those from the balance sheet that determine the firm's total asset turnover. As we know, the product of these two variables is the ROA, and the product of ROA and the equity multiplier is the ROE.

Again, the important point is that we can see that if ROE is inadequate, it is a result of one of two determinants:

1. Asset utilization, measured by ROA.
2. How the assets are financed, measured by the equity multiplier.

If a firm is doing an average job with its return on assets, it may still outperform other firms in terms of ROE by using more debt to finance its operations. This is equivalent to having a higher equity multiplier because one dollar of equity is supporting even more assets. Conversely, a firm with an industry-average equity multiplier but a higher-than-average ROE could be identified as doing an outstanding job with regard to return on assets.

If ROA is deemed to be inadequate, Figure 3–3 clearly shows the factors that can be changed to improve the ROA. On the income statement side, either sales will have to be increased or one or more of the expense categories will have to be reduced. On the balance sheet side, assets will have to be reduced unless sales can be increased, resulting in a higher total asset turnover.

▪ *Example*

If Syntex could increase its sales to the level of its assets, the asset turnover would be 1.0 and the ROA would be 22.5 percent instead of 21.1 percent. ▪

Limitations of Financial Statement Analysis

Financial analysis, particularly ratio analysis, is widely used by the firm's managers, its creditors, and potential investors in its stock. It is an important technique, and anyone wishing to have a complete understanding of managerial

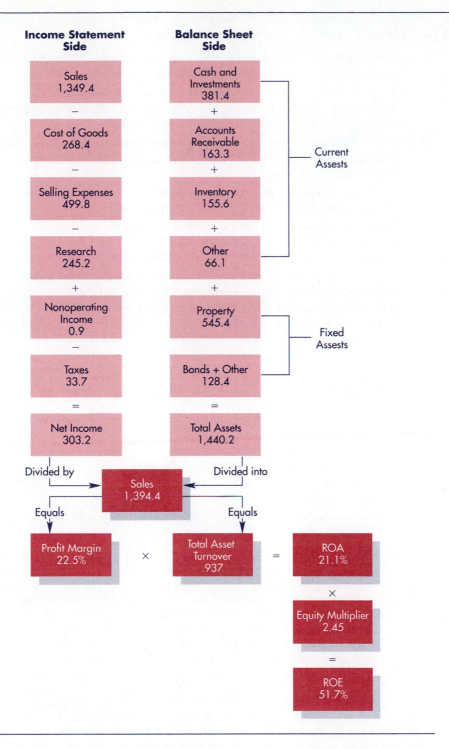

finance must be familiar with it. Nevertheless, financial analysis has limitations and potential problems, including the following:

1. Based as it is on accrual accounting data and historical costs, the current period's figures may not be closely related to cash flows.
2. Because of alternative accounting treatments, comparisons among firms may be difficult. Furthermore, one firm's accounting procedures may change over time, making trend analysis less reliable.
3. Many large corporations have multiple divisions operating in multiple industries, making difficult the compilation of the industry averages that will be used for a benchmark.
4. Inflationary periods can significantly distort a firm's recorded values relative to the actual market values. Both inventory costs and depreciation charges are well known in this regard, and both affect the calculation of profits. Inflation can distort the comparison of ratios for several firms, or one firm's ratios over time.
5. Financial analysis may be distorted by what is termed *window dressing,* whereby a firm attempts to make the financial statements look better for at least a short period of time. An example of window dressing would be borrowing long-term to improve the liquidity ratios at the end of the reporting period and repaying the loan shortly thereafter.

International Perspective

The increasing international operations of firms can make the job of financial analysis more difficult, and, clearly, the international aspect is increasing in importance. Obviously, financial managers, stockholders, and other interested parties will be increasingly affected by international considerations in the 1990s and must adapt accordingly. Consider the following facts:[15]

1. In 1989, the revenues from the foreign operations of the 100 largest U.S. multinationals increased 9 percent to $553 billion.
2. Exxon alone had $63 billion of foreign sales in 1989 out of total sales of $87 billion.

The foreign operations of U.S. companies produce, among other problems, complications in translating the results from abroad into dollars. The dollar amount of a firm's earnings in a foreign country ultimately depends on the exchange rate between that country and the United States. As the exchange rate fluctuates, the earnings figure in dollars also changes. Specifically, if the dollar is weak against a foreign currency, the foreign earnings will translate into more dollars, and if the dollar is strong, they will translate into fewer dollars. Exchange rates fluctuate constantly and cannot be predicted with certainty.

The Statement of Financial Accounting Standards No. 52, "Accounting for the Translation of Foreign Transactions and Foreign Currency Statements," dictates that a company use the primary currency in which the foreign subsidiary operates to translate the accounts at the exchange rate in effect on the date of the financial statements. It is important to note that any gains or losses resulting from the translation do not flow through to the income statement. Instead, they are reported separately on the parent's balance sheet as a part of stockholders' equity.

---

[15]These figures are taken from the *Forbes* international 500 survey, reported in the July 23, 1990 issue.

■ *Example*

In Table 3–1, the Syntex balance sheet, "cumulative translation adjustments" are reported for the three years 1987 to 1989 as $21.5 million, $18.2 million, and $18.7 million, respectively. ■

A Transition from Financial Analysis to Cash Flows

Financial analysis is conducted to identify the strengths and weaknesses of a firm and to assess its performance based on accounting data. As we can see in Figure 3–3, the DuPont system of analysis focuses on the determinants of ROA and, ultimately, ROE. Return on equity is an important component of a firm's profitability and deserves careful attention. Nevertheless, *ROE is only one step in the process leading to the determination of stock price and the maximization of shareholder wealth.* As such, it is not the key item of interest. ROE is one of two components of a firm's reported net earnings per share (EPS). The other is book value per share (stockholders' equity divided by shares outstanding). Thus:

$$\text{EPS} = \text{ROE} \times \text{Book value per share} \qquad (3\text{–}15)$$

$$= \frac{\text{Net income}}{\text{Stockholders' equity}} \times \frac{\text{Stockholders' equity}}{\text{Number of common shares outstanding}}$$

For Syntex:[16]

$$\text{EPS} = \frac{\$303.2}{\$587.2} \times \frac{\$587.2}{113,700,000}$$
$$= \$2.67$$

EPS is a very important variable in finance. Much attention is focused on the bottom line of the income statement, EPS, and rightly so. It is an important factor in helping to determine a stock's price. Recall that investors often refer to the P/E ratio, or the number of times earnings a stock is selling for. Furthermore, the dividend payout ratio suggests that dividends are paid out of earnings—that is, dividends are a percentage of earnings. This can be misleading, however, because companies may pay dividends while earnings are depressed or even negative.

■ *Example*

Dravo Corporation, a NYSE company, reported the following figures for three consecutive years:

Year	EPS	DPS	Cash Flow per Share
1	$(.68)	$.85	$1.87
2	(.65)	.50	1.58
3	(.84)	.50	1.32

■

---

[16]Rounding errors account for the one cent difference in calculations versus reported figures in tables.

In actuality, dividends can only be paid if there is cash available to pay them. Nevertheless, for the majority of companies a close relationship exists between dividends and earnings because dividends are paid out of earnings. The pattern of dividend payments across time tends to be considerably smoother than the pattern of earnings because, as we shall see in Chapter 16, dividends typically adjust with a lag to earnings. Therefore, if earnings are rising, dividends will rise also, but with a lag and more smoothly. If earnings are falling, dividends will eventually be cut, but, again, usually more gradually than the rate of earnings decrease.

Figure 3–4 shows the EPS and DPS for Syntex plotted from the mid-1970s through 1989. Notice that Syntex has enjoyed a strong upward growth in earnings, although not without some dips, such as in 1977 and 1984. Dividends, on the other hand, have either remained constant or grown at a slower rate, although the trend is clearly upward.

Finally, EPS is not the critical interest factor to the firm's stockholders and potential investors. Rather, the price of the stock is the central issue, and share price, as we will see in Chapter 6, is a function of the future cash payments to investors and the required rate of return demanded by investors. Therefore, we cannot stop at net earnings in our study of a firm's profitability and expected

■ *Figure 3–4*
Cash Flow per Share, EPS, and DPS for Syntex, 1974–1989

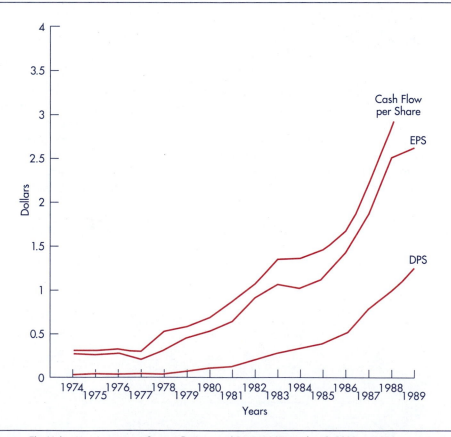

returns. We must go one step further and examine the cash flow of the firm. Although the two are related, net earnings and cash flow are not the same, and a firm's cash flows are very important in the valuation process because the cash payments to be received by stockholders will be paid out of the firm's cash flows. We now turn to an analysis of cash flows.

CASH FLOW

A firm can be profitable according to reported earnings and still go bankrupt because of a lack of cash; in other words, net income does not measure cash flow. This fact alone justifies the need for the financial decision maker to consider carefully the concept of **cash flow,** defined as the amount of cash inflows and outflows during a specified period of time.

cash flow
the amount of cash inflows and outflows during a specified period

The primary reason we are interested in the firm's cash flows is related directly to the objective of financial management that guides us throughout this text. The value of the firm depends on the present value of the cash payments (flows) investors expect to receive in the future. As we saw in Chapter 2, when we consider total return, the only two ways an owner of a stock can benefit financially is from stock dividends and/or the sale of the stock at a price higher than the purchase price. The only cash flows received directly by stockholders from the firm are dividends. Furthermore, as we shall see in Chapter 6, the dividend stream is the basis for a stock's value; because dividends are paid in cash, a firm's dividend payments depend ultimately on its cash flows rather than its reported earnings. As we saw earlier, although Dravo reported losses in EPS for each of three years, it was able to continue paying a dividend because of its cash flows.

Cash Flow versus Accounting Income

Cash pays bills and allows a firm to pay dividends to its stockholders. The continuing nature of any business means that the firm must be able to generate cash from its operations. The net earnings figure is an incomplete measure of the cash availability of a firm. Net income can increase while the cash figure becomes negative. On the other hand, earnings can be adversely affected by depreciation while cash flow is increasing.

■ *Example*

In an article on La Quinta Motor Inns, *Forbes* noted that earnings for that year were likely to be hit hard by high depreciation charges. But "earnings tell only so much," according to *Forbes*. La Quinta's cash flow increased from $1.59 per share to $2.14. Noting that La Quinta's debt ratio was considerably higher than that for other motel chains, *Forbes* argued that "La Quinta's cash flow is comfortably more than double its yearly interest expenses."[17] ■

Net income as reported on the financial statements is the result of a number of compromises, all under the general framework of GAAP. Net income is derived

[17]See Alan M. Field, "Hanging in for the Long Run," *Forbes,* June 16, 1986, p. 118.

after certain write-offs are taken. Typically, the largest two write-offs for a firm are depreciation and deferred taxes.

In accordance with GAAP, *depreciation* is a charge designed to reflect the wasting away of long-term assets such as plant and equipment. To calculate depreciation, the firm writes off a portion of the asset's cost each year, theoretically on the basis of the estimated useful life of the asset but operationally on the basis of depreciation schedules provided in the tax code.

The important point about depreciation is that it is not a cash outlay but rather a noncash charge. Depreciation itself creates no funds—it is only an accounting entry. However, to the extent it previously reduced net income, it should be added back. Depreciation mainly affects the amount of a firm's taxes. It reduces earnings before taxes and therefore the amount of taxes paid (which is a cash outflow).

The easy way to adjust for depreciation in a cash flow sense is to simply add back depreciation to the reported net income after-tax figure. However, this procedure leads one to think of depreciation as a source of funds. As we know, this is not a proper view because depreciation does not actually provide any funds. In Chapter 11, where we discuss the cash flows to be used in capital budgeting, we will use a better procedure that reflects the fact that depreciation is acting as a tax shield.

A second major item to be adjusted for is *deferred taxes*. This item arises because of differences between accounting procedures used for financial statements and those used for tax purposes. Firms often charge off more on their tax return than they do on their income statement, thereby paying less tax while reporting higher net income to the stockholder. That is, taxes paid are lower than taxes provided for on the income statement. The principal item generating this difference is depreciation.

Because the reported income does not reflect the benefit of the lower taxes actually paid, it is necessary to treat the increase in deferred taxes as a source of funds. Thus, we add it back to net income.[18]

For many firms, there is a close relationship between cash flow per share and earnings per share. Figure 3–4 indicates that this is true for Syntex.

Statement of Cash Flows

The statement of cash flows is prepared from consecutive balance sheets showing the beginning and ending amounts for the period and the current income statement (additional selected data may also be needed). The statement itself classifies cash receipts and cash payments into three categories: operating, investing, and financing activities.

- *Operating activities* involve income statement items including cash revenues, interest and dividends received, and cash outflows to suppliers, employees, government (taxes), creditors (interest), and so on.
- *Investing activities* involve cash flows that typically result from changes in long-term asset items, such as cash from the sale of securities of other firms and from the sale of plant and equipment.

---

[18]Other factors also can affect cash flow, including the method of inventory valuation, depletion, accrued expenses, and so on. For most firms, these items are relatively minor.

■ *Financing activities* involve cash flows that result from changes in long-term debt or stockholders' equity, such as the sale of equity securities (a cash inflow) and the payment of dividends (a cash outflow).

Table 3–4 shows the statement of cash flows for Syntex for 1989. The statement begins with Cash Provided from Operating Activities and proceeds with the other two major categories of adjustments—Cash Provided (Used) in Investing Activities and Cash Provided (Used) in Financing Activities. Each of these categories contains several items, both positive and negative. For example, under investing activities we see the capital expenditures made by Syntex for the year. Under financing activities we see both the funds raised by selling long-term debt and the repayment of some long-term debt. Additionally, dividends paid to stockholders must be subtracted in this category.

■ *Table 3–4*
Sample Statement of Cash Flows

SYNTEX CORPORATION AND SUBSIDIARY COMPANIES
Consolidated Statement of Cash Flows
For the Years Ended
July 31, 1989, 1988, and 1987
($ in millions)

	1989	1988	1987
Cash provided from operating activities			
Net income	$303.2	$296.6	$248.8
Items not requiring cash outlays, principally depreciation and amortization	54.4	50.6	40.3
Net effect of changes in			
Trade receivables	(1.3)	(17.7)	(33.2)
Inventory	(16.9)	7.0	(4.2)
Accounts payable	5.7	8.0	.5
Accrued liabilities	13.7	47.8	59.6
Other	(7.8)	(23.2)	(3.0)
Net cash provided from operating activities	351.0	369.1	308.8
Cash provided (used) in investing activities			
Capital expenditures	(143.1)	(111.5)	(84.3)
Purchases of short-term investments	(313.3)	(224.3)	(238.0)
Proceeds from short-term investments	227.8	241.7	168.0
Other investing activities	.9	1.1	15.6
Net cash used in investing activities	(227.7)	(93.0)	(138.7)
Cash provided (used) in financing activities			
Net change in short-term debt	22.4	99.2	11.5
Proceeds from issuance of long-term debt	120.5	2.6	4.2
Repayment of long-term debt	(31.4)	(2.7)	(15.0)
Payment of dividends	(154.4)	(127.4)	(103.0)
Common shares repurchased	(279.3)	(28.5)	(318.1)
Other financing activities	5.0	3.4	1.8
Net cash used in financing activities	(317.2)	(53.4)	(418.6)
Effect of exchange rate changes on cash	(.3)	.9	(1.3)
Net change in cash and cash equivalents	(194.2)	223.6	(249.8)
Cash and cash equivalents at beginning of year	383.9	160.3	410.1
Cash and cash equivalents at year-end	$189.7	$383.9	$160.3

Source: Syntex Corporation, *1989 Annual Report.*

Calculating a Firm's Cash Flow

Our primary interest here is understanding and calculating a firm's cash flows. A first cut at calculating a firm's cash flow involves combining the adjustments mentioned earlier (primarily, depreciation and deferred taxes) with the net earnings after tax. This is what many analysts traditionally have meant by cash flow. For Syntex, this calculation would be (in thousands):

Net income	$303.2
Items not requiring cash	
Depreciation and amortization	54.4
Net income after tax plus noncash charges	$357.6

This calculation shows the basic cash flow of the firm as the sum of its net after-tax income and noncash charges. Typically, the largest of these noncash charges is depreciation. According to these figures, in 1989 Syntex enjoyed a basic cash flow of about $358 million while its net earnings were $303 million—a substantial difference. Although many analysts have often stopped at this point in considering the firm's cash flows, the current approach to cash flow, utilizing the newly required financial statement of cash changes, goes further.

We next consider the *cash flow from operations,* or *net cash provided from operating activities.* This new measure of cash flow is found by adjusting net income (earnings from continuing operations) to cash flow provided from operations—that is, net income is adjusted for items that affect reported net income but do not affect cash. This is done by starting with the figure for net income after tax plus noncash charges, calculated above, and making certain adjustments. These adjustments involve changes in certain current-asset and current-liability accounts. For example, increases in assets such as accounts receivable and inventories must be financed, which requires the use of cash. These increases are shown as negative items in the adjustment. By contrast, increases in accounts payable are added back to net income.

Syntex shows the calculation of cash flow from operations in the top part of its statement of changes in financial position (see Table 3–4); this is repeated to show how this figure is derived.

Cash provided (required) by continuing operations	
Net income after tax plus noncash charges*	$357.6
Changes in	
Accounts receivable	(1.3)
Inventories	(16.9)
Accounts payable	5.7
Accrued liabilities	13.7
Other	(7.8)
	$351.0

*As previously calculated.

This calculation shows that Syntex enjoyed a cash flow provided from operations of about $351 million in a year when reported income after tax was

$303 million. Cash provided by continuing operations in 1988 and 1987 totalled $369 million and $309 million, respectively.

Table 3–4 shows that Syntex used more cash in investing activities than was provided from that source and used more cash in financing activities than was provided from that source. Thus, both of these totals were negatives, and their sum exceeded the net cash provided from operating activities. Therefore, Syntex had a negative change in cash and cash equivalents for the year. Subtracting this negative from the beginning cash and cash equivalents produced the ending cash and cash equivalents. In effect, in 1989 Syntex drew upon its large reserve of cash and cash equivalents to help finance its activities for that year.

What is the significance of these cash flow numbers? As Syntex itself noted in its *1989 Annual Report,* cash was provided by operating activities and short-term borrowing and was used to repurchase its own shares, to make capital expenditures, and to pay dividends to stockholders. And as we will see in Chapter 6, dividends are the basis for valuing common stocks.

In summary, the stock price depends on estimates of risk and expected return. Expected return is a function of the cash flows that investors expect to receive. These cash flows, in turn, depend ultimately on the cash flow provided by a firm's operations, of which net income is a primary, but not the only, component.

SUMMARY

- There are four basic financial statements: the balance sheet, the income statement, the statement of retained earnings, and the statement of cash flows (a new statement).
- The balance sheet shows what the firm owns (its uses of funds) and how it is financed (its sources of funds). The income statement measures performance over a particular time period (typically, one year).
- The bottom line of the income statement is earnings after tax, which on a per–share basis is a very important variable to investors. These earnings can be paid out as dividends and/or retained by the firm.
- The statement of changes in stockholders' equity shows how the components of stockholders' equity change from one period to the next.
- The statement of cash flows is an important new statement that shows a firm's cash receipts and payments, classified by sources and uses. It reflects the increased emphasis on cash flows and emphasizes the fact that net income is not the same as cash flow.
- Generally accepted accounting principles are used to prepare the financial statements.
- Financial analysis involves the study of the financial statements in order to learn more about a firm. It is often associated with ratio analysis, which examines the relationships among various financial statement accounts both at a point in time and over time.
- Traditionally, financial ratios have been divided into four categories: liquidity, activity, leverage, and profitability. A fifth category, market ratios, is useful to investors in assessing the value of the firm.
- Ratios must be compared with a standard (typically, industry averages) to have any meaning. Trend analysis, which looks at the ratios over time, also is useful.
- Like any other tool, ratios have limitations, including the standard used for comparison, differences in accounting methods, the impact of accounting, and the possibility of window dressing.
- A firm can be profitable and go bankrupt because of a lack of cash. Ultimately, we must focus on cash flows because net income reflects a number of compromises and is derived only after certain write-offs are taken.
- The value of the firm depends on the future cash payments investors expect to receive. We need to go beyond a firm's net income and consider its cash flow provided by continuing operations.

■ The statement of cash flows classifies cash receipts and cash payments into three categories: operating, investing, and financing activities. It shows the sources of cash during the period and how the cash was used.

KEY TERMS

annual report, p. 54
average collection period, p. 65
balance sheet, p. 55
book value, p. 56
cash flow, p. 77
current assets, p. 55
current liabilities, p. 57
current ratio, p. 63
debt-equity ratio, p. 66
debt-to-total-assets ratio, p. 66
depreciation, p. 58
dividend payout, p. 68
dividends per share, p. 58
dividend yield, p. 68
DuPont system of analysis, p. 69
earnings per share, p. 58
equity multiplier, p. 70
fixed-asset turnover ratio, p. 65

generally accepted accounting principles (GAAP), p. 60
income statement, p. 58
inventory turnover, p. 64
market value, p. 56
net income, p. 58
par value, p. 58
price-earnings ratio, p. 68
profit margin, p. 67
quick ratio, p. 64
ratio analysis, p. 62
retained earnings, p. 58
return on assets, p. 67
return on equity, p. 67
statement of cash flows, p. 60
stockholders' equity, p. 56
times interest earned, p. 66
total assets turnover ratio, p. 66

QUESTIONS

3–1. What constitutes a complete set of financial statements? What is the newest financial statement?

3–2. Explain the accounting definition that underlies the balance sheet. The income statement.

3–3. Explain how stockholders' equity is calculated on the balance sheet.

3–4. Explain, in general terms, how net after-tax income is calculated on the income statement. Where does cash flow appear on the income statement?

3–5. "Income is reported when earned." Give an example of this accounting principle where no cash flow is involved.

3–6. Can more than one set of financial statements be prepared? Explain.

3–7. What is the relationship between retained earnings and cash?

3–8. What is meant by the term *financial analysis*? What role does ratio analysis play in financial analysis?

3–9. Identify five categories of financial ratios and explain the purpose of each grouping.

3–10. What are the limitations of ratio analysis?

3–11. Leverage ratios like the debt-equity ratio and the debt ratio (debt/total assets) attempt to reflect a firm's financial risk. Unfortunately, there are some weaknesses in these two ratios. Identify and briefly discuss these weaknesses.

3–12. Financial ratios are based on historical data. Of what use are they in developing expectations about the future?

3–13. In comparing financial ratios of different companies, what factors other than major industry classification may be important?

3–14. In each of the following, give an example of how a supposedly good ratio value might, in fact, be indicating a trouble spot.
   a. Fixed–asset turnover ratio
   b. Current ratio

3–15. In what ways might common stockholders redefine return on equity and the debt–equity ratio to reflect their unique residual ownership position?

3–16. Suppose that a firm is interested in comparing its ratios with its industry average but finds that none of the financial ratio industry services carry data on the industry. What could the firm do to accomplish the comparison?

3–17. Explain how a firm with an inferior return on assets (relative to other companies in its industry) can show a superior return on equity. Explain how the opposite situation can occur.

3–18. With regard to the previous question, does a superior return on equity for Company A relative to Company B automatically lead to a higher share price for A? Why or why not?

3–19. What is meant by the *equity multiplier*? In what sense is this a measure of leverage?

3–20. Explain why net income is not the same as cash flow.

3–21. Give two examples of noncash charges that show up on many firms' financial statements. How are these items treated on the financial statements? How do they figure into the calculation of cash flow?

3–22. What exactly is meant by the term *cash flow from operations*? How is this figure determined?

3–23. Explain in general how the statement of cash flows is prepared. What does this statement show?

3–24. From a valuation standpoint, why is it important to know the figure for Cash Provided by Continuing Operations in addition to the reported earnings?

3–25. In valuing a company, what is the significance of the P/E ratio?

DEMONSTRATION PROBLEMS

Consider the following financial statements for Koler Plumbing Supplies for 1990.

KOLER PLUMBING SUPPLIES
Balance Sheet

Current assets	
Cash and equivalents	$_ _ _ _ _
Accounts receivable	424,055
Inventories	210,373
Other	55,040
Total current assets	$ 769,568
Property, plant, and equipment	
Land	$ 6,698
Buildings	103,613
Machinery	262,019
Less accumulated depreciation	241,260
Net property, plant, and equipment	$_ _ _ _ _
Other assets	
Marketable investments	$ 207,898
Other investments	180,109
Total other assets	$ 388,007
Total assets	$_ _ _ _ _
Current liabilities	
Short-term debt	$ 148,055
Accounts payable	116,738
Accrued expenses	230,192
Total current liabilities	$_ _ _ _ _
Long-term debt	$ 53,400
Deferred income taxes	$ 61,800
Stockholders' equity	
Common stock—$1 par value, 69,470 shares issued	$_ _ _ _ _
Capital in excess of par value	22,435
Retained earnings	593,575
Translation adjustments	(1,605)
Treasury stock	5,415
Total stockholders' equity	$_ _ _ _ _
Total liabilities and stockholders' equity	$_ _ _ _ _

KOLER PLUMBING SUPPLIES
Income Statement

Revenues	$3,118,708
Costs and expenses	
Cost of sales	$_ _ _ _ _
Selling, general and administrative expenses	378,510
Other expenses	24,912
Total costs and expenses	$2,916,325
Income before income taxes	$_ _ _ _ _
Provision for income taxes	63,750
Net income	$_ _ _ _ _

3–1. Complete the balance sheet for Koler Plumbing Supplies by calculating the missing items shown by the dotted lines.

3–2. Complete the income statement for Koler by calculating the missing items shown by the dotted lines.

3–3. Calculate for Koler Plumbing:
   a. EPS.
   b. DPS, assuming the dividend payout ratio was 28 percent.
   c. Book value per share.
   d. The dividend yield, based on a year-end price of $40.
   e. The price-earnings ratio, based on a price of $40.

3–4. Calculate the following ratios for Koler:
   a. Current ratio.
   b. Quick ratio.
   c. Inventory turnover.
   d. Average collection period.
   e. Fixed-assets turnover.
   f. Total-assets turnover.
   g. Debt ratio.
   h. Profit margin.

3–5. Calculate the following for Koler:
   a. ROA.
   b. ROE.
   c. Show how ROE is determined by ROA and leverage.

Solutions to Demonstration Problems

3–1. With regard to current assets, cash and equivalents must equal total current assets less all other current assets, or $769,568 − ($424,055 + $210,373 + $55,040) = $80,100.

   Similarly, net property, plant, and equipment is equal to all property, plant, and equipment less accumulated depreciation, or ($6,698 + $103,613 + $262,019) − $241,260 = $131,070.

   Total assets is the sum of total current assets, net property, plant and equipment, and other assets, or $769,568 + $131,070 + $388,007 = $1,288,645.

   Total current liabilities is the sum of short-term debt, accounts payable, and accrued expenses, or $148,055 + $116,733 + $230,192 = $494,985.

   The common stock account, at $1 par value and 69,470 shares issued, must be valued at $69,470.

   Total stockholders' equity is equal to the sum of common stock, capital in excess of par value, retained earnings, translation adjustments (which is a negative figure), and treasury stock (which must be subtracted, not added). Thus, $69,470 + $22,435 + $593,575 − $1,605 − $5,415 = $678,460.

   Total liabilities and stockholders' equity is equal to the sum of total current assets, long-term debt, deferred income taxes, and total stockholders' equity, or $494,985 + $53,400 + $61,800 + $678,460 = $1,288,645.

3–2. Cost of sales must be equal to total costs and expenses minus the sum of selling, general and administrative expenses and other expenses, or $2,916,325 − ($378,510 + $24,912) = $2,512,903.

   Income before income taxes is the difference between revenues and total costs and expenses, or $3,118,708 − $2,916,325 = $202,383.

   Net income equals income before income taxes less provision for income taxes, or $202,383 − $63,750 = $138,633.

3–3. *a.* EPS = Net income after tax/Shares issued
$$= \$138{,}633/69{,}470$$
$$= \$2.00$$
    b. DPS = $2.00(.28) = $.56
    c. Book value per share = Stockholders' equity/Shares issued
$$= \$678{,}460/69{,}470$$
$$= \$9.77$$
    d. Dividend yield = $0.56/$40 = .014, or 1.4 percent
    e. Price-earnings ratio = $40/$2.00 = 20

3–4. *a.* Current ratio = $769,568/$494,985 = 1.55
    b. Quick ratio = ($769,568 − $210,373)/$494,985 = 1.13
    c. Inventory turnover = $3,118,708/$210,373 = 14.8
    d. Average collection period = [$424,055(365)]/$3,118,708 = 50 days
    e. Fixed-assets turnover = $3,118,708/$131,070 = 23.79
    f. Total-assets turnover = $3,118,708/$1,288,645 = 2.42
    g. Debt ratio = Total debt/Total assets = $548,385/$1,288,645 = 42.6 percent
    h. Profit margin = $138,633/$3,118,708 = 4.45 percent

3–5. *a.* ROA = Net income after tax/Total assets = $138,633/$1,288,645 = 10.76 percent
    b. ROE = Net income after tax/Stockholders' equity = $138,633/$678,460 = 20.43 percent
    c. ROE = ROA × (equity multiplier)
$$= \text{ROA} \times (\text{Total Assets/Stockholders' equity})$$
$$= 10.76 \times 1.90$$
$$= 20.44 \text{ percent}$$

PROBLEMS

3–1. Given the following information, determine the total assets for the Billingsley Company:

Cash	=	$1,000
Inventory	=	$3,000
Gross fixed assets	=	$10,000
Accumulated depreciation	=	$5,000
Common stock	=	$15,000

3–2. Given the following information for the Wingler Corporation, calculate the stockholders' equity:

Cash	=	$100,000
Accounts receivable	=	$30,000
Inventory	=	$40,000
Accounts payable	=	$15,000
Notes payable	=	$22,000
Long-term debt	=	$120,000

3–3. Calculate the reported earnings for the Pettway Corporation for 1989 based on the following information:

Net sales	=	$4,800,863
Cost of goods sold	=	$3,439,160
Selling and administrative expense	=	$813,930
Interest expense	=	$13,810
Miscellaneous income	=	$1,183
Income taxes	=	$229,083

3–4. With reference to Question 3–3, calculate the following well-known accounting terms that appear in financial statements:
  a. Gross profit.
  b. Earnings before other income (expense) and income taxes.
  c. Earnings before income taxes.

3–5. Midwest Public Service Company has current liabilities of $5,500,000; a current ratio of 2.2; a quick ratio of 1.3; and sales of $44,550,000. What is its inventory turnover ratio?

3–6. Given the financial data shown below for Crystal Fixtures, determine the following:
  a. Current ratio.
  b. Quick ratio.
  c. Inventory turnover.
  d. Collection period.
  e. Fixed-assets turnover.
  f. Total-assets turnover.
  g. Debt-equity ratio.
  h. Times interest earned.
  i. Profit margin.
  j. Return on assets.
  k. Return on equity.

CRYSTAL FIXTURES
($ millions)

Assets		Income Statement	
Cash and securities	$ 250	Sales	$4,000
Receivables	200	Cost of goods sold	2,600
Inventories	300	Gross margin	1,400
Plant	1,250	Operating expense	1,200
Total assets	$2,000	Interest	50
		Taxes	50
		Net income	$ 100

Claims	
Payables	$ 200
Accruals	100
Bonds	1,000
Common stock	200
Retained earnings	500
Total claims	$2,000

3–7. Schreier Plumbing's most recent balance sheet and income statement are as follows:

SCHREIER PLUMBING
($ thousands)

Assets		Income Statement	
Cash	$ 100	Sales	$800
Receivables	200	Cost of goods sold	500
Inventory	600	Operating expenses	100
Plant	300	Interest	50
Total assets	$1,200	Taxes	50
		Net income	$100

Claims	
Payables	$ 400
Long-term debt	200
Common stock	200
Retained earnings	400
Total claims	$1,200

Find:
  a. Current ratio.
  b. Quick ratio.
  c. Inventory turnover.
  d. Collection period.
  e. Fixed assets turnover.
  f. Debt-equity ratio.
  g. Times interest earned.
  h. Profit margin.
  i. Return on assets.
  j. Return on equity.

3–8. From a return-on-assets profitability standpoint, which of the following situations is most preferable, and which is least preferable?
  a. Profit margin = 2 percent; total assets turnover = 3.0 times.
  b. Profit margin = 7 percent; total assets turnover = 2.1 times.
  c. Profit margin = 4 percent; total assets turnover = 3.0 times.

3–9. Given the following information about a company, find its return on equity:
  Fixed assets = (2)(Current assets)
  Current liabilities = $50
  Inventory = 0
  Long-term debt = Equity
  Quick ratio = 2
  Return on assets = 10 percent

3–10. Determine the return on equity of a firm with financial data given below:
  Current ratio = 4
  Profit margin = 10 percent
  Current liabilities = $1,000,000
  Inventory turnover = 2
  Stockholders' equity = 1.25 times current assets
  Quick ratio = 3

3–11. Midwest Supplies, Inc., with net sales of $10 million, has the following balance sheet:

Assets		Claims	
Cash	$ 250,000	Accounts payable	$ 300,000
Securities	250,000	Notes payable	900,000
Accounts receivable	500,000	Bonds	800,000
Inventory	2,000,000	Retained earnings	1,000,000
Plant and equipment	2,000,000	Common stock	2,000,000
Total assets	$5,000,000	Total claims	$5,000,000

Additionally, some relevant industry averages for companies in Midwest's line of business are these:

Current ratio	2.0
Quick ratio	1.0
Inventory turnover	10
Collection period	15 days

Evaluate how well Midwest Supplies appears to be managing its current assets.

3–12. Given the abbreviated balance sheet shown below for Central Systems Company, find the return on equity if the company's return on assets is as follows:
   a. 5 percent.
   b. 10 percent.

Total assets	$2,000,000
Current liabilities	200,000
Bonds (8%)	800,000
Preferred stock (6%)	500,000
Common stock ($100 par)	500,000
Total claims	$2,000,000

   c. If Central Systems Co. pays out half its earnings as dividends, determine earnings per share and dividends per share in *(a)* and *(b)*.

3–13. Given the following information for the R. Hill Company, calculate the indicated market ratios:
   Given: EPS = $3.00
          DPS = $1.50
   Current market price = $30
   Calculate: *a.* The payout ratio.
              b. The dividend yield.
              c. The P/E ratio.

3–14. Using the information for Syntex for 1987 as reported in Tables 3–1 and 3–2:
   a. Calculate:
      (1) Return on assets.
      (2) Return on equity.
      (3) The equity multiplier.
   b. Show that these three numbers are internally consistent.

3–15. Given the information in Question 3–14, and based on the identity that EPS = Book value per share × ROE: (average shares = 120.2 million)
   a. Calculate book value per share for Syntex for 1987.
   b. Using the above identity, show that the EPS were $2.07 for 1987.
   c. Explain how the factors affecting EPS as reported are related.

3–16. Based on the following information for General Microsystems:
   a. Calculate the EPS and DPS for the year 1988:

   Net earnings = $707.75 million
   Average number of common shares = 217.5 million
   Payout ratio = 49%

   b. Calculate the total amount of cash needed by the firm to make the dividend payments for the year.

3–17. Using the information in Question 3–16 and assuming that retained earnings was $2,310.25 million at the beginning of the year, calculate the retained earnings at the end of the year.

3–18. Using the following information for the Agrawald Company, calculate its basic cash flow, or net after-tax income plus noncash charges:

   Earnings from continuing operations before income taxes = $1,096,803
   Provision for income taxes = $334,205
   Depreciation = $240,100
   Deferred income taxes = $6,192

3–19. Given the following data for Scientific Imprints, calculate the cash provided (required) by continuing operations.

Net income after tax plus noncash charges	$1,077,348
Changes in	
Inventories	$ (91,655)
Accounts receivable	$ (191,525)
Other current assets	$ (19,030)
Other assets	$ (35,463)
Payables and accruals	$ 170,118
Income taxes payable	$ 193,813
Other	$ 7,490

SELECTED REFERENCES

Basic references on financial analysis include:

Fraser, Lyn M. *Understanding Financial Statements.* Reston, Va.: Reston Publishing Company, 1985.

Harrington, D. R., and B. D. Wilson. *Techniques of Financial Analysis.* Homewood, Ill.: Richard D. Irwin, Inc., 1987.

Harrington, D. R., and B. D. Wilson. *Corporate Financial Analysis.* Plano, Tex.: BPI, Inc., 1986.

Helfert, Erich A. *Techniques of Financial Analysis.* Homewood, Ill.: Richard D. Irwin, Inc., 1987.

APPENDIX 3–A   FINANCIAL RATIO ANALYSIS: AN EXAMPLE

As an example of financial ratio analysis, we will apply the ratios presented in Table 3–3 to Weirton Manufacturing Company. The chapter discussion of the ratios is appropriate and should be reviewed. Table 3A–1 shows the balance sheet for the company, Table 3A–2 the income statement. The reporting year for Weirton is $19+8$ and the current market price of the stock is $18.

Liquidity Ratios

The firm's current liabilities ($12,700,000 on Weirton's $19+8$ balance sheet) show those bills already incurred that will mature within the coming year, and the current assets show—to varying degrees—the liquid assets available to meet these obligations. The *current ratio* for Weirton and for the industry:

$$\text{Weirton's current ratio} = \frac{\$19,200,000}{\$12,700,000} = 1.5$$
$$\text{Industry average} = 1.9$$

Bearing in mind that industry averages are not magic numbers, Weirton's liquidity might be too low.

The *quick ratio* attempts to correct for the current ratio's implicit assumption that inventory is as liquid as marketable securities; in fact, inventory is typically the least-

WEIRTON MANUFACTURING COMPANY
Balance Sheet
at December 31, 19 + 8 and 19 + 7

Assets	Dec. 31, 19 + 8	Dec. 31, 19 + 7
Current assets		
Cash and marketable securities	$ 4,000,000	$ 3,000,000
Accounts receivable—net	6,900,000	6,100,000
Inventory	8,300,000	7,900,000
Total current assets	19,200,000	17,000,000
Property, plant, and equipment—at cost		
Land	11,000,000	9,000,000
Plant and equipment	43,500,000	40,000,000
	54,500,000	49,000,000
Less accumulated depreciation	22,400,000	20,400,000
Net fixed assets	32,100,000	28,600,000
Total assets	$51,300,000	$45,600,000
Liabilities and Owners' Equity		
Current liabilities		
Accounts payable	$ 6,700,000	$ 5,700,000
Notes payable	4,900,000	4,400,000
Taxes payable	1,100,000	1,000,000
Total current liabilities	12,700,000	11,100,000
Long-term debt		
Mortgage note—6%	10,000,000	10,000,000
Bonds—4%	10,000,000	10,000,000
Total long-term debt	20,000,000	20,000,000
Total liabilities	$32,700,000	$31,100,000
Owners' equity		
Preferred stock—5% ($100 par)	$ 2,000,000	$ —
Common stock ($10 par)	11,000,000	10,000,000
Capital in excess of par value	2,500,000	1,500,000
Retained earnings	3,100,000	3,000,000
Total owners' equity	18,600,000	14,500,000
Total liabilities and owners' equity	$51,300,000	$45,600,000

liquid component of current assets. Dropping inventory from the numerator of the current ratio:

$$\text{Weirton's quick ratio} = \frac{\$10,900,000}{\$12,700,000} = 0.9$$

$$\text{Industry average} = 1.1$$

Like the current ratio, the higher the quick ratio, the more liquid the firm's position. Weirton's quick ratio is below the industry average, which corroborates the current ratio comparison.

■ *Table 3A–2*
Sample Income
Statement

WEIRTON MANUFACTURING COMPANY
Income Statement
For the Years Ended
December 31, 19+8 and 19+7

	Dec. 31, 19+8	Dec. 31, 19+7
Income		
Net sales	$65,400,000	$65,000,000
Cost of goods sold	53,200,000	52,500,000
Gross margin	12,200,000	12,500,000
Operating expense		
Selling	4,000,000	4,100,000
General and administrative (Note A)	4,700,000	4,400,000
	8,700,000	8,500,000
Net operating income	3,500,000	4,000,000
Other expense and losses		
Interest expense	1,000,000	1,000,000
Net income before taxes	2,500,000	3,000,000
Income taxes	1,200,000	1,400,000
Net income	$ 1,300,000	$ 1,600,000
Earnings per common share		
Earnings before extraordinary items	$ 1.09	$ 1.60
Net earnings	1.09	1.60
Retained earnings		
Retained earnings at beginning of year	3,000,000	2,400,000
Net income	1,300,000	1,600,000
Total retained earnings	4,300,000	4,000,000
Deduct—cash dividends		
Preferred	100,000	—
Common	1,100,000	1,000,000
Retained earnings at end of year	$ 3,100,000	$ 3,000,000

Note A: Included in general and administrative expense are $2,000,000 depreciation in 19+8 and $1,900,000 depreciation in 19+7.

On balance, it appears Weirton's liquidity position is somewhat low. This does not necessarily mean it is too low, as there may be extenuating circumstances not reflected in the ratios. Weirton may, for example, have been very aggressive in managing its current assets. Alternatively, the industry average may be too high. But Weirton's low liquidity relative to industry competitors raises a red flag that warns the new management to investigate this area. The general rule of a financial ratio analysis is that ratios extremely divergent from industry norms on either side warrant further investigation.

Activity Ratios

Activity ratios, or *turnover ratios,* show how rapidly assets are being converted (turned over) into sales. Although generalizations can be misleading, high turnover ratios are usually associated with good asset management, and low turnover ratios with bad asset management.

Inventory turnover shows how efficiently the firm's inventory is being managed. It is a rough measure of how many times per year the inventory level is replaced (turned over).

$$\text{Weirton's inventory turnover} = \frac{\$65,400,000}{\$8,300,000} = 7.9$$
$$\text{Industry average} = 8.0$$

Keeping in mind that there are alternate ways to calculate inventory value—for example, *average inventory* and *ending* (end-of-period) *inventory*—Weirton's inventory turnover is approximately equal to the industry average, indicating that the firm's inventory management practices are about in line with the competition's.

The *collection period* indicates the efficiency of the firm's collection policy by showing how long it takes for accounts receivable to be cleared.

$$\text{Weirton's collection period} = \frac{(\$6,900,000)(365)}{\$65,400,000} = 39 \text{ days}$$
$$\text{Industry average} = 45 \text{ days}$$

The significance of the collection period figure is this: Assuming all sales are made on credit, how many days worth of sales are tied up in receivables?

Weirton's collection period is very low relative to the industry average. However, this is an example of where a ratio may be too good. A collection period this low in relation to the industry norm may mean that Weirton's credit policy is too restrictive. If Weirton relaxed its credit policy by extending credit to customers now on a cash basis, it might increase its sales and profits significantly.

The *fixed-asset turnover ratio* is a measure of how well the firm uses its long-term (fixed) assets and shows how many dollars of sales are supported by one dollar of fixed assets.

$$\text{Weirton's fixed-assets turnover} = \frac{\$65,400,000}{\$32,100,000} = 2.0$$
$$\text{Industry average} = 2.2$$

Higher-than-average fixed-asset turnover ratios reflect better-than-average fixed-asset management, and lower ratios poorer management. However, it is important to remember that book values of fixed assets may be considerably different from the market value, thus, the fixed-asset turnover may be deceptively low or high. Weirton's fixed-asset turnover is slightly below the industry average, which indicates the firm may not be utilizing its long-term assets as well as other members of its industry.

The *total-assets turnover ratio* indicates how many dollars of sales are supported by one dollar of total tangible assets. It is a measure of the firm's total-assets management.

$$\text{Weirton's total-assets turnover} = \frac{\$65,400,000}{\$51,300,000} = 1.3$$
$$\text{Industry average} = 1.4$$

Leverage Ratios

The *debt-equity ratio* is the ratio of the total debt in the firm, both long-term and short-term, to equity, where equity is the sum of common and preferred stockholders' equity.

$$\text{Weirton's debt-equity ratio} = \frac{\$32,700,000}{\$18,600,000} = 1.8$$
$$\text{Industry average} = 0.8$$

Any ratio over 1.0 means the firm has used more debt than equity to finance its investments. Obviously, Weirton has been much more aggressive than most of its industry competitors in using debt. Debt-equity ratios may vary considerably within an industry, but many analysts feel that a radical departure from the industry norm is dangerous, and Weirton may well have difficulty raising money through new long-term debt. This would restrict the firm's future financing mobility.

The *debt-to-total-assets ratio* indicates the percentage of assets financed by debt of all types, whether short-term or long-term. About 64 percent of Weirton's assets are financed by debt. As we know, Weirton is a heavy user of debt. About two-thirds of its assets are financed by debt; only one-third is financed by the owners.

Times interest earned is supposed to measure how ably the firm can meet its interest obligations by showing how many times the interest payments are covered by funds that are normally available to pay interest expenses. This does not include other financial resources that could be made available to meet interest expenses.

$$\text{Weirton's times interest earned} = \frac{\$3,500,000}{\$1,000,000} = 3.5$$
$$\text{Industry average} = 6.6$$

Weirton's times interest earned is considerably lower than the industry average, which reinforces our conclusion that Weirton has used much more debt than its typical competitor. Weirton's creditors and potential creditors may not be too happy with this situation, particularly in bad economic times. The degree to which they are displeased will affect Weirton's future borrowing possibilities. If lenders become too wary of the firm's ability to service its debt, it will be difficult for Weirton to borrow except at very high interest rates and/or with restrictive covenants (agreements between the firm and lender that protect the lender by restricting the firm's financial freedom).

Profitability Ratios

The *profit margin* shows the percentage of every sales dollar the firm was able to convert into net income.

$$\text{Weirton's profit margin} = \frac{\$1,300,000}{\$65,400,000} = 2.0\%$$
$$\text{Industry average} = 2.3\%$$

This is an important ratio because it describes how well a dollar of sales is squeezed into profit. In Weirton's case, on average, each dollar of sales is processed into two cents profit. However, Weirton's profit margin is comparatively low. The profit-margin numerator, net income, is sales less *all* expenses, including interest. Weirton has used debt more aggressively than most of its competitors and has larger interest expenses. It may be that, except for interest expenses, Weirton is doing all right. Many analysts prefer to call this equation net profit margin and define gross profit margin as the sales quantity less cost of goods sold divided by sales.

Return on assets relates net income to total assets; it measures how profitably the firm has used its assets.

$$\text{Weirton's return on assets} = \frac{\$1,300,000}{\$51,300,000} = 2.5\%$$
$$\text{Industry average} = 3.2\%$$

Weirton's relatively low return on assets suggests that the firm is not utilizing its assets as profitably as many of its competitors.

This low return on assets should be cause for some concern. According to the *DuPont system of analysis,* return on assets is the product of total-assets turnover and profit margin:[1]

$$\text{Return on assets} = (\text{Total assets turnover})(\text{Profit margin})$$
$$\text{Weirton's return on assets}^2 = (1.3)(2.0\%) = 2.6\%$$
$$\text{Industry average} = (1.4)(2.3\%) = 3.2\%$$

This breakdown of the return-on-assets formula emphasizes that Weirton is behind the industry in both asset utilization and profit margin. Weirton should find out why its total-assets turnover ratio is below the industry average. It may be that the firm has excessive fixed assets relative to its sales potential, or it may not be aggressive enough in its sales effort. In any event, the firm should investigate this area. The firm also should explore why its profit margin is low.

Return on equity indicates the rate of return earned on the book value of the owners' equity.

$$\text{Weirton's return on equity} = \frac{\$1,300,000}{\$18,600,000} = 7.0\%$$
$$\text{Industry average} = 5.7\%$$

It might seem puzzling that the firm's return on equity is better than the industry average when Weirton's profit margin and return on assets are both less than the industry average. This is due to Weirton's aggressive use of debt. While debt financing causes net income to decline because of interest expenses, it also means the firm issues less equity, which gives the equation a low denominator. This results in a high return on equity. Alternatively stated, the firm is borrowing money at a fixed cost, earning more on the borrowed money than the cost of borrowing, and passing the profit on to the equity holders.

Market Ratios

The income statement (Table 3A–2) provides two of the most interesting and useful items of information available to common stockholders: earnings and dividends. As with many financial variables, earnings and dividends have more meaning when reported on a per-share basis.

Earnings per share (EPS) were $1.09 in 19+8, down from $1.60 the previous year. Despite this decrease, the firm paid the same *dividend per share* (DPS), $1 (see Figure 3A–1). Notice from Table 3A–2 that the total dollar dividends increased by $100,000 because 100,000 new shares were issued, and these new shares also received the $1 per share dividend. Furthermore, the EPS figure was reduced by this additional common stock outstanding. That is, the EPS for 19+8 of $1.09 was determined by dividing $1,200,000 available for common ($1,300,000 − $100,000) by 1,100,000 shares. If the firm had not issued new common, but rather obtained the $2,000,000 from operations, EPS would have been $1,200,000/1,000,000 = $1.20. This reduction of EPS caused by broadening the equity base is called *dilution*.

EPS and DPS are important numbers and play a central role in financial management. In particular, the projections of expected EPS and DPS are very important. We also can analyze Weirton's recent EPS and DPS as time trends.

---

[1]Return on assets $= \dfrac{\text{Sales}}{\text{Total assets}} \times \dfrac{\text{Net income}}{\text{Sales}} = \dfrac{\text{Net income}}{\text{Total assets}}$

[2]The discrepancy between this calculated 2.6 percent return and the previously calculated 2.5 percent is due to rounding.

■ *Figure 3A–1*
EPS and DPS Time
Trends for Weirton

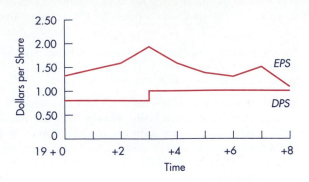

As Figure 3A–1 shows, the EPS time series has fluctuated. EPS rose from $19+0$ to $19+3$, but there seems to have been a declining trend in EPS from $19+3$ to $19+8$. Since EPS reflects the profitability of the firm from the common stockholders' viewpoint, this decline is an obvious concern to the company and stockholders.

The dividend-per-share series has been much steadier, reflecting Weirton's dividend policy. Typically, firms have fairly stable DPS patterns across time, and Weirton's case is no exception. Weirton raised dividends from $0.80 per share to $1 per share in $19+3$, but the current EPS of $1.09 now barely covers this dividend level. If the earnings picture worsens further in the future, Weirton may well reduce DPS. Later in the book we will investigate how firms establish their dividend policy and the effect of this policy on stockholder wealth.

The *dividend payout* ratio in $19+8$ was $1.00/$1.09, or 92 percent. The *dividend yield*, given a current market price of $18, was 5.6 percent. The *price-earnings ratio* was $18/$1.09, or 16.5.

Summary of Ratios

At this point, we may summarize the ratios and attempt to draw some rough conclusions. One of the main points to understand about ratio analysis is that all the information needed for a conclusive judgment about the company is not available in the financial statements. Such conclusions may require information that only management has. So the best an outside analyst can do with ratio analysis is identify areas where something unusual is happening. In fact, most analysts use ratio analysis to identify potential trouble spots. Also, as already noted, ratio analysis is most meaningful when a comparison of company and industry results is made. Table 3A–3 shows the firm's ratios and the companion industry averages.

First, as evidenced by current and quick ratios, Weirton's liquidity seems to be relatively low. This may be because the firm is purposefully aggressive in its working-capital management. However, creditors and even the stockholders may not like a relatively low liquidity position.

Second, Weirton's lower-than-average total-assets turnover indicates relatively inferior asset management. Weirton's inventory and fixed-assets turnover are both low. On the other extreme, Weirton's collection period is quite a bit faster than the industry average, which indicates a tight credit policy. This policy may be unduly restricting sales and could be a contributing factor to the firm's low turnover ratios. These questions certainly warrant investigation.

■ *Table 3A–3*
Ratio Summary for
Weirton Manufacturing

Ratio	Weirton	Industry Average
Current	1.5	1.9
Quick	0.9	1.1
Inventory turnover	7.9	8.0
Collection period	39 days	45 days
Fixed-assets turnover	2.0	2.2
Total assets turnover	1.3	1.4
Debt-to-equity	1.8	0.8
Debt-to-total assets	64%	40%
Times interest earned	3.5	6.6
Profit margin	2.0%	2.3%
Return on assets	2.5%	3.2%
Return on equity	7.0%	5.7%

Weirton obviously has used debt financing more liberally than most of its competitors. This extra debt has several effects. It makes the firm riskier. It also decreases the profit margin because of the requirement of making interest payments that reduce net income. This reduction of profit margin also causes the firm's return on assets to decline, because return on assets equals total asset turnover times profit margin. However, the firm's return on equity is increased by the debt financing. Weirton's profit margin and return on assets are less than the industry average, but the company's return on equity is greater than average. Both long-term lenders and common stock investors may feel that the company's financing policies include too much debt, and the new management should give some thought to this question.

This analysis of Weirton Manufacturing indicates that there are several things to investigate, perhaps including information not shown on the financial statements. These topics will be covered later in the book.

Analysis of Time Trends

Weirton's ratios for the past several years, along with companion industry averages, are shown in Figure 3A–2. For several years, Weirton's liquidity ratios have been lower than those of most members of its industry. Nevertheless, the company has been successful in borrowing, which indicates that creditors are not overly concerned with Weirton's liquidity, even though the company may be paying more for borrowing than its competitors.

The company's inventory turnover and collection period have been fairly constant. Weirton's inventory turnover has fluctuated around the industry average, and its receivables policy has been historically tighter than the industry average. Weirton's fixed-assets turnover ratio has been declining, which is partly explained by the decline in the industry average. The lower fixed-asset utilization has contributed to declining total-assets turnover both in Weirton's case and in the industry average. However, Weirton's deterioration in these ratios has been relatively more severe.

Weirton's debt usage is considerably higher than the industry average, but it has been for some time. This evidence, together with the previous trend analysis of liquidity ratios, indicates that Weirton has been very aggressive in its financing policies.

Both Weirton's and the industry's profit margins have been fluctuating, but in the past three years the company has fallen behind the industry. Part of this decline is due

■ *Figure 3A–2*
Trend Analysis for
Weirton

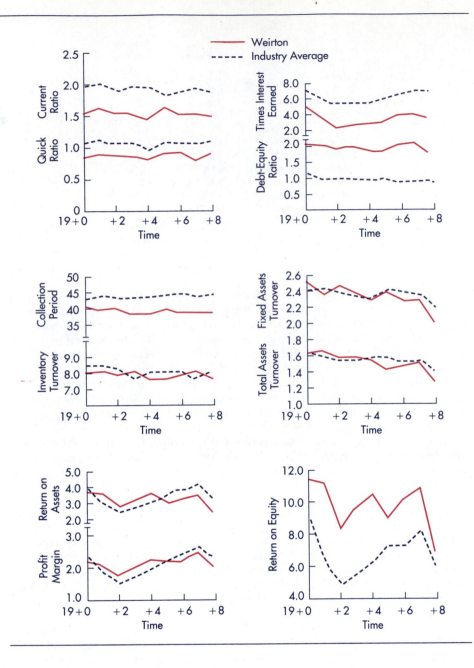

to Weirton's larger interest payments, but notice that Weirton used to have a higher margin than the industry despite its greater use of debt. This difficulty is further highlighted by Weirton's relatively poor return on assets the past three years. Weirton's worse-than-average performance in both profit margin and total-assets turnover has pulled the company below the industry average for return on assets. These difficulties clearly warrant further investigation. Weirton's return on equity has historically been higher than the industry's, which reflects the company's heavy reliance on debt financing.

In summary, there are disappointing trends in several of the company's ratios. Weirton's fixed-asset turnover ratio is trending downward faster than the industry average, and this has caused Weirton's total-assets turnover ratio to decline faster than the industry's average. Also, Weirton's profit margin has been below the industry's for the past few years. This fact, together with an inferior total-assets turnover, has caused Weirton's return on assets to slip below the industry average.

We also should note that our trend analysis has been very limited. We have looked at only eight years of data. If the company's policies have been fairly stable, it would be worthwhile to look at a longer time series to get a better picture of both the trend and the variability in the ratio time series. Where there have been major changes in policies, it may be useless to consider any trends prior to the change.

Time Value of Money

The Time Value of $3 Billion Dollars

In one of the most famous legal battles in corporate history, Pennzoil Company sued Texaco Inc. Pennzoil finally agreed to settle the case by accepting a cash settlement of $3 billion dollars from Texaco, payable on April 7, 1988. Such a massive amount of money moving in our payments system as a single payment from one party to another party is unsettling at best (for example, the most money that can be moved in a single wire transfer through the Federal Reserve System is approximately $1 billion dollars). More important, such a tremendous sum of money is not going to be left idle for any period of time because of the interest that can be earned on invested funds—that is, because of the time value of money.

On the day of the Texaco transfer to Pennzoil, three-month Treasury bills were yielding approximately 6 percent annual interest. Therefore, if Pennzoil were to invest the $3 billion for three months in these risk-free Treasury securities, it could earn $45,000,000. This means that a loss of one day in reinvesting these funds would cost Pennzoil approximately $500,000 in forgone interest in the single safest investment alternative available. If Pennzoil could use these funds in alternatives with higher returns, or reduce any liabilities carrying a higher financing cost, the gain would be even larger. Is it any wonder, then, that Pennzoil used the entire $3 billion within 30 minutes of the receipt of the funds at its commercial bank?

The goal of the firm is maximization of stockholder wealth. Given this goal, the financial manager should be aware of what investors demand compensation for so that they can plan accordingly. Financial theory asserts that stockholders require compensation for two reasons:

1. The time value of money.
2. Risk bearing.

In this chapter, we consider the time-value-of-money concept, and in Chapter 5 we analyze the concept of risk.

The Pennzoil example is a dramatic illustration of one of the most important concepts in finance: Money has a time value because of the opportunity to invest it at some rate of return, and cash flows received in the future are not as valuable as cash flows received today. Since most financial decisions will not involve a sum as large as the Pennzoil settlement, the forgone earnings from not investing immediately normally will not be as dramatic. Nevertheless, the time-value-of-money principle will always be true, and because money has a time value, cash flows received at various points in time are not additive. Adjustments must usually be made for cash flows that occur in different time periods.

The primary *chapter learning objectives* are:

1. To understand intuitively the meaning of the time value of money and why the timing of the cash flows is critical in finance.
2. To learn the mathematical techniques that will make cash flows expected to be available at different points in time equivalent to one another.

FUTURE VALUE

Assume you can earn 6 percent interest on money in your savings account. If a relative offers you a choice between a gift of $100 today or $100 a year from now, which is more attractive? To answer this question we must make the two sums *time equivalent*. If you had the $100 today, you could put it in your savings account and earn 6 percent interest for a year. The interest would be $6, and you would have $106 at year's end. So, with a 6 percent rate of return available, the choice between $100 now or one year later is the same as a choice between $106 next year or $100 next year. Any rational person would, of course, prefer the larger amount.

future value

the amount to which one or more payments will grow when compounded at a stated rate for a stated period

The $106 in this example is the **future value,** at the end of one year, of the original $100 investment. We find this future value by the following calculations:

$$\text{Future value at end of Period 1} = \begin{pmatrix} \text{Original sum of money} \end{pmatrix} + \begin{pmatrix} \text{Interest rate} \times \text{Original sum of money} \end{pmatrix}$$

$$= \$100 + (0.06)(\$100)$$
$$= \$106$$

We can generalize this problem using some symbols: Let PV_0 equal sum of money at time zero (that is, the original sum of money), FV_1 equal future value at end of period 1, and k equal interest rate per period.

Then

$$FV_1 = PV_0 + k(PV_0) \tag{4-1}$$
$$= PV_0(1 + k)$$

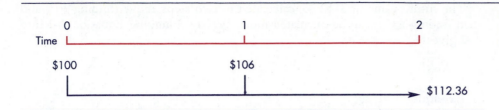

■ *Figure 4–1*
Future Value Time Scale
(k = 6 Percent)

The subscripts indicate what time period the money is in. PV_0 refers to a sum of money today (a present value). However, we will drop the zero subscript because present value usually means the value today (time period zero). FV_1 refers to a sum of money one period in the future (a future value), FV_2 refers to two periods in the future, and FV_n refers to n periods in the future.

Time-Scale Technique

At this point it is useful to introduce the *time scale,* which is a visual aid that will help illustrate time-value-of-money concepts. Time scales are diagrams that show the time equivalence of money sums. We will use time scales to illustrate several time-value-of-money concepts.

The time scale for our example is shown in Figure 4–1, and it indicates that at 6 percent interest, $100 today has a future value after one year of $106. It also shows, as we will see below, that $100 today has a value of $112.36 two years from now.

Compounding

In our previous example we looked only at the future value after one period, but we need procedures for calculating future values over longer periods. For example, what would the original $100 be worth after two years, assuming neither principal nor interest is withdrawn at the end of one year? The key to answering this question is to understand that the second year's interest is paid on both original principal and the interest earned in the first year. Paying interest on interest is called **compounding**. Since we already know the future value of the original $100 at year one ($106), we can easily find the future value at the end of Year 2, FV_2:

compounding
the mathematical process of computing the final value of one or more payments when compound interest is involved

$$FV_2 = FV_1 (1 + k) \qquad (4\text{–}2)$$
$$= \$106(1.06)$$
$$= \$112.36$$

Therefore, if the interest rate is 6 percent, $100 now is equivalent to (has a future value of) $112.36 after two years. Figure 4–1 illustrates this concept by showing that the $106 value at the end of period one is once again compounded at 6 percent, producing a value of $112.36 after two years.

The meaning of *equivalence* is worth emphasizing. The statement that $100 now is equivalent to $112.36 after two years does not mean that $100 equals $112.36. Equivalence simply means these two sums have the same value *after taking the difference in timing into account.*

The future value of $112.36, calculated in two steps above (finding FV_1 and then finding FV_2), can be calculated more directly. Plugging Equation 4–1 into 4–2 gives us:

$$FV_2 = PV(1 + k)^2 \qquad \textbf{(4–3)}$$

■ *Example*

$$
\begin{aligned}
FV_2 &= \$100(1.06)^2 \\
&= \$100(1.1236) \\
&= \$112.36
\end{aligned}
$$
                                                                                    ■

We could continue for three years, four years, and so on, but the generality should be apparent. The future value of a current sum of money at period n is FV_n:

$$FV_n = PV(1 + k)^n \qquad \textbf{(4–4)}$$

■ *Example*

The future value of $100 invested for 10 years at 6 percent interest per year is calculated as follows:

$$
\begin{aligned}
FV_{10} &= \$100(1.06)^{10} \\
&= \$100(1.791) \\
&= \$179.10
\end{aligned}
$$

This calculation is easy if we know that $(1.06)^{10}$, or 1.06 raised to the 10th power, is equal to 1.791. We will see shortly how these values can be determined. ■

We generalize this process for any future period n as:

$$FV_n = (PV)(FVIF_{k,n}) \qquad \textbf{(4–5)}$$

since

$$(1 + k)^n = (FVIF_{k,n})$$

The future value (compound) factor, $FVIF_{k,n}$, is simply the number that is multiplied times the original sum of money to obtain the future value. It is, in effect, the value of $1 at some future period if that $1 earns interest at k percent for n periods.

The Appendix at the end of this text contains the four mathematical tables that could be used in lieu of a calculator. Table A shows the future value (compound) interest factors, abbreviated as FVIF, for selected years ranging from 1 to 50 and for selected k's ranging from 1 to 30 percent. For purposes of illustration, Table 4–1 is an excerpt from that table. We use this table by looking up the compound factor corresponding to the number of periods and the interest rate with which we are working.

■ *Example*

Let $PV = \$2,000$, $k = 8$ percent per year, and $n = 5$ years. To solve this problem, we see from Table 4–1 that the intersection of five years and 8 percent, highlighted by the two dark bands across the five-year row and down the 8 percent column,

■ *Table 4–1*
Compound Factor Table*

Period (n)	Percent (k)				
	2	4	6	8	10
1	1.020	1.040	1.060	1.080	1.100
2	1.040	1.082	1.124	1.166	1.210
3	1.061	1.125	1.191	1.260	1.331
4	1.082	1.170	1.262	1.360	1.464
5	1.104	1.217	1.338	1.469	1.611
6	1.126	1.265	1.419	1.587	1.772
7	1.149	1.316	1.504	1.714	1.949
8	1.172	1.369	1.594	1.851	2.144
9	1.195	1.423	1.689	1.999	2.358
10	1.219	1.480	1.791	2.159	2.594

*For a more comprehensive set of compound factors, see Table A in the back of the book.

is an FVIF factor of 1.469. Multiplying by the beginning amount of $2,000 produces the correct answer of $2,938. ■

Most people today have access to inexpensive financial calculators, and these problems can be solved as easily, or more easily, using calculators than using compound interest tables. Perhaps more important, the calculator will solve for values not found in the tables, avoiding problems of interpolation. We will refer to calculator procedures whenever appropriate.[1]

Future Value of a Series of Payments

So far we have considered only the future value of a single payment made at time zero. In many instances we may be interested in the future value of a series of cash payments of C_1, C_2, C_3, and so on. If we think of the future value of this series of payments as the sum of the individual future values of the separate payments, we can follow the same procedures used with single payments. The future value at period n is FV_n:

$$FV_n = (C_1)(FVIF_{k,n-1}) + (C_2)(FVIF_{k,n-2}) + \ldots + (C_{n-1})(FVIF_{k,1}) + C_n \quad (4\text{–}6)$$

Notice that the first cash payment, C_1, compounds for *n − 1 periods* because one period has transpired when the payment is received and starts to earn interest; the second cash payment, C_2, compounds for n − 2 periods because two periods have transpired, and so on.[2] The next to the last cash payment, C_{n-1}, compounds for only one period, and the last payment earns no interest since the payment is made on the future value date. Figure 4–2 shows the receipt of these payments, and their respective subsequent compounding periods, on the time scale.

---

[1]**Calculator Tip**   To raise an interest rate to a power, enter the decimal equivalent of the interest rate and add 1.0. Then hit the "y×" button, and enter the number of years involved (which represents the power to which the number is to be raised). Finally, press the "=" button.

■ *Example*
Using the information above, enter .08 in the calculator and add 1.0, hit the "y×" button and enter a value of 5 for the number of years. This produces an answer of 1.469 (rounded off) as the interest rate factor. This is the same value obtained by looking in the compound factor table as above. ■

[2]The mathematical notation "+…+" in Equation 4–6 means "and so on."

▪ *Figure 4–2*
Time Scale for Future
Value of Series of
Payments

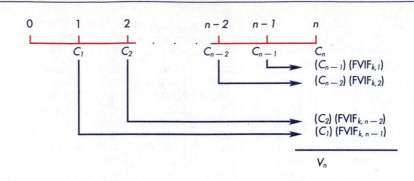

▪ *Figure 4–3*
Time Scale for Future
Value of Sample Set of
Payments (k = 6 Percent
per Year)

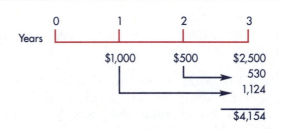

▪ *Example*

Find the future value at the end of three years of the following set of cash payments: C_1 = \$1,000, C_2 = \$500, and C_3 = \$2,500. The interest rate is 6 percent per year. Figure 4–3 shows the time scale for the problem. The future value of this series of payments is:

$$FV_3 = (\$1,000)(FVIF_{.06,2}) + (\$500)(FVIF_{.06,1}) + \$2,500$$
$$= (\$1,000)(1.124) + (\$500)(1.060) + \$2,500$$
$$= \$1,124 + \$530 + \$2,500$$
$$= \$4,154$$

Future Value of an Annuity

annuity
a series of payments
of a specified amount
for a specified period

A special type of future value problem involves an **annuity,** defined as a series of equal payments for a specified period of time.[3] An individual who receives an annuity could deposit each of the annuity payments in an interest-bearing account and accumulate a future sum of money based on compound interest principles. As in the previous discussion, the first payment is received at the end of the first

---

[3] The cash payments are equal: $C_1 = C_2 \ldots C_n = C$; that is, the payment in each period equals $= \$C$.

■ *Table 4–2*
Annuity Compound
Factor Table*

Period (n)	Percent (k)				
	2	4	6	8	10
1	1.000	1.000	1.000	1.000	1.000
2	2.020	2.040	2.060	2.080	2.100
3	3.060	3.122	3.184	3.246	3.310
4	4.122	4.246	4.375	4.506	4.641
5	5.204	5.416	5.637	5.867	6.105
6	6.308	6.633	6.975	7.336	7.716
7	7.434	7.898	8.394	8.923	9.487
8	8.583	9.214	9.897	10.637	11.436
9	9.755	10.583	11.491	12.488	13.579
10	10.950	12.006	13.181	14.487	15.937

■ *Table 4–2*
Annuity Compound
Factor Table*

*For a more comprehensive set of annuity compound factors, see Table B in the back of the book.

period and compounds for $n - 1$ periods, the second payment is received at the end of the second period and compounds for $n - 2$ periods, and so on. The future value of this series of equal payments is:

$$FVA_n = C(1 + k)^{n-1} + C(1 + k)^{n-2} + \ldots + C(1 + k)^1 + C(1 + k)^0 \quad \text{(4–7)}$$
$$= C[(1 + k)^{n-1} + (1 + k)^{n-2} + \ldots + (1 + k)^1 + (1 + k)^0]$$
$$= (C)(FVIFA_{k,n})$$

The *future value of an annuity factor (FVIFA)* is the factor that, when multiplied by the amount of the annuity, produces the **future value of an annuity.**

The future value interest factors for an annuity can be found in Table B of the Appendix. An abbreviated version of Table B is presented in Table 4–2. We read this table as before, searching for the intersection of the number of years and the appropriate interest rate to be earned on the funds. *This table, and most of the problems we will encounter, assumes that the payments start at the end of each period; therefore, the first payment comes at n = 1.* Such annuities are called **ordinary (deferred) annuities.** If the annuity started at the beginning of the period (with the first payment at n = 0), it would be called an **annuity due.** A lease contract often involves an annuity due. An annuity due is obviously more valuable than an ordinary annuity, everything else being equal, because the first payment is received immediately. An ordinary annuity factor can be converted to an annuity due factor by multiplying the factor by $(1 + k)$. Thus, the $FVIFA_{k,n}$ for an annuity due can be found by multiplying the $FVIFA_{k,n}$ for an ordinary annuity by $(1 + k)$. The same will also be true for the present value of an annuity considered below.

future value of an annuity
the dollar amount of a series of equal payments for a specified period when compound interest is involved

ordinary (deferred) annuity
an annuity whose first payment is to be received one period from now

annuity due
an annuity whose first payment is immediate rather than one period from now

■ *Example*

Calculate the future value of a six-year annuity of $10,000 per year if the interest rate to be earned is 8 percent. An examination of Table 4–2 shows that the intersection for six periods and 8 percent is 7.336. Consequently, the future value of a six-year annuity of $10,000 per year at an interest rate of 8 percent per year is $73,360 ($10,000 times 7.336). ■

It is useful to be able to use the future value of an annuity factor equation as well as the tables. This allows us to compute a *FVIFA* when tables are unavailable or for interest rates not shown in tables. The equation is:

$$FVIFA_{k,n} = \frac{(1 + k)^n - 1}{k} \qquad (4\text{--}8)$$

▪ *Example*

If *k* equals 6.5 percent, and *n* equals 10, then:

$$FVIFA_{.065} = \frac{(1 + .065)^{10} - 1}{.065} = \frac{1.877 - 1}{.065} = 13.494 \qquad ▪$$

PRESENT VALUE

present value
the value today (time period zero) of a future payment or payments discounted at a stated discount rate

Present value is the mirror image of future value. While future value shows how much a sum can become at some future date, **present value** shows what the value is today of future sums of money. Suppose, for example, you can buy a Treasury bond that can be sold back to the U.S. government in one year for a guaranteed $1,000. There are no interest payments to consider: you buy the bond today and you receive $1,000 one year later. If your time value of money is 8 percent per year, what would you be willing to pay for the bond today? Alternatively stated, What is the present value of $1,000 to be received one year from now if the time value of money is 8 percent per year?

Equation 4–4 was used to convert present sums into future values. This equation may be rearranged to solve for *PV*. Thus:

$$FV_n = (PV)(1 + k)^n \qquad (4\text{--}4)$$

and

$$PV = \frac{FV_n}{(1 + k)^n} \qquad (4\text{--}9)$$

▪ *Example*

The present value of the $1,000 to be received one year from now, if the time value of money (discount rate) is 8 percent, is

$$PV = \frac{\$1,000}{(1.08)} = \$926$$

A rational investor who can earn 8 percent per year would be indifferent to the choice between receiving $926 now or $1,000 in one year because the amounts are *time equivalent;* that is, the investor with $926 today could invest it at 8 percent and have $1,000 in one year. Figure 4–4 shows the time scale of the present value for this example. ▪

discounting
the mathematical process of reducing future values to present values

This process of reducing future sums by moving them back in time is called **discounting,** and *k* is called the discount rate. Discounting is the exact opposite of compounding and refers to the shrinking of sums of money as they are brought back to the present. Obviously, present values are less than their future values

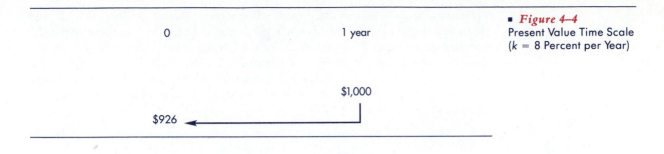

■ *Figure 4–4*
Present Value Time Scale
(k = 8 Percent per Year)

0   1 year

$1,000

$926

■ *Table 4–3*
Discount Factor Table*

			Percent (k)		
Period (n)	2	4	6	8	10
1	0.980	0.962	0.943	0.926	0.909
2	0.961	0.925	0.890	0.857	0.826
3	0.942	0.889	0.840	0.794	0.751
4	0.924	0.855	0.792	0.735	0.683
5	0.906	0.822	0.747	0.681	0.621
6	0.888	0.790	0.705	0.630	0.564
7	0.871	0.760	0.665	0.583	0.513
8	0.853	0.731	0.627	0.540	0.467
9	0.837	0.703	0.592	0.500	0.424
10	0.820	0.676	0.558	0.463	0.386

*For a more complete set of discount factors, see Table C in the back of the book.

because the present sum could be invested today at the rate k percent and compounded to the larger future value.

The discount factor for k percent interest and n periods is denoted as $PVIF_{k,n}$. It is important to note that the discount factor is simply the reciprocal of the compound factor. That is:

$$PVIF_{k,n} = \frac{1}{FVIF_{k,n}}$$

Knowing the future value factor, we can easily calculate the corresponding present value factor.

■ *Example*

Using the previous example of $k = 8$ percent, and $n =$ five years, where the future value factor is 1.469, the corresponding present value factor is 1/1.469 or .681. This figure can easily be verified by using the tables, as shown in the next section. ■

Discount Factors and Tables

As with compounding, tables of discount factors have been developed to ease the computational work. Table C in the Appendix contains a detailed present value table, while Table 4–3 contains an excerpt for expositional purposes. Note in the present value table that all the present value interest factors are less than 1.0, and that they decline as we read down a particular column (i.e., as time increases, holding interest rate constant) or as we read across a particular row (i.e., as the interest rate increases, holding time constant). We can verify from Table 4–3 that the present value interest factor for 8 percent and five periods is .681. When multiplied by the present value interest factor, the future value is converted to a present value. That is:

$$\text{Present value} = \frac{\text{Future value at}}{\text{period } n} \times \begin{array}{l}\text{Present value interest factor for}\\ k \text{ percent per period and } n \text{ periods}\end{array} \qquad \textbf{(4–10)}$$

$$PV = (FV_n)(PVIF_{k,n})$$

- ▪ *Example*

If the time value of money is 6 percent per year, Table 4–3 shows that the present value interest factor for 10 years is .558. Therefore, the present value of $500 to be received in 10 years is $279, or $500 × 0.558.[4] ▪

Effects of Time and Discount Rates on Present Value

Since $PV = (FV_n)(PVIF_{k,n})$, increases or decreases in the present value interest factor cause corresponding increases or decreases in the present value. In other words, variables that affect the present value interest factor also affect present value, and in the same direction. Two variables affect present value interest factors and consequently present values: the number of periods, n, and the discount rate, k.

Recall that the present value interest factor equals $1/(1 + k)^n$. As time increases, the denominator of the factor becomes larger, and therefore the factor (and present value) becomes smaller. Over time periods of 5, 10, 15, 20, and 25 years, using a discount rate of 4 percent, the present value interest factor declines as shown below:

Time, n (years)	5	10	15	20	25
Present value interest factor (4 percent discount rate)	0.822	0.676	0.555	0.456	0.375

Similarly, as the discount rate increases, the denominator of the present value interest factor increases and the factor (and present value) decreases. This is shown by present value interest factors for a 10-year period using discount rates of 2, 4, 6, 8, and 10 percent:

Discount rate, k (percent)	2	4	6	8	10
Present value interest factor (10-year time period)	0.820	0.676	0.558	0.463	0.386

---

[4]**Calculator Tip**   The present value interest factors can be calculated easily using the calculator by remembering that $PVIF_{k,n} = 1/(1 + k)^n$. Enter the interest rate as a decimal and add 1.0. Raise to the appropriate power using the "y^x" key, where the appropriate power is the number of periods being considered. Then take the reciprocal by hitting the "$1/x$" key. In the problem above, notice that .558 is equal to $1/(1 + .06)^{10}$.

This analysis indicates that:

- The more distant a sum of money, the less its present value.
- The greater the discount rate, the less a future sum is worth today.

The discount rate represents an **opportunity cost** of not having use of the future sum today. If the future sum were available today, a rate of return equal to the discount rate could be earned on the money. Because investors with high opportunity costs forgo high rates of return, the higher the discount rate, the less valuable a future sum of money is. Figure 4–5 shows some examples of the relationship among present value, time, and discount rate. The exception to the rule that present value decreases as time increases is the case of the 0 percent discount rate. When $k = 0$, the future value equals its present value no matter when the sum is received. Notice also in Figure 4–5 that for very large discount rates, present value drops off very quickly. A person with a 20 percent discount rate, for example, views $1.00 to be received in period 20 as being worth only about $0.026 today.

opportunity cost
the rate of return forgone on the next best alternative investment

Present Value of a Series of Payments

We now consider the present value of several cash flows, each received at a different time. The series is represented by C_1, C_2, C_3, and so on, where the subscripts indicate the time period when the sum arrives. The present value of such a series is simply the sum of the individual present values of the separate payments:

$$PV = \frac{C_1}{(1 + k)} + \frac{C_2}{(1 + k)^2} + \ldots + \frac{C_{n-1}}{(1 + k)^{n-1}} + \frac{C_n}{(1 + k)^n} \qquad \text{(4–11)}$$

The first payment is discounted one period, the second payment two periods, and so on. This process is illustrated in Figure 4–6. Equation 4–11 may be written more compactly by using the symbol Σ, meaning "to sum up" or "add together." So:[5]

$$PV = \sum_{t=1}^{n} \frac{C_t}{(1 + k)^t} \qquad \text{(4–12)}$$

To put Equation 4–12 in a more practical perspective, we can say that it is equivalent to:

$$PV = (C_1)(PVIF_{k,1}) + (C_2)(PVIF_{k,2}) + \ldots \qquad \text{(4–13)}$$
$$+ (C_{n-1})(PVIF_{k,n-1}) + (C_n)(PVIF_{k,n})$$
$$= \sum_{t=1}^{n} (C_t)(PVIF_{k,t})$$

As Equation 4–13 shows, the present value of a series of payments is the sum of the present value of each individual payment. The present value of any one payment is the payment times the appropriate discount factor. If the time value of

---

[5]This is a somewhat general form of the present value formula. It could be further generalized by allowing the discount rate to change in each period also, but we will not do that here. The problems dealt with in this book assume that k is constant from period to period.

■ *Figure 4–5*
Time and Discount Rate Effects on Present Value

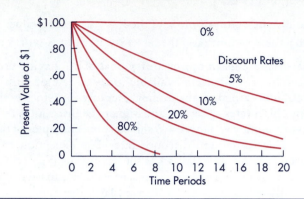

■ *Figure 4–6*
Time Scale for Present Value of Series of Payments

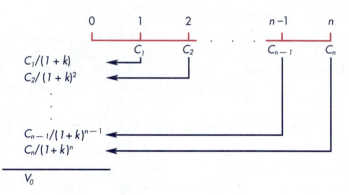

money is 6 percent per year, we can easily find the present value of a series of yearly payments, as shown in Figure 4–7:

$$PV = (\$1,000)(0.943) + (\$2,000)(0.890) + (\$1,000)(0.840)$$
$$= \$943 + \$1,780 + \$840$$
$$= \$3,563$$

The process is the same regardless of the number of payments. For example, with 20 different cash payments, we would find the present value of each one, multiplying together the amount and the appropriate *PVIF,* and add all 20 products together.

present value of an annuity
the dollar amount today of a stream of equal payments to be received for a specified period discounted at an appropriate discount rate

Present Value of an Annuity

We have previously defined an annuity as a series of equal payments of C dollars for a specified period of time. The **present value of an annuity** of n periods, PVA_n, is calculated as follows:

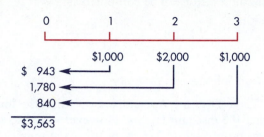

■ *Figure 4–7*
Calculating the Present
Value of a Set of
Payments (k = 6 Percent)

■ *Table 4–4*
Annuity Discount
Factor Table*

Period (n)	Percent (k)				
	2	4	6	8	10
1	0.980	0.962	0.943	0.926	0.909
2	1.942	1.886	1.833	1.783	1.736
3	2.884	2.775	2.673	2.577	2.487
4	3.808	3.630	3.465	3.312	3.170
5	4.713	4.452	4.212	3.993	3.791
6	5.601	5.242	4.917	4.623	4.355
7	6.472	6.002	5.582	5.206	4.868
8	7.325	6.733	6.210	5.747	5.335
9	8.162	7.435	6.802	6.247	5.759
10	8.983	8.111	7.360	6.710	6.145

*For a more comprehensive set of annuity discount factors, see Table D in the back of the book.

$$PVA_n = \frac{C}{(1+k)} + \frac{C}{(1+k)^2} + \cdots + \frac{C}{(1+k)^{n-1}} + \frac{C}{(1+k)^n} \quad (4\text{–}14)$$

$$= C\left[\frac{1}{(1+k)} + \frac{1}{(1+k)^2} + \cdots + \frac{1}{(1+k)^{n-1}} + \frac{1}{(1+k)^n}\right]$$

$$= C\sum_{t=1}^{n}\left[\frac{1}{(1+k)^t}\right]$$

The mathematical portion of Equation 4–14 is called the present value interest factor for an annuity, $PVIFA_{k,n}$. The product of this factor and the constant annuity payment, C, is the present value of the annuity:

$$PVA_n = (C)(PVIFA_{k,n}) \quad (4\text{–}15)$$

These factors are available in Table D in the Appendix, and an abbreviated version of Table D is shown in Table 4–4.

■ *Example*

Consider an annuity of $10,000 per year for six years when the interest rate (k) is 8 percent. Table 4–4 shows that the factor is 4.623 at the intersection of 8 percent and 6 periods. Therefore, the present value of this annuity is $10,000 × 4.623 = $46,230. ■

The annuity discount factor can be computed as:[6]

$$PVIFA_{k,n} = \frac{(1 + k)^n - 1}{k(1 + k)^n}$$ (4–16)

Present Value of an Infinite Life Annuity

A casual look at Table D in the Appendix shows that the longer an annuity is received, the higher the discount factors. However, the discount factor goes up more slowly as time progresses. In fact, as the life of the annuity becomes infinitely long ($n \to \infty$), the discount factor approaches an upper limit. It can be shown mathematically that this limit is $1/k$. The present value for an infinite life annuity is therefore:

$$PVA_\infty = (C)(PVIFA_{k,\infty}) = (C)\frac{1}{k}$$ (4–17)

$$= \frac{C}{k}$$

perpetuity
a series of equal payments that lasts forever

Equation 4–17 illustrates the concept of a **perpetuity,** defined as an annuity that continues indefinitely (i.e., forever). The present value of a perpetuity is easy to value because discount factors are not directly involved. It is very important to remember that the value of k in Equation 4–17 is put in decimal form, and that *k is not added to 1.0.* This is the exception to the rule for the time value of money calculations we will be doing throughout this text. Also note that the higher the value of *k,* the lower the value of the perpetuity because the numerator remains constant as the discount rate changes.

■ *Example*

If the discount rate is 15 percent per year, the present value of a perpetuity of $300 per year is $300/0.15 = $2,000. If the discount rate were to rise to 20 percent, the present value of this perpetuity would be $300/0.20 = $1,500. Conversely, if the discount rate were to decline to 10 percent, the value of the perpetuity would rise, in this case to $300/0.10 = $3,000. ■

Although most realistic problems do not have payments that last forever, assuming infinite life frequently leads to a close approximation of the more precise answer and saves time and effort.

Present Value of an Uneven Series of Payments

In a number of situations encountered in finance, the cash flows will not be identical; this identity is a requirement if we are to use the annuity procedure. In many cases, however, an annuity will be involved for part of the cash flows, and therefore the annuity calculation can and generally should be used. It is worthwhile to point out the obvious first. If each of the payments to be received in the future is different and if the present value of the entire set of payments is to be calculated, it is necessary to discount each of the cash flows separately and then add all of them together, as shown in Equation 4–13. Although laborious, this is not

---

[6]An alternative formula for calculating *PVIFA* is $\{1 - [1/(1 + k)^n]\}/k$.

difficult to do. It should also be obvious that if some of the payments are identical, this same process can be used. In summary, *the present value of any series of payments can always be determined by discounting each cash flow separately and adding the entire discounted set of cash flows together.*

What about the case where an annuity is involved for part of the period over which payments will be received? In this case, we use the present value of the annuity calculation, being careful to recognize the time period over which the annuity is to be received. For example, if the payments stream involves a six-year annuity to be received over the Years 3 to 8, we must take account of this fact. Since the first payment in this annuity is not to be received until Year 3, we cannot simply treat this annuity as we would one for which the first payment is to be received at the end of Year 1.

The solution involves subtracting from the *PVIFA* for the annuity itself the *PVIFA* for the number of years until the annuity starts. Therefore, for a six-year annuity starting in Year 2, subtract the one-year *PVIFA* from the six-year *PVIFA*. For a five-year annuity starting in Year 4, subtract the three-year factor from the eight-year factor.

▪ *Example*

Assume we wish to find the present value of the following stream of payments when $k = 10$ percent.

Year 0	1	2	3	4	5	6	7	8	9
Payment	$500	$600	$700	$700	$700	$700	$700	$800	$1,000

We could calculate the present value of each of these payments and add them together in the following manner:

$$
\begin{aligned}
\$\ 500 \times .909 &= \$\ 454.50 \\
\$\ 600 \times .826 &= \$\ 495.60 \\
\$\ 700 \times .751 &= \$\ 525.70 \\
\$\ 700 \times .683 &= \$\ 478.10 \\
\$\ 700 \times .621 &= \$\ 434.70 \\
\$\ 700 \times .565 &= \$\ 395.50 \\
\$\ 700 \times .513 &= \$\ 359.10 \\
\$\ 800 \times .467 &= \$\ 373.60 \\
\$1,000 \times .424 &= \underline{\$\ 424.00} \\
&\quad\ \$3,940.80
\end{aligned}
$$

Alternatively, note that this problem contains an annuity for the Years 3 to 7. Therefore, the present value of this annuity can be found by subtracting from the *PVIFA* for seven years the *PVIFA* for two years, in effect producing a *PVIFA* for a five-year period where the first payment is not received until Year 3:

$PVIFA_{.10,7} - PVIFA_{.10,2} = PVIFA$ for five years, starting in Year 3
$PVIFA_{.10,7} - PVIFA_{.10,2} = 4.868 - 1.736 = 3.132$

Present value of the five-year annuity of $700 starting in year 3 =
$700 × 3.132 = $2192.40

Total present value of the payments stream =
$454.50 + $495.60 + $2192.40 + $373.60 + $424 = $3940.00.

Except for rounding error, this procedure produces the same answer as discounting each of the cash flows as above. As the number of periods the annuity covers increases, the computational savings from using the annuity procedure becomes more obvious. ▪

SOME TIME VALUE OF MONEY MECHANICS
Solving for Annuity Payments

Instead of finding the future or present value of an annuity, we may be interested in calculating one of the following:

1. A loan amortization problem—what schedule of equal payments is required to pay off a loan by a designated time in the future?
2. A sinking fund problem—what schedule of payments is required to accumulate a certain sum by a designated time in the future?

Loan Amortization Problems

One of the most important type of problems to be solved with compound interest calculations involves the debt-service payments required to *amortize* (pay off in equal installments over some time period) a loan. Many loans require a series of equal payments; therefore, the annuity concept is applicable here. The present value of the annuity is equal to the original amount borrowed. Another way of stating the problem is to ask the question, What equal payment, C, is required to exactly recover a present value, PV, with interest k percent per period over n periods?

The calculation is, again, directed toward finding an annuity amount, but the annuity is one that will exactly recover a present sum with interest.[7] If, for example, the firm borrows $20,000 at 6 percent interest per year and is required to pay off this loan with 4 *equal* payments, what is the required payment? The answer is readily seen by recalling Equation 4–15:

$$PVA_n = (C)(PVIFA_{k,n})$$

Solving for C:

$$C = \frac{PVA_n}{PVIFA_{k,n}} \qquad (4\text{–}18)$$

▪ *Example*

For the problem described above:

$$C = \frac{\$20,000}{PVIFA_{.06,4}} = \frac{\$20,000}{3.465} = \$5,772.01$$

▪

---

[7]This kind of problem is faced most frequently by firms that lend money. For example, when a savings and loan institution makes a mortgage loan on a house, the monthly payment is set up to allow the savings and loan company to recover the amount lent, PV, with interest, by requiring the homeowner to pay back $$C$ per month.

By paying this equal dollar amount every year, the firm is repaying the principal of the loan ($20,000) and also paying interest at 6 percent per year *on the outstanding balance of the loan.* The **amortization schedule** for this loan is shown in Table 4–5. Notice the following points about an amortization schedule:

- The payments are constant each year because we are dealing with an annuity concept, which always involves equal payments. However, the allocation of each of these payments between interest and principal repayment varies each year because *interest is paid only on the outstanding balance of the loan for that year.* The first year interest must be paid on the entire amount borrowed, $20,000, which at a 6 percent rate is $1,200. The next year, however, interest must be paid only on the remaining loan balance outstanding. Note that the interest rate remains constant at 6 percent.
- The amount of interest paid each year declines, whereas the amount of principal repayment increases each year.
- The beginning balance for the loan is the amount borrowed. This amount decreases each year as a result of principal repayments until the ending balance in the final year of the payment schedule is zero. Obviously, as the loan is repaid, the borrowed amount decreases.

amortization schedule
a schedule showing the repayment details for a loan, including the amount of each payment apportioned to interest and to principal

Sinking Fund Problems

The sinking fund problem refers to this question: What equal payment, C, compounded at k percent per period, is required to provide a future sum, FV_n, n periods from now? For example, a firm may borrow money and then be required to make *sinking fund* payments each period so as to have enough money accumulated at the designated date (period n) to pay back the loan. The answer can be found by recalling Equation 4–7, which solves for a future value given the constant annuity cash payment, C:

$$FVA_n = (C)(FVIFA_{k,n})$$

Solving for the annuity payment:

$$C = \frac{FVA_n}{FVIFA_{k,n}} \qquad \text{(4–19)}$$

■ *Table 4–5*
Loan Amortization Schedule for a $20,000 Loan at 6 Percent for Four Years

(1) Year	(2) Beginning Balance	(3) Loan Payment*	(4) Interest [(2) × .06]	(5) Principal Repayment [(3) − (4)]	(6) Ending Balance [(2) − (5)]
1	$20,000.00	$ 5,772.01	$1,200.00	$ 4,572.01	$15,427.99
2	15,427.99	5,772.01	925.68	4,846.33	10,581.66
3	10,581.66	5,772.01	634.90	5,137.11	5,444.55
4	5,444.55	5,772.01	326.67	5,445.34	—**
		$23,088.04	$3,087.25	$20,000.79**	

*$20,000/PVIFA_{6,4} = $5,772.01.
**Slight differences are due to rounding errors.

- **Example**

Assume a firm borrows $1.2 million and the loan principal must be paid off three years from now. The firm can invest money to earn 8 percent per year. What annual payment must the firm make to ensure that the needed $1.2 million is available at the designated date?

$$C = \frac{\$1,200,000}{FVIFA_{.08,3}} = \frac{\$1,200,000}{3.246} = \$369,686$$

This annual deposit of $369,686 is called a *sinking fund payment*. ▪

Determining Discount Rates

Up to now, we have assumed the discount rate was given. We will spend considerable time later in the text, however, finding discount rates. The preliminaries to these tasks are introduced here. The crux of present value problems is as follows: given the future cash flows and the discount rate (k), find the present value (PV). Suppose, instead, we know both the future cash flows and the present value, but not the discount rate. How can we find this unknown rate?

There are three cases to consider:

1. There is only one future cash flow.
2. There is an annuity cash flow series.
3. There is a series of cash flows that is not an annuity.

As we will see, the first two cases are easy to deal with and the third case is more difficult.

Case 1: Only One Future Cash Flow

In this simplest of all cases, recall how to find the present value for one future cash flow (FV_n) from Equation 4–10:

$$PV = (FV_n)(PVIF_{k,n})$$

Solving for the discount factor:

$$PVIF_{k,n} = \frac{PV}{FV_n} \tag{4–20}$$

To find the discount rate that makes future and present values time equivalent, we need only find (in Table C) that rate that corresponds with the discount factor and is consistent with the stated time period n.

- **Example**

If $PV = \$200$ and $FV_9 = \$400$, $PVIF_{k,9} = \$200/\$400 = 0.50$, and from Table C we find the discount rate to be 8 percent per period. Note that this problem could also be solved by using the compound factor table, Table A. Look across the nine-year row for a factor of 2.000, which occurs (approximately) at 8 percent. We can do this because $FVIF_{k,n} = FV_n/PV$. ▪

Case 2: An Annuity Cash Flow Series

Let the size of the annuity be $\$C$ per period. Given the size and length of the annuity and its present value, how can we find the unknown discount rate? Recall that the present value of an annuity is:

$$PVA_n = (C)(PVIFA_{k,n})$$

Therefore:

$$PVIFA_{k,n} = \frac{PVA_n}{C} \qquad\qquad \text{(4–21)}$$

The procedure is the same as before, except that we use the present value of an annuity table.

■ *Example*

If a $300 annuity lasts eight years and has a present value of $1,500, $PVIFA_{k,8} = \$1500/\$300 = 5.0$, and from the present value of the annuity table, the discount rate is found to be approximately 12 percent per year. ■

Case 3: Uneven Cash Flow Series

A more difficult problem arises when there is a series of unequal payments. Suppose the present value of a series of future receipts—$100 in Year 1, $200 in Year 2, and $400 in Year 3—is $500. What discount rate is implied by these numbers? Since the payments are not equal, we cannot use the present value of the annuity table. However, we can set up the problem:

$$\$500 = (\$100)(PVIF_{k,1}) + (\$200)(PVIF_{k,2}) + (\$400)(PVIF_{k,3})$$

We find k by trial and error. First, choose a trial discount rate, say 20 percent. The present value of the series of payments at 20 percent is:

$$
\begin{aligned}
PV &= (\$100)(0.833) + (\$200)(0.694) + (\$400)(0.579) \\
&= \$83.30 + \$138.80 + \$231.60 \\
&= \$453.70
\end{aligned}
$$

Because this calculated present value does not equal the known present value, $500, we try another discount rate. We observe that the calculated present value of $453.70 is too low, so we choose a new discount rate that will raise the calculated present value. Since present value increases as the discount rate decreases, let us try 15 percent.

$$
\begin{aligned}
PV &= (\$100)(0.870) + (\$200)(0.756) + (\$400)(0.658) \\
&= \$87.00 + \$151.20 + \$263.20 \\
&= \$501.40
\end{aligned}
$$

This present value is not exactly equal to $500, but it is very close, so the correct discount rate is about 15 percent. The technique illustrated here will be used later. In work on investment decisions, we will refer to such a derived discount rate as an **internal rate of return.** In financing decision work, we will refer to these derived discount rates as the *cost of capital* or the *required rate of return*.

internal rate of return
the compound rate of return that equates the present value of the future cash flows from an investment to the present value of the cost of that investment

Interest Periods of Less than a Year

Compound factors, annuity compound factors, discount factors, and annuity discount factors all have one thing in common: they are determined by the number of interest periods, n, and the time value of money per period, k. Notice in particular that the definitions of n and k do not specify the length of the time period. In working examples throughout the chapter, we have focused on n in years and k in percentage per year; however, if the interest period is less than a year, we must acknowledge this fact in setting up and working problems.

Some of the most common interest periods less than a year are monthly, quarterly, and semiannual periods. The key to handling such problems correctly is always to keep in mind the generality of the definitions of n and k; they are per-interest-period concepts. It is also important to distinguish between the **stated annual interest rate,** which is the quoted interest rate stated in percentage form on an annual basis and used to determine the dollar interest payment, and the **effective annual interest rate,** which is the interest rate actually paid or earned.[8] A simple example illustrates the meaning of each.

stated annual interest rate
the nominal or stated interest rate

effective annual interest rate
the annual percentage rate that is actually being earned, taking the total compounding effect into account

Assume that an investor can earn money on a savings account at a stated annual interest rate (k) of 6 percent. At the end of one year, a $100 investment would grow to $106—the 6 percent tells us the dollar interest payment we receive. On the basis of annual compounding, this $106 would grow to $106(1.06), or $112.46, at the end of two years. The effective annual interest rate, on the other hand, takes into account the frequency of compounding during the year, such as quarterly or daily. It is calculated as follows:

$$\text{Effective annual interest rate} = (1 + k/m)^m - 1 \qquad \textbf{(4–22)}$$

where m is the number of compounding periods during a year.

▪ *Example*

If our $100 is invested on the basis of quarterly compounding instead of annual, the effective annual interest rate would be $(1 + .06/4)^4 - 1$, or:

$$(1.015)^4 - 1 = 1.06136 - 1 = 6.136\%$$

In other words, the $100 would compound as if it were invested at a rate of 6.136 percent per year instead of 6 percent. At the end of two years, the investment would have a value of $100(1.06136)^2 = $112.65. ▪

Obviously, the more frequent the compounding, the larger the effective annual interest rate. Table 4–6 shows the differences in effective rates for several frequencies of compounding if $k = 10$ percent. For a one-year horizon, the effective annual rate increases from 10 percent to approximately 10.52 percent under continuous compounding, which is the limit one can achieve.

As the compounding period is shortened and the number of compounding periods increases towards infinity, we reach the limit of compounding—continuous compounding. For a one year horizon, this limit is:

$$\text{Continuous compounding rate for one period} = e^k - 1.0 \qquad \textbf{(4–23)}$$

---

[8]The stated annual interest rate is sometimes called the nominal interest rate, and the effective rate is also called the true interest rate or the annual percentage rate (APR).

Nominal Rate	Frequency of Compounding	Equation		Effective Annual Rate
.10	Annual	$[1 + (.10/1)^1)]$	-1.0	.10
.10	Semiannual	$[1 + (.10/2)^2)]$	-1.0	.1025
.10	Quarterly	$[1 + (.10/4)^4)]$	-1.0	.1038
.10	Monthly	$[1 + (.10/12)^{12})]$	-1.0	.1047
.10	Daily	$[1 + (.10/365)^{365})]$	-1.0	.10516
.10	Continuous*	e^{kn}	-1.0	.10517

*e = 2.7183.

■ *Table 4–6*
Effective Annual Rates Using a 10 Percent Nominal Rate for Various Frequencies of Compounding

where the constant e is approximately equal to 2.71828 and k is defined as before.

■ *Example*

A stated annual rate of 12 percent continuously compounded is equal to $e^{0.12} - 1.0$, or $1.12750 - 1.0 = .12750$, or 12.75 percent.[9] ■

To calculate a future value for one period using a continuously compounded rate, we simply modify Equation 4–5 as follows:

$$FV_n = (PV)(e^k) \qquad (4\text{–}24)$$

■ *Example*

$200 invested for one year at a 10% continuously compounded rate would be worth $200 $(e^{0.10})$ = $200(1.1052) = $221.04. ■

Continuous compounding has several applications in the theory of finance and is a useful concept to know. On a practical basis, for a one-year horizon, as Table 4–6 illustrates, there is only the slightest of differences between daily compounding and continuous compounding. As the time horizon extends, however, the difference in the final results between these two frequencies of compounding becomes more dramatic.

To calculate FV_n when compounding occurs more frequently than once a year *and a multiple-year horizon is involved,* we can modify Equation 4–4, using what we learned in 4–22, as follows:

$$FV_n = (C)(1 + k/m)^{mn} \qquad (4\text{–}25)$$

We adjust for the number of years by multiplying the number of years by the frequency of compounding within a year.

■ *Example*

Suppose a firm is putting $1 million into a savings account that pays 8 percent interest compounded quarterly. The firm expects to leave the money in this

[9]**Calculator Tip** To compute this value, enter the stated rate as a decimal and hit the "e^x" key. Subtract 1.0 to obtain the rate.

account for five years. How much will be in the account at the end of the five years? Asked differently, What is the future value of the $1 million? We know that $FV_n = (PV)(FVIF_{k,n}) = (\$1,000,000)(FVIF_{k,n})$ and that we must adjust both the discount rate, which is a stated annual rate, and the number of periods because the interest paid is a quarter in this example.

$$k = \frac{\text{Stated annual interest rate}}{\text{Number of interest periods per year}}$$

$$n = (\text{Number of interest periods per year}) \times (\text{Number of years})$$

Therefore,

$$FV_{20} = (\$1,000,000)(FVIF_{.02,20})$$
$$= (\$1,000,000)(1.486) = \$1,486,000$$ ∎

▪ *Example*

As another example, let's find the present value of $2,000 due in five years if the time value of money is 6 percent, compounded semiannually. In this case, $k = 0.06/2 = 0.03$ and $n = (2)(5) = 10$. Therefore:

$$PV = (\$2,000)(PVIF_{.03,10}) = (\$2,000)(0.744) = \$1,488$$ ∎

It is important to remember in problems like these that neither the procedures nor the formulas have changed, but we must be careful in determining n and k. The key to working problems where the interest period is less than a year is to set the problem up so that n is the number of interest periods and k the interest rate per period.

We can easily adjust our continuous compounding formula for multiple periods as follows:

$$\text{Continuous compounding factor for multiple periods} = e^{kn} \quad \textbf{(4–26)}$$

and

$$FV_n = (PV)(e^{kn}) \quad \textbf{(4–27)}$$

▪ *Example*

Assume that you invest $200 for five years at a continuously compounded rate of 10 percent. The original $200 would grow to $200 $(e^{0.10(5)}) = \$200(e^{0.50}) = \$200(1.64872) = \$329.74$. ∎

SUMMARY

▪ The basic idea of the time value of money is that money received in the future is not as valuable as money received today. Development of the time-value-of-money concept permits comparison of sums of money that are available at different points in time.

▪ The future value, FV_n, of a present sum of money, PV, compounded for n periods at k percent per period is:

$$FV_n = (PV)(1 + k)^n = (PV)(FVIF_{k,n})$$

where $FVIF_{k,n}$ is the compound factor for n periods and k percent interest per period.

■ The future value of a series of payments is merely the sum of the individual future values of the separate payments. In the special case where all payments are equal, the series is called an annuity, and the future value of the annuity is:

$$FVA_n = (C)(FVIFA_{k,n})$$

where $FVIFA_{k,n}$ is the annuity compound factor for n periods and k percent interest per period, and C is the amount of the annuity payment.

■ If the time value of money is k percent, the present value of a sum of money to be received n periods from now is:

$$PV = \frac{FV_n}{(1 + k)^n} = (FV_n)(PVIF_{k,n})$$

where $PVIF_{k,n}$ is the discount factor for n periods and k percent discount rate.

■ The present value of a series of payments is equal to the sum of the present values of the individual payments:

$$PV = \sum_{t=1}^{n} \frac{C_t}{(1 + k)^t} = \sum_{t=1}^{n} (C_t)(PVIF_{k,t})$$

■ If the series is an annuity:

$$PVA_n = (C)(PVIFA_{k,n})$$

■ If the annuity has an infinite life, it is a perpetuity, and:

$$PV = \frac{C}{k}$$

■ For a loan amortization problem, divide the amount borrowed, PVA_n, by the $PVIFA_{k,n}$ to determine the equation payments, C, required to repay the loan.

$$C = PVA_n/PVIFA_{k,n}$$

■ For a sinking fund problem, the annuity payment, C, can be calculated by dividing the future amount, FVA_n, by the $FVIFA_{k,n}$.

$$C = FVA_n/FVIFA_{k,n}$$

■ The stated annual interest rate, k, is the quoted interest rate, while the effective annual interest rate is the interest rate actually paid or earned. It is calculated as:

$$(1 + k/m)^m - 1$$

where m is the number of compounding periods during a year.

■ To calculate FV_n when compounding occurs more frequently than once a year *and a multiple year horizon is involved:*

$$FV_n = (C)(1 + k/m)^{mn}$$

■ To calculate FV_n with continuous compounding:

$$FV_n = (PV)(e^{kn})$$

KEY TERMS

QUESTIONS

4–1. Explain the relationship between present value and compound value.

4–2. Explain how compound value factors can be determined using a calculator.

4–3. Define an annuity. Distinguish between an ordinary annuity and an annuity due.

4–4. Explain why all present value factors must be less than 1.0.

4–5. Explain the effects of time and discount rates on present values.

4–6. Under what condition is the future value always equal to its present value no matter when the sum is received?

4–7. Explain how, using the tables at the end of the text, you could determine when a sum of money doubles if you know the interest rate being earned on the money. Explain when it triples.

4–8. What is the upper limit of the discount factor as the life of an annuity becomes infinitely long?

4–9. In most time-value-of-money problems, we add 1.0 to the interest rate before doing anything else. What is the exception to this procedure?

4–10. Distinguish between the stated annual interest rate and the effective annual interest rate.

4–11. What is the future value of a perpetuity? What is the present value of a perpetuity?

4–12. How is a perpetuity related to an annuity?

4–13. What relationship exists between discount factors and annuity discount factors?

4–14. Explain the relationship between e^k and $(1 + k)$.

4–15. Explain why the value of e forms the basis of continuous compounding.

4–16. Explain how, under continuous compounding, we can obtain the effective rate of interest for a stated interest rate k.

4–17. Explain how we can express the present value of a given future amount under conditions of continuous compounding, for example, $PV = (FV_n)(e^{-kn})$.

4–18. If someone promised to pay you $1,000 five years from now, would you prefer that this be under the conditions of finite interest calculations or continuous compounding calculations? Assume your opportunity cost is 10 percent.

4–19. Two investors are contemplating buying a U.S. Treasury bill that promises to pay the owner of the bill $10,000 in 180 days. Investor A has a time value of money of 8 percent, and investor B has a time value of money of 10 percent.
  a. Which investor would be willing to pay more for the bill? Why?
  b. Suppose the bill were for 90 days. What would this change in maturity do to the price that either investor would be willing to pay?

4–20. Assume that an American chemical company has just purchased and paid for mineral rights to bauxite deposits in Africa. Under terms of the contract, the company may not have access to the bauxite until after the African government completes further geological exploration of the area. Other things being equal, what would the following conditions imply about the present value of the company's bauxite holdings? Explain your answers.
  a. During the interim for exploration, the firm's time value of money decreases.
  b. Because of weather difficulties and government planning priorities, the exploration is delayed for several months.

      c. Further exploration reveals that the deposit is smaller than originally thought.

      d. Because of a change of governments in the African country, the company is advised that, although it still has the right to extract the bauxite, the rate at which the mineral may be extracted will not be as fast as originally agreed upon.

4–21. Suppose that you are contemplating investing in one of two different stocks, A and B, that offer expected rates of return of 10 percent and 12 percent, respectively.

      a. What factors might cause this discrepancy in rates of return?

      b. Under what conditions might you prefer to purchase Stock A?

4–22. Explain how you would use the concept of the effective annual interest rate to determine what rate Bank X would have to pay you using annual compounding for you to be indifferent between it and Bank Y, which is using semiannual compounding.

DEMONSTRATION PROBLEMS

4–1. Find the future value of a $500 deposit at the end of 10 years if the interest rate to be earned is 15 percent. Find the present value of $2,023 to be received 10 years from now if the discount rate is 15 percent.

4–2. You have a choice of receiving 30 payments of $30,000 a year, with the first payment to be received one year from now, or $150,000 in cash today. If your opportunity cost is 20 percent, which would you prefer?

4–3. How much must you invest each year in a sinking fund to earn $50,000 after 15 years? The interest rate to be earned is 10 percent.

4–4. A firm borrows $200,000 at 15 percent interest and must pay off the loan in 10 years. What is the required annual payment?

4–5. You are offered an annuity contract today for a cost of $13,420 that will pay you $2,000 a year for 10 years (the first payment to be made one year from now). What is the rate of return implied by this contract?

4–6. If the nominal interest rate is 8 percent but compounding occurs quarterly, what is the effective annual interest rate? What would the rate be under continuous compounding?

Solutions to Demonstration Problems

4–1. The $FVIF_{k,n}$ factor for 10 years and 15 percent, is 4.046, which can be found by using Table A in the Appendix or by raising 1.15 to the 10th power on a calculator. Therefore:

$$FV_n = \$500(4.046) = \$2,023$$

The present value of the $2,023 to be received 10 years from now is found by looking up the $PVIF_{k,n}$ in Table C of the Appendix, or by taking the reciprocal of 1.15 raised to the 10th power and multiplying this factor by the $2,023. Therefore:

$$PV = \$2,023(.247) \approx \$500$$

We should realize instinctively that the present value of the $2,023 must be $500 because compounding and discounting are opposites of each other, and in this case all of the numbers are the same. (Rounding errors account for small differences.)

4–2. We can calculate the present value of the $30,000 annuity by looking up the $PVIFA_{k,n}$ factor for 30 periods and 20 percent in Table D of the Appendix and multiplying this factor by $30,000. This factor is 4.979. Therefore:

$$PVA_n = \$30,000(4.979) = \$149,370$$

Since $150,000 today is larger, we would prefer this alternative.

4–3. To solve this problem, we set the amount to be accumulated equal to the product of the annual payment and the annuity compound factor for the relevant number of years and interest rate as found in Table C. Therefore:

$$\$50,000 = C(FVIFA_{k,n})$$
$$\$50,000 = C(31.772)$$
$$C = \$1,573.71$$

4–4. This is a loan amortization problem. The formula is:

$$PVA_n = (C)(PVIFA_{k,n})$$
$$C = PVA_n/PVIFA_{k,n}$$
$$C = \$200,000/5.019 = \$39,848.58$$

4–5. In this problem the present value of the contract, $13,420, and the equal annual payments of the annuity, $2,000, are known. Therefore,

$$\$13,420 = \$2,000\ (PVIFA_{k,n})$$
$$PVIFA = \$13,420/\$2,000 = 6.710$$
$$k = 8 \text{ percent (from Table D, looking across the 10 year row)}$$

4–6. The effective annual interest rate $= (1 + k/m)^m - 1$. Therefore,

$$(1 + .08/4)^4 - 1 = (1.02)^4 - 1 = 1.0824 - 1 = .0824, \text{ or } 8.24 \text{ percent}$$

Under continuous compounding, the effective annual rate would be:

$$e^k - 1 = e^{.08} - 1 = 1.0833 - 1 = .0833, \text{ or } 8.33 \text{ percent}$$

PROBLEMS

4–1. If you place $5,000 in a savings account, what will be the amount in the account after four years if it earns 15 percent annual interest?
   a. Use the interest rate tables to solve this problem.
   b. Use a calculator to solve this problem.

4–2. Calculate the future value of a $1,000 deposit at the end of 20 years if the interest rate is 10 percent. Recalculate the future value if the interest rate is 20 percent, and compare your answers.

4–3. Find the future value of the following income stream as of Year 30, assuming that the appropriate interest rate is 15 percent per year.

Year	1	2--------9	10	11---------30
Income	$100	$100------$100	$100	$300-------$300

4–4. Calculate the future value of an annuity of $100 per year for 20 years if the interest rate is 10 percent. Recalculate the problem assuming the interest rate is 20 percent and compare the two answers.

4–5. Calculate the future value of an annuity of $500 per year for 10 years, assuming an interest rate of 25 percent, by using the formula to calculate the annuity compound factor.

4–6. Calculate the present value and then the future value at the end of Period 6 for each of the following cash flow streams. Assume an interest rate of 8 percent.

Period	1	2	3	4	5	6
A	$200	$200	$200	$200	$300	$300
B	150	150	150	150	150	150
C	150	180	210	70	125	90
D	300	300	−100	75	200	300

4–7. Calculate the present value of $5,000 to be received 20 years from now if the discount rate is 10 percent. Redo the problem assuming the discount rate is 20 percent and compare your answers.

4–8. Using your calculator, calculate the discount factor for 20 percent for 20 years. Also, calculate the discount factor for 20 percent for 40 years.

4–9. Having just won a crossword puzzle contest, you may take your prize in any of three cash flow patterns. If money is worth 20 percent per year to you, which pattern would you most prefer? Which pattern would you least prefer?

			Year		
Pattern	1	2	3	4	5
A	$200	$200	$ 200	$200	$200
B	0	0	1,000	0	0
C	0	0	400	400	400

4–10. Congratulations! You have won the Reader's Digress Sweepstakes. You have the choice of receiving 15 payments of $12,000 a year, first payment to be received one year from now, or $100,000 in cash today. If your opportunity cost is 10 percent, which should you choose?

4–11. Burley and Bright Tobacco Ltd. manufactures and sells a popular chewing tobacco. The company receives about a $20,000 cash flow each year from the product after all expenses, including taxes. Harris Cigars recently offered to buy the product for $160,000. Assuming Burley and Bright's discount rate is 10 percent, should they sell the product if they think its estimated life expectancy is:
   a. 15 years?
   b. Indefinitely long?

4–12. How much money must be invested each year in a sinking fund earning 7 percent per annum in order to have $20,000 accumulated after 10 years?

4–13. Fielitz Mining Company is establishing a sinking fund to pay off a $100,000 loan that matures on May 20, 19+9. Payments to the sinking fund must be made annually for 10 years on May 20; the first payment is due in 19+0 and the last in 19+9. Fielitz is required to make *equal* annual payments, and the company anticipates that money paid to the sinking fund will earn 8 percent per year. Determine the amount of the annual sinking fund payment.

4–14. Mr. Call is preparing to spend a lump sum of $17,000 now for an annuity that will pay him $2,000 per year for 15 years, beginning one year from now. What rate of return is implied by this contract?

4–15. Consider the following series of cash flows: $C_1 = \$200$, $C_2 = \$200$, $C_3 = \$200$, $C_4 = \$500$, $C_5 = \$500$. Find the present value of the series at $k = 0.20$.

4–16. With reference to Problem 4–15, if your company can acquire the series of cash flows for $1,000 today, what rate of return will your company earn on its investment?

4–17. A man must pay back a debt of $1,000 in a lump sum after five years. Suppose, instead, the loan were repaid in semiannual payments, the first due six months from now and the last at loan termination? What would be the amount of each installment if money is worth 10 percent compounded semiannually?

4–18. Find the present value of a series of 10 monthly payments of $500 each that begins next month. The nominal interest rate is 24 percent per year, compounded monthly.

4–19. You've just borrowed $10,000 to buy a car. You're going to make equal monthly payments beginning next month. How large a payment must you make if:
   a. You make 40 payments and $k = 0.02$ per month.
   b. You make 30 payments and $k = 0.02$ per month.
   c. You make 30 payments and $k = 0.01$ per month.

4–20. A company will borrow $50,000 today and is required to pay off this loan in equal quarterly installments. The lender's required rate of return is 8 percent compounded quarterly, and the length of the loan is five years.
   a. Find the amount of the quarterly payment.
   b. Suppose the loan is retired instead by a single payment at the end of the loan. How large a payment must be made at that time to repay the loan principal plus interest owed?

4–21. A firm is attempting to arrange a loan from a bank to purchase some equipment. The firm has talked to four different banks and gotten loan terms from ea '. Calculate the rate of return the firm would be paying in each case:
   a. Bank A loans $10,000 today to the firm; the firm pays the bank $15,38! the end of five years.
   b. Bank B loans $10,000 today; the firm pays the bank $3,500 per year at : end of each year for four years.
   c. Bank C loans $10,000 today; the firm pays $2,000 per year the first three ye: and then $4,000 per year for two more years (all payments at year-end).

4–22. A company buys a $100,000 piece of land by paying 20 percent down and t remainder in annual payments of $20,000 for five years, with a $50,000 payme... in year six. What interest rate is the company paying?

4–23. Your finance professor makes you the following offer: He will give you $500 at the end of every six months for the next five years if you agree to pay him back $500 every six months for the following 10 years. Should you accept this offer if your opportunity cost (discount rate) is 18 percent, compounded semiannually?

4–24. Mr. Joy is 60 years old, and a life insurance agent is trying to interest him in an annuity that would pay $1,000 per year (payable once a year) for 15 years.
   a. What would be the maximum amount Mr. Joy should pay for the annuity today, assuming his time value of money is 8 percent and the first payment begins in one year?
   b. How much should Mr. Joy spend if his first payment arrives in five years?
   c. Suppose that Mr. Joy buys the annuity that begins paying after one year. Immediately after receiving the eighth payment, he attempts to sell the remainder of the annuity to a third party. What is the minimum price Mr. Joy should accept if his time value of money is unchanged?
   d. What minimum price would be acceptable if he decided instead to sell the remainder of the annuity immediately *before* the eighth payment?

4–25. Given the following nominal interest rates, compounding frequencies, and lengths of time involved:

	Nominal Interest Rate (%)	Compounding Frequency	Time (Years)
A	16	Quarterly	6
B	8	Semiannually	9
C	10	Yearly	20
D	20	Daily	3
E	12	Monthly	5

    a. Find the interest rate per period, k, and the number of interest periods, m, in each case:

    b. Calculate the effective *annual* interest rate for each case.

    c. Assuming a beginning amount of $1,000, calculate the ending wealth, FV_n, for each of the five cases based on the effective interest rate.

4–26. A firm borrows $100,000 at 10 percent interest and is required to pay off the loan in five years.

    a. What is the required payment?

    b. Develop the amortization schedule for this loan.

4–27. Assume you invest $20,000 in an account for 8 years. What will you have at the end of that period if the account pays:

    a. Ten percent a year.

    b. Ten percent continuously compounded.

4–28. What is the effective annual interest rate under continuous compounding if the stated annual rate is 15 percent? 20 percent?

4–29. What is the present value of $1,000 to be received in five years if the rate is 9 percent compounded continuously?

4–30. Assume you will contribute $2,000 a year to an IRA account for the next 40 years, with the first payment due one year from now. How much will you accumulate if the interest rate earned on these funds is 10 percent? 15 percent?

4–31. Given the information in Problem 4–30, how much would the equal annual payments have to be to accumulate $1,000,000 in 40 years?

4–32. Assume you will contribute $5,000 a year to your retirement account, with the first payment being made immediately. You will earn 9 percent on these funds. How much can you expect to accumulate after 40 years?

5

Risk Concepts

The Nature of Risk

U.S. Sprint is the long-distance telephone company jointly owned since 1986 by GTE and United Tele-communications. Sprint was the end result of a large risk undertaken by GTE in 1983 to become a major player in the long-distance phone business upon the breakup of the dominant AT&T operation. The risk was that a massive investment by GTE—$3 billion in direct investment and almost $1 billion in pre-tax losses in five years—would pay off when a new, modern network was in place. GTE's stock price was adversely affected during those years, and United Telecom, which also suffered heavy losses in Sprint, experienced very little movement in its stock price.

By May 1988, a 20,000-mile optical-fiber phone network, the first of its kind, was installed. While more red ink was forecast—$250 million to $300 million—Sprint was also expected to turn a profit as early as mid-1989, with the real payoff after that.[1] Shortly thereafter, however, GTE agreed to sell United about a one-third interest in the joint venture, with an option to purchase the rest of GTE's portion through 1995. Both sales were to be at book value.

[1]See Robert T. Grieves, "Hold the Phone," *Forbes*, June 13, 1988, p. 52 and *The Value Line Investment Survey*, various issues.

Implicit in the work in the preceding chapter was the assumption that the outcome of any decision is known with certainty. In fact, the decisions of a financial manager are seldom, if ever, made under conditions of complete certainty. There is always a chance that the actual results will be different from those anticipated, as illustrated by the Sprint situation—GTE took a large risk and then apparently decided the potential payoff was inadequate. The financial manager must make actual real-world decisions under conditions that we refer to as *risk* or *uncertainty*.

Investors require compensation to invest money in ventures where returns are not certain, and the required compensation to induce investors to enter these risky investments is in addition to the compensation they require for the time value of their money. That is, investors require a rate of return that:

1. Reflects their time value of money.
2. Compensates them for the perceived risk.

The previous chapter developed the time-value-of-money concepts related to expected returns; this chapter develops risk concepts.

Primary *chapter learning objectives* are:

1. To understand the nature of risk and the calculation of risk measures.
2. To learn basic portfolio concepts, which incorporate the risk-return trade-off.
3. To understand the required rate of return through the use of asset-pricing models.

UNDERSTANDING AND MEASURING RISK

Suppose a financial manager for Chrysler can invest $100 million, and the return from the investment will be an unknown amount, *X*, at the end of the year. Upon investigation, she decides that the actual value of *X* will be determined by the general level of economic activity during the year. After looking at several forecasts of economic activity, she concludes there are three possible values for *X*: $8,000,000, $10,000,000, and $12,000,000, each with a one-third chance of occurrence. She now knows something about the possible values for *X* and how likely they are. But she still does not know what *X* will be; she does not have complete certainty concerning the outcome of the decision.

Risk and *uncertainty* are terms we use to describe situations where the outcomes of decisions are not known with complete certainty. For our purposes, we can define **risk** as the chance that the actual outcome will be unequal to the expected outcome. As a general proposition, the greater the chance of low (or negative) returns, the greater the risk of the investment.

Two important points must be remembered. First, some risk is present in any decision. A decision to invest $10 million in an asset similar to other assets a firm holds and has experience with almost certainly carries less risk than a decision to invest $10 million in a revolutionary process for extracting gold from sea water; nevertheless, some risk is always present.

Second, since risk cannot be avoided completely, the best strategy to account for its effect is to recognize it formally, measure it as best we can, and then make choices based on decision rules that incorporate the risk measure. The remainder

risk
the chance that the actual outcome will be unequal to the expected outcome

of this chapter is devoted to defining and developing the concept of risk. Later chapters develop decision rules that include risk considerations.

Probability Distributions

Consider UpJohn Pharmaceutical's prospects when deciding whether to launch an expensive campaign to promote their new, widely publicized product for baldness. One risk is the amount of total sales that may occur, but the main question is, Will sales be large enough to at least recover all costs? Suppose a market research study concludes that the odds are three to one in favor of a successful level of sales being achieved. This is equivalent to saying there is a 75 percent chance (0.75 probability) that sales will be satisfactory and a 25 percent chance (0.25 probability) that sales will not be satisfactory.

Probabilities are merely numbers that represent the chances of occurrence of different outcomes. These uncertain outcomes can be thought of as random variables, or numerical functions whose values depend on chance.

We need to recognize several facts about probabilities as used in the analysis of risk:

- All probabilities must be between 0 and 1.0. Impossible outcomes have 0 probability of occurrence; an outcome that is certain (a sure thing) has a probability of occurrence equal to 1.0.
- The sum of the probabilities of the possible outcomes equals 1.0, no more, no less. In the UpJohn example, the probabilities 0.75 and 0.25 sum to 1.0.
- When probabilities are assigned to various values of a random variable, the result is a **probability distribution,** which formally brings together all the possible outcomes and their associated probabilities.

probability distribution
the possible states of nature and their associated probabilities for a random variable

- *Example*

Assume UpJohn is considering investing $50,000,000 in additional inventory for its new drug. If this investment is made, the company can avoid some inventory shortages like those that have occurred lately. Based on some research, the rate of return to be earned on the new drug is believed to be directly related to how the national economy does in the near future. If the economic climate is good, company sales should be up, and the investment in inventory will enable the company to avoid shortages, thereby increasing profits. However, if the economic climate is poor, sales will slack off, UpJohn will have built up inventory unnecessarily, and the rate of return earned on the inventory investment will be low. Finally, if the economy is average, the rate of return will be about average.

Table 5–1 shows possible rates of return on this inventory investment, with estimates of probabilities added. In effect, this probability distribution is a simple description of the consequences of the inventory investment. As one example of how to interpret the distribution, notice that Table 5–1 shows that the probability of getting a 10 percent rate of return on this investment is 0.6. ■

A probability distribution of the type illustrated in Table 5–1 is a *discrete* distribution, which refers to the fact that probabilities are assigned to a finite number of specific outcomes. A different class of distributions, called *continuous*

■ *Table 5–1*
Probability Distribution
for Additional Investment
in Inventory

■ *Table 5–1*
Probability Distribution
for Additional Investment
in Inventory

State of Economy	Probability	Expected Rate of Return on Investment (%)
Bad	0.2	0
Average	0.6	10
Good	0.2	20

distributions, assigns probabilities to intervals between two points of a continuous graph.[2] In the real world, instead of probabilities of *exact* amounts (e.g., the 0.6 in Table 5–1), the probabilities of ranges are more commonly used. In cases where ranges of estimates are relevant, the *normal probability distribution*, often referred to as the *bell-shaped curve*, is commonly used.

■ *Example*

As an example of the difference in discrete distributions and continuous distributions, consider the distribution of actual total returns for Chrysler, UpJohn, and the Standard & Poor's 500 Composite Index, a widely used measure of stock market activity that reflects the performance of a broadly diversified portfolio of common stocks. In Figure 5–1 the actual distribution of returns for a recent multi-year period is shown by the bars of the histogram, and the appropriate normal distribution is superimposed. ■

The normal distribution is a mathematical function, completely defined by a specific mean and a specific standard deviation, concepts to which we now turn.[3]

Summary Statistics of Probability Distributions

By summary statistics we mean some property or characteristic of the function that conveys or describes something important about the distribution. We will investigate certain summary statistics of probability distributions and associate some of these features with important finance concepts. To assist us in this investigation, we will consider the prospects shown in Table 5–2 for two companies' stocks, UpJohn and Chrysler. Having examined the distribution of returns for UpJohn and Chrysler for the last several years, we are now attempting to estimate their expected return for the following year. Based on the information in Table 5–2, we are forecasting that for each company three outcomes—potential rates of return—are possible.

Central Tendency: Expected Rate of Return

One summary statistic of a probability distribution is the *central tendency*, which refers to the value that the outcomes tend to cluster around. There are several

---

[2]The area under a continuous curve adds up to 1. The probability that a particular outcome will be contained in a certain range is represented by the area under the curve over that range.
[3]Theoretically, there are an infinite number of different pictures of a normal probability distribution, dependent on the combination of the mean and standard deviation of the distribution.

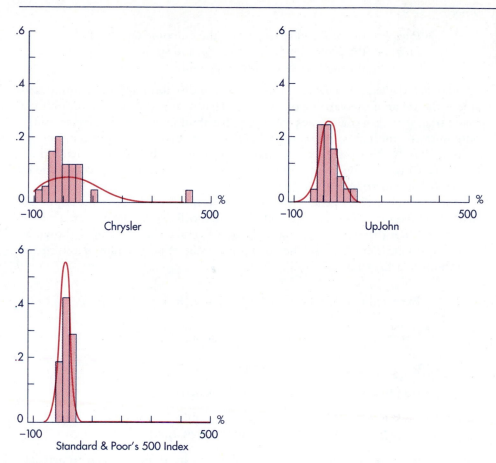

■ *Figure 5–1*
Total Returns for
Chrysler, UpJohn, and
the S&P 500, 1968–1988

■ *Table 5–2*
Example Investments

UpJohn Expected Rate of Return		Chrysler Expected Rate of Return	
(Percent)	Probability	(Percent)	Probability
0	0.2	−10	0.3
10	0.6	10	0.3
20	0.2	40	0.4
	1.0		1.0

measures of central tendency, but finance emphasizes the importance of a particular measure, called the *expected value* of a random variable, which is the proba-
bility-weighted average of the possible outcomes or the mean of the probability
distribution of random variable X.

For investment X:

$$\text{Expected value} = Prob_1X_1 + Prob_2X_2 + \ldots + Prob_nX_n$$

where:

$$Prob_1 = \text{the probability of getting the outcome amount } X_1$$
$$Prob_2 = \text{the probability of getting } X_2, \text{ and so on}$$
$$n = \text{the number of outcomes possible}$$

Note that the expected value of the probability distribution for a random variable is the value of the variable on average. That is, it is the average return over many trials. For each trial of the probability distribution in Table 5–2, one of three outcomes is expected to occur for Chrysler: -10 percent, 10 percent, and 40 percent. If only these three states of nature occur for each trial, over many trials the average outcome will be (as shown below) 16 percent, the expected value of the probability distribution.

**expected rate
of return**
the rate of return
expected for some future
(uncertain) period

Since our interest here generally is rates of return, we will analyze the **expected rate of return** instead of the expected value. We will denote the expected rate of return as $E(R)$; therefore, the expected rate of return for UpJohn is shown as $E(R_U)$, for Chrysler, $E(R_C)$. The equation for the expected rate of return for UpJohn, using the summation sign, Σ, is:

$$\text{Expected rate of return for UpJohn} = E(R_U) = \sum_{j=1}^{n} Prob_j \, X_j \qquad \textbf{(5–1)}$$

where $Prob_j$ is the probability of getting the amount X_j.[4]

- *Example*

The expected rates of return for these two stocks are:

$$E(R_U) = (0.2)(0) + (0.6)(10) + (0.2)(20) = 10\%$$
$$E(R_C) = (0.3)(-10) + (0.3)(10) + (0.4)(40) = 16\%$$

The expected rates of return for these distributions are 10 percent and 16 percent, respectively. In other words, UpJohn has an *expected* return of 10 percent for 1989, and Chrysler an *expected* return of 16 percent, representing the weighted average of the expected outcomes.[5] It is always important to remember that these are *expected* outcomes, and the risk is that the actual outcome will be different from the expected outcome. ▪

Other things being equal, investors are presumed to prefer distributions with large values of $E(R_X)$. That is, investors desire large expected rates of return. In the example above, Chrysler's expected rate of return is greater than UpJohn's expected rate of return. Other things equal, Chrysler is more attractive to investors than UpJohn. This does not mean, however, that if offered the choice of the two prospects, at the same price, investors would necessarily choose Chrysler over UpJohn. The meaning of *other things being equal* as used here requires that the two distributions be alike in all other important features. In reality, other things usually are not equal. Obviously, our two example distributions are not alike; investors may perceive, for example, that Chrysler is riskier than UpJohn.

---

[4] The summation sign, Σ, denotes the sum of all $Prob_j X_j$ values when j ranges from 1 to n.
[5] Note that the expected rate of return may be a number that does not correspond to any of the possible outcomes—this is true for Chrysler but not for UpJohn.

We turn now to a discussion of dispersion that will lead us to a formal consideration of risk.

Dispersion: Standard Deviation

Dispersion refers to spread or scatter in the probability distribution. Just as central tendency identifies a number that the outcomes tend to center on, dispersion measures how spread out or scattered the outcomes are. In other words, dispersion measures how likely it is that an outcome will vary from the central tendency. There are several dispersion measures, but finance has traditionally measured dispersion by variance and standard deviation.

The **standard deviation** of a random variable measures the variability around the expected value—that is, it measures the dispersion. It is based on the *variance,* which is the weighted dispersion of outcomes around the expected value, with probabilities serving as weights.[6] For investment X, involving an expected rate of return $E(R_X)$:

standard deviation
a statistical measure of variability or dispersion

$$\text{Standard deviation of } X = \{Prob_1[X_1 - E(R_X)]^2 + Prob_2 [X_2 - E(R_X)]^2 + \ldots + Prob_n[X_n - E(R_X)]^2\}^{1/2}$$

This expression is more compactly written using the symbol σ (sigma) for the standard deviation of a single variable and the summation sign, Σ:

$$\text{Standard deviation of } X = \sigma_X = \left\{ \sum_{j=1}^{n} Prob_j[X_j - E(R_X)]^2 \right\}^{1/2} \qquad \textbf{(5-2)}$$

The basic point about Equation 5–2 is that it reflects the likelihood that the *actual* value of X will vary from the *expected* return for X, and to what degree. The lower the standard deviation, the more likely it is that actual and expected values will be similar.

▪ Example

Using the data for UpJohn and Chrysler shown in Table 5–2, and recalling that $E(R_U) = 10$ percent and $E(R_C) = 16$ percent, the standard deviations for UpJohn and Chrysler are calculated as shown:

$$\sigma_U = [(0.2)(0 - 10)^2 + (0.6)(10 - 10)^2 + (0.2)(20 - 10)^2]^{1/2}$$
$$= (20 + 0 + 20)^{1/2} = 6.3\%$$
$$\sigma_C = [(0.3)(-10 - 16)^2 + (0.3)(10 - 16)^2 + (0.4)(40 - 16)^2]^{1/2}$$
$$= (202.8 + 10.8 + 230.4)^{1/2} = 21.1\%$$ ▪

---

[6]The standard deviation is simply the positive square root of the variance (*Var*), which is defined as:

$$Var_X = \sum_{j=1}^{n} Prob_j[X_j - E(R_X)]^2.$$

For comparing dispersion, standard deviation and variance provide identical results because the standard deviation is simply the square root of the variance. Thus, if the variance of distribution X is less than the variance of distribution Y, the standard deviation of distribution X is also less than that of Y. Note, however, that the variance is expressed in squared units of the variable, which generally has no intuitive meaning. The standard deviation, on the other hand, is expressed in the same units as the variable of interest, such as percentage. Therefore, it is usually more convenient to concentrate on the standard deviation.

As the calculations in the example indicate, Chrysler has much more variability in its distribution than UpJohn does. Of course, we know already from Figure 5–1 that Chrysler has shown much more dispersion than UpJohn in its past returns. Notice also that the distribution for the S&P 500 is much tighter than that for either stock alone, illustrating the beneficial effects on risk that can result from holding a combination of assets. We therefore need to consider this important principle involving portfolios.

PORTFOLIO CONCEPTS

portfolio
an investor's assets
taken as a unit

In our discussion so far we have considered the total risk of an investment opportunity. That is, we have implicitly assumed that each investment is held in isolation, with its own return and risk parameters to be assessed, and earned, independently. In fact, firms, like investors, hold a **portfolio,** or combination, of assets. This simple fact gives an important direction to financial management. The fundamental point to understand is that a financial management decision should not be made in isolation by focusing narrowly on that decision. Rather, the decision should be considered in the broad perspective of its effect on the total holdings (the portfolio of assets).

Our orientation in this book is to view the firm's management as a financial steward of its stockholders. For simplicity, let us call the firm's management *the firm*. From this perspective, the firm makes financial management decisions that affect that portion of the investor's wealth entrusted to the firm. Consequently, the firm's financial management decisions affect investors' total portfolio holdings, and it is important to understand basic portfolio concepts.

The two variables of interest to investors when holding a portfolio of financial assets, or to firms when holding a portfolio of real assets, are the expected returns from, and the risk of, those assets. Investors like returns but dislike risk. They know they cannot escape risk. If they are to attempt to earn larger expected returns, they must be willing to accept more risk. The relevant question, therefore, is how the expected return and risk of a portfolio of assets are determined. To answer this question, we must analyze the basics of portfolio theory by considering each of these two variables in turn.

The essence of portfolio theory can be simply stated. The two characteristics of interest are the *expected return* from the portfolio and the *risk*. Regarding the risk of the portfolio, the whole (the risk characteristics of the portfolio) is unequal to the sum of the parts (the risk characteristics of the individual assets).

Expected Portfolio Return

By expected portfolio return we mean the return that, on average, we should receive from the investment represented by the portfolio. This expected return is calculated by determining the expected return of each component of the portfolio and using these returns to compute a weighted average. The weights used are the portfolio weights, which describe how the portfolio's investment is weighted among the various assets.

Portfolio weights are percentages of the total dollar amount available to be invested in the portfolio and sum to 1.0, signifying that 100 percent of the amount available for investment is accounted for.

- *Example*

A portfolio consisting of four stocks held in equal amounts has portfolio weights of .25, .25, .25, and .25.[7] Of course, the weights do not have to be equal. For example, a portfolio may consist of three stocks held in the proportions .40, .20, and .40. ■

The important point is that the portfolio weights sum to 1.0. We will use W_j to represent the portfolio weights. The *expected return on a portfolio, E(R_p)*, is calculated as:

$$\text{Expected portfolio return} = E(R_p) = \sum_{j=1}^{n} W_j\, E(R_j) \qquad (5\text{–}3)$$

where

$$
\begin{aligned}
E(R_p) &= \text{the expected return on the portfolio} \\
E(R_j) &= \text{the expected return on asset } j \\
W_j &= \text{the portfolio weight for asset } j, \text{ where } \Sigma W_j = 1.0
\end{aligned}
$$

The expected portfolio return is a simple *weighted* average of the component assets' expected returns.[8] Other things being equal, higher values would be desirable. Again, it is important to note that we are talking about *expected* return here. The *realized* return for our portfolio example may turn out to be different from the expected return.

- *Example*

Consider a simple two-stock portfolio composed of the two stocks analyzed, Chrysler and UpJohn. Assume that the following data are given:

$$
\begin{aligned}
E(R_U) &= 10\% & E(R_C) &= 16\% \\
\sigma_U &= 6\% & \sigma_C &= 21\%
\end{aligned}
$$

The portfolio is composed of 50 percent Chrysler and 50 percent UpJohn. That is:

$$
\begin{aligned}
W_U &= 0.5 \\
W_C &= 0.5
\end{aligned}
$$

where:

W_U = percent of portfolio invested in UpJohn

$W_C = 1.0 - W_U$ = percent of portfolio invested in Chrysler

Thus:

$$
\begin{aligned}
\text{Expected portfolio return} = E(R_p) &= W_U[E(R_U)] + W_C[E(R_C)] \\
&= (0.5)(10) + (0.5)(16) = 13\%
\end{aligned}
$$
■

Notice that the expected portfolio return in our example is halfway between the expected returns of the two individual assets, since we assumed 50–50 weights. As discussed, the expected portfolio return is simply a weighted average of the

[7]If 10 stocks were held in equal amounts, the weights for each would be .10. For 100 stocks held in equal amounts, the weight for each would be .01.

[8]This will always be true, regardless of how many assets are in the portfolio or how the assets are weighted.

individual assets' expected returns. Thus, if the weight for Chrysler had been larger, the expected return on the portfolio also would have been larger.

Portfolio Risk

Total portfolio risk is measured by the standard deviation of the portfolio's rate-of-return distribution, which will be designated as $SD(R_p)$. As $SD(R_p)$ increases, portfolio risk increases; that is, as $SD(R_p)$ increases, the riskiness of the portfolio of assets rises. In comparing two investors' portfolios, if one investor's $SD(R_p)$ value exceeds the $SD(R_p)$ value of the second investor, the first investor has a riskier portfolio.

Unlike the expected return calculation, portfolio risk is not simply a weighted average of the individual security's standard deviations. That is:

$$SD(R_p) \neq \Sigma \; W_j SD(R_j)$$

Therefore, the contribution of each asset to portfolio risk is not simply $W_j \, SD(R_j)$. The reason is that movements in the returns among the various assets must be taken into account because in some cases they may move opposite to each other. For example, a bad return for Chrysler during a particular period could be offset by a good return from UpJohn during the same period. To take account of such movements, we will analyze two measures of co-movement, the correlation coefficient and the covariance.

Correlation Coefficient

correlation coefficient
a measure of the relative association between two variables

Co-movement refers to the association of movement between two variables. There are, of course, many ways that two variables may be associated, but the simplest form of association is a linear (straight-line) relationship. The **correlation coefficient** describes how much linear co-movement exists between two variables, say X and Y:[9]

Correlation coefficient between X and Y = $Corr_{XY}$

The correlation coefficient, $Corr_{XY}$, indicates something about the directionality of association between X and Y.

- If $Corr_{XY}$ is positive, the two variables tend to be large at the same time and small at the same time. Rates of return on common stocks are a good example of positively correlated variables. When rates of return are relatively high on any one stock (say, Ford), they are usually high on any other stock (say, General Electric). If X and Y are positively correlated, then values of X and Y, when plotted against one another, suggest a positively sloping straight-line graph, as shown in Figure 5–2A.
- If $Corr_{XY}$ is negative, relatively large values of X are associated with relatively small values of Y: the variables move in directions opposite to one another. An example of negatively correlated random variables are interest rates and the volume of new housing construction activity. When interest rates climb, building activity declines, and when interest rates go

---

[9]It is important in this discussion to keep in mind that we are talking about association, not causation. We are not saying that X causes Y or Y causes X.

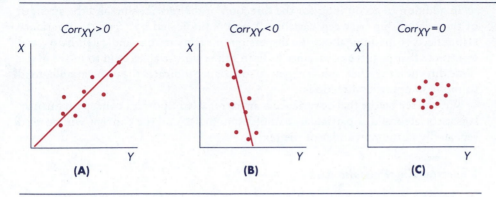

(A)   (B)   (C)

down, building activity increases. An example of negatively correlated variables is shown in Figure 5–2B.

■ When $Corr_{XY} = 0$, the variables are uncorrelated, and movements in one variable appear unrelated to movements in the other variable. For example, sunspot activity and stock market rates of return are uncorrelated. Uncorrelated variables have a plot as indicated in Figure 5–2C.

The sign of the correlation coefficient indicates the direction of the co-movement—whether it is positive or negative. The absolute value of the correlation coefficient indicates the *relative* strength of the co-movement. The range of values that $Corr_{XY}$ can be is:

$$-1.0 \leq Corr_{XY} \leq +1.0$$

The closer $Corr_{XY}$ gets to either $+1.0$ or -1.0, the stronger the association between X and Y. When $Corr_{XY} = +1.0$, the variables exhibit *perfect positive correlation*. When $Corr_{XY} = -1.0$, the variables exhibit *perfect negative correlation*.

Covariance

Another measure of co-movement, **covariance,** indicates how two variables covary. However, covariance is a more inclusive measure of co-movement than correlation because it expresses, not only how well two variables track with each other, but also how likely each variable is to vary from the expected value.

covariance
a measure of the absolute association between two variables

$$\text{Covariance between } X \text{ and } Y = Cov_{XY} = Corr_{XY}\sigma_X\sigma_Y \qquad (5\text{–}4)$$

where:

$Corr_{XY}$ = correlation coefficient between the returns of X and the returns of Y

σ_X and σ_Y = standard deviation of X and Y distributions, respectively

■ *Example*

Assume the correlation between Chrysler and UpJohn is $+0.2$, $\sigma_C = 21$ percent and $\sigma_U = 6$ percent. The covariance between their rates of return is:

$$Cov_{CU} = (0.2)(6)(21) = 25.2$$

■

In addition to accounting for the direction of the relationship and the strength of the relationship between variables X and Y (indicated by $Corr_{XY}$), covariance also reflects something about the dispersion of each variable (indicated by σ_X and σ_Y). Note that positive covariance indicates the two variables tend to move in the same direction together, while negative covariance indicates the two variables tend to move in opposite directions.

We will see below that covariance is an extremely important concept in finance. It is associated with a particular formulation of risk, and the concept will be used repeatedly in the remainder of the text.

Understanding Portfolio Risk

We are now in a position to understand portfolio risk, which is a function of each individual asset's risk plus the covariances between the returns on the individual assets. The formula is:

$$SD(R_p) = \left[\sum_{j=1}^{n} W_j^2 \, Var(R_j) + \sum_{j=1}^{n} \sum_{k=1}^{n} W_j W_k Cov_{j,k} \right]^{1/2} \quad j \neq k \qquad (5\text{--}5)$$

Equation 5–5 can be understood simply as the sum of the weighted variances and the weighted covariances for the assets in the portfolio. The first term is the weighted variance term and the second term is the weighted covariance term.

- If the second term is zero, portfolio risk would obviously be reduced relative to the case of positive covariance, where both terms would be added together. If the second term is negative, it would be subtracted from the first term, which measures the weighted individual assets' risk using their respective (weighted) standard deviations.
- Thus, the covariance among asset returns can add to the weighted individual risks, contribute nothing to weighted individual risks, or reduce the impact of weighted individual risks.

To better understand how the risk of a portfolio of assets is affected by the relationships among those assets, consider the simplest portfolio consisting of only two stocks. In the two-asset portfolio case, portfolio risk equals the square root of the sum of the weighted variances of the two component assets' returns plus twice their weighted covariance, as shown by Equation 5–6:

$$\text{Portfolio risk for the two–asset case} = \qquad (5\text{--}6)$$
$$SD(R_p) = [W_X^2 \sigma_X^2 + W_Y^2 \sigma_Y^2 + 2W_X W_Y Cov_{XY}]^{1/2}$$

- ### Example

Continuing the portfolio example involving UpJohn and Chrysler, use Equation 5–6 to solve for $SD(R_p)$. Using the data given: $\sigma_U = 6$ percent; $\sigma_C = 21$ percent; $Corr_{UC} = +0.2$; $W_U = W_C = .5$.

$$Cov_{UC} = (0.2)(6)(21) = 25.2$$

Therefore:

$$SD(R_p) = [(0.5)^2(6)^2 + (0.5)^2(21)^2$$
$$+ (2)(0.5)(0.5)(25.2)]^{1/2}$$
$$= (9 + 110.25 + 12.6)^{1/2}$$
$$= (131.85)^{1/2}$$
$$= 11.48\%$$

Now, what would happen if these two assets were correlated -0.2 rather than $+0.2$? In this case, the covariance term (the third term of Equation 5–6) would become negative because the covariance would be negative, reducing the risk substantially as shown by the following calculation. Notice that this calculation is exactly like the previous one except for the negative sign on the third term.

$$SD(R_p) = [(0.5)^2(6)^2 + (0.5)^2(21)^2$$
$$+ (2)(0.5)(0.5)(-25.2)]^{1/2}$$
$$= (9 + 110.25 - 12.6)^{1/2}$$
$$= (106.65)^{1/2}$$
$$= 10.33\%$$

As we can see, the change in sign from positive to negative reduced the risk of the portfolio by about 10 percent. Had the correlation been even more negative, such as -0.5 or -0.8, the risk of the portfolio could have been reduced even more. ∎

Risk-Return Combinations

It's worth reemphasizing that the portfolio standard deviation of rate of return is assumed to be an adequate measure of total risk for investors.[10] Consequently, the larger $SD(R_p)$, the riskier an investor's portfolio. Other things being equal, investors will prefer portfolios with low risk values. To acquire such portfolios, however, the investor must accept a lower expected return. To obtain a larger expected return, an investor must be exposed to a larger risk. This is what is meant by a *risk-return trade-off.* Given estimates of expected returns and risks for a set of stocks, the key to understanding portfolio theory is the weights. As the portfolio weights are changed, the portfolio's expected return and standard deviation also change.[11]

■ *Example*

Stock X has an expected return of 10 percent, and stock Y, 20 percent. Respective standard deviations are 5 percent and 10 percent. The expected return and risk of portfolio combinations can be calculated using Equations 5–3 and 5–6. Choosing different values of W_X and W_Y leads to different risk–return results. As W_Y ranges

---

[10]In finance it is commonly assumed that returns are log normally distributed and, therefore, the mean and standard deviation provide the necessary information.

[11]In fact, in constructing efficient (optimal) portfolios, it is the portfolio weights that are varied in the optimization program to produce different expected return–risk combinations.

■ *Figure 5–3*
Risk-Return Tradeoff

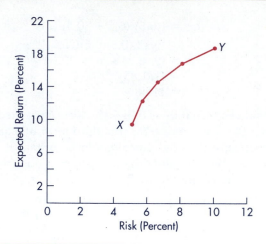

from its lower limit of zero to its upper limit of 1.0, $E(R_p)$ and $SD(R_p)$ both change. The point is that as the portfolio weights are changed, the portfolio's expected return and standard deviation also change. The following data show five (of many) possible weighting combinations, with $\text{Corr}_{XY} = +0.6$.

W_X	W_Y	$E(R_p)$ (%)	$SD(R_p)$ (%)
1.00	0	10.0	5.0
0.75	0.25	12.5	5.6
0.50	0.50	15.0	6.8
0.25	0.75	17.5	8.3
0	1.00	20.0	10.0

Figure 5–3 graphs the $E(R_p)$ and $SD(R_p)$ results for these five possible weighting combinations. ■

THE RISK OF AN ASSET WITHIN THE PORTFOLIO

It can be shown that as the number of assets, n, in the portfolio increases, the impact of the first term of Equation 5–5, the variance term, becomes smaller, approaching zero for large values of n.[12] The implication of this is that for well-diversified portfolios, portfolio risk is primarily due to the impact of the covariance relationships as captured by the second term in Equation 5–5.

---

[12]This is because the impact of the squared weight term, W_j^2, becomes small and approaches zero as n becomes large.

Consider now a single component within the portfolio: an individual asset. What is the proper measure of risk for this single asset within the portfolio?

Suppose we consider a new investment prospect for an investor's current portfolio. Let asset X be this new investment and let Y be the investor's current portfolio. The investor's new portfolio will be designated by Z. Notice we are setting up another simple portfolio problem where we combine two assets, X and Y, into a portfolio, Z. It so happens that Y, in this case, is itself a portfolio.

If investment X is added to the investor's current portfolio, Y, what will be the new portfolio's standard deviation of return $[SD(R_Z)]$? As we saw, the risk of a portfolio of two assets is given by Equation 5–6:

$$SD(R_Z) = (W_X^2\sigma_X^2 + W_Y^2\sigma_Y^2 + 2W_XW_YCov_{XY})^{1/2}$$

Notice there is nothing new here except that we are giving special attention to defining X and Y. The new asset being brought into the portfolio is asset X. Since we are viewing X from a portfolio perspective, the question is what impact asset X has on portfolio risk.

Equation 5–6 shows that three components together determine total portfolio risk:

1. $W_X^2\sigma_X^2$.
2. $W_Y^2\sigma_Y^2$.
3. $2W_XW_YCov_{XY}$.

Any term with an X subscript (like W_X^2) is a term that the asset X influences or wholly determines. On inspection, there are two such terms, the first and the third. The first, $W_X^2\sigma_X^2$, is called asset X's *own variance*. Term 3 is the covariance term. What we see by looking at Equation 5–6 closely like this is that asset X can contribute to total portfolio risk in only two ways: through its own variance term or through the covariance term.

As long as investors hold *well-diversified portfolios* of assets, the own–variance term is of less importance; therefore, the risk contribution of asset X must come through the covariance term. This is mathematically true, and we discuss this further below.

Well-Diversified Portfolios

The investor with a well-diversified portfolio has spread wealth over many assets so that none of them makes up a large part of the portfolio. Few people are willing to risk putting all their eggs in one basket because they know intuitively that the risk of doing so is too high.

In the context of Equation 5–5, holding well-diversified portfolios means two things. First, the old portfolio, Y, is itself a composite of many assets, none of which is a large fraction of that portfolio's total value. Second, the new asset, X, must be relatively small in comparison with the new portfolio, Z. This means that the relative weight of the new asset, W_X, must be small.[13] The impact of this is that when a small W_X is squared in the portfolio risk equation, W_X^2 becomes

---

[13]How small? As an upper bound, W_X would probably not exceed 0.10, that is, 10 percent, and in most cases it would be considerably smaller.

even smaller. This ensures that the own-variance term will always be insignificant when portfolios are well diversified.[14]

Notice now that W_X^2 is not in the covariance term in Equation 5–6. W_X is, but W_X^2 is not. Consequently, the covariance term will not automatically become negligible. This is reasonable since the covariance of the elements of a portfolio is central to its risk, as explained above.

Of course, in some instances the covariance term may also be small. Recall that covariance equals $Corr_{XY}\sigma_X\sigma_Y$. So $Corr_{XY}$, the correlation coefficient, strongly influences covariance. If $Corr_{XY}$ is relatively small, the covariance is correspondingly small. If $Corr_{XY}$ is negative, the covariance term is negative, and the covariance is subtractive in Equation 5–6. Thus, covariance may have either large or small positive effects on portfolio risk, or large or small negative effects, or a zero effect, depending on the correlation coefficient. But in any event, it is only the covariance of the asset's returns that substantially affects portfolio risk. The asset's own variance is always insignificant as long as W_X is small.

The conclusion we have just reached is an important one and deserves emphasis: *As long as an asset's weight in a portfolio is fairly small, the risk of that asset will be measured by its covariance with the rest of the portfolio.* We need to remember that point when we're describing the risk of a new investment. The new investment's risk will be the covariance of its rates of return with the rates of return of the rest of the portfolio.[15]

The Role of a Market Index

As we asserted above, investors are believed to be most concerned with risk at the portfolio level. Further, we assume that total portfolio risk is best measured by the standard deviation of return of the entire portfolio. When a new investment is added to an investor's portfolio, the appropriate measure of its risk is related to how it affects the portfolio. For well-diversified portfolios, which are the norm for most investors, the risk of the new component is best described by the covariance between the rates of return of the component and the investor's present portfolio.

It is important at this point to remember we are looking at finance from the firm's standpoint. Now the firm is making financial management decisions that will affect many investors' portfolios. However, from the risk perspective we have just developed, investors' decisions about new investments are related to the covariance of returns between a potential purchase and their portfolio. At this point, therefore, we have a thorny problem: How do we specify what the term *investors' portfolios* means, given millions of different investors, each with a different portfolio?

---

[14]Taking the upper bound of $W_X = 0.10$ as an example, $W_X^2 = 0.01$, a very small number. It is so small, in fact, that it will cause the own-variance term to be too small to worry about. For more realistic (that is, smaller) values of W_X, the own-variance term becomes even smaller.

[15]There is one last point to consider here. Our conclusion above depended on the important assumption that the new asset being considered for inclusion in the investor's portfolio was small in relation to the rest of the portfolio. What if that assumption is not true? If the new asset is relatively large, then our general conclusion that only covariance risk is important is no longer valid. We will then have to look at both the own-variance and the covariance terms. Certainly there are times when this extra complication needs to be considered. Our position in the rest of the book is that the normal case will be that covariance risk is a sufficient measure of a single investment's risk in a portfolio context.

Financial theory starts with a simplified view of the world and says that the average investor's expected rate of return and risk of the portfolio may be expressed in terms of a **market portfolio** that, in turn, is typically proxied by a well known stock market index such as the Standard & Poor's 500 Composite Stock Index.[16] That is, let:

$$E(R_M) = \text{Expected market index rate of return}$$

$$SD(R_M) = \text{Standard deviation of market index rate of return}$$

These two numbers are supposed to represent average investors' beliefs about expected return and risk of typical well-diversified portfolios. That is, when investors hold well-diversified portfolios, we can describe the expected return and risk of the average investor's portfolio as $E(R_M)$ and $SD(R_M)$, respectively.[17]

Once we equate the average investor's portfolio with a broad market index, we have a practical guide to the main question we have been addressing in this section: How do we measure the risk associated with a single asset within the portfolio? Consider Equation 5–6 again, but this time think of the investor's present portfolio as the market index, M, and the new investment, as before, as X. Rewriting Equation 5–6, we obtain:

$$
\begin{matrix}
\text{Standard deviation} \\
\text{of the rate of} \\
\text{return on the} \\
\text{new portfolio}
\end{matrix}
= SD(R_Z) = [W_X^2 \sigma_X^2 + W_M^2 \sigma_M^2 + 2W_X W_M Cov_{XM}]^{1/2}
\tag{5–7}
$$

where:

$$Cov_{XM} = Corr_{XM}\sigma_X\sigma_M$$

Equation 5–7 is just 5–6 rewritten to reflect the use of the market index as an approximation of average investors' well-diversified holdings. And by the same reasoning we have already used, the risk associated with asset X is directly related to the covariance between rate of return on X and on the market index, Cov_{XM}. The greater this covariance, the greater is the risk associated with asset X.

The conclusion of this analysis is that for an individual component of an investor's portfolio, the relevant measure of risk is, not the component's variance, but its covariance with a general wealth or market index. That is, the contribution of the component to total (portfolio) risk is through the covariance of the component's returns with the market's returns. In other words, the more an investment reflects the ups and downs of the market, the riskier that investment is. This conclusion is an extremely important one in finance.

> **market portfolio**
> the portfolio of all assets in the market in the proportions in which they actually exist

---

[16]The Standard & Poor's 500 Composite Stock Index is a market-value-weighted index of 500 of the largest and best known U.S. corporations. It is widely used by institutional investors as a proxy for the entire stock market.

[17]This simplification obviously assumes several things. It assumes that investors hold well-diversified portfolios and that the index is general enough to represent all kinds of assets. Both of these assumptions are oversimplifications, yet they are not so wild as to lead to conclusions about investor behavior that are greatly at odds with observed behavior. Investors do appear to hold very well diversified wealth portfolios including stocks, bonds, real estate, furniture, cars, jewelry, and so on, and the choice of an index can always be made that is roughly consistent with these holdings. Moreover, this simplification—assuming that the expected rate of return and standard deviation of rate of return of investors' portfolios can be roughly equated with $E(R_M)$ and $SD(R_M)$, respectively—permits us to make very powerful statements regarding the risk involved in the firm's financial management decisions.

Beta as a Measure of Covariance

We have now seen that covariance is the appropriate measure of risk for most individual financial management decisions. However, covariance is not a very intuitive concept. The notion of a covariance of 40, for example, lacks intuitive meaning. But we can relate covariance to an equivalent concept that does have some intuitive meaning. This is done through the beta concept.

beta
a measure of a stock's price sensitivity to that of a market index

The **beta** of an asset is defined as the covariance of the rates of return of that asset with those of the rest of the portfolio, divided by the variance of the rates of return of the rest of the portfolio. If we make the usual assumption that the average investor's portfolio is well approximated by a market index, then beta is the covariance of rates of return of the asset and those of the market index, divided by the variance of the market index rates of return:

$$\text{Beta of asset } X = \beta_X = \frac{Cov_{XM}}{\sigma_M^2} \qquad \text{(5–8)}$$

Since an asset's beta measures its risk in a well-diversified portfolio, for well diversfied investors:

$$\text{Risk of asset } X = \text{Beta of asset } X$$

Notice that an asset's beta and risk are directly related to covariance; the larger Cov_{XM} is, the larger risk and beta will be. Beta relates the asset's covariance to the variance of the market index and is a kind of relative covariance.

Consider three assets, *A, B,* and *C,* with beta values as follows:

$$\text{Beta}_A = 2.0$$
$$\text{Beta}_B = 1.5$$
$$\text{Beta}_C = 0.5$$

Given what we now know about the risk of individual assets in a portfolio context, it should be evident that *A* is the riskiest of the three because it has the largest beta, and *C* is the least risky because it has the smallest beta.

An important benchmark for betas is 1.0, which is the beta for the market index. Any asset whose beta is greater than 1.0 (such as *A* or *B*) is riskier (more volatile) than the market, and any asset whose beta is less than 1.0 (such as *C*) is less risky (less volatile) than the market. An average stock has a beta of 1.0 because an average stock will tend to move up or down in step with the general market. Knowing this benchmark for beta, one can easily see the impact of beta on the required rate of return for an asset. Other things being equal, the larger the beta, the larger the required rate of return.

▪ *Example*

If the market moves up (down) 5 percent, a stock with a beta of 1.0 will tend to move up (down), on average, 5 percent. On the other hand, if the beta for this stock were 2.0, it would tend to move up (down) 10 percent if the market moved up (down) 5 percent because it would be twice as volatile as the market. Given the greater risk of the stock with a beta of 2.0, the required rate of return also would be expected to be larger. ▪

Actual beta coefficients for a miscellaneous sample of stocks as of a point in time are shown in Table 5–3. These betas are calculated by, and reported in, *The*

Company	Beta	Price
AT&T	.90	$ 39
A&W Brands	1.50	33
Campbell Soup	1.00	58
CBS	1.05	196
Chrysler	1.40	16
Coca-Cola	1.00	44
Delta Airlines	1.05	74
Duke Power	.75	56
Empire Dis. Ele	.45	29
General Electric	1.10	69
General Mills	1.00	86
General Motors	.95	47
IBM	.90	118
Merck	.95	84
Owens-Corning	1.75	23
Reebok	1.25	18
Syntex	1.10	58
UpJohn	1.10	42
S&P 500 Composite Index	1.00	—

■ *Table 5–3*
Beta Coefficients for Selected Stocks

Source: *The Value Line Investment Survey*, Part 1, Summary & Index, July 6, 1990. Reprinted by permission.

Value Line Investment Survey, a well-known investment advisory service.[18] Also reported in Table 5–3 is the price of the stock at the time of the beta observation. It is obvious from an examination of the table that there is virtually no relationship between the price of a stock and its beta. For example, Reebok Shoes was selling for $18, and had a beta of 1.25, while Duke Power was selling for $56 and had a beta of .75.

Note in Table 5–3 that most of the companies have a beta close to 1.0, which is the beta for the stock market as a whole as represented, for example, by the Standard & Poor's 500 Composite Index, a well-known index of stocks often used to report what the market is doing. The three "generals" in the table—General Electric, General Mills, and General Motors—had betas of 1.10, 1.00, and .95, respectively, while IBM had a beta of .90, as did AT&T. Campbell Soup, General Mills, and Coca-Cola all had betas of exactly 1.00, which means that their price movements, on average, would be expected to correspond to the overall market. Therefore, if the market were to advance or decline 10 percent, the prices of each of these stocks would, on average, be expected to advance or decline 10 percent.

What about volatility considerably greater or less than the market? Notice that the beta for Owens-Corning was 1.75, meaning that this stock was 75 percent more volatile than the market, on average. Thus, if the market declined 20 percent, Owens would decline, on average, 35 percent. On the other hand, the same market decline would be expected to result in a decline in the price of Duke Power

[18]Betas can be obtained from a number of sources, such as brokerage houses and other investment advisory services.

of only 15 percent because of its beta of .75, and for Empire District Electric the decline, on average, would be only 9 percent because of its beta of .45.

Beta coefficients for stocks are typically estimated using regression analysis. The equation is $Y = a + bX + \epsilon$, where Y is the dependent variable, the total return for the stock, and X is the independent variable, the total return for the market. The a is the intercept term, or the value of the dependent variable when the independent variable has a value of zero. The b is the slope, or beta coefficient, for the stock. The ϵ is the random error term, or the difference between the actual return on a stock for some period and the return estimated for that period by the regression line. For purposes of estimating betas for stocks, monthly return data is often used, with 60 months being a common number of observations.

- **Example**

Using 60 months of total return data for UpJohn and a market index, the following regression results were obtained:

$$R_U = a + b(R_M)$$
$$R = .95 + 1.10(R_M)$$

These calculations indicate that the estimated a and b for UpJohn are .95 and 1.10, respectively. Thus, UpJohn is more volatile than the market, and on average if the market rises or falls 10 percent, we would expect UpJohn to rise or fall 11 percent. When the market return is zero, UpJohn has a unique return of .95 percent. ▪

A regression equation of the type referred to above is often called the *characteristic line* (see Figure 5–4). Thus, beta is the slope of the characteristic line.[19] Notice that the slope of this line is the estimated beta for UpJohn, and it measures the sensitivity of UpJohn's rate of return to the rate of return on the market index. The regression approach will reveal the historical association of a stock with the market. However, the contemporaneous beta may differ from the one obtained through regression as the company undergoes change.

Knowing that the benchmark for beta is 1.0, it is easy to see the impact of beta on the required rate of return for an asset. Other things being equal, the larger the beta the larger the required rate of return. To determine exactly how much larger, we need to consider the required rate of return in detail.

RISK AND THE REQUIRED RATE OF RETURN

Consider now an investor who is thinking about buying an asset. Given the riskiness of that particular asset, what is the minimum expected rate of return that would induce an investor to acquire it? We call that rate of return the **required rate of return.** It is also called the *discount rate.*

Three factors compose the required rate of return:

1. The real rate of interest.
2. A premium for expected inflation.

required rate of return
the minimum expected rate of return needed to induce an investor to purchase an asset

[19]Recall that the slope of a line can be estimated as the rise over the run. This ratio of rise over run is the same thing as the ratio of the change in the dependent variable over the change in the independent variable.

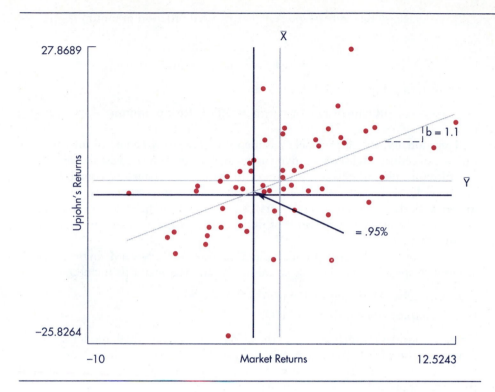

■ *Figure 5–4*
Characteristic Line for
UpJohn Pharmaceuticals

3. A premium for risk.

Required rate of return = Real rate of interest + expected   **(5–9)**
inflation premium + Risk premium

The real rate of interest is also called the *pure time value of money*. It is the rate earned on a perfectly safe investment (where there is no risk) when inflation is nonexistent. Historically, over many decades, the real rate of interest is thought by some economists to have been around 1 percent to 2 percent per year, although there have been large deviations from this average at times. In mid-1990 one well known investment advisory service was estimating the real rate of interest at about 4 percent per year.

The expected inflation premium is the extra rate of return over and above the real rate that investors require in deciding to commit their money to an investment. After all, who wants to invest money for the coming year at 4 percent—even in a perfectly safe investment—if inflation is expected to be 6 percent? Investors must have a required rate of return on safe investments (those where the risk premium is zero) that compensates them for the real rate of interest and expected inflation. Therefore, the **risk-free rate of return (RF)** used in finance theory is approximately equal to the real rate of interest plus some expected inflation premium, as explained in Chapter 2.[20]

**risk-free rate
of return**
the nominal rate of
return on an asset free of
default risk

---

[20]Actually, $(1 + RF) = (1 + RR)(1 + EI)$, where RR = real rate of interest and EI = expected inflation premium.

$$RF = \text{Real rate of interest} + \text{Expected inflation premium} \qquad \textbf{(5–10)}$$

where:

$$RF = \text{risk-free rate of return}$$

Substituting Equation 5–10 into 5–9:

$$\text{Required rate of return} = RF + \text{Risk premium} \qquad \textbf{(5–11)}$$

Traditionally, the finance field has identified the risk-free rate of interest with the rate of return (yield) on an investment that compensates investors for the real rate of return plus an inflation premium. In the United States, we equate *RF* with yields on U.S. Treasury bills, which are short-lived government securities. For longer periods (covering several years) we equate *RF* with yields on the longer-lived U.S. Treasury bonds. Both of these securities are discussed in more detail in later chapters.

Now consider the risk premium in Equation 5–11. Several finance models attempt to specify what the risk premium for an investment is, including:

- Capital asset pricing model (CAPM).
- Arbitrage pricing theory (APT).

There is considerable debate within the finance field about which model is a better representation of risk premiums. We will use the CAPM, which is older, for our work for reasons described below. The APT, a newer and still somewhat controversial approach, is discussed in Appendix 5–A.

CAPM and Risk

capital asset pricing model (CAPM)
a model that relates the required rate of return for a security to its risk as measured by beta

Under the **capital asset pricing model (CAPM),** the risk premium for asset (investment) X is:

$$\text{CAPM risk premium for investment } X = [E(R_M) - RF]\, \text{Beta}_X \qquad \textbf{(5–12)}$$

where:

$$RF = \text{risk-free rate of return}$$
$$E(R_M) = \text{required rate of return on the market index}$$
$$\text{Beta}_X = \text{risk (beta) of asset } X$$

Combining Equations 5–11 and 5–12 and placing the required rate of return into the context of asset X:

$$k_X = RF + [E(R_M) - RF]\, \text{Beta}_X \qquad \textbf{(5–13)}$$

where:

$$k_X = \text{required rate of return for asset } X$$

The intercept of Equation 5–13, *RF,* represents the required rate of return for an asset with a beta value of 0, that is, an asset with no risk. Since there is no risk, the appropriate required rate of return is the risk-free rate of return, *RF.*

The *required rate of return on the market index,* in a market in which assets are priced competitively, would equal the expected rate of return on the index. That is, in equilibrium, where market supply and demand forces have come to a stable position, the required rate of return on the market index is equal to $E(R_M)$. This equality does not mean that the two cannot change over time, for they do. It means that, on the average, expectations of market index rates of return and the requirements of investors who hold that index are approximately equal in competitive capital markets.

Equation 5–13 is the CAPM specification of how risk and required rate of return are related. The CAPM theory asserts a linear relationship between an asset's risk and its required rate of return. This linear risk–return relationship is shown in graphical form in Figure 5–5, which is called the **security market line.** Required rate of return, *k*, is on the vertical axis, and asset risk, beta, is on the horizontal axis. The slope of the line in Figure 5–5 equals the difference between the required rate of return on the market index and the risk-free interest rate. Assets like *A* with relatively high risk will have relatively large required rates of return. That is, investors will apply relatively large discount rates to those assets' cash flows. Assets like *C* with lower risk (lower betas) will have lower required rates of return.

The CAPM relationship is entirely consistent with our concept of risk. We will use the CAPM several times throughout the book. It is a most important concept in finance.

It is important to realize that the line in Figure 5–5 shows the required return and risk at a particular point in time. This line can, and does, change over time due to two factors:

1. Changes in the risk-free rate, *RF*.
2. Changes in the risk premium, which reflects investor psychology.

The risk-free interest rate of Equation 5–10 is a nominal interest rate and, therefore, is affected by inflationary expectations. An unanticipated increase in inflation could lead to an increase in *RF* that would cause the CAPM line to shift upward. This is shown in part A of Figure 5–6. Notice that the increase in the risk-free rate from *RF* to RF_1 causes a parallel shift upward in the line.

security market line
the graphical depiction of the CAPM

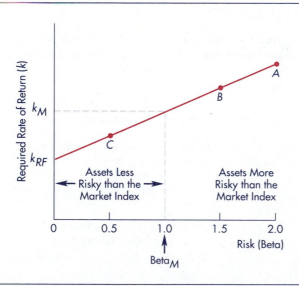

■ *Figure 5–5*
Required Rate of Return versus Risk

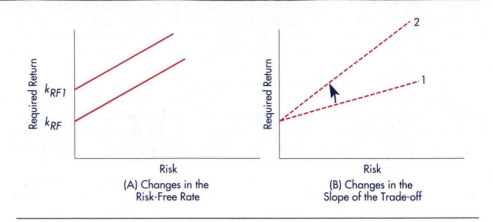

(A) Changes in the
Risk-Free Rate

(B) Changes in the
Slope of the Trade-off

A second change in the shape of the line results from a change in investor psychology. As investors become more pessimistic about investing, they demand a higher required rate of return for the same level of risk. This is shown in Part B of Figure 5–6, where the original line, 1, has rotated upward to the left (2). The steeper the slope of the CAPM, the greater the required rate of return for a given level of risk.

The slope of the risk–return trade-off line indicates the degree of *risk aversion*. Most investors are risk averse, meaning that they will not accept risk for its own sake but must be compensated to do so. The implications of risk aversion for the valuation of securities is that the higher a security's risk, other things being equal, the higher the expected return and the lower the price. In a market of risk averse investors, riskier securities must have expected returns that exceed that of lower-risk securities.

PROBABILITY OF FAILURE

We have emphasized that risk can be equated with the covariance (beta) concept. However, covariance does not adequately capture one dimension of risk: the risk of failure. For the whole firm, failure risk refers to its not being able to meet its obligations as they come due.

For an individual asset we might describe failure risk as the risk that the profitability of the asset is below some specified critical level.

$$\frac{\text{Probability}}{\text{of failure}} = \frac{\text{Probability that profitability is below}}{\text{some critical level}}$$
$$= Prob\ (X < X_{\text{critical}})$$

where:

$$X = \text{profitability outcome}$$
$$X_{\text{critical}} = \text{profitability failure level}$$

- *Example*

Suppose that a proposed investment project has a probability function of rate of return as follows (where X = rate of return):

Probability	X (%)
0.2	−10
0.5	20
0.3	30

Suppose, further, that we define failure here as the situation where the project has a negative rate of return. We find the probability of failure by identifying all the outcomes associated with failure and adding up their probabilities. In the example, the probability of failure = $Prob$ (X< 0) = 0.2.

Investors are said to be risk averse. They require large expected rates of return for investments that are risky in the beta sense. But many investors simply will not take on investments that are likely to fail, even if they carry very high rates of return. Many firms behave similarly. If an investment or financing plan has a high risk of failure, many firms will reject it.

Although our main emphasis in this book will be on covariability risk, we must also keep in mind this second dimension of risk. The risk of failure plays a particularly important role in working-capital management, where the firm must be especially careful to avoid running out of cash to pay its obligations as they come due.

SUMMARY

- Investors expect to earn a rate of return that compensates them for their time value of money and their risk exposure.
- Since future consequences of present decisions are not known with certainty, risk is present in almost all decisions.
- A probability distribution is a complete description of all possible outcomes and associated probabilities.
- The expected rate of return for a single random variable, like X, is $E(R_X)$:

$$E(R_X) = \sum_{j=1}^{n} Prob_j X_j$$

- To measure risk, we use the standard deviation. The standard deviation of a single random variable, like X, is:

$$\sigma_X = \left\{ \sum_{j=1}^{n} Prob_j [X_j - E(R_X)]^2 \right\}^{1/2}$$

- The standard deviation of a portfolio, σ_p, of two random variables, like X and Y, is:

$$\sigma_p = (W_X^2 \sigma_X^2 + W_Y^2 \sigma_Y^2 + 2W_X W_Y Cov_{XY})^{1/2}$$

where:

$$Cov_{XY} = Corr_{XY}\sigma_X\sigma_Y$$

and:

$$Corr_{XY} \text{ is the correlation coefficient}$$

■ Most investors hold well-diversified portfolios of assets, and a diversified portfolio can be approximated by a wealth or market index.
■ For most financial management decisions made by the firm, the appropriate measure of risk is the covariance of the rates of return associated with these holdings.
■ The required rate of return is the minimum expected rate of return necessary to induce someone to invest in an asset. The greater the risk of the asset, the greater the required rate of return demanded by investors.
■ The CAPM provides a way to calculate the required rate of return for an asset, given its beta, the expected return on the market index, and the expected risk-free rate of return.
■ An alternative method for specifying the risk premium is arbitrage pricing theory (APT), which views asset risk as better portrayed by relating an asset's returns with several indices. APT allows for more risk elements than only the market-related risk, but does not specify what these elements are. It is discussed in Appendix 5–A.
■ Another risk measure, the probability of failure, focuses on outcomes that are very undesirable.

KEY TERMS

arbitrage pricing theory (APT), p. 163
beta, p. 148
capital asset pricing model (CAPM),
  p. 152
correlation coefficient, p. 140
covariance, p. 141
expected rate of return, p. 136
market portfolio, p. 147

portfolio, p. 138
probability distribution, p. 133
required rate of return, p. 150
risk, p. 132
risk-free rate of return, p. 151
security market line, p. 153
standard deviation, p. 137

QUESTIONS

5–1. Risk is the chance that the expected outcome will be unequal to the actual outcome. Agree or disagree and explain your reasoning.

5–2. Describe three facts about probabilities as used in the analysis of risk.

5–3. In what way is expected value a weighted average? In what way is the expected value of a probability distribution similar to the expected return for a portfolio?

5–4. Since the expected value of a probability distribution is often different from any of the specified outcomes used to calculate the expected value, how can it be justified as a measure of the expected return from the investment?

5–5. What is the relationship between the dispersion in outcomes, risk, standard deviation, and variance?

5–6. Some financial analysts argue that investment alternatives whose returns are negatively correlated with market index rates of return are—other things being equal—very desirable investments. Explain this idea.

5–7. Explain why an investment's covariance with a market index is assumed to be a better measure of the investment's risk than the investment's variance.

5–8. In what situation would the variance of an individual asset's rates of return be an appropriate measure of the asset's risk?

5–9. Among Anderson Alloys's stockholders are two completely different investor types: Mr. Bold and Mr. Cautious. Mr. Bold has almost every penny of his wealth (except for a few clothes) invested in Anderson Alloys. Mr. Cautious holds a well-diversified portfolio of assets and consequently has only a small portion of his total wealth invested in Anderson Alloys. Both of these investors are presumed by financial theory to associate the risk involved with holding Anderson stock with the variability of rates of return on the stock, but they are presumed to have different perceptions of the kind of variability that is important.

Identify risk measures advocated by finance theory for these investors and contrast these risk measures, justifying why each is appropriate for the particular investor.

5–10. Ms. Boyette, who is well diversified, is talking to her finance consultant about a new investment prospect for her portfolio. She wants to know how risky the prospect is in relation to her current portfolio of holdings. The consultant says: "Well, if we computed a beta on this investment—using your current portfolio as the reference portfolio—we'd get a positive beta. On the other hand, if we look at *covariance,* the covariance of this investment would be *negative* in relation to your current portfolio."

What inferences should she draw from the consultant's statements?

5–11. Other things being equal, what would be the effect on the beta of UpJohn's stock if:
   a. The variance of the market index rate of return increased?
   b. The standard deviation of its rate of return decreased?
   c. The correlation between rates of return on UpJohn and the market index increased?

5–12. Why is beta a more-convenient measure to use than covariance?

5–13. What is meant by the term *market risk premium? Risk premium?*

5–14. What precisely is meant by the term *required rate of return?*

5–15. Using the CAPM as a guide, how would a change in each of the following affect the required rate of return for an asset?
   a. An increase in the risk-free rate of return.
   b. An increase in the beta for the asset.
   c. An increase in the market risk premium.
   d. A decrease in the expected return on the market index.

5–16. What estimates must be made to use the CAPM? How difficult are these estimates likely to be?

5–17. Given a plot of the CAPM:
   a. How would you expect it to change if the risk-free rate of return increases, other changes held the same?
   b. How would you expect it to change if investors' risk aversion increases, other changes held the same?

5–18. Explain the concept of APT (see Appendix).

5–19. What is meant when we say APT is a multifactor model?

5–20. Does the APT resolve the estimation problems inherent in the CAPM?

5–21. What happens to the average variance of assets in a portfolio as the number of assets increases?

5–22. Explain the following statement: "For an individual component of an investor's portfolio, the relevant measure of risk is not the component's variance."

5–23. Which dimension of risk does covariance not adequately capture? How can this risk be measured?

DEMONSTRATION PROBLEMS

5–1. Wylie Electronics is considering an investment in a new, improved chip-making machine. The company estimates that there is a 20 percent chance of a 30 percent loss, a 25 percent chance of a 6 percent loss, a 30 percent chance of a 25 percent return, and a 25 percent chance of a 40 percent return. What is the expected return from this investment?

5–2. Calculate the standard deviation of the investment that Wylie Electronics is considering in Problem 1.

5–3. The standard deviation for a project being considered is 24 percent, while the standard deviation for the market index is 20 percent. The correlation coefficient between the rates of return for the project and the market is .80. Calculate the beta for this project.

5–4. Wilson Graphics is considering a project with a beta of 1.6. The risk-free rate of return is 7 percent and the expected return on the market is 16 percent. What is the required rate of return on the project? What is the risk premium for this project?

Solutions to Demonstration Problems

5–1. The expected value (or expected return) of a probability distribution is always calculated as a weighted average of the possible outcomes and their associated probabilities. Therefore, we simply multiply each possible outcome by its associated probability and sum up the products. This is true whether there are two possible outcomes and probabilities, or 20, or 50.

Possible outcome	×	Probability of occurrence	=	Product
−30%	×	20%		−6.00%
− 6%	×	25%		−1.50%
25%	×	30%		7.50%
40%	×	25%		10.00%
			Sum =	10.00%

5–2. To calculate the standard deviation of a probability distribution, we start with the expected value (or return). From Problem 1 we know this is 10 percent. We then subtract each possible outcome from the expected value, square this difference, multiply the square by the associated probability for this outcome, and add together each of these products.

$$\sigma_X = \left\{ \sum_{j=1}^{n} Prob_j [X_j - E(R_X)]^2 \right\}^{1/2}$$

$$= [(0.2)(-30 - 10)^2 + (0.25)(-6 - 10)^2 + (0.30)$$
$$(25 - 10)^2 + (.25)(40 - 10)^2]^{1/2}$$

$$= (320 + 64 + 67.50 + 225)^{1/2}$$

$$= 26.01\%$$

5–3.
$$B_X = \frac{Cov_{X,M}}{\sigma_M^2}$$

and

$$Cov_{X,M} = Corr_{XM}\sigma_X\sigma_M$$

Therefore:

$$Cov_{X,M} = (20)(24)(.80)$$
$$= 384$$

Since Var_M or $\sigma_M^2 = (SD_M)^2$:

$$B_X = \frac{384}{(20)^2}$$
$$= .96$$

5–4. $k_X = RF + [E(R_M) - RF]\ Beta_X$
    $= 7 + (16 - 7)\ 1.6$
    $= 21.4\%$

The risk premium for any asset, using the CAPM, is the product of its beta and the market risk premium $[E(R_M) - RF]$. Therefore, the risk premium for this asset is:

$$9(1.6) = 14.4\%$$

PROBLEMS

5–1. A firm is considering some investments that offer the following rate of return probability functions: (rate of return $= X$). Find the expected rate of return of each investment.

A		B		C	
X (%)	Probability	X (%)	Probability	X (%)	Probability
−20	0.1	−40	0.4	−30	0.4
0	0.2	40	0.6	10	0.4
10	0.4			50	0.2
20	0.2				
40	0.1				

5–2. Using the information in Problem 5–1, find the standard deviation of rate of return of each investment.

5–3. An investment proposal has a rate-of-return (X) distribution as follows:

X (%)	Probability
−10	0.2
−5	0.2
−0	0.2
10	0.4

Find the investment's expected rate of return and standard deviation of rate of return.

5–4. Using your answers from Problem 5–3, assume the market index standard deviation of rate of return is 10 percent and the correlation coefficient between rates of return of the investment proposal and market index is $+0.8$. Find the proposal's beta.

5–5. A distribution of rates of return for project X and the market index M is shown below:

Probability	X (%)	M (%)
0.1	20	−10
0.7	10	10
0.2	0	20

Based on that distribution, compute:

a. $E(R_X)$ and $E(R_M)$.

b. σ_M

c. Beta_X, assuming $Cov_{XM} = -40$.

5–6. Compute Beta_X for each of the following situations:

a. $\sigma_X = 10\%$.

       $\sigma_M = 15\%$.

   $Corr_{XM} = +0.8$.

b. $\sigma_X = 10\%$.

       $\sigma_M = 15\%$.

   $Corr_{XM} = -0.3$.

c. $\sigma_X = \sigma_M$.

   $Corr_{XM} = +0.5$.

5–7. a. Given the following returns on four assets, compute the expected return on a portfolio if each security is equally weighted.

$$E(R_1) = 12\%$$
$$E(R_2) = 20\%$$
$$E(R_3) = 10\%$$
$$E(R_4) = 32\%$$

b. Calculate the expected return on the portfolio if the weights for the four securities are as follows:

$$W_1 = 5\%; \; W_2 = 30\%; \; W_3 = 15\%; \; W_4 = 50\%$$

5–8. The standard deviation for Security A is 20 percent and for Security B is 26 percent. The correlation coefficient between these two securities is -0.6. Calculate Cov_{AB}.

5–9. Given the information in Problem 5–8, assume that a portfolio is to consist of 40 percent in Security A and 60 percent in Security B. Calculate the risk of this portfolio.

5–10. You currently own a portfolio which has $E(R_Y)$ of 15 percent and a standard deviation of return (σ_Y) of 20 percent. You add a new security (X) to your portfolio and that security represents 10 percent of the total new portfolio. Compute the new standard deviation of portfolio return (σ_Z), given the following information on the new security:

Rate of Return (%)	Probability
−20	0.2
10	0.6
30	0.2

Assume that $Corr_{XY} = +0.4$.

5–11. The market index has an expected return of 12 percent and a standard deviation of 22 percent. Stock X has a standard deviation of 15 percent and a correlation with the market index of .35. Stock Y has a standard deviation of 35 percent and a correlation with the market index of .85.

Calculate the covariance of Stock Y with the market index.

5–12. The market index has a standard deviation of 22 percent. Stock J has an expected return of 12 percent, a standard deviation of 26 percent, and a beta of 1.2. Calculate the covariance of Stock J with the market index.

5–13. The risk-free interest rate is 10 percent and the required rate of return on the market portfolio is 15 percent. If an asset is 40 percent riskier than the market portfolio, what should be that asset's required rate of return?

5–14. Find k_X for each situation below:

Situation	k_M	k_{RF}	$Beta_X$
a	0.10	0.05	1.0
b	0.20	0.10	0.9
c	0.20	0.10	2.0
d	0.25	0.15	−0.5

5–15. Given the following information for Stocks A, B, and C, calculate each stock's risk premium.

Stock	Expected Return (%)	RF	$E(R_m)$	B
A	10	6%	12%	.8
B	14	6%	12%	1.0
C	18	6%	12%	1.1

5–16. Calculate the market's risk premium under each of the following two scenarios:

Scenario	$E(R_m)$ (%)	RF (%)
1	14	7
2	16	9

5–17. The historical risk premium for the market index has been about 7.5 percent, and this is expected to continue. Stock X has a correlation with the market index of .8. The standard deviation for stock X is 30 percent while for the market index it is 22 percent. The risk-free rate of return is 8 percent.

Calculate the required rate of return for stock X.

5–18. Financial theory asserts that any two assets that have the same risk must have the same required return, and vice versa. Grube Market Advisors, Ltd., a Kansas City market research firm, has lost some of the financial data it recently prepared, but it can make use of the risk-return idea expressed above to overcome the missing–data problem. Fill in the missing elements of the following table, assuming that $Beta_A = 2\ Beta_B$, that $\sigma_M = 10$ percent, and that $k_M = 10$ percent.

Stock	Required Return (%)	Standard Deviation of Return (%)	Covariance with Market Index	Beta
A	15	20	200	—
B	—	15	—	—
C	15	40	—	—

5–19. Consider investments A and B, which have distributions of rates of return as follows:

A		B	
Probability	Rate of Return (%)	Probability	Rate of Return (%)
0.05	−5	0.02	−10
0.10	0	0.03	−5
0.35	5	0.05	0
0.35	10	0.60	10
0.10	15	0.20	15
0.05	20	0.10	20

a. If an investor defines failure as suffering a loss of more than 5 percent, determine the risk of failure for each asset.

b. If an investor defines failure as earning less than a zero rate of return, which is riskier? Explain.

5–20. Mr. Hawk is considering the purchase of a strategically located apartment complex in a midwestern university town. He plans to purchase the property, hold it for one year, and then sell it, hoping for a profit. Hawk feels that his return will depend on the level of enrollment at the university. If enrollment expands next year, the need for additional housing will increase the demand for his property. Hawk estimates that his rate of return will be directly tied to the student enrollment level. Specifically, he thinks that for every 200-student enrollment increase (decrease) that occurs, he will make (lose) 1 percent in rate of return.

a. Given the following distribution of possible enrollment changes and their associated probabilities, what expected rate of return should Hawk make on this investment?

Enrollment Change	Probability
−4,000	0.10
0	0.10
1,200	0.50
2,000	0.20
4,000	0.10

b. Suppose this investment represents Hawk's total wealth. Calculate the appropriate measure of his total risk.

c. Hawk defines failure as earning a return of less than 7 percent. If he will tolerate at most a 15 percent probability of failure, will this investment be acceptable from a risk-of-failure standpoint?

SELECTED REFERENCES

A very readable treatment of risk and return concepts is:

Brealey, Richard A. *An Introduction to Risk and Return for Common Stocks.* 2nd ed. Cambridge, Mass.: MIT Press, 1983.

The classic book on portfolio theory is:

Markowitz, H. M. *Portfolio Selection: Efficient Diversification of Investments.* New York: John Wiley & Sons, Inc., 1959.

A reasonable discussion of the CAPM's use can be found in:

Mullins, D. W., Jr. "Does the Capital Asset Pricing Model Work?" *Harvard Business Review,* January–February 1982, pp. 105–14.

The basis of APT is contained in:

Roll, R. W., and S. A. Ross. "An Empirical Investigation of Arbitrage Pricing Theory." *Journal of Finance,* December 1980, pp. 1073–1104.

Ross, S. A. "The Arbitrage Theory of Capital Asset Pricing." *Journal of Economic Theory,* December 1976, pp. 341–60.

APPENDIX 5–A   ARBITRAGE PRICING THEORY: AN ALTERNATIVE TO THE CAPM

According to the CAPM (Equation 5–13), an asset's risk is expressed by the asset's beta, and the asset's required rate of return is directly related to the beta value. In recent years, an alternative theory to the CAPM has been developing in the advanced finance literature. This new theory is called the **arbitrage pricing theory (APT)**, and many finance scholars believe it is a better risk-return model than CAPM.

The word *arbitrage* means the purchase of an asset in one market and the simultaneous sale of an identical or highly similar asset in another market so as to make a profit on the two transactions. If, for example, you could buy a share of General Motors stock for $65 from an investor in California and immediately sell that share to another investor in Missouri for $67, you would have made a $2 arbitrage profit. Of course, everyone would like to play that game. So in an efficient market, which is characterized by a great deal of competition among investors, the arbitrage process will cause highly similar

arbitrage pricing theory (APT)
a theory stating that multiple factors explain the return on a security

assets to have equal prices. That is, if the prices of highly similar assets were not equal, the arbitrage process would work until price equality occurred. In the example above, shares of General Motors, being economically indistinguishable from each other, should all sell for the same price regardless of which state the buyer or seller lives in.

Stated differently, the arbitrage process leads naturally to the *law of one price,* which says that equivalent assets should be priced equally. This law also implies that equivalent assets should have equal expected and required rates of return. Using this arbitrage concept, a risk-return model has been developed that is today challenging the CAPM model as a theoretical and empirical foundation in finance. Recall from Equation 5–13 that the CAPM relates an asset's required rate of return with the asset's risk (beta), the risk-free interest rate (k_{RF}), and the market portfolio's rate of return (k_M):

$$k_X = RF + [E(R_M) - RF]\, \text{Beta}_X$$

Viewed abstractly, this equation can be rewritten as:

$$k_X = RF + (F_M)(\text{Beta}_X) \tag{5–14}$$

where:

$$F_M = \text{market factor} = E(R_M) - RF$$

Recall that Beta_X measures the risk of asset X relative to the market index. That is, the CAPM views asset X's risk as being entirely market related and equal, therefore, to a single beta value, Beta_X.

Essentially, the arbitrage pricing theory views the CAPM as being too simple in assuming an asset's risk is described completely by a single beta that is related to the market index. Rather, the APT views asset risk as better portrayed by relating an asset's returns with several indices. That is, an asset has several relevant betas, not just one.

A simple version of the APT is:[21]

$$k_X = RF + (F_1)(\text{Beta}_{X1}) + (F_2)(\text{Beta}_{X2}) + (F_3)(\text{Beta}_{X3}) \tag{5–15}$$

where F_1, F_2, and F_3 are the excess returns on broad factors that are important determinants of asset rates of return. Beta_{X1}, Beta_{X2}, and Beta_{X3} are the risk of asset X relative to each of the three factors, respectively. In this simple version of the APT, three broad factors affect risk and return. Therefore, three sensitivity coefficients (betas) convert these factors into a required rate of return for any given asset.

The APT is thus a more complex theory because it allows for more risk elements for asset X than only the market-related risk. Exactly what F_1, F_2, and F_3 and other factors economically stand for is unresolved today and is the subject of ongoing research. Some researchers have suggested unanticipated movements in inflation, industrial production, and the general cost of risk bearing. Other suggestions have leaned more toward a national economy factor and industry factors.

Proponents of the APT model argue that it is more general than the CAPM because the CAPM is a single-factor model but the APT is a multifactor model. APT proponents also say that the CAPM has not performed well in statistical verification tests. On the other side, testing of the validity of the APT has been performed only recently and remains unfinished. Evidence supporting the APT as being a better risk-return model than the CAPM is inconclusive and hotly debated at this time. It also bothers many finance scholars that the APT fails to state explicitly how many factors are important and exactly what those factors are.

It's too early to tell if the APT model will eventually replace the CAPM as the main theoretical model in finance. We will take the position that the CAPM is the best model we have today.

---

[21]In a more general version of the APT, there can be more (or less) than three factors.

6

Valuation and Financial Management

Valuing Two Competitors

Recently, CBS was selling for about $160 per share, having earned $5.21 the previous year while paying a $3.00 dividend. In contrast, Capital Cities/ABC was selling for about $314 per share, having earned $16.46 the previous year while paying a 20-cent dividend. The beta for CBS was 1.05, and the beta for Capital Cities was .95. The P/E ratio for CBS was 14; for Capital Cities, 13.9.

Earnings per share for CBS were estimated by *The Value Line Investment Survey* to more than double in the current year; the estimate for Capital Cities was for a 40 percent increase. Cash flow per share, as calculated by *Value Line*, was $7.90 a share in the previous year, with an estimate of $14.30 for the current year. Corresponding figures for Capital Cities were $27.01 and $33.75.

A *Forbes* magazine article published during this time contrasted CBS's value with that of rival Capital Cities/ABC. According to *Forbes*: "The stock market's judgment is clear. CBS's market cap is $1.7 billion . . . while . . . Capital Cities/ABC has a market cap, net cash, amounting to $6.7 billion. In revenues, Capital Cities is less than twice as big as CBS, but the market says it is worth almost four times as much."[1]

---

[1]See Subrata N. Chahravarty, "Behind All That Shuffling and Reshuffling at CBS," *Forbes*, August 8, 1988, pp. 77–78 and *The Value Line Investment Survey*, various issues.

We know that the firm is charged with the goal of maximizing stockholder wealth. Stockholders' wealth in the firm can be affected by two variables: changes in the number of shares owned and changes in the stock price. Since we assume that the number of shares owned is constant, the only determinant of stockholders' wealth is stock price.[2] Our emphasis in this chapter, therefore, is on stock price.

To achieve the goal of maximizing stock price, the financial manager must understand how the stock price actually is valued. In Chapter 1 we learned that the firm makes financial management decisions that can be broadly categorized as investment decisions and financing decisions. We assume that the financial manager will make the best financial management decisions possible. However, as we learned in Chapter 2, the manager must also consider the investor's perspective because investors, buying and selling stocks in the marketplace, collectively, and ultimately, determine the stock price. As we saw in Chapter 5, investors assess both the expected return and the risk for a stock, recognizing the upward-sloping trade-off that exists between these two determinants of value.

Thus, the fundamental issue in finance is one of *valuation:* How are securities prices determined? Was the market really saying that Capital Cities/ABC was worth four times what CBS was worth? If not, how should an investor go about valuing these two companies? This is the final step in a chain that ties the firm's goal to the fundamental decision areas of financial management—investment and financing—that we identified in Chapter 1.

Primary *chapter learning objectives* are:

1. To understand the concept of valuation.
2. To work through the mechanics of stock valuation models.
3. To review the valuation of other securities.

FOUNDATION CONCEPTS IN VALUATION

From a financial viewpoint, the basis of value for any asset, whether physical (such as a machine) or financial (such as common stock), is the cash benefits the owner of the asset expects to receive from it during the asset's life. If you decide to buy a share of stock, for example, what are you willing to pay for it? Traditional theory suggests that the amount you are willing to pay is determined by what you expect to receive from the stock in the future. The returns that the asset buyer receives are typically spread out over time. A prospective buyer or seller estimates the expected future cash benefits and discounts these back to today at an appropriate required rate of return. The resultant present value represents the value of the asset to the potential buyer or seller.

To summarize, an asset's value is derived from its *discounted expected cash flows:*

- The expected cash flows are based upon the profitability and cash flow prospects for the firm, as discussed in Chapter 3.

---

[2]If the firm should arbitrarily change the number of shares the stockholder owns by, say, splitting the stock or by issuing a stock dividend, the price of the stock will adjust proportionately to keep the stockholder's wealth the same. Thus, a two-for-one split would give the stockholders twice as much stock, but each share would be worth only about half as much as before the split, other things being equal. See Chapter 16.

- The discounting process is based on the present value techniques we developed in Chapter 4.[3]
- The discount rate is based on the required-rate-of-return concept, discussed in Chapter 5.

Putting all of these concepts together, the valuation process can be described as:

$$V_0 = \frac{C_1}{1+k} + \frac{C_2}{(1+k)^2} + \ldots + \frac{C_n}{(1+k)^n} = \sum_{t=1}^{n} \frac{C_t}{(1+k)^t} \qquad \textbf{(6-1)}$$

where:

$$V_0 = \text{estimated value of assets at time zero}$$
$$C_t = \text{expected cash flow in period } t$$
$$k = \text{required rate of return (discount rate)}$$
$$n = \text{life of the asset}$$

- *Example*

The cash flow from an asset is expected to be \$100 per year for 10 years, and the required rate of return is 10 percent. Using the present value of an annuity concept that we learned in Chapter 4:

$$V_0 = \sum_{t=1}^{10} \frac{100}{(1.10)^t} = (100)(PVIFA_{.10,10}) = (100)(6.145)$$
$$= \$614.50$$

An investor who uses a 10 percent discount rate would place a value of \$614.50 on an asset that promised \$100 a year for 10 years. However, an investor with a different discount rate and/or a different opinion of the future cash payments would evaluate the asset differently. For example, with a 15 percent discount rate the estimated value of the asset would be only \$501.90. ■

Market Value Is What's Important

The word *value* is used in many different contexts in business. For many assets, book value, an accounting concept discussed in Chapter 3, is only loosely related to the economic worth of the assets. Our concern in the valuation process is with economic worth. Moreover, we are concerned with economic worth in a marketplace environment where people can buy and sell assets.

Prospective buyers and sellers *individually* estimate an asset's future expected cash flows and discount these at their own required rate of return to arrive at the asset's **intrinsic value**—the estimated value (to them) of the asset. To the prospective buyer, the calculated intrinsic (present) value represents the maximum price he or she would pay to acquire the asset; to the prospective seller, the calculated intrinsic (present) value represents the minimum selling price.

intrinsic value
the estimated value of an asset

---

[3]The word *expected* in the phrase "expected cash flow" refers to an expected value as defined in Chapter 5. That is, C_t is the expected value of all possible cash flows in period t. We introduce no special mathematical notation to underscore this point, but we emphasize that C_t is indeed a mathematical average of the cash flows in period t. We are also careful to use the word *expected* throughout this chapter to remind the reader of this point. A more careful mathematical notation is used in Chapter 14.

In well-established markets, many *potential* buyers and sellers of the asset are evaluating its future expected cash flows and discounting these at their own appropriate rate. The result of the interaction between all these buyers and sellers is a kind of consensus price, called the *market value* of the asset. This price occurs at the intersection of the demand and supply schedules of potential buyers and sellers.[4] Market value is thus the price at which transactions take place between marginally satisfied buyers and sellers. When a financial asset has many competing buyers and sellers, an individual buyer or seller has little influence on the asset's price and is essentially a price taker, either buying or selling the asset at the given market price.

Market value stems from the cash flows expected by investors (who, in the aggregate, we call the market) and the required rate of return applied to these cash flows. These are the two parameters of valuation that we have referred to previously, and Equation 6–1 incorporates them into a general model of valuation applicable to any asset.

Risk and Return Relationships

We have studied risk and return in some detail, especially in Chapter 5. However, two simple points about return and risk need to be reemphasized because of their importance:

1. Investors have risk/return preferences.
2. Risk and return are closely related.

Investor Preferences

When we say that investors have risk/return preferences we mean that investors:

1. Like high returns.
2. Dislike high risk levels.

That is, given a choice—*and other things being equal*—investors would like to acquire assets with large rates of return and with low risk levels. As the next section shows, however, it's very difficult to find high-return/low-risk investments. On the most pragmatic level, then, to induce investors to accept higher risk levels when investing, they must be adequately compensated for the higher risk.

Finance theory is founded on the strongly held belief that investors will trade off risk and return when evaluating investments. An investor will be willing, for example, to invest in a slightly more risky venture if the return or payoff is commensurately greater. Finance theory presumes, in fact, that the risk/return trade-off can be modeled. The capital asset pricing model (CAPM), studied in Chapter 5, and arbitrage pricing theory (APT), described in Appendix 5–A, are two competing examples of risk/return specifications. Few people would argue that these or other models are perfect, but most finance theorists believe that these models provide important insights about investors' risk/return trade-off preferences.

---

[4]Figure 2–4 illustrates this concept.

Risk and Return Are Closely Related

Perhaps it is unnecessary to remind ourselves that risk and return are closely related. But it's surprising how often this elementary point is forgotten. In any case, finding investments that have high rates of return and low risk is very difficult. Why? Because of competition from other investors.

▪ *Example*

Assume you are considering buying an invention from the inventor. You intend to market the product yourself. You are convinced it is a fairly safe investment financially, and the rate of return prospects look great. That is, it looks today like a high-return/low-risk investment. Two kinds of competition will come into play, however. First, if other investors also have access to the inventor, they will be motivated to bid against you since everyone likes high-return/low-risk investments. This bidding competition will drive the invention's price (cost) up. And if your cost increases, your subsequent rate of return will decrease. Second, even if you beat all the other investors to this invention, if subsequent returns are large others will look for ways to produce the same product to compete with your investment. Unless you have perfect patent protection, you will find near-substitute products competing vigorously with yours. Think of the new products or services where exactly these sorts of competitive forces have been seen recently: film developers, video tape stores, frozen yogurt shops, copying and printing shops, and the list goes on. ▪

The point of the example is that risk and return go together, and we should not expect to find free lunches. That does not mean there are no attractive investments around, for indeed there are investments where the return is favorable relative to the risk level. We discuss this more fully next in "Market Efficiency." But you should always be skeptical of situations if the normal risk/return relationship seems out of line.

We studied the relationship between risk and the required rate of return in Chapter 5. The main point in that discussion and here is that *risk is reflected in the required rate of return.* Specifically, as risk increases, investors' required rate of return increases (i.e., the discount rate rises). That concept plays an important role in our valuation work in this chapter.

Market Efficiency

One of the most important principles in modern financial theory is that markets are efficient. By *market efficiency* we mean that prices of assets in the market reflect all the information that the market has about the asset. That is, through the interaction of many potential buyers and sellers in the marketplace, prices are established that are fully consistent with all information available to investors.

In an efficient market an asset's price should fully reflect the riskiness of the asset. Therefore, a buyer should only expect to earn a rate of return that is commensurate with that risk. A buyer would be mistaken, according to the **efficient market hypothesis,** to believe that he or she can acquire an asset at a bargain price and thereby earn an abnormally large rate of return. Thus, there are no bargain prices; there are only fair prices set by the efficient market. If the theory

efficient market hypothesis
the hypothesis that information about securities is quickly and, on average, accurately reflected in prices

is strictly true in all kinds of markets, the financial manager who operates in those markets will be frustrated in attempts to earn a rate of return in excess of a normal rate of return. As already discussed, a *normal rate of return* is a rate of return consistent with the asset's risk level.

Looking ahead, we'll draw two conclusions about market efficiency and consider two implications.

Conclusions about market efficiency:

1.   Real asset markets, where physical assets (like machinery and plant and equipment) are traded, are not fully efficient.
2.   Financial asset markets, where financial assets (like stocks and bonds) are traded, are generally very efficient.

Implications of market efficiency:

1.   Financial managers can exploit the inefficiencies in the real asset markets through good investment decisions.
2.   There is less chance that financial managers can add much to stockholder wealth through financing activities in the highly efficient financial markets.

The notion of an efficient market, where there are no price bargains or lemons, is an alien idea to most people when they first encounter it. Nevertheless, it is one of the foundation cornerstones of modern finance theory, and we need to be aware of this idea and consider its implications.

Competition and Arbitrage

Why should markets be efficient in the sense described above? A combination of intense competition and arbitrage work together to make markets efficient.

Consider a marketplace environment—like the stock markets—where investors are allowed to compete freely against each other for profits, which can be quite large. The magnitude of the potential profits to successful investors is a strong incentive for people to excel in this kind of investment. A great deal of effort will be expended by many men and women to achieve these profits: They will do research related to the market; they will talk to anyone who can provide them with an edge in their investment activities; they will study financial reports. They will also watch each other closely to see who is doing what and who seems to be winning the investment game—which fosters emulation of success in whatever form it takes. Further, no single investor or group of investors will be so successful that all other investors are dominated.

What has just been described is a highly competitive market. Large numbers of investors are scrambling for profits by seeking information about the assets. Those who can acquire relevant information first could use it to their advantage. Consequently, when new information becomes available, investors quickly assess it and then make their buy or sell decisions, which, in turn, affect prices. If the new information is considered unfavorable, the asset's price will fall. If the information is favorable, the price will rise. The important point is that information about the asset drives the asset's price to a proper, or fair, value. That is, at any point in time, the asset's price in an efficient market fairly represents all information then known about the asset.

A contributing factor in market efficiency is played by *arbitrage,* purchasing an asset in one market and simultaneously selling an identical or highly similar asset in another market in order to profit from price discrepancies.[5] We saw above that competition for profits causes information about assets to be quickly translated into asset prices, forcing prices to their fair levels. Arbitrage contributes to this by forcing assets within equivalent risk classes to have equal prices. If prices of equivalent assets were not equal, arbitrage opportunities would exist. Shrewd investors (called *arbitragers*) would take advantage of price differences between equivalent assets by purchasing the undervalued asset and selling the overvalued asset, reaping an instantaneous and riskless arbitrage profit equal to the difference between the two prices.[6]

Many people would like to play this game, and it will be played only so long as the price difference is greater than the cost of buying and selling the two assets. However, the game shouldn't last long. Buying pressure on the undervalued asset will push its price upward, and selling pressure on the overvalued asset will push its price downward. Eventually arbitrage would restore price equality. In an efficient market, arbitrage would occur quickly (in theory, instantaneously).

COMMON STOCK VALUATION

Common stock is merely a particular kind of asset; therefore, we can evaluate common stock using the general valuation principle discussed above. The first task is to identify the variables in Equation 6–1 when the asset is common stock. Let us develop this idea by steps, starting with a one-period horizon and progressing to a multiple-period horizon.

One-Period Valuation Model

Suppose an investor plans to buy a share of stock, hold it one year, and then sell. How will this investor value the share of stock? That is, what price will that person be willing to pay for it? The cash income the investor will receive from purchasing the stock is the dividend (if any) paid during the year plus the sale price at the end of the year.[7] Adapting valuation Equation 6–1 to this scenario:

$$P_0 = \frac{D_1}{1 + k_e} + \frac{P_1}{1 + k_e} \qquad \textbf{(6–2)}$$

where:

$$P_0 = \text{current price of the stock}$$
$$D_1 = \text{expected dividend in year one}$$
$$P_1 = \text{expected price of stock at end of year one}$$
$$k_e = \text{required rate of return on the firm's equity (stock)}$$

---

[5]Recall that we encountered the arbitrage concept in the previous chapter while briefly studying arbitrage pricing theory (APT) in Appendix 5–A.

[6]The profit is riskless because the investor makes his or her profits quickly and closes out the position. Also, the assets are equally risky.

[7]For simplicity, we assume the dividend is paid at the end of the year. In actuality, dividends for most companies are paid quarterly.

- *Example*

Assume the expected dividend for Micro Technology Inc. is 70 cents per share, the expected future price is $20 per share, and k_e is 15 percent. The value of the share to the investor is:

$$P_0 = \frac{\$0.70}{1.15} + \frac{\$20}{1.15} = \$18$$

Note the implications of the $18 price as calculated. If an investor buys this stock for $18 today, receives a 70-cent dividend, and sells the stock for $20 one year from now, the investor will earn the 15 percent rate of return that was required to invest. This shows why the discount rate is often called the required rate of return. It is the *minimum expected rate of return* the investor is requiring in order to make the investment. ■

Two-Period Valuation Model

Now suppose the investor plans to hold a stock for two years before selling. How is the value of the stock determined when the investment horizon changes? The answer is to incorporate the additional year's information.

- *Example*

Let the expected dividend for Micro Technology in the second year be 75 cents, the expected price at the end of the second year be $22.25, and the required rate of return remain 15 percent. The value today of this common stock to the investor would be:

$$P_0 = \frac{D_1}{1 + k_e} + \frac{D_2}{(1 + k_e)^2} + \frac{P_2}{(1 + k_e)^2} \qquad (6\text{--}3)$$

$$P_0 = \frac{\$0.70}{1.15} + \frac{\$0.75}{(1.15)^2} + \frac{\$22.25}{(1.15)^2} = \$18$$

By buying the stock for $18, receiving a $0.70 dividend next year and a $0.75 dividend the following year, and selling the stock for $22.25, the investor will earn a 15 percent rate of return. Alternatively stated, if the investor's required rate of return is 15 percent, the present value of the expected cash flow stream from Micro Technology is $18. ■

Indefinite-Period Valuation Model

We could add more years to the example, but the general idea should be evident because the principle is always the same. For an investor who plans to hold the stock for n periods and then sell, the value of the stock is:

$$P_0 = \frac{D_1}{1 + k_e} + \frac{D_2}{(1 + k_e)^2} + \cdots + \frac{D_n + P_n}{(1 + k_e)^n} \qquad (6\text{--}4)$$

$$P_0 = \sum_{t=1}^{n} \frac{D_t}{(1 + k_e)^t} + \frac{P_n}{(1 + k_e)^n}$$

Regardless of the number of periods of dividends, we must account for them and discount them back to today. The same is true of the expected price of the stock at the end of the holding period.

- **Example**

If an investor expects a $2 dividend for each of 10 years and a selling price of $50 at the end of 10 years, and the discount rate is 10 percent, the present value of the stock is:

$$P_0 = \sum_{t=1}^{10} \frac{\$2}{(1.10)^t} + \frac{\$50}{(1.10)^{10}} = (\$2)(PVIFA_{.10,10}) + (\$50)(PVIF_{.10,10})$$
$$= (\$2)(6.15) + (\$50)(0.386) = \$31.60 \qquad \blacksquare$$

Dividend Discount Model

There is one last generalization to make about deriving a stock valuation formula. Many investors do not contemplate selling their stock in the near future but are long-term holders. Since a common stock has an infinite life, we need to accommodate the potentially endless series of dividends that may be received in the future on the stock. Furthermore, we need not continue to directly account for the stock price, which clearly is unknown today, at some future time. The reason is that the stock price at any future time, say n, can be expressed as the sum of dividends from $n + 1$ to ∞. So:[8]

$$P_n = \sum_{t=n+1}^{\infty} \frac{D_t}{(1 + k_e)^t}$$

Substituting this equation for P_n in Equation 6–4, and simplifying,

$$P_0 = \sum_{t=1}^{\infty} \frac{D_t}{(1 + k_e)^t} \qquad \text{(6–5)}$$

Equation 6–5 is a more general form of the stock valuation model. It is often referred to as the **dividend discount model** because it shows the current price of the stock as determined by the discounted future expected dividends. It is an extremely important equation. In fact, it is the foundation for the valuation of common stock.

dividend discount model
a model that states that the intrinsic value of a stock is equal to the discounted value of all future dividends

Notice the similarity of Equation 6–5 to the general valuation equation, 6–1. The value of the stock is its current price (P_0), the expected cash flows are the expected future dividends (D_t), and the discount rate applied to the dividends (k_e) is called the *required rate of return on equity*. The time horizon in Equation 6–5 is infinitely long, indicating that the firm is a going concern and there is no foreseeable termination date on the stock.[9]

Two points about Equation 6–5 invariably bother students. First, suppose the firm pays no current dividend. Does this mean that the current price of the stock is zero? The answer is no because the current price of the stock depends on future

---

[8]Recall that $n = \infty$ stands for an infinitely long time (see Chapter 4).

[9]The same points about value discussed earlier in this chapter hold for common stock valuation. P_0 is the intrinsic value of the stock, or the estimated value. Market value is the price at which transactions occur between marginally satisfied buyers and sellers.

expected dividends. In addition, even if the expected dividends in the next 10 or 20 years were zero, this does not mean $P_0 = 0$. The current price of the stock is determined by expectations of *all* future dividends, not just the near ones. Only if a stock were expected never to pay dividends would $P_0 = 0$ in Equation 6–5.

The second point concerns the infinity sign, which, in effect, asks us to account for every expected dividend between now and infinity (a long time by anyone's standards). This really presents no insurmountable problem, however, if we can efficiently model the expected dividend stream. Even before we do that, however, recall from Chapter 4 that we know from the present value tables that a dollar to be received 30 to 40 years from now, at any reasonable discount rate, is worth very little today (that is, its present value is close to zero).

■ *Example*

Using a discount rate of 12 percent, one dollar to be received in 30 years is worth only 3.3 cents today, and after 40 years it is worth only 1 cent today. On a practical dollar basis, therefore, the infinity sign is not a problem. ■

To implement the dividend valuation model, which requires that we discount the entire future stream of expected dividends, we must model the *expected growth rate* of dividends. That is, if we can classify the company to be valued as falling into a particular expected-growth-rate category, and if each of these categories has well-defined procedures to follow, we can value the stock. Fortunately, this situation prevails. Techniques are available for each growth rate category. Furthermore, we only need three categories to cover all stocks for which the dividend valuation model can be used. We will discuss each of these three categories in turn.

No Growth

Some companies have future dividend patterns anticipated to be very stable, with little expectation of growth. This situation implies a steady or no-growth future dividend stream where $D_1 = D_2 = \ldots = D_\infty = D$. Notice the two conditions implied here: (1) unchanging cash flows (2) forever. When these conditions occur, Equation 6–5 mathematically reduces to a much simpler form, called the constant-dollar dividend, or no-growth model:

$$P_0 = \frac{D_0}{k_e} \qquad \text{(6–6)}$$

Current stock price, P_0, equals the current (and unchanging) dividend divided by the required rate of return. This is a special case of valuation known as a *perpetuity* (discussed in Chapter 4), which is simply an annuity that continues forever. It is very important to note again that in this special case of a perpetuity, the 1.0 is not added to k_e.

■ *Example*

If dividends for Taconite Trust are expected to be constant at $1.50 per share forever and if the required rate of return on equity is 10 percent, $P_0 = \$1.50/0.10 = \$15$ per share. ■

Technically, this simplification of the more complex valuation model shown in Equation 6–5 is valid only when the assumptions of both a constant-dollar dividend and an infinite time horizon are strictly satisfied. Although these two strict conditions hold in few examples, Equation 6–6 is still very useful because it frequently gives good approximations even when the two assumptions are not met. However, as n gets smaller and/or the expected dividend stream departs from constancy, the approximation becomes worse.

Constant Growth

Many companies have expected dividend streams that can be roughly described as growing at a constant rate for long periods of time. For these companies, Equation 6–5 can be mathematically reduced:[10]

$$P_0 = \frac{D_0(1 + g)}{k_e - g} \qquad \text{(6–7)}$$

Or, equivalently, since $D_1 = D_0(1 + g)$:

$$P_0 = \frac{D_1}{k_e - g} \qquad \text{(6–8)}$$

where:

D_0 = current dividend
D_1 = expected dividend in Year 1
g = expected percent growth in dividends (expressed in decimal form)

Certain assumptions are used in deriving Equation 6–8 from Equation 6–5.

- The *expected dividend growth rate, g,* is constant from year to year.
- This constant growth is forever ($n = \infty$).
- $k_e > g$.[11]

As with the previous no-growth case, at first glance the assumptions of the constant-growth case appear unrealistic. But they are only abstractions from reality, and Equation 6–8 is actually an extremely useful valuation formula that affords good approximations in many situations where the assumptions are not strictly met. We will make extensive use of Equation 6–8 in the cost-of-capital work in Chapter 14.

- **Example**

Suppose the market (1) expects UpJohn to pay a $1.78 dividend next year, (2) anticipates that dividends will grow at 10 percent per year for the foreseeable future, and (3) has a required rate of return of 16 percent. Then:

$$P_0 = \frac{D_1}{k_e - g} = \frac{\$1.78}{0.16 - 0.10} = \$29.70$$

---

[10]The derivation is presented in Appendix 6–A.

[11]If this condition were not true, we could get some nonsense results about P_0 from using Equation 6–8.

Variable Growth

A firm's current situation often does not reflect its long-term prospects. For example, a company currently paying uneven or zero dividends may be expected to show a long-term pattern of no growth or constant growth. Many firms have periods when they pay no dividends. New firms, typically, pay no dividends initially, conserving their cash flow for investment purposes. The same is true for firms in trouble. By contrast—and more important for valuation work—some firms may be going through explosive or supergrowth periods. In both cases, *the dividend stream typically reverts to constant growth or no growth at some later date.* We will consider each of these cases separately.

1. *Delayed no growth or delayed constant growth.* The question is, How do we find today's price (P_0) of a stock with delayed no growth or constant growth? This situation can be handled by the valuation model with only a few adjustments to cope with the real-world complications. We use a combination of our valuation model and an elementary technique we learned in Chapter 4 when we were studying the time value of money. The steps involved are these:
   a. Find the price of the stock one year before the no-growth or constant-growth period begins.
   b. Find the present value of the price found in Step 1, plus the present value of any dividends expected prior to the no-growth or constant-growth period.

Performing these steps will reduce these more complicated dividend patterns to a current market price, P_0.

▪ *Example*

Consider Vichie Springs Bottled Water Company, a company paying no dividends on its common stock currently but expected to begin paying a dollar a share four years from now. Assume further that the expected dividends in subsequent years are also one dollar a share. Vichie's required rate of return is 10 percent. Notice that this is a case of three years of zero dividends followed by a (delayed) no-growth period of indefinite length. The time line for this situation is shown in Figure 6–1. Notice that in doing Step 1, one year prior to the start of the no-growth period is year 3.[12] Also, there are no intermediate dividends between years 1 and 3 to worry about in Step 2. The two steps are as follows:

Step 1:

$$P_3 = \frac{D}{k_e} = \frac{\$1}{0.10} = \$10$$

Step 2:

$$P_0 = P_3 \,(PVIF_{.10,3}) = (\$10)(0.751)$$
$$= \$7.51$$

2. *Supernormal growth.* Many firms go through life cycles with very rapid growth in the early years followed by a growth rate that approximately matches the economy's growth rate. Personal computer manufacturers

[12]The end of Year 3 is the same point as the beginning of Year 4.

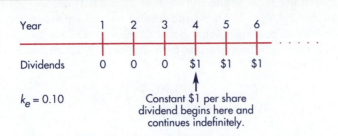

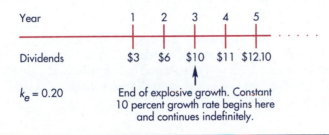

■ *Figure 6–2*
Example of Explosive
Growth Followed by
Constant-Growth
Dividend Pattern

and suppliers (software, components, etc.) are a good recent example of these *supernormal growth* firms. The distinguishing characteristic of a supernormal growth company is that it has at least two different growth rates—it can have more, but it must have at least two.

Regardless of the particular rate of explosive growth in the early years, the valuation procedure for a supernormal growth rate company is identical to that of any other company using the dividend valuation model: find the present value of the expected future dividends. This procedure involves the following steps:

a. Calculate the present value of all dividends expected during the supernormal growth period.

b. Calculate the price of the stock at the end of the supernormal growth period—when the company has become a constant growth stock (use Equation 6–8)—and discount this price back to time period zero. (In discounting the price back to today, *it is important to realize that the end of year* n *is, for our purposes, the same as the beginning of year* n + 1. Thus, if supernormal growth is expected for a period of 10 years, followed by normal growth, we solve for the price at the beginning of year 11, which is actually P_{10} using our notation. We then discount this price back 10 periods, not 11.)

c. Add the values found in Steps 1 and 2.

■ *Example*

Sunbelt Storage Systems, a maker of hard disks for a new model of microcomputer, is expected to have a short period of explosive growth in dividends, followed by a return to a lower, sustainable constant growth rate. The time line for this example is shown in Figure 6–2. Notice that Step 1 calls for solving the constant growth model as of the end of Year 2, and that this calculation involves the dividend during Year 3, D_3. In the second step, the price at the end of Year 2 and the dividends paid up to that point are discounted back to Time Period 0 and added together, resulting in an estimated price for Sunbelt of about $76, which is found as follows:

$$P_2 = \frac{D_3}{k_e - g} = \frac{\$10.00}{0.20 - 0.10} = \$100$$

$$P_0 = \frac{D_1}{1 + k_e} + \frac{D_2}{(1 + k_e)^2} + \frac{P_2}{(1 + k_e)^2}$$
$$= (\$3)(0.833) + (\$6)(0.694) + (\$100)(0.694)$$
$$= \$2.50 + \$4.16 + \$69.40$$
$$= \$76.06$$

As in the case of delayed growth, the key to solving a supergrowth problem is to account for the entire stream of dividends from Time Period 1 to infinity and discount this stream back to Time Period 0. Regardless of how many different dividends are involved, or when the growth rate becomes constant, the process is always the same.

Required Rate of Return on Equity

Equations 6–6 and 6–8 are simple but useful valuation expressions. Notice that Equation 6–8 is the more general of the two, because by setting $g = 0$ in 6–8, we get 6–6. Let's consider Equation 6–8 in more detail. In particular, consider a turned around version of 6–8, found by rearranging the equation to solve for k_e, the required (or expected) rate of return on equity:

$$\text{Required rate of return on equity} = k_e = \frac{D_1}{P_0} + g \qquad \textbf{(6–9)}$$

Equation 6–9 is merely 6–8 rearranged. In this form, the equation says the required (expected) rate of return on equity equals the dividend yield (next year's dividend divided by current stock price) plus the expected growth rate in dividends.

■ *Example*

In early 1989, Newhall Land was selling for $53 per share, was expected to pay a $1.20 per share dividend over the next year, and had an expected dividend growth rate of about 12 percent per year:

$$k_e = \frac{\$1.20}{\$53} + 0.12 = .143 = 14.3\%$$

Equation 6–9 is an important formulation used widely in finance. It provides us with one way to calculate k_e, the required (or expected) rate of return on equity. As we will see in Chapter 14, the calculation of the cost of capital, which involves the cost of equity capital, is a complex and controversial topic.

Small Firm Considerations

The dividend discount model discussed above is the conventional model applied to companies when estimating the value of their shares. Each of the variations of the model assumed either that the firm was paying a dividend or would start to pay a dividend. What about small firms that pay no dividends? How do we value them?

The typical life cycle for a firm is to start out paying no dividends because all earnings are needed to finance the growth of the firm. The major source of equity financing is retained earnings as the firm plows back everything it earns in order to finance its growth. In addition, it borrows money from available sources, typically banks. Access to capital markets is limited for small firms, and the costs on a percentage basis of raising funds through securities offerings, even if buyers are readily available, are prohibitive.

The expectation for most small firms that are successful and growing is that they eventually will pay a dividend at some time in the future. Therefore, one way to value these firms is to estimate when such dividends will begin and the expected stream of dividends thereafter. Applying the dividend discount model then produces an estimated value for the stock. The Vichie Springs example, presented above, of a company not expected to pay a dividend for four years and then to pay a constant dividend, is one instance of this procedure. However, the delayed payment of dividends may be followed by any number of patterns of future dividends, including a constant growth rate or, perhaps more likely, explosive growth for a few years followed by a constant growth rate.

■ *Example*

Assume that the King Software Company, which is developing several new products expected to be widely received by PC users, is currently not paying a dividend. Given the rapid growth forecasted for earnings, King is expected to pay a dividend after three years. The dividend will start at 50 cents per share and increase by 25 cents through year eight, after which the company is expected to slow down and grow at a constant rate of 9 percent per year. The required rate of return for firms in this risky business is estimated to be 20 percent per year. The value of King Software shares would be estimated as:

$$P_0 = \frac{\$0.0}{(1.20)} + \ldots + \frac{\$0.0}{(1.20)^3} + \frac{\$0.50}{(1.20)^4} + \frac{\$0.75}{(1.20)^5} + \frac{\$1.00}{(1.20)^6} + \frac{\$1.25}{(1.20)^7}$$
$$+ \frac{\$1.50}{(1.20)^8} + \frac{\$1.50(1.09)}{.20 - .09} \left(\frac{1}{(1.20)^9} \right)$$
$$= \$4.46 \qquad ■$$

CHANGES IN EXPECTED CASH FLOWS AND REQUIRED RATE OF RETURN

Consider what happens to a firm's stock price as, inevitably, things change over time. To illustrate what's happening, we will work with Equation 6–8 and make a useful substitution. Equation 6–8 is:

$$P_0 = \frac{D_1}{k_e - g}$$

Now, consider what the dividend actually represents. Conceptually, D_1 is the cash flow paid from the firm to the common stockholders, and g is the expected growth in investors' cash flows. Recall that k_e is the required rate of return on equity. Therefore, a useful teaching version of Equation 6–8 is:

$$P_0 = \frac{\text{Next year's cash flow}}{\begin{array}{cc}\text{Required rate of} & \text{Expected growth rate}\\ \text{return on equity} & \text{in cash flows}\end{array}} \qquad (6\text{–}10)$$

This version of the stock valuation model clearly points to what causes stock price, P_0, to change:[13]

1. Changes in expected cash flows (both next year's and—through the growth rate—future years').
2. Changes in the required rate of return on equity.

The following causes and effects are specifically related:

Cause	Effect on P_0
Expected Cash Flows	
Increase	Increases
Decrease	Decreases
Required Rate of Return	
Increases	Decreases
Decreases	Increases

- ## *Example*

Suppose investors have the following expectations about Brassfield Industries stock:

Next year's cash dividend = $3.00 per share
Expected growth rate in cash flows = 6%
Required rate of return = 16%

Therefore, from 6–10:

$$P_0 = \frac{\$3.00}{0.16 - 0.06} = \$30.00$$

Now suppose investor expectations change:

Next year's cash dividend = $3.00 per share
Expected growth rate in cash flows = 8%
Required rate of return = 17%

Therefore:

$$P_0 = \frac{\$3.00}{0.17 - 0.08} = \$33.33$$

Both the expected growth and the required rate of return increased. The net effect on Brassfield's stock price was an increase of $3.33. In this case the increased expected growth overpowered the increase in k_e, but if k_e had risen to 19 percent

---

[13]By changes in P_0 we actually mean major changes. P_0 fluctuates continually as buyers and sellers interact. The changes we refer to are not these minor fluctuations.

while the growth rate was rising to 8 percent, the stock price would have dropped to $27.27. ▪

Many combinations of k_e and cash flow could occur. In the example above, the two effects were opposing one another. This is a common situation, for reasons described below.

Impact of Financial Management Decisions on Stock Price

Equation 6–10 is important because it identifies the two variables the firm should be most concerned with as it makes its major financial management decisions, broadly categorized as investment decisions and financing decisions. Since the firm's goal is to maximize stockholder wealth, and since Equation 6–10 shows that stock price and, hence, stockholder wealth are determined by the expected cash flows and k_e, the firm should carefully consider what impact its financial management decisions have on the expected cash flow stream and k_e. We will consider this impact on each of the two determinants of value.

Expected Cash Flows

In the long run, the expected future cash flows are determined mainly by the firm's investment policy. The cash flows are determined by the profitability of the firm's investments, and profitability depends on how well the firm chooses its investments. But choosing investments is simply the investment-decision aspect of financial management. Therefore, the chain is as follows: the firm makes investment decisions that establish the firm's profitability, and this expected profitability determines the expected cash flows anticipated by investors.

The firm's financing decisions also influence the expected cash flows. Whether or not the firm uses debt and how much debt is used affect the size of the expected cash flows. There is considerable controversy, however, concerning the exact impact financing decisions have on the profitability of the firm, and the main determinant of expected cash flows is the firm's investment policy.

Required Rate of Return

The required rate of return on any asset is the rate of return the market requires in order to hold the asset. We saw in Chapters 4 and 5 that investors require compensation for both the time value of money and their risk exposure. We account for both of these requirements in the discount rate. That is, the discount rate, k_e (or required rate of return), equals the risk-free rate of return plus an appropriate risk premium:[14]

$$k_e = \frac{\text{Riskless rate}}{\text{of return}} + \text{Risk premium} \qquad (6\text{--}11)$$

Equation 6–11 consists of two components. Because of its importance, we review the following material from Chapter 5.

---

[14]It's worth emphasizing once more that not all investors have the same required rate of return, and we are oversimplifying by equating k_e with *the* required rate of return. That is, k_e is the equilibrium or market required rate of return.

1. *Risk-free rate of return.* If an investor could buy stock that carried no risk, its required rate of return would be a function only of the *risk-free* (or *riskless*) interest rate. In Chapter 5 we saw that this rate is usually associated with U.S. government securities and is denoted *RF*.[15]

2. *Risk premiums.* Since common stock investments are not riskless, investors require a *risk premium* when they invest. For any given investor, the size of the premium depends on how much risk the firm's stock would add to (or subtract from) the investor's portfolio.

In Chapter 5 we showed that the risk of a single asset depended on that asset's covariance with a suitable market index. Beta was found to be a good intuitive measure of covariance. The *capital asset pricing model* (CAPM), presented in Chapter 5, relates the required rate of return to beta. It is repeated here to emphasize its importance as a concept.[16]

$$k_e = RF + [E(R_M) - RF]\text{Beta} \qquad (6\text{--}12)$$

where:

$$RF = \text{the risk-free interest rate}$$
$$E(R_M) = \text{the required rate of return on the market index}$$
$$\text{Beta} = \text{a measure of the covariance between rates of return on the market index and the firm's common stock}$$

Notice that Equation 6–12 is merely a more detailed version of Equation 6–11, where:

$$RF = \text{Riskless rate of return}$$
$$[E(R_M) - RF]\text{Beta} = \text{Risk premium}$$

Notice also that the risk premium has two components:

1. $E(R_M) - RF$, the market risk premium; that is, the excess return the market index offers in comparison to the risk-free rate.

2. Beta, the covariance between rates of return on the market index and the firm's stock.

A specific stock i has a risk premium, $B_i[E(R_M) - \text{RF}]$, which may be greater or smaller than the market risk premium, depending on the degree to which it covaries with the market. The greater the covariance, the greater the multiplier that determines the additional risk premium.

This covariance risk premium is, in turn, determined by the firm's financial management policies. A firm's policies, reflected in either investment or financing decisions, may affect its stock's covariance with the market. **Business risk** is the covariability caused by the kinds of investments the firm makes, and **financial risk** is the extra covariability caused by the firm's financing policies. Business and

business risk
the risk caused by the type of business the firm is in

financial risk
the risk to the firm induced by the use of debt to finance its assets

---

[15]Actually, even for government securities there is some risk present. Inflation risk is present because interest received with certainty sometime in the future may not have the purchasing power it is expected to have.

[16]We also saw in Chapter 5 that there was a competing risk/return model to that of the CAPM equation. The arbitrage pricing theory relates required rates of return to k_{RF} and three risk factors, each factor having its own companion beta. We will not review that alternative model in its k_e version here. Its central point regarding valuation is that, as in the CAPM case, various kinds of risk affect k_e, which, in turn, directly affects P_0.

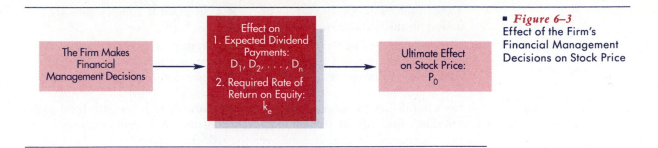

financial risk interact to determine beta. We will explore these topics more fully in later chapters.

In conclusion, *the financial management decisions made by the firm cause the expected cash flow and* k_e *to change, and hence cause* P_0 *to change.* The process is shown schematically in Figure 6–3. Which investments the firm chooses and how it finances these investments are the main determinants of the stock's required rate of return, the expected cash flows, and P_0. Good financial management decisions are those that would be expected to increase P_0, and poor financial management decisions are those that would be expected to decrease P_0.

THE VALUATION OF OTHER SECURITIES

Because the firm's goal is to maximize stockholders' wealth, our valuation emphasis has been focused on the firm's common stock. However, we can apply the basic valuation concepts introduced at the beginning of this chapter to other financial assets as well. In doing so, we set the stage for our work on cost of capital later in the book.

BOND VALUATION

Bonds are long-term sources of borrowing. A company issues (sells) bonds to investors, and it is instructive to see how these financial securities are valued in the marketplace. First, we need to define some terms:

Par value: Face value of the bond. It is the price at which the bond will be redeemed by the issuing company at the end of the life of the bond. For most bonds, and for all instances considered in this text, the par value is $1,000.

Coupon rate: The annual interest rate paid on the par value of the bond. The bond's annual coupon (interest) equals the **coupon interest rate** times par value.[17]

Maturity: The length of time the bond will be outstanding. The issuing company redeems the bond on its maturity date.

coupon interest rate
the contractual interest
rate on a bond when it
is issued

---

[17]Actually, for most bonds, semiannual coupons are paid every six months, each equal to one half of the annual coupon amount.

yield to maturity
the compound annual
average rate of return
that will be earned if a
bond is purchased today
and held to maturity

Market value: The bond's current price. It is the price at which bonds are trading in the marketplace.

Yield to maturity: The bond's required rate of return. The **yield to maturity** is the discount rate that equates the bond's market value with the present value of the future interest payments and redemption of par value.

Since bonds have a contractual payment stream, there is less risk for a firm's bondholders than for its stockholders. The possibility of default causes bondholders to require a risk premium over the risk-free interest rate, which means the required rate of return on the bonds exceeds the risk-free interest rate. However, the required rate of return on a firm's bonds, k_i, will always be less than the required rate of return on the firm's stock because the bonds are safer than the stock. Differences in required rates of return among bonds of different companies are caused by differences in default risk and other technical features added to the bond.

Solving for Price

Adapting the general valuation equation, Equation 6–1, to bonds, we have:

$$B_0 = \sum_{t=1}^{n} \frac{I_t}{(1 + k_i)^t} + \frac{P_t}{(1 + k_i)^n} \tag{6–13}$$

where:

B_0 = current market price of the bond (recall that the subscript zero refers to current time)
P_t = expected principal repayment in year t
I_t = expected interest payment in year t
k_i = required rate of return for bond i
n = maturity of bonds (number of periods remaining before retirement of bonds)

When bonds are first issued by the company, the coupon rate is usually set very close to the interest rate prevailing in the marketplace for bonds of similar risk and maturity. That is, the bond's coupon rate is set approximately equal to the bond's required rate of return (yield to maturity). This practice causes the bond's market value (at time of issue) and par value to be roughly equal. Let's look at an example.

■ *Example*

In early 1989 Boise Cascade Corporation, a major timber company, issued some new $1,000-par-value bonds due to mature in 2001. The bonds carried a rate of 9⅞ percent and were sold at par. This indicates that bonds of similar risk and maturity required rates of return of about 10 percent at that time. Thus, at time of issuance, the required rate of return on these Boise Cascade bonds was approximately 10 percent. Consequently, and being exact in our calculations:

$$\text{Annual interest} = (\text{Coupon rate})(\text{Par value}) \tag{6–14}$$
$$= (0.09875)(\$1,000)$$
$$= \$98.75$$

Equation 6–14 shows that each of the 20 annual interest payments will amount to \$98.75. We know that the par value of \$1,000 will be redeemed in the year 2001 and that the required rate of return (yield to maturity) is 9.875 percent. Therefore, the market price of these bonds at time of issue will be determined as follows, based on annual coupons:

$$
\begin{aligned}
B_0 &= (\$98.75)(PVIFA_{.09875,12}) + (\$1,000)(PVIF_{.09875,12}) \\
&= (\$98.75)(6.8556) + (\$1,000)(0.323) \\
&= \$677 + \$323 \\
&= \$1,000
\end{aligned}
$$

Because the coupon rate and required rate of return are equal at time of issue, the bond's current market price (B_0) equals its par value. ▪

What happens to the bond's market value after the bond is issued? That depends partly on what happens to market interest rates. The bond's required rate of return will reflect market conditions. If interest rates rise, the bond's required rate of return will rise; if interest rates fall, the bond's required rate of return will fall. The bond's market value is a present value, and we learned in Chapter 4 that present values move in the opposite direction from interest rates. Let's look at this further.

▪ *Example*

Suppose that after five years, interest rates have risen, and the required rate of return on the Boise Cascade bonds has changed to 12 percent. Then the price of the bonds at that time (with 7 years of life remaining) would be calculated as:

$$
\begin{aligned}
B_0 &= (\$98.75)(PVIFA_{.12,7}) + (\$1,000)(PVIF_{.12,7}) \\
&= (\$98.75)(4.5638) + (\$1,000)(0.4523) \\
&= \$450.68 + \$452.30 \\
&= \$902.98
\end{aligned}
$$

Since the required rate of return has risen, present value (the market value of the bond) has fallen.

On the other hand, suppose that after five years interest rates have fallen, so the required rate of return is 8 percent. Now the price of the bonds (with 7 years life remaining) is calculated as shown:

$$
\begin{aligned}
B_0 &= (\$98.75)(PVIFA_{.08,7}) + (\$1,000)(PVIF_{.08,7}) \\
&= (\$98.75)(5.2064) + (\$1,000)(0.5835) \\
&= \$514.13 + \$583.50 \\
&= \$1,097.63
\end{aligned}
$$

Since the required rate of return has fallen, present value (the market value of the bond) has risen. ▪

So, the course of a bond's market value is heavily influenced by market interest rates, which pull the bond's required rate of return along with them. Of course, if the bond's risk were to change appreciably at some point, that too could have a dramatic impact on its required rate of return and, therefore, on its market price.

Another strong influence on the bond's market value is the remaining maturity of the bond. When maturity is a long way off, the required rate of return will play a dominant role in establishing market value. As maturity approaches, however, the present value of the par value will loom larger and will play an ever more important role in determining the present value of the bond. By a few weeks before maturity, no matter what the market rate of interest, the price of the bond will be about equal to par value. By the maturity date, the market price of the bond will converge to its face value of $1,000.

■ *Example*

Assume that the Boise bonds are one year from maturity and, as in the previous example, the discount rate is 8 percent. The price of the bonds would be:

$$
\begin{aligned}
B_0 &= (\$98.75)(PVIF_{.08,1}) + (\$1,000)(PVIF_{.08,1}) \\
&= (\$98.75)(.9259) + (\$1,000)(.9259) \\
&= \$91.43 + \$925.90 \\
&= \$1,017.33
\end{aligned}
$$

Semiannual Coupon Payments

We have assumed in the previous examples that interest is paid annually. In reality, bond interest is typically paid semiannually.

This creates no fundamental problem, for we have worked problems like this back in Chapter 4. What we do is simply note that, since payments are semiannual:

1. There are twice as many payment periods as there are years.
2. The bond's semiannual interest payment is one half of the annual coupon payment.
3. The bond's semiannual required rate of return is (approximately) one half of the annual required rate of return.[18]

With these adjustments, we can work any bond problem we're faced with.

■ *Example*

Suppose we wish to find the current market value of a $1,000-par-value, 8 percent coupon bond that matures in five years, and the yield to maturity is 10 percent per year. Then:

$$
n = (2)(5) = 10
$$

$$
\text{Semiannual interest} = \frac{(0.08)}{2}(\$1,000) = \$40
$$

$$
\text{Semiannual } k = \frac{0.10}{2} = 0.05
$$

Therefore:

$$
\begin{aligned}
B_0 &= (\$40)\,(PVIFA_{.05,10}) + (\$1,000)\,(PVIF_{.05,10}) \\
&= (\$40)(7.222) + (\$1,000)(0.614) = \$309 + \$614 \\
&= \$923
\end{aligned}
$$

---

[18]We use the word approximately because the actual relationship between the semiannual and annual required rates of return involves two-period compounding.

Solving for Yield to Maturity

The yield to maturity is the compound annual average rate of return that will be earned from a bond investment if the bond is purchased today and held to maturity. It is also the discount rate that equates the bond's market value with the present value of the future interest payments and redemption of par value. Thus, in solving for the yield to maturity, we know the current market price of the bonds, as well as the cash flow stream on the right side. What remains is a trial-and-error process to find the discount rate that will make the cash flow stream on the right side equal to the current market price on the left. Many calculators and computer programs are set up to solve for the yield to maturity. The following example shows conceptually what is involved.

▪ *Example*

Suppose the price of the Boise bonds is currently $872.06 and 11 years remain to maturity. We wish to find the yield to maturity on these bonds. Note that since the market price is less than $1,000, the discount rate must be above the coupon rate of 9.875 percent. To find the *YTM,* we must solve this equation:

$$\$872.06 = (\$98.75)(PVIFA) + (\$1,000)(PVIF)$$

We would solve this equation by trying a discount greater than 9.875 percent, for example, 11 percent, and seeing if the present value was less than or greater than the price of $872.06. At 11 percent we would find the present value greater, meaning that a higher discount rate is necessary. Next, we could try 12 percent (based on semiannual discounting of six percent for 22 periods and a semiannual coupon of $49.375).

$$\begin{aligned}\$872.06 &= (\$49.375)(12.0416) + (\$1,000)(.2775)\\ &= \$594.55 + \$277.50\\ &= \$872.05\end{aligned}$$

Perpetuities

If bonds have very long lives ($n \to \infty$) and interest payments are constant ($I_1 = I_2 = \ldots = I$), then Equation 6–13 reduces to a simpler form:

$$B_0 = \frac{I}{k_i} \qquad (6\text{--}15)$$

where I = the constant interest payment.

This formula is analogous to Equation 6–6, used to value no-growth common stock.

▪ *Example*

If a perpetuity pays $90 each year forever and if k_i = 10 percent:

$$B_0 = \frac{\$90}{0.10} = \$900$$

Estimating the Required Rate of Return

As in the case of common stock, we are often interested in estimating a bond's required rate of return. Equation 6–15 is a particularly useful approximation formula for this task. Rearranging 6–15 to solve for the bond's required rate of return (yield to maturity), k_i, we see that:

$$k_i = \frac{I}{B_0}$$

(6–16)

This equation assumes, of course, perpetual bonds with a constant interest payment.

▪ *Example*

If interest payments on the perpetuity are $90 per year and if the bond's market price is now $800:

$$B_0 = \frac{\$90}{\$800} = 0.1125 = 11.25\%$$

▪

PREFERRED STOCK VALUATION

Preferred stockholders receive dividends, which are discounted at the rate of return required for preferred stock. This rate is less than that for common stock because preferred is less risky. Its claims are paid before those of common stock, both in normal times and in bankruptcy. Since preferred stock's dividends and claims on assets are more secure, its rate is less likely to fluctuate than that of common stock. Therefore, the preferred rate of return is less likely to covary with the market index. But the preferred is riskier than the firm's bonds, and the required rate of return on the preferred, k_p, is therefore greater than that of the bonds.

Adapting valuation Equation 6–1 to preferred stock, we see that:

$$P_0 = \sum_{t=1}^{\infty} \frac{d_t}{(1 + k_p)^t}$$

(6–17)

where:

P_0 = current market price of preferred stock
d_t = expected preferred dividend in year t
k_p = market discount rate applied to expected preferred stock dividends

We're assuming the preferred has no maturity date ($n = \infty$). If future dividends are expected to be constant ($d_1 = d_2 = \ldots = d_n$), then 6–15 reduces to:

$$P_0 = \frac{d}{k_p}$$

(6–18)

▪ *Example*

In early 1989, one of Alabama Power Company's preferred stock issues paid a $9 dividend and the market discount rate was 9.8 percent. Since there is no maturity date, the market value of the preferred stock was calculated as shown:

$$P_0 = \frac{\$9}{0.098} = \$91.84$$

Note also that by rearranging Equation 6–18:

$$k_p = \frac{d}{P_0} \qquad\qquad \textbf{(6–19)}$$

    ■

SUMMARY

■ Valuation is a present value concept that involves estimating future cash flows and discounting them at a required rate of return to determine a security's intrinsic value.

■ Financial markets are assumed to be efficient, meaning that security prices quickly and, on balance, accurately reflect information.

■ Stock price may be expressed as a function of the expected future dividends and a discount rate that represents the required rate of return on equity.

■ The dividend discount model:

$$P_0 = \sum_{t=1}^{\infty} \frac{D_t}{(1 + k_e)^t}$$

shows how P_0 depends on the expected future dividends and the discount rate.

■ An increase in expected dividends would cause P_0 to increase, and a decrease in expected dividends would cause P_0 to decrease. Likewise, an increase in k_e would cause P_0 to decrease, and a decrease in k_e would cause P_0 to increase.

■ The dividend discount model is implemented by estimating the future growth rate in dividends. There are three growth rate cases: constant dollar dividend, constant growth rate, and variable growth rates.

■ The financial management decisions that the firm makes determine the risk/return characteristics of the firm, which establish the expected dividend stream and k_e and, ultimately, P_0.

KEY TERMS

business risk, p. 182
coupon interest rate, p. 183
dividend discount model, p. 173
efficient market hypothesis, p. 169

financial risk, p. 182
intrinsic value, p. 167
yield to maturity, p. 184

QUESTIONS

6–1. According to valuation theory, what general factors determine stock price?

6–2. Other things being equal, what would be the qualitative effect on the stock price of the BAR Company if the following changes occurred? Explain your answers.

    a. The firm's future earnings prospects increased.

    b. The covariance between market index rates of return and BAR stock rates of return decreased.

    c. The correlation between market index rates of return and BAR stock rates of return decreased.

    d. The standard deviation of BAR stock's rate of return distribution increased.

    e. The firm's required rate of return on equity decreased.

6–3. Under what conditions could the following valuation models justifiably be used?
   a. $P_0 = D_1/(k_e - g)$.
   b. $P_0 = D/k_e$.

6–4. Explain why the required rate of return on a firm's common stock is greater than the required rate of return on its preferred stock.

6–5. "Many stocks do not pay current dividends; therefore, it is not valid to evaluate them using the dividend-valuation model." Comment on this statement.

6–6. Suppose an investor possesses inside information (information the general public does not have) about new investments the firm recently made that will dramatically increase earnings. Use Equation 6–5 to explain how knowledge of this information is valuable to the investor.

6–7. Suppose you own stock in a privately held corporation where there is no public market for the stock and hence no readily observable market value for the stock. How might you go about determining the market value of the stock?

6–8. While reading the financial pages one morning, you notice that Rendleman Citrus, Inc., has just invested heavily in new orchards in a very arid part of Texas where there is also little irrigation water. Rendleman's executives forecast the new orchards will eventually be very profitable and will cause earnings to increase substantially in the future. However, the next day you also observe that Rendleman's stock price drops five points in unusually heavy trading. Explain this drop in stock price using the dividend valuation model.

6–9. Explain why the equation for the dividend discount model, Equation 6–5, does not contain the future price of the stock as a term.

6–10. Using k_e as determined by the CAPM, explain what would happen to k_e if
   a. Inflation decreased.
   b. Investors' risk aversion increased.
   c. Interest rates increased.

6–11. For any two investors valuing the same stock, what differences in results (the price that is determined) would you expect if Investor A's holding period is three years while Investor B's holding period is six years?

6–12. From a valuation perspective, in what circumstances would the valuation process for a bond, a preferred stock and a common stock be identical?

6–13. Summarize the differences in procedure between valuing bonds on an annual interest basis and on a semiannual interest basis.

6–14. Explain two methods for determining the required rate of return on a common stock.

6–15. What is meant by the term *normal rate of return*?

6–16. What are the implications to a financial manager if the efficient market hypothesis is strictly true in all types of markets?

6–17. What is meant by the *intrinsic value* of an asset?

6–18. In what sense can the market value of an asset be considered a *consensus price*?

6–19. What is the relationship between risk and the required rate of return?

6–20. Is the efficiency of real asset markets likely to be the same as that for financial asset markets?

6–21. Based on your answer to the preceding question, what are the implications for financial managers?

6–22. Based on the dividend discount model, what would be the value of a stock that never planned to pay a dividend?

6–23. Define precisely the term *required rate of return*.

6–24. How would you calculate the required rate of return for a no-growth common stock?

6–25. What condition must exist to have a supergrowth valuation situation?

6–26. Explain conceptually how to value a supergrowth company.

DEMONSTRATION PROBLEMS

6–1. Find the price of a preferred stock which pays a dividend of $8 per year if the required rate of return is 12 percent.

6–2. Find the price of a stock if the dividend expected to be paid next period is $5, the expected growth rate in dividends is 6 percent, and the required rate of return is 14 percent.

6–3. Ferris Metals, currently selling for $60 a share, recently paid a dividend of $1.50 and has an expected dividend growth rate of 7 percent. What is the required rate of return for this stock?

6–4. Johnson Baby Products is undergoing rapid growth; dividends are expected to grow for the next three years at 25 percent a year, after which they will grow at 6 percent a year for the indefinite future. The company is currently paying $1.00 per share in dividends. The required rate of return is 12 percent. What is the price of Johnson Baby Products?

6–5. A bond has 10 years to maturity and a coupon rate of 10 percent. Bond interest is paid semiannually. The required rate of return on this bond is now 12 percent. What is its price?

Solutions to Demonstration Problems

6–1. For any perpetuity, such as a preferred stock, finding the price is simply a matter of dividing the fixed dollar dividend by the required rate of return. Therefore:

$$P_0 = \$8/.12 = \$66.67$$

6–2. Recognizing the fact that a constant growth rate in dividends is stated in the problem, we apply the constant-growth version of the dividend discount model.

$$P_0 = D_1/(k - g)$$
$$P_0 = \$5/(.14 - .06)$$
$$= \$62.50$$

6–3. We apply the rearranged form of the constant-growth version of the dividend discount model. We must compound D_0 to D_1 by multiplying D_0 by $(1 + g)$; therefore, $D_1 = \$1.50 (1 + .07) = \$1.61$, and:

$$k = D_1/P_0 + g$$
$$= \$1.61/\$60 + .07$$
$$= 9.7\%$$

6–4. This is a supergrowth company because it has two different growth rates. We must first determine dividends for Years 1, 2, and 3, and discount them back to today at the required rate of return. We must then solve for price at the beginning of Year 4, using the constant growth model and D_4 in the numerator, and discount this price back to today using the three-year present value factor. We then add these two components together.

	Dividend	Present Value Factor @ 12%	Present Value
D_0			
$D_1 = D_0(1 + g) = \$1.25$		.893	$1.12
$D_2 = D_1(1 + g) = 1.56$		.797	1.24
$D_3 = D_2(1 + g) = 1.95$		.712	1.39
			$3.75

$$
\begin{aligned}
P_3 &= D_4/(k - g) \\
&= \$1.95(1 + .06)/(.12 - .06) \\
&= \$2.07/.06 \\
&= \$34.50 \\
P_0 &= P_3 \times .712 = \$34.50 \times .712 = \$24.56 = \text{present} \\
&\quad \text{value of } P_3 \\
\text{Price} &= \text{Present value of the first 3 years of dividends } + \text{ Present} \\
&\quad \text{value of } P_3 \\
&= \$3.75 + \$24.56 = \$28.31
\end{aligned}
$$

6–5. To solve a standard bond price problem, we must find the present value of the interest payments, the present value of the face value to be received at maturity, and add these two numbers together. Because of the semiannual interest, we must divide the coupon and required rate of return in half and double the number of periods. The dollar coupon is $100, or 10 percent of $1,000.

$$
\begin{aligned}
\text{Present value of the interest payments} &= \$50 \times 11.470 = \$573.50 \\
\text{Present value of the face value (\$1,000)} &= \$1,000 \times .312 = \underline{\$312.00} \\
&\qquad\qquad\qquad\qquad\qquad\quad \$885.50
\end{aligned}
$$

Notice that the interest payment part is solved using the *PVIFA* factor for 6 percent, 20 periods. The face value part is solved using the *PVIF* factor for 6 percent, 20 periods.

PROBLEMS

6–1. An asset with an expected life of four years has the following expected cash incomes, C_t:

t	C_t
1	$ 1,000
2	1,000
3	2,000
4	10,000

Assuming that an appropriate discount rate is 15 percent, calculate the asset's theoretical market value.

6–2. An asset with an anticipated life of six years has the following anticipated cash incomes:

t	1	2	3	4	5	6
Income	$200	300	600	1,000	1,400	2,000

Find the asset's worth to an investor with these discount rates:
a. 10 percent.
b. 20 percent.
c. 40 percent.

6–3. Find the current price of a share of common stock for the following circumstances:

Case	k_e	D_1	g
a	0.10	$ 5	0.0
b	0.25	10	0.0
c	0.20	20	0.10
d	0.30	6	0.20
e	0.25	2	0.10

6–4. The Mitchell Corporation pays a current dividend of $2.50 per share, which is expected to continue indefinitely at the same amount. If the required rate of return is 10 percent, what is the value of Mitchell's stock?

6–5. Assume that investors are currently expecting that National Financial Company will pay a constant $5-per-share stream of dividends forever and that the required rate of return on equity is 25 percent.
a. Determine the current stock price.
b. What will the stock price be if dividend expectations increase by a dollar a share and if the required rate of return on equity stays at 25 percent?
c. After the change described in (b) has occurred, what will happen to the stock price if the required rate of return on equity changes to 30 percent?

6–6. A stock is expected to pay a 50-cent dividend in Year 1, a 75-cent dividend in Year 2, and a $1.00 annual dividend thereafter for the foreseeable future. How much would you pay for such a stock if your required rate of return were 12 percent per year?

6–7. An investor buys a share of KRJ stock and expects to receive an annual dividend of $6 indefinitely. The first dividend is due in one year.
a. If the investor has a 30 percent required rate of return, what would he or she be willing to pay for the stock now?
b. What would he or she be willing to pay for the KRJ stock now if the first dividend were not due until year five?

6–8. The Ferret Company's last dividend was $2.00 per share, which is expected to grow at a constant rate of 8 percent per year. The required rate of return is 12 percent. What is the price of Ferret common?

6–9. The Finley Corporation is expected to pay a dividend of $3.00 per share next year, and this dividend is expected to grow at a constant rate of 10 percent for the foreseeable future. If the required rate of return is 14 percent, what is the price of the stock?

6–10. Poindexter Consulting Services is currently selling for $50 per share. It is expected to pay a dividend of $2.00 per share next year. If the required rate of return is 10 percent, what is the expected growth rate for Poindexter?

6–11. Kathryn's Tape Shoppes has a current price of $60 per share. It recently paid a dividend of $1.50 per share. If the growth rate for this firm is expected to be constant at 8 percent per year, what is the required rate of return?

6–12. An investor expects to receive a $10-per-share dividend from JKL stock every year for the foreseeable future. According to *The Wall Street Journal*, the current market price of JKL is $50 per share. What is the current required rate of return on equity of this stock?

6–13. Using the data in Problem 6–12, assume that JKL dividends were expected to stay at $10 per share per year for 10 years and then increase to $15 per share for each year thereafter. What would we expect JKL stock to sell for today if the market's required rate of return stayed the same as that calculated in Problem 6–12?

6–14. Determine the theoretical value per share of the common stock of the CSK Company if anticipated dividends are $2 per year for an indefinitely long time and if the required rate of return on equity is 20 percent per year.

6–15. Given the answer to Problem 6–14, assume there are 200,000 shares of common stock outstanding. What would be the new theoretical value per share of the common stock if the firm accepted a group of projects whose net present value is $400,000?

6–16. Shown below are beta values for five different common stocks.

Stock	Beta
A	0.0
B	1.5
C	1.0
D	0.5
E	2.0

a. If the risk-free interest rate is 12 percent and if the required rate of return on the market is 16 percent, find k_e for each stock.

b. Rank the stocks according to risk.

c. How does each stock compare in risk to the market index portfolio?

6–17. The D. Brock Company is a conservatively managed company. The expected common dividend for the next period is $3 per share, expected dividend growth is about 6 percent per year, and the required rate of return on the stock is 9 percent. However, in response to stockholder pressure, the board of directors replaces the management of the company with a team of recent business school graduates who have been well trained in finance. This new management team is considering alternative financial policies that would be expected to have the results shown below. Determine the anticipated effect on stock price of each plan, and identify the best plan. Explain why the identified plan is best.

Plan A: Adopt a set of investment opportunities that would increase the expected dividend growth rate to 9 percent and the required rate of return to 11 percent.

Plan B: Adopt new investment and financing plans that would reduce the expected dividend growth rate to 5 percent and the required rate of return to 8 percent.

Plan C: Eliminate some relatively unprofitable investments the firm owns and rearrange the firm's capital structure. The result would be an expected dividend growth rate of 10 percent and a required rate of return of 15 percent.

Plan D: Adopt a set of investment opportunities that would increase growth to 7 percent and the required rate of return to 10 percent.

6–18. The Wilson Corporation recently paid a dividend of $1.00 per share. This dividend is expected to grow at 25 percent a year for the next five years, after which the dividend is expected to grow at a rate of 7 percent for the indefinite future.

The required rate of return for Wilson is 18 percent. What is the price of the stock?

6–19. The 4F Company is expected to enjoy explosive growth in dividends for the next three years, at a rate of 30 percent per year. The dividend growth rate is then expected to "slow" to 20 percent a year for the next five years. Finally, the dividend growth rate is expected to be constant at 6 percent a year thereafter. The last dividend paid was $2.00 per share, and the required rate of return for 4F is 20 percent. What is the price of the stock?

6–20. Buschmann Bancorp, Inc., has common stock outstanding with a beta of 1.6. The expected return on the market index is 20 percent, and the risk-free interest rate is 15 percent. Buschmann pays a $4.60-per-share dividend, and no growth in dividends is expected. What is your best estimate of the current price of Buschmann's stock?

6–21. A $1,000 bond pays an annual coupon rate of 6 percent. Interest payments are annual. Find the current market price of the bond if its required rate of return is 5 percent per year and if its maturity is now 20 years. Assume the next interest payment is due one year from now.

6–22. Zee Company has a $1,000 bond that will mature in 10 years. The coupon rate is 8 percent, and the bond pays interest semiannually. If the bond's required rate of return is 12 percent compounded semiannually, what is its current market value?

6–23. *a.* If an investor can buy a share of stock for $50 on the expectation of receiving $8 in dividends every year for an infinitely long time period, what required rate of return is the market imposing on the stock?

b. Suppose that the dividend expectation on the stock changes to $10 per share for an infinitely long time and that the required rate of return does not change. What should the new market price of the stock be?

6–24. Given the data in Problem 6–23, assume that the dividend expectation is $10 per share for the next five years, and then $11 per share thereafter, and that the stock's required rate of return is 18 percent. What should the market price of the stock be?

6–25. The Lummer Corporation has preferred stock outstanding that pays a dividend of $2.00 per share annually. Required rates of return on preferred of this risk category recently rose from 10 percent to 12 percent. What will the new price of this preferred stock be?

6–26. The Wilder Company has an issue of preferred stock outstanding that pays a dividend of $1.50 per share. The current price of this preferred stock is $15. What is the required rate of return on this security?

6–27. The Stengel Company has outstanding an issue of common stock, an issue of preferred stock, and an issue of mortgage bonds. The company's common stock sells for $50 per share and is expected to pay a dividend next year of $1.60 per share. Investors expect these dividends to grow at an annual rate of 7 percent.

Stengel's preferred stock was issued in perpetuity and pays an annual dividend of $3. Its current market price is $35. Stengel's $1,000-face-value mortgage bonds mature in 30 years. They pay an annual interest rate of 9 percent and currently are selling for $1,248.

a. What implied required rates of return are investors demanding on each of these securities?

b. From the investors' standpoint, which set of securities is the riskiest of the three? Least risky? Explain how you reached your conclusions.

6–28. Determine the price of each of the securities in Problem 6–27 if required rates of return increase by 100 percent in each case.

6–29. Dot Company has a $1,000 bond that will mature in 20 years. The coupon rate is 8 percent, and the bond pays interest semiannually.

If the market price of the bond is $699, what is its required rate of return?

6–30. *a.* The ABE Company also has a $1,000 bond outstanding that matures in 20 years and pays a 10 percent coupon, interest paid semiannually. If this bond is viewed by investors as being equally as risky as the Dot Company bond in Problem 6–29, what should the market price of the ABE bond be?

b. If required rates of return stay the same, what should the market prices of the bonds be 10 years from now?

c. If interest rates for bonds like Dot and ABE changed to 16 percent compounded semiannually, and maturity is 20 years away, what would the current market prices of these bonds be?

SELECTED REFERENCES

Historical estimates of the risk and return on equities can be found in:

Carelton, Willard T., and Josef Lakonishok. "Risk and Return on Equity: The Use and Misuse of Historical Estimates." *Financial Analysts Journal*, January–February 1985, pp. 38–47, 62.

The real world use of the dividend discount model is discussed in:

Rappaport, Alfred. "The Affordable Dividend Approach to Equity Valuation." *Financial Analysts Journal*, July–August 1986, pp. 52–58.

APPENDIX 6–A   DERIVATION OF THE CONSTANT-GROWTH MODEL

To derive the constant-growth model, we start with the dividend valuation model and expand it out n periods.

From Equation 6–5, expanded out for n periods:

$$P_0 = \frac{D_1}{1 + k_e} + \frac{D_2}{(1 + k_e)^2} + \ldots + \frac{D_n}{(1 + k_e)^n}$$

But, for a constant growth in dividends of g percent per period:

$$D_1 = D_0(1 + g)$$
$$D_2 = D_0(1 + g)^2$$

$$\cdot$$
$$\cdot$$
$$\cdot$$

$$D_n = D_0(1 + g)^n$$

Substituting these into the equation above gives:

$$P_0 = \frac{D_0(1 + g)}{1 + k_e} + \frac{D_0(1 + g)^2}{(1 + k_e)^2} + \ldots + \frac{D_0(1 + g)^n}{(1 + k_e)^n} \qquad \text{(6A–1)}$$

$$\therefore P_0 = D_0\left[\frac{1 + g}{1 + k_e} + \frac{(1 + g)^2}{(1 + k_e)^2} + \ldots + \frac{(1 + g)^n}{(1 + k_e)^n}\right]$$

Multiplying both sides of Equation 6A–1 by $[(1 + k_e)/(1 + g)]$ gives:

$$\frac{P_0(1 + k_e)}{1 + g} = D_0\left[1 + \frac{1 + g}{1 + k_e} + \ldots + \frac{(1 + g)^{n-1}}{(1 + k_e)^{n-1}}\right] \qquad \text{(6A–2)}$$

Subtracting 6A–1 from 6A–2 gives:

$$\frac{P_0(1 + k_e)}{1 + g} - P_0 = D_0\left[1 - \frac{(1 + g)^n}{(1 + k_e)^n}\right] \tag{6A–3}$$

Now, if n approaches infinity and $k_e > g$, the last part of the bracketed term of 6A–3 will approach zero. Therefore:

$$\frac{P_0(1 + k_e)}{1 + g} - P_0 = D_0 \tag{6A–4}$$

Solving for P_0:

$$P_0 = \frac{D_0(1 + g)}{k_e - g} = \frac{D_1}{k_e - g} \tag{6A–5}$$

Short–Term
Financial Management

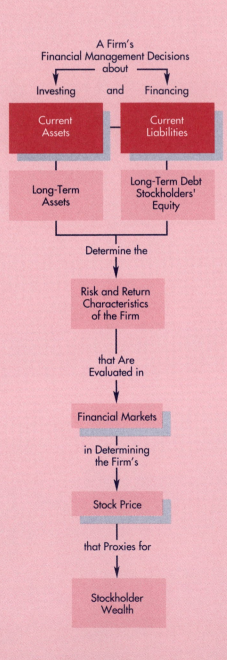

A Firm's
Financial Management Decisions
about

Investing   and   Financing

Current Assets   **Current Liabilities**

Long-Term Assets   Long-Term Debt Stockholders' Equity

Determine the

Risk and Return Characteristics of the Firm

that Are Evaluated in

Financial Markets

in Determining the Firm's

Stock Price

that Proxies for

Stockholder Wealth

We begin our study of financial management decisions by examining the top half of the balance sheet, combining the investment and financing decisions. In the next four chapters, we analyze the management of the firm's current assets and current liabilities, where *current* is defined as having a life or maturity of one year or less. Current assets are mainly cash, marketable securities, accounts receivable, and inventory, while current liabilities are mainly accounts payable, notes payable, and accruals. Management of current assets and liabilities, traditionally called working-capital management, is part of the broader concept of short-term financial management. This part of the financial management process is concerned with all of the firm's decisions affecting cash flows in the short term.

The management of working capital involves routine, daily administration of, and decisions about, current assets and current liabilities. The importance of this topic is underscored by the fact that current assets constitute about 40 percent of the total assets of manufacturing firms. Working capital management activities consume a significant portion of the financial manager's time; moreover, although these decisions lack the glamour and attention of major long-term investment and financing decisions, they are critical to the success of a firm, particularly small firms.

The diagram accompanying this opening discussion illustrates both the valuation process we deal with throughout this book and that portion of the process discussed in these four chapters.

Working–Capital Management

The Importance of Working Capital

The oil industry suffered severe shocks in the 1980s as the price of oil dropped sharply in the face of a seeming surplus of oil. All segments of the industry were hurt, as were oil-producing regions such as Texas. The oil- and gas-drilling industry was impacted severely. For example, Parker Drilling Company had suffered six years of consecutive operating losses by 1988, with the expectation by some analysts of at least two more years of losses. The company lost over $300,000,000 in net profits from 1983 to 1987 alone. Total assets in 1987 amounted to only $355,000,000.

Despite these severe losses, Parker Drilling held up reasonably well through all this difficulty. One strong aspect of its operations was its management of working capital. Although cash declined in each year from 1984 through 1987, Parker had some $56 million in cash at the end of 1987. Its current ratio (current assets divided by current liabilities) was a respectable 2.6 at the end of 1987, down from 4.5 in 1986 (it was 2.6 in 1982, when Parker showed a net profit of $76,000,000). Although current assets declined each year during this period, current liabilities in 1987 were very close to their lowest level in more than 10 years. Nor was this liquidity purchased with long-term debt, which in 1987 was the lowest it had been since 1981. Parker sold common stock in 1987 to be used at least partially for working-capital purposes, and it was expected to do so again within the next few years.

Clearly, Parker Drilling faced enormous financial strains during the 1980s. Nevertheless, it appears to have survived some of the most troubled years in memory for the oil-drilling industry, thanks in no small part to the sound management of its liquidity, or working-capital, position. The same is not true for Global Marine, once one of the world's largest offshore oil rig operators. It was forced to seek protection under the bankruptcy laws because of its losses as oil prices declined.

short-term financial management
a firm's decisions that affect its short-term cash flows

working capital
defined as current assets

net working capital
defined as current assets minus current liabilities

working-capital management
the management of both current assets and current liabilities—the top half of the balance sheet

Consistent with our emphasis throughout this text on valuation, which is dependent on cash flows, **short-term financial management** is concerned with all of the firm's decisions that affect its short-term cash flows. The term *working-capital management* is often used to denote the decisions a firm must make about its current assets and liabilities. Technically, **working capital** is defined as current assets, and **net working capital** as current assets minus current liabilities, but the terms are used interchangeably. When we speak of **working-capital management** in this text, we mean the management of both current assets and current liabilities—the top half of the balance sheet. Working-capital management is the major part of the broader short-term financial management process, which is concerned with all decisions affecting cash flows.

Working-capital management involves decisions about the level of current assets to be held, the composition of those assets, and how current assets are to be financed. The Parker Drilling example shows the importance of the topic in helping a firm survive adverse circumstances.

Our purpose in this chapter is to address the broader issues associated with short-term financial management. The primary *chapter learning objectives* are:

1. To understand the nature and importance of short-term financial management.
2. To relate short-term financial management to the valuation of the firm.
3. To analyze the investment decision in current assets.
4. To analyze the financing decision for current assets.

AN OVERVIEW OF SHORT-TERM FINANCIAL MANAGEMENT

Short-Term versus Long-Term Financial Decisions

As we learned in Chapter 1, financial decisions can be divided into investment decisions and financing decisions. Traditionally, in the study of managerial finance, the analysis of current assets has been separate from the analysis of fixed assets (capital budgeting). Furthermore, the analysis of short-term financing has been separate from the analysis of long-term financing (capital structure). The end result is that, in the study of managerial finance, individual current assets and current liabilities are organized and analyzed as a unit under a title such as *working-capital management* or *short-term financial management*. Entire books are now devoted to the subject.[1] Similarly, long-term investment decisions (i.e., capital budgeting decisions) are widely recognized as a body of knowledge and are taught in several areas, including accounting, economics, and industrial engineering, again with entire books devoted to this subject.

Conceptually, the separation between short-term financial decisions and long-term investment and financing decisions is artificial. To see this, think about the flow of cash through the firm. Figure 7–1 uses cash as the focal point to relate the two halves of the firm's operations—the short-term half and the long-term half.

---

[1]See, for example, Frederick C. Scherr, *Modern Working Capital Management: Text and Cases* (Englewood Cliffs, N.J.: Prentice Hall, Inc., 1989).

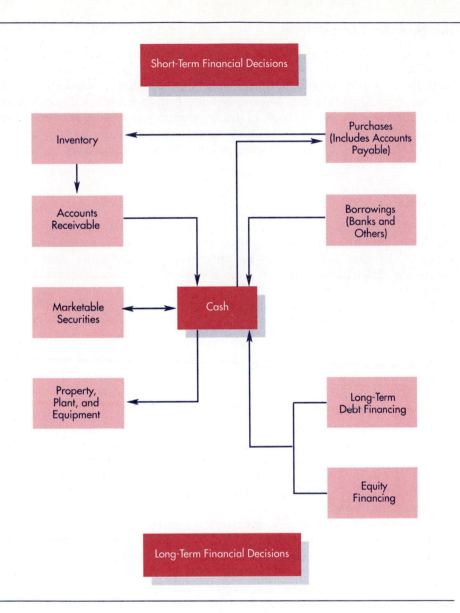

As we can see from Figure 7–1, both halves are important in affecting cash flow through the firm and, ultimately, affecting stockholder wealth, and it is clear that both halves are closely related. Cash has to be allocated to both short-term assets and long-term assets, and financing can be obtained on both the short-term and long-term sides.

Many short-term financial-management decisions have to be made, and most have to be made on a continuing basis. In fact, relative to total cash flow, as depicted in Figure 7–1, the activity, or turnover, on the short-term side is quite high relative to the long-term side.

The Need for Current Assets

As we saw in the case of Parker Drilling, current assets provide the firm with liquidity, thereby protecting it during difficult periods. In effect, such liquidity helps the firm deal with the problem of risk (or uncertainty), which we studied in Chapter 5. As an ongoing concern, business firms are interested in enhancing stockholder wealth, and this requires steady generation of profits. Profits, in turn, require a successful sales program, and current assets are necessary to ensure the smooth functioning of the sales program. At the heart of the need for current assets is the operating cycle.

The Cash-Conversion Cycle

The *working-capital cash flow cycle* refers to the process of purchasing materials and labor, producing a product, selling the product on credit, and receiving payment. Various cash outflows and inflows occur during this time period. Short-term financial management concerns the efficient management of these cash flows.

cash-conversion cycle
the time necessary to convert cash into inventory, inventory into receivables, and receivables into cash

We will use the term **cash-conversion cycle** to refer to the length of time necessary to complete the following sequence of events:[2]

1. Convert cash into inventory.
2. Convert inventory into receivables.
3. Convert receivables into cash.

The cash-conversion cycle can be visualized in a broad way by referring to Figure 7–1 and following the movement from cash. Whether spent immediately or used to service accounts payable, cash is used, in effect, to produce inventory. For manufacturing firms, this phase would start with the purchase of materials and would conclude with the delivery of manufactured goods to inventory.[3] In other words, cash is used to pay for purchases that go through the production process and end up in inventory.

In the next phase of the cycle, inventory is converted into receivables as sales are made to customers.[4] In the last phase, receivables are collected, and the cycle is complete. The firm has moved from cash to inventory to receivables to cash again.

Thus, the firm by necessity must invest funds in current assets. Cash is needed to pay bills not perfectly matched by current cash inflows, and firms hold marketable securities (such as short-term government notes) to have funds available as needed. Firms carry inventory to ensure having ample products to sell, and they issue their customers credit (hold accounts receivable) for competitive sales reasons. An adequate level of current assets assures a smooth, uninterrupted sales process.

---

[2]The cash-conversion cycle emphasizes cash flows rather than operating events. For a discussion of the model, see Verlyn D. Richards and Eugene J. Laughlin, "A Cash Conversion Cycle Approach to Liquidity Analysis," *Financial Management,* Spring 1980, pp. 32–38.

[3]Wholesalers and retailers would not have a manufacturing portion of this phase, but would have a direct conversion of cash into inventory. Service firms may have no inventory.

[4]Firms that offer no credit (cash-and-carry firms) would not have this phase.

To see the cash-conversion cycle in a different perspective, consider Figure 7–2. Here, what is sometimes called the *operating cycle* can be seen to be the sum of:

1. The *inventory-conversion period*, or the average number of days necessary to make and sell the product.
2. The *receivables-conversion period*, or the average number of days needed to collect credit sales.

The operating cycle spans a broad scope of activities within the working-capital management area. For example, when purchases are made, most will be on credit, giving rise to accounts payable, an important source of short-term financing. When the purchases are paid for, the firm must make a cash outlay. The time between these cash outlays and the subsequent cash inflows is the cash-conversion period.

Because of our emphasis on cash flows, we are concerned primarily with the cash-conversion cycle part of Figure 7–2, which we will consider in more detail in Chapter 8 when we analyze cash management. The cash-conversion cycle is the net time period (in days) between the firm's actual cash expenditures on productive resources and the actual receipt of cash from the sale of its products. This measure takes into account what is called the *payables deferral period*, which is the time period between the purchase of raw materials and labor and the actual payment in cash for these items. Subtraction of the payables deferral period from the operating cycle results in the cash-conversion cycle, which is the actual time between cash outflows and cash inflows.

In effect, the cash-conversion cycle measures the time during which the firm has funds invested in working capital. An increase in the cash-conversion cycle would indicate a worsening of the firm's basic liquidity, and a decrease would indicate an improvement in the firm's liquidity.

Permanent and Temporary Current Assets

It might appear that the need for current assets is reduced as the operating cycle ends; therefore, we must distinguish between permanent and temporary current assets. If the firm is a going concern, it will have a continuous need

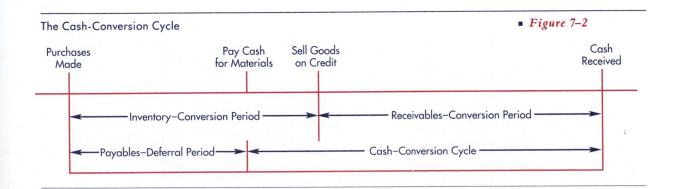

The Cash-Conversion Cycle   ■ *Figure 7–2*

Purchases Made — Pay Cash for Materials — Sell Goods on Credit — Cash Received

Inventory–Conversion Period — Receivables–Conversion Period

Payables–Deferral Period — Cash–Conversion Cycle

for some minimum level of current assets that is as permanent as the firm's fixed assets.

- The minimum level of current assets that is always needed is called *permanent current assets*.
- Any amount above the permanent current assets level is referred to as *temporary current assets*.

Both facilitate the sales process through the operating cycle, but temporary current assets are held to meet liquidity needs expected to last only temporarily as a result of seasonal and other factors.

Figure 7–3 illustrates the basic distinction between permanent and temporary current assets. The permanent level stays fairly constant, but with an allowance for growth over time as the firm becomes larger, while temporary current assets fluctuate quite widely depending on operating needs, seasonal factors, and so on.

The Importance of Short-Term Financial Management

The importance of short-term financial management to the firm can scarcely be exaggerated. Each day, it absorbs most of financial managers' efforts. Most firms undertake significant fixed-asset projects—build new plants or make acquisitions—only periodically. On the other hand, almost all firms constantly face changes in their current assets and current liabilities, and short-term cash flows are continually changing.

To gain some perspective on the importance of short-term financial management, Table 7–1 shows, in percentage form, the assets and liabilities for all manufacturing corporations. Notice first that for all manufacturers, current assets accounted for an average of almost 40 percent of total assets. Therefore, regardless of the fact that, in general, the critical earning assets of the firm are its plant, equipment, and so on, a very large percentage of all assets have maturities of one year or less and must be properly managed if the stockholders' wealth is to be maximized.

Table 7–1 shows that, on average, current liabilities make up about 25 percent of total liabilities and stockholders' equity. This percentage slightly exceeded that on long-term debt, often thought of as a major source of financing. Thus, while

■ *Figure 7–3*
Permanent and Temporary Current Assets

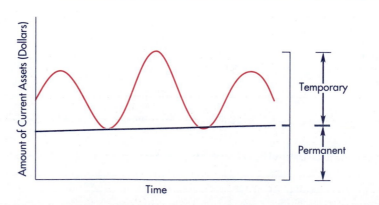

■ *Table 7–1*
Balance Sheet Ratios
for Manufacturing
Firms by Size, 1989

Selected Balance Sheet Ratios	All Manufacturing*	All Manufacturing* Assets under $25 Million
Total cash, U.S. government and other securities	4.9	10.6
Trade accounts and trade notes receivable	14.6	25.9
Inventories	14.8	25.2
Total current assets	37.7	65.4
Net property, plant, and equipment	33.2	28.2
Short-term debt including installments on long-term debt	5.9	11.4
Total current liabilities	25.6	32.8
Long-term debt	24.0	19.1
Total liabilities	59.5	54.0
Stockholders' equity	40.5	46.0

*During the first quarter of 1988, a number of companies were reclassified by industry.

Source: Adapted from *Quarterly Financial Report for Manufacturing, Mining, and Trade,* Federal Trade Commission, Washington, D.C., Fourth Quarter, 1989.

total long–term sources of financing, including in particular stockholders' equity, are more important in total than current liabilities, it is obvious that firms cannot afford to pay insufficient attention to one-fourth of their total financing.

Small Firm Considerations

Short-term financial management easily constitutes the majority of the financial activities of many small firms. They are acutely attuned to the flow of cash through the firm because their survival depends on a proper balancing. Small firms have fewer alternatives than do large firms in raising funds, and fewer safety nets on which to rely. Regardless of a small, successful firm's profitability outlook, failure to pay the bills will result in bankruptcy. Large firms can report accounting losses for a quarter or a year, or more, and continue in business because they have enough cash flow or because they can raise the financing needed to carry them through. But small firms often are unable to do this, and, in fact, the opposite often applies—small firms can report positive accounting earnings, or the expectation thereof, and still face a crisis or go bankrupt because of a lack of cash with which to continue operating.

Table 7–1 also shows selected balance sheet ratios for those manufacturing firms with assets under $25 million (one standard for identifying small firms). Notice that, on average, current assets are 65 percent of total assets, a very significant contrast to the percentage cited earlier for all firms. Current liabilities are 33 percent of the total, considerably higher than for all firms taken together. Clearly, small firms must pay particular attention to short-term financial management.

SHORT-TERM FINANCIAL MANAGEMENT AND THE VALUATION OF THE FIRM

As we saw in the discussion above, a significant part of a firm's total assets are allocated to current assets. Furthermore, it seems reasonable to assume that as the level of current assets varies, current liabilities will also vary. Obviously, proper attention must be paid to the management of the firm's short-term assets and liabilities if the firm's goal of maximizing the stockholders' wealth is to be achieved.

It sometimes seems more difficult to associate decisions about short-term financial management with maximizing the price of the stock than it does in the case of specific fixed-asset decisions or long-term financing decisions. Nevertheless, while this association may be more difficult at times, the finance principles involved remain the same. We need to understand and make short-term financial-management decisions on the basis of the overall valuation of the firm.

As we learned in Chapter 6, the valuation concept involves an upward-sloping trade-off between the firm's risk and expected return. Short-term financial-management decisions are simply a subset of the total financial decisions made by the firm, all of which interact to affect a firm's expected return and risk. This is illustrated in the figure accompanying the opening of Part III. This figure depicts, in balance sheet terms, both the short-term and long-term financial decisions made by a firm that impact its return and risk parameters, which are evaluated by the financial markets in determining the stock price, which, in turn, is directly related to the stockholders' wealth.

There are two ways to maximize stockholder wealth:

1. *The net present value (NPV) approach.* As we shall see in Part IV on capital budgeting, a firm's projects can be valued by discounting the cash flows to be generated by the project, a process known as the net present value approach. Accepting projects with positive NPVs benefits the stockholders and can lead to stockholder wealth maximization. Although this approach is directly applicable to short-term financial-management decisions, it is somewhat more abstract and difficult to implement.
2. *Cost minimization.* Rather than focus on maximizing net present values, we can talk of cost minimization, which also benefits the stockholders. A reduction of costs, whether the cost of financing the firm's assets or the general cost of doing business, will contribute directly to maximizing the stockholders' wealth. This approach, typically, is easier to focus on when analyzing short-term financial-management decisions.

Given the risk-return nature of the overall financial management process, it is appropriate to consider the risk/return trade-off involved in short-term financial management.

The Risk/Return Trade-Off

In the specific case of short-term financial management, return can be thought of as the firm's profitability as measured by the return on assets, or ROA (see Chapter 3). Risk in this situation is not the covariance form of risk we have discussed previously, but rather a kind of failure risk, discussed at the end of Chapter 5. Specifically, risk here refers to *technical insolvency,* the inability to pay bills as they come due. This risk is related to the net working capital of the firm, or the current ratio, discussed in Chapter 3. Recall that the current ratio measures a firm's liquidity, or ability to pay current obligations, by dividing current assets by current liabilities.[5]

---

[5]Alternatively, the quick ratio measures liquidity by removing inventories from current assets because, typically, they are the least liquid of current assets. Thus, this is a more stringent test—an acid test—of the firm's ability to pay its current bills.

Like other financial management areas, working-capital management involves investment decisions and financing decisions. Therefore, we will consider the risk/return trade-off involved in working-capital management by focusing on each of these two decisions in turn.

The Investment Decision

As the firm expands its sales volume, usually it is necessary to increase investment in both fixed assets and current assets; therefore, the levels of sales, current assets, and fixed assets are all related. A firm generally expects to earn more on fixed assets, which are the critical earning assets of the firm, than on current assets. This means that the firm must make a specific policy decision about the amount of current assets to hold for any given level of sales.

If the firm maintains a relatively high level of current assets, it will have more cash to pay bills as they come due and more inventory to fill sales orders. However, profitability is affected by both sales and costs. There is a cost associated with maintaining a comfortable liquid position because money will be tied up in current assets at the expense of fixed assets. To the extent that this investment is idle—only the marketable securities portion of current assets earns a direct return—profitability will suffer. On the other hand, the risk of the firm will decline because the current ratio, our proxy for risk, will be higher under a policy of maintaining a high level of current assets.

One way to think of the risk/return trade-off involving the investment decision is to analyze the cost to the firm of having a particular ratio of current assets (CA) to total assets (TA), or CA/TA ratio, which is a useful way to express the firm's level of current assets. Dividing current assets by total assets gives the CA/TA ratio:

$$\text{CA/TA} = \frac{\text{Current assets}}{\text{Total assets}} \tag{7–1}$$

The higher the CA/TA ratio, the larger the relative investment in liquid (current) assets. However, we must be careful here not to compare apples and oranges. The nature of some industries dictates relatively high or low CA/TA ratios, and it is usually best to compare firms in similar lines of business. Generally, wholesalers and retailers, by the nature of their business, have higher CA/TA ratios than most other kinds of companies. Manufacturing companies tend to have somewhat lower ratios.[6]

In general, for any particular sales level, the greater the firm's CA/TA ratio, the lower the risk and the lower the expected return. Conversely, the smaller the firm's CA/TA ratio, the greater the risk and the greater the expected return. This risk-and-return trade-off is crucial (a) in determining optimal levels of current assets in the aggregate and the individual components of current assets in particular and (b) in affecting the stockholders' wealth. If we minimize costs by minimizing the investment in current assets, the attendant risk may be more than enough to offset the cost savings, driving down the price of the stock and, therefore, decreasing stockholder wealth. On the other hand, if we maximize liquidity by maintaining a high level of current assets, the costs of doing so may more than

---

[6]Service company CA/TA ratios tend to be even lower, and transportation and utility companies have the lowest CA/TA ratios.

offset the value to the stockholders of lower risk, once again driving down the price of the stock and decreasing stockholder wealth.

▪ Example

The C.B. Turner Company is considering three different levels of investment in current assets. One plan is fairly conservative, another moderate, and the third aggressive. The level of fixed assets in the three plans is the same. Details are as follows:

$$\text{Fixed assets} = \$100,000$$

$$\frac{\text{Expected earnings before}}{\text{interest and taxes (EBIT)}} = \$30,000 \text{ per year}$$

$$\text{Plan A current assets} = \$100,000 \text{ (conservative)}$$

$$\text{Plan B current assets} = \$\ 75,000 \text{ (moderate)}$$

$$\text{Plan C current assets} = \$\ 50,000 \text{ (aggressive)}$$

The effects of these differing levels of investment in current assets are shown in Table 7–2.

As Table 7–2 shows, profitability—measured here by EBIT/total assets—is highest under the aggressive plan (C) and is progressively lower under the moderate (B) and conservative (A) plans. That is:

$$\frac{\text{Return of}}{\text{Plan C}} > \frac{\text{Return of}}{\text{Plan B}} > \frac{\text{Return of}}{\text{Plan A}}$$

Notice also, however, that measuring insolvency risk by the CA/TA ratio:

$$\frac{\text{Risk of}}{\text{Plan C}} > \frac{\text{Risk of}}{\text{Plan B}} > \frac{\text{Risk of}}{\text{Plan A}}$$

Not surprisingly, the greater the risk, the higher the rate of return, and the lower the risk, the lower the rate of return. This general proposition is true of all financial decision making. The financial manager of the Turner Company would have to decide if the higher expected return of Plan C was large enough to more than offset the higher risk of Plan C in terms of the likely reaction of the financial markets. ▪

The Financing Decision

The right side of a balance sheet shows the firm's total sources of financing. A firm typically finances with both current liabilities and long-term liabilities, and

▪ *Table 7–2*
Current Asset
Risk/Return Example—
Turner Company Data

	Anticipated Results		
	A	B	C
Current assets	$100,000	$ 75,000	$ 50,000
Fixed assets	100,000	100,000	100,000
Total assets	$200,000	$175,000	$150,000
EBIT/total assets	15%	17%	20%
Current assets/total assets	0.50	0.43	0.33

it must choose the balance between these two. As in the case of the investment decision above, the financing decision, or choice between current liabilities and long-term liabilities, will affect the risk and return characteristics of the firm and, therefore, the price of the stock.

As we will see, increasing current liabilities at the expense of long-term liabilities *normally* will increase the firm's profitability because short-term debt financing is generally considered to be less expensive than long-term debt financing. At the same time, an increase in current liabilities, holding current assets constant, by definition decreases the current ratio and, therefore, increases the firm's risk. Even if current assets are not held constant, short-term financing involves more risk, as will be explained in the last part of this chapter. Thus, a trade-off exists between profitability and risk within the financing-decision component of working-capital management.

The trade-off between risk and return involved in the financing decision may be demonstrated by thinking of the risk involved in the financing mix as being measured by the following ratio:

$$\text{CL/TF} = \frac{\text{Current liabilities}}{\text{Total financing}} \qquad (7\text{--}2)$$

This ratio relates the firm's total financing to current liabilities.[7] Our previous discussions imply that, other things being equal, the greater the CL/TF ratio, the more risk the firm has. As we know from above, however, returns should also be higher, resulting in a trade-off. An example can show how return and risk are related in this situation.

- *Example*

A newly formed company, Poindexter Printing, is considering three alternative financing plans. Plan A is conservative; it makes relatively heavy use of long-term financing. Plan B is an in-between plan that uses both sources of financing in a substantial way. Plan C is more aggressive, in that it makes relatively heavy use of short-term financing. Poindexter will use payables and accruals to the fullest extent possible and will have the same net worth and EBIT under each of the plans.[8] The financing alternatives are as follows:

Plan	Short-Term Debt (6%)	Long-Term Debt (10%)
A (conservative)	$100,000	$400,000
B (matching)	300,000	200,000
C (aggressive)	500,000	0

All other data and the results of the analysis showing the effect of the choice of financing plan on risk and return are shown in Table 7–3.

---

[7]The ratio is conceptually similar to the CA/TA ratio (Equation 7–1), which measures how much of the firm's total assets are current assets.

[8]Recall that EBIT = earnings before interest and taxes.

■ *Table 7–3*
Financing Risk-Return
Trade-Off Example—
Poindexter Printing

	Plan A (Conservative)	Plan B (Matching)	Plan C (Aggressive)
Current assets	$ 400,000	$ 400,000	$ 400,000
Fixed assets	600,000	600,000	600,000
Total assets	$1,000,000	$1,000,000	$1,000,000
Payables and accruals	$ 100,000	$ 100,000	$ 100,000
Short-term debt (6%)	100,000	300,000	500,000
Current liabilities		$ 200,000	$ 400,000
Long-term debt (10%)	400,000	200,000	0
Equity (10,000 shares)	400,000	400,000	400,000
Total financing	$1,000,000	$1,000,000	$1,000,000
EBIT	$ 120,000	$ 120,000	$ 120,000
Interest	46,000	38,000	30,000
EBT	74,000	82,000	90,000
Tax (40%)	29,600	32,800	36,000
Net income	$ 44,400	$ 49,200	$ 54,000
EPS*	$4.44 per share	$4.92 per share	$5.40 per share
Return on equity**	11.1%	12.3%	13.5%
CL/TF***	0.2	0.4	0.6

*EPS = earnings per share.
**Return on equity = net income/equity.
***CL/TF = current liabilities/total financing.

Earnings per share and return on equity are highest under the aggressive plan and lowest under the conservative plan. The Plan B results are between these extremes. That is:

$$\frac{\text{Return under}}{\text{Plan C}} > \frac{\text{Return under}}{\text{Plan B}} > \frac{\text{Return under}}{\text{Plan A}}$$

However, financing risks (measured by CL/TF) are similarly ordered:

$$\frac{\text{Risk of}}{\text{Plan C}} > \frac{\text{Risk of}}{\text{Plan B}} > \frac{\text{Risk of}}{\text{Plan A}}$$

This illustrates the financing risk/return trade-off. Heavier reliance on cheaper short-term financing provides greater returns, but it is riskier. Once again, the financial manager would have to decide which trade-off to take. Does the higher return under Plan C more than compensate for the higher risk under Plan C? If it does, other things being equal, the stockholders should benefit. ■

Interaction of Current-Asset and Current-Financing Levels

Although we analyzed the risk/return trade-off for different levels of current assets separately from the risk/return trade-off for different levels of current liabilities, they are clearly interrelated. These interactions need to be accounted for in making financial decisions.

The CA/TA ratio measures the relative liquidity of the firm's asset structure, and other things being equal, the greater the CA/TA ratio, the less risky and the less profitable the firm will be. Similarly, the CL/TF ratio measures the relative liquidity of the firm's financial structure, and other things being equal, the greater the CL/TF ratio, the more risky and profitable the firm will be. In describing a firm's working-capital policy, we should bear in mind that at the broadest level, working-capital policy has these two dimensions:

1. Relative asset liquidity (CA/TA).
2. Relative financing liquidity (CL/TF).

These two dimensions can reinforce each other or offset each other. For example:

- A high CA/TA ratio combined with a low CL/TL ratio is doubly conservative.
- A low CA/TA ratio combined with a high CL/TL ratio is doubly aggressive.
- A high CA/TA ratio combined with a high CL/TL ratio is at least partially offsetting, as is a low CA/TA ratio combined with a low CL/TA ratio.

Another example of this interaction is when the firm chooses to offset a somewhat risky asset structure, caused by the firm's line of business, with a conservative financing policy. This applies to both short-term and long-term financing strategies.

This discussion illustrates one of the main features of working-capital management: the interaction between asset and financing mixes. Our work in the following three chapters will necessarily focus on individual aspects of current-asset and current-liability management. But these two topics are fundamentally related, and both also are related to the long-term investment and financing decisions the firm makes.

Conclusions

In summary, like every other type of financial decision made by a firm, short-term financial management involves trying to find the optimal trade-off between profitability and risk that will maximize the shareholders' wealth. Excessively high levels of current assets reduce a firm's risk but also lower its return on investment, while excessively low levels of current assets increase the firm's profitability and its risk. Improper current-liability management can be costly and, in rare cases, fatal. For example, the Penn Central Railroad defaulted on a short-term liability, commercial paper, forcing bankruptcy.

It is important in this analysis of the role of working-capital management in the valuation of the firm to recall our discussion in Chapter 2 about the role of the market in determining the price of the stock. The impact of working-capital decisions on the value of the firm ultimately depends on how the market views the firm's policies. The financial manager's task is to make the best decisions possible regarding the firm's level and composition of current assets and current liabilities. Finally, however, the value of the firm will depend on the market's reaction to the actions of the financial manager. Market preferences for expected returns and the accompanying risk will, as always, be the basis of valuation. Working-capital policies that seem clearly to increase returns, or to decrease risk, should have a positive impact on the stock price. The problem is that most working-capital policies involve a trade-off between return and risk, with both either increasing together or decreasing together. In the end, the market must determine if the benefits outweigh the costs.

INVESTING IN CURRENT ASSETS

The optimal level of current assets is that level most consistent with the goal of stockholder wealth maximization. It depends on several factors, including the variability in sales and cash flows, the level of assets, the particular industry, and the unique characteristics of the company. Clearly, no one working-capital policy is best for all firms. Table 7–4 shows some actual CA/TA ratios for 10 randomly selected firms. As we can see, the range is wide, from 68 percent for Hewlett-Packard to 18 percent for Hershey Foods (1987 figures). Table 7–4 also shows, for comparison, the current liabilities/total financing (CL/TF) ratio for these same firms, which will be discussed below.

How does a firm determine the optimal level of current assets to hold? The answer comes directly from economics—invest in current assets until the marginal benefit on the last dollar of investment is equal to the marginal cost. This is an important principle that underlies most of the decisions in finance. As we will see, it is exactly the principle we use to decide how much to invest in fixed assets.

Marginal analysis as applied to the determination of the optimal investment in current assets is illustrated in Figure 7–4. The downward-sloping curve shows the marginal benefit of investing in current assets. As more dollars are invested, the marginal benefit declines. On the other hand, the marginal cost of investing in current assets increases as the level of investment in current assets increases. The point of optimal investment is the point where the two curves intersect—where the marginal benefit equals the marginal cost. At this point, the net contribution of the marginal investment is zero, and profits are at their highest level.

To implement marginal analysis operationally, we will need to study each category of current assets, which is done in the following two chapters. However, it is helpful at the outset to discuss the basic idea of an optimal level of current assets by relating this level to total assets. As noted, the objective is to find the optimal trade-off between profitability and risk.

■ *Table 7–4*
CA/TA and CL/TF Ratios for 10 Selected Nonfinancial Firms

Company	Current Assets/Total Assets			Current Liabilities/Total Assets		
	1987	1986	1985	1987	1986	1985
Bethlehem Steel	0.3082	0.2540	0.2319	0.2420	0.2017	0.1966
Goodyear	0.3936	0.3531	0.3679	0.2548	0.2489	0.2312
Chrysler	0.3094	0.3725	0.4215	0.3328	0.3556	0.3752
Hershey Foods	0.1822	0.0375	0.0270	0.2947	0.1638	0.1631
Hewlett Packard	0.6750	0.6066	0.5884	0.3363	0.2415	0.2423
Inter. Paper	0.2483	0.2074	0.1830	0.1729	0.1697	0.1250
Ford	0.4890	0.4866	0.4434	0.3958	0.4119	0.4043
McDonnell Douglas	0.6322	0.0134	0.0101	0.5620	0.5444	0.5546
Northern Telecom	0.4110	0.5513	0.5403	0.2938	0.2512	0.2728
Pepsico	0.3258	0.3119	0.4768	0.3018	0.2769	0.3132

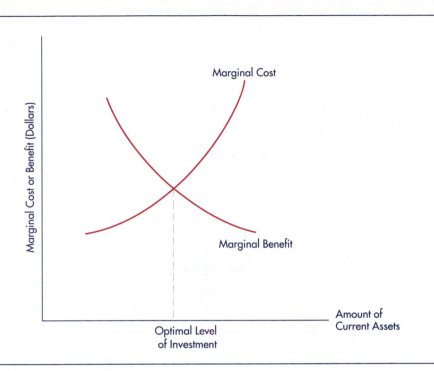

Current Assets and Total Assets

There are significant differences between investing in fixed assets and investing in current assets. Investments in current assets often are reversible. The firm can liquidate, or at least reduce, the investment with little or no cost. For example, Treasury bills can be sold immediately for cash, and inventory can usually be sold fairly quickly, although price concessions may be necessary. Fixed investments, on the other hand, are not easily reversed quickly. At the very least, costs, often significant, will be involved. Furthermore, current asset investment is not "lumpy"—that is, it does not usually occur in large, periodic chunks. For example, if $10,000,000 is required to build a new plant, this much must be spent—after all, half a plant makes no sense. By contrast, current assets are more divisible. The optimal levels of current assets may be $10,100,000 or $9,900,000. The firm attempts to achieve the optimal level by equating marginal benefits to marginal costs.

Two different kinds of costs are involved in deciding on a CA/TA ratio. First is the *cost of liquidity*. If the firm carries excessive amounts of current assets, its rate of return on total assets will suffer. As the firm's CA/TA ratio increases, the cost of liquidity increases.

Second, there is the *cost of illiquidity,* which is the cost of having too little invested in current assets. The consequences of having too little cash, inventory, and so on, all have costs, and these illiquidity costs increase as the firm's CA/TA ratio declines, other things being equal.

In selecting an optimal level of current assets, the firm must balance these two costs, seeking a minimum cost position. This concept is illustrated in

■ *Figure 7–5*
Trade-Off between Cost
of Liquidity and Cost of
Illiquidity

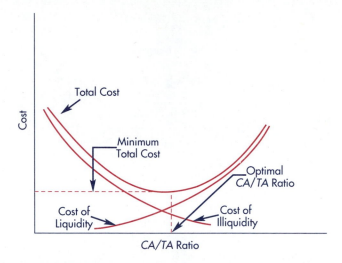

Figure 7–5. As the CA/TA ratio increases, the cost of liquidity increases, but the cost of illiquidity declines. As the firm's CA/TA ratio decreases, the cost of liquidity decreases, but the cost of illiquidity increases. The total cost of maintaining a particular working-capital policy is the sum of these two costs, and the firm is interested in finding the minimum point on the total cost function.

Determinants of Current Asset Changes

In managing its current assets, the firm should always be aware of two problems: having too much in current assets and having too little. Balancing the costs involved in these two positions is important in determining optimal levels for the various classes of current assets. However, suppose for the moment that the firm is at some satisfactory level of current assets. What would cause the firm to change this level?[9] There are three primary reasons: (1) changes in levels of sales and/or operating expenses, (2) policy changes, and (3) changes in technology.

As sales increase, larger amounts of cash, accounts receivable, and inventory are needed to facilitate this growth. Similarly, as operating expenses rise (even without a sales increase), more funds must be tied up in current assets. The opposite effect occurs when sales or operating expenses decline.

Why do sales and/or operating expenses change? There may be *long-run trends* at work. The cost of an important raw material may change over time. Trends of such long duration would mainly affect the need for permanent current assets. A second source of change is *cyclical change* in the economy and/or industry, which influences current-asset levels, both permanent and temporary. A third source of change is *seasonality* in sales patterns. Because of their line of business, many firms have peak sales seasons, which cause peak cash, inventory, and receivables needs. Seasonality is the main source of variation in temporary current-asset levels.

---

[9]Most of the variation in the level of current assets occurs in accounts receivable and inventory.

Policy changes are instituted by management. If a company historically has had a conservative current-asset policy—it keeps relatively high levels of current assets for its sales volume—a conscious managerial decision to have a less conservative policy will have an obvious impact on the firm's level of current assets.

Technological changes can be an important factor also. If a brewing company finds a way to speed up the brewing process, for example, it can reduce its operating-cycle duration and lower its commitment of funds to current assets by decreasing its investment in goods in process.

FINANCING CURRENT ASSETS

Investment in current assets requires financing, and this is an appropriate place to consider an overview of the main issues involved in financing current assets.

Short-Term versus Long-Term Financing

Our attention in this portion of the chapter is directed to the pros and cons of financing current assets with either short-term or long-term financing. The features of various short-term and long-term sources of financing have substantial differences. It is thus an abstraction to speak of short-term versus long-term financing as if each of these categories contained financing alternatives with homogeneous features. However, the various short-term sources of financing do share some fundamental risk-and-return commonalities, as do the several long-term sources of financing.

Since *the choice of a current-assets financing plan ultimately reduces to a risk/return trade-off,* it seems helpful to contrast short-term and long-term financing in a general way despite the fact that important differences exist among short-term financing sources and among long-term financing sources. This contrast can be made on the basis of cost considerations and risk considerations. We will derive two important conclusions for the firm and its stockholders about the pros and cons of financing current assets with either short-term or long-term borrowing:

1. Short-term financing typically is cheaper than long-term financing (cost considerations).
2. Short-term financing is more risky than long-term financing (risk considerations).

Cost Considerations

Most typically, *the cost of short-term financing is less than the cost of long-term financing.* At one extreme, accruals and accounts payable are relatively cheap (see Chapter 10). Even ignoring these two sources, the cost of short-term borrowing is usually less than the cost of long-term borrowing, which, in turn, is considered the least costly of all the long-term financing alternatives.

Figure 7–6 shows the annual long- and short-term rates as they apply to corporate borrowing. Notice that while the short-term rate typically is below the long-term rate, this is not always the case. For example, the short-term rate exceeded the long-term rate in the late 1970s, peaking in 1980. On the other hand, on an annualized basis the short-term rate was below the long-term during the 1980s.

■ *Figure 7–6*   Short and Long Interest Rates, 1970–89

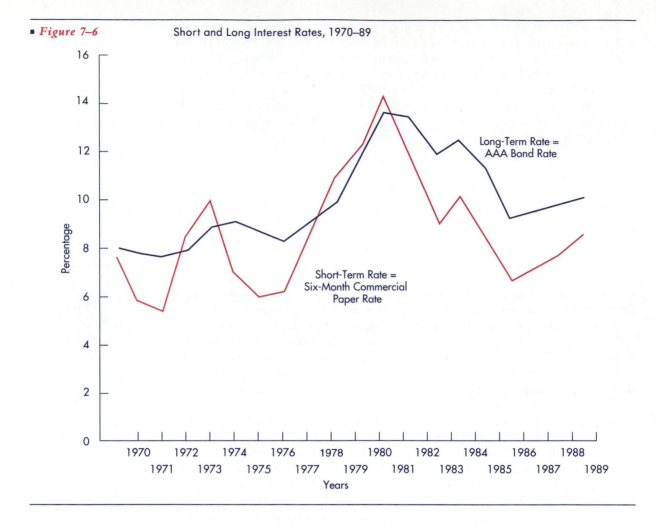

term structure
of interest rates
the relationship between
the maturity of debt and
its yield

The relationship between the maturity of debt and its yield (cost) is called the **term structure of interest rates.** The term structure of interest rates can be displayed in a *yield curve*. The yield curve has taken on several shapes in past years, but the most common is the *upward-sloping* yield curve shown in Figure 7–7. In this figure, interest rates increase with time: the longer the maturity of the debt, the greater the interest rate. The increase in interest rates is usually most pronounced among the shorter-lived maturities, a phenomenon that emphasizes the cost differential between short- and long-term interest rates. It is usually cheaper to borrow short term than long term.

Sometimes the yield curve has been flat and sometimes it has sloped *downward*. However, the most common shape historically has been an upward slope, such as that shown in Figure 7–7, which is consistent with long-term rates being higher than short-term rates.[10]

[10]There is actually no such thing as "the" long-term or short-term rate. There are *many* such rates. The rates shown in Figure 7–6 are representative examples. The long-term rate shown is the Aaa Moody's bond interest rate, and the short-term rate is the prime commercial paper rate. These rates are for comparable, high-quality corporate debt obligations.

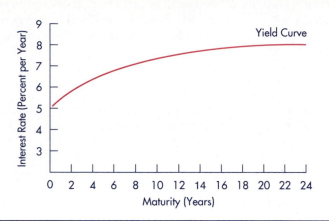

One of the most frequent explanations given for the fact that long-term interest rates are higher than short-term interest rates is the *liquidity-preference theory*. This theory says that since lenders are risk averse, and risk generally increases with length of lending time (because it is more difficult to forecast the more distant future), more lenders would prefer to make short-term loans. These lenders— says the theory—can be induced to lend for longer periods of time only by granting them higher interest rates. Hence, the usual upward-sloping yield curve.

A competing theory to explain yield curve shapes is the *expectations theory* of the term structure of interest rates. This theory asserts that yield curves reflect investors' expectations of future short-term interest rates. Downward-sloping yield curves are explained as situations where future short-term interest rates are expected to decline; flat yield curves are explained as situations where future short-term interest rates are expected to be about the same as they are now; upward-sloping yield curves are explained as situations where future short-term interest rates are expected to rise. While there is not total agreement, the majority opinion today is that the term structure is best explained by a theory that uses features of both competing theories.

The effect of higher long-term financing costs relative to short-term costs is to make the rate of return on equity higher when the firm chooses short-term financing. Thus, from a *return* standpoint, short-term financing is usually (but not always) preferable.

Risk Considerations

The other major consideration in comparing short-term and long-term financing is that *short-term financing involves more risk*. If the firm uses long-term financing to build up current assets, there will be less risk involved in renewing the borrowing. This is most evident in financing permanent current assets, which we defined as the minimum level of current assets the firm requires. Suppose the firm finances its permanent current assets with short-term debt. As the short-term debt matures, the firm must arrange new short-term borrowing. This periodic refinancing exposes the firm to the possibility that there may be times when it is difficult to borrow new money, particularly if the firm is experiencing hard times. At the extreme, the firm may be unable to acquire new financing and will face the prospect of disruption of its operating activities, or possibly even failure. If the firm finances with long-term debt instead, there will be fewer refunding occasions. This means that a long-term financing plan contains less risk, other things being equal.

■ *Example*

Southmark Corporation, a real estate and financial services concern, acknowledged in a filing with the Securities and Exchange Commission that because of its liquidity problems, it faced the prospect of having insufficient cash to meet its obligations.[11] The company indicated that its bank lenders were not renewing some credit lines as they matured. Such actions forced the company to pay down about $100 million of bank debt. ■

Therefore, *while short-term is usually less costly than long-term financing, short-term financing also typically involves more risk*. We have a risk/return trade-off involved in the choice between short- and long-term financing of current assets. The more short-term financing is used, the greater the firm's profitability, but the greater the risk.

Financing Needs

At any point, the firm's financing need is the sum total of financing needed for the firm's investment in current and fixed assets. Figure 7–8 shows a diagram of the firm's financing needs. Current-asset requirements are divided into permanent and temporary components.

Alternative Financing Plans

The current-asset financing plan may be readily related to the broader issue of the financing plan for all the firm's assets. The firm has a wide variety of financing policies from which to choose, and the fact that short-term financing usually is less costly, but involves more risk, than long-term financing plays an important part in describing the degree of aggressiveness or conservatism of the firm's financing policy.

In comparing financing plans, we should distinguish between three different kinds of financing:

1. Long-term financing.
2. Negotiated short-term financing.
3. Spontaneous short-term financing.

Long-term financing, covered in Chapters 18 to 20, includes (in addition to cash flow from operations), common and preferred stocks, bonds, leases, and term loans. Negotiated short-term financing refers to sources of short-term credit the firm must arrange in advance to obtain. These are covered in Chapter 10 and include short-term bank loans, commercial paper, and factoring of receivables.

---

[11]See Michael Totty, "Southmark Says Liquidity Woes Are Worsening," *The Wall Street Journal,* December 21, 1988, p. B2.

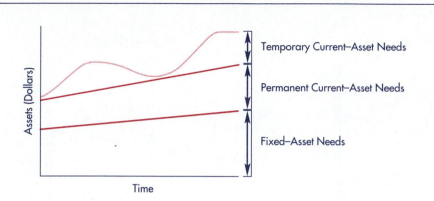

Spontaneous short-term financing refers to short-term funds the firm may acquire almost automatically without formal negotiation. The major forms of short-term spontaneous financing, also covered in Chapter 10, are trade credit (accounts payable) and accruals (wages and taxes). Since spontaneous short-term financing normally is cheap, most firms will attempt to use it as much as possible; therefore, spontaneous financing will increase and decrease as the firm's need for financing current assets increases and decreases. Because spontaneous short-term financing is so desirable, we may safely assume that the firm will always use it to the fullest extent possible. Consequently, we will omit spontaneous short-term financing and that portion of current assets supported by it from the following discussion of the relative desirability of long-term versus short-term financing. In effect, we focus on the negotiated sources of financing (both long-term and short-term).

A Matching Approach

One financing plan involves *maturity matching*—matching the expected life of assets purchased with the expected life of the financing raised to pay for the assets. The rationale for matching is that because the purpose of financing is to pay for assets, when the asset is expected to be relinquished, the financing should also be relinquished. Arranging financing for longer periods than the assets require is costly because the financing is not needed for the full period. Similarly, arranging financing for shorter periods than the assets require is also costly in that there will be extra transaction costs involved in continually arranging new short-term financing. Also, there is always the risk that new financing cannot be obtained in times of economic difficulty, or can be obtained only at a higher cost because of fluctuating interest rates. A matching approach reduces the risk that the firm will be unable to meet its obligations as they come due.

Under a matching approach, fixed assets and permanent current assets would be financed with long-term financing, and temporary current assets would be financed with short-term financing.[12] Figure 7–9A shows the firm's investment

---

[12]Recall that we are not including spontaneous short-term financing and the current assets supported by spontaneous short-term financing in this and the following discussions.

■ *Figure 7–9*   Financing Plans

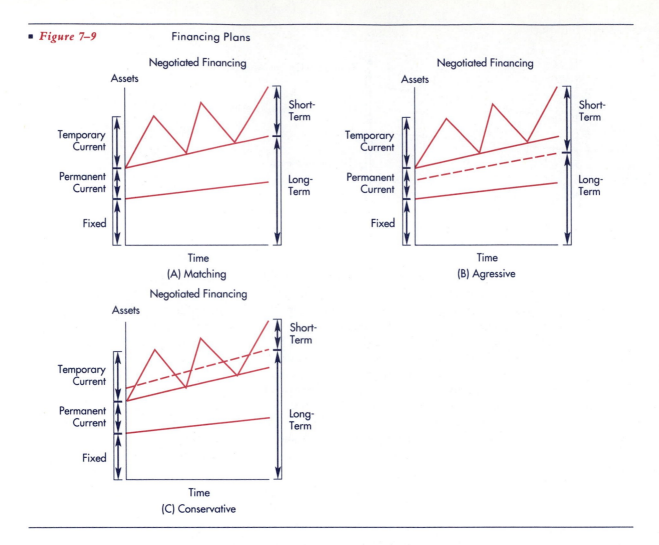

(A) Matching

(B) Aggressive

(C) Conservative

and financing patterns over time under a maturity matching plan. As the firm's fixed-asset and permanent current-asset levels increase, the long-term financing level also increases. When temporary current-asset levels increase, short-term negotiated financing increases, and when the firm has no temporary current assets, it also has no short-term negotiated financing.

Aggressive Approaches

The firm's financing plan is said to be aggressive if the firm uses more short-term negotiated financing than is needed under a matching approach (see Figure 7–9B). The firm is no longer financing all its permanent current assets with long-term financing. The more short-term financing used relative to long-term financing, the more aggressive the financing plan. Some firms even finance part of their long-term assets with short-term debt, which would be a highly aggressive plan.

Conservative Approaches

Conservative financing plans use more long-term financing than is needed under a matching approach (see Figure 7–9C). The firm is financing a portion of its temporary current-asset requirements with long-term financing. In periods when the firm has no temporary current assets, the firm has excess financing available that will be invested in marketable securities. These plans are conservative because they involve relatively heavy use of (less risky) long-term financing.

Implications

The choice of a financing plan will directly affect the stockholders' wealth. If an aggressive plan is chosen, the risk of the firm will be higher than under the other two plans, but the expected return will also be higher. If a conservative plan is chosen, the risk of the firm will be lower, but so will the expected return. The financial manager must decide which posture to take, based on assessments of the market's reactions. It is perfectly legitimate to assume risk as long as the expected return is large enough to compensate for the risk and the firm is not taking an unreasonable chance of insolvency. Furthermore, there is no reason to assume that a matching policy is best for maximizing the stockholders' wealth. Such a policy may, for a particular firm, be too conservative, and the market may penalize the price of the stock because the firm is not realizing its potential. The point here is that the financial manager must recognize that these choices exist and then must attempt to determine which of these policies would be most likely to maximize the stockholders' wealth, given the valuation process in the financial markets that determines the price of the stock.

SUMMARY

- Short-term financial management is concerned with all of the firm's decisions that affect its short-term cash flows.
- Working-capital management refers to the management of the firm's current assets and current liabilities.
- The primary working-capital policy questions are deciding the optimal level and composition of current assets to hold and how to finance the current assets held.
- The need for current assets is related to the firm's cash-conversion cycle, which is the length of time necessary to convert cash to inventory, inventory to receivables, and receivables to cash.
- In general, the greater the level of current assets, the less profitable and less risky the firm will be. Thus, there is a trade-off between return and risk when deciding the level of current assets to hold.
- Choice of a financing plan for supporting the firm's current assets also involves a risk/return trade-off. If the firm makes relatively heavy use of short-term borrowing, the firm will be more profitable but also riskier.
- Overall, working-capital management is concerned with both the choice of current-asset levels and the financing of these levels. The two problems are interrelated, and the risk/return trade-offs involved in each may be used to reinforce or offset each other.

KEY TERMS

cash-conversion cycle, p. 204   term structure of interest rates, p. 218
net working capital, p. 202   working capital, p. 202
short-term financial management, p. 202   working-capital management, p. 202

QUESTIONS

7–1. Describe what effects the following situations would have on the firm's level of current assets:
   a. The company's inventory-management skills increase because of a successful training program.
   b. Most economists agree that there will be a "liquidity crunch" in the next few months and that cash will be a scarce commodity.
   c. The firm has just finished its peak sales season.
   d. Management believes that the company's return on assets is too low and that the firm needs to manage all assets more efficiently.

7–2. Financial analysts are studying two companies, A and B. A has the higher CA/TA ratio and the lower CL/TF ratio. However, the analysts conclude that B has less working-capital management risk than A. How could you explain this finding?

7–3. Lynn Thorne, an analyst, is comparing two companies, A and B, that are in the same industry. In writing up her report, she notes that B has a greater current-asset to total-asset ratio than A.
   a. Other things being equal, what effect would this finding probably have on the analyst's assessment of the relative risk and return of the two companies?
   b. In summarizing her report, she concludes that B's working-capital management policy seems to be more aggressive than A's. Is this conclusion necessarily inconsistent with the information given in the problem? Explain.

7–4. Classify the following as either spontaneous or negotiated sources of short-term financing:
   a. Accounts payable.
   b. Notes payable.
   c. Commercial paper.
   d. Accrued taxes.

7–5. Explain the advantage of a matching financing plan relative to a financing plan that extensively uses:
   a. Long-term financing.
   b. Negotiated short-term financing.

7–6. Typically, yield curves are observed to slope upward; however, they also take other shapes. Suppose that some yield curve data are as follows:

Maturity (years)	1	5	10	20
Yield to maturity (percent)	6	20	15	12

Is it possible to explain this type of yield curve using only the liquidity-preference theory? Briefly justify your answer.

7–7. Explain why many economists argue that short-term borrowing costs are usually less than long-term borrowing costs.

7–8. Assume that two companies, X and Y, are competitors in the same industry. They are very similar in size and sales volume. At any given time, in fact, they tend to have equal amounts of long-term assets, inventory, receivables, and sales. They both only use three kinds of financing: accounts payable, short-term

borrowing, and common stock. Firm X uses a matching financing plan, while Y is more conservative. In the long run, which company will tend to have the following?
  a. A larger amount of accounts payable.
  b. A greater amount of short-term borrowing.
  c. A lesser amount of current assets.

7–9. Which is riskier to a borrower, long-term borrowing or short-term borrowing? Explain your answer.

7–10. Explain how working-capital decisions affect a firm's stock price.

7–11. What role does the term *structure of interest rates* play in deciding between short-term and long-term financing?

7–12. Describe the expected impact on a firm of pursuing an aggressive financing plan versus a conservative financing plan.

7–13. Explain why the choice of a current-asset financing plan ultimately reduces to a risk/return trade-off.

7–14. What is meant by *the cost of liquidity*?

7–15. What is the usefulness of the CA/TA ratio? Can comparisons using this ratio be misleading?

7–16. Assume that a firm will experience cash flows with no uncertainty. How would this affect its working-capital policy? What if, in addition to the elimination of uncertainty, all cash inflows and outflows were perfectly synchronized. How would this affect its working-capital policy?

7–17. Explain the concept of the operating cycle and describe its components.

7–18. Which is longer, the operating cycle or the cash-conversion cycle? Why?

DEMONSTRATION PROBLEMS

7–1. Roenfeldt Motors anticipates sales of $4,000,000 next year, with an EBIT of 15 percent of sales. Fixed assets total $2 million. The company is considering three possible levels of current assets: (1) $600,000, (2) $800,000 or (3) $1,000,000. For each of these three possibilities, calculate:
  a. CA/TA ratios.
  b. EBIT/TA ratios.
  c. Rank the plans on both risk and profitability.

7–2. The V. Smith corporation has a fixed asset/total asset ratio of 0.5 and a current ratio of 2.0. Calculate the CA/TA and CL/TF ratios after completing the following balance sheet.

Current assets	_____	Current liabilities	_____
Fixed assets	$100,000	Long-term debt	$ 50,000
		Equity	_____
Total	_____	Total	_____

Solutions to Demonstration Problems

7–1. a. Calculate the CA/TA ratios:

Plan 1   600,000/2,600,000 = 23.1%
Plan 2   800,000/2,800,00 = 28.6%
Plan 3 1,000,000/3,000,000 = 33.3%

   b. Calculate the EBIT/TA ratios:

$$\begin{aligned}
\text{EBIT} &= .15(4{,}000{,}000) = 600{,}000 \\
\text{Plan 1} \quad & 600{,}000/2{,}600{,}000 = 23.1 \\
\text{Plan 2} \quad & 600{,}000/2{,}800{,}000 = 21.4 \\
\text{Plan 3} \quad & 600{,}000/3{,}000{,}000 = 20.0
\end{aligned}$$

   c. Ranking on risk, the higher the CA/TA ratio, the lower the risk. Plan 3 has the lowest risk. Ranking on profitability, the lower the CA/TA ratio, the higher the EBIT/TA ratio. Therefore, Plan 1 has the largest profitability.

7–2. To complete the balance sheet based on the ratio analysis of Chapter 3, we first compute total assets, based on a FA/TA ratio of 0.5. Total assets must be $200,000, given this ratio and fixed assets of $100,000. Current assets must be $100,000 since current assets plus fixed assets must equal total assets.

Current assets	$100,000	Current liabilities	$ 50,000
Fixed assets	100,000	Long-term debt	50,000
		Equity	100,000
Total	$200,000	Total	$200,000

We now know that total financing is equal to $200,000. Since the current ratio is 2.0, current liabilities must equal $50,000. Equity must equal $100,000 for the right-hand side to balance. Therefore:

$$\begin{aligned}
\text{CA/TA} &= \$100{,}000/\$200{,}000 = .5 \\
\text{CL/TF} &= \$ 50{,}000/\$200{,}000 = .25
\end{aligned}$$

PROBLEMS

7–1. An analyst has attempted to estimate the costs of liquidity and the costs of illiquidity for her company for different ratios of current assets to total assets. These costs are shown below. Use these to determine the firm's optimal ratio of current assets to total assets.

	Cost of	
CA/TA	Liquidity	Illiquidity
0.1	$ 5,000	$80,000
0.2	10,000	60,000
0.3	20,000	40,000
0.4	40,000	30,000
0.5	80,000	25,000
0.6	150,000	20,000

7–2. Entries for Jackson Cleaner's balance sheet have been jumbled out of order. Using the information shown on the next page, compute the firm's ratios of current assets to total assets and current liabilities to total financing.

Balance Sheet
($000)

Accounts payable	$ 200	Common stock	$3,000
Plant	6,000	Cash	700
Inventory	1,000	Accruals	400
Bonds	1,000	Equipment	2,000
Retained earnings	1,500	Notes payable	900
Accounts receivable	300	Preferred stock	3,000

7–3. Pratt-Lyons anticipates an $800,000 sales volume next year. Normally, for every dollar in sales the firm generates, 10 cents in earnings before interest and tax will result. Pratt-Lyons's fixed-asset investment is $1 million, and the company will maintain current assets at one of three levels: (1) $300,000, (2) $250,000, or (3) $200,000. Determine for each of the three plans:
   a. CA/TA ratios.
   b. EBIT/TA ratios.
   Rank the plans from most risky to least risky and from most profitable to least profitable. Indicate the basis of your rankings.

7–4. If a firm's current ratio is 2, use the balance sheet below to determine the CA/TA and CL/TF ratios.

Investments		*Financing*	
Current assets	___	Current liabilities	___
Fixed assets	$200	Long-term debt	___
		Equity	$100
Total	___	Total	$300

7–5. Holcomb Enterprises has the abbreviated income statement shown below. The firm's comptroller has suggested that the firm is keeping too much inventory and cash. Furthermore, a $200,000 reduction in inventory and cash would allow the firm to forgo renewing a $200,000 note payable that matures soon. That is, the firm would reduce both its current assets and current liabilities by $200,000.

EBIT	$2,600,000
Interest	450,000
EBT	2,150,000
Tax (0.4)	860,000
Net income	$1,290,000
EPS (2,000,000 shares)	$0.645 per share

---

   a. Determine the price of the stock if Holcomb's ratio of price to earnings (P/E) is 10.
   b. If the $200,000 note to be renewed has a 10 percent interest rate, determine the interest saving the firm would realize by adopting the comptroller's suggestion.

c. Assuming that EBIT is unaffected by the reduction in current assets and current liabilities, determine EPS if the comptroller's suggestion is adopted. Determine the new stock price if the P/E ratio remains at 10.

d. An analyst argues that EBIT may suffer because the firm may lose some sales due to low inventory levels if the suggestion is adopted. The analyst estimates the probable loss in EBIT at $30,000. Determine the EPS if the analyst's forecast is accurate. Assuming a P/E ratio of 10, estimate stock price.

e. If there is a 50-50 chance that the $30,000 EBIT loss would occur, calculate the expected price if the comptroller's suggestion is adopted. Based on this calculation, would you agree with the recommended change?

7-6. XYZ Company has the abbreviated balance sheet shown below. This balance sheet reflects a period where XYZ's permanent current assets equal 50 percent of its total current assets. At any given time, XYZ can finance about 40 percent of its current assets with accounts payable. Fill in the financing portion of the balance sheet, assuming XYZ uses a matching financing plan, and that permanent current assets and fixed assets are at constant levels.

Investments		Financing	
Current assets	$120	Accounts payable	____
Fixed assets	100	Bank loans	____
Total	$220	Long-term financing	____
		Total	____

7-7. Analysts at Fixup Services, Inc., feel the firm will have a permanent current-asset level during the next two years of $3 million. Temporary current-asset levels are seasonal. Total current-asset levels and fixed-asset levels in millions of dollars during the next two years, by quarter, are as follows:

	Year 1 (Quarters)				Year 2 (Quarters)			
	1	2	3	4	1	2	3	4
Total current assets	5	4	3	4	5	4	3	5
Fixed assets	10	10	10	10	10	11	11	11

The company operates under the following guidelines:

a. Each one-dollar increase (decrease) in temporary current assets will cause spontaneous short-term financing to increase (decrease) by 60 cents.

b. Any increase (decrease) in temporary current assets not financed (disfinanced) by spontaneous short-term financing is financed (disfinanced) by negotiated short-term financing.

c. Any increase (decrease) in fixed assets will be financed (disfinanced) by equity.

Given these instructions, fill out the financing sections of the balance sheets on the next page.

	Year 1 (Quarters)				Year 2 (Quarters)			
	1	*2*	*3*	*4*	*1*	*2*	*3*	*4*
Short-term financing								
Spontaneous	2	—	—	—	—	—	—	—
Negotiated	1	—	—	—	—	—	—	—
Long-term debt	3	—	—	—	—	—	—	—
Equity	9	—	—	—	—	—	—	—

SELECTED REFERENCES

General discussions of working–capital management can be found in:

Amihud, Yakov, and Haim Mendelson. "Liquidity and Asset Prices: Financial Management Implications." *Financial Management,* Spring 1988, pp. 5–15.

Crum, Roy L.; Darwin D. Klingman; and Lee A. Tavis. "An Operational Approach to Integrated Working Capital Planning." *Journal of Economics and Business,* August 1983, pp. 343–78.

Gilmer, R. H., Jr. "The Optimal Level of Liquid Assets: An Empirical Test." *Financial Management,* Winter 1985, pp. 39–43.

Lambrix, R. J., and S. S. Singhui. "Managing the Working Capital Cycle." *Financial Executive,* June 1979, pp. 32–41.

Shulman, Joel M., and Raymond A. K. Cox. "An Integrative Approach to Working Capital Management." *Journal of Cash Management,* November–December 1985, pp. 64–67.

Two recent books dealing with working–capital management are:

Smith, Keith V., and George W. Gallinger. *Readings on Short-Term Financial Management.* St. Paul, Minn.: West Publishing Company, 1988.

Vander Weide, James, and Steven F. Maier. *Managing Corporate Liquidity: An Introduction to Working Capital Management.* New York: Wiley, 1988.

Cash and Marketable Securities

Managing the Cash Position

Schlumberger Ltd. is a worldwide leader in the petroleum industry, providing wellsite and contract drilling services. It is well known for its wireline service, which provides information to drillers seeking oil discoveries. Like other companies in the oil-related industries, Schlumberger suffered from the drop in oil prices during the 1980s. However, the company has an unusual cash and marketable securities position, which has enabled it to not only withstand adverse conditions but also to undertake a share repurchase program, buy other companies, and pay stockholders a relatively constant dollar amount of dividends.

From 1983 through 1987, Schlumberger's cash and marketable securities totalled $3.2 billion, $4 billion, $4.6 billion, $3.8 billion, and $2.6 billion, respectively. As *The Value Line Investment Survey* noted at the time, "The company is still earning a tidy sum of interest income on its $2.6 billion in cash holdings."[1] According to the 1987 annual report, interest income for 1985 to 1987 was, respectively, $443 million, $356 million, and $235 million. Thus, in three years Schlumberger earned more than $1 billion in interest income by managing a large cash and marketable securities position.

---

[1] *The Value Line Investment Survey*, June 10, 1988, p. 1605.

In Chapter 7 we introduced the general concepts associated with managing the firm's current-asset and current-liability positions. In this chapter we look in more detail at the problems involved with managing two very important components of current assets: cash and marketable securities. Cash includes currency and checking accounts kept at commercial banks. **Marketable securities** are the primary component of *near-cash* assets that serve as a backup pool of liquidity, providing cash quickly when needed while offering a short-term investment outlet for excess cash. The Schlumberger example illustrates how important liquidity can be during times of financial stress and how such liquidity, properly managed, can contribute to a firm's operating earnings.

marketable securities
marketable financial assets characterized by short maturity, high liquidity, and low risk and paying competitive market rates

Primary *chapter learning objectives* are:

1. To understand the firm's *cash-management* activity, which includes cash flow management, cash budgeting, and estimation of optimal cash and marketable securities levels.

2. To consider the features of marketable securities that can be held by the firm.

AN OVERVIEW OF CASH MANAGEMENT

Reasons for Holding Cash

Firms have various reasons for holding cash and marketable securities. They must have cash to pay bills and, in most cases, to maintain compensating balances, and they may carry cash to guard against the unexpected and to speculate. There are two major reasons why firms carry cash:

1. *Transactions purposes.* Firms must be able to meet their bills as they come due.[2] If the firm's cash receipts and cash payments were perfectly synchronized so that whenever the firm had to pay out $X,$ that amount in cash receipts was forthcoming, there would be no need to hold cash or marketable securities for transactions reasons. However, cash inflows and outflows are never fully synchronized. Firms may also keep marketable securities for transactions purposes.

2. *Compensating balances.* Modern businesses depend on commercial banks for many services, some of which are paid for by direct fees. Others are paid for indirectly as a result of the bank requiring a firm to keep **compensating balances**, minimum demand deposit levels the firm agrees to maintain at the bank.

compensating balance
a minimum checking account balance that a firm agrees to maintain at its bank

There are at least two other possible reasons why firms may hold cash.

- *Precautionary motives.* Large unanticipated net cash outflows may occur. Several bills may be presented for cash settlement earlier than expected, anticipated cash receipts from previous sales could be unexpectedly delayed, or customers who are unhappy with the merchandise may cancel the sale.

- *Speculative motives.* The firm may speculate on interest rate movements by buying securities when interest rates are expected to decline.[3]

---

[2]A firm's transaction balance is the cash balance needed by the firm to conduct its daily business.
[3]Recall that when interest rates decline, fixed-income securities, such as bonds, rise in price.

Alternatively, the firm can also delay materials purchasing, holding cash on the anticipation that materials prices will decline in the near future. Most firms do not regularly hold cash and securities for speculative reasons but instead use a line of credit (explained later) from a bank.

Cash and Marketable Securities Balances

Table 8–1 provides a perspective on the size of cash and marketable securities for manufacturing firms. For all manufacturers, cash and demand deposits amounted to 1.5 percent of total assets and time deposits (including CDs) another 1.2 percent, for a total of 2.7 percent. Other short-term investments amounted to 2.7 percent of assets. Thus, about 5.6 percent of an average manufacturer's total assets is in the form of cash and marketable securities. This percentage is roughly doubled when small firms are considered, with cash itself accounting for more than half of the total.

The second and fourth columns of Table 8–1 indicate that cash and marketable securities account for approximately 15 percent of total current assets for the average manufacturing firm regardless of size. Notice, however, that cash as a percentage of current assets is twice as important for small firms, compared to all firms, and other short-term investments is half as important.

Cash-Management Activity

We use the term **cash management** activity to refer to a combination of activities:

1. Speeding up collections while controlling disbursements.
2. Determining cash needs.
3. Making cash forecasts.
4. Investing excess cash effectively.

cash management
a combination of activities involving the estimation, handling, and investment of the firm's cash

We include both cash and marketable securities in this definition because the management of cash itself—that is, currency and demand deposits—is closely related to the management of near-cash assets, particularly marketable securities. The management of marketable securities is the other side of the coin from managing cash. The two logically cannot be separated in discussing cash management because proper management of one necessarily involves interaction with the other.

	All Manufacturing		Assets Less Than $25 Million	
	Percent of Total Assets	*Percent of Current Assets*	*Percent of Total Assets*	*Percent of Current Assets*
Cash and demand deposits	1.5	3.7	5.4	8.0
Time deposits, including CDS	1.2	3.0	2.5	3.8
Total cash	2.7	6.7	7.9	11.8
Other short-term investments	2.9	7.3	2.5	3.7
Total cash and securities	5.6	14.0	10.4	15.5

Source: Federal Trade Commission, Third Quarter, 1988.

■ *Table 8–1*
Cash and Marketable Securities Ratios for Manufacturing Firms by Size, 1988

■ *Figure 8–1*
Cash Management
Activity

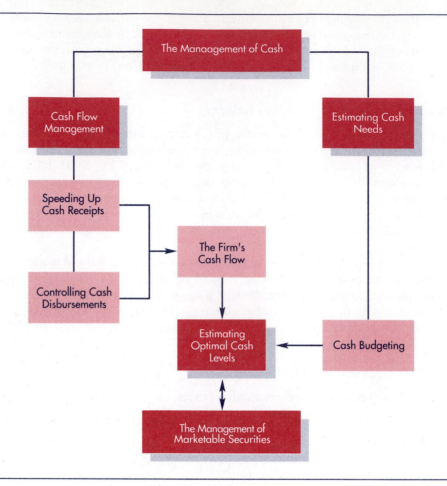

Figure 8–1 diagrams the basic cash-management activity, which consists of several closely interrelated components, separated for organizational purposes into the management of cash and the management of marketable securities. First, the financial manager is concerned with the efficient flow of cash throughout the firm. As shown on the left side of Figure 8–1, this involves, within reasonable limits, speeding up cash receipts while controlling cash disbursements. The reason for the importance attached to this *cash flow management* is obvious upon reflection—cash is a nonearning asset (it earns no interest).[4] Therefore, the objective is to minimize the amount of cash held, without adversely affecting the firm's operations.

Simultaneous with the efficient management of cash flow, the financial manager must estimate cash needs as a part of its general budgeting (forecasting) process. This cash budgeting process allows the manager to forecast the level of cash flow for the firm from month to month.

---

[4]Note, however, that cash can, in a sense, earn a return. For example, cash is needed for compensating balances which, in turn, are used to pay banks for services rendered.

Given the operating expectations of the cash budget, which shows the projected cash inflows and outflows over a specified period, the optimal cash level can be estimated. This target cash level, in turn, serves as a guide for deciding when to invest idle cash in earning assets such as marketable securities and when to sell these securities to replenish the cash balance. Thus, the last step in Figure 8–1 is the management of marketable securities, which must be coordinated with those activities involving the management of cash.

Cash Management and the Valuation Process

The objective of cash management is to minimize the level of cash and marketable securities while ensuring adequate liquidity for the firm with the ultimate goal of contributing to shareholder wealth maximization. Effective cash management is crucial to effective financial management and the success of the firm. If the level of cash and marketable securities is too high, the return on investment will be affected adversely, as will the return on equity. However, a low level of cash and marketable securities increases the firm's risk exposure. Once again, we see that the decisions to be made involve a trade-off between return and risk.

THE MANAGEMENT OF CASH

As shown in Figure 8–1, one aspect of overall cash-management activity is efficient management of the firm's actual cash flow. This task is closely related to the cash-budgeting process because the cash budget must reflect anticipated cash inflows and outflows. Both of these activities will influence the establishment of an optimum cash balance. We will consider each of these three activities in turn.

Cash Flow Management

Cash flow management techniques are based on an understanding of the working-capital cash flow cycle, described in Chapter 7. Recall that the cash-conversion cycle, a part of the firm's operating cycle, takes account of the due date for accounts payable, when the firm must pay for the raw materials purchased to produce the inventory. The **cash-conversion cycle** is the number of days between the cash outflows associated with paying the accounts payable and the cash inflows associated with collecting the receivables.

cash-conversion cycle
time between outlay of cash for purchase of raw materials and receipt of cash from sale of finished product

- *Example*

Assume that raw materials for Universal Chair Company are purchased on Day 0, and an accounts payable by the firm is generated. This accounts payable must be paid on the due date, which is assumed to be 30 days later. On Day 90, Universal's finished goods are sold to a buyer on credit, generating an accounts receivable for the firm. The average collection period for Universal is assumed to be 45 days. Therefore, the accounts receivable will be converted into cash 135 days from the day raw materials were purchased. The cash-conversion cycle will cover 105 days, the time between the payment of cash by Universal for its purchases and the receipt of cash by the firm for its sales. ∎

Given the activities involved in purchases, sales, and so forth, it is obvious that several different parts of a firm are involved in the activities that generate the firm's cash flows. All of these parts go together to influence short-term cash flows, and from a financial standpoint, it is up to the financial officers of the firm to see that these activities are conducive to the maximization of stockholder wealth. Figure 8–2 shows the impact of the various individuals on the timing and amount of a firm's cash flows.

In Figure 8–2, the selling firm is shown separately from the buying firm. We can think of this figure as illustrating separate firms or simply the two sides of the same firm. On the sell side, the particular positions that come into play are credit manager and marketing manager; on the buy side, it is the purchasing manager and the payables manager. In both cases, the financial officers of the firm are involved, including the treasury manager and the controller. Note that on the sell side, the key concern for cash flows is the time between the receipt of a check from a customer and the availability of funds to the firm. On the buy side, the key consideration is the time between the mailing of the check to pay for purchases

■ *Figure 8–2*
The Cash Flow Lines and Individual Responsibilities

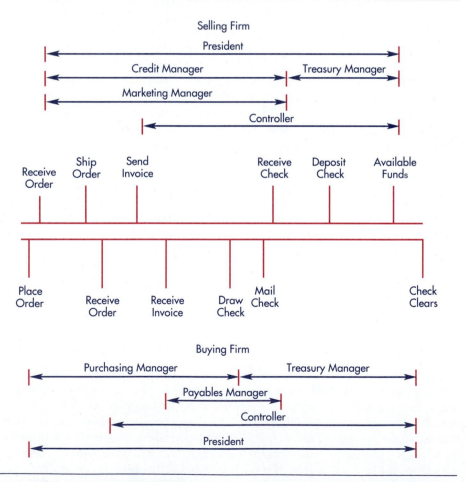

and the clearing of the check, representing the loss of cash to the firm. As we shall see below, part of the cash-management process is to coordinate the functions involving the receipt and dispersal of cash to best serve the interests of the firm.

The *cash turnover* is calculated by dividing the cash operating cycle into the number of days in the year. The higher the cash turnover, the less cash required. The objective of cash flow management is to establish an optimal cash-conversion cycle and cash turnover—the maximum cash turnover and the minimum cash-conversion cycle consistent with sound and proper practices regarding the payment of bills (accounts payable) and the collection of receipts (accounts receivable). The more effective the management of the cash operating cycle, the less the need for external financing with its associated costs and risks.

The firm should use basic, obvious strategies for optimizing the cash-conversion cycle. These include paying accounts payable at the latest date possible consistent with the taking of cash discounts and the maintenance of a firm's credit rating, managing inventory as efficiently as possible (the highest turnover possible without costly runouts), and collecting accounts receivable as soon as possible consistent with good customer relations. Each of these strategies is designed to free up as much cash as possible without adversely affecting the firm. This allows the firm to support more transactions with less cash, freeing additional funds for investment.

The financial manager can use a variety of techniques to increase the efficiency of cash flow management. These techniques can be divided into those involving the speeding up of cash receipts and those involving the efficient control of cash disbursements.

Speeding Up Cash Collections

The traditional payment system in the manufacturing and service sectors is, of course, checks, as opposed to cash in the retail sector. Therefore, the financial manager's objective here is to reduce **float,** that is, the interval from the time a customer places a payment check in the mail to the time the firm has use of the money. Within this time interval are three sources of delay, each giving rise to **collection float,** which refers to dollars tied up in the collection process:

> **float**
> funds tied up in checks written but not yet collected

> **collection float**
> the amount of funds tied up in the collection process

- *Mail float* refers to money tied up in the mailing process.[5]
- *Processing float* refers to funds received by the firm but not yet deposited at its bank.
- *Availability float* refers to checks deposited but not yet cleared through the banking system.[6]

Efficient cash management is aimed at reducing all three forms of float. Several techniques exist for doing this.

1. *Optimizing collection points.* One way to reduce mail float is to efficiently locate the collection points. Suppose a Boston firm makes sales all over the country. A check written by a customer in San Francisco may take four days to arrive in Boston. If the firm had a collection center on the

---

[5]Technically, *mail time* is the difference between when a check is mailed and when it is received at the firm's processing center. *Mail float* is the product of mail time and the total dollars collected.

[6]The clearing process amounts to presenting the check back to the customer's bank and having that bank accept the check, thus signifying that it has sufficient funds to cover the check.

West Coast, however, mailing time would be reduced. By setting up carefully chosen collection centers around the country, the Boston firm can reduce mail float. Two principal methods of establishing a decentralized collection network are lockboxes and field collections.

lockbox system
system designed to reduce float by having customers remit to nearby post office boxes, which are emptied one or more times daily by the firm's bank

a. A lockbox is simply a post office address handled by the firm's bank. In a **lockbox system,** the firm bills its customers with instructions to mail payments to a post office box in a designated city. The firm authorizes a local bank (called a *lockbox bank*) to collect checks from the box (as often as 20 times a day) and to process them through the bank's clearing system, notifying the firm of the payments. At time of deposit, the clearing process begins, resulting in lower processing float because the checks are being deposited before the firm's accounting department processes the payments. The bank charges the firm for this service, typically around 40 cents to $1.00 per payment, through either direct fees or compensating balances. Because these arrangements are relatively expensive, the firm normally will have relatively few lockbox banks. As long as interest rates are high, multiple lockbox locations can be cost-effective because they minimize a check's mail time.

Lockboxes significantly reduce the in-transit time of an average check and the internal processing float. In fact, for many banks, the complete lockbox processing cycle now averages two to three hours. Many companies save about one full day in processing float, and several days through the reduction in mail, availability, and processing float.

concentration banking
a payment collection system involving the firm's collection mechanism, depository banks, and one or more concentration banks

b. In a **concentration banking** system, the firm collects payments itself, through field sales offices or the like. Like lockboxes, this system has the advantage of placing collection centers close to the customers, thereby reducing mail float. Payments received by the sales offices are recorded and then deposited at a local bank (called a *depository bank*). These are more likely to be small banks since field offices are often in small cities. Many firms have several dozen depository banks, and some have hundreds. The time required, too, for the check to clear can be reduced because the check is often drawn on a local bank.

Funds collected and deposited in depository banks are transferred to the firm's *concentration banks*. Transfers are made by depository checks and wire transfers, as explained below. The cash manager will use the funds at the concentration banks to pay the firm's bills and/or invest surplus balances. In effect, the local (depository) banks serve as a feeder system for the firm's primary disbursement accounts at the concentration banks.

In deciding whether a lockbox or a concentration banking system or some combination of the two is worthwhile, the firm must compare marginal benefits from speeding collections with the marginal costs incurred.

■ *Example*

Epsom Computers is comparing the costs and benefits of setting up a lockbox system or a concentration banking system in place of the company's present arrangement, which involves checks being mailed to headquarters. The lockbox system generates more benefits—in the form of higher opportunity cost savings because of a lower float—than the alternative system because the operating bank is more efficient and the configuration of cities used is better. But the lockbox system is more expensive to operate. Epsom's analysis of the situation looks like this:

Assumptions

Interest rate: 12 percent per year.
Lockbox system: Would free up an additional annual average of $5 million float over the current system. Total marginal cost would be $300,000 per year.
Concentration banking system: Would free up an additional annual average of $3 million float over the current system. Total marginal cost would be $200,000 per year.

Calculations

$$\frac{\text{Net benefit of lockbox system}}{\text{over current system}} = \frac{(0.12)(\$5,000,000) - \$300,000 = \$300,000}{\text{per year}}$$

$$\frac{\text{Net benefit of concentration banking}}{\text{system over current system}} = \frac{(0.12)(\$3,000,000) - \$200,000 = \$160,000}{\text{per year}}$$

Both systems offer improvements over the current system, but the lockbox system appears to be the better arrangement. ∎

2. *Cash concentration.* Once deposits have been made, the firm is interested in quickly transferring surplus funds (funds above any target balance) to its disbursement accounts at its concentration banks, which are usually at money center banks or banks that provide the firm with its credit line. These are the control banks for the entire system, assisting the firm in efficiently managing its cash.

There are several ways to transfer funds:

a. *EFTS.* There are two broad classes of payments: paper and electronic. Paper-based payments include checks and drafts (as well as credit cards). Electronic payment is a general term denoting a funds transfer or payment mechanism that relies primarily on computer systems. **Electronic funds transfer (EFT)** refers to mechanisms for transferring payments electronically.[7]

The two major categories of electronic payments are wires and automated clearing house (ACH) transfers:

(1) *Wire payments.* Wire transfers involve virtually instantaneous transfer of payment data by a two-way computer-to-computer network. Many banks use the Federal Reserve Bank's **Fedwire** system, a large-dollar, time-critical funds transfer service. The average value of a Fedwire payment is $2.6 million. Another major wire system is the Clearing House Interbank System (CHIPS), involving same-day settlement for banks.[8]

electronic funds transfer (EFT)
electronic system for transferring funds between firms

Fedwire
a wire payment system for large-dollar, time-critical funds transfers

---

[7]EFT systems include those systems designed primarily for businesses as well as consumer-oriented systems. The latter include the automated clearing house (ACH), automated teller machine (ATM), and point-of-sale (POS) systems.

[8]The Society of Worldwide Interbank Financial Telecommunications (SWIFT) is a message system for international transfers through many banks worldwide.

Funds may be transferred in a matter of minutes, and many firms have arranged for standing instructions with their local (collection) banks to wire automatically any surplus funds to the concentration bank. Wiring is fairly expensive, however, and wiring very small amounts of money would be uneconomical. Total sending and receiving charges for domestic wires typically range from $10 to $20 per wire. Corporations use wire transfers when they require fast payment or rapid confirmation of the payment.

(2) *Automated clearing house (ACH)*. This is a computer-based alternative to the check-collection system. The ACH sorts check-like electronic images and exchanges electronic records in a manner that parallels how a paper-based clearing house sorts checks by institution and exchanges them. This system makes possible next-day settlement for small transactions.

b. *Depository transfer checks*. Local sales offices use Depository Transfer Checks (DTC), a nonnegotiable check payable to the concentration bank, to speed deposits made at depository banks to concentration banks. Under the traditional mail system, the field agent simultaneously deposits the daily receipts at the local field depository bank and mails a depository transfer check to the concentration bank along with a deposit slip for the funds deposited in the local bank. This system of depository transfer checks obviously is not as fast as wire transfers, but it is very inexpensive.

Under an electronic DTC system, a collection center receives and processes the firm's deposit information. This information is transferred several times a day to the concentration bank, which sends a DTC to the local depository bank for payment. This electronic system provides one-day clearing, is inexpensive, and eliminates mail float.

Table 8–2 shows the key characteristics of the three principal methods of payment: wire, ACH, and check. The key point about EFT transactions in this discussion is that it speeds up the collection of cash. The efficient handling of cash necessitates that it be moved from the local deposit banks to the concentration bank, and the ACH system facilitates this. The float is reduced or eliminated.

While the receiver of the funds will prefer this reduction of the float, the payer probably will not like losing the advantage of float normally gained by sending checks in the mail. This loss of "float disbursement" is a serious impediment to the adoption of EFTs nationwide. In fact, EFT has not fulfilled the expectation by some that it would become the substitute for paper checks. Total EFT mechanisms accounted for only 1.2 percent of total noncash payments by 1987, with total volume growth rates apparently declining.[9] (Note, however, that this figure is the number of transactions and not the value of the transactions). It is important to recognize, moreover, that the check system is changing. Costs are probably falling, service is improving, and users are probably more satisfied. Total check collection float has declined in recent years. Under current conditions, a strong

---

[9]See Bruce J. Summers, "Electronic Payments in Retrospect," *Economic Review,* Federal Reserve Bank of Richmond, March–April 1988, pp. 16–19.

Characteristic	Wire	ACH	Check
Cost	Very high	Low; could be very low	Low
Notification	Yes	No	No
Confirmation	Yes	No	No
Transfer execution time	Within day	Next day	Generally next day or later
Transaction type	Single or small group	Batch	Batch
Message	Limited	Limited (CCD) Extensive (CTP) Extensive (CTX)	Limited on check but extensive via attachment of remittance advice.
Economics	Very high fixed cost and peak-load limited.	High fixed cost but no peak-load problem; very low variable cost.	Moderate fixed cost but relatively high variable cost.
Security	Crucial	Important	Important

■ *Table 8–2*
Key Characteristics of Wire, ACH, and Check Payments

Source: Bernell K. Stone, "Electronic Payment Basics," *Economic Review*, Federal Reserve Bank of Atlanta, March 1986, p. 10.

disincentive for converting from checks to EFT will continue because of the float benefit from writing checks.

Controlling Disbursements

While the firm is interested in collecting cash as rapidly as possible, it is also interested in controlling its disbursements. In doing this, the firm is subject to ethical considerations and the constraint that its credit standing is not impaired. While there are several techniques for legally slowing disbursements, the firm should be aware that whatever slows down its disbursements also slows down the cash collection of those being paid. The firm's suppliers and creditors may object to practices that blatantly slow the firm's disbursements.

1. *Avoidance of early payments.* Business credit information services, such as Dun & Bradstreet, collect the trade experiences of many companies. As discussed in the next chapter, credit grantors consider this data in deciding whether to grant credit to another firm. Firms that do not pay promptly will tend to have relatively poor credit ratings. This can create difficulties in securing ample trade credit, so there are definite advantages to making payments on time. However, there are no advantages— unless a cash discount is offered (see Chapter 10)—to paying early. If a payment is due on the 30th of the month, the firm should not pay prior to the 30th.

2. *Remote disbursing.* Remote disbursing is one method of playing the float game, generating *disbursement float*. Remote disbursing involves paying bills from banks that are far distant from the payee, thereby increasing clearing and mail float. For example, a firm could set up a system where there are two main disbursement accounts, one on each coast. East Coast bills are paid with checks drawn on the West Coast bank, and West Coast bills are paid with East Coast bank checks. An advantage of having few disbursement accounts is that fewer checking accounts need be

maintained, which allows a smaller total cash balance. Ethical and legal issues are involved in systems of this type, and the financial manager should proceed cautiously.

3. *Zero-balance accounts.* A zero-balance account system can be established at the firm's concentration bank to control disbursement activity. As the name implies, these accounts contain no funds; that is, they have a zero balance. When checks are presented to these accounts for payment, a negative balance is incurred during the day. At the end of the day the accounts are restored to zero by a transfer of funds from a central control account which is located in the same bank. In turn, the firm may need to buy or sell marketable securities in order to maintain the proper balance in the central control account.

   Zero-balance accounts are an effective means of controlling cash disbursements. They provide overall control while simultaneously permitting intra-firm flexibility, which is needed in the case of a firm with several divisions, each of which needs its own disbursing account.

4. *Bank drafts.* When a check issued by the firm is presented to the bank, the firm's checking account is immediately reduced. However, a bank draft, which is an order to make payment drawn by the firm upon itself, must be sent back to the firm by its bank for approval before payment is made. After acceptance, the firm deposits the necessary funds to cover payment, which means that cash does not have to be available until the firm is presented with the draft and approves its payment. However, not all suppliers accept drafts, and service charges for processing drafts are higher.

Cash Budgeting

Planning for and controlling the use of cash are extremely important tasks. Failure to properly anticipate cash flows can lead, on the one hand, to idle cash balances and a lower rate of return and, on the other, to cash deficits and possible failure. The starting point for a sound cash-management program is a properly prepared cash budget.

cash budget
a statement showing cash inflows, outflows, and cash balances over some period of time

A **cash budget** is basically a worksheet used to show cash inflows, outflows, and cash balances over some projected time period. It is a device to help the financial manager plan for and control the use of cash.

One of the main purposes of the cash budget is to estimate the firm's cash balance in future time periods. The time horizon of a cash budget is fairly short, typically 6 to 12 months. Within this time framework, the firm will forecast cash inflows and outflows and cash balances, typically on a monthly or weekly basis. Additionally, most firms use daily cash budgets for the next one or two weeks to keep close control of imminent cash flows and balances.

Elements of the Cash Budgeting System

Many cash budgeting systems are set up to handle all cash flows, regardless of their nature; other firms prefer to prepare two separate cash budgeting systems, one handling operating cash flows and balances and the other handling financial cash flows and balances. Table 8–3 illustrates the major categories of cash flows included in the cash budget. Numerous other items appear also.

Cash Inflows	Cash Outflows
Operating	Operating
Cash sales	Payroll payments
Receivables collections	Payables payments
	Capital expenditures
Financial	Financial
Interest receipts	Dividend payments
Sale of marketable securities	Interest payments
Issuance of new securities	Redemption of securities
	Loan repayments
	Purchase of marketable securities
	Tax payments

**Lessie Packaging
Sales Worksheet
($000)**

	Nov.	Dec.	Jan.	Feb.	Mar.
Past sales	$480	$450			
Estimated future sales			$450	$500	$500
Estimated sales-related receipts:					
Cash sales (10 percent of current month sales)			45	50	50
Receivables collections:					
50 percent of last month sales			225	225	250
40 percent of sales from two months ago			192	180	180
Total receivables collections			$417	$405	$430
Estimated sales-related expenditures:					
Payables payments (50 percent of current-month sales)			$225	$250	$250

An example will help illustrate the preparation of a cash budget. Lessie Packaging is a small container manufacturer. In early January, the company's comptroller prepares to update the firm's cash budget. She routinely uses a three-month time horizon, subdivided into monthly periods, because she feels this is about as far ahead as she can accurately forecast cash flows. Currently, she is estimating cash flows and end-of-month cash balances for the months of January, February, and March.

The comptroller begins her analysis with the sales worksheet, illustrated in Table 8–4. The starting point of the worksheet is the recording of sales for the past two months (November and December) and the projection of sales for the coming three months.[10]

Although Lessie's policy on credit sales is to grant 30 days from the date of sale for customers to pay their bills, a large portion of credit customers do not

[10]Many techniques are used to forecast sales, ranging from management consensus and intuition to sophisticated time-series techniques such as regression analysis.

pay their bills promptly. Specifically, past experience leads the comptroller to expect that about 10 percent of any month's sales will be cash sales, about 50 percent will be credit sales that will be collected during the subsequent month, and the remaining 40 percent are credit sales that will be collected during the second subsequent month.

Using these projections and the sales estimates shown in Table 8–4, Lessie's comptroller can estimate cash sales and receivables collections for the coming three months (these estimates are also shown in Table 8–4). Notice that collection of the $450,000 estimated January sales is spread over a three-month period: 10 percent ($45,000) will be collected as cash sales in January, 50 percent ($225,000) will be collected in February, and the remaining 40 percent ($180,000) will be collected in March.

Accounts payable are also related to the sales volume, reflecting the ordering of material and supplies in anticipation of future sales. Lessie's production schedule is such that the company orders materials and supplies on the basis of next month's sales forecast. On average, the cost of these orders runs about 50 percent of sales. The firm receives 30-day credit from its suppliers, so payments on accounts payables are made in the month that the sales occur. For example, based on the forecast of a $500,000 sales level in February, the firm will order $250,000 worth of material and supplies in January. However, the $250,000 cash disbursement will not be made until February. The sales worksheet shows that estimated cash payments on the firm's payables each month will be 50 percent of that month's estimated sales.

Next, the comptroller is ready to prepare the cash budget, which has three parts: the estimated cash inflows section, the estimated cash outflows section, and the estimated cash surplus or shortage position section. Lessie's cash budget is shown in Table 8–5.

The estimated cash inflows section itemizes all anticipated cash inflows for each month in the planning period. Included here are the estimates of cash sales and cash receivables collections determined from the sales worksheet. Lessie also has some interest receipts, $150,000 worth of marketable securities that mature in February, and some other cash receipts.

The estimated cash outflows section itemizes all anticipated cash disbursements during the planning period, including the estimated payables payments determined from the sales worksheet. Another major cash expenditure item is payroll. In addition, Lessie has minor capital-expenditure payments scheduled in January and February and a major capital expenditure of $100,000 planned in March. The company also has to make a quarterly income tax payment of $75,000 in January, a $60,000 quarterly cash dividend payment, a $200,000 loan repayment in March, and other cash disbursements of about $20,000 per month.

The difference between estimated cash inflows and outflows is the estimated net cash flow. As Table 8–5 shows, estimated monthly net cash flows are −$95,000, +$63,000, and −$319,000, respectively. The large negative estimated net cash flow for March is caused by the $100,000 capital expenditure and the repayment of the $200,000 loan.

The last section of the cash budget shows the calculation of the estimated cash surplus or shortage position of the firm, given the estimated net cash flows for the planning period. *Included in these calculations is the firm's minimum cash balance level.* This minimum cash balance represents that level of cash ($1 million here)

■ *Table 8–5*
Lessie Packaging—
Cash Budget

**Lessie Packaging
Cash Budget
($000)**

	January	February	March
Estimated cash inflows			
Cash sales	$ 45	$ 50	$ 50
Receivables collections	417	405	430
Interest receipts	3	3	2
Sale of marketable securities	0	150	0
Other cash receipts	10	15	13
Total cash inflows	$ 475	$ 623	$ 495
Estimated cash outflows			
Payroll payments	$ 230	$ 220	$ 240
Payables payments	225	250	250
Capital expenditures	20	10	100
Tax payments	75	0	0
Dividend payments	0	60	0
Interest payments	0	0	4
Repayment of loan	0	0	200
Other cash disbursements	20	20	20
Total cash outflows	$ 570	$ 560	$ 814
Estimated net cash flow for month	−$ 95	$ 63	−$ 319
Estimated cash surplus (shortage)			
Beginning-of-month cash balance	$1,050	$ 955	$1,018
Estimated net cash flow for month	− 95	63	− 319
Estimated end-of-month cash balance	955	1,018	699
Less: Minimum cash balance	1,000	1,000	1,000
Estimated cash surplus (shortage)	−$ 45	$ 18	−$ 301

that Lessie does not want to go below. We discuss the determination of the minimum cash balance level later in this chapter.

At the end of December, when the planning period begins, Lessie has a cash balance of $1,050,000. If the firm were to make no working capital corrections during the planning period, the firm's estimated end-of-month cash balance would be $955,000 in January, $1,018,000 in February, and $699,000 in March. That is, relative to the desired $1 million minimum cash balance, the firm would have a $45,000 cash shortage at the end of January, an $18,000 cash surplus at the end of February, and a $301,000 cash shortage at the end of March.

The cash budget shown in Table 8–5 is incomplete; it does not include the effect of any financial management actions the cash manager may take to eliminate the anticipated cash surpluses and/or shortages.[11] There are many solutions for balancing the budget. The simplest is to borrow the amount of any cash shortage and invest any surplus. Lessie would borrow $45,000 in January, invest $18,000

---

[11]The type of cash budget shown in Table 8–5 is often called an unbalanced cash budget.

in February, and borrow $301,000 in March.[12] Notice that there are some complications even in this simple solution. First, these new borrowing and investing plans will entail interest cash flows that should be included in the cash budget. Second, if the amounts borrowed and invested mature within the planning period, the repayment of any loan principal and the receipt of any investment principal must also be included in the cash flow section of the budget. If, for example, Lessie borrows $45,000 in January for 30 days to cover its estimated January cash shortage, the $45,000 loan repayment and attendant interest payments must be included in the February estimated cash outflows section.

What makes the cash budget problem particularly difficult and challenging is the vast array of ways to balance the budget, each of which has interactive effects on estimated cash flows. At one extreme, the firm may choose to reduce cash outflows by delaying payment on its accounts payable. Another alternative is to attempt to speed up cash inflows by applying pressure on those credit customers who are slow payers. A third alternative is to sell in January the $150,000 of marketable securities maturing in February. There are many other alternatives.

The point is that in addition to estimating the size of the anticipated cash surplus or shortage, there is also the associated problem of how to balance the cash budget, which involves considering all the dimensions of working-capital management. Actually, the problem can also involve long-term decisions. For example, Lessie may consider postponing its $100,000 March capital expenditure because of the large cash outflow anticipated in that month. Usually, however, the cash flows associated with long-term investment decisions are taken as given, and the cash manager is charged with the responsibility of arranging the firm's working capital such that a satisfactory cash balance is maintained and the firm's long-term investment plans are unimpeded.

Sensitivity Analysis and Optimistic/Pessimistic Forecasts

The example in Table 8–5 is also incomplete in that it is based on only one set of estimated cash inflows and outflows. These figures might comprise *expected* cash flows or even most probable values, but the analysis throughout Table 8–5 did not allow for alternative cash flow estimates. That is, we need to consider the possibility of errors or variability in cash flow estimates.

Variability in cash flow analysis is usually handled through *sensitivity analysis* or through *optimistic/pessimistic forecasts*. Sensitivity analysis, which will be considered in more detail in Chapter 13, is concerned with answering what-if questions. What if Lessie's cash sales were 20 percent higher, or lower, than estimated in Table 8–5? Questions like this can be addressed through sensitivity analysis. A computer is particularly advantageous for this analysis.

To make optimistic/pessimistic forecasts, the analyst prepares a cash budget that is purposely optimistic and/or pessimistic. Why do this? Because extreme deviations from expectations are the very circumstances for which we should have contingency plans. This is particularly true on the pessimistic side. A cash budget prepared under the assumption of very poor cash flow conditions can be very useful indeed.

[12]The planned investment and borrowing in February and March, respectively, would only be planned actions; when the comptroller prepares her updated cash budget at the beginning of February, she may well have new expectations of estimated cash inflows and outflows based on events that transpired in January. These new expectations could affect the estimated cash surplus or shortage positions.

Estimating Optimal Cash Levels

When the firm keeps cash on hand, it suffers an opportunity cost in that resources are tied up in a nonearning asset. But if too little cash is held, the firm will continually incur the transactions costs of acquiring cash. Planning for the optimal cash level begins with a projection of future net cash flows over a near-term planning period. This period, usually a month or less, is normally shorter than the cash budget planning period discussed above.

First, the firm should separate anticipated cash flows into *known* and *uncertain* categories. Known cash flows are those that are reasonably foreseeable; management knows the size and timing of these cash flows with some degree of certainty. A previously declared dividend that will be paid in two weeks is an example. Uncertain cash flows are those whose size and timing are estimated with less precision. Cash sales are a good example. A list of the major known and uncertain cash flows looks like this:

Major Known Cash Flows	*Major Uncertain Cash Flows*
Proceeds from issuing new securities	Cash sales
Payroll payments	Receivables collection
Capital expenditures	Payables payments
Tax payments	
Dividend payments	
Interest receipts and payments	
Loan repayments	

Because the size and timing of uncertain cash flows are much less predictable, the cash-management problems associated with them are more difficult. In the following analysis, we address only the uncertain cash flow components. Since cash balances are usually held for transactions and compensating balance purposes, we concentrate only on these two motives for holding cash.[13]

The main problem in determining how much cash to hold for transactions purposes involves a cost trade-off. Holding cash incurs an opportunity cost, or the amount of forgone return the firm could have earned by investing the cash. At some point, the firm will want to invest excess cash in short-term interest-earning assets, such as marketable securities. This will incur a transfer cost. On the other hand, if the firm keeps too little cash, there will be a need to sell some securities or borrow funds, either of which also incurs a transfer cost. These transfer costs include brokerage fees, time and expenses of arrangements, long-distance calls, clerical expenses, and other expenses attributable to the cash manager's efforts during the transfer.

Figure 8–3 shows how the transactions cash balance fluctuates as net cash flows randomly fluctuate. When the transactions cash balance hits zero, the firm must either sell some marketable securities or borrow to restore the cash balance to level z. At the other extreme, when the cash balance has grown to level h, the firm will want to reduce the cash balance back to level z by investing $h - z$ amount of dollars in marketable securities.

---

[13]Most firms do not regularly keep cash or securities for speculative reasons, and most of them keep their precautionary liquidity balances in the form of marketable securities.

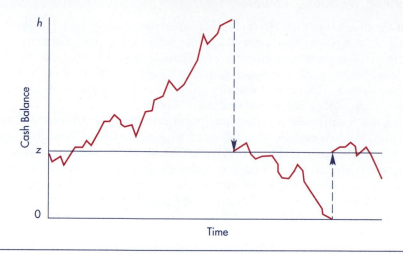

The problem becomes a search for the values of z and h that will minimize the expected total cost of maintaining a transactions balance, which is the sum of opportunity costs plus transactions costs. The procedure for solving this problem involves some complex mathematics, but one solution, worked out by Merton Miller and Daniel Orr, is explained in Appendix 8–A.[14]

THE MANAGEMENT OF MARKETABLE SECURITIES

As noted when we discussed the cash-management activity, the management of marketable securities is the other side of the coin from managing cash. Therefore, we do not need to elaborate its importance.

One important aspect of the investment problem in marketable securities is what amount to maintain. Stated differently, What is the optimal level of investment in marketable securities? The second major aspect of the problem is, Which marketable securities should the firm invest in? That is, What should be the composition of the firm's portfolio of marketable securities? Very many types and maturities are available.

The Optimal Level of Marketable Securities

Firms invest in securities to meet such known cash flow drains as dividend payments. Also, cash that has temporarily accumulated and can be used by the firm elsewhere in the near future may be invested in securities.

When its cash account hits the determined minimum level, the firm may liquidate some securities, so it will want to ensure that it has enough marketable securities to make any necessary cash replenishments. Failure to have enough

---

[14]Equations 8A–1 and 8A–2, from the chapter appendix, apply to the special case where there is a 0.5 probability of an increase in the daily cash balance and a 0.5 probability of an equal decrease in the daily cash balance. Optimal z and h values for other situations are presented in M. Miller and D. Orr, "A Model of the Demand for Money by Firms," *Quarterly Journal of Economics,* August 1966, pp. 413–35.

securities on hand when needed will require the firm to make other arrangements, like borrowing, and such interruptions have *stockout costs* associated with them. On the other hand, the firm will not want to hold too large a level of securities. Since the rate of return earned on securities is usually less than the rate of return on other assets, an opportunity cost is incurred in holding marketable securities.

Marketable Securities and Shareholder Wealth

The greater the firm's investment in marketable securities, the greater the expected opportunity cost and the less the expected stockout cost. Conversely, the smaller the investment in marketable securities, the smaller the expected opportunity cost and the greater the expected stockout cost. As with virtually every other financial decision, a trade-off is involved in this portion of short-term financial management.

The firm's problem is to find that level of marketable securities where the expected total cost—the sum of expected opportunity and stockout costs—is minimized. Thus, the management of marketable securities can be thought of as a cost minimization problem, as described in Chapter 7.

Solutions to the problem of expected total cost usually come from models that are more complicated versions of inventory control models, like the simple transactions cash balance model we studied earlier in this chapter, or linear or dynamic programming models. Some major banks and consulting services sell solutions to client firms.

Characteristics of Marketable Securities

In choosing a portfolio of marketable securities, the firm will be particularly interested in their risk, marketability, and maturity. Differences in these features are the primary determinants of the yield differences among securities and explain why firms select certain kinds of securities for short-term investments.[15]

Risk

Other things being equal, the firm would like to receive the highest possible yield on its investment in marketable securities. However, as we have seen repeatedly, seeking higher rates of return leads to accepting larger amounts of risk. Since the firm keeps marketable securities for precautionary reasons and to meet known, scheduled outflows of cash, the firm will tend to invest in very safe marketable securities. Firms tend to buy the highest-yielding marketable securities they can find, subject to the constraint that the securities have an acceptable risk level. Risk in this context refers to risk of failure; however, failure can have more than one meaning here. At one extreme, a security could default: the issuer might fail to redeem the security according to the contract terms. In a less severe sense, the price of the security could fall at a time when the firm needs to sell it. If the firm sells the security for less than the needed amount, this too is a kind of failure. To minimize these possibilities, firms tend to restrict their securities investments to certain classes of safe financial instruments.

---

[15]Another factor is taxability. Interest income from most municipal (state and local) securities is tax-exempt; therefore, these securities have lower returns. A firm must adjust the returns on taxable securities by its marginal tax rate before it can compare taxable and tax-exempt alternatives.

Maturity

The longer the maturity of a security, the more likely are price fluctuations prior to maturity. Since downside price fluctuations are undesirable, the firm will prefer short-term securities. At the long end of the maturity spectrum, firms prefer marketable securities whose remaining life is no greater than six to nine months. At the short end of the spectrum, firms can and do invest funds overnight.

Marketability

Marketability refers to how readily the security can be liquidated into a cash position prior to maturity. Highly marketable securities are those for which there is an active secondary market. This ensures that securities can be liquidated quickly and that there need be no major price concessions made to facilitate the sale. Firms tend to purchase securities that are highly marketable. Securities with restricted marketability may be acceptable, however, if they have very short maturities.

Yields

Yields (that is, rates of return) on marketable securities are a function of the characteristics of the securities described earlier. For example, T-bills are the safest, most marketable financial assets in the world and their yields reflect that fact.

Yield calculations can be complex, but the general idea is not complicated:[16]

$$\text{Yield} = \left(\frac{\text{Interest}}{\text{Market price}}\right)\left(\frac{365}{\text{Days to maturity}}\right) \qquad \textbf{(8–1)}$$

This particular yield equation is appropriate for short-term interest-bearing securities that are held to maturity and have only one interest payment, which is paid at maturity. More complicated yield formulas are needed for more complicated situations.

Equation 8–1 can also be used for discount securities by substituting the amount of the discount for the interest amount. The amount of the discount equals the security's face value (what it will be redeemed for) minus the security's market price:

$$\text{Discount} = \text{Face value} - \text{Market price} \qquad \textbf{(8–2)}$$

One particularly confusing aspect of yields is that yields quoted in the financial press often are not the yield calculated from Equation 8–1. Many quoted yields are based on a 360-day year and a face value base rather than a 365-day year and a market value base. Treasury bills (T-bills) are one such example. Quoted yields for T-bills are not consistent with Equation 8–1.

■ *Example*

Suppose a 90-day $10,000 face value T-bill has a $200 discount. The quoted yield will be stated as:

$$\text{Quoted yield} = \left(\frac{\$200}{\$10,000}\right)\left(\frac{360}{90}\right) = 0.0800 \text{ per year}$$

---

[16]For a thorough treatment, see Marcia Stigham, *Money Market Calculations: Yields, Break-evens and Arbitrage* (Homewood, Ill.: Dow Jones-Irwin, 1981).

But the actual yield (from Equation 8–1) is:[17]

$$\text{Yield} = \left(\frac{\$200}{\$9,800}\right)\left(\frac{365}{90}\right) = 0.0828 \text{ per year}$$

Why do traders and money managers use the wrong formula in quoting yields? It's the traditional way to calculate T–bill (and some other) yields, and tradition seems hard to break. Money managers need to know the exact definition of quoted yield for every security being considered in their portfolio and how to convert those *quoted* yields to *actual* yields. Otherwise, what appears to be an inferior yield may be a better yield.

Types of Marketable Securities

Firms invest in many types of marketable securities. For the most part, however, they are very safe, short–term, and highly marketable. *Interest-bearing securities* pay a stated interest rate, called the *coupon rate*. Interest is paid periodically and/or at maturity. Interest is not paid on discount securities. Instead, the investor earns a rate of return from buying the security at a price below—discounted from—par (face value) and selling the security at par value on the maturity date.

U.S. Treasury Bills

Treasury bills are short–term discount securities issued by the U.S. government. The market for these securities is the largest and most liquid of the U.S. money markets.

Like all Treasury securities, bills are thought of as being free of default risk since they have the full financial backing of the U.S. government. Because Treasury bills are safe and readily marketable, they tend to have lower yields than other marketable securities. U.S. Treasury securities historically have been the marketable securities most widely held by corporations.

> **Treasury bills**
> short-term marketable debt of the U.S. Treasury, issued on a discount basis for maturities up to one year

Federal Agency Securities

In recent years, many U.S. government agencies have raised funds by issuing securities. These **federal agency securities** have maturities ranging from one month to several years and have been widely purchased by corporations because of their marketability and relative safety. Secondary markets for these securities are strong, although not equal to the Treasury securities market. The securities are guaranteed by the agencies themselves rather than the U.S. government. Their slightly lower marketability and safety in comparison to Treasury securities causes them to have slightly higher yields. Some prominent examples of agency issues are Federal Intermediate Credit Banks, Federal National Mortgage Association, Federal Land Banks, Federal Home Loan Banks, Government National Mortgage Association, and Banks for Cooperatives. Called *agencies,* these securities are interest bearing.

> **federal agency securities**
> securities issued by several government agencies and government-sponsored agencies, with yields somewhat higher than Treasury securities

---

[17]If the discount is $200, the T-bill's market price is ($10,000 minus $200) = $9,800.

Negotiable Certificates of Deposit

certificate of deposit (CD)
negotiable instrument issued by banks representing the deposit of a specified amount, with yields based on size and maturity

A **certificate of deposit (CD)** is an interest-bearing security that certifies that a specified amount of money placed in a bank will receive a stated amount of interest for a stated amount of time. Banks have effectively used CDs to induce business firms to invest their short-term funds with them. The safety of the CDs is guaranteed by (and hence is related to the strength of) the issuing bank, and CDs may be sold prior to maturity. A fairly strong secondary market has developed for CDs issued by banks in New York, Chicago, and other major financial centers. Yields on CDs tend to exceed Treasury securities yields. Major banks normally issue CDs in denominations of $500,000 or more, but smaller banks issue CDs in smaller denominations. This effectively means that the highest-quality CDs are available only to large firms.

Commercial Paper

commercial paper
short-term, unsecured promissory note issued by corporations with good credit ratings

Commercial paper refers to unsecured promissory notes by companies to raise short-term financing. When a firm invests in commercial paper, it is essentially lending to the issuing company. Commercial paper is rated according to its safety, which depends on the financial strength of the issuing company. The highest quality paper is rated "prime 1." Yields on commercial paper are related to rating and maturity, and initial maturities usually range from five days to nine months. There is no active secondary market for commercial paper, so most purchasers will hold the paper until maturity. However, issuing firms and dealers often will agree to repurchase commercial paper prior to maturity, at a discount, on request. The combination of limited marketability and extra risk causes commercial paper yields to exceed Treasury securities yields. Commercial paper is usually issued in units of $25,000 or more. It is a discount type of security.

Banker's Acceptance

banker's acceptance
short-term, marketable security representing a guarantee by a bank of a transaction by a firm

Time drafts drawn on and accepted by banks are called **banker's acceptances.** They are used to facilitate trade and are particularly useful in export-import businesses. Since acceptances are guaranteed by the participating bank, they are as safe as that bank's guarantee. The secondary market for acceptances is active, with New York as its primary location. Primary participants are banks and principal dealers. Initial maturities on these discount securities are usually no longer than 180 days, and yields are usually higher than on Treasury securities of similar maturity. Banker's acceptances are normally issued in units of $25,000 or more.

Repurchase Agreements

repurchase agreement
an agreement by a bank or securities dealer to sell specific securities and to repurchase them at a specified price and time

The purchase of short-term securities by an investor from a government-bond dealer, and the subsequent repurchase of the securities by the dealer, is referred to as a **repurchase agreement** (or repo). Government-bond dealers are agents who actively buy and sell government securities, and they have used the repo technique to help them finance their large inventories of government securities. Offering packages of safe government securities with a guaranteed repurchase enables dealers to procure funds from the corporate sector of the economy. Repos are interest bearing, so the firm receives a specified interest rate on the

Summary of Investment Characteristics for Major Marketable Securities   ■ *Table 8–6*

Type of Security	Original Maturity	Discount (D) or Interest Bearing (I)	Typical Minimum Denomination	Type of Secondary Market	Risk
Treasury bills	3, 6, 9, 12 months	D	$ 10,000	Excellent	Lowest
Federal agencies	Few months to many years	I	$ 1,000	Good	Slightly more than Treasury bills
Negotiable CDs	30 days to 1 year	I	$100,000	Good	A function of issuing bank
Commercial paper	Up to 270 days	D*	$100,000	Limited	A function of issuer
Banker's acceptance	30 to 180 days	D	$ 25,000	Good	More than agencies
Repurchase agreements	Overnight to several days	I**	$ 10,000	Very limited	More than Treasury bills

*Sometimes I.
**Sometimes D.

arrangement, which is basically a short-term loan to the dealer, and the repurchase date is arranged to suit the needs of the firm. There is no active secondary market for repos, but maturities are very short, ranging from one day to a few weeks. Since most repos involve Treasury securities, yields on repos are competitive with yields on other Treasury securities handled by dealers (who charge a fee for their services).

The investment characteristics of these major securities are summarized in Table 8–6.

SUMMARY

■ The term *cash-management activity* refers to a combination of activities involving forecasting cash needs, managing the inflows and outflows of cash, and investing excess cash effectively. The objective is to minimize the level of cash and marketable securities while earning adequate liquidity.

■ Firms primarily hold cash and securities for transactions and for precautionary, speculative, and compensating balance motives.

■ One important aspect of cash management is the conscious speeding up of cash collections and slowing down of cash disbursements. Another important aspect is the *cash budget,* a worksheet used to show cash inflows, outflows, and cash balances over some projected time period, which helps the financial manager estimate the firm's cash balance in future time periods.

■ Optimal cash levels must be estimated, including maximum, minimum, average, and return cash balances. These procedures account for the firm's needs both to cover transactions and to keep compensating balances.

■ A firm's portfolio of *marketable securities* is held mainly for precautionary reasons and to meet scheduled cash outflows. These securities are characterized by the qualities of very short maturity, very low risk, and high marketability.

■ The most widely used marketable securities are U.S. Treasury obligations. Other marketable securities include Federal agencies, negotiable CDs, commercial paper, banker's acceptances, and repurchase agreements.

KEY TERMS

banker's acceptance, p. 252
cash budget, p. 242
cash-conversion cycle, p. 235
cash management, p. 233
certificate of deposit, p. 252
collection float, p. 237
commercial paper, p. 252
compensating balances, p. 232
concentration banking, p. 238

electronic funds transfer, p. 239
federal agency securities, p. 251
Fedwire, p. 239
float, p. 237
lockbox system, p. 238
marketable securities, p. 232
repurchase agreements, p. 252
Treasury bills, p. 251

QUESTIONS

8–1. Explain what is meant by *cash management*. What is its objective?

8–2. Identify in each of the following situations which of the four motives for holding cash explains the increase in cash described.
  a. The firm's new management orders that the checking account level be permanently raised to make the chance of a cash stockout less likely.
  b. The bank requires that the firm increase its checking account level before a current loan is renewed.
  c. The vice president–controller directs that the cash balance be built up to allow the firm to take advantage of some possible merger opportunities that are expected to arise within the next few months.
  d. Cash balances increase as a cyclical increase in sales begins.

8–3. Other things being equal, what effect would the following events have on the average cash balance that the firm keeps for transactions purposes? Explain your answers.
  a. Interest rates decrease.
  b. It becomes more expensive to transfer funds from cash to securities and vice versa.
  c. The variability of daily net cash flows decreases.

8–4. In the transactions cash balance model, contrast the average cash balance and the return point.

8–5. The owner of J.C.'s Tuxedo Rentals is negotiating a loan of $400,000 at an Atlanta bank. During negotiations the bank's lending officer insists that a compensating balance be maintained, but that it does not matter whether it is an absolute minimum of $40,000 or a minimum average of $40,000. The officer further says that the interest rate and all other features of the loan will be the same under the two alternatives. Given these facts, explain whether either arrangement is more favorable to J.C.'s.

8–6. Compare the cost and the speed of collection of wire transfers, depository transfer checks, and special handling procedures.

8–7. Explain the difference between an unbalanced cash budget and a revised cash budget.

8–8. Define and contrast mail float, processing float, and deposit float.

8–9. How is the cash-conversion cycle related to the operating cycle?

8–10. What is meant by cash flow management? What is the cash turnover?

8–11. What is meant by playing the float?

8–12. Why do you think that EFTs have not become more popular?

8–13. Some marketable securities are called *discount securities,* and others are called *interest-bearing securities*. Briefly distinguish between these two types of securities.

8–14. In what sense can Treasury bills, commercial paper, and negotiable certificates of deposit be thought of as IOUs?

8–15. Rank the expected yields on 90-day Treasury bills, commercial paper, and negotiable certificates of deposit from lowest to highest. Use the current issue of *The Wall Street Journal* to determine the accuracy of your ranking.

DEMONSTRATION PROBLEMS

8–1. Waddell Graphics is analyzing a lockbox system to replace its field collection system. The lockbox system would reduce the average annual cash float by $1,000,000 at a cost of operating of $100,000. The field collection system costs $40,000 to operate and reduces the average annual cash float by $500,000.
   a. If interest rates are expected to average 15 percent, what should Waddell do?
   b. If interest rates are expected to average 10 percent, what should Waddell do?

8–2. Hall Dental Supplies has annual sales of $100 million, which are uniform during the year (365 days). Its deposit float is four days' worth of sales (on average). An alternative system, which would reduce deposit float to two days' worth of sales, has been suggested.
   a. Calculate the average dollar value of deposit float under each system.
   b. The cost of the alternative system is $75,000. If money has an opportunity cost of 10 percent annually, determine if Hall should make the change to the alternative system.

8–3. Complete the cash budget, given the following information:

	January	February	March
Estimated net cash flow for month	−4,000	2,000	−2,000
Beginning-of-month cash balance	12,000		
Estimated end-of-month cash balance			
Minimum cash balance	6,000	8,000	10,000
Estimated cash surplus (shortage)			

Solutions to Demonstration Problems

8–1. *a.*
$$\text{Net benefit of lockbox system} = (.15)(\$1,000,000) - \$100,000$$
$$= \$150,000 - \$100,000$$
$$= \$50,000$$
$$\text{Net benefit of field collection system} = (.15)(\$500,000) - \$40,000$$
$$= \$75,000 - \$40,000$$
$$= \$35,000$$

Therefore, the lockbox system would provide a net gain.

b.
$$\text{Net benefit of lockbox system} = (.10)(\$1,000,000) - \$100,000$$
$$= \$100,000 - \$100,000$$
$$= 0$$
$$\text{Net benefit of field collection system} = (.10)(\$500,000) - \$40,000$$
$$= \$50,000 - \$40,000$$
$$= \$10,000$$

Therefore, the field collection system should be retained.

8–2. Average sales/day = $100,000,000/365 = $273,973.
   a. The average dollar value of deposit float:

$$current system = \$273,973 \times 4 = \$1,095,892$$
$$alternative = \$273,973 \times 2 = \$547,946$$

   b. Opportunity cost savings per year = Reduction in deposit float × Annual interest rate
$$= \$547,946 \times .10 = \$54,795/year$$

   Since the cost of the alternative system is more than the cost savings, Hall should not implement the alternative.

8–3.

	January	February	March
Estimated net cash flow for month	−4,000	2,000	−2,000
Beginning-of-month cash balance	12,000	8,000	10,000
Estimated end-of-month cash balance	8,000	10,000	8,000
Minimum cash balance	6,000	8,000	10,000
Estimated cash surplus (shortage)	2,000	2,000	−2,000

PROBLEMS

8–1. Wingler Corporation is considering initiating either a lockbox system or a field collection system. Interest rates are in the range of 20 percent per year. Annual marginal benefits and costs relative to Wingler's current system are:

	Lockbox Collection System	Field Collection System
Average annual reduction in cash float	$500,000	$250,000
Annual marginal cost	$ 40,000	$ 15,000

   a. What decision should Wingler make?
   b. What decision should Wingler make if annual interest rates were in the 5 percent range?

8–2. Lacey's Stores has annual sales of $73 million. The company uses a centralized billing system, and on average, the firm's deposit float is about five days' worth of sales. A financial consultant has suggested that Lacey's should consider going to a field collection system. This would reduce deposit float to about three days' worth of sales.
   a. Assuming uniform sales during the year (365 days), determine the firm's average sales per day.
   b. Calculate the average dollar value of deposit float under the centralized billing system and the field collection system.
   c. If money can be risklessly put to work at 15 percent annual interest, determine whether Lacey should change to a field collection system if the cost of the field collection system will be $40,000 per year.

8–3. Leaseco Corporation uses depository transfer checks in field collection situations where the daily volume of collections is not sufficient to justify a wire transfer. Assume that a single, end-of-day wire transfer would save Leaseco two days over a depository transfer check, and that the cost of attaining this gain would be an extra $3 per wire. How large must the daily collection volume be to justify a wire transfer system if the interest rate is 15 percent per year?

8–4. Complete the unbalanced cash budget shown below:

Cash Budget ($000)

	April	May	June
Estimated net cash flow for month	−200	100	−100
Beginning-of-month cash balance	600	___	___
Estimated end-of-month cash balance	___	___	___
Absolute minimum cash balance requirement	300	400	500
Estimated cash surplus (shortage)	___	___	___

8–5. Redwood Outbackers, Ltd., is preparing a sales worksheet for the coming six months. Monthly sales for each of the next three months (April, May, and June) are anticipated to be $90,000. Sales are then anticipated to rise to $100,000 in July before falling to $60,000 in August and $40,000 in September. The firm has no cash sales; 20 percent of any month's sales are collected in the following month, 30 percent the second month, 30 percent the third month, and 20 percent four months after the initial sale. Payables for a given month are 40 percent of the previous month's sales. Sales data on the past four months: December, $50,000; January, $50,000; February, $60,000; and March, $80,000.

   a. Set up a sales worksheet for the next six months showing estimated sales-related cash receipts and expenditures.

   b. Determine Redwood's sales-related net cash flow for each month.

8–6. Given the following distribution of daily net cash flows, determine the expected daily net cash flow and variance of daily net cash flows.

Net cash flow	−$20,000	−$10,000	$10,000	$20,000
Probability	0.2	0.2	0.3	0.3

8–7. Lubber's Grocery Stores' analysts are preparing a cash budget for the months of October, November, and December. Estimated sales for those months are $830,000, $860,000, and $900,000, respectively. Sales in the just-completed month of September were $840,000. Lubber's has a small chain of grocery stores in small towns; about 70 percent of sales are cash, and the other 30 percent are credit sales collected the month following the sale. Lubber's settles its payables, which run at about 40 percent of sales, one month after the sales month.

   Payroll expenditures for Lubber's for the coming three months are expected to be $300,000 per month. Also, Lubber's has capital expenditure cash payments scheduled equal to $50,000 in November and $200,000 in December, and a $400,000 note payable due in November. A previously declared dividend of $80,000 is to be paid in October, and miscellaneous expenditures are estimated to be $10,000 per month.

   a. Prepare a sales worksheet for Lubber's for the next three months.

   b. Assuming that the October 1 cash balance was $500,000 and that Lubber's has a minimum absolute cash balance requirement of $500,000, prepare a cash budget for Lubber's for the next three months. The last line of the budget should show the estimated cash surplus or shortage for each month.

   c. As the cash manager for the firm, explain to the president the reason for any estimated cash shortages that appear imminent.

8–8. Shannon Kentucky Stables has just completed the sale of some thoroughbred horses to a wealthy businessman in Africa. The buyer has indicated that he will pay the bill of $1.6 million by check on the 13th of the month. If the check is sent through the mail, there is a 20 percent chance it will arrive by the 19th, a 60 percent chance it will arrive by the 20th, and a 20 percent chance it will arrive by the 21st. Alternatively, Shannon can send a courier to pick up the check. Airfare is $1,000, and other expenses (including the time not spent on other duties by the courier) are about $200 per day. If all goes smoothly, the courier would be gone two days. But there may be disruptions in the courier's schedule. For example, the African businessman may wish to entertain the courier, and reluctance to accept the invitation may appear rude and would jeopardize any possible future sales. Such a disruption would probably cause a one-day delay, and there is a 50-50 chance that the disruption would occur.

a. Determine the expected cost of sending a courier after the money.

b. Determine the expected opportunity cost savings the firm would realize by sending a courier and reducing transit time if the current annual interest rate on money lent risklessly for short periods of time is 12 percent.

c. What recommendations would you make about sending a courier?

SELECTED REFERENCES

Electronic fund transfers and related concepts are discussed in:

Frisbee, Pamela S. "The ACH: An Elusive Dream." *Economic Review,* Federal Reserve Bank of Atlanta, March 1986, pp. 4–8.

Stone, Bernell K. "Electronic Payment Basics." *Economic Review,* Federal Reserve Bank of Atlanta, March 1986, pp. 9–18.

An assessment of corporate practices in this area can be found in:

Kamath, Ravindra R., et. al. "Management of Excess Cash: Practices and Developments." *Financial Management,* Autumn 1985, pp. 70–77.

The classic article on determining optimal cash balance levels is:

Miller, Merton H., and Daniel Orr. "The Demand for Money by Firms: Extension of Analytic Results." *Journal of Finance,* December 1968, pp. 735–59.

For an overall discussion of cash management and corporate liquidity, see:

Stone, Bernell K. "Corporate Perspectives of Cash Management." In *Payments in the Financial Services of the 1980s.* Westport, Ct.: Quorum Books, 1984, pp. 40–58.

Vander Weide, James, and Steven F. Maier. *Managing Corporate Liquidity.* New York: John Wiley, 1985.

APPENDIX 8–A   THE MILLER-ORR MODEL

$$\text{Transactions balance return point} = z = (3b\sigma^2/4i)^{1/3} \tag{8A–1}$$

and:

$$\text{Transactions balance upper bound} = h = 3z \tag{8A–2}$$

where:

$$b = \text{transfer cost per transfer}$$
$$i = \text{daily interest rate}$$
$$\sigma^2 = \text{variance of daily net cash flows}$$

Using the variance concept developed in Chapter 5, the variance of the daily net cash flows can be determined from the daily net cash flow distribution:

$$\sigma^2 = \sum_{j=1}^{N} (Prob_j)(NCF_j - \overline{NCF})^2 \qquad \textbf{(8A–3)}$$

where:

$$NCF_j = \text{the } j\text{th net cash flow outcome}$$
$$Prob_j = \text{the probability of occurrence of the } j\text{th outcome}$$
$$\overline{NCF} = \text{the average net cash flow}$$
$$N = \text{the number of possible outcomes}$$

Also from Chapter 5, recall the expected value (average) definition:

$$\overline{NCF} = \sum_{j=1}^{N} (Prob_j)(NCF_j) \qquad \textbf{(8A–4)}$$

If the firm follows the policy of using optimal z and h values, its average transactions balance will be:

$$\text{Average transactions balance} = (4/3)z \qquad \textbf{(8A–5)}$$

■ *Example*

Let us assume that the near-term planning period is a month, and that net cash flow per day is the relevant unit. Past net cash flow records can be of great value to the cash manager in estimating the future net cash flow activity of the firm.

Consider the problem facing the cash manager for the Kelso Company. He is preparing to estimate how much cash the firm should plan on maintaining during the coming month of November. He has compiled the net cash flow probability distribution shown in Table 8A–1. This distribution is based on net cash flows that have occurred during November in the past few years.

To the extent that this historical distribution reflects the future, it can be used as an indicator of the distribution of future net cash flows. Kelso's cash manager feels that this upcoming November's net cash flow distribution will be very similar to the distribution shown in Table 8A–1, as the firm's sales level is at approximately the same level

Probability	Daily Net Cash Flow ($)	
0.3	−2,000	■ *Table 8A–1*
0.4	0	Kelso Daily Net Cash
0.3	+2,000	Flow Distribution
1.0		

that is has been in the past. Because of the seasonal nature of the firm's business, Kelso's cash manager has not included data from other months. If there were no seasonal cash flow elements involved, the firm could use data from other months in preparation of the above distribution.

The daily net cash flow distribution for Kelso is shown in Table 8A–1. Therefore:

$$\overline{NCF} = (0.3)(-2,000) + (0.4)(0) + (0.3)(2,000) = 0$$
$$\sigma^2 = (0.3)(-2,000 - 0)^2 + (0.4)(0 - 0)^2 + (0.3)(2,000 - 0)^2$$
$$= \$2,400,000$$

Kelso's cash manager has also determined that the transfer cost is $50 and the current annual interest rate is 10 percent. Therefore:

$$b = \$50$$
$$i = 0.10/365 = 0.000274 \text{ per day}$$

and

$$z = \left[\frac{(3)(50)(2,400,000)}{(4)(0.000274)} \right]^{1/3} = \$7,000$$

and

$$h = 3z = \$21,000$$

The transactions balance return point, $7,000, is the cash position Kelso should come back to when the upper or lower bound is hit. To handle its transactions cash needs, Kelso should carry no more than $21,000 during the planning period (November). Whenever the cash balance reaches $21,000, the firm should transfer $(h - z)$, or $14,000, into marketable securities or a savings account. When the cash account is exhausted, Kelso should transfer $7,000 from marketable securities or from its savings account into the cash account. The average transactions balance is given by Equation 8A–5 as:

$$\text{Average transactions balance} = (4/3)z = (4/3)(\$7,000) = \$9,333 \qquad \blacksquare$$

Compensating Balances

Most firms keep much larger cash balances in the bank than are necessary for transaction needs. These are compensating balances. The amount of the compensating balance depends on the amount of bank services provided and the amount of loans outstanding; it will be the subject of negotiation between the firm and the bank. Obviously, the firm would like to keep as small a compensating balance as possible. The point at which the balance is finally set will depend on the negotiating strengths of the two parties.

Minimum compensating balances are usually established in one of two ways. First, there may be an absolute minimum balance requirement below which the firm's bank account may not go without penalty. The other arrangement is to have a minimum average balance; the firm need only keep its average bank balance above the stipulated minimum.

■ *Example*

Suppose the minimum compensating balance is established at $400,000. If this is an absolute minimum, the firm's checking account can never be less than $400,000. If, on the other hand, the $400,000 is a minimum average balance, the firm's checking account can be less than $400,000 on any given day so long as the average daily balance for some agreed period of time (such as a month) is not less than $400,000. Obviously, the former is a much stricter requirement. ■

Total Cash Balances

We are interested in determining optimal total cash balance levels. While the firm's cash balance will not be constant over time, we can investigate what the optimal minimum, maximum, and average cash balances over a designated time interval should be. Also, we will establish the optimal cash return point. All of these determinations refer to the firm's total cash balance, which should be enough to cover both transactions and compensating balances.

- *Example*

Suppose that, using techniques described earlier, the Cubic Company decides that for transaction purposes, its optimal cash return point is $z = \$150,000$, which implies that:

$$\text{Maximum transaction balances} = h = 3z = \$450,000$$

and:

$$\text{Average transactions balance} = (4/3)z = \$200,000$$

Furthermore:

$$\text{Minimum transactions balance} = \$0$$

Assume also that the Cubic Company must keep a \$400,000 compensating balance. What will be Cubic's optimal minimum, maximum, and average cash balances, and the optimal cash return point? The answers depend on the type of compensating balance that is required. We will assume that Cubic's compensating balance must never go below a specified minimum amount.

When there is an absolute minimum compensating balance requirement, that requirement becomes the firm's minimum cash balance level. For the Cubic Company example, minimum cash balance = \$400,000. Establishing the minimum cash balance also determines the other cash balance results:

$$
\begin{aligned}
\text{Cash return point} &= \text{Minimum cash balance} + z \\
&= \$400,000 + \$150,000 = \$550,000 \\
\text{Maximum cash balance} &= \text{Minimum cash balance} + h \\
&= \$400,000 + \$450,000 = \$850,000 \\
\text{Average cash balance} &= \text{Minimum cash balance} + \text{average transactions balance} \\
&= \$400,000 + \$200,000 = \$600,000
\end{aligned}
$$

Notice that in each of these calculations, the basic building block is the amount of the minimum cash balance. Cubic's total cash balance will not be allowed to go below \$400,000, and when that level is reached, \$150,000 should go into the cash account, building it up to \$550,000. Whenever the cash account reaches the upper limit of \$850,000, the firm will invest \$300,000 in marketable securities, reducing the cash account back to \$555,000. The average cash balance over the planning period should be \$600,000. ▪

PROBLEMS FOR APPENDIX

8A–1. In considering its transactions cash balances needs, the firm has decided that the optimal return point, z, is \$200,000. Determine the average transactions balance associated with this optimal return point.

8A–2. Considering only the transactions demand for cash, a firm has determined that the cash balance should never exceed \$300,000. Additionally, the firm must meet an absolute minimum compensating cash balance of \$300,000. Determine:

    a. The transactions balance return point.

    b. The total cash balance return point.

    c. The optimum average total cash balance.

8A–3. The cash manager for Krider & Associates is preparing to estimate the transactions balance needed by the firm during the next few weeks. Ignoring all other motives for holding cash, determine the optimal return point, the maximum cash balances, and the average cash balance expected if the following conditions exist:

Situation	Variance of Daily Net Cash Flows ($)	Transfer Cost ($)	Annual Interest Rate (%)
A	7,000,000	30	10
B	7,000,000	30	5
C	10,000,000	40	7
D	40,000,000	50	6
E	1,000,000	50	10

9

Accounts Receivable and Inventory

Receivables and Inventory Problems

MiniScribe Corporation makes disk-drives for personal computers. Sales rose from $114 million in 1985 to over $600 million in 1988, and earnings grew for several straight quarters. However, an industry-wide slump hit in 1988. According to analysts, MiniScribe did not cut back production until accounts receivable and inventory rose to unusually high levels. According to some estimates, accounts receivable were running at an average of 122 days, compared to an industry average of 70 days. The ratio of inventory to sales rose to 43 percent, compared to an industry average of 24 percent.

MiniScribe reported a loss in the fourth quarter of 1988 of about $15 million. During 1988 the price of the stock rose as high as $13 but closed for the year at $7.75. By late February of the following year the price had declined to $4.

In early 1989, the chairman and chief executive officer, who had been credited with saving MiniScribe when he took control in 1985 by cutting costs and raising new capital, resigned in the face of new problems. According to him, the new chairman would, among other moves, "have to correct the short-term imbalances in the working capital assets."[1]

---

[1]See Michael Allen, "MiniScribe's Wiles, Once a 'Dr. Fix-It,' Resigns Top Posts at Disk-Drive Maker," *The Wall Street Journal,* February 23, 1989, p. B7, and *Annual Reports* and filings, MiniScribe Corporation.

In this chapter we study the two remaining major components of current assets: accounts receivable and inventory. These two items typically constitute the bulk of a firm's current assets. Thus, successful management of a firm's current asset position requires careful attention to these two assets. As the MiniScribe example clearly illustrates, adverse developments in these current assets can result in severe repercussions for the firm and direct losses in stockholder wealth.

Primary *chapter learning objectives* are:

1. To understand the nature of credit policy and how credit policy decisions are made.
2. To understand the benefits and costs of holding inventory.

THE FINANCIAL MANAGEMENT OF ACCOUNTS RECEIVABLE AND INVENTORY

In this chapter, we consider the two largest components of a typical firm's current assets, accounts receivable and inventory. We do so from a financial-management standpoint, concentrating only on the financial considerations of managing these assets. Obviously, other aspects of their management are extremely important, such as the production side of inventory management. It should be understood that while we do not always make it explicit, the financial activities of the firm must be coordinated with marketing, production, and other activities of the firm. For example, higher inventory levels will enable the firm to purchase larger (and presumably more economical) quantities and help to avoid interruptions in the production process. More lenient credit terms may enable the firm to increase sales. These objectives of the production and marketing groups, respectively, typically conflict with those of financial management, and they will have to be resolved by management.

The importance of these two components of current assets to all firms should be noted. Table 7–1 showed that for all manufacturing firms, trade accounts and trade notes receivable constituted roughly 40 percent of current assets, as did inventories. Thus, almost 80 percent of firms' current assets are tied up in these two items, and almost 30 percent of their total assets.

Maximizing Stockholder Wealth

The decision to grant credit is, in effect, an investment decision. The firm is investing in a current asset as part of its overall activities, with the objective, as always, of maximizing shareholder wealth. We will study investment decisions for long-term assets in Part IV, but the basic rule that always applies can be stated simply: if the expected returns from the additional investment in receivables exceeds the expected costs, invest—if the expected costs exceed the expected benefits, do not. This is the basis of the NPV rule discussed in Chapter 7. Implementation of this procedure, based as it is on discounted cash flows at the required rate of return, can lead to stockholder wealth maximization.

The essential objective of inventory management from a financial standpoint is to provide the necessary inventory for efficient operations at the minimum cost. Preventing lost sales because of stockouts, preventing losses due to obsolescence and deterioration, minimizing the funds tied up in inventory so that they can be used elsewhere, and so forth, will raise the firm's profit margin and asset turnover and, therefore, raise the return on investment (see Chapter 3's discussion of the DuPont analysis). In turn, other things being equal, the higher return on assets will contribute to a higher stock price, which is the objective of inventory management in particular and financial management in general.

THE MANAGEMENT OF ACCOUNTS RECEIVABLE

The most common and important form of receivables is *accounts receivable,* which is debt owed to the firm by customers for the firm's goods or services sold to them in the ordinary course of business.[2] When the firm makes a sale and does not receive cash payment, the firm grants **trade credit,** which creates an account receivable. Most credit sales are made on *open account,* without any formal acknowledgment of debt obligation through a financial instrument. Our interest in this portion of the chapter will be on the analysis of investment in accounts receivable. Since most ordinary business sales in the United States are credit sales, most business firms have substantial investments in receivables.

trade credit
a sale made on credit, generating an accounts receivable

Credit Terms

Credit terms are specifications of the conditions under which the firm extends credit to its customers. There are two primary parts: the *credit period* and any *cash discount terms* offered.

Credit Period

The credit period is the length of time the firm extends credit on a sale; it is usually stated in terms of a due date, or net date, the date by which the supplier expects payment. Credit periods tend to be fairly uniform within an industry.

Cash Discounts

Many firms offer cash discounts to induce customers to pay their bills early.[3] This discount can be taken only if the buyer pays by a certain date, the discount date, which is earlier than the due date.[4] If the bill is not paid by the discount date, the right to take the cash discount is lost, and the buyer is expected to pay for the merchandise by the due date.[5] If a discount is offered, the credit terms will reflect the amount of the discount and the discount period, which is the length of time the discount is offered.

---

[2]There are several categories of receivables, including notes and acceptances receivable, which are distinguished as out of the ordinary. They do not arise from the firm's normal sales efforts.

[3]A cash discount is different from a quantity discount. Both are price discounts, but the latter is a price concession made to large-quantity purchasers.

[4]Both due date and discount date are stated as being so many days from a starting date. Terms of 2/10, net 30, for example, presuppose some agreed-upon starting date from which the 10-day discount period and 30-day net period commence.

[5]The cash discount is expressed as a percentage, so a 2 percent discount means buyers who take the cash discount pay only $0.98 for each dollar owed.

Specification of Credit Terms

A complete specification of the firm's credit terms has three parts: (1) the amount of cash discount, (2) the discount period (or date), and (3) the due date (credit period).

- ### Example

Assume a 3 percent discount, a 15–day discount period, and a 60–day credit period; in this case, the terms would be 3/15, net 60. Any customer who pays by the 15th day receives a 3 percent discount. All other customers are expected to pay the full amount of the bill by the 60th day. ■

Determinants of Credit Terms

Credit terms in U.S. industry range from liberal to stringent. In general, there are three broadly defined determinants of credit terms: general economic conditions, industry factors, and company factors.

- When money and credit are tight (difficult to obtain), credit terms will be more stringent. Suppliers will have more difficulty procuring funds themselves and may be more reluctant to continue offering credit at the same terms. In extreme cases, suppliers may not be able to offer credit at all to their slow payers. This is why most firms try to keep a good credit rating.

- Another important determinant of credit terms is the prevailing practices in the industries in which the buyer and seller operate. First, the credit period is a function of the durability of the commodity. Perishable items like food have fairly short credit periods, while nonperishable items such as manufactured goods have longer credit periods. Another industry factor is buyer and seller competition, which has classical economic demand and supply effects. Vigorous competition for sales by a large number of sellers promotes more liberal credit terms, whereas few sellers and many buyers leads to less liberal credit terms. The buyer's line of business also strongly influences the amount of risk involved in granting credit and, consequently, the credit terms. Failure rates are not the same in all industries, and companies in risky industries will receive less favorable credit terms.

- In addition to general economic and industry considerations, certain factors are unique to the company. One is the financial strength of the buyer and seller. A financially strong buyer is more likely to receive liberal credit terms because there is less risk the supplier will not be paid. Similarly, if the seller is financially strong, it is more able to acquire funds and may offer more liberal credit terms. Relatively weak buyers need more liberal terms but will be unable generally to command them unless there is strong sales competition. Perhaps the dominant company consideration is the buyer's credit history. Firms that have been prompt payers in the past are more likely to have liberal credit terms extended to them than firms that are slow payers.

CREDIT POLICY: AN OVERVIEW

The expression *credit policy* refers to the firm's decisions that will affect the amount of trade credit it will grant. Although general economic conditions and industry practices have strong impacts on levels of receivables, the firm's investment in receivables is also affected by its own credit policy decisions.[6] Moreover, the firm can change credit policies in response to changing economic conditions.

Any credit policy may be broadly defined as being somewhere in the range of tight to loose. Firms with tight credit policies tend to have relatively short credit periods and to sell on credit only to those customers who have the highest-quality credit ratings. Firms with loose credit policies tend to have relatively long credit periods and to sell on credit to a broader array of customers, including those with relatively low credit ratings.

Credit policies can have a major impact on the firm's sales, costs, and profitability. Other things being equal, firms with relatively loose credit policies will tend to have higher sales levels but also will tend to have higher costs. Thus, as with most financial management decisions, the decision to commit funds to accounts receivable involves a trade-off. Certain benefits will accrue to the firm from establishing a particular trade credit policy, and certain costs will be incurred. The firm's problem is to compare the costs and benefits involved to determine its best level of receivables.

Benefits of Extending Trade Credit

The firm grants trade credit because it expects the investment in receivables to be profitable. (Also, the firm typically must grant trade credit in order to be competitive with other firms granting credit.) The immediate impact of granting trade credit shows up in the firm's sales level, and the motivation for investment in receivables may be oriented toward either sales expansion or sales retention. The former refers to granting more trade credit (1) to increase sales to present customers and/or (2) to attract new customers. The second motivation, sales retention, refers to granting trade credit to protect the firm's sales from competition. For example, if a competitor offers customers better credit terms, the firm may choose to match these terms in an effort to protect its sales.

Costs of Extending Trade Credit

Trade credit involves five kinds of costs. We will consider each of these in turn.

1. Production, selling, and administrative costs.
2. Cash discounts.
3. Bad–debt losses.
4. Taxes.
5. Required rate of return (opportunity cost).

---

[6]The firm may choose to limit the amount of credit any customer may receive by imposing a line of credit limit. This means the seller limits the amount of accounts receivable allowed to the customer. When the limit is reached, future credit sales are denied until the customer's accounts receivable are reduced sufficiently to accommodate the new order.

Production, Selling, and Administrative Costs

Unless the credit sales are being made to liquidate inventory, production and selling costs will be associated with the sales expansion. Any incremental administrative costs should also be included in the cost calculations. There are two major kinds. First, any incremental credit-checking expenses should be included. Second, incremental collection costs, which are monies spent on trying to collect tardy accounts, are a relevant consideration. If an increase in accounts receivable does not cause a corresponding increase in either credit checking or collection costs, no administrative expenses should be charged. This situation may occur when the firm's credit department is operating below capacity.

Cash Discounts

Cash discounts act as inducements for customers to pay their bills early. If payment is made by the discount date, the buyer can pay less than the full amount of the invoice, which in effect is a cost to the firm.

▪ Example

Suppose a firm offers its customers a 2 percent discount if they pay by the discount date. Suppose further that $30 million of the firm's sales are expected to be paid by the discount date. The cost to the firm will be $30,000,000 \times 0.02 = \$600,000$ per year. In return, the firm receives an acceleration of receipts and a reduced level of receivables. The firm may also realize a higher level of sales because of the effective price decrease, although that is not the usual intent of the cash discount. ▪

Bad-Debt Losses

These are sales receipts the firm cannot collect.[7] One important determinant of the size of bad-debt losses is general economic conditions. As the economy worsens, bad-debt losses will increase. The important discretionary determinant of the size of a firm's bad-debt losses is the quality of customer credit accounts. As the firm loosens its credit standards and sells to less-reliable customers, bad-debt losses will increase; conversely, as the firm tightens its standards, bad-debt losses will decrease. It is worth emphasizing, however, that the firm should not let its credit standards be oriented toward minimizing bad-debt losses, myopically focusing on the size of bad-debt losses (or any other cost). If relaxed standards lead to sales gains that generate profits greater than associated costs—including additional bad-debt losses—then the relaxation is financially desirable.

▪ Example

Suppose a firm expects sales to be $40 million and bad-debt losses will be 2 percent of sales. Then bad-debt losses will be $(0.02 \times \$40,000,000) = \$800,000$, and net sales will be $39,200,000. ▪

---

[7] The effect of bad-debt losses is to reduce the amount of sales revenue received. Thus, we can distinguish between total sales and net sales.

Taxes

We also want to account for the tax obligations of the profit on the sales. For computation purposes we will not deduct any noncash charges (like depreciation) before figuring taxes. They are presumably accounted for elsewhere by the firm.[8] Given these considerations:

$$\text{(9--1)}$$

$$\text{Taxes} = \frac{\text{Tax}}{\text{rate}} \left[\text{Sales} - \frac{\text{Production, selling, and}}{\text{administrative costs}} - \frac{\text{Cash}}{\text{discounts}} - \frac{\text{Bad-debt}}{\text{losses}} \right]$$

Required Rate of Return

In Chapter 5, we discussed a required rate of return (discount rate) to be used in valuation analysis. Investments in receivables also have a required rate of return. Alternatively stated, there is an opportunity cost associated with investing in receivables. That opportunity cost is the required rate of return on the investment in receivables. We handle this concept by applying the required rate of return, k, to the relevant cash flows associated with the investment in receivables. Because the timing of these cash flows is often a matter of days, it will be helpful to use a daily required rate of return:

$$k_{\text{daily}} = \frac{k_{\text{annual}}}{365} \qquad \text{(9--2)}$$

- ### Example

If the annual required rate of return is 20 percent, the daily required rate of return is $0.20/365 = 0.00055$ per day. ∎

This daily required rate of return is used to determine discount factors that are applied to the cash flows associated with credit policy decisions. These discount factors depend on how many days from time zero (time of initial investment in the receivable) the relevant cash flows occur.[9] *As an approximation,*

$$\text{Discount factor} = \frac{1}{\left(1 + \dfrac{\text{Daily required}}{\text{rate of return}} \times \dfrac{\text{Number of days}}{\text{from } t_0}\right)}$$

That is:

$$\text{Discount factor} = \frac{1}{(1 + kt)} \qquad \text{(9--3)}$$

---

[8]This treatment is actually a consequence of assuming that fixed production costs do not increase because of the credit-granting decision, because if they did, depreciation would also increase, and this change should be included in the calculations.

[9]Equation 9–3 is actually an approximation formula, since $1/(1 + kt)$ is not exactly equal to $1/(1 + k)^t$. We use this approximation formula, which is a reasonably good one, for ease of exposition and because the daily discount rates are too small to allow use of our end-of-book discount factor tables. In the example above, the solution would require calculation of $(1.00055)^{30}$.

where:

$$k = \text{daily required rate of return}$$
$$t = \text{number of days from } t_0 \text{ (time zero)}$$

■ *Example*

Extending the above example involving an annual required rate of return of 20 percent, or a daily discount rate of 0.00055, assume a cash flow occurs 30 days from t_0:

$$\text{Discount factor} = \frac{1}{[1 + (0.00055)(30)]}$$
$$= \frac{1}{1.0165} = .984$$

MAKING CREDIT POLICY DECISIONS

Making optimal credit policy decisions requires identification of the credit-granting decision framework. There are four major components:

1. Setting credit standards.
2. Developing credit terms.
3. Evaluating receivables management.
4. Establishing a collection policy.

Credit Standards and Analysis

credit standards
designate the standards that a customer of the firm must meet in order to be granted credit

Credit standards designate the standards a customer of the firm must meet to be granted credit. They require a subjective judgment of the customer's likelihood of paying the debt incurred.

Establishment of credit standards will determine the type of customers to whom the firm will make credit sales. Credit standards traditionally have been depicted in terms of the three "Cs" of credit:

1. *Character* refers to the willingness of the customer to pay; that is, the probability that the customer will attempt to honor the implied promise to pay represented by the credit transaction. This can be assessed partially by looking at the customer's past payment practices.
2. *Capacity* refers to the ability of the customer to pay. It is a subjective judgment based on what the customer has done, as well as the current and prospective situation. Capacity involves trying to assess the customer's current and future financial condition.
3. *Conditions* refers to the present economic conditions. A general recession will affect borrowers across the board. Localized conditions, such as the oil slump in Texas in the mid-1980s, can severely affect specific geographical areas.

Sources of Credit Information

When an order is received from a new customer, a decision must be made whether credit will be extended. The firm would like to gather as much information as possible about the applicant, but the search will be limited by the time and cost involved.

Credit-rating agencies. These are important sources of credit information. Dun & Bradstreet is the best known and most widely used service; the company sells reference books containing credit data on several million businesses. In addition, more detailed information about a company's credit can be obtained by ordering a credit report. Other credit reporting agencies provide similar services.

Financial statements. The applicant's financial statements also provide credit information. The firm can write directly to the applicant for a copy of the statements and can then analyze the company financially.

The firm may also use its bank to check out credit applicants. Credit departments of banks across the country exchange information, and a manufacturer in San Diego, for example, can use its bank to collect credit information on a new customer in Seattle. Typically, firms will use their banks to collect information only on their larger new orders; otherwise, the costs of acquiring information may be prohibitive.[10]

Credit Risk Classes

Typically, credit standards are stated in terms of what risk class of customers the firm will extend trade credit to. Customer credit ratings are frequently designated by both estimated financial strength (net worth) and the credit appraisal supplied by credit-rating agencies. For example, Dun & Bradstreet uses a combination of letters and numbers to classify companies by estimated financial strength and composite credit appraisal. For example, if a company is rated CC2, net worth is estimated to be between $75,000 and $125,000, and its composite credit rating, according to Dun & Bradstreet, is good.[11]

Based on such information, many firms classify current and potential customers into risk classes. Statistical techniques such as regression analysis and discriminant analysis are also used to categorize credit applicants into risk classes.[12]

Setting Credit Standards

How does a firm analyze the profitability of extending credit to individual applicants or of changing the firm's credit standards? The procedure is to account for all cash costs and benefits as they occur, and then discount them at the daily required rate of return. This is the same procedure that we have used, and will continue to use, throughout this text: estimate cash flows and find their net present value.

■ Example

The Cupertino Computer Company currently has credit terms of 2/10, net 30 and grants credit to any applicant with a high or good credit rating from Dun & Bradstreet. Cupertino is now considering changing its credit standards to include

---

[10]In addition to the sources of information just listed, trade associations, chambers of commerce, and even competitors may be able to provide useful information.

[11]A high credit appraisal carries a 1, and a limited credit appraisal carries a 4.

[12]Financial ratios have been found to be useful predictors of a firm's financial strength. See Kung H. Chen and Thomas A. Shimeda, "An Empirical Analysis of Useful Financial Ratios," *Financial Management*, Spring, 1981, pp. 51–60.

■ *Table 9–1* Setting Credit Standards Data—Cupertino Computer Company	Sales increase	$7,300,000 per year or $20,000 per day
	Collection period	60 days
	Percentage of new sales that will take the cash discount	0
	Cost increases	
	1. Production, selling, and administrative costs	80% of increased sales: (0.80)(20,000) = $16,000 per day
	2. Cash discounts	2% of sales that take discount: (0.02)(0)(20,000) = $0 per day
	3. Bad-debt losses	10% of increased sales: (0.10)(20,000) = $2,000 per day
	4. Taxes	40% of (increased sales − increased production, selling, and administrative costs − increased cash discounts − increased bad-debt losses): (0.40)(20,000 − 16,000 − 0 − 2,000) = $800/day
	5. Required rate of return	20% per year 0.20/365 = 0.00055 per day

applicants with fair credit ratings. In considering this change, Cupertino has estimated a payments pattern schedule. It has also estimated the data relating to this decision shown in Table 9–1.

We make three other assumptions:

1. All net sales receipts (net of taxes) are received on the collection period date (which is Day 60 in the example).
2. All production, selling, and administrative costs are incurred at day zero.
3. Fixed costs have not been increased (so there are no increased depreciation expenses).

This credit standards problem has now been simplified to where it can be viewed as a simple investment problem with an initial investment (production, selling, and administrative costs) at day $t = 0$, and a return, or net benefit, on day $t = 60$ (the collection period). There are several different, but approximately equivalent, ways to set up this analysis. We will use a fairly simple approach. The analysis is based on one day's sales. If the net present value of one day's sales is positive, the company should extend credit to applicants from the *fair* group. In the Cupertino example (see Table 9–1):

$$\text{Initial investment} = \begin{array}{l}\text{Production, selling, and}\\ \text{administrative costs}\end{array} \tag{9–4}$$

$$= \$16,000 \text{ per day}$$

$$\text{Benefit} = \text{Sales} - \frac{\text{Cash}}{\text{discount}} - \frac{\text{Bad-debt}}{\text{losses}} - \text{Taxes} \tag{9–5}$$

$$= \$20,000 - 0 - \$2,000 - \$800$$

$$= \$17,200/\text{day}$$

That is, the problem looks like the time-scale picture shown in Figure 9–1. Now, Table 9–1 shows that the required rate of return is 0.00055 per day,

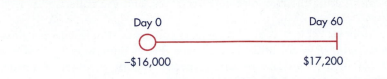

■ *Figure 9–1*
Time Scale of Credit
Standards Problem

and from Equation 9–3, we see that the discount factor for the 60-day collection period is:

$$\text{Discount factor} = \frac{1}{1 + (0.00055)(60)} = 0.968$$

We can use this discount factor to apply the discounting process that we studied in Chapter 4. By discounting the benefit back to time period zero and netting it against the initial investment (which occurs at time period zero), we arrive at the *net present value* (NPV), which was defined in Chapter 7 and is explained in detail in Chapter 12.[13]

$$\text{NPV} = -\$16,000 + (0.968)(\$17,200) = \$650/\text{day}$$

The net result is a positive \$650 NPV per day, which indicates Cupertino should be willing to offer credit to applicants from this group.

Also, it is possible to add more precision to our analysis by estimating cash payment schedules in more detail. This would entail estimating what percentage of the increased sales would pay by Day 10, Day 30, and so on. Other possible adjustments would include making a more precise estimate of when taxes are paid. ■

Developing Credit Terms

In the previous example, we focused on whether it would be advantageous to *change* credit *standards*. Now consider the issue of *changing* credit *terms*. Or, looked at from a different perspective, What is the optimal set of credit terms?

When the firm changes its credit terms, there can be two effects. Suppose the change is to more liberal terms. Sales should increase, as new customers are attracted and old customers are induced to buy more. But there should also be a change in the payments pattern of the old customers as they react to the new terms. Our analysis should account for both of these effects. The information used to investigate these kinds of issues is of the same kind we have been developing. Let us continue to use Cupertino Computer Company as an example.

■ *Example*

Cupertino has collected the information shown in Table 9–2 for its present credit terms of 2/10, net 30, and a set of proposed credit terms of 2/10, net 60. Note there are several effects of moving to more liberal credit terms: sales increase, the

---

[13]The net present value is the difference between the discounted benefits and the discounted costs of a proposal or project. In effect, all costs and benefits are discounted back to time period zero and netted together. A positive NPV indicates an acceptable project, and the larger the NPV, the better.

percentage of sales taking the cash discount decreases, and the collection period lengthens.

The information in Table 9–2 can be used to construct simplified cash flow streams and resulting NPVs for both sets of terms. From Equations 9–4 and 9–5 we get the initial investment and return, respectively, for each set of terms; the discount factors are found from Equation 9–3. Tax calculations are made using Equation 9–1. The complete analysis of the Cupertino example is shown in Table 9–3.

As Table 9–3 shows, the NPV results are better for the present terms, so Cupertino should not change to the proposed set. Of course, there may be other

---

■ *Table 9–2*
Credit Terms Data

	Present Terms (2/10, Net 30)	Proposed Terms (2/10, Net 60)
Daily sales	$100,000	$110,000
Production, selling, and administrative costs	(0.8)(sales)	(0.8)(sales)
Tax rate	40%	40%
Required rate of return	0.00055 per day	0.00055 per day
Bad-debt loss	(0.05)(sales)	(0.05)(sales)
Collection period	30 days	60 days
Percentage of sales taking cash discounts	40%	35%

■ *Table 9–3*
Credit Terms Analysis

Present Terms (2/10, net 30)	
Initial investment (@ $t = 0$) = (0.8)(100,000)	$ 80,000 per day
Sales	100,000 per day
Less	
Cash discounts (0.40)(0.02)($100,000)	800 per day
Bad-debt losses (0.05)($100,000)	5,000 per day
Taxes (0.40)($100,000 − $80,000 − $800 − $5,000)	5,680 per day
Benefit (@ $t = 30$)	$ 88,520 per day

$$\text{Discount factor for 30 days} = 1/[1 + (0.00055)(30)] = 0.984$$

$$\text{NPV} = -\$80,000 + \$88,520(0.984) = \$7,104 \text{ per day}$$

Proposed Terms (2/10, net 60)	
Initial investment (@ $t = 0$) = (0.8)(110,000)	$ 88,000 per day
Sales	110,000 per day
Less	
Cash discounts = (0.35)(0.02)($110,000)	770 per day
Bad-debt losses = (0.05)($110,000)	5,500 per day
Taxes = (0.40)($110,000 − $88,000 − $770 − $5,500)	6,292 per day
Benefit (@ $t = 60$)	$ 97,438 per day

$$\text{Discount factor for 60 days} = 1/[1 + (0.00055)(60)] = 0.968$$

$$\text{NPV} = -\$88,000 + (0.968)(\$97,438) = \$6,320 \text{ per day}$$

credit terms that *are* more desirable. Terms of 2/10, net 45, for example, may be better than the present terms. The credit manager should attempt to find the best possible credit terms. One thing the firm must be very careful of, however, is the competition's reaction to such moves. If the firm's competitors relaxed their credit periods to protect their sales, the firm's increased sales could be substantially lower than predicted, and the firm might suffer a loss from its decision to relax credit. ▪

Evaluating Receivables Management

The control function is an important part of the financial management area. This idea also applies to receivables, and the firm should continually check on how well it manages its investment in receivables.

Collection Period

The collection period is defined as:

$$\text{Collection period} = \frac{(\text{Accounts receivable})(365)}{\text{Sales}} \qquad (9\text{–}6)$$

One method of evaluating the accounts receivable management is to compare the collection period to the stated credit terms. If terms are 2/10, net 30, and the collection period is 60 days, something seems wrong. Also, the time pattern of the collection period can be analyzed to see if there have been major changes that would indicate difficulties. However, the collection period is very sensitive to sales fluctuations and the period over which sales are measured, so it may give misleading signals about the status of the receivables management during periods when sales are changing.

Aging Schedule

The *aging schedule* shows what volume and percentage of the accounts receivable have been outstanding for various lengths of time. The following is an example of an aging schedule:

Period Outstanding	Amounts of Accounts Receivable Outstanding	Percentage of Total Accounts Receivable
Less than 30 days	$2,500,000	62.5%
30 days to 60 days	1,000,000	25.0
60 days to 90 days	300,000	7.5
90 days to 180 days	160,000	4.0
Over 180 days	40,000	1.0
Total	$4,000,000	100.0%

If significant amounts of accounts receivable have been outstanding longer than the firm's stated credit terms, they will be identified by an aging schedule. While the aging schedule provides more information than the collection period, it, too, is subject to giving misleading signals when sales change. Rising sales will create more receivables in the "near" categories; falling sales have the opposite effect.

Collection Experience Matrix

The main problem with the two monitoring procedures discussed above is that they focus on aggregated accounts receivable. The key to resolving the problem is to develop a procedure that works with disaggregated accounts receivable data. The *collection experience matrix* is a matrix of accounts receivable information that does just that. We can demonstrate the technique with an example.

▪ *Example*

Assume that today is June 1 and that credit sales for the past five months look like this:

Month	January	February	March	April	May
Sales ($000)	200	100	100	200	300

Notice the considerable sales variation. Next, we prepare a matrix that relates the sales in each of these five months to the accounts receivable levels over subsequent months. These data would be obtained from the firm's accounts receivable ledgers. The matrix of sales-related receivables levels is shown in Table 9–4. ▪

To interpret Table 9–4, take the month of February as an example. February sales were $100,000. Reading down the February column, we find that $89,000 in receivables were outstanding at the end of February ($11,000 had been collected). At the end of March, $60,000 of the February receivables were still outstanding; at the end of April, $30,000 of the February receivables remained outstanding; and by the end of May, all February receivables either had been collected or written off. Other months are interpreted similarly. Reading down the column describes the receivables levels over time that are attributable to the sales of the month at the top of the column.

We can convert Table 9–4 to a collection experience matrix by dividing the accounts receivable levels in each column by the sales amount at the top of that column. The result states accounts receivable as a percentage of original sales. The resultant collection experience matrix for the example is shown in Table 9–5. At the end of February, for example, the percentage of February sales still outstanding was 89 percent ($89,000/$100,000). At the end of March, 60 percent ($60,000/$100,000) of the February sales were outstanding, and so on.

The diagonal arrows in Table 9–5 are drawn to indicate that we compare results along the diagonals. The top diagonal shows, over time, how well the company

---

▪ *Table 9–4*
Monthly Sales and Subsequent Accounts Receivable Levels ($000)

	January	February	March	April	May
Sales amount	200	100	100	200	300
Accounts receivable level at end of month					
January	180				
February	120	89			
March	60	60	90		
April	0	30	58	182	
May	0	0	30	120	270

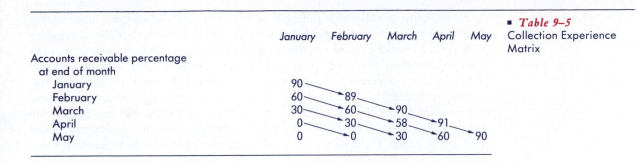

collects the current month's credit sales. The next topmost diagonal relates to receivables one month older, and so on.

If receivables collection patterns are relatively stable over time, we should see relatively constant percentages connected by the arrows. This is the case in the example: receivables as a percentage of month-of-origination sales are, on average, at 90 percent at the close of the sale month, at 60 percent one month later, at 30 percent two months later, and at 0 percent three months later. If the percentages increase as we move down any diagonal, the firm's collection experience is worsening, and this may require an investigation. If the percentages decrease down the diagonals, receivables collection is getting better (faster).

The advantage of disaggregating data into a collection experience matrix is that the result disentangles the confounding joint effects of (1) sales changes and (2) changes in receivables collection patterns.

Establishing a Collection Policy

A certain portion of the firm's customers will be tardy or nonpayers. Collection policy is directed toward (1) speeding up collections from tardy payers and (2) limiting bad-debt losses.

A well-established collection policy will have clear-cut guidelines for the sequence of collection activities. After the credit period is over and the receivable is identified as tardy, the first step in the sequence is usually a letter reminding the customer the account is overdue. If the receivable remains tardy, other letters are sent, progressively more stern in tone. Eventually, a telephone call or perhaps a personal visit by a representative of the firm's credit department will be made. If payment is still not made, the firm may turn over the account to a collection agency. These agencies aggressively pursue collection and typically work for a fixed charge plus a percentage of what they collect. Finally, legal action may be undertaken.

Most creditors realize that different collection procedures may be necessary for customers in serious financial difficulty than for those who are just habitually slow payers. Vigorous pursuit of receivables from a customer on the verge of bankruptcy may only help cause bankruptcy. This would further jeopardize collection of the account because bankruptcy proceedings usually take considerable time, and most bankruptcy debts are never fully satisfied. It is often better in such situations to be more patient, or even to take reduced payment in settlement of the account.

Establishing a collection policy that will indicate the optimal progression through this sequence of events is no easy task. Inflexibility in the collection policy is harmful. Basically sound customers who become temporarily slow payers because of economic conditions or special financial problems may become offended at hard-nosed collection procedures, and the firm may lose their business permanently. But if the collection policy is too lenient, receivables costs will mount, and profitability will suffer. The optimal collection policy will not necessarily induce fastest payment and/or lowest bad-debt losses—such a policy may incur prohibitive costs. The optimal collection policy will provide the highest expected annual profit, which is more consistent with stockholder wealth maximization. Determining the optimal collection policy thus requires comparing both costs and benefits of collection procedures.

▪ *Example*

Suppose that a particular $2,000 account is delinquent and that the firm's credit department is considering whether it is worthwhile to pursue collection further. A credit analyst estimates it will cost $200 plus 50 percent of the amount collected to pursue the collection. The analyst also estimates the amounts likely to be collected ultimately and the probabilities of collecting them as:

Amount Collected (x_j)	Probability
$ 0	0.4
500	0.3
1,000	0.2
2,000	0.1

Expected amount collected = $\Sigma \, Prob_j x_j$ = $550
Expected cost = $200 + (0.5)($550) = $475
Expected net benefit   = $ 75

Since the expected collection is greater than the expected cost, the firm should pursue the account, other things being equal. ▪

THE MANAGEMENT OF INVENTORY

Inventory Management and Shareholder Wealth

Audiovox Corporation achieved success by becoming an early seller of Japanese car radios.[14] Sensing an opportunity in cellular telephones, Audiovox made a deal with Toshiba to become an exclusive U.S. distributor. The company quickly seized a major market share in cellular phones, which soon accounted for nearly one half of its sales.

Audiovox made large inventory commitments to Toshiba, helping to pay for the inventory by raising funds in a public offering of its stock. Faced with a possible congressional cutoff of phones from Toshiba as a result of that company's

---

[14]See Fleming Meeks, "Trouble on the Line," *Forbes*, July 11, 1988, pp. 84–85.

controversy over selling secrets to the Soviet Union, Audiovox increased its supply from Toshiba by an amount considerably above sales projections. However, the cutoff did not occur, and phone prices plunged sharply. The value of Audiovox's surplus phone inventory decreased significantly, along with accounts receivable. The company was forced to share markdowns with the dealers who sold the phones. The gross profit margin was adversely affected, as were earnings. The stock price dropped sharply, wiping out half of the initial investor's capital.

There are several kinds of inventory. *Raw materials* are inputs used in the product that have been purchased but not yet utilized. *Goods-in-process* inventories are partially completed products. *Finished-goods* inventories are products ready for sale that have not yet been sold. By their nature, most manufacturing firms have substantial levels of all three kinds of inventories, while retail and wholesale firms have mostly finished-goods inventories.[15]

Financial Management of Inventory

Functional area managers in the purchasing, production, and sales departments typically have considerable managerial control of various inventories. Unfortunately, because of the nature of their jobs, they may not view inventory management from a financial management perspective. The purchasing department, for example, may focus too much on quantity discounts offered for large purchases, which can lead to excessive inventories of raw materials. Production managers may encourage excessive inventory accumulation by their desire to minimize production problems. Likewise, sales and marketing departments will prefer large inventories of finished goods so that all sales orders can be filled promptly.

These pressures are persistent facts of life. But just as too little inventory is undesirable, so also is too much. From a financial-management viewpoint, the costs and benefits of holding inventories must be balanced. As we have learned, seeking an optimal balance between benefits and costs is a key part of the process of maximizing stockholder wealth.

Benefits of Holding Inventory

For most firms, the investment in inventory is substantial because maintaining inventory allows the firm to independently perform the key activities of (1) purchasing, (2) production, and (3) selling. Without adequate inventory, the first two activities would be completely controlled by the firm's sales schedule. If sales increased, the purchasing and production activities also would have to increase. Similarly, if sales decreased, purchasing and production activities would decrease.

There are, however, compelling reasons for not rigidly tying purchasing and production schedules to sales.

- Taking quantity discounts—significant cost savings may be obtained by purchasing in larger quantities than needed for a particular sales level.
- Inventory speculation—the firm may wish to purchase raw materials before an announced or anticipated price increase.

---

[15]A fourth inventory, *supplies*, refers to materials regularly used by the firm, but not directly in the production process, such as office supplies, plant-cleaning materials, fuel, and the like.

- Cost reduction—acquisition costs may be reduced through inventory purchasing since fewer orders need be made.
- Efficient production—production runs may be accomplished more efficiently since inventory permits least-cost production scheduling.
- Avoidance of stockouts—lost sales are less likely since an adequate inventory of finished goods reduces the possibility of a stockout.

The basic function of inventories, then, is to uncouple the purchasing, production, and selling activities so that each may operate at its most efficient rate. In the long run, purchasing and production activities are, and should be, tied to the firm's sales activity. But in the short run, it is incorrect to force these activities to be rigidly related. Inventories permit this short-run uncoupling so that each activity may be pursued in the best manner.

Costs of Holding Inventory

There are three main categories of inventory cost:[16]

1. *Ordering costs* are incurred in requisitioning, purchase ordering, setting up, trucking, receiving, and storage placement. The more often acquisitions of inventory are made, the higher the firm's ordering costs. So, if the firm keeps relatively large inventory levels, fewer acquisitions will be made, and ordering costs will be relatively small.

2. *Carrying costs* (both out-of-pocket and opportunity) are related to holding a given quantity of inventory. Major carrying cost categories are opportunity cost of funds, insurance, taxes, storage, and obsolescence risk. Inventory carrying costs and inventory levels move in the same direction. If inventory levels increase, carrying costs do too, other things being equal.

3. *Stockout costs* are related to running out of inventory and include lost sales, less efficient production, and emergency procurement costs. In general, these components are more difficult to estimate than acquisition or carrying costs because they are either hypothetical (such as lost sales) or contingent on other events (such as emergency procurement costs, whose size may depend on the inventory level of the firm's suppliers at the time of a stockout). Larger inventory levels mean lower stockout costs, other things being equal.

INVENTORY CONTROL MODELS

As discussed above, benefits and costs are associated with inventory. The firm must seek efficient policies with regard to the level of inventory investment if stockholder wealth is to be maximized. The firm can choose from several inventory control models designed to determine the optimal inventory level of each item carried.

One issue in managing inventory effectively is the classification problem. This refers to the task of identifying which inventories the firm should spend most

---

[16]As in other cost-benefit analyses, an important thing to bear in mind is that only *marginal costs* should be included; costs not actually affected by inventory-level decisions should be excluded.

effort in controlling. Even modest-sized firms may have several hundred items in inventories; however, it is seldom justified, for example, to have the same degree of inventory control on all items. Rather, the firm will be well advised to emphasize control on those items with the greatest market value. Classification techniques identify items that are most important in value.

Some studies have shown that for the average manufacturer, the inventory breakdown by number of items is by far the most important from a value standpoint, so the firm should direct most of its inventory-control efforts to these items. Other items should not be ignored, of course, but they do not warrant the same attention.

Inventory control models can be *deterministic* or *probabilistic*. The simpler deterministic models assume that demand is known with certainty. The more complex probabilistic models assume that demand is a random variable with a probability distribution.

The Economic Ordering Quantity (EOQ) Model

The Order Quantity Problem

The order quantity problem is concerned with how much inventory to add when stock is replenished. There are several ways to attack this problem, ranging from fairly simple to very sophisticated, and most methods are oriented toward a cost-minimizing procedure. The presentation here will focus on one of the simpler methods because our purpose is to illustrate the financial parameters of inventory management, not the actual procedures for doing so. In other words, we deal with inventory as a financial problem, not as a production problem.

The task is to find the best quantity to order, given certain levels of demand for inventory and the associated costs of (1) ordering, (2) carrying, and (3) stockouts. For the moment, we ignore stockout costs, which will be discussed below.

Assume that the demand for inventory is known with certainty and is steady (constant) over some relevant planning horizon and that unit ordering and carrying costs are constant over the range of possible inventory levels being considered.[17] Given these assumptions, the inventory level over time would look like that shown in Figure 9–2. Beginning inventory is at level Q; this stock is used steadily until it reaches zero, when inventory is restored to level Q again. Thus, the vertical lines represent the (instantaneous) replenishment of the inventory, while the sloped lines represent the use of the item. Because the order quantity is Q and the inventory varies between Q and 0, the average inventory is one half the order quantity, or Q/2.

Economic Order Quantity

The optimal quantity, or **economic order quantity (EOQ),** will be that level of inventory that minimizes the total cost associated with inventory management. Since we are not considering stockout costs here, total cost equals carrying cost plus ordering cost:

$$\text{Total cost} = \text{Carrying cost} + \text{Ordering cost} \qquad (9\text{–}7)$$

economic order quantity (EOQ)
level of inventory that minimizes the total cost associated with inventory management

---

[17]This assumption means there are no seasonal fluctuations.

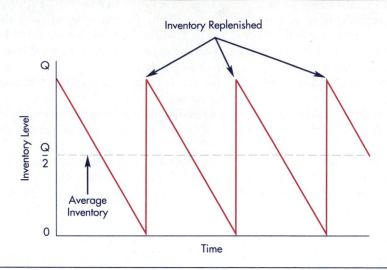

Carrying cost is the product of the average inventory carrying cost per unit. As discussed, Figure 9–2 shows that average inventory is $Q/2$. Therefore:

$$\text{Carrying cost} = (\text{Average inventory})(\text{Carrying cost per unit}) \qquad \textbf{(9–8)}$$

$$= \frac{Q}{2}(C)$$

$$= \frac{QC}{2}$$

where:

$$Q = \text{order quantity}$$
$$C = \text{carrying cost per unit}$$

The ordering cost is the number of acquisitions of inventory made during the planning period times the cost per acquisition. If D is total demand (total usage) over the planning period, and inventory is replenished in lots of size Q at each ordering, there will be D/Q acquisitions during the planning period. Therefore:

$$\text{Order cost} = (\text{Number of orders})(\text{Cost per order}) \qquad \textbf{(9–9)}$$

$$= \frac{D}{Q}(A)$$

$$= \frac{DA}{Q}$$

where:

$$D = \text{Total demand}$$
$$A = \text{Cost per order}$$

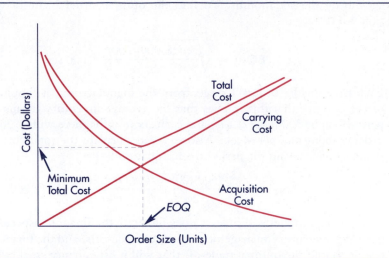

Substituting Equations 9–9 and 9–8 into Equation 9–7, we get:

$$\text{Total cost} = \frac{QC}{2} + \frac{DA}{Q} \tag{9–10}$$

Written this way, the total cost function reflects the trade-off between carrying and order costs in determining the optimal order quantity. Figure 9–3 illustrates this trade-off. As order size increases, carrying costs increase because the average inventory level increases. However, order costs decrease because a larger average inventory means there will be fewer acquisitions. Figure 9–3 also shows that at the optimal order quantity (EOQ), total cost is minimized. It is this optimal order quantity we are trying to determine. Solving mathematically for EOQ results in:[18]

$$\text{EOQ} = \sqrt{\frac{2DA}{C}} \tag{9–11}$$

The greater the total demand for the item, D, the greater the EOQ value. Also, as C, the carrying cost, increases, EOQ decreases. And as order costs, A, increase, EOQ increases.

■ *Example*

Pichler Brothers Wholesalers sells TV sets to retail outlets in the Midwest. The inventory-planning period is six months, and estimated demand over this period is 18,000 sets. Order costs are $200 per order, and carrying costs are $20 per

---

[18]Mathematically, we find the EOQ by differentiating Equation 9–10 with respect to Q, setting this differential equal to zero, and solving for the optimal value of Q, EOQ.

set during the six months. To find the optimal order quantity we use Equation 9–11:

$$EOQ = \sqrt{\frac{(2)(18,000)(200)}{20}} = 600 \text{ sets}$$

Each time Pichler orders TV sets from the manufacturer, it should order in lots of 600. Notice that this implies that the average inventory during the planning period will be 300 (600/2) sets, and each six months there will be 30 (18,000/600) orders, about one per week. Also, we can calculate the total cost of inventory management during the period from Equation 9–10:

$$\text{Total cost} = \frac{(600)(20)}{2} + \frac{(18,000)(200)}{600} = \$12,000 \qquad \blacksquare$$

While this model is simple, it does illustrate the financial aspects of inventory ordering. Inventory management involves trade-offs, and the financial manager's task is to find the optimal trade-off that will most enhance stockholder wealth.

The most limiting assumption of the model is that demand is known with certainty. Since demand is almost never known with certainty, firms carry safety stocks.

Safety Stocks

We determined the EOQ by balancing off order and carrying costs, but we ignored uncertainty. The presence of uncertainty creates a need for inventory *safety stocks* so that if demand is greater than anticipated, the firm will have an inventory buffer. The acknowledgment of uncertainty and the addition of safety stock changes the inventory level diagram shown in Figure 9–2 to a diagram like Figure 9–4.

The slope of the line in Figure 9–4 measures the expected rate of sales. However, the actual level of sales can vary and, therefore, the safety stock is used as an inventory buffer to reduce stockout possibilities. Determining the optimal level

■ *Figure 9–4*

Inventory Level over Time with Safety Stock

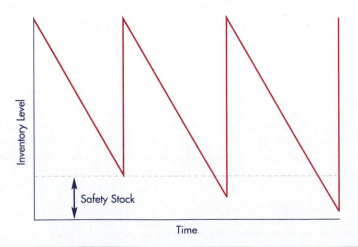

of safety stock involves comparing stockout costs with the cost of carrying safety stock. In other words, a trade-off is involved, as in virtually all other financial management decisions, and a decision must be made on a financial basis.

A firm would initially order the sum of the EOQ and the safety stock. It would presumably reorder the EOQ whenever the inventory level falls to the sum of the safety stock and the amount of usage that is expected to occur while awaiting delivery of an order.

Just-in-Time Inventory Management System

A significant development in inventory management is the **just-in-time inventory management systems.** These systems are based on the idea expressed in the name—required inventory items should be supplied to the production process as needed, in both a time sense and a quantity sense. The purpose of these systems is to reduce the inventory investment, decrease the operating cycle (discussed in Chapter 7), and increase efficiency.

The just-in-time was introduced by Toyota a number of years ago. It is very well suited for production processes involving large-scale, repetitive operations, such as auto manufacturing. By having its supplies located close by, the auto manufacturers can achieve short-notice delivery of the needed items as an average. Obviously, careful coordination is needed between user and suppliers.

just-in-time inventory management system required inventory items should be supplied to the production process as needed, in both a time sense and a quantity sense

Evaluating Inventory Management

One widely used method of evaluating inventory management is to analyze the inventory turnover ratio, defined as:

$$\text{Inventory turnover} = \frac{\text{Sales}}{\text{Inventory}} \qquad \textbf{(9–12)}$$

Presumably, the higher (lower) the inventory turnover, the more (less) efficiently inventory is managed. However, *inventory turnover has meaning only when compared to competitors' ratios and/or with the firm's ratios in previous years.* The analyst must also bear in mind that there may be perfectly logical reasons for low inventory turnover ratios that may not be apparent from the financial data. Also, extremely high inventory turnover ratios may be an indication of future problems: inventory levels may be too low to support future sales.

Another method of evaluating inventory management and control is a detailed breakdown of inventory costs. This breakdown should be complete in the sense that all relevant costs are accounted for, whether acquisition, carrying, or stockout. Also, the cost breakdown should reflect only marginal costs, as we have emphasized before. As with turnover ratios, costs have meaning only in a comparative sense.

SUMMARY

- Investment in accounts receivable is made by granting trade credit and is motivated by a desire for sales expansion and/or sales retention.
- Granting trade credit involves several kinds of costs, including bad-debt losses; production, selling, and administrative expenses; taxes; the cost of funds; and any cash discounts offered.

- Sales gains made by changes in credit policy must be compared against the costs of the changes in determining optimal credit policies.
- The firm's credit policy formulation begins with establishment of credit standards using the cost-benefit principle. The other two aspects of credit policy are receivables monitoring and collection procedures.
- The primary purpose of inventory is to permit the uncoupling of purchasing, production, and sales activities, allowing each to proceed at its optimal pace.
- Establishment of the most profitable inventory policies involves balancing off acquisition, carrying, and stockout costs.
- The order quantity problem is concerned with how much inventory to add when stock is replenished.
- The economic order quantity (EOQ) is that level of inventory that minimizes the total cost associated with inventory management.

KEY TERMS

credit standards, p. 270
economic order quantity (EOQ), p. 281

just-in-time inventory management
   system, p. 285
trade credit, p. 265

QUESTIONS

9–1. What is the relationship between trade credit and accounts receivable? What is meant by *open account*?

9–2. What are the primary components of *credit terms*?

9–3. List the five types of costs involved in extending trade credit.

9–4. What probable effects would the following changes have on the level of the company's accounts receivable?
   a. The firm changes its credit terms from 3/10, net 30, to 2/10, net 30.
   b. Interest rates increase.
   c. Production costs associated with the firm's product decrease.
   d. The economy worsens, and the country slips into a mild recession.

9–5. In assessing how well the firm's receivables are being managed, what advantage does the aging schedule offer in comparison to the collection period calculation?

9–6. At a staff meeting, the controller criticizes the credit manager for what appears to be a deterioration in the management of the firm's receivables. The controller says that bad-debt losses have increased considerably lately, and the collection period has also increased. Describe the conditions under which this criticism may be unjustified.

9–7. Assume that the Cupertino Computer Company is considering setting new credit standards to include another risk class of customers. Outline the steps that would be involved in making this decision.

9–8. What role does the calculation of the collection period ratio play in helping to evaluate the management of accounts receivable?

9–9. Given the facts of the MiniScribe situation, described at the outset of the chapter, what are the implications for the company's sales forecasts during that period?

9–10. Parr Shipping has decided to change its credit terms from the industry standard— 2/5, net 40—to 2/5, net 50. No changes in credit standards have been planned. Discuss what impact this change will have on Parr's sales and collection period:
   a. In the short run.
   b. In the long run.

9–11. In analyzing accounts receivable to set credit standards, it is common practice to assess administrative costs. A typical assumption is that these costs are incurred at date of sale.
  a. What are the main components of administrative costs?
  b. How appropriate is it to assume that all administrative costs are incurred at date of sale?

9–12. Briefly explain the difference between stockout costs and carrying costs.

9–13. Explain the three main categories of inventory costs.

9–14. Explain the concept of the EOQ.

9–15. Mitchell Cereals is attempting to determine its EOQ level for grain. Would the following events tend to raise or lower this EOQ? Explain.
  a. Purchase ordering costs decrease.
  b. Interest rates decrease.
  c. Trucking costs decrease.
  d. Sales increase.

9–16. What are safety stocks? Why are they necessary, given the EOQ model?

DEMONSTRATION PROBLEMS

9–1. Old Milwalkee Breweries' credit department is considering extending credit to a new group of applicants. After gathering some credit background information, a company analyst estimates that if credit is extended to the members of this group, the collection period will be 60 days. Bad-debt losses of 2 percent will be incurred, and none of the customers will take advantage of the cash discount offered. The required rate of return is 20 percent per year, and the tax rate is 40 percent. Production, selling, and administrative costs are 86 percent of the sales value of the product. If estimated sales to this group are $1,000 per day, determine whether Old Milwalkee should offer credit to this group of applicants.

9–2. Minnesota Minerals estimates that during the next planning period, the demand for its product will be 40,000 units. Acquisition costs are $50 per order, and carrying costs are $4 per unit.
  a. Calculate the EOQ.
  b. Using the EOQ from part (a), calculate the total inventory cost during the planning period.

Solutions to Demonstration Problems

9–1. Initial investment = $(0.86)(\$1,000) = \$860$ per day
  Bad debt losses = $(0.02)(\$1,000) = \$20$ per day
  Taxes = $(.40)(\$1,000 - \$860 - \$20) = \$48$ per day

Therefore:

Benefits = $\$1,000 - \$20 - \$48 = \$932$
$k = .20/365 = .000548$
Discount factor = $1/[1 + (.000548)(60)] = 0.968$

Therefore, NPV = $-\$860 + (.968)(\$932) = \$42$ per day

9–2. a.
$$EOQ = ((2DA)/C)^{1/2}$$
$$= \left[\frac{(2)(40,000)(\$50)}{\$4} \right]^{1/2}$$
$$= 1,000,000^{1/2}$$
$$= 1,000 \text{ units}$$

b.

$$\text{Total cost} = QC/2 + DA/Q$$
$$= \left[\frac{(1,000)(\$4)}{2} \right] + \left[\frac{(40,000)(\$50)}{1,000} \right]$$
$$= \$2,000 + \$2,000$$
$$= \$4,000$$

PROBLEMS

9–1. Whitenight Clothing, Inc., which has over $1 million in delinquent receivables, has been approached by a collection agency offering to attempt to collect the receivables. The charge to Whitenight would be $150,000 plus 50 percent of all receivables collected. Based on previous experience with collection agencies, Whitenight estimates there is a 50 percent chance that $100,000 would be collected, a 30 percent chance that $300,000 would be collected, and a 20 percent chance that $500,000 would be collected. Should Whitenight accept the agency's offer?

9–2. Find the appropriate daily discount factor for the following situations:

Situation	Annual Required Rate of Return (Percent per Year)	Number of Days
A	20	30
B	30	60
C	10	45
D	25	90

9–3. A customer owes Ajax Plumbing a $2,000 receivable due in 30 days. Find its present value today if the current annual interest rate is 25 percent.

9–4. A new customer has applied for credit approval to our company. If the application is approved, we will probably sell about $10,000 worth of merchandise to the customer per year. Production, selling, and administrative costs would be about $9,500 per year, no cash discounts would be offered, and there is no real chance of a bad–debt loss. However, the customer is known to be a slow payer. We estimate about a 90-day collection period for the account. Should the application be approved if the tax rate is 40 percent and k is 20 percent per year?

9–5. Sylla Manufacturing uses a collection experience matrix to monitor its receivables. Given the data below, prepare the matrix for Sylla and comment briefly on any apparent trends in efficiency regarding receivables management.

Receivables Levels at End of	Month of Sales			
	December	January	February	March
December	70	—	—	—
January	35	90	—	—
February	10	60	130	—
March	5	20	70	100
April	0	10	50	80
May	0	0	20	40
June	0	0	10	30
Total sales	100	100	150	120

9–6. A firm currently offers net 30 credit terms and is considering changing to net 60 terms. Neither set of terms includes a cash discount. The firm does not contemplate selling to lower-quality customers, but if the change is made, the firm believes that more sales can be made to current customers and to new customers of the same general credit caliber. Because there will be no relaxation of credit quality, the percentage of bad-debt losses on the new sales should stay the same as on current sales, 3 percent. Incremental production, selling, credit checking, and collection costs are 90 cents per dollar of sales and are expected to remain constant over the range of anticipated sales increases. The required rate of return is 15 percent per year. Current annual credit sales are $36.5 million, and the current level of accounts receivable is $4 million. If the change in credit terms is made, credit sales are expected to increase to $42 million, and the credit manager estimates the new terms will cause the collection period to increase by 30 days. Assume a zero tax rate. Determine the present collection period and the collection period under the proposed credit terms change.

9–7. Given the information in Problem 9–6, determine if the new credit terms are desirable. Show all work.

9–8. Anderson Minerals regularly inventories boxcar loads of crushed limestone. In a typical planning period, Anderson needs about 50,000 boxcar loads. The carrying cost is about $200 per boxcar, and the cost per acquisition is $20. Determine Anderson's total acquisition cost for the planning period, assuming that EOQ lot sizes are ordered.

9–9. A senior inventory analyst has just received a report from a beginning analyst whom she is helping train. The purpose of the report was to determine how many units of inventory of a certain machine part should be purchased when orders are placed. The new analyst said the answer to the EOQ problem was 5,000 units. However, some other data (shown below) that were cited by the new analyst in his report cause the senior analyst to suspect an error in the calculations. Is there an error? (Ignore safety stock considerations.)

Other Data Cited	
Total cost of managing inventory during planning period	$65,000
Carrying cost	$10 per unit
Acquisition cost	$100 per order

9–10. Given the following data, calculate the EOQ: The planning period is six months, the estimated demand during this period is 36,000 units, acquisition costs are $400 per order, and carrying costs are $40 per unit during the six months.

9–11. During the coming planning period, demand for a company's product is estimated to be 10,000 units. Acquisition costs are $50 per order, and carrying costs are $1 per unit. Determine the EOQ.

9–12. Using the information from Problem 9–11, calculate the total inventory cost during the planning period using the optimal order quantity calculated from 9–11. What cost has not been accounted for in these calculations?

SELECTED REFERENCES

A collection of recent articles on short-term financial management, including 14 articles on trade credit management and 11 articles on inventory management, can be found in:

Smith, Keith V., and George W. Gallinger. *Readings on Short-Term Financial Management.* St. Paul, Minn.: West Publishing Company, 1988.

For a discussion of monitoring accounts receivable, see:

Gentry, James A., and Jesus M. De La Garza. "A Generalized Model for Monitoring Accounts Receivable." *Financial Management,* Winter 1985, pp. 28–38.

For a discussion of the just-in-time inventory system, see:

Walleigh, Richard C. "What's Your Excuse for Not Using JIT?" *Harvard Business Review* March–April 1986, pp. 38–54.

10

Short-Term Financing

Short-Term Financing Alternatives

EG&G is a diversified manufacturer of advanced scientific and technical products, with revenues in one recent year of slightly over $1 billion. Its balance sheet for that year showed working capital of $109 million, cash and marketable securities of $115 million, and a current ratio of 1.55. Current liabilities amounted to $198 million, of which about 47 percent came from accrued expense items, a spontaneous source of short-term financing. About 30 percent of the current liabilities consisted of short-term debt and current maturities of long-term debt. According to notes in the financial statements, this amount consisted primarily of commercial paper with maturities of less than 90 days and interest rates averaging 1.3 percentage points below the prime rate for that period. EG&G also had a $150 million multicurrency credit agreement with a banking group at rates below prime to serve as a backup facility for commercial paper borrowing.

Emery Air Freight Corporation, which delivers packages overnight by air, also had revenues of slightly over $1 billion in the same year. Emery had $20 million of working capital, cash and marketable securities of about $57 million, and a current ratio of 1.06. Current liabilities amounted to $334 million, about 28 percent of which came from short-term debt (the remainder came from accounts payable and accrued expenses, which were not separated). In contrast to EG&G, Emery Air Freight raised its short-term debt from bank financing and other borrowings, primarily Salomon Brothers Holding Company (SBHC), rather than from commercial paper. According to the notes accompanying the financial statements, the bank financing bears interest at the London Interbank Offered Rate plus 2.5 percent, while borrowing under the SBHC loan at that time carried a rate of prime plus 7 percent.

In this chapter we analyze short-term sources of financing. Recall that the distinction between short-term and long-term financing is whether repayment is to be made within one year. As the EG&G and Emery Air examples demonstrate, the cost of short-term funds can vary widely; therefore, firms must carefully assess both the benefits and the costs of short-term financing.

There are two broad classes of short-term financing:

- Spontaneous financing refers to sources of funds that arise almost automatically and do not require much formal arrangement by the firm. In a sense these sources seek out the firm.

- Negotiated financing sources require (more or less) intensive effort by the firm that must negotiate for them; the firm must seek out the funds.

We analyze the spontaneous sources of short-term funds first, followed by the negotiated sources of short-term funds.

Primary *chapter learning objectives* are:

1. To review spontaneous and negotiated sources of financing.
2. To consider the advantages and disadvantages of the alternative sources of short-term financing.

SPONTANEOUS SOURCES OF SHORT-TERM FINANCING

The two main categories of spontaneous short-term financing are trade credit and accruals, which we consider in turn.

Trade Credit

As discussed in Chapter 9, most of a firm's purchases do not have to be paid for immediately, and this deferral of payment is a short-term source of financing called **trade credit.**[1] Keep in mind that in Chapter 9 we examined trade credit from the standpoint of a firm granting trade credit to other firms. Now we are examining the same trade credit, but from the standpoint of the firm using trade credit.

trade credit
debt between firms arising from credit sales between firms

A major source of funds for U.S. business firms, trade credit traditionally provides approximately 5 percent to 25 percent of the firm's total financing, depending on the kind of business the firm is in and the size of the firm.[2] Based on the data underlying Table 7–1, for all manufacturing firms trade accounts and trade notes payable provided about 8 percent of total financing (including stockholders' equity).

Small Firm Considerations

Small companies tend to rely on trade credit more than large ones (as a percentage of total credit) because they are generally less able to access the capital and money markets, whereas trade credit can be obtained readily by any firm with a reason-

---

[1]Trade credit is recorded as an account payable for the buyer and as an account receivable for the seller.
[2]Wholesale and retail companies have historically been heavy users, as have manufacturers.

able financial record.[3] For example, Table 7–1 showed that small manufacturers (assets less than $25 million) had about 13 percent of their total financing supplied by trade accounts and trade notes payables.

Types of Trade Credit

As noted in Chapter 9, in an *open account* sale the seller ships the merchandise to the buyer, and the trade credit simply appears on the buyer's books as an account payable. The seller's confidence in entering this kind of arrangement usually comes from checking the credit worthiness of the buyer and/or the history of previous business transactions with the buyer. Because open-account transactions are the most widely used type of trade credit, a firm would be in trouble if its credit rating deteriorated to the point where this kind of credit became difficult to obtain.

When the buyer signs a promissory note to obtain trade credit, it shows up on the buyer's balance sheet as a *trade note payable*.[4] The note will have a specified future payment date and is typically used when the seller is less sure the buyer will pay for the delivered goods. Although a more formal arrangement than the open account, it is actually no more legally binding. It does, however, document the debt and, when presented for collection through a bank, gives the seller more leverage in forcing collection.[5] Trade notes payable are used routinely in some industries that deal with extremely expensive merchandise, like furs and jewelry.

Credit Terms

Reviewing from Chapter 9, the expression *credit terms* refers to the conditions under which credit is granted.[6]

The three major items of the credit terms—due date, cash discount, and discount rate—are usually stated as follows:

$$x/y, \text{ net } z$$

where x is the cash discount (percent), y is the discount date (days), and z is the due date (days).

---

[3]This dependence on trade credit by small companies is quite important during tight money periods when raising funds from negotiated sources is difficult for all companies, but particularly so for small ones.

[4]Other notes payable that are not trade notes payable are notes issued to banks, employees, officers, and stockholders.

[5]A *trade acceptance* is an alternative method of formally acknowledging the debt the buyer owes the seller. The seller draws a bank draft (trade acceptance) on the buyer. This draft is a legal instrument proclaiming that the buyer will pay the bank the amount of the bill on some specified future date. The seller sends the merchandise after the buyer signs the draft; on the due date, the bank asks for payment and forwards this payment (less a service fee) to the seller.

Using trade acceptances has several advantages for the seller. As with notes payable, the seller has forced the buyer to acknowledge in writing that a debt exists. More important, the seller has employed the bank to make collection, and most companies would be much more hesitant about not paying an acceptance to the bank promptly than about not paying an open-account trade credit to the supplier promptly. Last, if the buyer has a reasonably good credit rating, the trade acceptance is marketable and may be sold at a discount (for less than face value) to investors.

Most of these advantages to the supplier, however, are disadvantages to the buyer, and competition among suppliers for sales has caused the use of trade acceptances to be somewhat rare in recent years.

[6]By definition, credit implies a deferred payment date; unless the supplier permits a deferred payment, no credit is actually extended. Consequently, the familiar COD (cash on delivery) and the less familiar CBD (cash before delivery) are not really credit sales because no deferred payment date is offered the buyer.

■ *Example*

Consider the following two examples of credit terms:

Credit Terms	Interpretation
2/10, net 30*	A 2 percent cash discount is allowed if the bill is paid by the 10th day. If the discount is not taken, the full amount of the bill is due by the 30th day.
3/15, net 60	A 3 percent cash discount is allowed if the bill is paid by the 15th day. If the discount is not taken, the full amount of the bill is due by the 60th day.

*These are the most common credit terms in the United States.

The buyer who wishes to take the cash discount must pay the bill—less the discount—by the discount date. A buyer of $1,000 worth of merchandise who is offered terms of 2/10, net 30, for example, may pay $980 any time up to the 10th day. There is no advantage in paying before the 10th day, however. Indeed, because of the time value of money, it would not make *financial* sense to do so without some inducement being offered. If the discount is not taken, $1,000 is due by the 30th day. Again, if the discount is not taken (or if none is offered), it would not make financial sense to pay before the due date. ■

Advantages of Trade Credit

Trade credit has several advantages:

- *Availability*. Except for firms in financial trouble, trade credit is almost automatic, and no negotiations or special arrangements are required to obtain it. This availability is particularly important to smaller companies that may have difficulty obtaining funds elsewhere.
- *Flexibility*. If the firm's sales increase, causing its purchases of goods and services to increase, trade credit will grow automatically. Likewise, if the firm's sales decrease, causing purchasing needs to drop, trade credit will likewise decrease.
- *Few or no restrictions*. In general, trade credit terms are much less restrictive than those of negotiated sources of funds.[7] As we will see, when the firm negotiates for short-term funds, it may have restrictions imposed on its financial activities by the lenders.

Costs of Trade Credit

In discussing the cost of trade credit, it is important to distinguish between *visible* and *hidden* costs. By visible costs we mean those costs that can be readily measured. Hidden costs are more difficult to determine. A good example of a hidden cost is deterioration in the firm's credit rating. It can be extremely difficult to put a dollar value on such a cost, but certainly a cost is involved in any significant deterioration, and proper financial decision making must recognize such costs if the stockholders' wealth is to be maximized.

[7]Restrictions may also be placed on trade credit in some instances, but this is far less common.

	Prompt Payment	Delayed Payment
Visible Costs	None	1. Cost of Forgoing Cash Discount 2. Penalty Charge for Late Payment
Hidden Costs	Costs Passed on to Buyer by Seller for: 1. Carrying Costs 2. Credit Checking 3. Bad-Debt Losses	Cost of Paying Late

■ *Figure 10–1*
Trade Credit Use and Costs

We can also distinguish between *prompt* and *delayed payment* practices. By prompt, we mean those situations in which the firm pays off the trade credit exactly on time. There are two such possibilities. If a cash discount is offered, paying on time means paying on the discount date. If a cash discount is not offered, prompt payment means paying on the due date. However, if a cash discount is offered but not taken, or if the full bill is not paid by the due date, the firm is making a delayed payment.[8]

Figure 10–1 shows a cross-classification of visible versus hidden costs and prompt versus delayed payment practices. Our discussion will address each of the four quadrants of the figure.

1. *Prompt payment—visible costs*. The northwest quadrant of Figure 10–1 shows there are no visible costs to the firm associated with prompt payment. That is, if the firm pays its suppliers exactly on time, taking all cash discounts on their discount date and paying all other bills on the due date, trade credit has no *visible* costs. This does not mean that there are no trade credit costs; it only means there are no visible costs.

2. *Prompt payment—hidden costs*. There may be hidden costs associated with prompt payment. To see these better, consider the suppliers. Some credit sales will result in bad-debt losses. The suppliers also have to pay for the funds used to produce products; consequently, they can scarcely afford to grant credit (funds) to customers costlessly. In addition, the credit-granting procedure usually involves some credit-checking operation, which suppliers either perform themselves or purchase from a credit-checking agency.

   Suppliers try to cover all of these costs by pricing the product higher than if there were only cash sales. How successful they are depends largely on how competitive the industry is. The aggregate demand for the product and the competition for sales among sellers will determine how much of these costs can be passed on to the buyer.

---

[8]A delayed payment does not necessarily imply a late or tardy payment. If the buyer ignores the discount offered, payment is delayed, but not late.

3. *Delayed payment—visible costs.* There are two kinds of costs to consider here:

> The cost of forgoing a cash discount offered.
> Penalty charges for late payment.

a. *Cost of forgoing cash discount.* We have already seen that if the firm takes the cash discount by the discount date, there are no visible costs of credit. However, if the firm fails to take the discount, it may incur a substantial visible cost. An easy way to examine this cost is to put the decision to take the discount or not into a simple loan framework. On the discount date the customer firm may (1) forgo the discount and pay the full amount of the bill on the due date, or (2) take the discount.[9]

■ *Example*

Suppose the terms on a $100 credit sale are 2/10, net 30. The customer firm is faced effectively with a loan problem with the following cash flows:

Day	(A) Forgo Discount (Delayed Payment)	(B) Take Discount (Prompt Payment)	(C) A − B
10	0	−$98	+$ 98
30	−$100	0	−$100

Column C reflects the cash flow differences between the two alternatives. By netting A − B, we have set up the problem as a loan problem. That is, by forgoing the discount, the customer firm receives a $98 loan for 20 days, which is repaid along with $2 interest at the end of the 20-day loan period. Considering the 20-day interval from Day 10 to Day 30 as one period, the interest rate the firm is paying when it forgoes the discount is found as follows:

$$\$98 = \frac{\$100}{1 + r}$$

Solving for *r:*

$$r = \frac{2}{98} = .0204 \text{ or } 2.04\%$$

However, this rate of return is for a 20-day period, and there are 18.25 (365/20) such 20-day periods in a year. Therefore:

$$\text{Visible annual cost of forgoing cash discount} = (2.04)(18.25) = 37.2\%$$

---

[9]The full amount may be paid after the due date; we consider this possibility later.

When working problems, we can simply calculate the annual cost in the following manner:

$$
\begin{array}{l}
\text{Visible} \\
\text{annual cost} \\
\text{of forgoing} \\
\text{cash discount}
\end{array}
= \frac{\text{Percent cash discount}}{100\% - \text{Percent cash discount}} \times \frac{365}{N}
\qquad \textbf{(10–1)}
$$

where

$$N = \text{number of days between due date and discount date}$$

- ### Example

Using the numbers in the previous example:

$$
\begin{array}{l}
\text{Visible annual cost of} \\
\text{forgoing cash discount}
\end{array}
= \frac{2}{98} \times \frac{365}{20} = 37.2\%
$$

Seeing the solution in this form reinforces the statement that the problem is a standard loan problem. The 2/98 term is interest ($2) divided by loan principal ($98), and the result of this division is a 20-day interest rate. The 365/20 term converts the 20-day interest rate to an annual interest rate. ∎

b. *Penalty charge on late payment.* Often the terms of trade will include a late payment penalty, similar to an interest charge. An example would be terms of net 30, 2 percent per month late charge. If invoices are not paid promptly by the due date (net 30), a late payment charge (2 percent per month) will be assessed. To annualize the visible cost of any late penalty, we go through a process similar to that in Equation 10–1:

$$
\begin{array}{l}
\text{Visible} \\
\text{annual cost of} \\
\text{penalty charge}
\end{array}
=
\begin{array}{l}
\text{(Percentage penalty)(Number of periods} \\
\text{per year)}
\end{array}
\qquad \textbf{(10–2)}
$$

- ### Example

Let's apply Equation 10–2 to the example above where the terms are net 30, with a 2 percent per month late charge.[10] To find the visible *annual cost* associated with the penalty charge, we must make an assumption about how late the invoice will be settled. Consider two alternatives:

1. Pay one month after the original due date (but before another 2 percent penalty is incurred).
2. Pay one week after the original due date.

Cost calculations for these two alternatives are:

Alternative	Visible Annual Cost of Penalty Charge
1	(2%) (12 months per year) = 24%
2	(2%) (52 weeks per year) = 104%

---

[10] We are explicitly presuming here that our firm has not paid the invoice by the due date.

These percentages are not a direct, explicit cost to the firm that it would likely pay under most conditions. Rather, these percentages should be interpreted as the *annualized* cost of having taken an additional month to pay and an additional week to pay, respectively, given a 2 percent penalty, if the firm were to repeat this action over and over during the year.

This example illustrates that by normal interest rate standards (i.e., within the historical range of about 5 percent to 20 percent) both alternatives are expensive. They are purposely expensive. Trade creditors impose high penalty charges to induce prompt payment by their customers. Consequently, for customers who can raise money from other sources, like their banks, at lower interest rates, it is clearly disadvantageous to pay late when there are penalty charges. That is, the annualized penalty charge is usually a very expensive way for firms to finance their payables. We'll look at that problem again below. ▪

4. *Delayed payment—hidden costs.* The firm could reduce the *visible* cost of forgoing cash discounts by not paying the full amount of the bill by the due date. Equation 10–1 may be generalized to include payment on dates other than the due date.

$$\text{Visible annual cost of forgoing cash discount} = \frac{\text{Percent cash discount}}{100\% - \text{Percent cash discount}} \times \frac{365}{N'} \tag{10–3}$$

where:

N' = number of days between discount date and date the bill is paid

▪ *Example*

Suppose the firm doesn't pay the $100 bill, in the earlier example involving 2/10, net 30, until Day 40, 10 days after the due date. Then:

$$\text{Visible annual cost of forgoing cash discount} = \frac{2}{98} \times \frac{365}{30} = 24.8\%$$ ▪

By stretching out the payment date, N' is increased, and the *visible* cost of forgoing the cash discount is reduced; the longer the firm stretches the payment date, the lower the visible cost. Whether failing to pay trade credit on time, or *stretching accounts payable,* is a wise decision is another matter. First, ethical considerations are involved. A firm reasonably can be expected to honor its obligations, which includes paying its bills on time.

Second, although this practice reduces the visible cost of forgoing cash discounts, as shown above, it increases the hidden cost that arises because of the possible deterioration of the firm's credit rating. If a firm becomes known as a slow payer, its suppliers may offer less-favorable trade credit terms (they may even stop granting credit), particularly when money is tight. Less-favorable credit terms are part of the hidden costs associated with stretching the payables. Their size depends mainly on the competitive conditions that exist between buyers and suppliers, with a dominant buyer more able to successfully stretch payables. But the main point is that stretch-ing the payables is not costless, and the supplier will attempt to pass all costs associated with such practices on to the buyer.

Relevant Cost Comparisons

From an economic standpoint, the purpose of calculating the cost of either for-going a cash discount or incurring a late payment penalty is to make cost com-parisons with other alternatives. Is it better to forgo a cash discount or to borrow the needed money and take the cash discount? Is it ever economically worthwhile to suffer a late-payment penalty? To answer such questions, we need to compare the interest rates (costs) associated with the alternatives involved in the problem and choose that alternative with the lowest interest rate.[11]

Suppose the question is whether to forgo a cash discount. The two alternatives are:

1. Forgo the cash discount (thereby borrowing from the supplier).
2. Take the cash discount (thereby borrowing from some other lender, like a bank).

To resolve the issue, we compare the interest rates of the two alternatives. The interest rate for the first alternative is the visible annual cost of forgoing the cash discount, possibly adjusted for hidden costs as described below.

Equations 10–1 through 10–3 deal only with *visible* costs. As we saw earlier in this chapter, *hidden* costs can also be important. Hidden costs increase the *total* cost of cash discounts forgone or late payment penalties:

$$\begin{matrix} \text{Total cost of} \\ \text{forgoing cash discounts} \\ \text{or late payment penalties} \end{matrix} = \begin{matrix} \text{Visible} \\ \text{cost} \end{matrix} + \begin{matrix} \text{Hidden} \\ \text{cost} \end{matrix} \qquad \textbf{(10–4)}$$

Hidden costs, although not measurable, manifest themselves in possible credit rating deterioration. Sometimes hidden costs can be effectively incorporated into the analysis even though they are not quantifiable. Suppose a manager is com-paring the visible cost of a late-payment penalty with a bank loan interest rate, and they are approximately equal. Equation 10–4 shows that the bank loan would be preferable here because the total cost of the late-payment alternative will be higher due to the hidden cost.

Accruals

An even more automatic source of short-term funds than trade credit is **accruals,** also known as accrued expenses. Since—by definition—accruals permit the firm to receive some service before paying for it, accruals are a form of short-term funds supplied to the firm at no explicit cost. Furthermore, accruals expand au-tomatically as the firm's operations expand. The main components of accrued expenses are wages and taxes.[12]

accruals
continually recurring liabilities representing services received for which payment has not been made

---

[11]It doesn't matter whether we compare before or after tax costs (interest rates), so long as we are consistent.

[12]Another accrual results from the institutional practices associated with interest payments. The firm has a con-tractual obligation to repay interest on its borrowings, but while the firm has continuous use of the borrowed funds, interest payments are made periodically at the *end* of agreed-upon time periods. This deferred, rather than continuous, payment of interest also provides short-term funds to the firm.

Accrued Wages

From an accounting standpoint, the firm incurs a liability the instant labor is furnished. But employees are paid afterward, usually at some fixed interval like two weeks or a month. In effect, the firm's employees are supplying the firm with short-term funds by receiving deferred wages and salaries. The longer this payment interval, the greater the amount of funds provided by the employees.

■ *Example*

To further illustrate this point, consider the following example, which assumes seven-day weeks and ignores any weekend payment problems:

Daily wages for McEnally Motorcycle Co. = $1,000

McEnally Motorcycle Pays Wages	Average Annual Financing Provided to McEnally Motorcycle by Wage Accruals
Daily	0
Weekly	(6 days)($1,000/day) ÷ 2 = $3,000
Monthly	(29 days)($1,000/day) ÷ 2 = $14,500
Yearly	(364 days)($1,000/day) ÷ 2 = $182,000

If McEnally Motorcycle pays its employees at the end of every workday, then McEnally Motorcycle's employees provide it with no financing through wage accruals. In all other cases, some accruals financing is being provided. Take the weekly case as an example. Every day except the last day of the week, there is some financing from accruals. In fact, six days' financing (seven days minus the last day) would have been provided if all the work had been done on the first day of the week. Since the work and wages are spread out over the week, we divide by two to account for the fact that, except for the first day of the period, any single day's accruals are not provided to the firm for the entire period. That is, dividing by two results in the annual average amount of financing provided. ■

Accrued Income Taxes

While the government has a percentage tax claim on each dollar the firm earns, the bulk of these taxes are paid only after profits have accumulated. This, too, is a deferred payment of an obligation of the firm and is a form of short-term capital provided to the firm. Corporate income taxes are calculated annually but are paid quarterly during the year in which the income is earned.

NEGOTIATED SHORT-TERM FINANCING

In the first part of this chapter, we investigated short-term (less than a year) sources of financing that are spontaneous (automatically available), provided the firm is not in trouble. Now we consider short-term sources of financing whose receipt requires the firm's negotiation.

Short-Term Bank Loans

A commercial bank receives money from customers in exchange for checking accounts (demand deposits) and savings accounts (time deposits). It lends these funds to individuals (consumer loans), to businesses (commercial loans), and to governments (by buying government securities). A short-term bank loan is a business loan from a commercial bank that will be repaid within one year.

Short-term bank loans are an important source of negotiated short-term financing for many firms. Whenever firms have a short-term need for funds that can't be satisfied with trade credit and internally generated funds, they often turn first to bank credit, which also serves as a financing reserve. The figures on which Table 7–1 are based indicate that bank loans with original maturity of one year or less provided about 2 percent of the total financing for all manufacturers, and about 7 percent for small manufacturers.

Establishing a Bank Relationship

When a firm engages in financial transactions with a bank, it establishes a banking relationship or connection. Large firms, because of the size of their short-term financing needs and/or because of their diversified geographical operations, may have connections with several banks; small firms, normally, deal with only one bank. The first step in the process of establishing this relationship is to choose among the competing banks. From the firm's standpoint, the following questions need to be answered:

1. Are the bank's loan costs competitive with those of other banks?
2. Is the bank large enough to service expected borrowing needs?
3. Are the bank's lending policies consistent with the firm's borrowing needs? That is:
   a. Does the bank have conservative or liberal lending policies?
   b. Does the bank understand and is it prepared to help with borrowing needs that are peculiar to the type of business the firm is in?

A firm should do certain things to keep its bank happy. Generally, it should keep the bank well informed on the firm's operations and financial position and be honest with the bank about the use of the borrowed funds. Specifically, the firm's management should establish business friendships with some of the bank officers, having them personally visit the firm to become more familiar with its operations. Banking relationships are the same as other relationships, and personal friendships between bank and company officers will help in securing future credit.

Management also needs to provide the bank full information on the firm's current operations and financial position. In particular, the firm should notify the bank of any major changes in the firm's operations or financial status and why they occurred. Banks are very interested in any future cash flow projections made by the firm.

Finally, the firm must comply with the loan agreement, use the loan proceeds only for their intended purpose and meticulously observe all loan restrictions and covenants.

Loan Analysis

The bank's analysis of the loan application is primarily directed to an appraisal of the firm's integrity, the intended use of the loan, and repayment prospects. The bank lends money on the expectation of repayment. While the bank has legal recourse to recapture its investment, loan defaults are not profitable to the bank. In assessing the likelihood of default, the bank will make a judgment on the character, or willingness to pay, of the applicant firm. The firm should cultivate business friendships with the bankers for exactly this reason—it is an excellent way for the firm to establish a reputation for integrity.

One of the first questions the bank will ask the firm is why it needs the loan. The most common uses of short-term funds are for inventory expansion and for financing accounts receivable. Banks prefer these kinds of short-term loan applications and look less favorably on long-term uses of the money.

A loan won't be granted unless the bank is reasonably certain of repayment; the bank will carefully assess the sources and possible timing of repayment. Banks look favorably on *self-liquidating* loans, which are loans used to acquire assets that will pay themselves off, such as inventory or accounts receivable. However, banks make loans for many investment proposals that are not self-liquidating, and in these cases the bank will look to the long-run profitability of the firm. Another source of repayment is the infusion of new permanent capital into the firm in the form of either debt or equity.

To protect itself against the prospect of loan default, the bank may require collateral—pledging assets for the settlement of the loan. This is discussed in more detail below. The bank will also be impressed by financial contingency plans formulated for possible trouble situations. These plans assure the bank that the company has considered the possibility that its investments may be disappointing and has formulated plans for loan repayment should this situation develop.

In general, banks reject commercial loan applications for several reasons.[13] The most frequent explanation for loan denial is poor credit evaluation. One of the most common reasons for a poor credit evaluation is insufficient owner's equity in the firm. Lenders view equity as a cushion or protection for their loans to the company. If the firm should fail, the greater this equity cushion, the more likely the lenders are to recover their entire loan, since debt holders get first claim on the firm's assets.[14]

The next most common reason for loan rejection is inconsistency with a bank's loan policy. A bank may say that a requested loan is at odds with its policy because its proposed duration is too long, there is no established deposit relationship with the bank, the bank doesn't handle the type of loan requested, or the bank's portfolio (its total collection of loans) already has enough loans of the kind requested.

Types of Short-Term Bank Loans

There are several kinds of short-term bank loans. We will discuss the well-known types.

---

[13]Some loans are refused because of banking restrictions. This usually happens when the loan is large.

[14]Other factors causing loan rejection because of a poor credit evaluation are an inferior earnings record, questionable managerial talent, insufficient collateral, and a poor credit history or none at all (as in the case of a new firm).

■ *Single loans (notes).* A single, or transaction, loan, often referred to as a *note,* is the traditional type of short-term bank loan, familiar to most people. The length of these loans may extend to one year, but often are in the range of 30 to 90 days. Characteristics of single loans include:

Negotiated and administratively handled on an individual basis.

Made for a specified use.

Evidenced by a promissory note.

Typically repaid in a single (lump sum) payment on the due date stated on the promissory note; alternatively, the loan can be renewed.

This type of loan is used most often by borrowers with relatively infrequent needs for short-term bank loans.

■ *Lines of credit.* Many firms use short-term bank loans so frequently that the single loan is administratively cumbersome. They use instead a **line of credit,** an agreement that permits the company to borrow up to some specified maximum amount from the bank during the life of the agreement. This arrangement minimizes the negotiation effort and provides the firm with a very flexible source of financing: the firm does not actually use, or draw down, its line of credit until it needs to, and when money is needed, the process is more automatic than with a single loan. Note, however, that the bank is not under a legal obligation to extend credit.[15]

line of credit
an agreement permitting a firm to borrow up to some specified maximum amount from a bank

A line of credit is often used to arrange seasonal financing needs. The firm will estimate its peak seasonal cash needs and then add a safety factor. For example, if the firm estimates it will need $200,000 cash to expand its inventories and accounts receivable during its peak season in September, it probably will add a safety margin, say, $25,000, and ask for a line of credit of $225,000.

Lines of credit must be negotiated, with renewals renegotiated. A typical agreement period is one year. The borrower must supply the bank with its current and projected financial information, including a cash budget for the coming year. The agreement will spell out the interest rate to be charged (typically, the prime rate plus some risk premium), any compensating balance requirement, and any other protective covenants. Most agreements contain a "clean-up" clause which requires the borrower to not owe any money on the line of credit for some period of time during the year, often 30 to 90 days. The bank does this to ensure that the borrower is using the line of credit for seasonal purposes, as opposed to permanent financing.

■ *Revolving credit.* With a **revolving credit agreement,** a formal arrangement, the bank is legally committed to provide credit, up to the maximum limit established, on demand by the firm. The firm pays a commitment fee, usually between .125 percent and .5 percent per year, on the unused portion of the line (the maximum limit established less the amount borrowed). If no funds are borrowed during the year, the

revolving credit agreement
a formal agreement by a bank, legally requiring it to provide credit up to some maximum established limit

---

[15]Except for situations where the firm or bank has encountered financial difficulties, however, the bank almost always does. The line-of-credit arrangement is periodically reviewed, commonly after the firm's annual report is published, so that the bank can use this audited report in analyzing the firm's position.

commitment fee must be paid on the full borrowing limit established in the agreement.[16] Of course, the firm must pay interest on any amount borrowed at any time. Most revolving agreements carry a floating interest rate (discussed below) pegged to a well-known open-market interest cost such as the Treasury bill rate. Thus, the cost of borrowed funds will vary over time as interest rates vary.

Revolving credit lines, typically, are negotiated for longer periods than lines of credit, such as two or three years, with extensions possible. During the agreement period the firm knows that it can rely on this source of funds if it needs to.

▪ *Example*

In its *1988 Annual Report,* General Mills noted that it had entered into a $150 million fee-paid revolving credit agreement for three years, extendable to five years at the company's option. ▪

Short-Term Loan Features

The particulars of the loan depend on the financial strength of the borrower, the loan policies of the bank, and general credit conditions.

Collateral refers to assets the firm pledges to turn over to the bank should default occur. Some firms are financially strong enough that the bank feels the loan is safe without requiring collateral. But the riskier the loan looks to the bank, the more likely will collateral be required. Any assets may be pledged, but short-term loans are usually secured by short-term assets: cash, securities, accounts receivable, and inventories. If the loan is unsecured (i.e., if no collateral is required), the bank becomes a general creditor, and its claims, if the firm declares bankruptcy, are the same as those of other general creditors. We will discuss collateral from the broader perspective of both bank and nonbank lenders at the end of this chapter.

Compensating balances (discussed in Chapter 8) refer to some minimum balance, typically 10 to 20 percent of the loan, that the borrower must keep in its checking account with the lending bank. Compensating balances ensure that the borrower will maintain an account with the lending bank, which is an important consideration for the bank. They also provide the bank with the right of offset against the firm's checking account balances should the loan default.[17] Compensating balances raise the effective interest rate the bank earns on the loan because the firm does not have the use of the entire amount of the loan.

When the bank extends a line of credit, it is expressly granting short-term credit to help the firm meet emergencies or seasonal financing needs. A credit line is not extended for permanent financing purposes. One way the bank has of ensuring that the credit line is being used as intended is to have a *cleanup clause* in the loan agreement. This requires that the firm be completely out of debt to the line of credit for one or more months.[18]

---

[16]The situation is actually more complex than this. Fees are assessed in several ways, and obligations can be satisfied, similarly, in several ways.

[17]This means the bank can recover the firm's checking account balance without sharing it with other creditors.

[18]If the firm is unable to comply with this clause, the bank will infer that the line of credit is being used as permanent capital and may suggest the firm secure long-term capital for its long-term needs.

In a *fixed-rate* loan, the interest rate remains constant during the life of the loan. Recently, inflation has often increased unexpectedly and eroded the purchasing power of outstanding loans. Lenders of fixed-rate loans had no way of recouping this loss since they could not raise interest rates to compensate for inflation. As a result, many lenders specify *floating rates* on loans. Under this arrangement, the loan interest rate is tied to some widely used market interest rate and is changed at agreed-upon intervals as the benchmark market interest rate changes.

Cost of Short-Term Bank Loans

Short-term bank loans, like all other financing sources, have a cost. Three factors determine the cost of short-term loans: the nominal interest rate, the method used by the bank to compute and collect the interest, and the firm's tax rate. The *nominal interest rate* is the annual interest rate stated on the loan agreement and reflects the general credit conditions prevailing in the economy and the creditworthiness of the applicant firm. It is similar to the coupon rate on a bond. As we know from Chapter 4, this is rarely equal to the *effective annual interest rate*. We will consider each of these rates in turn.

The **prime rate** has traditionally been thought of as the nominal interest rate banks charge their most creditworthy corporate borrowers. It used to be considered the lowest short-term interest rate the bank charged. In the 1970s, however, as interest rates skyrocketed, banks began to make loans to their best customers at rates below the prime rate. Thus, the prime rate now serves more as a reference rate for other interest rates.

> **prime rate**
> a published interest rate on loans from commercial banks to their most-valued corporate borrowers

Like other interest rates, the prime rate is determined by supply and demand in the marketplace for funds. When the economy is expanding, firms need funds to make investments, and this competition bids up interest rates. But when the economy is contracting, lenders bid down interest rates because there is less demand for funds—assuming demand for funds to finance a federal deficit does not keep rates at a high level. The prime rate tends to fluctuate with other interest rates, reflecting general economic conditions—it increases in periods of inflation and decreases in periods of deflation. Note, however, that the prime rate is set by bankers rather than by demand and supply conditions in an open market.

Firms that don't qualify for prime rate loans are considered less creditworthy and are charged a higher interest rate. Loans for such firms may be made at a rate equal to the prime rate plus some additional risk premium. This premium will increase as the perceived creditworthiness of the firm decreases. In general, small firms pay larger interest rates than large firms since small firms fail more often and are hence riskier.

The effective annual interest rate is the actual annual interest rate on the loan. It is the (before tax) annual rate of return that the lender is earning (and the borrower is paying) on the loan. To understand how the effective interest rate is calculated, we must first look at how the bank determines the dollar interest on the short-term loan. The bank figures simple interest on the loan as follows:

$$I = (L)(i)(t) \qquad \textbf{(10–5)}$$

where:

I = interest (dollars)
L = loan principal (dollars)
i = nominal interest rate (percent per year)
t = time (years)

The effective annual interest rate is calculated using the procedures discussed in Chapter 4. Since our primary concern here is the other aspects of the cost of bank loans, we will *approximate* the effective annual interest rate with the following equation.[19]

$$r = \frac{I}{L_0}(m) \qquad (10\text{--}6)$$

where:

r = effective interest rate (percent per year)
L_0 = net proceeds (dollars)
m = the number of time periods per year

Multiplying by *m* in Equation 10–6 *annualizes* the interest rate.

▪ *Example*

Suppose the McEnally Motorcycle Company has negotiated a 180-day, $200,000 loan with the Fourth National Bank. The nominal interest rate is 8 percent, and the interest and principal are due on the maturity date.

$$\text{Interest} = (\$200{,}000)(0.08) \times \frac{180}{365} = \$7{,}890$$

$$r = \frac{\$7{,}890}{\$200{,}000} \times \frac{365}{180} = 8\%$$

The firm in the example receives $200,000 net proceeds at the time of the loan, and 180 days later pays the bank $207,890. In this simplified case, nominal and effective interest rates are equal because the loan principal and net loan proceeds are equal. However, commercial banks discount loans, require compensating balances, and use the banker's year on commercial loans. These practices raise the effective interest rate and, therefore, the cost of bank loans. We will consider each of these three factors in turn.

1. *Discounting a loan* means to collect the interest at the start of the loan rather than at the end.

   ▪ *Example*

   Using the McEnally Motorcycle example again:

$$\text{Interest} = (\$200{,}000)(0.08) \times \frac{180}{365} = \$7{,}890$$

$$\text{Net loan proceeds} = \$200{,}000 - \$7{,}890 = \$192{,}110$$

$$r = \frac{\$7{,}890}{\$192{,}110} \times \frac{365}{180} = 8.33\%$$

The firm receives $192,110 net loan proceeds at the time of the loan and pays the bank $200,000 six months later. The total dollar amount of interest ($7,890) is the same as in the earlier example, but by charging the interest

---

[19]The reader should review in Chapter 4 the formulas for exact calculations.

at the start of the loan, the bank reduces the net loan proceeds, which means the firm has lower proceeds to work with over the life of the loan ($192,110 instead of $200,000). Consequently, the firm pays a higher effective interest rate.

2. *Compensating balances* effectively increase the cost of loans.

■ **Example**

Using the McEnally Motorcycle example, assume that in addition to an 8 percent discount the bank requires a 10 percent compensating balance:

$$\text{Interest} = (\$200,000)(0.08) \times \frac{180}{365} = \$7,890$$

$$\text{Net loan proceeds} = \$200,000 - \$7,890 - \$20,000 = \$172,110$$

$$\text{Compensating balance} = (\$200,000)(0.10) = \$20,000$$

$$r = \frac{\$7,890}{\$172,110} \times \frac{365}{180} = 9.30\%$$

■

Compared to the previous example, the effective interest rate and cost have been increased by requiring a 10 percent compensating balance. This is because $20,000 is now tied up in the firm's checking account, reducing the net loan proceeds from $192,110 to $172,110. And the bank is charging McEnally interest on this unusable $20,000.[20]

3. The *banker's year* is a 360-day year, and its use by the bank raises a loan's effective interest rate and cost. The banker's year changes the number of days assumed to be in a year in Equation 10–5 from 365 to 360.[21]

■ **Example**

Consider the last version of the McEnally example using the banker's year:

$$\text{Interest} = (\$200,000)(0.08) \times \frac{180}{360} = \$8,000$$

$$\text{Compensating balance} = (\$200,000)(0.10) = \$20,000$$

$$r = \frac{\$8,000}{\$172,000} \times \frac{365}{180} = 9.43\%$$

■

Using the banker's year increases the dollars of interest charged, which causes the effective interest rate (r) to increase.

Open-Market Loans

Open-market loans are funds obtained through the impersonal national and international money market, where funds are borrowed and lent for periods of less

---

[20]Of course, if McEnally already had $20,000 in its Fourth National checking account, it would use that money as its compensating balance and have the use of the full $192,110, reducing the effective interest rate and cost back to their previously determined levels.

[21]Notice that although we substitute 360 for 365 in Equation 10–5 to get the dollars of interest the firm must pay the bank, we do not make a similar substitution in Equation 10–6 to compute r. Why not? Because 10–6 converts the interest calculation into an effective interest rate based on the actual number of days in the year, which is 365.

than one year. The primary feature of this market is the negotiable financial instrument created because of the loan. We will consider only commercial paper in this discussion.[22]

commercial paper
short-term, unsecured promissory notes issued by corporations with high credit ratings

Commercial paper is a form of unsecured promissory note, with maturities from 3 to 270 days, that firms issue to raise short-term money. In Chapter 7, we analyzed commercial paper from the standpoint of investing in it as a marketable security. Here, we need to analyze commercial paper from the standpoint of the issuer.

The commercial paper market is a blue-chip market; only the financially strongest and most creditworthy companies can issue commercial paper. This is because the lenders in this market (the buyers of the commercial paper, mainly other businesses, insurance companies, pension funds, and banks) are primarily interested in investing excess cash for a short time without exposing themselves to any appreciable risk of loss.

Commercial paper is an important source of short-term financing for large corporations. This market is dominated by financial companies, which account for more than three fourths of all paper issued. In recent years, some nonfinancial companies have aggressively used commercial paper for partial financing of long-term assets. Typically, commercial paper remains outstanding until it matures.

Paper is issued either through a *dealer* or via *direct placement*. A dealer is a special agent who handles commercial paper for a fee. Dealers may either buy the paper outright from the firm or sell the paper on commission. An alternative to the dealer market is direct placement of the paper to investors. This route has been used particularly by large sales-finance companies such as General Motors Acceptance Corporation.[23] Directly placed paper now dominates dealer-placed paper issued by financial companies.

The interest yield on commercial paper is largely a function of its maturity, interest rates on alternative investments, the reputation of the issuer, and the rating of the paper provided by rating services.[24] As Figure 10–2 shows, interest yields on commercial paper are generally below the prime rate posted by banks, which is why paper is an attractive financing alternative to bank borrowing.

The issuing firm pays no interest on the paper but sells it at a discount from face value, with the difference between selling price and redemption at face value providing the investors' return.[25] The interest yield is found as follows:[26]

$$\text{Interest yield} = \frac{\text{Face value} - \text{Sale price}}{\text{Sale price}} \times \frac{365}{\text{Days to maturity}} \qquad \textbf{(10–7)}$$

---

[22]Banker's acceptances are an important form of short-term financing for firms in the import-export trade. They are discussed in Chapter 22.

[23]In deciding whether to use a dealer or the direct placement market, the firm will compare the dealer's fee with the cost of setting up a staff to market the commercial paper. Smaller companies will not be able to justify the staff expense and will tend to use dealers, especially since they are also less well known in financial circles.

[24]The two best known rating services are Standard & Poor's and Moody's. All rating services have three-point rating schemes, with the safest paper rated 1 and the riskiest, 3. Moody's rating scheme, for example, is Prime-1, Prime-2, and Prime-3.

[25]This return is designated as interest for tax purposes.

[26]In computing the sale price in Equation 10–7, the firm must net all the flotation costs associated with issuing paper. These include (1) fees to the dealer if a dealer is used, (2) fees to the rating services, (3) fees to the bank that serves as agent for collection and payment of the paper, and (4) the costs of a backup line of credit from a bank. To market commercial paper successfully today, the issuer must have the backup credit line to show clearly the ability to redeem the paper at its maturity. The costs of this backup take two forms: a commitment fee and a compensating balance.

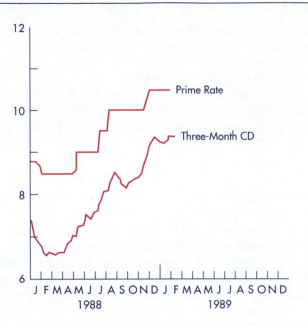

■ *Figure 10–2*
Prime Rate and Three-
Month CD Rate, 1988–89
(Percent, Weekly
Averages)

Source: Adapted from *Economic Trends*, Federal Reserve Bank of Cleveland, February 1989, p. 15.

This expression is identical in form to Equation 10–6. The first term divides the interest (face value less sale price) by the amount of the investment (sale price). The second term annualizes this interest rate.

■ *Example*

Assume 90–day paper sold at $97.50 net:[27]

$$\text{Interest yield} = \frac{2.50}{97.50} \times \frac{365}{90} = 0.104 = 10.4\%$$

■

The principal advantage of using commercial paper is its low cost in comparison to bank borrowing rates. A second major advantage is the availability of commercial paper during periods of tight bank credit. This reason has, in fact, led many companies into the commercial paper market.

The main disadvantage of using commercial paper stems from the impersonal nature of the paper market. If the firm encounters financial difficulties and can't redeem its paper, it will be hard to get extensions of time from the investors who hold the firm's paper. Banks are more inclined to help the firm work things out in time of distress. Some firms feel that heavy use of commercial paper by them will damage their bank relationships so much that their bank, which values customer loyalty, will not treat them as preferred customers during the periodic credit squeezes that occur. At the other extreme, some firms believe they are better off not having to worry about treatment by their bank since they can turn to the paper market.

---

[27]Prices of commercial paper are stated per $100 of face value. The $97.50 net means the firm receives (nets) $0.975 on each dollar of paper sold.

Secured Loans

Short-term loans may be divided into unsecured loans, for which no collateral is put up by the firm, and secured loans. The riskier the loan, the more likely that the lender will require collateral. Therefore, interest rates on secured borrowing are usually greater than interest rates on unsecured borrowing. Any of the firm's assets may be used as collateral: current assets—either financial (marketable securities) or nonfinancial (accounts receivable and inventory)—or long-term assets (plant and equipment). Our discussion of secured lending will be directed toward the more common practice of using accounts receivable and inventory as security.

Lending Agents

As we saw earlier in this chapter, banks often make unsecured loans when the loan looks safe enough. On riskier loans, the bank will require collateral.

Finance companies are specialized lending agents. There are three kinds. Consumer finance companies (such as Household Finance Corporation) lend to consumers for a wide variety of consumer purposes. Sales finance companies specialize in buying installment loan contracts that retailers have made with consumers. They also finance retailers' inventories, for example, those of car dealers. Business finance or commercial finance companies specialize in lending to business firms.

Factoring Receivables

One way the firm can acquire short-term financing is to sell its accounts receivable to a company that specializes in buying this kind of asset. These companies are called *factors,* and this procedure is called *factoring.*[28]

The firm may use factoring in two ways: (1) as a continuous process or (2) on an ad hoc basis. Typically, factoring is a continuous process, but the procedure is similar in both instances and is shown in Figure 10–3. Under a normal factoring arrangement, when the firm receives a credit sales order, it forwards the order to the factor, which performs a credit check. If the factor refuses to accept the order, the firm will refuse to sell the goods on credit. If the factor approves the order, the goods are shipped. Payment is then made to the factor by the customer and is remitted to the firm, less the factor's fees.[29]

While having the customer pay the factor directly is the usual arrangement, some firms fear that the customer may interpret these instructions as an indication the firm is in financial trouble. Also, some customers apparently do not like to have their bill sold to someone else, regardless of the reasons. Consequently, it is not uncommon for the firm to arrange its billing procedures in such a way that the customer does not realize the payment is going directly to the factor.

---

[28]Sometimes these companies are called *old-line factors* to distinguish them from factors that lend to the firm, using receivables as collateral, but that don't buy the receivables outright.

[29]There are variations on this procedure. The firm may request to receive payment from the factor prior to payment by the customer. Under this arrangement, the factor pays the firm the amount of the receivables less (1) the factoring fee, (2) interest on the advance payment, and (3) a reserve the factor sets aside for bad-debt losses. The size of this reserve depends on the factor's opinion of the quality of the receivable, and can range from an 80 percent or so advance of the invoice for high-quality receivables to only a 50 percent advance for lower-quality receivables. The factor owns these receivables and cannot look to the firm to cover any bad-debt losses. The factor is said to have purchased the receivables *without recourse.* When the customer pays for the shipment, the factor remits the reserve to the firm.

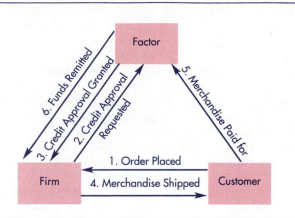

There are two cost components involved in factoring: (1) the commission and (2) the interest on any advance paid to the firm. Depending on how risky the factor feels the receivables are, the commission will usually be between about 1 and 3 percent of the invoice. The interest rate on the advance depends on prevailing interest rate levels and normally ranges from 4 percent to 6 percent higher than the prime bank rate.

Factors perform three functions for the firm: (1) credit checking, (2) financing, and (3) risk bearing. Firms need not use all three services, but to the extent they do, factoring offers a convenient packaging of services. Moreover, once the factoring arrangement has been established, it provides very flexible financing. As sales grow—assuming no deterioration in the quality of receivables—additional financing through factoring is readily available.

There are two principal disadvantages. First is the administrative burden of the constant shuffle of information between factor and firm. Second, there has been a long-standing reluctance to use factoring because it has been perceived as a sign of financial weakness. This perception is apparently changing in view of recent periodic tight credit situations, and more firms now view factoring as a normal means of securing short-term financing.

Pledging Receivables

Pledging receivables refers to using accounts receivable as collateral for a loan, but unlike factoring, the legal ownership of the receivables remains with the firm. In essence, the lender is buying the receivables *with recourse;* if the receivables turn out to be uncollectible, the lender can turn to the firm to make good the loan. Except that receivables are normally paid directly to the firm under this arrangement, the procedures, costs, and good and bad features are much the same as those of factoring.

Inventory Loans

Inventory is another common source of loan collateral. Because it is fairly liquid, which is one of the primary conditions for short-term collateral, banks and finance companies willingly accept most standard types of inventories as collateral. Extremely unusual inventory or perishable inventory will be less acceptable. In

---

- - -

FINANCIAL MANAGEMENT INSIGHTS

The International Aspects of Short–Term Financing

Universal Matchbox Group Ltd. is a leading designer, manufacturer, and marketer of toys in more than 120 countries. It also is a contract manufacturer for other major toy companies. Its stock is traded on the New York Stock Exchange while it has design and manufacturing facilities in several countries. Universal Matchbox earned 21 cents in 1988 after a loss of $3.67 the previous year.

In 1988 net sales increased approximately 14 percent. As a result of the higher sales, accounts receivable increased, as did inventories. This resulted in a higher level of net working capital for the year. Short-term bank borrowings increased significantly in order to provide the higher level of working capital. Of a total of $191 million in liabilities and shareholders' equity, some $82 million was in the form of short-term bank borrowings, and total current liabilities amounted to $127 million.

Universal Matchbox has an international flavor in its working capital approach and short-term financing operations. The company maintains a "syndicated working capital facility" in Hong Kong dollars, U.S. dollars, and British Sterling. This facility was arranged for a three-year period, and the company had a commitment from

The Hongkong and Shanghai Banking Corporation, its principal banker, to renew the arrangement. Any borrowings from this facility carry an interest rate of 1¼ percent above the London or Hong Kong Interbank Offering Rate. Commitment fees are charged at three tenths of one percent of the unused available credit. Some restrictive covenants apply under this arrangement, primarily involving the payment of dividends. Universal Matchbox had to provide security for the facilities, including the pledge of shares owned by Universal in its major subsidiaries.

Universal's subsidiaries in the United States and United Kingdom have agreements, renewable annually, to factor and finance their trade facilities. Under the U.S. factoring agreement, a fee of .875 percent of the gross amount factored is charged, with an interest rate calculated at 1.25 percent over the Singapore Interbank Offered Rate for amounts advanced under the financing agreement. Any advances under this agreement are secured by the factored accounts receivable and are limited to 80 percent of the amount of such receivables. For its United Kingdom operations, the company has a separate factoring agreement with different terms.[30]

[30]This information is based on Universal Matchbox Group, Inc., *Annual Report,* 1988.

obtaining a loan based on inventory, the points of negotiation are what percentage of inventory value the lender will make the loan on, the cost of the loan, and what kind of control the lender expects.

The lender will usually lend from about 40 percent to 90 percent of the value of the inventory, depending on its quality and liquidity. As with any collateral, the lender is concerned with the ease of converting the assets to cash if the loan fails. The percentage loan offered by the lender depends on the answers to such questions as, What can the assets be sold for? How quickly can they be sold? Are they perishable? Because such questions have judgmental answers, the percentage loan offered by competing lenders may vary considerably, and the firm may find it worthwhile to shop around.

The cost of inventory loans has two parts: (1) an interest rate and (2) a service charge. The service charge is imposed because the lender may have substantial costs associated with keeping tabs on the inventory to ensure the loan is indeed backed by some collateral. These costs are directly related to the kind of legal security or control the lender and borrower negotiate.

Banks and finance companies are not equipped physically to keep the inventory themselves. Therefore, they need a system to hold the firm accountable for the inventory. There are two systems, one entrusting the collateral goods to the firm, the other entrusting them to an independent third party.

Borrower entrustments are in the form of either a blanket lien or a trust receipt. A *blanket lien* is an all-inclusive lien that gives the lender recourse to all the firm's inventories. This arrangement will be unsatisfactory from the firm's standpoint if it only wants to pledge a portion of its inventory. Also, it may be unsatisfactory from the lender's standpoint because there is no real control over the inventory. If inventory is reduced because of sales, for example, the collateral is also reduced.

A *trust receipt* is a pledge by the firm that it will keep the identified inventory as collateral for the lender until its sale, at which time the proceeds of the loan will be returned to the lender. This form of entrustment is commonly used where the inventory is easily identifiable, as with cars. Like blanket liens, however, this arrangement offers the lender incomplete control since inventory counts can be, and occasionally are, falsified.

Independent third parties are warehouse storage companies that attest to the physical presence of inventory and control the flow of inventory. A *terminal warehouse* is a public warehouse, where, for a fee, goods are stored. Under a terminal warehouse receipt loan, inventory may be removed from storage only on approval of the lender, providing the lender good control over the loan collateral. There is an unsatisfactory aspect to this arrangement from the firm's standpoint, however. Inventory must be physically moved from the firm's production and/or storage facilities to the warehouse. To alleviate this problem, field warehousing arrangements have been developed.

A *field warehouse* is an arrangement that establishes a warehouse on the firm's property. The warehousing company physically sets off the pledged inventory in an area that can be controlled (this may be done with a fence or by using a temporary building), and the warehousing agent polices this inventory, releasing any or all of it only on directions from the lender.

Other Sources of Short-Term Financing

There are other sources of short-term financing, all of which require negotiation.[31] Private lenders also provide short-term capital, mostly to small businesses. We can classify these lenders into two groups. Personal private lenders include family and friends. Impersonal private lenders include individuals, usually found in larger cities, who make loans to businesses. In this latter group, interest rates are extremely high, and sometimes organized criminal elements are behind the operation.

Some companies obtain short-term financing by persuading customers to make advance payments. Usually, these arrangements are a matter of industry practice.

---

[31]Under certain situations, the firm may obtain special credit from its suppliers by negotiation. One situation is in a financial emergency. In such a crisis, the firm may attempt to get supplier approval to let the firm delay payment without any increase in price of future purchases or diminution of future credit terms. At the extreme, the firm may be negotiating with its suppliers to prevent seizure of the purchased goods.

For example, aircraft manufacturers have traditionally received progress payments from the airline companies as plane construction proceeds.

SUMMARY

- Spontaneous sources of short-term funds are almost automatic in the sense that companies do not usually have to negotiate with the supplier for them.
- Trade credit is the major spontaneous source of funds and results when suppliers "carry" the buyers by accepting deferred payment on sales.
- The major determinants of credit terms are general economic conditions, industry factors, and company factors. The main advantages of trade credit are its ready availability, the flexibility it offers the firm, and its less-restrictive terms.
- The credit terms specify the conditions of the credit sale.
- There are two kinds of costs associated with trade credit. Visible costs are expenses whose dollar value can be readily determined. All other costs are hidden costs.
- The cost of forgoing cash discounts can be quite large.
- The other spontaneous source of short-term funds is accruals, principally involving wages and taxes, which arise because of the practice of paying some continuously occurring liabilities at fixed deferred time intervals.
- The most prominent short-term sources of financing the firm must negotiate is bank loans. Loans are rejected primarily because of a poor credit evaluation.
- Commercial paper is a form of unsecured promissory note issued by the most creditworthy firms. It is a substitute for bank loans for many large firms.
- Collateral comprises assets pledged to the lender in case of loan default. Collateral on short-term loans most frequently consists of either accounts receivable or inventory.

KEY TERMS

accruals, p. 299
commercial paper, p. 308
line of credit, p. 303

prime rate, p. 305
revolving credit agreement, p. 303
trade credit, p. 292

QUESTIONS

10–1. What is the main advantage of using trade notes payable rather than open-account sales? The main disadvantage?

10–2. Even when the firm's credit terms lead to a high annual cost of forgoing the cash discount, many customers still forgo the discount. If we were to survey these customers, what reasons might they give to explain their actions?

10–3. How does stretching the payables affect the cost of trade credit?

10–4. In what sense are accruals a more automatic source of short-term funds than trade credit?

10–5. The McEnally Motorcycle Company operates in an industry where the typical credit terms are 3/10, net 60. Mr. A, a credit analyst with McEnally Motorcycle, thinks that if the company changed its credit terms to 3/10, net 75, the company's sales would increase significantly. Ms. B, another analyst with McEnally Motorcycle, argues that this sales increase would be only temporary and that in the long run the firm could not increase its sales level by changing its credit terms. "Why?" asks A. "Because," says B, ". . . ." Give her answer.

10–6. If credit sales were prohibited, what would probably happen to the overall level of invoice prices? Explain your answer.

10–7. Two firms, X and Y, both buy raw goods from the same supplier, who offers them credit on 2/10, net 30 terms. When X is short of cash, it forgoes the discount and often stretches the payables. When Y is short of cash it borrows for 30 days from the bank at a rate that is usually between 10 percent and 15 percent. X thinks Y foolish to borrow at these rates to take advantage of a 2 percent discount. How would you explain Y's "foolishness" to X?

10–8. Briefly explain the difference between visible and hidden costs of trade credit.

10–9. What main points of analysis will a bank perform on a loan application?

10–10. Explain the reason for including a cleanup clause in a loan agreement.

10–11. Under what conditions would a firm prefer to seek a single loan from a bank rather than a line of credit?

10–12. What effect would the following conditions have on the cost of short-term bank borrowing?
  a. Nominal interest rates decrease.
  b. The bank begins the practice of discounting all loans.
  c. The bank lowers its compensating balance requirement.
  d. Tax rates are increased.

10–13. Explain the advantages and disadvantages to the firm of factoring its receivables.

10–14. Explain the difference between factoring and pledging receivables.

10–15. What types of firms sell commercial paper? Why?

10–16. Under what conditions would a firm prefer to borrow short term from its bank rather than sell commercial paper?

10–17. Commercial paper is a current asset for some firms and a current liability for others. Explain this statement.

10–18. Is it possible for a firm to borrow at less than the prime rate?

DEMONSTRATION PROBLEMS

10–1. Find the visible cost of forgoing the cash discount for terms of 3/30, net 90, assuming the firm stretches payables 30 days.

10–2. Cardinal Transportation, Inc., gets credit terms from its various suppliers that, on average, are net 30. However, as a matter of historical policy, Cardinal settles its payables in 10 days. Assuming that Cardinal's annual purchases are $730,000 and that Cardinal can invest short-term funds at 15 percent a year, what is the annual cost in dollars of continuing this policy rather than paying on the due date?

10–3. Determine the cost of a bank loan given the information shown:

Tax rate	40%
Principal	$200,000
Term	180 days
Quoted interest rate	15%
Compensating balance	10%
Banker's year	360 days

Solutions to Demonstration Problems

10–1. $(3/97)(365/(60 + 30)) = 12.5\%$

10–2. Annual purchases = \$730,000

$$\text{Purchases/day} = \frac{\$730,000}{365} = \$2,000/\text{day}$$

Average payables under current policy = (\$2,000/day)(10 days) = \$20,000
Average payables under pay-on-due-date policy = (\$2,000)(30) = \$60,000
Difference = \$60,000 − \$20,000 = \$40,000
Annual cost of keeping current policy = interest loss = (\$40,000)(.15) = \$6,000

10–3. Interest = (\$200,000)(.15)(180/360) = \$15,000
Compensating balance = (.10)(\$200,000) = \$20,000
$r = (\$15,000/\$180,000)(365/180) = .169$
After-tax $r = (.169)(.60) = 10.14\%$

PROBLEMS

10–1. Determine the annual percentage interest cost of forgoing the cash discount under each of the following terms of sale, assuming the firm pays on the due date.
    a. 2/5, net 30.
    b. 5/2, net 20.
    c. 2/15, net 30.

10–2. DJ Corporation has an annual labor payroll of about \$146 million. DJ currently pays its labor force at the end of each seven-day workweek, but DJ will soon change this policy to one of paying at the end of every two weeks.
    a. How much average annual financing do labor wage accruals currently provide?
    b. How much average annual financing will labor wage accruals provide under the new plan?
    c. How much interest will be saved annually by the change if the annual interest rate is 13 percent?

10–3. Boarsback, a small retail leathercraft store, has periodic cash flow problems that sometimes make it hard for the firm to pay bills from its leather supplier. Over lunch one day, Mr. Goulet, the owner of Boarsback, who is untrained in finance, tells you he has two alternatives when these difficulties arise. He can borrow from a local commercial lending company, or he can forgo the trade discount his supplier offers him. Because of his somewhat-shaky financial position, he would never attempt to stretch the payables for fear the supplier would cease offering trade credit to him.
    Which of the two alternatives available would you recommend to him if the following conditions prevail?

Situation	Cost of Loan from Commercial Lending Company (%)	Credit Terms
A	18	2/15, net 60
B	20	3/10, net 60
C	15	2/10, net 50

10–4. A new firm is considering how best to set up credit terms, and one important feature is how quickly the customers will pay their bills. Three plans have been suggested: Plan A, 2/5, net 30; Plan B, 3/10, net 50; Plan C, 3/10, net 40.

Other things being equal, which plans would encourage speediest customer payment habits? Which would encourage slowest customer payment habits? Explain your answers.

10–5. Brown Company can borrow from its bank at about 13.5 percent per year. Credit terms from Brown's suppliers offer a cash discount of x percent if Brown will pay within five days of invoice receipt. Otherwise, Brown must pay within 60 days of invoice receipt. Find the x that makes Brown indifferent between (1) taking the cash discount and (2) forgoing the discount and paying on the due date.

10–6. A firm receives credit terms of 1/10, net 40, from a supplier. In times of tight money, the firm can either forgo the cash discount or take out a bank loan. If the firm forgoes the cash discount, it will stretch the payables. However, when the firm stretches its payables, a 1 percent penalty interest charge is made for any bill overdue from 1 to 30 days. After 30 days, the supplier would refuse to provide future trade credit. Assuming the firm will be careful not to overstep the 30-day stretch period, which would be financially more attractive, stretching payables 30 days or taking out a bank loan that costs 15 percent on an annual basis?

10–7. Knapper Knickers Company is experiencing some temporary cash flow problems. The company has been refused further short-term loans from financial institutions: thus, Knapper has decided to forgo cash discounts from its clothing suppliers. Knapper is now taking the cash discount. Credit terms from these suppliers are 2/10, net 20. Annual clothing purchases by Knapper are about $200,000.
   a. Determine Knapper's present level of accounts payable to its clothing suppliers.
   b. Determine Knapper's new levels of clothing supplier accounts payable if Knapper pays its clothing supplier payables on the due date.
   c. Repeat (b) and assume that Knapper stretches its clothing supplier payables by 10 days.

10–8. As a matter of policy, Lorenzi Lawn Furniture forgoes the cash discount offered by its major supplier. The due date is 30 days after the discount date, and Lorenzi regularly stretches its payables by 30 days. If the visible cost of forgoing the cash discount (including the stretching) is about 32 percent, how large a cash discount is Lorenzi offered by the supplier?

10–9. Find the interest payment, effective interest rate, and cost of the following bank loans. The loans are discounted, a 10 percent compensating balance is required, and the banker's year is used.

Situation	Principal	Term	Nominal Interest Rate	Firm's Tax Rate
A	$100,000	180 days	0.08	0.5
B	$ 60,000	90 days	0.10	0.4
C	$ 75,000	270 days	0.12	0.46

10–10. A firm takes out a $500,000 loan for 60 days at a nominal interest rate of 8 percent. If the loan is discounted and if a 10 percent compensating balance is required, determine the after-tax cost of the loan if the firm's tax rate is 30 percent. The banker's year is not used.

10–11. A firm is borrowing $100,000 for 90 days from a bank. A 10 percent compensating balance is required, and a loan origination fee of 2 percent of the loan is charged. The loan is discounted, and the bank uses the banker's year. The simple interest rate charged is 16 percent. Determine the effective interest rate the firm is paying.

10–12. Northeast Financial Company has just issued 60-day commercial paper in $10,000 face value denominations. The interest yield on the paper is 16.25 percent. What did investors pay to receive a $10,000 face value amount of this paper?

10–13. Given the following information about an issue of commercial paper, determine its cost:

Maturity	60 days
Net proceeds per dollar of paper sold	98.3¢
Tax rate	38%

10–14. Chemgreen Lawn Service Company is talking to two banks about borrowing $10,000 for 90 days. Carleton State Bank would charge 10 percent simple interest with no discounting of the loan, and would not require Chemgreen to keep a compensating balance. Pringle National Bank would charge 9 percent simple interest, would discount the loan, would require a 10 percent compensating balance, and uses the banker's year to compute interest. Neither bank charges a loan origination fee. Determine which loan is more advantageous to Chemgreen. Show all work.

10–15. A firm wants to acquire a 73-day short-term bank loan. The bank will lend the firm $L at a 10 percent interest rate. The loan will be discounted, and a compensating balance equal to 10 percent of L must be maintained. Find L if the firm wants to net $75,000 cash proceeds when the loan is first taken. The banker's year is not used.

10–16. Allison Sales and Service needs to raise $1 million net in 90 days to finance an expansion of inventory and accounts receivable. The company's analysts are evaluating the merits of obtaining a six-month loan from the bank versus issuing six-month commercial paper. Since the company is financially strong, it will be able to borrow from the bank at the prime rate in effect when the loan is negotiated.

If Allison issues commercial paper, it has decided on a direct placement with a local insurance company to save on issue expenses. Allison's analysts estimate that the net proceeds of the sale will depend on the prime rate prevailing at the time of issue. The following estimates have been prepared:

Prevailing Prime Rate	Probability	Proceeds of Commercial Paper Sale* (per $100 of Paper)	Probability
8%	0.2	$96.85	0.1
		96.75	0.6
		96.60	0.3
8.5%	0.5	$96.60	0.3
		96.00	0.5
		95.80	0.2
9%	0.3	$95.35	0.1
		95.25	0.7
		95.10	0.2

*After issue expenses.

    a. On an expected-value basis, how much commercial paper will Allison be required to issue to receive the needed $1 million net if the prime rate is as follows?
      (1) 8 percent.
      (2) 8.5 percent.
      (3) 9 percent.
    b. Determine the expected interest rate of the commercial paper for all three prime rates.
    c. Under what conditions would the firm prefer to issue commercial paper? To borrow from the bank?

SELECTED REFERENCES

A discussion of the cost components in credit borrowing is contained in:

Hill, Ned C.; William L. Sartoris; and Sue L. Visscher. "The Components of Credit Borrowing Costs." *Journal of Cash Management,* October–November 1983, pp. 56–64.

A discussion of accounts payable as related to shareholder wealth maximization can be found in:

Gentry, James A., and Jesus M. De La Garza. "Monitoring Accounts Payable." *The Financial Review,* November 1990, pp. 559–76.

A summary discussion of the management of short-term liabilities can be found in:

Scherr, Frederick C. *Modern Working Capital Management: Text and Cases.* Englewood Cliffs, N.J.: Prentice Hall, Inc., 1989, Chapter 11.

Long–Term Investments

In these three chapters we investigate how the firm should make its capital budgeting (long-term investment) decisions. As we well know by now, these decisions should be made in light of the goal of the firm. The stockholders have entrusted the firm with their money and expect the firm to invest this money wisely. Therefore, investment decisions should be consistent with the goal of maximizing stockholder wealth.

In fact, a clear and important relationship exists between the valuation process we studied in Part II and the capital budgeting techniques we will study here. In valuation, investors estimate the present value of expected cash flows, adjust these cash flows for the time value of money and for risk, and decide if the asset should be purchased. In capital budgeting, a firm estimates the present value of the expected cash flows from a long-term asset, adjusts these cash flows for the time value of money and for risk, and decides if the asset should be purchased.

In capital budgeting, a firm calculates an investment proposal's net present value (NPV), or the net benefit of the expected cash flows. Accepting projects with positive NPVs has a *direct* impact on the value of the firm and, therefore, on the stockholders' wealth. A firm can increase the value, and the stockholders' welfare, by accepting projects with positive NPVs.

11

Capital Budgeting and Cash Flow Principles

Evaluating Cash Flows

Geothermal Resources International is a small company that has worked to prove the viability of geothermal energy, which uses heat from the earth to produce steam for running turbines and generating electricity.[1] Geothermal plants at the Geysers, north of San Francisco, have been producing for many years and are among the lowest-cost plants Pacific Gas & Electric has.

Geothermal Resources feels that the process has proven itself, and after many years of work it is ready to capitalize on the technology with large-scale investment projects. Several geothermal wells will supply steam to a new power project at Coldwater Creek. The cost to the company will be more than $100 million, with expected annual cash flows of $20 million for a long period of years. The company was also working on a project to develop a geothermal field at a cost of $160 million. The power will be sold to California Edison under a 30-year contract, producing millions of dollars a year in cash flows. Finally, the company sought to acquire Thermal Power Company, which includes a minority interest in the operation that supplies geothermal steam to most of Pacific Gas & Electric's power plants at the already developed Geysers site. The cost of this project was $140 million. The company viewed it as a cash flow acquisition that would provide a revenue stream of millions of dollars annually for many years.

---

[1]See James Cook, "The True Believer," *Forbes*, January 11, 1988, pp. 43–44, and annual reports.

The typical financial manager must identify and evaluate numerous investment alternatives on an ongoing basis. These capital expenditures will provide cash inflows over a period of years. As always, the objective is to choose projects that will most enhance the stockholders' wealth. And as always, the firm faces a risk/return trade-off. Some capital projects may be potentially very lucrative, but they may also carry large risks, in some cases sufficient to bankrupt the firm if the project is unsuccessful.

The capital budgeting process involves several components, including:

- Project development and classification.
- Estimation of cash flows.
- Decision rules.
- Risk considerations.

After considering an overview of capital budgeting and project classification, we will concentrate on cash flows in this chapter, followed by decision rules in Chapter 12 and risk considerations in Chapter 13.

The most important step in the capital budgeting process is the estimation of cash flows. Unfortunately, according to several surveys of executives, it is also the most difficult step because of the problems involved in obtaining accurate estimates of the expected costs and revenues associated with investment proposals.[2] The potential for error is large.

The primary *chapter learning objectives* are:

1. To understand the importance and nature of cash flows as used in capital budgeting decisions.
2. To examine in detail the three parts of a cash flow stream for a typical capital project.

LONG-TERM INVESTMENT IN FIXED ASSETS

What Is Capital Budgeting?

Business firms must regularly evaluate investment opportunities involving *fixed (permanent) assets*. Because these decisions effectively determine a firm's future success or failure, their importance cannot be overstated. Fixed assets are the true earning assets of the firm, directly earning a return for the firm. Remember, current assets do not directly earn a return, except for marketable securities.

capital budgeting process of determining if capital projects should be included in the firm's capital budget

The phrase *capital budgeting* is used repeatedly in this group of chapters. **Capital budgeting** is the process of analyzing and evaluating projects to determine if they should be included in the capital budget.[3] A *capital budgeting project* is a proposed investment in some long-term asset (such as machinery, trucks, or plant) that the firm can make if it chooses. Therefore, when we talk about capital budgeting, or *project analysis,* we are referring to the firm analyzing the economic desirability of the prospective investment.

Capital budgeting projects originate within the firm. Proposals come from several sources, including suggestions by employees about how production can

---

[2]See David F. Scott Jr. and J. William Petty II, "Capital Budgeting Practices in Large American Firms: A Retrospective Analysis and Synthesis," *The Financial Review,* March 1984, pp. 111–23.
[3]The capital budget describes the planned expenditures on fixed assets.

be done more cheaply, marketing information that a new product is desired by customers, the necessity to build plants abroad for competitive reasons, and so forth. Larger firms assign staff from, for example, accounting, marketing, engineering, research and development, and strategic planning to identify and analyze capital expenditures. Generally, a formalized procedure exists to facilitate the identification and analysis of potential capital expenditures.

Classifying Projects

We can categorize long-term investments in various ways, but most fall into two categories:[4]

1. Replacement projects.
2. Expansion projects.

Replacement Projects

Replacement projects are cost-reduction or revenue-maintenance investments that usually add no revenues to the firm; the purpose of the investment is to reduce costs or maintain current operations as equipment wears out. Assets wear out or become outdated, and the firm must decide whether to replace them with new assets. This often involves replacing worn-out equipment necessary to continue profitable production. In such cases, generally, an involved decision-making process is not necessary because the firm must have the assets to continue in business.

- ### Example

Hershey Foods Corporation has traditionally classified replacement projects as *profit maintaining,* meaning that they were intended only to ensure that profits remain constant. Minimal economic, market, and competitive analysis was necessary in these situations.[5] ▪

In other situations, this involves replacing working equipment with newer equipment having lower operating costs. For example, replacing the printing equipment used in the manufacturing of greeting cards with a newer, more efficient machine is a cost-reduction investment. The savings will show up as increased cash flow, but the firm's revenue will not increase.

Some investments both expand income and reduce costs. For example, if the firm is considering replacing an old machine with a new machine of greater capacity, there may be both revenue and cost effects.

Expansion Projects

Projects designed to expand revenue usually (*a*) expand present operations or (*b*) develop new product lines. When a company expands present operations, it adds capacity to existing product lines. For example, a greeting card company

---

[4]Other categories could include safety or environmental projects, a timely topic in today's business world, and miscellaneous projects such as employee recreational facilities, parking lots, and so on.

[5]This point was drawn from Panel Discussions on Corporate Investment, "Capital Budgeting," *Financial Management,* Spring 1989, pp. 10–17.

increases its plant size to provide more card-production capacity. Development of a new product line is also income expansionary, but it requires a new kind of production activity within the firm. If the card company invests in new plant and equipment to produce candles, which the firm has not manufactured previously, this represents new product line development. In either case, the investment is expected to bring additional revenue to the firm.

Project Classification and Forecasting Errors

The accuracy of estimation of cash flows varies according to the type of capital investment. A survey of the cash flow estimation practices of firms (discussed in detail later in the chapter) indicates that cash flows for strict replacement projects are relatively easy to forecast. About 60 percent of the respondents reported forecast errors of 10 percent or less for these cash flows. For expansion projects, however, only 40 percent of respondents attained the same level of accuracy.

Capital Budgeting Decisions and Valuation

Long-term investment (capital budgeting) decisions are valuation problems. All valuation problems require estimation of cash flows and required rates of return, and identification of appropriate decision rules. Recall from Chapter 6 that when we value a common stock, we must:

1. Estimate the cash flows, as in the dividend discount model.
2. Apply a required rate of return or discount rate to the estimated cash flows.
3. Compare the resulting estimate of the value of the stock, or intrinsic value, to the current market price for the stock in deciding if the stock is undervalued or overvalued.

Capital budgeting decisions are directly analogous; in accordance with its goal of shareholder wealth maximization, the firm must perform three tasks in evaluating projects:

1. Estimate the cash flows involved with the project.
2. Estimate a required rate of return or discount rate for the project. As we shall see, this discount rate will be the *cost of capital* and is designated k.[6]
3. Apply a decision rule to determine if an investment is good or bad.

In this chapter, we concern ourselves only with the first element: defining and estimating cash flows. In Chapter 12, we consider decision criteria for making capital budgeting decisions. The fact that cash flows are not usually known with certainty is an unfortunate and important fact of life, but in developing the principles of cash flow estimation, we ignore the uncertainty problem. We'll explore the effect of uncertainty on capital budgeting decisions in Chapter 13. We defer until Chapter 14 a complete discussion of the cost-of-capital concept.

---

[6]The required-rate-of-return concept was explained in Chapter 5.

UNDERSTANDING CASH FLOWS

As explained in Chapter 3, cash flow differs from income statement profits (earnings) in that the latter also includes noncash charges such as depreciation. Cash flows represent *cash* transactions. For any year, for each project being considered:

$$\text{Cash flow}_t = \text{Cash receipts}_t - \text{Cash payments}_t \qquad \text{(11--1)}$$

In most years, cash revenues will exceed cash payments, and there will be a net cash inflow to the firm. In some years (most typically at time of investment, $t = 0$), cash payments will exceed cash receipts, resulting in a cash outflow for the firm. Thus, we have the following cash flow conventions:

> When cash receipts > cash payments, cash flow is positive
> When cash receipts = cash payments, cash flow is zero
> When cash receipts < cash payments, cash flow is negative

Why Use Cash Flows?

It is imperative to understand that in capital budgeting decisions, cash flows, as opposed to accounting income, is the concept used. These two figures are often quite different. Although accounting income certainly plays a prominent role in the life of a firm, cash flows are more important when deciding which projects to invest in.

There are two compelling reasons to evaluate investment opportunities in terms of cash flows rather than accounting earnings.

1. Cash flows are a theoretically better measure of the net economic benefits or costs associated with a prospective project.
2. Use of cash flows minimizes accounting ambiguities.

Regarding the first point, the firm is really interested in estimating the economic value of a project. This value is a function of the economic outflows (costs) and inflows (benefits) the firm will experience if the project is accepted. The firm must pay for a purchased asset with cash, which represents a forgone opportunity to use the cash in other productive ways. Consequently, the firm should measure the future *net* benefits (revenues minus costs) in cash terms also.

If accounting practices were attuned to reporting cash transactions, there would be no problem. But standard financial accounting practices are oriented more toward allocating investment costs across useful economic life than toward placing cash costs at the point of incurrence. Thus, when the firm makes a new investment, traditional accounting procedures spread out the initial investment by (1) capitalizing it over the life of the asset and then (2) reducing future net benefits by subtracting an annual depreciation charge. But this accounting treatment reflects neither the original need for cash at the time of investment nor the actual size of the net cash inflows or outflows in later years.

A second reason why it is better to base an investment analysis on cash flows rather than on earnings pertains to accounting ambiguities in determining earnings. There are many ways to value inventory, allocate costs, and choose a depreciation schedule to calculate earnings, all of which are permissible under generally accepted accounting practices. Thus, different earnings numbers could be developed for the same project, depending on the accounting procedures followed. But only one set of cash flows is associated with the project; the firm pays the initial investment and has a single stream of future cash flows. The cash flow stream has far fewer ambiguities. This more pragmatic reason reinforces the need to use cash flows.

Being Precise about the Cash Flows to Use

The capital budgeting process requires that we estimate the cash flows involved with a particular project. This means that we are concerned with *cash flows,* not accounting profits. It also means that certain other considerations must be taken into account. Capital budgeting has its own procedures and guidelines, which are enumerated below.

1. *Cash flows are measured incrementally.* In evaluating capital projects, it is critical to note that the firm must be concerned only with cash flows directly involved with a particular project—that is, cash inflows and cash outflows that occur because a project is undertaken. The question to be asked is, What cash flows will result for a firm if it accepts a particular project it is considering or if it rejects that project? This is equivalent to identifying a firm's *net change* in total cash flows from undertaking a particular project—that is, we identify all changes in the firm's revenues and costs that would result if the project under consideration was accepted. The terminology used to refer to the *net* cash flows attributable to an investment project is **incremental cash flows.**

    incremental cash flows
    difference in cash flows between two investment alternatives in a replacement decision

    a. With expansion projects, the incremental cash flows are straightforward because they are simply the outflows and inflows associated with the project.

    b. With replacement projects, the incremental cash flows, or *additional* cash flows the firm would receive if it replaces one project with another, are calculated by netting together the cash flows for the two projects.

    ■ *Example*

    As an example of incremental cash flows in a replacement analysis, assume that Craft Corporation is considering replacing an existing packaging machine that generates $3,000,000 of operating cash flows annually with a new machine that generates $4,000,000 of operating cash flows annually. The incremental annual operating cash inflow for Craft is $1,000,000. Other things being equal, its total cash inflows would change by $1 million per year if the existing machine was replaced by the new machine since it could continue to generate $3 million in operating cash flows simply by operating the existing machine. ■

2. *Sunk costs are irrelevant and should be excluded from this analysis.* Sunk costs are costs already made or committed and should not affect the current accept/reject decision. The only relevant costs for a current decision are those that will be made from this point forward if a project is undertaken.

- *Example*

Most consumers are familiar with Wal-Mart Stores, a chain that has ex-perienced rapid growth in the last few years and that continues to add new stores at a rapid rate. Suppose that in 1990 Wal-Mart paid a company that specializes in evaluating possible new store locations $200,000 for analyzing a site for a proposed store in Columbia, South Carolina. Wal-Mart charged off this cost in 1990 but did not build a new store on this location. In 1991 Wal-Mart, once again evaluating the possibility of opening a store on the Columbia site, analyzed the costs and benefits of doing so. Regardless of the decision to build, the $200,000 had already been spent and could not be recovered. Therefore, this cost was not relevant in making the current cap-ital budgeting decision. ■

3. *Frequently, there are opportunity costs that should be included in the investment.* These costs account for the money the firm might have earned had it used its resources differently. Instead, the firm gave up these opportunities by choosing the proposed investment. If, for example, a firm uses some land it owns to store surplus equipment, the company should be aware of what it might have earned by selling or renting the land or using it for some other purpose. If relevant opportunity costs are associated with an investment proposal, they should be included.

   In some situations, an existing piece of equipment may have an estimated salvage value at the end of its useful life in addition to a current salvage value. Such opportunity costs must be included as a negative in the ter-mination cash flows. An example of this situation is shown in Table 11–6.

4. *Cash flows must be measured on an after-tax basis.* Cash flow after tax (CFAT) refers to the specific cash flow the firm receives or pays out after all cash payments, including taxes, have been accounted for. Long-term investment projects last more than one year, and for each year there is an expected cash flow after tax.

$$\text{CFAT}_t = \text{CFBT}_t - \text{Tax}_t \qquad \qquad \textbf{(11–2)}$$

where:

$$\text{CFAT}_t = \text{cash flow after tax in year } t$$
$$\text{CFBT}_t = \text{cash flow before tax in year } t$$
$$\text{Tax}_t = \text{tax in year } t$$

Equation 11–2 is the foundation for cash flow determination. We first de-termine cash flows without tax considerations and then deduct tax charges to arrive at cash flows after tax.

A Brief Primer on Taxes

The tax laws require that we recognize the technical distinction between ordinary income and capital gains.

- *Ordinary income* is income the firm receives mainly from its routine business operations. Ordinary income is taxed at the company's ordinary income tax rate.

- If the firm sells an asset, a part of the sale proceeds may be a *capital gain*. If a capital asset is sold for more than its purchase price, the difference between the sale price and the purchase price is considered a capital gain and must be classified as such.

Until 1986, capital gains were taxed at a lower rate than ordinary income. The Tax Reform Act of 1986 eliminated this differential taxing for corporations, although the terminology and classification of capital gains is retained under the law.[7] Because capital gains are now added to ordinary corporate income and taxed at regular corporate rates, our discussion below will be simplified by taxing all gains at the same rate.

What are the corporate tax rates? Ordinary income is taxed as follows:

1. 15 percent on the first $50,000.
2. 25 percent on the next $25,000.
3. 34 percent on the amount over $75,000 plus a surcharge on amounts up to $335,000.[8]

- The *average tax rate* is defined as the total tax liability divided by taxable income.
- The *marginal tax rate* is the rate at which additional income is taxed, and for taxable income in excess of $335,000, it is 34 percent.

The marginal tax rate is the appropriate tax rate to use in making financial decisions.

THE THREE TYPES OF CASH FLOWS

Three types of cash flows can occur for each investment project:

1. Initial investment.
2. Operating cash flows.
3. Termination cash flows.

- The *initial investment* is the sum of the cash outlays associated with an investment project. These outlays typically, but not always, occur at $t = 0$. Because they are outlays, these cash flows are shown with negative signs.
- *Operating cash flows* are associated with the normal operation of the project after the initial investment, usually from $t = 1$ to the end of the asset's life at $t = n$; although typically positive, negative flows can occur.
- *Termination cash flows* represent the cash flows, if any, the firm receives on disposal of the project at $t = n$. These cash flows are typically positive.

For a number of important reasons, accountants, tax advisors, and managers often think in terms of the *calendar* year, which begins on January 1 and ends

---

[7]Maintaining the distinction will facilitate matters if future tax revisions reinstate differential tax rates for ordinary income and capital gains. A minor charge was made in 1990 for capital gains.

[8]For amounts between $100,000 and $335,000, a business firm must pay, in addition to the above, the lesser of $11,750 or 5 percent of the taxable income in excess of $100,000.

on December 31. However, when analysts are estimating the timing of the cash flows associated with a prospective project, they tend to use what might be called *analysis* time.

In analysis time:

- The project's initial investment is located at time zero ($t = 0$).
- The subsequent operating cash flows are located at periods (years) from $t = 1$ to $t = n$.
- Any termination cash flows are placed at year n.

The time scale we developed in Chapter 4 is a picture of analysis time. The analyst attempts to locate all the project's cash flows on the time scale to capture the most important features of their timing. All cash flows for a given year are assumed to occur at the end of the year.[9] This framework has evolved over the years to reflect an effective balance between excessive detail and oversimplification and, in general, this approach is a very effective way to depict the cash flow patterns of investments.

Table 11–1 shows three examples of cash flows using a time scale, or analysis time.

- Part A shows the standard pattern of cash flows most often observed in a capital budgeting problem. An outflow (negative cash flow) occurs at $t = 0$ when monies are paid to invest in a project; therefore, II (initial investment) is shown as a negative. Operating cash inflows occur in Years 1 through n, the life of the project; furthermore, there is a termination cash flow in Year n when the project is liquidated. The operating cash flows and the termination cash flow usually are positive, although negative amounts can occur.

- Part B shows the cash flow pattern when the initial investment period is prolonged for several years. The construction of a building would be a good example. The initial investment occurs in Years 0, 1, and 2, and in each case represents an outflow of cash. Operating cash flows begin in Year 3 and continue through Year n.

- Part C shows a first year operating cash flow loss, a deferred termination (the project is terminated one year after the last operating year), and a loss in the year of termination (it costs more to haul the old equipment away than the scrap is worth). This example illustrates how cash flow patterns can take numerous forms, both with regard to timing and to sign. In the final analysis, however, the concepts are exactly the same—the amount of each of the three possible types of cash flow must be classified as to timing and sign.

We are now in a position to consider in detail the three types of cash flows for an investment project. We will do so in order.

---

[9]Rarely will a depiction perfectly capture the timing because of the inherent crudeness of the typical time scale, which uses one-year intervals. This will be true particularly when we discuss the timing of working-capital investment and depreciation. Bear in mind then that our simple time scale (or analysis time) framework is only an approximation of reality.

■ *Table 11–1*
Example Cash Flow
Patterns

A. Standard Pattern: II @ t = 0
                    All OCF $\geq$ 0
                        TCF > 0

Year	0	1	2	3	$\cdots$	$n-1$	n
Cash Flow	$-II$	OCF_1	OCF_2	OCF_3	$\cdots$	OCF_{n-1}	$OCF_n + TCF$

In this standard pattern, the initial investment is made at time period 0, the operating cash flows (inflows) occur in subsequent years starting with Year 1 and continuing through Year n, and the project is terminated in Year n, at which time there is a termination cash flow in addition to the regular operating cash flow.

B. Prolonged Initial Investment Period (for Two Years)

Year	0	1	2	3	$\cdots$	$n-1$	n
Cash Flow	$-II$	$-II_1$	$-II_2$	OCF_3	$\cdots$	OCF_{n-1}	$OCF_n + TCF$

In this variation of the standard pattern, an initial investment is made at the time period 0 as before. Additional investment is required in Years 1 and 2. The operating cash flows (inflows) commence in Year 3 and continue through Year n, at which time there also is a termination cash flow.

C. First operating cash flow is negative, project is terminated one year after operating phase has ended, and termination cash flow is negative.

Year	0	1	2	3	$\cdots$	$n-1$	n
Cash Flow	$-II$	$-OCF_1$	OCF_2	OCF_3	$\cdots$	OCF_{n-1}	$-TCF$

In this more complex variation, all of the initial investment occurs at time period 0 as in case A. However, the operating cash flow for the first year is a negative number rather than the normal positive number. The operating cash flows terminate in Year $n-1$, and the project is terminated one year later, with the termination cash flow being a negative.

Key: II = Initial Investment
       OCF = Operating Cash Flow
       TCF = Termination Cash Flow

Initial Investment

The initial investment (net initial cash outflow) is the relevant cash outflow at time zero. It is calculated by netting together all relevant cash inflows at time zero with all relevant cash outflows at time zero (we assume here for simplicity that these cash outflows occur at time zero).[10] Several well-known components are typically incorporated in an analysis of the initial investment, as explained below. In addition, the initial investment may include such costs as software and associated debugging expenses, the implementation of new operating procedures in accounting, purchasing, and so forth.

---

[10]If they occur later, they would be netted against any cash inflows for that later period since cash outflows carry a negative sign.

The three most typical components of initial investment are:

1. Acquisition price (including installation costs).
2. Change in net working capital.
3. Salvage proceeds of old asset being replaced.

It bears emphasizing that these are potential components. An initial investment need not include all of them.

Acquisition Price

An asset's *acquisition price* is its purchase price plus any installation and freight costs. It is typically the largest part of the initial investment, and it provides the basis for tax depreciation. That is, the acquisition price is usually equal to the asset's *depreciable basis*.

Net Working-Capital Change

New investment in long-term assets may often create the need for increased investment in net working capital, which as we learned in Part III is the difference between current assets and current liabilities. Whether increased long-term investment causes increased investment in net working capital depends on the nature of the project. Recall the distinction at the beginning of this chapter between revenue-expansion and cost-reduction projects. If the project expands company revenues, usually there would be an increased need for cash and inventory, and higher levels of accounts receivable. However, if the project is of the cost-reduction type, there should be no increased investment in the firm's cash, inventory, and receivables accounts.

We use net working capital because a part of any change in current assets is offset by a change in those current liabilities (accounts payable, for example) that automatically change when firm revenues expand. We net the change in current assets and current liabilities to obtain the net working-capital change, if any, that occurs during the initial investment phase of the project.[11] We will account for the recovery of any change in net working capital at project termination.

It is also possible for working capital to decrease as a result of new investment in long-term assets. For example, installing a production line that uses just-in-time inventory procedures would decrease the net working capital requirement. In this case, the net working capital change would be subtracted in computing the initial investment.

Salvage Proceeds of Replaced Asset

If a new asset is used to replace an existing asset, an initial-period cash inflow may result from the disposal of the replaced asset. This type of transaction has varying tax implications, which we will illustrate with a set of examples. As you study these examples, it is essential to remember that the tax laws permit the firm to recover the acquisition cost through depreciation charges with no tax liability.

---

[11]There are no tax consequences to compute here; they are handled in the operating cash flow section.

book value
depreciable basis
minus accumulated
depreciation

We will call the original cost (or depreciable basis of an asset for tax purposes) the acquisition price.[12] The **book value** of an asset is the acquisition price minus the accumulated depreciation. The market value of an asset whose present use is terminated is termed the *salvage proceeds*. The book value in any year can be calculated as:[13]

$$\text{Book value} = \text{Depreciable basis} - \text{Accumulated depreciation}^{14}$$

- *Example*

Consider the sale of an old asset that is being replaced. Suppose the following data pertain to the sale of the old asset:

Depreciable basis = acquisition price	$30,000
Accumulated depreciation	20,000
Book value	$10,000

Depending on the relationships between the asset's salvage proceeds and book value, the salvage proceeds may be subject to tax, may not be taxable, or may produce a tax loss. Using the example data, we will illustrate each of these situations.

Case A: Salvage proceeds = book value. If the old asset is sold for $10,000, there is no tax on this sale because there is no taxable income—the firm is merely recovering its unrecovered cost, which is the remaining book value. There is no tax effect on the initial investment because the firm is entitled to recover the remaining book value of an asset either through the remaining depreciation charges scheduled to be taken or through salvage proceeds equal to the remaining book value.

Case B: Salvage proceeds > book value. If the old asset is sold for more than book value, the gain is taxable.[15] Suppose the salvage proceeds are $15,000. The $5,000 difference between the $15,000 salvage value and the $10,000 book value would be taxed at the company's marginal tax rate.

Case C: Salvage proceeds < book value. If the old asset is sold for less than its book value, say $5,000, the loss on the asset is treated as a depreciable income loss.[16] In the example, the book value is $10,000 and the salvage value is $5,000,

---

[12]The acquisition price typically is the depreciable basis.

[13]It is important to distinguish between depreciable personal property—such as machinery—and real estate because tax laws are more complicated on real estate. Technically, this discussion pertains only to personal property assets.

[14]The book value may be increased by capital improvements.

[15]The difference between salvage value and book value is taxed as ordinary income because it represents *recaptured depreciation*. The Internal Revenue Service, arguing that the firm took too much depreciation, taxes the gain over adjusted basis at the ordinary income tax rate. If the old asset is sold for more than the depreciable basis (say, $35,000), the difference ($20,000) between depreciable basis ($30,000) and book value ($10,000) is taxed as ordinary income since it represents recaptured depreciation; the difference between salvage value and depreciable basis ($35,000 − $30,000 = $5,000) is treated as a capital gain, which under the 1986 tax act is taxed as ordinary income.

[16]If the asset is not depreciable or not used in the business, the loss can be used only to offset capital gains.

(Depreciable Basis = $30,000, Book Value = $10,000)

Case	(1) Salvage Value (CFBT)($)	(2) Taxable Income ($)	(3) Tax Rate (%)	(4) Tax($)*	(5) CFAT($)** = (1) − (4)
A	10,000	0	40	0	10,000
B	15,000	5,000	40	2,000	13,000
C	5,000	−5,000	40	−2,000	7,000

*Tax = tax rate × taxable income.
**CFAT = CFBT − tax.

resulting in a loss of $5,000. This leads to a negative taxable income (tax loss) on salvage value of − $5,000. The tax savings would be equal to the product of the tax loss and the marginal tax rate. ■

We can summarize the cash flow treatment of the replaced asset's salvage value by referring to Table 11–2. It shows the taxable income results, determined above, plus the tax calculations using those taxable incomes (for simplicity and ease of calculation, the presumed tax rate is 40 percent) plus the determination of the after-tax cash flow associated with the disposal of the old asset. Remember that it is the CFAT numbers shown along the right-hand side of Table 11–2 that are the main output of the salvage analysis. These CFAT results were obtained by subtracting the tax from the CFBT, where CFBT is simply the salvage value. Notice this uses the cash flow identity, Equation 11–2.

Operating Cash Flows

Determining operating cash flows requires that we calculate cash flows before tax, calculate tax payments, and then net the two to get cash flows after tax. In calculating operating CFAT numbers, a tabular approach is very useful in helping to understand the problem.

■ *Example*

Consider the following calculations associated with Year 6 of an investment project being considered by DorFin Inc.:

Year	(1) Cash Revenues	(2) Cash Operating Expenses	(3) (1) − (2) CFBT	(4) Depreciation	(5) (3) − (4) Taxable Income	(6) T* × (5) Tax	(7) (3) − (6) CFAT
6	$500	$300	$200	$100	$100	$40	$160

*T = tax rate. The example assumes a marginal tax rate, T, of 40%.

This short example illustrates the way operating CFAT numbers are constructed.

1. Cash operating expenses are netted from cash receipts to get CFBT.[17]
2. Depreciation charges (discussed below) are deducted from CFBT to arrive at taxable income.
3. The amount of tax owed is determined by multiplying taxable income base by the firm's tax rate.
4. Subtract the amount of tax from CFBT to get CFAT; that is, CFAT = CFBT − tax. ∎

Operationally, to calculate CFAT numbers we can use a formula that is derived from our basic definition that CFAT = CFBT − tax.[18] It is stated as:

$$CFAT = (CFBT)(1 - T) + (Dep)(T)   \textbf{(11-3)}$$

where:

$$T = \text{tax rate}$$
$$Dep = \text{depreciation expense}$$

Applying Equation 11–3 to the DorFin example above:

$$CFAT = (200)(.6) + (100)(.4) = \$160$$

Equation 11–3 is a quick computational method and, furthermore, directly emphasizes the role that depreciation plays in project cash flow construction. The effect of being able to deduct noncash charges (such as depreciation) for tax purposes is to make taxable income less than CFBT; that is, depreciation deductions shield income from taxation, creating a *tax shield*. The tax shield is equal to the product of the depreciation amount and the tax rate.

Financing Costs Not Included

Look again at the example above. Note in particular that financing costs are not included, in either CFBT or CFAT calculations. Financing costs are payments made to those parties who provide the financing used to buy the project (the initial investment). There are no deductions for interest (debt financing), common dividends (common stock financing), or any other kind of financing in the example. Financing costs are not included in the cash flow analysis because in our approach they are incorporated into the determination of the project's required rate of return. We show how this is done in Chapter 14. But for our purposes here, remember that financing costs are not included in the cash flow analysis.

Taxing Operating Cash Flows

Operating cash flows represent taxable income. In analyzing a project, the analyst must adjust the taxable income at the proper tax rate. For large firms with no tax complications, the 34 percent rate applies.

---

[17]Cash operating expenses are frequently denoted as *fixed* or *variable*. Fixed operating expenses will be unaffected by the project's production levels. On the other hand, variable operating expenses are directly related to the project's production levels.

[18]CFAT = CFBT − Tax
   Tax = (CFBT − Dep)(T)
   CFAT = CFBT − (CFBT − Dep)(T) = (CFBT)(1 − T) + (Dep)(T)

The estimated taxable income for the year will occasionally be negative for a project. If the firm as a whole is profitable, then its taxable income is reduced by the loss on the project.[19] Mechanically, we handle negative taxable incomes exactly like positive taxable incomes, preserving the algebraic sign of the answer.

- *Example*

Assume that CFBT is $100 for a particular year for a proposed project, depreciation is $200, and the firm's tax rate is 40 percent. The project's taxable income for the year will be − $100, and the income tax associated with the project will be − $40. CFAT for the project that year will be $100 − (− $40) = + $140. Notice that, mechanically, we are doing nothing new, but we are careful to preserve the negative sign on taxable income and income tax calculations. ∎

Depreciation Methods

Depreciation charges, *which are not cash flows,* enter into the operating cash flow series because depreciation is deducted from annual operating CFBT to arrive at taxable income. **Depreciation** can be defined as the systematic allocation of an asset's cost over a time period longer than one year. This allocation of historic cost based on accounting principles implies nothing directly about the asset's current market value, which could be rising even as the asset's depreciated value declines over time.

depreciation
systematic allocation of an asset's cost over a period of more than one year

Historically, the two principal types of depreciation schedules are *straight-line* and *accelerated*. Accelerated schedules allow higher depreciation in the earlier years of the project. This decreases taxable income and increases CFATs in the project's early years, with the reverse being true for later years. Since money has time value, this transfer of CFAT from later to early years makes projects more desirable.

The Economic Recovery Tax Act of 1981 dramatically changed the methods of computing depreciation, creating a depreciation system called the *accelerated cost recovery system* (ACRS).[20] The Tax Reform Act of 1986 modified the manner in which the ACRS system is used, creating the **modified accelerated cost recovery system (MACRS),** which is currently used in computing annual depreciation for assets acquired in 1987 or later. This act increased the depreciable lives of most assets, a tax disadvantage to the firm, but allows most depreciable assets to be written off using a more favorable method.

modified accelerated cost recovery system (MACRS)
depreciation system in current use, based on specified class lives and recovery percentages per year

Under the Tax Reform Act of 1986, MACRS involves standard recovery percentages based on accelerated depreciation over specified class lives. A *class life,* or recovery period, is the number of years over which a specific class of assets may be depreciated for tax purposes. As Table 11–3 indicates, these recovery periods range from 3 years up to 20 years.[21] Most equipment is found in the 7-year class life. The actual depreciation percentages shown in Table 11–3 are

---

[19]In evaluating projects, we will assume the firm as a whole is profitable.

[20]The two depreciation systems replaced by the ACRS were called the *general guidelines* and the *asset depreciation range* (ADR). Assets purchased prior to 1981 will still come under those systems, but we will not study them. The new system introduced by the 1981 Act actually referred to *cost recovery* rather than to depreciation; however, because the effects of cost recovery and depreciation are identical, we retain the use of the commonly used term *depreciation*.

[21]This applies to assets other than real property, for which the recovery periods are 27.5 years and 31.5 years.

■ *Table 11–3*
MACRS Class Lives

MACRS Life (Years)	Depreciation Method
3, 5, 7, and 10	200% declining balance
15, 20	150% declining balance
27½ (residential buildings)	Straight-line
31½ (nonresidential buildings)	Straight-line

based on a declining-balance method, with a switch to straight-line depreciation at the optimal point.[22]

Tax legislation limits the amount of depreciation that can be taken in the year an asset is bought or sold, through the use of an *averaging convention*. The **half-year convention** requires that personal property be treated as being placed in service or disposed of at mid-year. The effect is to allow a half-year of depreciation for both the first year and the last year of service relative to what otherwise could be taken under a declining-balance method.[23] The result of the half-year convention is that the number of years of depreciation charges is equal to the asset class life plus 1. For a three-year asset, depreciation must be taken over four years, for a five year asset it must be taken over six years, and so forth.

half-year convention
tax law requirement that property be treated as being placed in service or disposed of at mid-year

■ *Example*

To illustrate the MACRS depreciation system, consider an asset with a cost of $100,000 purchased on January 1, 1989. Assume this asset is classified as a five-year life asset under MACRS, although its economic life could be several years longer.[24] Although the asset may have a salvage value at the end of its economic life, this is not considered when calculating MACRS depreciation—the asset is depreciated to a zero value at the end of its MACRS life. Table 11–4 shows the annual dollar depreciation for the asset, and the following points are noteworthy:

- The asset's cost is recovered over a six-year period because of the half-year convention.
- Because of the half-year convention, the depreciation amount for the first year is only one half of what the 200 percent declining balance would indicate.

[22]The depreciation method allowed for assets classified as 3-year, 5-year, 7-year, and 10-year is the 200 percent declining-balance method, with the 150 percent declining-balance method to be used for assets with 15-year and 20-year lives. Straight-line depreciation applies to real property.

To calculate the MACRS depreciation deduction, take the straight-line depreciation rate and double it for 200 percent declining-balance or multiply it by 1.5 for 150 percent declining-balance. This rate is applied to the undepreciated value (book value) of the asset at the beginning of the year, which is the difference between the asset's historical cost and the depreciation accumulated to the beginning of that year. The half-year convention must be taken into account. Firms may switch over to straight-line depreciation in any year where this method provides a larger deduction than the MACRS percentage.

[23]For real property (e.g., buildings), the *mid-month convention* is used. A half-month of depreciation is allowed for the month an asset is placed in service or disposed of.

[24]Under MACRS, an asset's economic life often varies considerably from the period prescribed for depreciation. In particular, the cash flows for the project may extend years beyond the end of the depreciation period. In capital budgeting, cash flows must be projected over the economic life of the project, not the prescribed depreciation period.

Illustration of MACRS and Straight-Line Depreciation for a $100,000 Asset
with a Five-Year Life   ■ *Table 11–4*

Year	Effective Calculation of Depreciation	Amount of Depreciation	Explanation	Depreciation Rate by Year	Rounded Depreciation Rates
1	$100,000 × 40% × .5	$ 20,000	Half-year convention	20%	20%
2	($100,000 − 20,000)* × 40%	32,000	Double declining balance	32	32
3	($100,000 − 52,000)* × 40%	19,200	Double declining balance	19.2	19
4	($100,000 − 71,200)* × 40%	11,520	Double declining balance	11.52	12
5	$17,280/1.5	11,520	Switch to straight-line	11.52	12
6	$11,520/2	5,760	Straight-line	5.76	5
		$100,000		100%	100%

Straight-Line		
Year		
1	$ 10,000	(Half-year convention)
2	20,000	
3	20,000	
4	20,000	
5	20,000	
6	10,000	(Half-year convention)
	$100,000	

*The second figure in parentheses is the adjusted basis—the first is the original basis.

- In Year 5, the switch is made to straight-line depreciation because the amount of depreciation under this method, $11,520, is greater than what it would be when using the double-declining-balance method, $6,912.[25]
- The full cost of the asset is recovered. ■

For exposition convenience, the MACRS depreciation percentages by year are often rounded. For a five-year recovery period, the effective percentages in Table 11–4 would be rounded to 20 percent, 32 percent, 19 percent, 12 percent, 12 percent, and 5 percent. For a three-year recovery period, the effective percentages are rounded to 33 percent, 45 percent, 15 percent, and 7 percent.

In lieu of MACRS, a firm can choose to use straight-line depreciation for any asset (regardless of asset class). **Straight-line depreciation** allocates an asset's historical cost over its class life using equal annual percentages calculated as 1/(class life). A firm using straight-line depreciation must use the number of years shown for that particular asset class and the half-year convention.

straight-line depreciation
depreciation of an asset based on an equal amount per year

■ *Example*

Assume the same $100,000 asset illustrated above with a life of five years. The normal straight-line depreciation would result in a charge of $20,000 per year.

[25]In Year 5, the adjusted basis is $100,000 − ($71,200 + $11,520) = $17,280. Under the double-declining-balance method, depreciation in Year 5 would be $17,280 × .40 = $6,912. Under straight-line depreciation, one and one-half years remain; therefore, the depreciation charge would be 2/3 × $17,280, or $17,280/1.5, which is $11,520.

Because of the half-year convention, only $10,000 can be taken in the first year, and the remaining $10,000 must be taken in Year 6. The year-by-year depreciation charges are shown in the bottom part of Table 11–4. ■

Summary

Operating cash flows represent the after-tax cash flows associated with a project. The cash flow after tax for a given year is found by netting the cash receipts and cash expenses and allowing for the tax shield generated by depreciation. Repeating Equation 11–3, it can be calculated as

$$CFAT = (CFBT)(1 - T) + (Dep)(T)$$

Termination Cash Flows

The termination cash flows are those associated with the end of the project; that is, termination cash flows are the after-tax cash flows, excluding operating cash inflows, that occur in the final year of the project. They are of two types:

1. Salvage proceeds of the asset.
2. Recovery of net working capital investment.

Salvage Proceeds of the Asset

Despite the Tax Reform Act of 1986, MACRS depreciation procedures in general have shortened the *depreciable lives* of most assets. This means that the normal recovery period is typically less than the asset's useful *economic life*. When an asset's economic life is terminated, there is frequently some value still left in the asset. What we try to do in practice is estimate what the salvage proceeds will be when the project is terminated; that is, we want to estimate the CFAT result of disposing of the asset.

The first step in this analysis is to estimate the sale proceeds of the used asset (net of disposal costs) as of the time $t = n$. This amount represents the cash flow before tax from the salvaging. We then compare the sales proceeds with the asset's depreciable basis to determine the tax liability. If the asset has been depreciated to zero under MACRS, the total sales proceeds represent a gain and are taxable. These calculations are exactly like those performed earlier in the chapter when the sale of a used asset was considered in the project's initial investment phase.[26]

Recovery of Net Working-Capital Investment

Recall that when we were doing a cash flow analysis of the initial investment stage of a revenue expansion project, any required change in net working capital was added (or subtracted) to the initial investment. At project termination, this investment is recovered, or added back. The recovery (add back) is tax free because the tax considerations were accounted for in computing the taxes on cash flows during the period of operating cash flow.

---

[26]It is worth emphasizing that when Year *n* arrives, the *actual* salvage proceeds will probably not equal the *estimated* salvage proceeds we determined here. Or the project may be terminated earlier or later than originally planned. But those possibilities need not bother us now; we can worry about them later. In some situations it is useful to consider a series of alternative salvage dates. Such an analysis leads to *abandonment decision* considerations. However, that analysis is beyond this book's scope.

SIMPLIFIED CFAT WORKSHEETS

We can summarize the CFAT analysis by combining the three parts:

- Initial investment.
- Operating cash flows.
- Termination cash flows.

We use simplified CFAT worksheets that will be extended in Chapter 12 to include economic analysis of the cash flows. We will consider as an example Biotech Labs, which is considering (independently) both an expansion project and a replacement project.

Expansion Projects

Consider a proposed project by Biotech that will expand the firm's revenue—the purchase of some new automated equipment used in the manufacture and packaging of its medical products. Financial data for the project are shown in the top part of Table 11–5 and include:

- An acquisition price of $20,000.
- An estimated life of four years.
- A $2,000 increase in net working capital.
- Salvage value on the new machine in four years of $5,000.
- Cash receipts of $22,000 per year.
- Cash operating expenses starting at $10,000 and increasing by $2,000 per year thereafter.
- Marginal tax rate of 34 percent.

Given these estimates, the complete CFAT stream is determined by using the CFAT worksheet shown in the bottom part of Table 11–5. Notice that the CFAT for the last year is the sum of the $4,436 operating cash flow plus the $5,300 termination cash flow.

In summary, for Biotech's proposed expansion project, we have analyzed the three types of cash flows—the initial investment, the operating cash flows, and the termination cash flows. These cash flows are shown in time scale form in Figure 11–1. Notice that the initial investment in time period zero is shown as a negative, representing an outflow, and the operating cash flows are shown for each year of estimated life of the project. The termination cash flows are also shown for the last year of the project, Year 4, as an additional cash flow to be added to the operating cash flow. Armed with this information, we could make a decision on the desirability of this project using the decision criteria explained in Chapter 12.

Replacement Projects

Suppose Biotech is also considering replacing some of its equipment in order to cut costs. For identification purposes, call the currently owned equipment the *old equipment*, and call the proposed replacement the *new equipment*. The financial data for the project are presented in Part A of Table 11–6.

■ *Table 11–5*
CFAT Worksheet for Biotech's Expansion Project

Revenue-Expansion Project Data:
  Estimated life: 4 years
  Depreciation basis = acquisition price: $20,000
  Use MACRS standard recovery for 3-year class life: half-year convention applies—
    percentages are 33%, 45%, 15%, and 7%
  Increased net working capital: $2,000
  Cash receipts: $22,000 per year
  Cash operating expenses: $10,000 the first year, increasing by $2,000 per year thereafter
  Salvage value in 4 years: $5,000

The Three Types of Cash Flows

I. Initial Investment

Acquisition price	− $20,000
Net working capital increase	− 2,000
Total initial investment = $CFAT_0$	− $22,000

II. Operating Cash Flows

Year	Cash Revenues	−	Cash Expenses	=	CFBT	−	Depreciation[a]	=	Taxable Income	Tax[b]	CFAT = (CFBT − Tax)
1	$22,000		$10,000		$12,000		$6,600		$5,400	$1,836	$10,164
2	22,000		12,000		10,000		9,000		1,000	340	9,660
3	22,000		14,000		8,000		3,000		5,000	1,700	6,300
4	22,000		16,000		6,000		1,400		4,600	1,564	4,436

III. Termination Cash Flows

	CFBT	Tax	CFAT
Salvage	$5,000	$1,700[c]	$3,300
Recovery of net working capital	2,000	0	2,000
			$5,300

Year	Percentage Rate × Cost = Depreciation[a]
1	(0.33)($20,000) = $ 6,600
2	(0.45)($20,000) = 9,000
3	(0.15)($20,000) = 3,000
4	(0.07)($20,000) = 1,400
	$20,000

Note: the percentages used here are rounded from the actual percentages, which are 33.33%, 44.44%, 14.82%, and 7.41%.

---

[a]Depreciation schedule using MACRS three-year recovery period.
[b]$Tax_t = (0.34)(\text{taxable income}_t)$.
[c]$Tax = (0.34)(\$5,000 − 0) = \$1,700$.

■ *Figure 11–1*
Time Scale of Cash Flows for Biotech's Expansion Project

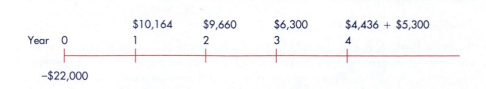

Part A: Replacement Project Data

Old Equipment
  Depreciable basis = acquisition price: $800,000
  Book value: $400,000
  Depreciation: $100,000 per year (until book value = 0)[a]
  Operating costs: $200,000 per year
  Remaining useful life: 4 years
  Current salvage value: $500,000
  Salvage value in 4 years: $200,000

New Equipment
  Acquisition price = depreciable basis: $900,000
  Depreciation method: MACRS straight-line with 3-year recovery period
  Useful life: 4 years
  Operating costs: $100,000 per year
  Salvage value in 4 years: $400,000

Other Data
  Ordinary tax rate: 0.34
  No net working capital increase is necessary if the replacement is made

Part B: Replacement Project CFAT Worksheet

The Three Types of Cash Flows for an Investment Project
I. Initial investment:

Acquisition price of new asset	−$900,000
Proceeds from sale of old asset[500,000 − (0.34)(500,000 − 400,000)]	+$466,000[c]
▲$CFAT_0$[b]	−$434,000

II. Operating cash flows:

Year	(1) ▲CFBT (Operating Cost Savings)	−	(2) ▲Depreciation[a]	=	(3) ▲Taxable Income	(4) ▲Tax = (3) × .34 (T = 0.34)	(5) ▲CFAT = (1) − (4)
1	$100,000		$197,000		−$ 97,000	−$32,980	$132,980
2	100,000		305,000		− 205,000	− 69,700	169,700
3	100,000		35,000		65,000	22,100	77,900
4	100,000		− 37,000		137,000	46,580	53,420

III. Termination cash flows (@ t = 4):

Proceeds from sale of new asset [400,000 − (0.34)(400,000 − 0)]	$264,000[d]
Forgone sale, old asset [200,000 − (0.34)(200,000 − 0)]	− 132,000
▲CFAT	$132,000

Depreciation Schedules for Assets[e]

Year	New	−	Old	=	▲Depreciation
1	$297,000	−	$100,000	=	$197,000
2	405,000	−	100,000	=	305,000
3	135,000	−	100,000	=	35,000
4	63,000	−	100,000	=	− 37,000
	$900,000		$400,000		

[a]Purchased before 1986 and depreciated on a straight-line basis with no half-year convention.

[b]▲ = change in.

[c]Old asset is sold for $100,000 more than book value. This gain is fully taxable at 34%, resulting in a tax of 34% or $34,000. Subtracting this tax of $34,000 from the $500,000 proceeds results in a net gain, CFAT, of $466,000.

[d]The $400,000 is fully taxable because the asset has been fully depreciated. Multiplying the $400,000 by the marginal tax rate of 34% results in a tax of $136,000. Subtracting this amount from the $400,000 proceeds leaves a CFAT of $264,000.

[e]For new asset, based on rounded MACRS depreciation rates of .33, .45, .15, and .07 and a depreciable basis of $900,000. For old asset, straight-line depreciation of $100,000 per year with no half-year convention.

Important points to note in Part A of Table 11–6 are that the book value ($400,000) is less than the current salvage value ($500,000), resulting in Biotech owing taxes on the $100,000 differential, and that the stated salvage value in four years for the old equipment is $200,000. This represents an *opportunity cost* if the new equipment is chosen, and it must be accounted for as such in the termination cash flows. Also note that the new equipment will save $100,000 per year in operating costs.

Given that information, we can construct the CFAT stream for this proposed replacement. In doing this, we net the cash flows between the new and old equipment alternatives; that is, we do an *incremental analysis* between the firm's current situation and what the situation would be if it buys the new equipment. We employ our standard analysis as follows:

$$\blacktriangle CFAT = CFAT \text{ of new} - CFAT \text{ of old} \qquad (11\text{–}4)$$

Since the CFATs are netted, ▲CFAT represents the incremental cash flow the firm would realize by replacing old equipment with new. This netting process is shown in the replacement CFAT worksheet in Part B of Table 11–6.

Each year's cash flows are netted and represent the effect of replacing the old equipment with the new. The initial investment is reduced by salvage proceeds from the immediate sale of the old equipment. As compensation for this new investment, operating cash flows increase by $100,000 per year. Depreciation deductions increase, lowering taxes. Finally, there is an increase in salvage value in the last year if the new equipment is purchased.

Notice that three salvage values are pertinent:

1. The current sale of the old asset.
2. The future sale of the new asset.
3. The loss of future salvage proceeds of the old asset caused by selling it now (the opportunity cost of selling the old equipment now is the $200,000 that could have been received in year four).

In summary, we have analyzed Biotech's proposed replacement project by once again considering the three components of a capital budgeting project. In this case, we did an incremental analysis to recognize the fact that only the change in cash flows is relevant. Figure 11–2 shows the time scale for the cash flows involved in this project. As before, the initial investment is a negative figure in Year 0. Operating cash flows occur in each of the first four years, and a large termination cash flow also occurs in Year 4. Because this is a replacement project, all of these cash flows are incremental, representing the difference between the old asset and the new.

■ *Figure 11–2*
Time Scale of Cash
Flows for Biotech's
Replacement Project

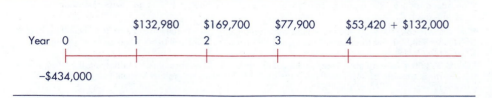

FOCUS ON CORPORATE PRACTICE

Unlike some other areas of managerial finance where accurate information about actual business practices is relatively scarce—for example, short-term financial management—considerable information is available about capital budgeting practices, procedures, and techniques as used by firms. Therefore, we can consider some of this evidence in this chapter and the next.

A recent survey analyzed the issue of how firms actually generate the cash flow information needed to make capital budgeting decisions.[27] It was based on 232 usable responses from the 1985 Fortune 500 listing.

Key points of the survey are the following:

1. A majority of the firms have annual capital budgets of over $100 million, and about two thirds prepare cash flow estimates for over 60 percent of their capital expenditures.

2. A majority of the firms generate *detailed* projections for proposals costing $40,000 or more.

3. Only 10 percent of respondents require detailed cash flow estimates for replacement of equipment, 31 percent require such estimates for facilities expansion, and 25 percent require them for new equipment.

4. Two thirds of the respondents indicated that an individual (or individuals) in the firm was responsible for coordinating/supervising the firm's cash flow estimation process. The positions that oversee the process include staff accountant, financial analyst, treasurer, vice president, department manager, controller, division director, assistant controller, or assistant treasurer.

5. More than two thirds of the respondents said that they have standard company procedures for estimating capital-spending cash flows.

6. The reported average length of the forecasting period was found to be almost identical to the average economic life of the projects.

7. A majority of the respondents used four forecasting methods: management's subjective estimates (90 percent), sensitivity analysis (69 percent), consensus of experts' opinions (67 percent), and computer simulation (52 percent).[28]

8. Seventy-five percent of respondents compare actual to forecasted cash flows. For the three components of cash flows discussed in the chapter, 95 percent make comparisons for initial investments, 68 percent for salvage values, and 100 percent for operating cash flows.

9. Initial investment has the largest percentage (68 percent) of the respondents claiming a 90 percent estimation accuracy, and annual operating cash flows has the smallest percentage (43 percent).

---

[27]This discussion is based on Randolph A. Pohlman, Emmanuel S. Santiago, and F. Lynn Markel, "Cash Flow Estimation Practices of Large Firms," *Financial Management,* Summer 1988, pp. 71–79.

[28]These methods are discussed in Chapter 13.

SUMMARY

- Capital budgeting involves the decision to acquire fixed (permanent) assets. A capital budgeting project is a proposed investment in some long-term asset.
- Most long-term investments can be classified as either expansion projects or replacement projects.
- In either case, the firm must perform three tasks: (1) estimate cash flows, (2) estimate a required rate of return (k), (3) apply a decision rule to determine if an investment proposal is acceptable or not.
- Estimating cash flows is an essential part of evaluating long-term investment proposals. Cash flows are a better measure of the net economic benefits or costs associated with a prospective project and minimize accounting ambiguities.
- The financial analyst must estimate the incremental cash flow after tax (CFAT) associated with the proposed projects:

$$\text{Cash flow after tax} = \text{CFAT} = \text{CFBT} - \text{Tax}$$

or:

$$\text{Cash flow after tax} = (\text{CFBT})(1 - T) + (\text{Dep})(T)$$

- The CFAT stream has three distinct parts: (1) initial investment, (2) operating cash flows, (3) termination cash flows.
- The initial investment is the relevant cash outflow at Time 0 and includes any of the following components: acquisition price, increase in net working capital, opportunity costs, and the salvage proceeds of the old asset being replaced.
- In formulating operating cash flows, we analyzed the half-year convention and the new MACRS method based on specified recovery periods, ranging from 3 to 20 years, for property other than real property.
- Depreciation deductions shield income from taxation, creating a tax shield.
- Termination cash flows associated with the end of the project include (1) salvage proceeds of the asset, (2) recovery of net working-capital investment, and (3) opportunity costs.

KEY TERMS

book value, p. 334
capital budgeting, p. 324
half-year convention, p. 338
incremental cash flows, p. 328

depreciation, p. 337
modified accelerated cost recovery system (MACRS), p. 337
straight-line depreciation, p. 339

QUESTIONS

11–1. In the absence of corporate taxation, write the equation for cash flow after tax in terms of cash receipts, cash payments, and depreciation.

11–2. Explain the distinction between investments for expansion and for replacement.

11–3. What role does opportunity cost play in capital budgeting?

11–4. The Townes Corporation is considering some new investments in a less-developed foreign country. Congress has attempted to encourage such investment by passing a law stating that all revenue earned on projects in that country will be tax exempt; furthermore, there will be no foreign taxes to pay. A junior analyst, who is helping a senior analyst prepare the CFAT schedule for a proposed investment in this foreign country, notices that the senior analyst failed to prepare a depreciation schedule for the investment. The senior analyst says it is not necessary to prepare a depreciation schedule for this particular investment, but the junior analyst does not understand why. Explain the reason.

11–5. A firm usually has some latitude in establishing depreciation schedules for new assets. Describe this latitude. In what sense may we say that a particular depreciation schedule is an optimal schedule?

11–6. An older piece of machinery will soon be sold for scrap. Of what importance is the asset's adjusted basis at the time of scrapping?

11–7. Explain why it is more appropriate to use cash flows than earnings in evaluating investment projects.

11–8. Kemp Industries is in the middle of preparing cash flow estimates for a proposed foundry in Texas. During this preparation phase, several events occur that might make Kemp's analysts want to change some of their cash flow estimates. Evaluate the impact of the following events on each of the three distinct parts of the CFAT schedule (initial investment, operating cash flows, and termination cash flows):

a. Congress raises the ordinary income tax rate.
b. The labor union representing foundry workers wins a new wage contract that will cause labor costs associated with the new venture to increase.
c. Depreciation guidelines are liberalized so that more depreciation can be taken in the early years of an investment.

11–9. Suppose that the firm is considering replacing an old machine with a new one. The firm does not anticipate that any new revenues will be created by the replacement since demand for the product generated by either machine is the same. However, in the CFAT worksheet used in evaluating the proposal, the analyst shows positive CFBTs in the operating cash flow section. What creates operating CFBTs in this situation?

11–10. Can cash flows equal accounting earnings? Why or why not?

11–11. An increase in the corporate tax rate, T, would increase the value of the depreciation tax shield. Would this increase the profitability of a project? Explain your answer.

11–12. Identify the three parts of the CFAT stream.

11–13. Explain the two types of termination cash flows. Why do many assets have a salvage value if they are fully depreciated?

11–14. Explain the concept of incremental cash flows. When would it be correct to state the capital budgeting decision in terms of total cash flows?

11–15. Why are sunk costs not relevant in cash flow analysis?

11–16. What is MACRS? What is a class life?

DEMONSTRATION PROBLEM

11–1. An existing piece of machinery could be sold today for $2,000. Its original basis is $4,000 and its present adjusted basis is zero. Operating costs for the machinery are $5,000 per year. If a new piece of machinery were purchased today to replace the older machinery, the gross investment would be $5,000. The new machinery would be depreciated by using a three-year class life. Estimated salvage value four years from now is $1,000. Operating costs for the new machinery would be half those of the old machinery. The ordinary tax rate is 40 percent. Prepare the ▲CFAT stream for this proposed replacement project.

Solution to Demonstration Problem

11–1.

Initial Investment

Gross investment, new asset	$= -\$5,000$
Sale, old asset $= \$2,000 - (.4)(\$2,000 - 0) =$	$+\$1,200$
$CFAT_0$	$= -\$3,800$

Operating Cash Flows

Year	$\blacktriangle CFBT$	$-$ $\blacktriangle Depreciation$	$= \blacktriangle TI \times .4 =$	$\blacktriangle Tax$	$\blacktriangle CFAT^*$
1	$2,500	(.33)($5,000) =	$ 850	$340	$2,160
2	2,500	(.45)(5,000) =	250	100	2,400
3	2,500	(.15)(5,000) =	1,750	700	1,800
4	2,500	(.07)(5,000) =	2,150	860	1,640

$^*\blacktriangle CFAT = \blacktriangle CFBT - \blacktriangle Tax$

Termination Cash Flows

Sale, new asset $= 1,000 - (.4)(1,000 - 0)$ $=$ $+600$

Summary of CFAT

Year 0	Year 1	Year 2	Year 3	Year 4
$-\$3,800$	$\$2,160$	$\$2,400$	$\$1,800$	$\$2,240$

PROBLEMS

11–1. A freight company has decided to purchase a new light-duty truck for its fleet. Determine the depreciation schedule for this investment under the MACRS method. The recovery period for light-duty trucks under MACRS is five years. Use the half-year convention.

11–2. The original basis of a piece of equipment is $300,000. If the ordinary income tax rate is 40 percent, determine the amount of tax owed and the CFAT the firm will receive from sale of the equipment in the following situations:

Case	Sales Price of Equipment	Adjusted Basis of Equipment
A	$200,000	$ 0
B	200,000	100,000
C	100,000	100,000
D	160,000	180,000
E	50,000	100,000
F	300,000	200,000
G	500,000	50,000

11–3. The original basis of an asset is $30,000, and its life classification is three years. Determine the depreciation schedule using the following methods and the half-year convention:

a. MACRS recovery percentages.

b. Straight-line depreciation.

11–4. The Okleshen Company is investigating the possibility of diversifying into a new product line—the manufacture of carbon-treated zwidgets. Equipment for this investment would cost $10,000 and would last four years; its expected salvage value is zero. The firm expects to sell 10 million zwidgets per year at a price of 80 cents per 1,000. Expected operating costs are 40 cents per 1,000. The ordinary income tax rate is 40 percent. A $3,000 increase in net working capital at the beginning of the project will be required.

Determine the CFAT schedule assuming a three-year class life and MACRS depreciation percentages.

11–5. Prepare the CFAT stream for an investment proposal, given the following information:

Useful life: eight years.

Class life: five years.

Purchase price: $9,700.

Installation and shipping cost: $300.

No old machine is being replaced.

Increase in net working capital: $500.

Estimated salvage value of the machinery in eight years is $1,000.

Depreciation uses MACRS standard recovery percentages.

Tax rate: 40 percent.

Cash receipts: $6,000 per year.

Cash operating expenses (not including taxes): $2,000 per year for the first five years; $4,000 per year for the last three years.

11–6. Bluemart is considering replacing an older piece of equipment with a newer model. The original basis of the older machine when it was first purchased was $50,000; the adjusted basis is zero. Preliminary investigations have indicated that the old equipment could be sold today for $10,000. The cost of the proposed new asset is $80,000, and an increase in net working capital of $2,000 is required if the replacement is made. The ordinary income tax rate is 40 percent. The new asset's class life is 10 years. Determine the initial investment associated with the replacement decision.

11–7. Several years ago, Westford built a plant for $1,800,000. The adjusted basis of this plant is now zero; however, the plant is still serviceable for another five years. Salvage proceeds at the end of this period are estimated at $200,000. Alternatively, the plant could be sold now for $600,000. If the old plant were sold now, a new one would be built for $2,500,000. The new plant would be expected to last five years, at which time its anticipated salvage value would be $500,000. Its depreciation class life is five years also. Straight-line depreciation with a five-year recovery period would be used on this new plant, and the firm would realize operating cost savings of $500,000 per year by replacing the old plant with the new plant. The ordinary tax rate is 40 percent. Determine the replacement CFAT stream.

11–8. The initial investment for a new project is $10,000. Included in that amount is a $1,000 buildup of net working capital. The project will have zero salvage value in five years; straight-line depreciation with a five-year recovery period (and half-year convention) is used; the tax rate is 40 percent; and the operating CFBT stream is as shown below. Determine the CFAT stream for the project.

Year	1	2	3	4	5	6
CFBT	$2,000	$3,000	$4,000	$4,000	$1,000	$1,500

11–9. The DeMong Mining Company is considering the purchase of a new milling machine costing $2,000,000. It would replace an existing machine that is now three years old, cost $1,000,000, is being depreciated on a straight-line basis *with no half-year convention* over a five year period, and has a useful life of six years. The new milling machine has a useful life of three years and has a three-year class life under MACRS. The new machine is expected to increase cash flows by $500,000 per year before taxes. The old machine has a current salvage value of $600,000, and an expected salvage value at the end of its useful life of $20,000. The new machine has an expected salvage value of $300,000 at the end of its useful life. Using an assumed tax rate of 40 percent for DeMong Mining, calculate the initial investment.

11–10. Using the information in 11–9, calculate the expected cash inflow for the new project in Years 1 and 2.

11–11. Using the information in 11–9, calculate the expected cash inflow for the project in Year 3.

11–12. Using the information in 11–9, calculate the expected terminal cash flows for this project.

SELECTED REFERENCES

A discussion of the issues in generating and monitoring cash flows can be found in:

Ang, J. S.; J. S. Chua; and R. Sellers. "Generating Cash Flow Estimates: An Actual Study Using the Dolphin Technique." *Financial Management,* Spring 1979, pp. 64–67.

Logue, Dennis E., and T. Craig Tapley. "Performance Monitoring and the Timing of Cash Flows." *Financial Management,* Autumn 1985, pp. 34–39.

An example of the difference between accounting figures and cash flows can be found in:

Kroll, Yoram. "On the Differences between Accrual Accounting Figures and Cash Flows: The Case of Working Capital." *Financial Management,* Spring 1985, pp. 75–82.

Examples of problems and biases that can occur in capital budgeting can be found in:

Pruitt, Stephen W., and Lawrence J. Gitman. "Capital Budgeting Forecast Biases: Evidence from The Fortune 500." *Financial Management,* Spring 1987, pp. 46–51.

Rappaport, Alfred, and Robert A. Taggart, Jr. "Evaluation of Capital Expenditure Proposals under Inflation." *Financial Management,* Spring 1982, pp. 5–13.

Statman, Meir, and Tyzoon T. Tyebjee. "Optimistic Capital Budgeting Forecasts." *Financial Management,* Autumn 1985, pp. 27–33.

12

Capital Budgeting Techniques

Evaluating a Gold-Mining Investment

Inco. Ltd. of Canada gave Echo Bay Mines an option to develop a gold site it had discovered in the early 1960s at Lupin, south of the Arctic Circle.[1] The option cost Echo about $5 million (Canadian) in cash and future royalties. To build a mine and mill, Echo had to raise $145 million, resulting in a total investment of about $150 million including the option cost.

The cash flows to be received from this project depend on the price of the gold when it is sold. Rev-

enues could range from as little as $45,000,000 a year if the price of gold averaged $300 per ounce to as much as $90,000,000 per year if gold averaged $600 per ounce. Echo Bay conservatively estimated that the mine had nine years of reserves, with output estimated to average 150,000 troy ounces. The net returns on this project also depend on the costs of mining the gold, and if Echo Bay could cut production costs, net returns would increase.

---

[1]See Howard Rudnitsky, "A New Klondike?", *Forbes*, July 16, 1984, pp. 132–133, and *The Value Line Investment Survey*, various issues, and annual reports for Echo Bay Mines.

When evaluating projects, the firm needs to:

1. Estimate the project's cash flows.
2. Establish an appropriate discount rate.
3. Formulate decision criteria consistent with the goal of maximizing shareholder wealth.

In Chapter 11, we investigated how to estimate a project's cash flows. Our concern in this chapter is with formulating criteria for making investment decisions. To accomplish this objective in a straightforward manner, we assume equivalence between the risk of the firm's current projects and the risk of the proposed projects. In Chapter 13, we will examine procedures that allow for risk differentials while considering the discount rate in a general way. Details on how the discount rate is actually estimated will be covered in Chapter 14.

Proper capital budgeting techniques are based soundly on economic theory. A bedrock principle of economics is to take action up to the point where the marginal benefit is equal to the marginal cost. This action is exactly what capital budgeting is all about. The criteria we will discuss in this chapter take into account both the discounted benefits and the discounted costs, allowing us to make proper capital budgeting decisions up to the marginal point.

Primary *chapter learning objectives* are:

1. To understand investment decision logic and the nature of capital budgeting decisions.
2. To analyze the investment decision criteria and learn how they can be used to make the three types of capital budgeting decisions.

CAPITAL BUDGETING DECISIONS

As we know from Chapter 11, capital budgeting is the process of making decisions regarding long-term investments. There are three basic types of capital budgeting decisions:

1. The accept-reject decision.
2. The mutually exclusive choice decision.
3. The capital-rationing decision.

Accept-Reject Decisions

The accept-reject decision is the fundamental decision of whether to invest in a proposed project. Every asset the firm acquires must successfully pass the accept-reject decision. The problem is defined thus: Given a proposed project, should the firm invest in it? If the answer is yes, the firm accepts (invests in) the project; if no, the firm rejects it.

Mutually Exclusive Choice Decisions

The mutually exclusive choice problem is defined thus: Given a set of competing investment alternatives, only one of which may be selected, which should the firm take? If, for example, Georgia-Pacific is considering buying a new pulp machine and there are three competing makes, the three machines represent mutually exclusive alternatives—only one may be selected. This choice among alternatives involves ranking them, and the selection rule will be to choose the acceptable proposal that is ranked best. As we will see, *best* refers back to the goal of the firm.[2]

Capital-Rationing Decisions

Capital rationing refers to the situation where the firm has many acceptable investment projects, but insufficient funds to undertake all of them at once. This amounts to having a budget constraint in one or more time periods during which the firm is choosing investments. The problem is defined thus: Given a set of investment alternatives and budget constraint(s), which group of investments should the firm select? The emphasis here is on the selection of a group of assets. This decision is usually more difficult to resolve than choosing a single alternative.

INVESTMENT DECISION CRITERIA AND THE ACCEPT-REJECT DECISION

We need to establish decision criteria and decision rules that help resolve the three types of capital budgeting decisions posed above. The criteria are evaluation techniques that indicate how attractive an investment is. A decision rule is a way of using the criteria to make decisions.

There are numerous investment decision criteria, but we will study only a few—those most frequently used as well as those consistent with the goal of shareholder wealth maximization. We can divide these criteria into two broad categories related to discounted cash flow (DCF): non-DCF criteria and DCF criteria. *Discounted cash flow* is an important concept that provides the distinction between the two sets of criteria: DCF methods use discounted cash flows, and non–DCF methods do not.

A principal issue here is, Which criteria are good and which are bad? *A criterion is good or bad depending on how well it relates to the firm's goal, which is to maximize shareholder wealth.* The firm should select only those investments the stockholders would make themselves, had they the opportunity to make the decision. What would the stockholders require of any potential investment? As discussed in the chapters on valuation, investors require compensation for their time value of money and for risk exposure. Consequently, any proposed technique should account, at a minimum, for time value and risk considerations. We will do so by focusing on a required rate of return, designated k.

Non–DCF criteria are popular in practice because they are easy to understand and use. Surveys of capital budgeting practices among large firms indicate that they continue to use non–DCF techniques (primarily as a supplementary criterion).[3] Although they can be useful guides, and are often used in conjunction with

---

[2]It is very important to remember that sometimes none of the mutually exclusive alternative proposals should be accepted. If evaluation of all the competing proposals results in a reject decision in each instance, none of the proposals should be accepted.

[3]See Marc Ross, "Capital Budgeting Practices of Twelve Large Manufacturers," *Financial Management,* Winter 1986, p. 22.

DCF methods as supplementary information, non-DCF techniques do not fully conform with the goals of the firm, as do DCF techniques. DCF methods, which also are widely used, according to surveys, do fully conform and should be used in making capital budgeting decisions.

We will examine four decision criteria below, a non-DCF technique followed by three DCF techniques.[4] For each technique, we will also describe its associated accept-reject rule. For ease of exposition, *we will consider only the accept-reject decision here*. Mutually exclusive choice and capital-rationing problems will be deferred to later sections of the chapter.

In presenting the four capital budgeting criteria below, we use the following problem. This example contains a simple and basic set of cash flows, with the initial outflow followed by a set of inflows. Recall from Chapter 11 that we can graph the cash flows on a time scale.

- *Example*

The Wilson Graphics Company is considering investing in a new printer. The complete stream of estimated cash flows after tax (determined by procedures developed in Chapter 11) is:

Year	0	1	2	3	4
CFAT	−$10,000	$4,000	$4,000	$3,000	$3,000

Payback

payback
number of years necessary to recover a project's cost through incremental cash inflows

Payback, the best-known non-DCF criteria, is defined as the number of years it takes to recover a project's net investment through incremental cash inflows. It is the point when the cash inflows equal the net initial investment or cash outflows.

$$\text{Payback} = \text{Number of years to recover initial investment} \qquad \textbf{(12–1)}$$

- *Example*

For the Wilson Graphics example given above, payback is the number of years it takes to recover $10,000:

$$\text{Payback} = 2\tfrac{2}{3} \text{ years}^5$$

The payback is determined by finding the point when the net investment cash outflow has been recovered through the cash inflows. In this example, as we can see in the diagram below, $11,000 will be recovered by the end of Year 3. Since the payback occurs when the net investment of $10,000 is recovered, and $8,000

---

[4] *The average rate of return (ARR),* a non-DCF method, is not discussed with the other techniques. It has several alternative definitions and names. One name and definition is average return on investment, defined as average cash flow after tax divided by initial investment. Alternatively, average annual profits after tax divided by the average investment in the project is called the accounting rate of return. The ARR is compared to a required or minimum acceptable ARR that has been established previously by the decision maker. The ARR, like payback, fails to meet the minimum requirement that any good investment yardstick must: it does not account for the timing of the cash flows. Unlike payback, however, it is a measure of profitability.

[5] This assumes the CFAT accumulates in a steady inflow. Thus, in Year 3, $1,000 flows in every one-third of the year.

is recovered after two years, we need only two thirds of Year 3 (shown as the double bar on the horizontal time line) to recover the remaining $2,000.

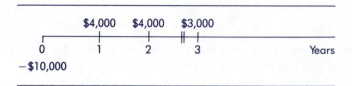

Accept-Reject Decision Rule

To use payback in the accept-reject decision, the firm states a minimum, or required, payback standard. Projects with expected paybacks shorter than this standard are accepted, and projects with expected paybacks longer than this standard are rejected.[6]

> If payback < required payback standard, accept the project
> If payback > required payback standard, reject the project

If the required payback standard is three years, the printer project will be accepted. But if the payback standard is two years, the project will be rejected. Sometimes the standard is related to the project's estimated life. The firm may require, for example, that the project reach payback by no later than one half of its estimated life. In the example, the required payback would be two years, and the project would be rejected.

The payback criterion has three glaring deficiencies:

1. *The payback standard can be determined only subjectively.* It cannot be explicitly specified in terms of the goal of the firm of maximization of shareholder wealth.

2. *The payback does not account for the timing of the cash flows that occur within the payback period.*

■ *Example*

Suppose the estimated CFAT stream in the Wilson Graphics example had been:

t	0	1	2	3	4
CFAT	− $10,000	$6,000	$2,000	$3,000	$3,000

This is the same example as before except that the pre-payback CFATs are rearranged ($2,000 has been shifted from Year 2 to Year 1). The payback is still two and two-thirds years, although this alternative CFAT stream is clearly more desirable because it provides an accelerated CFAT stream. Payback ignores the timing of pre-payback period cash flows. ■

3. *A decision made solely on the basis of payback completely ignores any cash flows that occur after the investment is recouped.*

---

[6]If payback = required payback, the firm is indifferent to whether the project is accepted. In all of the other decision criteria discussed below, a comparable indifference point occurs where the calculated and required criteria values are equal; however, we will concentrate only on the accept-reject portions of the decision rule.

■ *Example*

Suppose the estimated CFAT stream were:

t	0	1	2	3	4
CFAT	$-\$10,000$	$\$4,000$	$\$4,000$	$\$3,000$	$\$10,000$

There is a very large cash inflow in Period 4, after the investment is recovered, but payback remains two and two-thirds years. ■

In summary, payback does not account for the timing of the pre-payback cash flows, and it ignores post-payback cash flows. These deficiencies detract from the accuracy of the payback method of evaluation. Furthermore, payback is not a measure of profitability. Instead, it measures the speed of capital recovery rather than the return on capital.

The advantages of the payback method are that it can be quickly calculated and is easily understood. Also, it provides a kind of rough-and-ready risk screen. Long-lived projects are risky partly because of the difficulty of estimating distant-future cash flows. Requiring fairly short payback periods ensures that the firm will not invest in many extremely risky projects. In this sense, payback reflects a project's *liquidity*. Of course, if the firm wishes to earn high returns, it will have to make some risky investments. Choosing investments on the basis of the payback period may effectively block many profitable but risky opportunities.

Many firms use payback as a supplementary technique to one of the DCF criteria. For small projects, a number of firms "severely simplify their DCF analysis and/or rely primarily on simple payback."[7]

Net Present Value

We now consider three major DCF techniques based on the present value concept of Chapter 4. Each of these techniques is consistent with the goal of the firm—maximizing the value of the stockholders' wealth.

net present value (NPV)
difference between the discounted cash outflows and the discounted cash inflows for an investment project

Net present value (NPV) refers to netting the present value of the initial investment, which is negative, against the present value of the subsequent CFATs, which are usually positive. That is, the NPV for a project is the discounted value of the entire cash flow stream for that project, with the discounting done at the required rate of return, k. NPV is stated in dollars.

The equation for NPV can be written as:[8]

$$\text{NPV} = \sum_{t=1}^{n} \frac{\text{CFAT}_t}{(1 + k)^t} - \text{CFAT}_0 \qquad (12\text{--}2)$$

where:

$$k = \text{the required rate of return}$$

---

[7]Ross, "Capital Budgeting Practices," p. 22.
[8]An alternative expression for Equation 12–2 is:

$$\text{NPV} = \sum_{t=0}^{n} \frac{\text{CFAT}_t}{(1 + k)^t}$$

In this case, CFAT_0 represents the cash outflows and carries a negative sign.

The required rate of return specifies the minimum rate required by the firm's investors—in effect, it is the minimum rate of return that must be earned on a project to leave the firm's market value (or shareholders' wealth) unchanged. It is also called the *discount rate* or *hurdle rate,* and it is discussed in more detail in Chapter 13. Also, the required rate of return can usually be thought of as the firm's marginal cost of capital, a concept discussed in detail in Chapter 14.

■ *Example*

For the Wilson Graphics problem:

$$NPV = -\$10,000 + \frac{\$4,000}{1 + k} + \frac{\$4,000}{(1 + k)^2} + \frac{\$3,000}{(1 + k)^3} + \frac{\$3,000}{(1 + k)^4}$$

Recall that $1/(1 + k)^t$ is the discount factor for k percent in period t. These discount factors could be calculated with a calculator or found in a present value table (see Table C at the end of the text). If $k = 10$ percent, the NPV of the project is found as shown in Table 12–1, where $PVIF_{.10,t}$ refers to the respective annual present value interest factors at 10 percent. ■

The process of calculating NPV for Wilson Graphics is illustrated in Figure 12–1. Here we can see that each cash flow is discounted back to time period zero,

Year	0	1	2	3	4
CFAT	−$10,000	$4,000	$4,000	$3,000	$3,000

$k = .10$

t	CFAT	× $PVIF_{.10,t}$	=	$PV_{.10}$
0	−$10,000	1.000		−$10,000
1	4,000	0.909		3,636
2	4,000	0.826		3,306
3	3,000	0.751		2,253
4	3,000	0.683		2,049
			NPV =	$ 1,244

■ *Table 12–1*
Calculating NPV for the Wilson Graphics Project

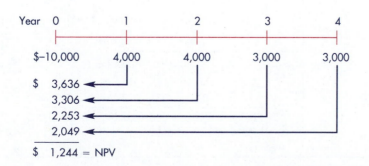

■ *Figure 12–1*
NPV for Wilson Graphics Example at $k = .10$

using the appropriate discount factor for each year, and netted against the initial investment of $10,000.

Accept-Reject Decision Rule

The investment rule is:

> If NPV > 0, accept the project
> If NPV < 0, reject the project

Since the example proposal has NPV > 0, it should be accepted.

Notice that the net present value method explicitly accounts for the timing of the cash flows. If the CFAT stream were accelerated, the project's NPV would increase. If the timing of the CFAT schedule were changed in any way, the project's NPV would reflect the change; therefore, the NPV method meets the requirement of properly accounting for cash flow timing.

Net Present Value Profile

net present value profile
graph of net present value (vertical axis) and the discount rate used for a project (horizontal axis)

It should be obvious, based on our discussion of discounting in Chapter 4, that the NPV for this project would decrease if k were greater than 10 percent, and increase if k were less than 10 percent. The relationship between the NPV for a project and the discount rate used to evaluate the project can be shown graphically with a **net present value profile,** which is a graph of the relationship between the NPV of a project (the vertical axis) and the discount rate (the horizontal axis). Figure 12–2 shows the net present value profile of the Wilson Graphics project.

When k = 10 percent, the example project's NPV = $1,244. Now notice that as k increases, the project's NPV decreases. This is shown in Figure 12–2 by the declining profile of net present value. The net present value profile cuts the horizontal axis of the graph at that discount rate that makes the NPV of the project equal to zero. This point, which is the project's IRR, is discussed below.

■ *Figure 12–2*
Net Present Value
Profile of a
Conventional Project

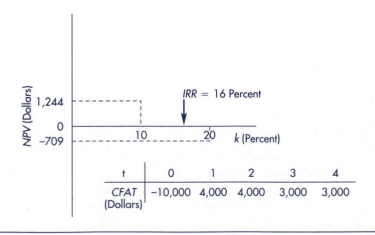

Understanding NPV

It is very important in studying the NPV concept to understand that NPV measures the net dollar gain from a project after full compensation for the time value of money and for the risk involved. Another way of thinking about this is to understand that if a firm accepts a project with an NPV of zero, it expects to be fully compensated for the time value of money and the risk involved but realizes that nothing additional will be added to the value of the stockholders' wealth. The firm is larger as a result of the project, but the value of the stock, and therefore stockholders' wealth, is unchanged.

■ **Example**

Figure 12–3A illustrates the case of NPV = $0 for Wilson Graphics. Assume that the required rate of return for Wilson Graphics is 16 percent. Part A demonstrates that discounting the cash flows at a rate of 16 percent results in an NPV of $0. Did the firm earn anything on its $10,000 investment? Yes! It earned the required rate of return of 16 percent on its investment. To see this, think of the firm's stockholders advancing the firm $10,000 to invest in capital projects. The stockholders require 16 percent per year on their investment. At the end of four years,

---

(A) NPV for Wilson Graphics Example at k = .16

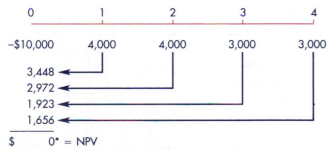

$$\$ \quad 0^* = \text{NPV}$$

*Rounding accounts for the $1 difference.

(B) Ending Values for Cash Flows If Compounded at 16 Percent

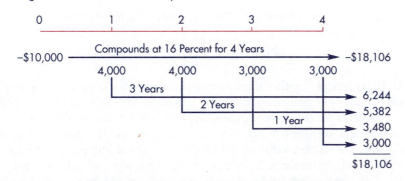

■ *Figure 12–3*
Understanding the NPV Calculation

therefore, they require $(1.16)^4 \times \$10,000 = \$18,106$. In other words, the firm must have available a total of \$18,106 by the end of four years if it is to provide the stockholders with their required rate of return on their initial investment of \$10,000.

Figure 12–3B illustrates the logic of the NPV calculation. If each of the Wilson Graphics cash flows received is reinvested to earn a 16 percent rate of return, the firm will have exactly \$18,106 at the end of four years. The first cash flow compounds for three years, the second for two years, the third for one year, and the final cash flow is received at the terminal date. Although stockholders will have been compensated for their required rate of return or the time value of money and the risk involved, their wealth will not have increased *beyond this required return*. However, if the firm failed to earn the 16 percent required return, stockholders would be worse off for having advanced the \$10,000 because the required return is an opportunity cost. ▪

NPV measures the "goodness" of a project. The larger the NPV, the better the project is. The maximum price a firm should pay for a project is that price at which the NPV is zero. The NPV of a project is zero when the present value of the inflows from a project equals the present value of the cost of that project. NPV, therefore, measures the difference between the maximum price the firm could pay and break even, and the actual price that it must pay. Obviously, the larger this difference the better, other things being equal.

NPV and the Valuation of the Firm

The importance of the NPV method of evaluating prospective investments goes beyond the merits already stated. *The NPV method is logically consistent with the firm's goal of maximizing stockholder wealth, or maximizing stock price.* Recall from Chapter 6 that the current market price of the firm's stock, P_0, is the present value of the expected future dividends:

$$P_0 = \sum_{t=1}^{\infty} \frac{D_t}{(1 + k_e)^t}$$

where:

$$k_e = \text{the investors' required rate of return on equity}$$
$$D_t = \text{the expected dividend in period } t$$

In comparison, the net present value of a proposed investment is:

$$\text{NPV} = \sum_{t=1}^{n} \frac{\text{CFAT}_t}{(1 + k)^t} - \text{CFAT}_0$$

Both processes involve discounting the net cash flows at a required rate of return. The NPV evaluation of a new project is logically tied to the firm's goal of shareholder wealth maximization because NPV is the dollar change in stockholder wealth resulting from an investment project. If a proposed project has NPV > 0, the market value of the firm's stock should be increased by the firm's acceptance of the project. Similarly, if the firm were to accept a project with NPV < 0, the market value of the firm's stock would be expected to decrease.

This also explains why the firm could accept a project with NPV = 0: The firm expects to earn its required rate of return from the project, although there is no expected increase in stock value.

■ *Example*

As a very simplified illustration of this relationship between the NPV evaluation of a new investment proposal and the firm's stock price, consider the Brown Company with 100 shares of stock outstanding. The market price is $10 per share for a total market value of $1,000. If Brown invests in a new project whose NPV = $50, the total market value of the stock would be expected to increase $50 to $1,050, and the stock price would be expected to rise to $10.50 per share. Acceptance of this new project because its NPV > 0 is thus consistent with the firm's goal. ■

Conclusions

The NPV evaluation technique is more than simply a good investment criterion. For accept-reject problems, the NPV always provides theoretically correct decisions, and we will see that for mutually exclusive choice problems, the NPV method is the best decision criterion.

Internal Rate of Return

The **internal rate of return (IRR)** is defined as that *discount rate* that equates the present value of a project's expected cash inflows (which begin in Period 1 or later) with its initial cost or the present value of the outflows. The IRR can be stated as:[9]

internal rate of return (IRR) discount rate that equates the cash inflows of an investment project with its cash outflows

$$CFAT_0 = \sum_{t=1}^{n} \frac{CFAT_t}{(1 + IRR)^t} \qquad (12\text{-}3)$$

Actually, calculating the IRR involves procedures we learned in Chapter 4 in determining discount rates. There are two possibilities:

1. The CFAT inflow stream is a *series of equal payments (an annuity)*. In this case, divide the initial cost by the constant annual operating CFAT to determine a $PVIFA_{k,n}$. Find the closest $PVIFA_{k,n}$ in Table D from the row appropriate to the number of years.

2. The CFAT inflow stream is a *series of unequal payments*. Here a trial-and-error procedure is involved: we pick a discount rate and check to see if the net present value of the project is zero at that discount rate. If not, we continue in an iterative (repeating) fashion until we find such a discount rate.

---

[9]This is equivalent to:

$$\sum_{t=1}^{n} \frac{CFAT_t}{(1 + IRR)^t} - CFAT_0 = 0$$

Example

For the Wilson Graphics example, we wish to solve the following equation for IRR:

$$-\$10{,}000 = \frac{\$4{,}000}{(1 + \text{IRR})} + \frac{\$4{,}000}{(1 + \text{IRR})^2} + \frac{\$3{,}000}{(1 + \text{IRR})^3} + \frac{\$3{,}000}{(1 + \text{IRR})^4}$$

In a trial–and–error approach, it helps to make a good first guess at what IRR is. If the CFAT stream were a constant $4,000 in all four years, the IRR would be approximately 22 percent.[10] Since the CFAT stream tails off to $3,000 per year in the last two years, let us try a slightly lower guess, say 20 percent.

At a 20 percent discount rate, NPV = −$706. Recall from Chapter 4 that as the discount rate decreases, NPV goes up. Since the NPV is negative at 20 percent, we choose a lower discount rate, say 15 percent, which will probably make NPV positive. At a 15 percent discount rate, NPV = $191. We now have a bracket on the IRR (one positive and one negative NPV), and we could interpolate to find IRR, which is approximately 16 percent. ■

In actual practice, of course, the IRR can be easily calculated by computer or calculators with a built-in IRR function. Many firms have computerized capital budgeting programs that automatically generate the IRR as part of the output. For our purposes, spreadsheet programs for personal computers have an IRR function that can easily solve these types of problems.[11]

Accept-Reject Decision Rule

After calculating IRR, which is the return on invested capital, the firm would then compare it with a required rate of return or cost of capital to determine the acceptability of the project.[12] Let k = the required rate of return (or cost of capital) as established by the firm:

If IRR $> k$, accept the project

If IRR $< k$, reject the project

Assuming the cost of capital is 10 percent, the project will be accepted.

The IRR explicitly takes into account the timing of the CFAT stream. Any change in the amount of timing of the cash flows will result in a change in the IRR; therefore, this criterion meets the standard for the minimum requirement of a good investment. Furthermore, like the NPV criterion, the IRR can be related to the firm's objective. If IRR $> k,$ a surplus remains after capital costs. This surplus accrues to the stockholders, increasing the value of the stock. Finally, it directly measures the rate of return on invested capital. Most financial decision

---

[10]If CFAT is $4,000 a year in each of the four years, −$10,000 + $4,000 PVIFA$_{\text{IRR},4}$ = 0. Then solving for PVIFA, PVIFA = $10,000/$4,000 = 2.5 and IRR ≈ 22 percent. If this calculation seems mysterious, review the material in Chapter 4 on determining discount rates.

[11]Using a program such as Lotus 1-2-3® or Quattro®, enter the cash flows for the Wilson Graphics project in one column. The first number, the initial investment of $10,000, is negative, followed by the four cash inflows. For example, if we are using Column A of the spreadsheet, we have now filled cells A1 through A5. In cell A6, we enter @IRR(.20,A1..A5). The .20 is our initial guess, and in this example it is the number we used as our first guess. The computer will solve for the correct IRR, .16.

[12]This required rate of return is sometimes referred to as a project's *hurdle rate,* which is defined in Chapter 13.

makers are accustomed to dealing with rate-of-return concepts, and they find the IRR an understandable and comfortable concept.

Conventional versus Nonconventional Projects

Investment projects may be classified as *conventional* or *nonconventional* based on the pattern of their cash flows (these concepts are discussed in more detail in Appendix 12–A). A conventional project has an initial investment followed only by positive cash flows. If projects are conventional, the IRR method will always give an accept-reject decision that agrees with the NPV method. We can illustrate why by returning to the net present value profile for the Wilson Graphics example shown in Figure 12–2. By definition, the intersection of the net present value profile and the horizontal axis is the project's IRR. Why? Because at $k = $ IRR, the project's NPV = 0, and the horizontal axis represents the zero NPV line. In the example, the IRR = 16 percent.

We can now see why the IRR and NPV methods agree when making an accept-reject decision for conventional projects. The NPV of the project for all costs of capital less than (to the left of) the IRR is positive, indicating the project should be accepted. But similarly, any time the IRR is greater than the cost of capital, the project should be accepted. Thus, when IRR $>k$ in Figure 12–2, the NPV and IRR method both indicate the project should be accepted. Likewise, when IRR $<k$ (as, for example, when $k = 20$ percent), the IRR rule rejects the project; Figure 12–2 shows NPV < 0, and the NPV rule would also reject the project.

The conclusion from considering both NPV and IRR for evaluating projects on an accept-reject basis is that for conventional, independent projects, both methods always give a correct accept-reject decision. The NPV method avoids the potential problem of multiple IRRs that can occur with nonconventional projects. The IRR, on the other hand, appears to have one advantage over NPV: it is easier to understand. Business executives and nontechnical people understand the concept of a rate of return much more readily than the concept of NPV. They may not understand the formal definition of IRR—see Equation 12–3—but they do understand the general meaning; it seems to be a culturally acquired concept, whereas NPV is not.

▪ Example

In a panel discussion on capital budgeting, an executive of Hershey Foods was quoted as saying: "There is a tendency in major Fortune 500 firms to not use NPV. Senior management prefers to use rates of return. I can tell you whether a 10 percent rate of return is good."[13] ▪

Surveys of business decision makers consistently have shown a preference for the use of the IRR despite its problems, actual and potential. A recent survey of capital budgeting practices found that in 7 of 10 studies identifying individual criteria, the IRR was the most favored.[14] As this survey concluded, "Despite the

[13]See Panel Discussions on Corporate Investment, "Capital Budgeting," *Financial Management,* Spring 1989, p. 17.
[14]See David F. Scott, Jr., and J. William Petty III, "Capital Budgeting Practices in Large American Firms: A Retrospective Analysis and Synthesis," *The Financial Review,* March 1984, p. 115.

difficulties associated with the internal rate of return model, as viewed by academics, it is very popular with practitioners."[15]

Problems with the IRR

Unfortunately, problems exist in using the IRR. One of these problems, multiple internal rates of return, is discussed in Appendix 12–A along with a detailed discussion of conventional and nonconventional projects. A nonconventional project is one that has more than one change in sign in the CFAT series.

When a project is nonconventional, the possibility exists that more than one discount rate equates NPV to zero.[16] In some instances nonconventional investments have only one IRR, but verifying this requires a laborious check. And if the check indicates multiple rates of return, finding a straightforward answer to the question of whether to accept or reject is not very likely. To avoid such problems as multiple IRRs, it is preferable to use the NPV method on all accept-reject decisions, whether the project is conventional or nonconventional. The NPV method is unambiguous and straightforward. There is no requirement to check for sign changes or for the possibility of multiple rates.

Profitability Index

profitability index (PI)
present value of the future cash inflows for a project divided by its initial investment

The **profitability index (PI)** is a DCF method similar to NPV. It is defined as the present value of future cash inflows divided by the initial investment:[17]

$$\text{Profitability index} = \text{PI} = \frac{\sum_{t=1}^{n} \text{CFAT}_t/(1 + k)^t}{\text{CFAT}_0} \qquad (12\text{–}4)$$

- **Example**

In the original example problem, if $k = 10\%$:

$$\text{PI} = \frac{\$4,000/1.10 + \$4,000/(1.10)^2 + \$3,000/(1.10)^3 + \$3,000/(1.10)^4}{\$10,000}$$

$$= \frac{\$3,636 + \$3,306 + \$2,253 + \$2,049}{\$10,000} = \frac{\$11,244}{\$10,000} = 1.12$$

Accept-Reject Decision Rule

The decision rule is:

> If PI > 1.0, accept the project
> If PI < 1.0, reject the project[18]

The reference point for PI numbers is 1.0, and for NPV it is 0. If the present value of the inflows is exactly equal to the present value of the outflows, the PI is exactly

---

[15]Ibid., p. 116.

[16]Note that while multiple sign changes are necessary for multiple IRRs, the magnitude of the cash flows also determines their existence.

[17]Since the future cash flows are typically positive, this criterion is also called the *benefit-cost ratio*.

[18]If PI = 0, NPV = 0 and IRR = k.

1.0 and the NPV is exactly 0.0. Since the example project's PI exceeds 1.0, it should be accepted.

The PI of 1.12 in the above example indicates a 12 percent return on the initial investment of $10,000. This means that the project is expected to return the initial investment, $10,000, plus an NPV equal to 12 percent of the initial investment.

Like the NPV and IRR methods, this technique explicitly accounts for the time value of money, which is a minimum requirement of a good investment criterion. It is very closely related to the NPV technique, simply presenting the same information in a different format by providing the dollar amount of present value per dollar invested. That is, it divides the present value of the cash inflows by the present value of the cash outflows, whereas the NPV subtracts the latter from the former.

The PI will always give the same accept-reject decision as the NPV analysis; however, in some mutually exclusive choice problems, the NPV and PI methods will disagree. In those instances, NPV is a better evaluation technique. However, in some capital-rationing situations, PI could be a better evaluation technique than NPV. These points are discussed below.

PI also suffers the same disadvantage as NPV. Many people have no intuitive feel for PI numbers and have difficulty understanding them. Therefore, sometimes it is more difficult for financial analysts (who prepare the investment proposals) to explain to senior executives (who approve financial outlays) why an investment is good just because its PI is greater than 1.

CHOOSING AMONG MUTUALLY EXCLUSIVE PROJECTS

When firms evaluate investment proposals, the first step is to determine if the projects are independent of each other. Our discussion of criteria thus far has assumed that projects are independent of each other—selecting one project does not affect the acceptance or rejection of another project. Except for the IRR problems we discussed, the three DCF criteria (NPV, IRR, and PI) provide good guidance on accept-reject decisions because they account for the time value of money.

We now investigate how the DCF criteria compare in evaluating mutually exclusive projects, where the acceptance of one project precludes the acceptance of another. *When dealing with mutually exclusive projects, financial managers must rank-order projects.* However, NPV and IRR do not always lead to the same ranking. This is in contrast to independent, conventional projects where both criteria lead to the same accept-reject decision.

We contrast NPV and IRR, then NPV and PI. In both comparisons NPV will be shown to be a better technique for evaluating mutually exclusive projects.

Decision Rules

We first must specify the decision rule used with each criterion to pick the best among several mutually exclusive projects.

Net Present Value (NPV)

The decision rule for NPV is to accept the project with the largest positive NPV. If none of the proposals has a positive NPV, none will be accepted.

Internal Rate of Return (IRR)

The decision rule for IRR is to accept that proposal with the largest acceptable IRR, where *acceptable* means greater than the cost of capital, k.[19] If none of the competing proposals has an IRR greater than k, all will be rejected.

Profitability Index (PI)

The decision rule for PI is to take the project with the largest acceptable PI, where an acceptable PI is greater than 1.0. If none of the projects has a PI greater than 1.0, none will be accepted.

NPV versus IRR

Recall that problems can arise with the IRR method when cash flow patterns are nonconventional. In this comparison between the IRR and NPV, we consider only conventional investments. Even for this group of investments, NPV is a better technique for selecting between mutually exclusive choices because, once again, problems can arise with the use of the IRR.

In many instances NPV and IRR will give consistent rankings, but at times conflicts in rankings between the two will occur.

- *Example*

Consider the two mutually exclusive investment proposals, A and B, shown in Table 12–2. At a 9 percent required rate of return the NPV of B is greater than the NPV of A, indicating B is the better project. However, the IRR of A is larger, indicating A is better. ▪

The conflict between NPV and IRR rankings can be shown graphically by comparing net present value profiles for the two investments. Figure 12–4 shows the profiles for Projects A and B on the same graph by relating the NPV for the two projects to the firm's cost of capital. Since both projects are conventional, both have only one IRR.

On the basis of IRR comparisons, A is the better project, but the net present value profile clearly shows that at some required rates of return, A is better and at others B is better. Since the required rate of return is stated to be 9 percent in the example, Project B is definitely better at that rate. If k had been 14 percent, then the NPV method would have pointed to A as a better project. However, the IRR decision is always to take Project A over B since A's IRR is higher. This criterion ignores the fact that different required rates of return affect the competing projects differently.

The point at which the net present value profiles of A and B cross in Figure 12–4 is referred to as the *crossover rate*. As long as k is greater than the crossover rate, both the IRR and NPV methods will result in the same decision for mutually

---

[19]Actually this is a naive IRR decision rule. A more sophisticated IRR rule, called the incremental IRR, can be specified that will surmount the ranking problems this naive IRR will be shown to have. The incremental IRR decision rule can be found in more advanced texts.

t	A	B
0	−$35,000	−$35,000
1	20,000	5,000
2	15,000	10,000
3	10,000	15,000
4	5,000	25,000
NPV (at k = 9%)	$ 7,237	$ 7,297
IRR	20%	16%

■ *Table 12–2*
Data for Two Mutually
Exclusive Investment
Projects

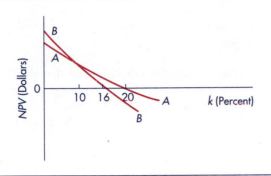

■ *Figure 12–4*
Net Present Value
Profiles of Mutually
Exclusive Projects
A and B

exclusive projects. However, if k is less than the crossover rate, potential conflicts can arise between the two methods.

Conflicts in Rankings

The conflicts in rankings can arise because of:

1. Scale differences.
2. Timing differences.

Scale Differences   Scale differences are differences in the size of initial investment. Such differences can cause a conflict in rankings by the two methods. (Notice, however, that because the initial investments of A and B in the example in Table 12–2 are equal, the conflict is not caused by size disparity. To see the conflict easily, consider the choice between a 100 percent rate of return on a $1 investment versus a 10 percent rate of return on a $100 investment. The IRR would rank the smaller project higher. The IRR ignores the relative sizes of the initial investments, but the NPV does not.

■ *Example*

For a more concrete example, consider mutually exclusive Projects C and D in Table 12–3. Project D costs twice as much as Project C. The IRR for C is 16.7 percent and for D, 14.9 percent, and the respective NPVs are $4,763 and $7,040

■ *Table 12–3*
Two Mutually Exclusive
Projects with Different
Initial Investments

Year	Project C	Project D
0	− $40,000	− $80,000
1	18,000	35,000
2	18,000	35,000
3	18,000	35,000
IRR	.167	.149
NPV @ .10	$ 4,763	$ 7,040

at a k of .10. Therefore, if these two projects are ranked by the IRR criterion, C is preferable, but a ranking on the basis of NPVs would indicate that D is preferred. ■

In thinking about scale differences, keep in mind that the IRR is expressed as a percentage and, therefore, cannot be directly related to the increase in stockholders' wealth. On the other hand, we have seen that NPV is measured in dollars and represents the dollar change in stockholder wealth resulting from investment in a project.

Timing Differences   Timing differences arise when most of the cash flows for one project occur in the early years, whereas for the other project, most occur in the later years. Depending on the exact nature of the timing differences between two projects, they may be ranked differently. Thus, even if the initial investment for two projects is identical, they may be ranked differently by the NPV and IRR if the timing differences are significant enough.

■ *Example*

As an example of the time disparity problem, consider Projects E and F in Table 12–4. The initial investment for each is identical, $50,000. Project E has low CFATs at the beginning and a large CFAT at the end of the project life; Project F shows the opposite. Project E's IRR is 33.3 percent; Project F's, 65 percent. NPV for E is $35,056 and for F is $30,917. Therefore, on the basis of IRRs, Project F is ranked higher, whereas on the basis of NPVs, Project E is ranked higher. ■

The conflict between IRR and NPV rankings in both the scale difference and time disparity examples above results ultimately because the two methods make different assumptions about the *reinvestment rate* (the implicit compounding of interest). The capital budgeting process, by construction, assumes that intermediate cash flows generated by the project during its life are reinvested at some rate of return. These reinvested cash flows will earn some assumed rate of return, known as the *reinvestment rate*.

■ NPV implicitly assumes that all the opportunity cost of funds for all cash flows invested in the intermediate period (Years 1, 2, and 3 in the example) are reinvested at the required rate of return, k.

Year	Project E	Project F
0	– $50,000	– $50,000
1	1,000	70,000
2	20,000	20,000
3	90,000	1,000
IRR	33.3%	65%
NPV @ .10	$35,056	$30,917

■ *Table 12–4*
Two Projects with a
Time Disparity

- The IRR method assumes that the opportunity cost of funds for all such flows is the computed IRR rate for the particular project. This means that for projects with a high IRR, a high reinvestment rate is assumed, and for projects with low IRRs, low reinvestment rates are assumed.

Which assumption is better? Most people are more comfortable with using k as the reinvestment rate. It is related to what the firm pays to acquire capital for that project; furthermore, since k is a marginal rate, it is the rate the next project can be assumed to earn.[20] This seems a more appropriate approximation of the firm's reinvestment rate than the project's IRR. Use of the required rate of return as the opportunity cost of funds is consistent with our objective of shareholder wealth maximization.

Conclusions

When faced with mutually exclusive projects, choose the project with the largest positive NPV because it will have the most beneficial effect on stockholder wealth. It is not surprising that the NPV method is the better criterion—the firm's goal is also formulated in terms of net present value. Furthermore, as we learned earlier, nonconventional projects can present unique difficulties for the IRR method.

NPV versus PI

Because NPV and PI are so closely related, for most mutually exclusive choice problems, NPV and PI will select the same best alternative. However, in some situations it is possible to get a conflict of rankings. Because the NPV method nets the original cost from the present value of the future cash flows whereas the PI method divides the present value of future cash flows by original cost, projects with different initial investments (different scales of investment) may have different rankings under the two evaluation methods.

■ *Example*

Consider the following two mutually exclusive investments.

---

[20]This assumes that the next project has risk equal to that of the firm as a whole.

t	Project G	Project H
0	−$1,000	−$700
1	800	600
2	800	600
$NPV_{.15}$	$ 301	$276
$PI_{.15}$	1.3	1.4

Notice that both projects are acceptable if the required rate of return is 15 percent, as both have NPV > 0 and PI > 1. However, when they are ranked by NPV, G is more attractive, whereas H is better when they are ranked by PI. ∎

When there is a conflict in rankings, which project should the firm accept? The NPV technique is superior, and Project G is a better project (when $k = 0.15$). The reason is the same as that given in the comparison of NPV and IRR techniques. The best project will add the most dollars to stockholder wealth, and this is the one with the highest positive net present value. Since the NPV method by definition always selects the project with highest positive net present value, *the NPV method is better than PI for evaluating mutually exclusive choices.* If there were never any situations where NPV and PI gave conflicting results, the firm could use the PI method, with the assurance it would always choose the correct alternative. But since there are instances in which PI does not select the correct investment, there is some danger to using the PI method.

Unequal Lives

In doing capital budgeting analysis, we encounter many situations where alternative investments have unequal lives—for example, one sort of equipment can be expected to wear out before another. When dealing with independent projects, unequal lives usually present no problem because each project is evaluated on its own on an accept-reject basis. When mutually exclusive projects have unequal lives, however, none of the DCF criteria provide reliable accept-reject decisions unless the projects can be evaluated for equal periods of time (or approximately equal periods—for example a 19-year project and a 20-year project could probably be compared with little harm done because the differential one year would have little effect on the present value calculations).

∎ *Example*

As an example of the unequal-life problem, assume that Masco Products, which manufactures trailers, is considering investing in extrusion-molding equipment as part of its manufacturing process. Masco has identified two good investment alternatives, I and J, which are mutually exclusive. Project I requires an initial investment of $140,000 and has a four-year life; Project J requires an initial investment of $135,000 and has a life of eight years. Annual after-tax cash flows for each project are shown in Table 12–5. The required rate of return (k) is 10 percent.

Table 12–5 indicates that the NPV of project I is $2,716, and the NPV of project J is $3,623. Analysis to this point would indicate that Project J should be chosen over Project I. However, the projects are not comparable because their lives are unequal. Therefore, a valid decision cannot be made at this point. ∎

Year	Project I Cash Flow	Factor	Present Value	Project J Cash Flow	Factor	Present Value
0	−$140,000		−$140,000	−$135,000		−$135,000
1	50,000	.909	45,455	60,000	.909	54,545
2	40,000	.826	33,058	40,000	.826	33,058
3	40,000	.751	30,053	30,000	.751	22,539
4	50,000	.683	34,151	10,000	.683	6,830
5				10,000	.620	6,209
6				10,000	.564	5,645
7				10,000	.513	5,132
8				10,000	.466	4,665
		NPV = $2,716			NPV = $3,623	

■ *Table 12–5*
Analysis of Projects
with Unequal Lives

One method of dealing with the problem of unequal lives is the *replacement chain* approach. To implement this procedure, we create a replacement chain for Project I, the shorter-lived project.

■ *Example*

Masco estimates that at the end of four years, a similar piece of equipment can be purchased for the same cost, $140,000, because manufacturing efficiencies will keep the nominal cost the same (the inflation-adjusted price will be lower). The after-tax cash flows for the following four years (Years 5 through 8) are estimated to match those for Years 1 to 4. ■

Table 12–6 shows the cash flow pattern for this replacement chain technique. The cost of the second project at the end of Year 4 must be discounted back to time period zero, as must the sum of the present values of the cash inflows for Years 5 to 8. (Note that the cost of the second project, $140,000, is netted against the cash inflow at the end of Year 4, $50,000, producing a net negative figure of −$90,000.)

This new analysis indicates that the net present value for Project I is $4,570, which is now larger than the net present value for Project J, which remains $3,623. Thus, Project I should be chosen over Project J on the basis of this replacement chain analysis.[21]

At times it is difficult to work out a replacement chain analysis that will make the life of the shorter project exactly equal to the life of the longer project. For example, if Project A had a life of 9 years and Project B a life of 11 years, the lowest common denominator would be 99 years, and the analysis would become quite tedious. In such cases, the firm either recognizes and accepts a discrepancy

---

[21]Table 12–5 was calculated using a spreadsheet program to demonstrate how such a program can simplify these calculations. Notice that the column labelled *factor* is calculated by adding 1.0 to k, or .10, and raising this sum to the appropriate power. Thus, the second-year factor is $(1.10)^2$, the third-year factor is $(1.10)^3$, and so on. We need only divide each year's cash flow by its respective factor to determine the present value. This is true because the present value factor for year t is calculated as $1/(1+k)^t$. Also note that since all outflows are negative numbers and all inflows are positive numbers, NPV can be calculated by having the spreadsheet sum all the present values in the present value column—in other words, this nets inflows against outflows, producing NPV.

Year	Project I			Project J		
	Cash Flow	Factor	Present Value	Cash Flow	Factor	Present Value
0	−$140,000		−$140,000	−$135,000		−$135,000
1	50,000	.909	45,455	60,000	.909	54,545
2	40,000	.826	33,058	40,000	.826	33,058
3	40,000	.751	30,053	30,000	.751	22,539
4	− 90,000	.683	− 61,471	10,000	.683	6,830
5	50,000	.620	31,046	10,000	.620	6,209
6	40,000	.564	22,579	10,000	.564	5,645
7	40,000	.513	20,526	10,000	.513	5,132
8	50,000	.466	23,325	10,000	.466	4,665
		NPV = $4,570			NPV = $3,623	

(for example, lives of 16 and 18 years), or uses an alternative technique, as explained below. If the discrepancy is small, such as one or two years, or if the discrepancy occurs far in the future when present values are less, it probably will not present a significant problem. After all, estimating the life of various projects is hazardous at best, and often is little more than speculation.

An alternative approach that is often used is the *equivalent annual annuity* (EAA) approach. With this procedure, each project's NPV over its initial life is calculated, and the annuity cash flow that has the same present value as each project's NPV is determined. In other words, we determine an annual cash flow whose discounted value has a present value equivalent to the project's NPV. The project with the higher annuity cash flow stream would be preferred.

To calculate an equivalent annual annuity:

1. Determine the NPV for each project over its initial life.
2. Determine the annuity cash flow with a present value equal to the project's NPV. This is equivalent to finding the annual equal payments that the project would provide if it were an annuity.
3. Choose the project with the highest equivalent annual annuity.

■ *Example*

Using our Masco data, we have determined that the NPV for Project I is $2,716 and for Project J, $3,623. Using these NPVs as PVs on a financial calculator, and $k = 10$ percent, we solve for the payments that, when discounted back over the life of each project, have a present value equal to the NPV for that project. Doing this, Project I has an EAA of $856.82, and Project J has an EAA of $679.11. Thus, we would choose Project I. ■

In the final analysis, these two methods will result in the same decision if comparable assumptions are used in each case. The EAA method has the advantage of quick and easy calculations, while the replacement chain method may be easier to visualize as a concept.

In summary, when we consider mutually exclusive projects, we should use analytical techniques that give the investments comparable lives. Of course, if assets need not be replaced, such special handling is unnecessary. For all independent projects, NPV automatically accounts for timing differences. Selection of independent projects with the largest NPV is a correct decision without regard to the question of unequal lives.

Finally, it should be noted that no asset need be held until it is economically exhausted. An asset may be worth more to someone else than to us, and we may prefer to sell it early. This notion of premature termination of the asset is referred to in the finance literature as the *abandonment decision;* it is discussed in more advanced texts.

CAPITAL RATIONING

Capital rationing refers to the situation where a budget ceiling is imposed on the size of the capital budget, and the firm may not invest in all acceptable projects. This is in contrast to the situation where all independent projects that meet the criterion are accepted regardless of the total number of projects or the amount of funds needed to finance them.

capital rationing
imposition of a budget ceiling on the size of the capital budget, preventing the firm from investing in all acceptable projects

Many firms do not have unlimited funds for investment; they often place an upper limit on the amount of funds that can be used for capital budgeting projects. As the Ameritech executive cited in Chapter 11 stated, "It's simply unrealistic to think that a company can take on every single project with a positive NPV and provide them with the amount of funding their developers desire."[22] Some firms have a policy of financing all capital budgeting projects with internal funds only—they will not raise funds in the financial markets to finance projects. A large company with multiple divisions may impose a budget constraint for capital expenditures on each of its divisions.

Given the set of projects that are acceptable, what subset of projects should the firm select in the face of a budget constraint? In this situation the firm is still trying to maximize stockholders' wealth, so it should invest in that group of projects that collectively has the largest net present value consistent with the imposed budget constraint. To do this, it may be preferable to invest in several smaller projects that better utilize the budget available than in one or more larger projects that leave a significant part of the budget uninvested.

Should we simply use the NPV method, our preferred DCF technique? The answer is, not necessarily. Quoting again from the Ameritech executive: "When ranking by NPV, you have to make sure that you don't pick one project with a return of say $150 over two projects with a return of say $100 each. You have to maximize shareowner wealth."[23]

How do we identify the best group? That is, what investment criterion will identify this group? Let us answer this question with an example. Because of the problems with IRR, we compare only NPV and PI methods.

- *Example*

Consider the investment alternatives shown in Table 12–7. All are acceptable, but because of a $200,000 budget constraint on this period's spending, not all of them

---

[22]See Panel Discussions on Corporate Investment, "Capital Budgeting," p. 16.
[23]Ibid.

■ *Table 12–7*
Capital Rationing
Example ($200,000
Budget Constraint
and *k* = 10 Percent)

Project	Initial Investment ($)	PV of Future Cash Flows* ($)	NPV ($)	PI
A	$ 50,000	$ 65,000	$15,000	1.30
B	50,000	61,000	11,000	1.22
C	50,000	58,000	8,000	1.16
D	50,000	56,000	6,000	1.12
E	100,000	150,000	50,000	1.50
F	100,000	120,000	20,000	1.20

*PV of future cash flows = $\sum\limits^{n} \dfrac{CFAT_t}{(1 + k)^t}$

may be accepted. If projects are ranked separately by NPV and PI, and a cutoff is made when the firm fully expends the $200,000 budget, the resultant rankings and project selections will be as shown in Table 12–8. The NPV method selects Projects E and F, whose combined net present value is $70,000. The PI method selects Projects E, A, and B, with a combined net present value of $76,000. ■

This example shows that the NPV method is not necessarily the best selection criterion under capital rationing. The PI method will select the optimal group of projects provided:

1. The capital rationing is for one time period.
2. The entire budget can be consumed by accepting projects in descending order of PI, down to the budget constraint.

The first condition means there is a budget constraint in only one time period. The second avoids problems that arise when the various combinations of this initial investment do not fit neatly into the investment budget. These instances are referred to as *project indivisibility* problems since fractions of projects may not be purchased, only whole projects. For example, if Project A cost $55,000 rather than $50,000, the proposed selection of the PI method could not be implemented, and any other combination involving Project A would not use up the entire budget but would leave part of its resources unproductive. The NPV method, therefore, would have selected the best group. In general, when indivisibilities exist, there is no way of knowing which of the two methods will work better.[24]

It is important to understand the meaning of our assertion that the PI method is the best method when there is one-period capital rationing with no budget indivisibility problem. It is best because it selects the group of projects with the largest group net present value. That is, the overall goal of attaining the largest positive net present value is still relevant, but we are using a technique other than the NPV method (namely, the PI method) to attain that goal.

Theorists argue that it is unwise for the firm to impose capital rationing on itself. Such a decision leads to suboptimal decisions because the firm is unable to obtain its maximum value. If the firm can raise capital at the required rate of

---

[24]In addition, if the firm must budget in several time periods (multiperiod capital rationing), the problem is best handled by linear programming techniques.

Ranking		NPV Method		PI Method
1		E*		E*
2	Budget line	F*		A*
3		A	Budget line	B*
4		B		F
5		C		C
6		D		D
NPV of group of projects selected		= $70,000		$76,000

■ *Table 12–8*
Project Selection under Capital Rationing

*Project included in budget.

return, it should invest in all projects with positive NPVs. Such a policy should maximize the stockholders' wealth over the long run.

If, in the example in Table 12–7, the firm had accepted all six investments, the NPV of the group would have been $110,000, which is $34,000 more than the group of three projects selected by the PI method. This $34,000 is the opportunity cost of rationing capital. By limiting investment to $200,000, the firm is passing up the chance to increase total stockholders' wealth by an additional $34,000.

FOCUS ON CORPORATE PRACTICE

Surveys indicate that five techniques are widely used by corporations to evaluate investment projects: the non-DCF techniques (payback and average rate of return), and the DCF techniques (net present value, internal rate of return and profitability index).

A 1960 survey of corporate capital budgeting practices indicated that only 30 percent of the surveyed firms used discounted cash flow techniques to evaluate at least some of their projects. A 1978 survey, however, showed that some 86 percent of surveyed firms did so. According to a recent study of capital budgeting practices, post 1969 studies consistently indicate that at least 57 percent of surveyed firms use discounting techniques.[25]

Although the movement toward DCF methods is clear, the extent of use remains in question. A 1978 study indicated that although 86 percent of responding firms used either the NPV or IRR, only 16 percent did so without also using non-DCF models.[26] The use of non-DCF methods as supplementary criteria appears to be widespread.

According to a compilation of the evidence, managements prefer the IRR over the alternatives.[27] Thus, while textbooks (including this one) point out the problems with IRR and recommend NPV, the IRR remains popular in practice.

[25]See David F. Scott, Jr., and J. William Petty II, "Capital Budgeting Practices in Large American Firms: A Retrospective Analysis and Synthesis," *The Financial Review,* March 1984, p. 114.

[26]Lawrence Schall, Gary Sundem, and William Geysbeck, Jr., "Survey of Analysis of Capital Budgeting Methods," *Journal of Finance,* March 1978, pp. 281–87.

[27]Scott and Petty, "Capital Budgeting," pp. 115–16.

According to the evidence, the NPV and PI are the least-popular capital budgeting techniques. Clearly, based on actual practice, non-DCF methods cannot be ignored. And the IRR, despite all its problems and limitations, remains the preferred DCF method.

Capital Budgeting Criteria and the Small Firm

The DCF criteria we have discussed in this chapter are appropriate and correct criteria for firms to use, under the conditions explained, when making capital budgeting decisions. They permit firms to make the correct decisions because they account for the necessary factors, such as the time value of money. Conceptually, these criteria apply to all firms and should be used by all firms because they are directly related to the wealth maximization goal that firms should pursue, whatever their size. From a financial standpoint, all firms are seeking to maximize the owners' wealth.

In practice, small firms often do not use the techniques we have discussed. A very large percentage appear to rely on non-DCF techniques, in particular, the payback method. Quite a few may employ no formal methods at all. Several explanations for this have been advanced.

First, many managers of small firms often lack the expertise to make the necessary calculations. They may not understand the time-value-of-money techniques, they may be unable to calculate an IRR, and so forth. Furthermore, the managerial resources in a small firm may be such that the decision makers are simply unable to take the time necessary to learn and use the more sophisticated methods. In addition, doing so is costly in terms of ongoing time and costs associated with data collection, preparation, and analysis.

A second and perhaps more important reason for the use of such techniques as the payback is that small firms typically must place a very high priority on the flow of cash within the firm. They have limited access to the financial markets, and their alternatives for raising cash are limited. The payback method emphasized the time element of cash flows, showing when the initial investment will be recovered. In the final analysis, this aspect of a capital investment may be more important to a small firm than the level of profitability.

SUMMARY

- Three different capital budgeting problems were identified:

    1. *Accept-reject decision.* Should the firm invest in a new project?
    2. *Mutually exclusive choice decision.* Which of the competing proposals (if any) should the firm invest in?
    3. *Capital-rationing decision.* Without violating the budget constraints, which set of investment proposals should the firm select?

- Four investment criteria were defined. Each can be categorized as either a discounted cash flow (DCF) or a nondiscounted cash flow (non-DCF) technique. Only the DCF techniques explicitly account for the crucial concept of the time value of money.

    1. Non-DCF methods:

$$\text{Payback} = \text{The number of years before the initial investment is recovered}$$

2. DCF methods:

$$\text{Net present value (NPV)} = \sum_{t=1}^{n} \frac{\text{CFAT}_t}{(1 + k)^t} - \text{CFAT}_0$$

$$\text{Internal rate of return (IRR)} = \sum_{t=0}^{n} \frac{\text{CFAT}_t}{(1 + \text{IRR})^t} = 0$$

$$\text{Profitability index (PI)} = \frac{\sum_{t=1}^{n} \dfrac{\text{CFAT}_t}{(1 + k)^t}}{\text{CFAT}_0}$$

- Table 12–9 summarizes the strengths and weaknesses of the four investment criteria.
- Assessing which criteria work best in which situations, we reached these conclusions:

1. *Accept-reject decision.* The NPV and PI methods are the best. They always give correct, identical accept–reject decisions.

2. *Mutually exclusive choice decision.* The NPV technique is best. It always identifies the correct alternative.

3. *Capital-rationing decision.* The PI method is best for simplified, one-period budget problems when the costs of the various alternatives do not create difficulties with completely expending the budget. Multiperiod capital-rationing problems are best resolved with linear programming methods.

KEY TERMS

payback, p. 354
net present value (NPV), p. 356
net present value profile, p. 358

internal rate of return (IRR), p. 361
profitability index (PI), p. 364
capital rationing, p. 373

Method	Good Features	Bad Features	
Payback	Easily understood Easy to calculate Provides a crude risk screen	Doesn't account for the time value of money of pre-payback cash flows Completely ignores post-payback cash flows	**■ Table 12–9** Strengths and Weaknesses of Various Investment Criteria
NPV	Relatively easy to calculate Best method for mutually exclusive ranking problems Tied for best method for accept-reject decision problems (with PI)	Hard to understand May not work well in capital-rationing problems	
IRR	Easily understood Has intuitive economic meaning Works OK on simple accept-reject problems, which are the most common investment problems	Can be tedious to calculate May not work well on nonsimple accept-reject problems (multiple rates), mutually exclusive choices, or capital-rationing problems	
PI	Relatively easy to calculate Best method for one-period capital-rationing problems Tied for best method for accept-reject decision problems (with NPV)	Hard to understand May not work well in some mutually exclusive choice situations	

QUESTIONS

12–1. Under what condition would the internal rate of return and net present value always give a similar accept-reject decision on a project?

12–2. Following are CFAT schedules for several different investments. Indicate which investments are conventional and which are nonconventional.

Year	0	1	2	3	4
A	−$100	$20	$ 40	$ 60	$ 80
B	− 200	− 20	− 100	100	400
C	− 25	10	10	20	30
D	− 100	10	− 10	50	50
E	− 50	10	10	10	20
F	− 85	10	10	− 15	150
G	− 250	75	100	20	− 50

12–3. Suppose that a capital budgeting project has two internal rates of return, 40 percent and 70 percent. Furthermore, the project's NPV at a 50 percent discount rate is +$2,000. Would this project be acceptable if the cost of capital is the following?
a. 60 percent.
b. 20 percent.
c. 75 percent.
Justify your answers.

12–4. What role, if any, does the accept-reject decision play in mutually exclusive investment decisions?

12–5. Given the net present value profiles of three mutually exclusive investments (A, B, and C) shown in the figure below, what investment decision should be made if the cost of capital, *k,* is equal to the following?
a. k_1.
b. k_2.
c. k_3.
d. k_4.

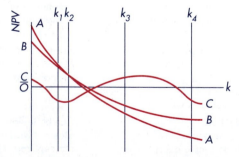

12–6. For most of the firm's investment decisions, net present value is either a superior decision criterion or is at least as good as competing techniques. In what investment situation is the profitability index *better* than net present value? Enumerate the conditions associated with this situation.

12–7. In evaluating a project by the NPV criterion, if NPV > 0, the project is accepted, and if NPV < 0, the project is rejected.

a. What decision should the firm take if NPV = 0? Explain your answer.

b. What is the analogous IRR situation?

12–8. Despite the well-known problems of evaluating projects on the basis of internal rate of return, the ABC Company uses this method exclusively in its capital budgeting analyses. What consequences are likely to arise over time in ABC's fixed-asset investment program, assuming ABC is not in a capital-rationing situation?

12–9. Explain the concept of the required rate of return as it is used in both the IRR and NPV methods.

12–10. What is the proper discount rate to use when time has no value?

12–11. Under what circumstances can conflicts in rankings arise between the NPV and IRR methods?

12–12. How can the problem of unequal lives be treated?

12–13. Describe the problems that can arise with the payback method.

12–14. What is the single most important strength of the NPV method?

12–15. Why should a firm be said to be indifferent to accepting a project with an NPV of $0—after all, nothing is being earned on the project?

12–16. A project with an initial investment of $20,000 has a PI of 25 percent. Does the company expect to earn 25 percent on its investment? What does it expect to earn on an NPV basis?

DEMONSTRATION PROBLEM

12–1. Finn Crab Company is analyzing some new investment proposals. The after-tax cash flows for three of these proposals are shown below.

	Year				
Proposal	0	1	2	3	4
A	−$100	$40	$40	$40	$40
B	− 50	25	25	25	—
C	− 90	20	30	40	50

Compute for each project:

a. Payback.

b. NPV at 20 percent.

c. IRR.

d. PI at 20 percent.

Solution to Demonstration Problem

12–1.

a. Payback$_A$ = 2.5 years
Payback$_B$ = 2 years
Payback$_C$ = 3 years

b. NPV$_A$ = −100 + 40(PVIFA$_{.20,4}$) = −100 + 104 = 4
NPV$_B$ = −50 + 25(PVIFA$_{.20,3}$) = −50 + 53 = 3
NPV$_C$ = −90 + 20(PVIF$_{.20,1}$) + 30(PVIF$_{.20,2}$) + 40(PVIF$_{.20,3}$) + 50(PVIF$_{.20,4}$)
= −90 + 17 + 21 + 23 + 24 = −5

c. A: $-100 + 40(\text{PVIFA}_{\text{IRR},4}) = 0$

$\quad$ $\text{PVIFA}_{\text{IRR},4} = 2.50$

$\quad$ $\text{IRR}_A = 22\%$

$\quad$ B: $-50 + 25\ \text{PVIFA}_{\text{IRR},3} = 0$

$\quad$ $\text{PVIFA}_{\text{IRR},3} = 2.0$

$\quad$ $\text{IRR}_B = 23.375\%$ (exact solution via calculator)

$\quad$ C: By trial and error, $\text{IRR}_C = 17\%$

d. $\text{PI}_A = 104/100 = 1.04$

$\quad$ $\text{PI}_B = 53/50 = 1.06$

$\quad$ $\text{PI}_C = 85/90 = .94$

PROBLEMS

12–1. Calculate the IRR and NPV for Projects X and Y. Assume that $k = .10$.

	0	1	2	3
X	$-\$ 80,000$	$36,000	$36,000	$36,000
Y	$-$ 160,000	70,000	70,000	70,000

12–2. Maris and Company can purchase an asset that costs $1 million and returns $150 thousand per year for 10 years. Both costs and returns are on an after-tax basis. Assuming that the required return is 10 percent, determine the following:

$\quad$ a. Payback.

$\quad$ b. IRR.

$\quad$ c. NPV.

$\quad$ d. PI.

12–3. Fatemi, Inc., must choose between two mutually exclusive projects with the following after-tax net cash flows:

	Year		
Project	0	1	2
A	$-\$3,000$	$ 0	$4,100
B	$-$ 3,000	2,900	800

$\quad$ a. Determine the IRR for each project.

$\quad$ b. What investment decision should Fatemi make with respect to these alternatives if the appropriate discount rate for both projects is 10 percent? Justify your answer.

12–4. Proposals A and B are mutually exclusive investment alternatives that the firm is considering. Their after-tax cash flow patterns are shown below. The cost of capital is 5 percent.

$\quad$ a. Calculate each project's internal rate of return.

$\quad$ b. Calculate each project's net present value.

$\quad$ c. Determine which project the firm should take and justify your choice.

Year	Proposal A ($)	Proposal B ($)
0	−70,500	−70,500
1	40,000	10,000
2	30,000	20,000
3	20,000	30,000
4	10,000	50,000

12–5. Dimkoff Tennisworld, Inc., has 4 million shares of common stock outstanding, currently selling for $15 per share. The company is considering undertaking some new investments that are listed below with their initial investment costs and estimated profitability indices.

Investment Prospect	Initial Investment	PI
A. Expand clothing lines	$2,000,000	1.5
B. Open up European retail outlets	3,000,000	1.6
C. Begin producing aluminum rackets	800,000	2.0
D. Increase tennis ball production	1,500,000	1.4
E. Increase advertising budget	500,000	2.8

    a. Which investment will add the most value to stockholders' wealth? Justify your answer.

    b. What would Dimkoff's theoretical stock price be if the company undertook all five investments?

12–6. An engineer has calculated the profitability index for a new proposal to be 1.025. The proposal's initial investment is $800,000, termination CFAT = 0, and annual operating CFAT = $x per year for five years. Find x if the project's required rate of return is 7 percent.

12–7. Financial analysts for the Kolbe Mining Company are considering the following set of investments, which are *not* mutually exclusive. Each project's initial investment is $100,000.

Proposal	PV of Future CFATs ($)
1	$123,000
2	139,000
3	134,000
4	264,000
5	180,000
6	418,000
7	424,000
8	170,000
9	143,000
10	74,000

    a. Which projects should the firm select if it has unlimited funds?

    b. Which projects should the firm select if it must limit capital expenditures this year to $500,000?

12–8. The OMJ Corporation is currently analyzing a proposed new investment. Additional after-tax cash flows anticipated from the new investment would be $17,000 per year for 20 years. The investment would cost $110,000 (after tax) at the outset, and $k = 0.15$. Evaluate the proposed investment.

12–9. Investment X costs $6,000 (after tax) at time zero. A mutually exclusive alternative, Y, costs $4,000. Investment X has CFATs of $1,800 per year for five years, and Y has CFATs of $1,250 per year for five years.
  a. Compute the IRR and $NPV_{.10}$ for each investment.
  b. Indicate which investment decision should be made with respect to X and Y and why.

12–10. As the financial analyst for the Ozark Can Company, you have been requested to evaluate the following prospective investments, which are *not* mutually exclusive. The company's cost of capital is 8 percent.

Project	Description
I	Replace data processing equipment. Cost $300,000. Expected life six years. Expected CFAT, $72,680 per year.
II	Install safety program. Cost, $100,000. Expected life, three years. Expected CFAT,, $46,566 per year.
III	Develop nonpolluting container. Cost $100,000. Expected life, five years. Expected CFAT, $27,047 per year.
IV	Develop plastic can. Cost $200,000. Expected life, four years. Expected CFAT, $69,444 per year.
V	Convert to metric system. Cost $200,000. Expected life, seven years. Expected CFAT, $36,496 per year.
VI	Add 6,000 square feet of manufacturing space. Cost $300,000. Expected life, eight years. Expected CFAT, $57,421 per year.

  a. Which projects would you recommend if the company has unlimited funds? Note: Round off present values to nearest thousands of dollars here and in (b). What is their total net present value?
  b. Which projects would you recommend if the company must limit capital expenditures this year to $600,000? What is their total net present value?
  c. How much do the firm's stockholders lose from the capital-rationing constraint?

SELECTED REFERENCES

Actual capital budgeting practices are discussed in:

Brick, Ivan E., and Daniel G. Weaver. "A Comparison of Capital Budgeting Techniques in Identifying Profitable Investments." *Financial Management,* Winter 1984, pp. 29–39.

Gurnani, C. "Capital Budgeting: Theory and Practice." *Engineering Economist,* Fall 1984, pp. 19–46.

Ross, Marc. "Capital Budgeting Practices of Twelve Large Manufacturers." *Financial Management,* Winter 1986, pp. 15–22.

Scott, Jr., D. F., and J. W. Petty. "Capital Budgeting Practices in Large American Firms: A Retrospective Analysis and Synthesis." *The Financial Review,* May 1984, pp. 111–23.

The IRR is discussed in:

Dorfman, Robert. "The Meaning of the Internal Rate of Return." *Journal of Finance,* December 1981, pp. 1010–23.

Emery, Gary W. "Some Guidelines for Evaluating Capital Investment Alternatives with Unequal Lives." *Financial Management,* Spring 1982, pp. 15–19.

The payback is discussed in:

Narayanan, M. P. "Observability and the Payback Criterion." *Journal of Business,* July 1985, pp. 309–23.

Capital budgeting under inflation is discussed in:

Mehta, Dileep R.; Michael D. Curley; and Hung-Gay Fung. "Inflation, Cost of Capital and Capital Budgeting Procedures." *Financial Management,* Winter 1984, pp. 48–54.

Rappaport, Alfred, and Robert A. Taggart, Jr. "Evaluation of Capital Expenditure Proposals under Inflation." *Financial Management,* Spring 1982, pp. 5–13.

APPENDIX 12–A   CONVENTIONAL AND NONCONVENTIONAL CFATS AND MULTIPLE IRRs

Conventional and Nonconventional Investments

The IRR may give unreliable investment decision signals if the cash flow stream is somewhat unusual. We can envision two different types of project cash flow streams: *conventional* and *nonconventional*.

Conventional patterns have cash outflows early in the life of the project, followed by a series of cash inflows in subsequent years. If we made a series out of the signs of the CFAT stream we would have a series composed of negative signs followed by positive signs. If there were an initial investment followed by a stream of expected cash inflows beginning in Year 1 and ending in Year 4, this series of signs would be − + + + +. If the investment required an initial outlay in Time 0 and a further net outlay in Time 1 followed by expected net cash inflows for three years, the series of signs would look like − − + + +. These two conventional series have two things in common: both have net cash outlays in the initial time periods followed by net cash inflows in the last time periods, and only one sign change, from − to +.

Nonconventional investments have more than one change of sign in the CFAT series. Suppose a proposed project has an initial investment at $t = 0$, a series of net cash inflows, and a final net cash flow that is negative. This sequence might arise with a logging operation where there is an initial land purchase cost followed by a series of net cash inflows, concluded by a reforestation cost at the end. The cash flow stream would have a series of signs that looked like this: − + + + + −. Notice that two sign changes occur. Any time cash flows change signs more than once, the investment is nonconventional. Other examples of nonconventional investments are − + + − + −, − + + + − −, − + − + −, and − + + + + − + + −. There are many more, but the common characteristic is that the first positive sign is followed by one or more subsequent negative signs.

Multiple Rates of Return

For nonconventional investments the two criteria may not agree. One problem is that for nonconventional cash flow patterns there may be more than one IRR; that is, there may be *multiple internal rates of return*. These multiple IRRs can occur whenever a non-conventional cash flow series occurs.

■ *Example*

Suppose a proposed logging investment has the CFAT stream shown in Figure 12–A1. There is an initial investment, a large cash inflow in Year 1, and an equally large cash outflow in the second year as the firm is required to restore the land. This is a nonconventional cash flow stream since there is more than one sign change. Figure 12–A1 shows there are two IRRs: 25 percent and 400 percent.[28] From looking at the NPV profile in Figure 12A–1, we see clearly that if the project's cost of capital is between 25 percent and 400 percent, the NPV of the project is positive, and the project should be accepted. If the cost of capital is less than 25 percent (a very likely possibility) or greater than 400 percent (an unlikely possibility), the project should be rejected because its NPV < 0. ■

Applying the IRR criterion to this proposal leads to difficulties. Suppose the cost of capital (*k*) equals 15 percent. Both IRRs are greater than 15 percent, and the IRR rule says that if IRR > *k*, accept. But Figure 12–A1 shows that at *k* = 15 percent, the project's NPV < 0. So the IRR gives an incorrect signal. Now suppose *k* = 30 percent. The analyst who discovers that IRR = 25 percent in the trial-and-error procedure may erroneously conclude that the project is unacceptable because IRR < *k*.

■ *Figure 12–A1*
Net Present Value Profile
of a Nonsimple Project

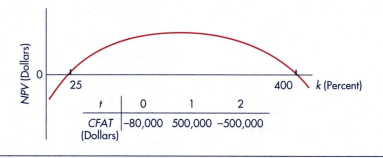

t	0	1	2
CFAT (Dollars)	−80,000	500,000	−500,000

---

[28]The maximum possible number of IRRs is the number of sign changes in the cash flows.

13

Capital Budgeting and Risk

The Risk of Investment Projects

Miller Brewing enjoyed great growth in the demand for its products, with beer volume up tremendously in one decade while the industry volume was up only modestly. In 1980, Miller decided to construct a new brewery in Ohio. The new plant was completed in 1982, about when the growth in beer sales flattened out for the first time in many years. To make matters worse, archrival Anheuser-Busch decided to launch an expensive capital expansion project and triple its advertising outlays. In five years, the sales volume of Miller High Life declined sharply. Miller Brewing never opened the brand new, fully equipped brewery—instead, it took a multi-million dollar write-off.

In 1981, Caterpillar broke ground on a very large parts distribution center in Illinois as a key part of its reinvestment plans in plant and equipment. Coinciding with the start of this construction, oil prices dropped, a recession hit, and the dollar rose. Caterpillar, whose non-United States sales account for a large portion of its business, lost $180 million in 1982, the first of several years of consecutive losses. In 1984, the company wrote off $212 million, much of this amount represented by the still-uncompleted parts distribution center.[1]

[1]See John Merwin, "A Billion in Blunders," *Forbes*, December 1, 1986, pp. 97–111; *The Value Line Investment Survey*, various isues; and annual reports.

In the first part of Chapter 11, we stated that three tasks were necessary in making long-term investment decisions:

1. Estimate the cash flows.
2. Estimate an appropriate discount rate (required rate of return).
3. Select and apply an investment criterion.

Chapter 11 was devoted to cash flow estimation principles, and Chapter 12 to a consideration of investment criteria. These topics were developed under the assumptions that the risk of a proposed project was equivalent to the risk of the assets currently held by the firm and that the proper discount rate to use was k, the firm's required rate of return. In this chapter, we specifically consider risk in investment analysis by analyzing the nature of the risk and by examining methods for adjusting for risk.

Primary *chapter learning objectives* are:

1. To understand the importance of considering the risk inherent in investment proposals.
2. To review methods for assessing the risks of investment projects.

CAPITAL BUDGETING AND RISK

The basic fact of life in finance is that the future is uncertain. Unless we can foresee the future, we must be prepared for the risk involved in all investment decisions. Up to this point we have assumed that a firm's exposure to risk was essentially the same for all projects under consideration and that therefore risk was not an issue in making the capital budgeting decision. Clearly, this is unrealistic.

In Chapter 5, we defined risk as the chance that the actual outcome of an investment may not be equal to the expected outcome. Thus, investors who assume risk in the pursuit of higher expected returns must understand that their realized return after some holding period may be less than what they expected or anticipated when they undertook the investment. Of course, the actual outcome could turn out to be larger than what was expected. Such is the nature of risk.

Similarly, the actual return from a firm's investment project will probably turn out to be different from the financial manager's expectation. As we noted in Chapter 11, cash flow estimation is a very difficult task subject to substantial error. Capital projects often extend over a period of years. A major expansion project, involving a new market or technique with which the firm is unfamiliar, is not comparable in risk to a simple replacement decision involving a machine with which the firm has years of experience.

Investment in new and unfamiliar areas of activity can be particularly risky because of a lack of information on which to base the decision. A good example is the acquisition of one firm by another because the purchaser can view the firm being purchased as an investment project. On the other hand, risk is a two-edged sword. While large risks may lead to large losses, they may also lead to large returns. The rewards for taking risks can be very large. Both the successful and unsuccessful sides of risky investments are illustrated in the following "Financial Management Insights."

...

FINANCIAL MANAGEMENT INSIGHTS

Risky Investments

The Unsuccessful Side of Risky Investments
Standard Oil Company of Ohio (Sohio), realizing the full production results of the great oil discovery in Prudhoe Bay by 1980, began spending its cash for acquisitions.[2] It bought Kennecott Corporation, a mining concern, in 1981 for $1.8 billion at $62 per share. The day prior to the acquisition announcement, Kennecott closed at $27. Sohio spent hundreds of millions on capital outlays for Kennecott. By 1986, this acquisition had generated more than $700 million of operating losses. Furthermore, in 1986 Kennecott's copper mines in Arizona and New Mexico were sold for $220 million, generating hundreds of millions in losses from the sale. The chairman of Sohio said that the company's new strategy was to return to its pre–Alaskan-project profile as a refiner and marketer of oil and gas.

The Successful Side of Risky Investments
In 1968, Merck & Company acquired Calgon Corporation, a producer of granular activated carbon. By 1980, Calgon's sales exceeded $100 million, but production relative to capacity remained low, and by 1982 Calgon earned only $6.6 million on sales of about $100 million. Merck decided to sell Calgon. The general manager wanted to buy the company but lacked the necessary financing. By 1985, the manager had arranged a complex financing arrangement amounting to $110 million, involving borrowed funds from several sources, including Merck itself. The manager and four other insiders, along with an investment banker, purchased $1 million in equity.

This was a risky investment. In the year of purchase Calgon's interest cost alone constituted a large percentage of its cash flow. Success depended on the manager's optimistic projections of declining production costs, stabilizing prices, and a favorable financial environment.[3] As it turns out, the projections proved conservative. Within 18 months the company had a surplus of cash, nearly three times the projections, and in 1987 sales hit $171 million. Sales in 1989 were over $250 million, and estimated 1991 sales were over $300 million.

[2]See Kerry Cooper and R. Malcolm Richards, "Investing the Alaskan Project Cash Flows: The Sohio Experience," *Financial Management,* Summer 1988, pp. 58–70.
[3]See Fleming Meeks, "Perfect Timing," *Forbes,* June 13, 1988, pp. 58–59; *The Value Line Investment Survey;* and annual reports.

Risk and the Valuation of the Firm

How does the firm deal with the risk inherent in capital budgeting? The first and most important step is to remind ourselves that the goal of financial decision making is to maximize stockholders' wealth. This is accomplished by maximizing the net present value of the firm. Therefore, the firm should attempt to accept projects with positive NPVs after assessing risk and, if necessary, adjusting for risk.[4] We know that such actions should increase the stock price. What is important to remember is that the use of the NPV technique is crucial to the success of financial management actions and that we must recognize risk differences.

The risks involved in capital budgeting arise from two primary sources, each of which has a number of components:

[4]Use of NPV is subject to any Chapter 12 caveats, such as the problem of capital rationing.

1. The actual net cash flows may differ from those estimated.
2. The correct required rate of return (k) may differ from that used by the financial manager.

Therefore, financial managers, who intuitively recognize that some investment proposals are more risky than others, will assess the risk of the proposals and either adjust the cash flow estimates or change the discount rate if risk adjustments are deemed necessary.

Several alternatives exist for dealing with project selection under conditions of risk. We will discuss commonly used methods, involving both the cash flows and the required rate of return, that are quite well known and, according to a survey of capital budgeting practices to be discussed below, are typically used by firms in actual practice.

At the outset we should note that many firms engage in risk analysis as it relates to capital budgeting because they are keenly aware of its importance. Nevertheless, it remains a difficult, unsettled issue whose development continues to evolve. As a Du Pont executive concerned with capital budgeting noted, "We really don't do a very good job of dealing with uncertainty when evaluating business plans."[5] The approaches discussed below, while sound in concept, have their limitations; however, they can be, and often are, used in practice to assess and quantify risk exposure.

RISK-ADJUSTED DISCOUNT RATES

One way to adjust for the risk of capital budgeting projects is to adjust the discount rate used in the analysis. The discussion in Chapter 12 involved the firm's required rate of return, which we have referred to as k. Recall from Chapter 12 that this k was used as the discount rate to calculate NPV, or as the standard against which to compare the calculated IRR. Let us reemphasize that there are several ways to say the same thing:

$$k = \frac{\text{Discount}}{\text{rate}} = \frac{\text{Required rate}}{\text{of return}} = \frac{\text{Cost of}}{\text{capital}} \qquad \textbf{(13–1)}$$

We will use these phrases interchangeably; they all mean basically the same thing. We will consider the concept of k in detail in Chapter 14.

Thus far we have used k, the firm's required rate of return, to evaluate projects having the same risk as a firm's average project. This is sensible because the average risk of a firm's projects is a primary determinant of the rate of return that security holders require. As we shall see in Chapter 14, k is a marginal rate reflecting the additional cost of raising funds to be used in projects under consideration. If the firm accepts a project having risk similar to that of the firm as a whole and uses a required rate of return equal to the marginal cost of capital, security holders will earn their required rates of return. If the project earns more (less), the stock price will rise (fall).

What if the risk level differs from the risk of a firm's average project? In this case, discount rates can be made to vary from one project to another in order to account for the riskiness of a project. Relatively risky projects would have rela-

---

[5]See Panel Discussion on Corporate Investment, "Capital Budgeting," *Financial Management* (Spring 1989), p. 11.

tively high discount rates, and relatively safe projects would be assigned relatively low discount rates. These differential required rates of return are called **risk-adjusted discount rates.** Figure 13–1 illustrates the main idea: as project risk increases, the discount rate (the required rate of return) used on the project should also increase.

Operationally, what is a project's required rate of return? It is a **hurdle rate** applied to the investment. A hurdle rate is a minimum rate of return required for project acceptance. In other words, if a proposal "crosses the hurdle" by exceeding this rate, or cutoff, it should be accepted, other things being equal. That is, if a project's net present value is positive, using the required rate of return as the discount rate, the project should be accepted. Otherwise it should be rejected. If the project's IRR exceeds the chosen hurdle rate, accept the project; if not, reject.

What should this hurdle rate represent in an economic sense? It should represent the firm's cost of acquiring the capital used to pay for the project. There are several ways to estimate risk-adjusted discount rates. We will consider two.

1. Use the firm's required rate of return, *k,* adjusted for risk.
2. Use the capital asset pricing model (CAPM).

risk-adjusted discount rate
discount rate that reflects the risk of a particular capital budgeting project, with higher-risk projects having higher discount rates and lower-risk projects having lower discount rates

hurdle rate
minimum rate of return required for project acceptance

k Adjusted for Risk

The symbol *k* represents the cost of capital. In principle, *k* represents what it costs to raise new investment capital in proportions that the firm establishes for itself as optimal over the long run. A particular asset being evaluated may have risk characteristics considerably different from those of the typical project on which *k* is based. Adjusting *k* for differential riskiness allows the asset's risk-adjusted discount rate to be expressed as follows, where k_X is the risk-adjusted discount rate for Project X:

$$\text{Risk-adjusted discount rate for Project X} = k_X^* = k \pm \text{Risk adjustment for Project X} \quad \text{(13–2)}$$

That is, a project's required rate of return can be thought of as the company's average cost of capital (or overall required rate of return), *k,* plus or minus a risk adjustment. If we think of *k* as being an appropriate required rate of return for a

■ *Figure 13–2*
Discount Rates for
Different Risk Classes
of Projects

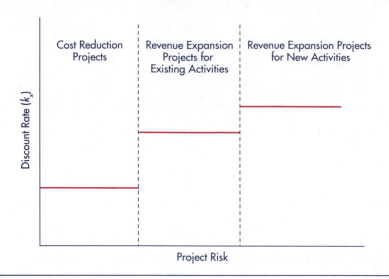

firm's projects of normal risk, then projects with greater (less) risk would have required rates of return, k^*, greater or less than k.

Unfortunately, we have little guidance on procedures for estimating the risk adjustments for projects. Some firms establish risk classes for capital projects. Each risk class has its own k^* (risk-adjusted discount rate). For example, a typical replacement project may have a $k^* = k$, the overall required rate of return. A revenue expansion project into an area with which the firm has experience might call for a k^* of a few percentage points above k. This would reflect a small risk premium for accepting a somewhat riskier project than normal. A revenue expansion into a totally new area would call for a substantially higher risk premium and, correspondingly, a substantially higher k^*. The concept of discount rates for different risk classes of projects, using the three risk classes just discussed, is illustrated in Figure 13–2. In the final analysis, the number of risk classes, and the assignment of individual projects to those risk classes, calls for subjective judgments by the decision maker.

Capital Asset Pricing Model (CAPM)

We first encountered the CAPM in Chapter 5 when we were developing fundamental risk concepts. Because the CAPM theoretically links up an asset's risk with its required rate of return, it can be used to estimate the risk-adjusted rate of return for an asset. The CAPM can be stated as:

$$\text{Risk-adjusted discount rate for asset X} = k_X = k_{RF} + (k_M - k_{RF})\text{Beta}_X \qquad \textbf{(13–3)}$$

where:

$$k_{RF} = \text{risk-free interest rate}$$
$$k_M = \text{required rate of return on the market index}$$
$$\text{Beta}_X = \text{the risk of asset X}$$

Figure 13–3
CAPM: k_X versus $Beta_X$

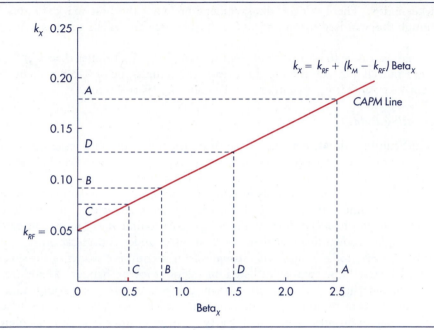

Equation 13–3 states that the risk-adjusted discount rate for a proposed project is the sum of the risk-free interest rate and the risk premium associated with the project. Moreover, this risk premium is a function of covariance with the market, as represented by beta, which is the appropriate financial management risk measure, as established in Chapter 5. The CAPM is illustrated in Figure 13–3.

The riskier the project, the greater the discount rate applied to the project's expected cash flows by the market. Similarly, the less risky the project, the smaller the discount rate applied to the project's expected cash flows. If a proposed project had a beta of zero, there would be no risk associated with the project, and the appropriate discount rate for evaluating the project would be the risk-free interest rate, k_{RF}.

To use Equation 13–3 we need estimates of k_{RF}, k_M, and $Beta_X$. Once we have this information, we can estimate k_X.

Estimating k_{RF}

We are trying to assess the economic attractiveness of *long-term* investments. Consequently, when we estimate k_{RF}, we want a long-term interest rate. How long? As a working approximation, we can use the anticipated life of the project. Since k_{RF} is supposed to represent a risk-free interest rate, we can estimate it using a U.S. government bond of approximately the same life as the proposed project. Of course, recognition of the fact that we are estimating k_{RF}, which is supposed to be known with certainty, indicates that we are only approximating the CAPM theory.

Estimating k_M

In comparison with k_{RF}, it is harder to estimate k_M. Interest rates on U.S. government bonds are observable, but there are no observable *expected* returns on the market index. There is even disagreement on what the best market index is, although the Standard & Poor's 500 Composite Index is widely used as a market index.

It may be easier to estimate the yield spread $(k_M - k_{RF})$ rather than k_M. Some recent research indicates these yield spreads are in the range of 6 to 8 percent. We certainly know that k_M should exceed k_{RF} since k_{RF} is risk free.

Estimating Beta$_X$

It is difficult to estimate beta values because that, too, requires guessing at unobservable variables. However, over time, analysts may develop a feel for the beta values of projects so that they can estimate these values fairly accurately.

Some analysts estimate betas by looking at common stocks of companies whose main business line corresponds with the project being analyzed. This is referred to as the *pure-play technique*. Ideally, the analyst tries to find one or more companies with a single-product line that matches the project under consideration.

It is very easy today to get beta estimates for the common stocks of the several hundred largest U.S. companies listed on major stock exchanges. Therefore, if we are considering a real estate investment project, we can get a rough idea of this project's beta by looking at the common stock betas of companies whose principal line of business is in real property. Common stock betas are also determined by the companies' capital structures (the mix of financing sources), so we must be careful in making such comparisons. But this is a useful approach to help us estimate betas.

■ *Example*

Suppose that we have estimated the following market data:

$$k_{RF} = 0.07$$

$$k_M - k_{RF} = 0.06 \text{ (Note: this implies } k_M = 0.13)$$

Furthermore, we have estimated the beta for Project A as:

$$\text{Beta}_A = 2.5$$

Then:

$$k_A = k_{RF} + (k_M - k_{RF}) \text{ Beta}_A = 0.07 + (0.06)(2.5) = 0.22$$

The appropriate discount rate for Project A is therefore .22, or 22 percent. ■

Now consider other investment projects. The market parameters (k_M and k_{RF}) used in the example above will also apply to these projects. The following list shows the estimated Beta$_X$ and calculated k_X values for several such projects (these values of Beta$_X$ and k_X are all shown in Figure 13–3):

Project	Beta$_X$	k_X
B	0.8	0.118
C	0.5	0.10
D	1.5	0.16

As Figure 13–3 shows, each project has its own risk-adjusted discount rate, which is determined by market parameters (k_M and k_{RF}) common to *all* projects and the risk (Beta$_X$) peculiar to the project. Thus, all project-risk and risk-adjusted discount rate values fall on the CAPM straight line. In effect, the CAPM converts the risk of projects into a risk-adjusted discount rate for each project.

Using the CAPM in Capital Budgeting

The CAPM model offers useful insights into the problem of risk adjustment in capital budgeting. It directly quantifies the risk premiums involved—the greater the risk of a project, as given by its beta, the greater the required rate of return. Thus, it can greatly facilitate the calculation of multiple hurdle rates for a firm.

As Figure 13–3 demonstrates, the CAPM approach shows if projects are acceptable or not. All projects with IRRs above the CAPM line are acceptable (the acceptance region), while all projects with IRRs below the CAPM line are rejected (the rejection region).

Unfortunately, a number of problems exist in trying to use the CAPM in capital budgeting. As we saw, it is difficult to estimate the parameters of the model; for example, how can betas for individual projects be obtained? A major theoretical problem involves the use of the single-period CAPM in a multiperiod setting—the capital budgeting process. A change in risk over time is difficult to incorporate into a capital budgeting framework using a CAPM approach.[6]

Risk-Adjusted Discount Rates versus k

Many firms use *k*, the average cost of capital, on all their investment projects. Unfortunately, this fairly widespread practice is not consistent with the fundamental notion that projects with different degrees of risk should be evaluated with discount rates that reflect those risk differences. Adjusting k_{AVG}, however imperfectly, for risk differences is a better approach than simply using *k* for all projects. This is illustrated in Figure 13–4, which shows the use of k_{AVG} versus the use of risk-adjusted discount rates.

We can see in Figure 13–4 that k_{AVG}, the firm's overall required rate of return or cost of capital, is represented by a horizontal straight line. The CAPM is used in Figure 13–4 to represent risk-adjusted discount rates. Projects A and B are being evaluated. Both would be acceptable using k_{AVG} because they are above the line. However, Project B is unacceptable using the CAPM to determine risk-adjusted discount rates because its return is less than its required rate of return, given its beta. Thus, when projects differ significantly in their riskiness, the use of k_{AVG} can result in improper acceptance decisions.

Total Risk versus Market Risk

We have examined two techniques for adjusting for risk: the adjustment of *k* for risk differentials and the CAPM model. Which model should be used by the firm?

---

[6]An analysis similar to the one just completed for the CAPM could be performed for the APT, a concept considered briefly in Chapter 5. However, the empirical aspects of arbitrage pricing are not yet fully enough developed to afford us very reliable estimates of market premiums comparable to the ($k_M - k_{RF}$) premium of the CAPM. We will not, therefore, apply the APT in this area.

■ *Figure 13–4*
Average Required Rate
of Return versus Risk-
Adjusted Discount Rates

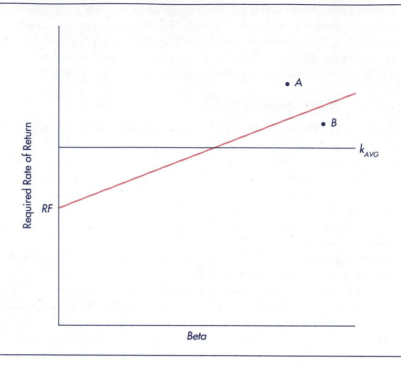

Under the CAPM framework, security risk can be divided into two parts:

$$\text{Total security risk} = \text{Market risk} + \text{Nonmarket risk} \qquad (13\text{–}4)$$
$$= \text{Nondiversifiable risk} + \text{Diversifiable risk}$$

Individual investors holding diversified portfolios can reduce or eliminate the diversifiable risk of securities, leaving only the market (nondiversifiable) risk as measured by beta.

If we apply this concept to capital budgeting, we can state an analogous identity:

$$\text{Total project risk} = \text{Market risk} + \text{Nonmarket risk}$$
$$= \text{Nondiversifiable risk} + \text{Diversifiable risk}$$

Total project risk is measured by standard deviation. In the case of a capital budgeting project, total project risk can be thought of as the variance, or standard deviation, of the expected future cash flows for the project. *Market risk* (or portfolio risk) for a project would be measured by the project's beta.

If the CAPM framework is applicable to capital budgeting, the total risk for a project is not the relevant consideration because diversifiable risk is eliminated by the holding of portfolios of assets. Instead, a new project should be considered solely on the basis of its market or nondiversifiable risk. Thus, each project should be evaluated on the basis of expected return and risk, as always, but with risk measured by the beta for the individual project. At least for the all–equity–financed firm, beta is the relevant measure of risk for a capital project. The CAPM then provides a very useful framework for capital budgeting decisions because it adjusts for risk by adjusting the required rate of return, k^*, for each investment project.

Projects riskier than average will have higher betas and, therefore, higher required rates of return.

In theory, it is not clear that beta is the proper measure of risk for an investment project in all circumstances. First, if lack of diversification is a problem, total risk is the better measure. Undiversified stockholders are concerned more with total risk than with market risk.

Second, if a firm can properly be viewed as a portfolio of assets and projects, portfolio diversification and firm diversification are perfect substitutes. In less-than-perfect capital markets, however, the two may not be perfect substitutes. In such cases, the nature of the cash flows is of prime importance to all parties concerned—stockholders, creditors, employees, and so on. A threat of bankruptcy elevates the question of the stability of cash flows to top priority. Even without an immediate threat of bankruptcy, interested parties are vitally concerned with low profits or substantially erratic profits.

Finally, the CAPM model, as an explanation of the pricing of risky assets in financial markets, remains a controversial topic. It is possible that investors consider factors other than market risk when setting required rates of return, whether well diversified or not. In practice, the CAPM has been found wanting. It is quite difficult to determine the beta for an individual project.

In summary, the CAPM holds that stockholders, being well diversified, judge project risk by its contribution to the risk of their total portfolio because a new project is simply an addition to their portfolio. Since the portfolio is diversified and contains primarily (or only) market risk, the contribution of a new project is measured by its beta. To the extent that this situation does not hold for investors in practice, and to the extent that serious implementation problems exist in actually using the CAPM in capital budgeting, other risk adjustment techniques are important and should be considered.

EXPECTED NET PRESENT VALUE

Once the risk-adjusted discount rate is estimated, it may be used to evaluate the desirability of the proposed project:

$$\overline{NPV} = \sum_{t=0}^{N} \frac{\overline{CFAT_t}}{(1 + k^*)^t} \tag{13-5}$$

where:

$$\overline{NPV} = \text{expected NPV}$$
$$\overline{CFAT_t} = \text{expected CFAT in year } t$$
$$k^* = \text{risk-adjusted discount rate}$$

Equation 13–5 is consistent with the original valuation equation (Equation 5–1), developed in Chapter 5. Projects are evaluated on the basis of future cash flow projections and an appropriate discount rate. Equation 13–5 emphasizes that estimated future cash flows are expected values, and the discount rate reflects the degree of risk in the project.

Expected CFAT

In generating cash flow estimates for use with Equation 13–5, we often find it useful to relate these estimates to the economic climates that may prevail. At the simplest level, we can think of the outcomes as bad, average, and good. A bad year may indicate recession, an average year normal economic activity, and a good year may indicate an economic boom. Probabilities can be attached to these economic states, and the analyst can estimate CFAT outcomes for each year of a proposed project's life.

▪ Example

Suppose that Brown and Rowland Electronics is considering an investment in a chip-making machine that is expected to last three years. The CFAT in each year has been related to the economy, and the resultant schedule of CFATs and associated probabilities is shown in Table 13–1. The anticipated initial investment is $50,000, and by setting the probability equal to 1.0, the company is saying this investment cost is known with certainty and is unrelated to the state of the economy. Future CFATs are not known with certainty, so their probabilities are less than 1.0. In Year 1, if the economy is bad, the estimated project CFAT is $20,000, and the associated probability is 0.2. If the economy is average, the estimated project CFAT is $25,000, and the probability of this state is, in the analyst's opinion, 0.6. Last, if the economy is good, the project's estimated CFAT is $30,000, and the estimated probability of this is 0.2. And so on, for the other two years.

Given these estimates of CFAT and associated probabilities, Brown and Rowland can now calculate expected cash flows. Using the expected-value equation from Chapter 5, adapted to cash flows:

$$\text{Expected CFAT in year } t = \overline{\text{CFAT}}_t = \sum_{j=1}^{N} (Prob_{tj})(\text{CFAT}_{tj}) \qquad \textbf{(13–6)}$$

where:

$$\begin{aligned}
\text{CFAT}_{tj} &= \text{cash flow after tax in year } t \text{ of the } j\text{th outcome} \\
Prob_{tj} &= \text{probability associated with the } j\text{th outcome in year } t \\
N &= \text{number of outcomes}
\end{aligned}$$

▪ **Table 13–1**
Estimated CFAT Schedule

Year	State of Economy	Estimated Project CFAT ($)	Probability
0	Any state	−50,000	1.0
1	Bad	20,000	0.2
	Average	25,000	0.6
	Good	30,000	0.2
2	Bad	20,000	0.4
	Average	30,000	0.2
	Good	40,000	0.4
3	Bad	10,000	0.4
	Average	20,000	0.2
	Good	30,000	0.4

Each year has an expected CFAT. Therefore:

$$\overline{CFAT_0} = (1.0)(-\$50,000) = -\$50,000$$

$$\overline{CFAT_1} = (0.2)(\$20,000) + (0.6)(\$25,000) + (0.2)(\$30,000)$$
$$= \$25,000$$

$$\overline{CFAT_2} = (0.4)(\$20,000) + (0.2)(\$30,000) + (0.4)(\$40,000)$$
$$= \$30,000$$

$$\overline{CFAT_3} = (0.4)(\$10,000) + (0.2)(\$20,000) + (0.4)(\$30,000)$$
$$= \$20,000$$

Assume further that $k^* = 0.25$ for this project. Then, using Equation 12–2, we find that:

$$\overline{NPV} = -\$50,000 + \frac{\$25,000}{1.25} + \frac{\$30,000}{(1.25)^2} + \frac{\$20,000}{(1.25)^3}$$

$$= -\$50,000 + \$20,000 + \$19,200 + \$10,240 = -\$560$$

Since $\overline{NPV}$ is negative, Brown and Rowland Electronics should reject this project. ▪

Notice that nothing is really new in this approach. The only difference between this technique and the NPV technique of Chapter 12 is that we have explicitly accounted for the fact that future cash flows are not certain.

That this technique is used by some firms is illustrated by Ameritech, a regional telephone holding company. According to an executive of the firm, "We asked (the people in the field) to just take the cash flows and come up with three adjustments—the best case, the worst case, and the most likely."[7]

Certainty Equivalents

A well-known but little-used technique for incorporating risk into capital budgeting decisions is that of *certainty equivalents*. Under this approach, the decision maker attempts to adjust the expected cash flows to reflect the project's risk—in effect, converting a risky $CFAT_t$ into a smaller but certain equivalent. This technique is difficult both to understand and to implement and, in fact, is seldom used in practice, according to survey findings discussed below.

Certainty equivalents are briefly discussed in Appendix 13–A.

WORST-CASE ANALYSIS

One thing prudent managers and analysts should do regularly is consider what the worst outcome may look like. That is, give Murphy's Law full throttle and investigate the case where cash flows are poor, project life is shorter than expected, and so on, and then take these worst-case estimates and see what net present value or rate of return looks like. Focusing attention on the worst case does not imply the manager or analyst expects the worst outcome to occur. But considering what the worst outcome looks like is useful for many reasons.

---

[7]See Panel Discussions on Corporate Investment, "Capital Budgeting," *Financial Management*, Spring 1989, p. 15.

First, worst-case analysis tells management how bad things could be if the worst outcome does occur. Therefore, everyone will go into the project, if it's undertaken, with their eyes open. There will be fewer surprises at the end of the process, and the surprises that do occur should be less shocking to management than if no worst-case preparation had taken place.

A second advantage of worst-case analysis is that it will tend to temper forecasting optimism. It is a fact of life that many analysts are overly optimistic in preparing projects for economic evaluation. A survey of Fortune 500 companies evaluated various aspects of bias in capital budgeting forecasts. The results indicated that such forecasts are optimistically biased by people with work experience—that is, people actually making the decisions.[8]

Actually, there are plausible reasons for optimism. People have pet projects and lose sight of important negative features of those projects when only the expected outcomes are considered. Also, there can be a great deal of excitement generated by some proposed capital projects, and it is easy to be caught up in that excitement to the point where estimates of project parameters are biased.

Then, too, there are often incentives for optimism. Units within a firm compete with other units for budget dollars, and the more aggressive units will capture a larger share of those dollars—until, of course, their excessive optimism is revealed by chronic failures. Optimistic forecasts are consistent with aggressive budgetary competition.

Another incentive for optimism is job enhancement. Optimism in project evaluation will lead to more activity, enlarged staffs, and possibly greater advancement prospects—particularly if some of the projects are very successful. This personal-incentive problem is yet another instance of what finance theory calls the agency problem. Recall from Chapter 1 that the agency problem arises when hired personnel have personal gain incentives that may be at odds with the owners' incentives. Given the incentives some managers and analysts have to be optimistic in project evaluation, this optimism can be detrimental to the goal of stockholder wealth maximization. In that context, the main point here is that worst-case analyses will tend to dampen optimism.

Optimism difficulties aside, the third advantage of performing worst-case analyses is that a realization of what the worst case involves may cause some projects to be rejected for the reason that the worst case is totally unacceptable. This possibility seems most likely for projects that are large enough to affect the firm materially. If, for example, a project to double the firm's manufacturing capacity were to end disastrously, the firm's existence might be threatened. The likelihood (probability) of this worst-case outcome no doubt also enters the deliberations. For situations where the worst case is bad enough and its likelihood large enough, it is easy to imagine management will turn down projects where the expected net present value is positive. To paraphrase an old saw: We must take care we don't drown in a river whose average depth is three feet; we can do this by looking for and avoiding the deepest (worst) part of the river.

It is also true that everything has its price, and there is a price to pay for performing worst-case analyses, too. By bringing attention to the worst outcome, we may magnify it to the point where we overemphasize it. We may become

---

[8]See Stephen W. Pruitt and Lawrence J. Gitman, "Capital Budgeting Forecast Biases: Evidence from the Fortune 500," *Financial Management* Spring 1987, p. 51.

mesmerized by how bad the worst outcome is and fail to appreciate that the likelihood of occurrence is very small, maybe trivially small. Consequently, the firm may reject projects that, all things considered, should be accepted. Thus, too much skepticism can be as bad as too little.

On balance, the price we pay here seems fair. Performing worst-case analysis seems very appropriate, and the bigger the risk, the more appropriate worst-case analysis becomes. In doing a worst-case analysis, sensitivity analysis, the next topic in our discussion, is very useful.

SENSITIVITY ANALYSIS

In making capital budgeting decisions, firms estimate the key components of a project: expected cash inflows, net cash outflow, and project life. These parameters are only estimates of what will occur and are subject to error. Most of the variables that determine a project's cash flows are based on probability distributions. Presumably, more experienced financial analysts will make better estimates of the future than less experienced analysts, but since the future is always uncertain, there will be estimation errors regardless.

A basic way to systematically investigate the effect of estimation errors on a project's NPV is through **sensitivity analysis.** In the context of NPV, sensitivity analysis provides information regarding the sensitivity of the calculated NPV to possible estimation errors in operating cash flows, the initial investment, the termination cash flows, and project life.

sensitivity analysis method of systematically investigating the effect of estimation errors on a project's NPV

In effect, sensitivity analysis involves a two-step process:

1. Express NPV in terms of its determinants.
2. Calculate the results of changing the value of one of the determinants.

The firm will have as a starting point forecasts of the determinants of NPV, primarily expected revenues and expected costs from which net expected cash flows are derived. A *base case* is established using the expected values for each determinant. The estimate of NPV from this analysis is referred to as the *base case NPV*.

By considering optimistic and pessimistic estimates for the key variables, the decision maker can then assess the effect of deviations in the forecasts on the base case NPV. This is *what-if analysis*—what happens to the NPV of the project if the operating cash flows turn out to be 10 percent less than forecast, the initial investment turns out to be 15 percent more than forecast, and so on. In effect, the decision maker examines the sensitivity of a project's return to changes in one of the variables that determine NPV.

■ *Example*

Suppose a proposed project has an estimated initial cost (after tax) of $75,000 and an estimated expected CFAT stream of $20,000 per year for seven years. The estimated k is 15 percent.

$$\overline{NPV} = -\$75,000 + (\$20,000)(\text{PVIFA}_{.15,7})$$
$$= -\$75,000 + (\$20,000)(4.160)$$
$$= \$8,200$$

The project should be accepted. Now, what if the analyst overestimated expected annual CFAT by $3,000? That is, what if expected CFAT were $17,000 per year?

$$\overline{NPV} = -\$75,000 + (\$17,000)(4.160) = -\$4,280$$

If the analyst overestimates expected CFAT by $3,000 per year, the project will have negative $\overline{NPV}$. Similarly, the analyst can determine the sensitivity of $\overline{NPV}$ to estimation errors in project life and in cash outflows. A sensitivity analysis would be particularly helpful for large projects that have a substantial impact on the firm. ■

By identifying the determinants of $\overline{NPV}$ and assessing the effects of changes in any one variable, the decision maker can identify how sensitive the $\overline{NPV}$ is to possible changes in each of the determinants. This, in turn, could suggest areas to concentrate on in obtaining better or more information.

Sensitivity analysis can be illustrated in the form of graphs. Each of the determinants of $\overline{NPV}$ that is analyzed in the sensitivity analysis can be graphed, with $\overline{NPV}$ as the vertical axis and deviations from the base case for that variable on the horizontal axis. Figure 13–5 illustrates two sensitivity graphs, one for CFAT and one for cost of capital. Notice that the base case is the reference point in each case, and that the horizontal axis is expressed in terms of deviations from the base case.

In the case of the CFAT sensitivity graph, the relatively steep slope of the line indicates that, as we would expect, the $\overline{NPV}$ is very sensitive to changes in CFATs (the steeper the slope of the line, the more sensitive the $\overline{NPV}$ to a change in the variable shown). The cost-of-capital sensitivity graph, on the other hand, shows that the project's $\overline{NPV}$ is not very sensitive to the cost of capital—the line is relatively flat. Similar graphs could be constructed for each of the variables important in determining the NPV for a project.

■ *Figure 13–5*   Examples of Sensitivity Graphs

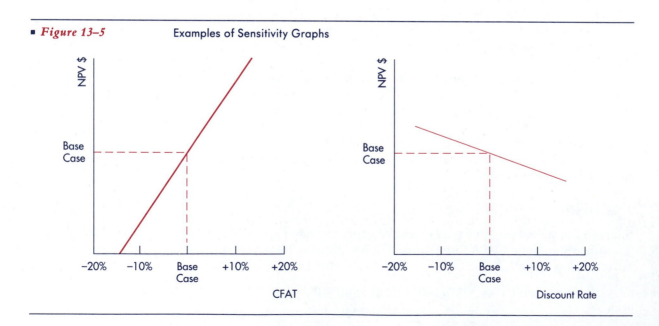

Using Spreadsheets

Sensitivity analysis can involve numerous calculations and recalculations, most of them straightforward but tedious. For example, if we wish to assess the effects of a change in the CFAT stream by +5 percent, or −5 percent, we must work through the results of this one change on NPV or IRR. Obviously, this type of analysis is ideal for a computer.

Financial-modeling programs are used to do this type of analysis—calculating the results of changing assumptions. In particular, spreadsheet programs such as Lotus 1–2–3® and Quattro®, referred to in Chapter 12, are widely available for use on microcomputers and are ideal for doing sensitivity analysis.

To carry out a spreadsheet analysis, the base case is determined and entered in the spreadsheet. Next, dozens (or hundreds) of what-if questions are asked. Each time a new question is asked, the spreadsheet can quickly recompute each period's net cash flows and a new NPV.

SIMULATION

Another method used by corporations to evaluate risky investment proposals is **simulation,** which can be defined as testing the results of an investment decision before it takes place.[9] As applied to investment analysis, simulation typically involves using a model and probability information to determine the distribution of net present value (or internal rate of return). In effect, it brings together sensitivity analysis and the probability distributions for each of the variables determining NPV.

A well-known simulation model by Hertz used nine factors to estimate the earnings for the firm.[10] Using management's assessment of the likely outcomes, probability distributions can be derived for each of the factors. A random combination of the factors is chosen, and the average rate of return from this combination calculated. A computer is used to simulate trial values for each of the factors and to calculate the resultant return. Repetition of the process—each run is referred to as an iteration—produces a frequency distribution from which the expected return and the dispersion in this return can be calculated.

simulation
in capital budgeting, a computerized technique that tests the results of an investment decision before it takes place. Many iterations are used to simulate trial values for each of the factors that affect the outcome

■ *Example*

Suppose the firm has estimated project probability distributions for initial investment, revenues and operating costs, life, and salvage value, as illustrated in Figure 13–6. The simulation proceeds as follows:

1. Randomly select a value of each variable from its distribution.
2. Take these values and other given information (tax rate, type of depreciation used, and so on) and calculate the project's NPV or IRR.
3. Repeat steps one and two many times (for example, 1,000 times).
4. Prepare the NPV or IRR distribution (see Figure 13–6).

---

[9]This is often referred to as Monte Carlo simulation.
[10]See David Hertz, "Risk Analysis in Capital Investment," *Harvard Business Review,* January–February 1964, pp. 95–106.

■ *Figure 13–6*
Simulation Approach

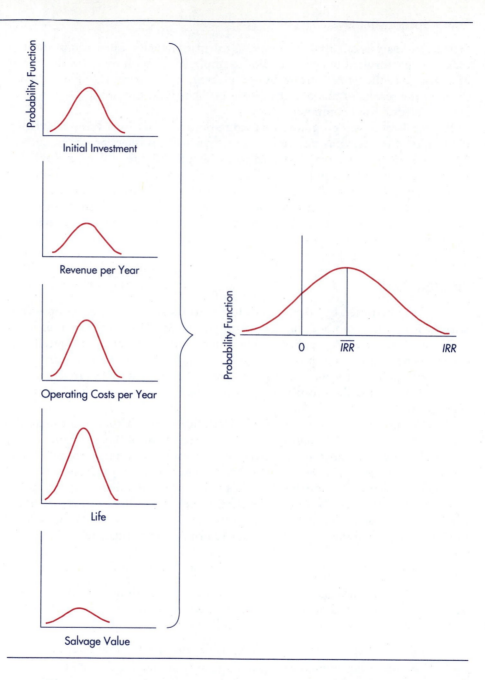

The result of the simulation is the distribution of NPV or IRR. The IRR is shown in Figure 13–6 (alternatively, it could be an NPV distribution). From the information used to prepare the distribution the analyst can also determine the standard deviation of the project's IRR, which is used in determining project risk. ■

One of the main advantages of simulation is that it shows the range of possible outcomes associated with the project rather than a point estimate—the outcome associated with expected values. The output of the simulation analysis is an expected NPV and a probability distribution for this value, which is helpful in estimating project risk. Consequently, it identifies possible extremely bad outcomes that might happen if the project is accepted. The analyst can also compute the probability of achieving an NPV that is greater than a specified value, or less. This can be very useful information.

One of the problems in using simulation in actual practice is that of obtaining probability distributions for the variables used. Furthermore, the simulation process assumes that the variables are independent of one another, when, in reality, some are almost certainly correlated with each other. If dependencies exist among the variables, they should be accounted for in determining the probability distributions.

Overall, simulation offers a very powerful approach to the analysis of risk. It is able to deal with the many interactions among the variables that determine NPV. Because of the time and data requirements of a simulation, however, it is most appropriate for large projects.

International Perspective

As previously noted, the basic principles of financial management are the same regardless of whether they are used in a domestic setting or in multinational operations involving foreign countries. This certainly applies to the area of capital budgeting, where the basic principle of capital budgeting applies: Invest if the discounted value of the cash inflows is greater than the discounted value of the cash outflows. That principle does not change simply because capital budgeting analysis must be done in a foreign country. Nevertheless, financial managers of multinational companies must recognize special differences that are apparent in making investments abroad.

The primary difference in capital expenditures made in the United States and those made abroad is that the expected cash flows estimated to be received by the foreign subsidiary from the project may, in the final analysis, not be received by the parent firm. There are several possible reasons for this.

1. The foreign country may prevent the operating subsidiary from repatriating funds back to the parent in the United States. Funds effectively not available to the parent for their most efficient use cannot be counted in the same manner as unrestricted funds.

2. Foreign investments are subject to political (sovereignty) risk. Assets can be appropriated under circumstances that U.S. financial decision makers normally do not even have to consider. The instability that exists in many countries makes this a significant and ever-present factor with which to contend.

3. Exchange rate risk is always present in transactions between countries. Since the cash flows to be received from the operating subsidiary are in the foreign currency, they must be converted into dollars to be transferred to the United States. When actually doing the capital budgeting analysis, the firm will have to incorporate expected future exchange rates. This is when sensitivity analysis or simulation can be

■ *Table 13–2*
Actual Use of Techniques
to Assess Risk

Method	Percent Using Ranged from	No. of Studies
Risk-adjusted discount rate	15–90	7
Changing the payback period	10–61	6
Adjusting cash flows by use of quantitative probability factors	13–32	4
Sensitivity analysis	10–55	2
Simulation	27	1

Source: David F. Scott, Jr., and J. William Petty III, "Capital Budgeting Practices in Large American Firms: A Retrospective Analysis and Synthesis," *The Financial Review*, March 1984, p. 118.

particularly useful since both permit the decision makers to estimate the effects of various exchange rates that may pertain in the future.

Exchange rate risk will be discussed in more detail in Chapter 22.

FOCUS ON CORPORATE PRACTICE

We noted at the outset of this chapter the difficulty of dealing with risk in capital budgeting analysis. Nevertheless, it is important to recognize the risk inherent in project analysis and to attempt to deal with it. In order to distinguish between theory and practice, we can consider how business firms actually handle the problem of risk.

According to an analysis of capital budgeting practices, a 1972 study found that about 40 percent of firms surveyed used a formal method of risk analysis. But a 1978 study found about 36 percent of firms using a quantitative technique to assess risk, and another 60 percent using subjective adjustments, for a total of 96 percent of respondents using some type of risk adjustment.[11] The conclusion of this analysis is that it is safe to assume that more than two thirds of large U.S. firms are significantly concerned with project risk.

What types of risk adjustments are used? Table 13–2 shows the risk adjustment techniques most frequently used, and the range in percentages of respondents from various studies that use a technique. In reading Table 13–2, note that the results of seven different studies are reported for five different techniques. All seven studies report the percentage of respondents using risk-adjusted discount rates, only two studies report the percentage using sensitivity analysis, and only one study reports on simulation.

It is clear from Table 13–2 that risk-adjusted discount rates are the most common technique used in making risk adjustments. As for other techniques, roughly one fourth of the companies surveyed apply probability distributions to forecasted cash flows. The results for the payback period adjustment approach are so varied that it is difficult to infer how popular this technique actually is. Finally, note that sensitivity analysis and simulation appear in the table and, according to the authors, "are coming into their own as risk assessment techniques."[12]

---

[11]See David F. Scott, Jr., and J. William Petty III, "Capital Budgeting Practices in Large American Firms: A Retrospective Analysis and Synthesis," *The Financial Review*, March 1984, p. 118.

[12]Ibid., p. 119.

SUMMARY

▪ It is desirable to analyze the riskiness of an investment project to obtain a feel for the nature of the risk present.

▪ The terms *discount rate, required rate of return,* and *cost of capital* are, for our purposes, interchangeable.

▪ A firm needs to assess a project's required rate of return, or hurdle rate, which represents the marginal cost of acquiring the capital used to pay for the project.

▪ In the risk-adjusted discount method, the firm adjusts for project risk by adjusting the discount rate: the greater the risk, the higher the discount rate.

▪ Two ways to estimate risk-adjusted discount rates are the firm's cost of capital adjusted for risk and the capital asset pricing model.

▪ The adjusted k_{AVG} method takes the firm's average cost of capital, k_{AVG}, and adjusts it up or down for the riskiness of the project:

$$k_X = k_{AVG} \pm \text{Risk adjustment}$$

▪ The CAPM method uses the capital asset pricing model. The project's risk equals its beta, which measures the covariance of returns of the project with the returns of the market.

▪ An important part of many risky investment decision models is determining expected cash flows:

$$\overline{\text{CFAT}}_t = \sum_{j=1}^{N} (Prob_{tj})(\text{CFAT}_{tj})$$

▪ The firm calculates an expected net present value using expected cash flows and the risk-adjusted discount rate, k:*

$$\overline{\text{NPV}} = \sum_{t=0}^{N} \frac{\overline{\text{CFAT}}_t}{(1 + k^*)^t}$$

▪ Worst-case analysis should be a regular part of a financial analysis. It will reduce surprise, temper forecasting optimism, and can help keep the firm from investing in projects whose downside risk is too great.

▪ A sensitivity analysis for a project can show what effect estimation errors will have on expected NPV, which may lead the firm to reject an otherwise acceptable project or to spend resources to gather more reliable project information prior to accepting the project.

▪ Simulation is useful because it reveals the bad outcomes as well as the expected-value outcomes.

▪ All these methods involve estimation of future outcomes, and since the future is always unknown, these estimates will be erroneous to some extent.

KEY TERMS

risk-adjusted discount rate, p. 389
hurdle rate, p. 389

sensitivity analysis, p. 399
simulation, p. 401

QUESTIONS

13–1. What is sensitivity analysis? How does it differ from simulation?

13–2. Explain how payback could be considered by some to be an effective risk-screening device.

13–3. What should be the relationship between a project's risk-adjusted discount rate and its beta?

13–4. What is the principal advantage of using simulation analysis on capital budgeting problems?

13–5. Other things being equal, what effect would the following events have on the risk-adjusted discount rate for a proposed purchase of mineral rights to a new iron ore deposit?

    a. An increase in the covariance between the project and the market index rate of return.

    b. A decrease in the required rate of return on the market index.

13–6. The vice president for finance of Barron Industries is being closely quizzed by some other members of Barron's board of directors at a board meeting. The firm's financial staff, which is headed by the finance vice president, has provided the board with an estimate that the firm's average cost of capital is currently 12 percent. However, a finance staff member has just completed a presentation concerning a proposed investment that the finance staff has thoroughly analyzed. The staff's recommendation is to accept the project even though its expected rate of return is only 10 percent. Equally puzzling, the vice president for marketing remarks that one of his division's pet projects, which had an expected return of 15 percent, was rejected last week by the finance staff. How might the finance vice president explain the fact that a project with an expected rate of return less than k_{AVG} is being recommended for acceptance, and a project with an expected rate of return greater than k_{AVG} has been rejected?

13–7. What are the advantages and disadvantages of using the CAPM in capital budgeting?

13–8. In what sense can a project's required rate of return be referred to as a *hurdle rate?*

13–9. How does the use of a CAPM framework for capital budgeting decisions change the consideration of risk?

13–10. What are *risk classes?* How are they used?

13–11. How can betas for projects be estimated?

13–12. How is total project risk measured? What are its two components?

13–13. How can sensitivity analysis be useful in doing a worst-case analysis?

13–14. Distinguish between total risk and market risk. How can market risk for a project be measured?

13–15. What is the relationship between the average cost of capital and risk-adjusted discount rates?

DEMONSTRATION PROBLEMS

13–1. A project has the following information associated with it:

    Life = 10 years.

    $CFAT_t$ = $600 each year (from operations).

    Initial investment = $2,000.

    Expected salvage = 0.

    $k = 0.20$.

    a. Find NPV.

    b. Which would be worse? To have the life shortened by 10 percent? Or to have the annual CFAT reduced by 10 percent?

13–2. International Communications uses the CAPM to determine risk-adjusted discount rates. The risk of each of three projects has been related to a market index, with betas as follows:

Project A	0.8
Project B	1.0
Project C	1.3

The risk-free rate is 9 percent, and the expected return on the market index is 15 percent. Determine the risk-adjusted discount rates for these three projects.

Solutions to Demonstration Problems

13–1. *a.* $\overline{NPV} = -\$2,000 + \$600 \text{ (PVIFA}_{.20,10})$

          $= -\$2,000 + \$2,515$

          $= \$515$

    b. If life is reduced by 10 percent:

$$n = (.9)(10) = 9 \text{ years}$$
$$\overline{NPV} = -\$2,000 + \$600 \text{ (PVIFA}_{.20,9})$$
$$= -\$2,000 + \$2,419$$
$$= \$419$$

    If $\overline{CFAT}$ is reduced by 10 percent:

$$\overline{CFAT} = (.9)(600) = \$540/\text{yr.}$$
$$\overline{NPV} = -\$2,000 + \$540 \text{ (PVIFA}_{.20,10})$$
$$= -\$2,000 + \$2,264 = \$264$$

13–2. The CAPM is applied to each of the projects, using the beta of each individual project.

$$k_A = 9\% + .8 (15\% - 9\%) = 13.8\%$$
$$k_B = 9\% + 1.0 (15\% - 9\%) = 15\%$$
$$k_C = 9\% + 1.3 (15\% - 9\%) = 16.8\%$$

PROBLEMS

13–1. You have been asked to evaluate an investment project under uncertainty. All the cash flow information necessary to evaluate the project is given below.

Period 0		Period 1		Period 2	
Probability	CFAT	Probability	CFAT	Probability	CFAT
1.0	−$300	0.40	$100	0.40	$100
		0.30	200	0.30	200
		0.20	300	0.20	300
		0.10	400	0.10	400

 a. Determine the expected CFAT stream for the project.
 b. If the risk-adjusted discount rate appropriate for this project is 15 percent, determine whether the proposal is acceptable.

13–2. Messere Communications' economists have estimated that the expected rate of return for the market for the next 10 years is about 14 percent. They have also observed the following market yields on 10–year bonds: 8 percent on government bonds, 9 percent on high-grade corporate bonds, 12 percent on low-grade corporate bonds. Given this information, determine the risk-adjusted discount rate for each of the following proposed 10–year new investments, whose beta risk measures are as shown:

Project	1	2	3	4	5	6
Beta	1.4	0.7	1.0	2.1	0	−1.0

13–3. Chance Aircraft Company analysts are preparing to determine the risk-adjusted discount rate for some investment projects the firm is considering. Some market data pertinent to this task are shown below. The risk of each project has been expressed in relation to a market index. Determine the risk-adjusted discount rate for each project.

Market Data

Required rate of return on the market index is 12 percent.
Risk-free interest rate is 6 percent.

Risk Data

Project A is about two times as risky as an investment in the market index.
Project B is about one half as risky as an investment in the market index.
Project C is about as risky as an investment in the market index.

13–4. The Anderson Mining Company is considering two mutually exclusive investment prospects. Projects A and B have expected cash flows after tax as shown below:

t	A ($)	B ($)
0	−350,000	−350,000
1	75,000	50,000
2	75,000	55,000
3	75,000	65,000
4	75,000	75,000
5	75,000	80,000
6	75,000	70,000
7		60,000
8		60,000
9		60,000
10		60,000

The company uses the risk-adjusted discount rate to evaluate risky projects. It selects the appropriate discount rate by determining the project payback through use of the following table:

Project Payback	Discount
Less than 1 year	0.06
1 to 5 years	0.08
5 to 10 years	0.10
Over 10 years	0.12

Which project should Anderson invest in?

13–5. Amalgamated Great Southern is evaluating two mutually exclusive investment possibilities. Each proposal costs $3,000 and is expected to last three years. Estimated cash flows for the proposed projects depend on the kind of economic climate that prevails each year and appear to be as follows:

Economic Climate	Probability	CFAT per Year ($) A	B
Bad	0.2	0	2,400
Average	0.6	3,000	3,000
Good	0.2	7,500	3,600

Amalgamated has decided to evaluate the riskier project at $k = 10$ percent and the less–risky project at $k = 8$ percent.

a. Calculate the expected annual cash flow for each project.

b. Determine the expected net present value of each project if Amalgamated equates risk with the standard deviation of annual cash flows after tax.

c. What should Amalgamated decide about these two projects? Justify your answer.

13–6. The firm is in the process of evaluating some new projects. It does this by comparing each project's risk–adjusted discount rate from CAPM with the project's expected rate of return. Given the information below, determine which projects are acceptable and which are not.

Project	Beta
A	1.0
B	1.2
C	−0.5
D	2.0

Required rate of return on market index = 8%.
Risk-free interest rate = 5%.

Possible rates of return and associated probabilities of the projects are as follows:

Probability	Rates of Return (%) A	B	C	D
0.3	10	−5	5	−10
0.6	15	10	4	10
0.1	20	15	3	30

13–7. A proposed investment project is expected to cost $200,000 initially after all tax considerations have been determined. The subsequent expected CFATs for the project are $100,000 per year, and the estimated life of the investment is four years. The firm has also determined that the appropriate risk-adjusted discount rate for this proposal is 10 percent.

   a. Determine the expected net present value of the project.

   b. If all other estimates stay the same, determine the project's NPV if:

      (1) The initial cost is 50 percent higher than originally estimated.

      (2) The annual CFAT is 50 percent lower than originally estimated.

      (3) The discount rate is 50 percent higher than originally estimated.

      (4) The project's life is 50 percent shorter than originally estimated.

   c. To which of these four estimation errors is the NPV of the project most sensitive? Justify your answer.

13–8. Culbertson Manufacturing is evaluating a project with a beta of 1.5. This project has expected CFATs of $2,000 per year for five years, with an initial investment of $9,000. The risk-free rate is 8 percent and the market risk premium is 8 percent.

   a. Calculate the risk-adjusted discount rate for this project.

   b. Determine if the project should be accepted or rejected.

13–9. A proposed project for Vetter Diesels has the estimated CFATs shown below with states of the economy and probabilities. The company plans to use a risk-adjusted discount rate of 25 percent.

   a. Calculate the expected CFAT for each year.

   b. Calculate the expected NPV.

Year	State of Economy	CFAT ($)	Estimated Project Probability
0	—	−250,000	1.0
1	Bad	100,000	0.2
	Average	125,000	0.6
	Good	150,000	0.2
2	Bad	100,000	0.4
	Average	150,000	0.2
	Good	200,000	0.4
3	Bad	50,000	0.4
	Average	100,000	0.2
	Good	150,000	0.4

SELECTED REFERENCES

General discussions of risk analysis in capital budgeting can be found in:

Ang, James S., and Wilbur G. Lewellen. "Risk Adjustment in Capital Investment Project Evaluations." *Financial Management,* Summer 1982, pp. 5–14.

Fama, Eugene F. "Risk-adjusted Discount Rates and Capital Budgeting under Uncertainty." *Journal of Financial Economics,* August 1977, pp. 3–24.

Hodder, James E., and Henry E. Riggs. "Pitfalls in Evaluating Risky Projects." *Harvard Business Review,* January–February 1985, pp. 128–35.

Use of the CAPM in capital budgeting is discussed in:

Graver, Robert R. "Investment Policy Implications of the Capital Asset Pricing Model." *Journal of Finance*, March 1981, pp. 127–41.

APPENDIX 13–A   CERTAINTY EQUIVALENTS

A formalized method for adjusting the cash flows is called the *certainty equivalent method* (CE); the riskiness of the project is handled, not by adjusting the discount rate but by adjusting the expected cash flows. The proponents of this method argue that the two important concepts accounted for in the valuation process—the time value of money and risk—should be separated. Specifically, use of a discount rate that lumps together the risk-free interest rate and a risk premium is wrong; discounting for the futurity of cash flows should include only time value considerations, not risk considerations. Adding the risk premium into the discount rate leads to a compounding of risk over time.

Let:

$$CE_t = \text{certainty equivalent CFAT in year } t$$

The certainty equivalent in any year represents the CFAT that investors would be satisfied to receive for certain in lieu of the distribution of CFATs that are possible for that year. In effect, the certainty equivalent converts the project's expected CFAT for the year into a certain amount investors consider equivalent to the project's calculated CFAT for the year. There is an inverse relationship between the risk of the expected CFAT and the certainty equivalent—the higher the risk, the smaller the certainty. Certainty equivalents are calculated as:

$$\text{Certainty equivalent} = \text{Risky cash flow} \times \alpha_t$$

where α_t is a certainty equivalent factor between 0.0 and 1.0. It is the ratio of the certain return to a risky return.

Once the certainty equivalents have been estimated, the certainty equivalent method computes NPV:

$$\overline{\text{NPV}} = \sum_{t=0}^{n} \frac{CE_t}{(1 + k_{RF})^t} \tag{13–A1}$$

where:

$$k_{RF} = \text{the risk-free interest rate}$$

NPV decision rules here are the same as with the risk-adjusted discount rate above. Recall that the risk-free interest rate, k_{RF}, can be approximated by the interest rate on U.S. government bonds.

The risk-adjusted-discount-rate approach is an intuitively appealing method. It seems very logical to apply a higher required rate of return to more risky proposals and a lower one to less risky proposals. Also, the theory is well developed and provides some concrete guidance about how to find risk-adjusted discount rates; thus, the method is both plausible and operationally tractable. On the disadvantage side, some argue that the method equates discounting for time with discounting for risk. This seems to imply that risk increases with time.

Because the certainty equivalent method can easily handle cash flow patterns that do not exhibit increasing risk with time, it seems to some a more flexible and general approach. On the negative side, the certainty equivalent method is not as intuitively appealing as the risk-adjusted-discount-rate method. It is more difficult to understand

and to explain the certainty equivalent adjustment. Also, implementation is more difficult. The certainty equivalent method requires the analyst to estimate a certainty equivalent for each year.

In summary, both methods have good and bad features. The essence of the difference between the two methods is that the risk-adjusted-discount-rate method accounts for risk by adjusting the discount rate in the *denominator* of the expected-net-present-value formula, while the certainty equivalent method accounts for risk by adjusting the expected cash flows in the *numerator* of the expected-net-present-value formula.

The valuation formula developed in Chapter 6 and used throughout the text is a risk-adjusted-discount-rate method. This fact does not imply that the certainty equivalent method is wrong, but it certainly reflects the far more widespread use today of the risk-adjusted-discount-rate approach.

PROBLEM FOR APPENDIX

13A–1. Given the following information, use the certainty equivalent method to determine if the proposed project is acceptable:

Year	Expected Cash Flow	Certainty Equivalent
0	−$100	−$100
1	60	48
2	60	48

U.S. government bond rate = 6%.
Cost of new corporate debt = 7%.
Average cost of capital = 10%.

The Cost of Capital, Capital Structure, and Dividend Policy

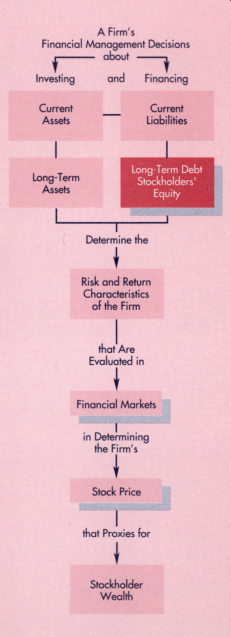

Part V analyzes critical long-term financing issues that every firm faces. Since the last three chapters discussed the long-term investment decisions that must be made, it is now appropriate to consider the long-term financing side. Every firm must decide how much its funds cost, how best to raise those funds, and how much of its after-tax profits should be reinvested in the firm and how much should be paid out directly to the stockholders. The issues discussed in Chapters 14 through 16 are among the most important in financial management.

Chapter 14 discusses the cost of capital, which plays a crucial role in the firm's financial decisions. In Chapters 11 through 13, we assumed we knew the cost of capital or discount rate to use in the capital budgeting process. In fact, it has to be calculated by the firm at the same time the investment decisions are made (for simplicity, we address these issues in a sequential fashion). The firm's financial managers must understand the subtle and subjective issues involved in making these calculations because improper estimates will have significant adverse implications for the firm. In calculating the cost of capital, we will use the concepts introduced in Chapter 6's discussion of valuation.

The cost of capital cannot be considered in isolation because it is directly affected by a firm's capital structure. Accordingly, Chapter 15 considers capital structure and addresses the issue of whether there is one optimal capital structure for each firm. As part of this analysis, we address the concept of leverage—the use of fixed-cost financing—in some detail because it is a natural part of any capital structure discussion. As is true of other financial decisions, the use of leverage involves a trade-off between return and risk, and firms must carefully consider the impact of leverage on their operations.

In Chapter 16 we consider the important issue of dividend payments to the stockholders. While a firm's earnings per share belong to its stockholders, the typical firm does not pay out all of its earnings in a period in the form of dividends, choosing instead to retain part of this amount. An important financial issue currently being debated involves the payment of dividends to stockholders. Should a firm pay dividends, and, if so, how much? After years of controversy, this issue remains unsettled. We will consider the various aspects of the controversy and observe prevailing beliefs and practices. We also consider stock repurchases made by a firm and the issue of stock dividends and stock splits.

14

Cost of Capital

Lowering the Cost of Capital

As discussed in Chapter 1, UtiliCorp United is an electric and gas utility company operating in seven states through five divisions, and in one Canadian province through a subsidiary. Total recent year-end capitalization and liabilities amounted to almost $1 billion.[1] The company's long-term financing consisted of 44 percent equity, 4 percent preference stock, and 52 percent long-term debt (also, of course, it used external short-term financing, primarily commercial paper and bank loans).

According to the *Annual Report:* "To lower our cost of capital, all 320,000 outstanding shares of the company's $4.125 Series of preference stock were called for redemption as of June 1 at $29.56 per share. This issue had cost the company 15.7 percent and was replaced with short-term debt incurring interest at only about 7.5 percent." The report continues: "We are considering issuing some type of permanent securities [next year] to retire existing short-term debt. The amount and timing will depend on the conditions of financial markets." Meanwhile, the company sold 2,000,000 shares of common stock for a net of $33 million, and the redemption of the preference stock had a total transaction value of about $9.5 million.

---

[1]Quotations and facts about UtiliCorp are taken from its 1987 *Annual Report.*

A firm's cost of capital plays a crucial role in the firm's financial decisions. The cost of capital is typically used as the discount rate (the k in Chapters 12 and 13) in capital budgeting decisions. More generally, we know that the firm's goal is to maximize stockholders' wealth. To achieve this, it should minimize the cost of all inputs, including capital. The financial manager, therefore, must focus on developing a sound estimate of the firm's cost of capital.

Referring to the Utilicorp statements and events, what did the company mean by the statement "to lower our cost of capital"? Replacing preferred stock costing 15.7 percent with short-term debt costing 7.5 percent obviously reduces Utilicorp's cost of financing, but what about the sale of the new shares of common stock—how did that transaction affect Utilicorp's cost of financing? This chapter will enable us to evaluate such statements and financial transactions, and understand the important concept of cost of capital.

The primary *chapter learning objectives* are:

1. To understand the meaning, importance, and use of the cost of capital.
2. To learn basic calculation procedures, concentrating on how to estimate the cost of capital assuming the firm's capital structure (the mix of financing sources being used) is relatively stable.[2]

UNDERSTANDING THE COST OF CAPITAL

The concept of a required rate of return was developed in Chapter 5. Suppliers of funds to a firm expect to be compensated for the time and risk involved; that is, they have a required rate of return they *expect* to earn on their investment. This rate reflects the *opportunity rate* that such funds could earn elsewhere, holding risk constant.

From the standpoint of the firm using funds, the required rate of return becomes the *minimum* acceptable expected rate to be earned from new investment opportunities. Since the required rate of return is an opportunity cost, the suppliers presumably could earn the required rate of return from comparable alternatives elsewhere, and they are going to demand that the firm earn at least this much. The firm, therefore, should not accept projects earning less.

cost of capital
composite cost of a firm's financing sources

The **cost of capital,** or required rate of return for a firm, can be defined as the composite cost of the firm's financing components. Like any other input the firm uses, capital has a cost. The total capital of a firm typically consists of several components, and each component has its own cost. The idea of a cost of capital is to bring these component costs together in one number the firm can use for decision-making purposes. Two very important uses of the cost of capital stand out in particular.

- The cost of capital is an important link in achieving the financial goal of the firm—maximizing the stockholders' wealth by maximizing the firm's equity value. Maximization of the firm's value is closely tied to minimization of all input costs, and capital is an important input.

---

[2]In the next chapter, we will relax the assumption that the capital structure is stable and see how this affects both the cost of capital and, what's more important, the value of the common stock.

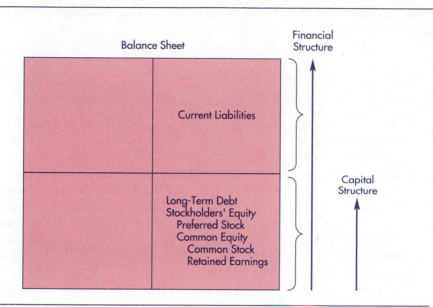

■ *Figure 14–1*
Sources of Capital
for the Firm

- The cost of capital is used to make capital budgeting decisions. It is important to use the correct minimum acceptable rate of return on new investments when making these decisions.[3]

To simplify, we assume that new investment projects will have the same level of risk as the firm's current investment projects, and that any new projects will be financed with the same proportions of each long-term financing component as is currently used. The cost of capital must reflect the overall financing activity of the firm—that is, over time, the firm is going to raise capital from several sources and use this capital to finance the firm. Though a particular project may be financed solely with the proceeds of a debt issue, it would be inappropriate to declare that the cost of the debt is the cost of capital for that project. The reason is that over time a firm will raise capital from several sources, and over the long run the funds raised by the firm will represent a composite, or weighted average, of sources.

What are these sources of funds for a company? They can be found on the right side of the balance sheet, as depicted in Figure 14–1. The entire right side of the balance sheet is referred to as the *financial structure,* and the long-term sources of financing as the **capital structure.** Our concern here will be with the capital structure. As we can see from Figure 14–1, this primarily involves long-term debt, preferred stock, and common stock.

capital structure
long-term sources of
financing for a firm

As noted, it is best to view the firm as an ongoing concern where the cost of capital (k) is a weighted average of the individual sources used over a period of years. To calculate this weighted average, the firm estimates the cost of each

---

[3]Sometimes risk adjustments are necessary, as explained in Chapter 13.

source of capital to be used and the percentage of the total financing that each source constitutes.

CALCULATING THE COST OF CAPITAL

In calculating the cost of capital, certain points should be noted:

- The cost of capital, like valuation, is a forward-looking concept. We are concerned here with future costs, not historical costs. Previous financing costs have no direct impact on the costs of new financing.
- The cost of capital is a market-based concept. Funds are raised in the capital markets, where rates of return are set on the basis of demand and supply conditions, and the cost of capital must reflect this. As a required rate of return, the cost of capital measures the *opportunity cost*—the rate that these funds could earn outside the firm if invested in alternatives with the same level of risk. The opportunity-cost concept is very important in understanding the cost of capital.
- Capital costs must be calculated on an after-tax basis. This makes them consistent with cash flows, which also are calculated on an after-tax basis.

Calculating the cost of capital is a three-part process:

1. Estimate the specific costs of capital.
2. Determine the weights or capital structure proportions.
3. Combine costs and weights to obtain an estimate of the cost of capital, *k*.

We will examine each of these three parts of the process of calculating a cost of capital in turn.

ESTIMATING SPECIFIC COSTS OF CAPITAL

By *specific costs of capital* we mean the costs of capital of each of the various parts, or components, included in the weighted cost of capital. Before turning to the details of the analysis, let's make sure the general features of the process are clear. The process of raising capital goes like this:

- *At time zero* ($t = 0$): The firm issues financial claims on itself (stock, bonds, etc.) to investors (the capital source), and the firm receives capital (cash) it desires from the investors.
- *At later time periods* ($t = 1, \ldots n$): The firm pays cash benefits (dividends, interest payments, etc.) to investors who hold the financial claims that were issued at $t = 0$.

The details of this process will change as we consider different specific sources of capital, but its general nature is always the same: the firm receives cash now in exchange for either future cash payments to the capital providers or the investors' expectation of a future price for the security higher than that paid for the security, or both.

It will be helpful to separate our work into two parts. Finding a specific cost of capital may be thought of as a two-step process:

1. Find the investors' required rate of return associated with the capital source.
2. Adjust the investors' required rate of return found in Step 1 into a specific cost of capital for the firm by considering:
   a. The firm's tax situation.
   b. The flotation costs the firm may incur in acquiring the capital.[4]

In practice, we need not perform these steps separately. But focusing on the two-step process at the beginning of our work is useful because it emphasizes an important point. A specific cost of capital for the firm is basically the rate of return required by investors *adjusted for the firm's tax and flotation cost particulars*. We will consider each of these two concepts in turn.

Investors' Required Rate of Return

We learned about the required rate of return in Chapter 6 when we studied valuation. The term *investors* here refers to the market, or all investors in aggregate; therefore, we are interested in what rate of return the market would require as compensation for providing capital to the firm. We know from Chapters 5 and 6 that required rates of return are conceptually related to risk—that is, there is always a trade-off between required rate of return and risk for sources of financing. As investors perceive greater risk from a financial instrument, they will expect, and therefore seek, a higher required rate of return.

The trade-off between risk and required rate of return, which underlies all of finance, is illustrated in Figure 14–2. The vertical intercept of the upward-sloping trade-off is the risk-free rate, RF, which generally is taken to be the rate of return on short-term, default-free Treasury securities. Long-term Treasuries, though also default-free, expose investors to interest-rate risk, that is, the risk that the price of the bonds could drop if interest rates rise. Therefore, these securities will plot on the trade-off line above RF. Corporate bonds, which carry varying degrees of default risk, will plot higher on the line than long-term Treasuries. Note that corporate bonds rated BAA, which have a higher probability of default than AAA corporates, are above the AAA bonds—higher risk, therefore higher required rate of return.

Preferred stock carries somewhat more risk than corporate bonds because of a lower priority of payment to the stockholders. Finally, common stock is the riskiest security we discuss here, and therefore it plots at the highest position. The risk to the owners is the highest because the future price of the stock is unknown and because the firm may or may not pay a dividend, a decision it can change at any time. Even if it pays a dividend, the stockholder is last in line as a claimant on the firm's income stream, after the bondholders, who come first, and the preferred stockholders, who come second. Another way of looking at it is that the firm has obligated itself to make specific payments to the holders of these securities, including a legal obligation to pay the bondholders, but the common stockholders have no such commitment.

[4]Flotation costs are initial expenses the firm incurs in acquiring the capital from investors.

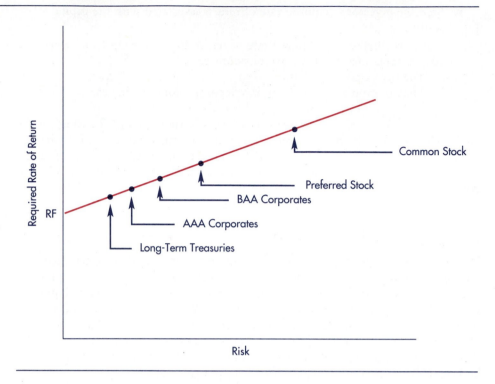

■ *Figure 14–2*
Trade-Off between Risk
and Required Rate of
Return for Sources
of Financing

Consider a particular source of capital, say source j: In present-value terms, investors' required rate of return for capital source j is the discount rate that satisfies this equation:

$$C_0 = \frac{C_1}{1 + k_j} + \ldots + \frac{C_n}{(1 + k_j)^n} = \sum_{t=1}^{n} \frac{C_t}{(1 + k_j)^t} \qquad \text{(14–1)}$$

where:

$$C_0 = \text{cash (price) paid by investors at } t = 0$$
$$C_t = \text{expected cash payments from firm to investors in year } t$$
$$n = \text{expected life of capital}$$
$$k_j = \text{investors' required rate of return for capital source } j$$

In a formal sense, solving 14–1 for k_j could be tedious, possibly involving a lengthy trial-and-error solution (see Chapter 6). For ease of exposition, approximation formulas will be introduced below at appropriate times.

The Firm's Cost of Capital

As noted earlier, in most cases the specific cost of capital for source j will not equal k_j since tax consequences and flotation costs relevant to the firm's situation may be important. A definition of the cost of capital for source j is:

$$k_J = \begin{array}{l} \text{The } \textit{after-tax, after-flotation expenses} \text{ rate of return the firm pays} \\ \text{to acquire capital from source } j. \end{array}$$

A comparison of the definitions of k_j and k_J shows the close linkages between the two concepts. We see that k_j is the investors' required rate of return. It is the price investors charge for letting the firm use their money. On the other hand, k_J is the actual cost the firm incurs. Differences between k_j and k_J can occur because of the firm's taxes and flotation costs. Some examples of these differences are illustrated below.

Debt

The cost of debt is calculated the same whether it is in any of several forms of bonds or bank loans. The features that distinguish one form of debt from another are primarily nonfinancial, and we can analyze the cost of debt as if only one type existed.

Investors' Required Rate of Return on Debt

Adapting Equation 14–1 to the debt situation, we would solve the following equation for k_d:

$$B_0 = \sum_{t=1}^{n} \frac{I_t + B_t}{(1 + k_d)^t} \qquad (14\text{–}2)$$

where:

$$k_d = \text{investors' required rate of return on debt}$$
$$B_0 = \text{initial price (proceeds) of debt}$$
$$I_t = \text{interest paid in period } t$$
$$B_t = \text{principal repayment in period } t$$
$$n = \text{maturity date}$$

This is equivalent to solving for the *yield to maturity* on the debt. It is the rate of return investors demand to purchase the new issue of debt.

Cost of Debt

Two adjustments, one major and one minor, need to be made to Equation 14–2 to compute the firm's cost of debt:

$$\text{Cost of debt} = k_D = \frac{(1 - T)}{(1 - f)} k_d \qquad (14\text{–}3)$$

where:

$$T = \text{corporate tax rate}$$
$$f = \text{flotation cost as a percentage of } B_0$$
$$k_d = \text{investors' required rate of return on debt}$$

Notice first that the cost of debt, k_D, is simply the investors' required rate of return on debt, k_d, adjusted for the firm's tax rate and flotation cost. We must adjust the cost of debt to an after-tax basis because our concern is with after-tax cash flows. It is important that cash flows and rates of return (or costs) be comparably based. Since a firm can deduct interest payments before computing its taxes, the firm's effective annual interest charges are only $(1 - T)$ times the annual interest payment. For moderate-sized and larger U.S. firms, the marginal corporate tax rate is 34 percent.[5] In effect, at this marginal rate the government is subsidizing about one third of the cost of debt financing.

The flotation cost adjustment works in the other direction. As the flotation cost increases, the cost of debt rises. For many debt situations the flotation cost as a percentage of the proceeds raised is very small, which leads many analysts to ignore it.

■ *Example*

Suppose the Timberlake Shoe Company is preparing to issue some new 10 percent coupon, 20-year bonds. Investors will pay $1,000 per bond when they are issued if the annual interest payments by the firm are $100 (a 10 percent coupon). The firm's tax rate is 34 percent, and flotation costs are 2 percent. Then:

$$\text{Cost of debt} = k_D = \frac{0.66}{0.98} \times \frac{\$100}{\$1000} = 0.0673 = 6.73 \text{ percent} \quad ■$$

Debt has the lowest cost of any source of capital available to the firm for two primary reasons:

1. The cost of debt is low relative to other sources because, *from an investor's viewpoint,* debt is the safest financial asset the firm can issue. This results from the priority of debt when the firm pays its sources of capital and in case of financial difficulty or bankruptcy. Because there is less risk in buying debt (compared to other financial instruments), investors will accept a lower rate of return on the debt.
2. Interest payments on debt are tax deductible, unlike dividend payments to either preferred or common stockholders.

Preferred Stock

The firm sells preferred stock to investors and compensates them in subsequent years by paying preferred dividends. These dividends are paid before common shareholders receive payment. Preferred stock carries a stipulated dividend rate, usually a percentage of the preferred's par value.[6]

Investors' Required Rate of Return on Preferred Stock

Since preferred stock is an equity security with constant dividend payments, we can employ the perpetuity version of Equation 14–1:

$$\text{Investors' required rate of return on preferred stock} = k_p = \frac{d}{P_0} \quad \textbf{(14–4)}$$

where:

$$d = \text{expected (constant) preferred dividend}$$
$$P_0 = \text{sale price of preferred stock}$$

---

[5]This is the federal tax rate. State tax rates would raise the marginal tax rate.
[6]Therefore, unlike the par value for a common stock, a preferred stock's par value is an important issue.

As Equation 14–4 shows, investors' required rate of return on preferred stock is the stock's annual dividend divided by the issue (or sale) price. The ratio of dividend to price is the *dividend yield* for the preferred.

Cost of Preferred Stock

Unlike interest payments, preferred dividend payments are not tax deductible to the company, so one dollar of preferred stock dividends actually results in one dollar of after-tax cash outflow from the firm. Therefore, there is no tax adjustment to make in converting k_p into the company's cost of preferred (k_P). There is, however, a flotation cost adjustment, resulting in:

$$\text{Cost of preferred stock} = k_P = \frac{d}{(1-f)P_0} = \frac{k_p}{(1-f)} \qquad \textbf{(14–5)}$$

■ *Example*

If investors are willing to pay $100 per share for the preferred stock of Timberlake Shoes that pays a 12 percent dividend, and flotation costs are 5 percent:

$$\text{Cost of preferred stock} = k_P = \frac{.12}{(0.95)} = 0.126 = 12.6\%$$

The cost of preferred is higher than Timberlake's previously calculated cost of debt (6.73 percent). This is because the preferred dividends are not tax deductible, as interest payments are, and because the preferred is a riskier investment *for an investor* than debt because the bondholder must be paid before the preferred stockholder can be paid. ■

Equity

The two sources of new equity capital are common stock and retained earnings. Common stock equity, or external equity, refers to proceeds from the sale of new common stock. Retained earnings, or internal equity, is the new equity funds raised within the firm by keeping a portion of *current* earnings. In effect, this source of equity is provided by the current stockowners in the form of forgone dividends.[7]

Investors' Required Rate of Return on Equity, k_e

The required rate of return on equity reflects the opportunity cost that stockholders can earn outside the firm. Investors' required rates of return on common stock (externally provided equity) and on retained earnings (internally provided equity) are equal. Therefore, we may refer to both or either as the required rate of return on equity, k_e.

Why do common stock and retained earnings have equal required rates of return? It should seem reasonable that investors would require the same return on additional investment in the firm in the form of retentions as they would on an investment in new common stock. By retaining earnings, the firm is denying its stockholders the use of these funds. What could the stockholders do with these

---

[7]*Earnings available to common shareholders* consist of dividends paid to common stockholders plus retained earnings.

monies? One option would be to buy more common stock in the firm. What kind of return would the investor require on this additional investment? The same as on the stock, k_e! Therefore, retained earnings have an opportunity cost, which is k_e.

Does it sound strange that stockholders should receive a return on their investment of retained earnings? It shouldn't. After all, the money retained is not being paid out to shareholders. The key to this puzzle is future earnings. Stockholders in companies that reinvest heavily expect the retained earnings to result in rapid growth. Therefore, earnings should increase substantially, and the company should have a rising dividend pattern. Today's forgone dividends should be rewarded by higher returns in the future.

Consider next the problem of estimating k_e. A good financial analyst often has several ways to do this, but two methods are particularly important.[8]

1. Dividend Discount Model Approach   This approach is consistent with the general definition given in Equation 14–1. For illustration purposes, consider the firm's issue of new common stock. The share price represents investors' outlay of funds. Cash payments to the stockholders are paid as common dividends, which are not tax deductible to the company; thus, every dollar paid results in a one-dollar expense after tax. Unlike preferred stock, however, common stock has no promised dividend rate. Investors estimate the future dividend rate by what is being paid on current shares and through any statements the company makes during the promotion of the new issue. Once new stock is issued, it has the same rights, privileges, dividends, price, risk, and so on, as the current stock, unless the new stock is some special form of common.

Because stockholders often expect dividend growth, using a perpetuity model such as Equation 14–4 for common stock is usually inappropriate. Instead, we should use a model that allows for future growth. We developed such a model in Chapter 6 (Equation 6–8), assuming that dividends were growing at an estimated annual rate of g percent each year for a very long period. This model is referred to as the *constant-growth version* of the dividend discount model.

$$\begin{array}{l} \text{Investors' required} \\ \text{rate of return} \\ \text{on equity} \end{array} = k_e = \frac{D_1}{P_0} + g \tag{14–6}$$

where

D_1 = next year's expected dividend per share
P_0 = current common stock price
g = expected constant dividend growth rate (in decimal form)

Equation 14–6 presumes a growth rate in expected dividends at g percent forever. This may seem extremely unrealistic, but Equation 14–6 is nonetheless very useful. Many firms do have dividend growth rates that are expected to be approxi-

---

[8]A third alternative is sometimes used, although it probably is best thought of as a quick, rough approximation. This method, called the *risk premium on debt technique,* calls for adding the average equity risk premium to a company's current debt cost. Historically, the equity premium risk has averaged 7 percent to 8 percent. These numbers are appropriate for a firm of average riskiness (that is, a beta approximately equal to that of the market, 1.0). Firms with smaller betas, such as utilities, would use correspondingly smaller equity risk premiums, such as 3 percent to 4 percent. Conversely, firms with betas larger than the market would use correspondingly larger equity risk premiums.

mately constant for several years, and for such firms, Equation 14–6 provides good estimates of k_e.

When the firm calculates the required rate of return on debt, the future expected interest payments and principal repayments are usually fixed in amount and may therefore be estimated with a very high degree of accuracy.[9] In addition, although future preferred dividends are not contractual obligations, they are fixed by terms stated on the preferred instrument and they also may be estimated relatively accurately. Common stock dividends, however, are paid at the discretion of the firm. Future dividend payments depend on the future earnings stream, and it is extremely difficult to estimate future earnings. Generally, the firm's earnings prospects will follow economy and industry trends, but it is equally difficult to predict such trends.

Note that g is the *expected* growth rate in dividends, not the historical growth rate. Although investors may use past growth rates to form expectations about future growth rates, they must ultimately estimate the expected future growth rate. What matters is the market's expectation of the growth rate. A good source of information is analysts' forecasts, obtainable from brokerage houses and investment advisory services such as *The Value Line Investment Survey*.[10] Some research suggests that analysts' estimates are more accurate than those of mechanical models.

▪ *Example*

To illustrate the procedures of using the dividend discount model to estimate the required rate of return on equity as well as the use of expected growth rate data, consider two New York Stock Exchange companies, Hawaiian Electric and Hershey Foods. Assume that Equation 14–6 is applicable for these two companies. Using late 1990 issues of *The Value Line Investment Survey,* the following data were obtained:

	Dividend Yield	Estimated Dividend Growth 1993–1995
Hawaiian Electric	7.4%	4.0%
Hershey Foods	2.5%	13.0%

Assuming that the constant growth version of the dividend discount model is appropriate for each of these companies and that *The Value Line Investment Survey* is reasonably accurate (i.e., reflects the market's beliefs) in estimating the dividend growth rate, the estimated required rate of return would be 11.4 percent for Hawaiian Electric and 15.5 percent for Hershey Foods. ▪

Finally, we need to reemphasize that Equation 14–6 applies to both common stock and retained earnings. That is:

[9] For floating-rate debt, however, interest payments in the future will change as interest rates change.

[10] The Institutional Brokers' Estimate Service (IBES) summarizes the earnings forecasts made by over 2,000 analysts representing more than a hundred brokerage firms. IBES covers some 3,500 stocks, providing such information as the highest and lowest estimate for each period, the amount of variation among the forecasts provided by different analysts, and the long-term (five-year) expected rate of growth in earnings.

| Investors' required rate of return on common stock | = | Investors' required rate of return on retained earnings | = | Investors' required rate of return on equity | = k_e |

2. The CAPM Approach   The required rate of return on equity (k_e) is the most difficult to estimate of the several required rates of return. One difficulty in using Equation 14–6 is the unreliability of estimates of the dividend growth rate (g). Different estimates of the expected growth rate in dividends for a company typically exist at any given time.

One potential way to avoid the inherent difficulties of future dividend estimation is to use the *capital asset pricing model* (CAPM) we used first in Chapter 5 and again in Chapter 13 as a risk adjustment method. Recall that this model expresses the relationship between the required rate of return and the risk of an asset. The firm's stock is a financial asset, so we can apply the CAPM to the problem of determining k_e, the required rate of return on equity.

In this context:

$$k_e = k_{RF} + (k_M - k_{RF})\text{Beta} \qquad \text{(14–7)}$$

where:

$$k_{RF} = \text{risk-free rate of interest}$$
$$k_M = \text{expected rate of return on the market index}$$
$$\text{Beta} = \text{beta (covariability) risk of the equity.}$$

In principle, k_{RF} is observable in the marketplace, and k_M (or the difference $k_M - k_{RF}$) can be estimated. What remains is to estimate beta.

As we know from Appendix 5–A, the most common method of estimating beta is through *regression analysis*. Rates of return on the firm's stock (R_s) and rates of return on a market index (R_m), for example, a stock market index, are collected. Typically, about five years of monthly returns are used to estimate beta. R_s values are then statistically related to R_m values through the following straight-line regression equation (it may be desirable to review Appendix 5-A):

$$R_s = a + bR_m \qquad \text{(14–8)}$$

The result of this statistical work is that beta equals the slope of this straight line:

$$\text{Beta} = b$$

■ *Example*

Figure 14–3 illustrates the CAPM approach to estimating the required rate of return on equity. It shows the same two companies from above, Hawaiian Electric and Hershey Foods, using their betas as estimated by *The Value Line Investment Survey*. Notice that Hawaiian Electric, as would be expected because it is a relatively stable electric utility, has a lower beta, .65, and therefore a lower required rate of return when read off the trade-off that the CAPM represents between risk (beta) and required rate of return. Hershey, on the other hand, had a higher beta, 1.10, and, therefore, a higher required rate of return. Once the *securities market line* (the plot of the CAPM) is plotted, the required rates of return for various securities can be determined on the basis of their betas. ■

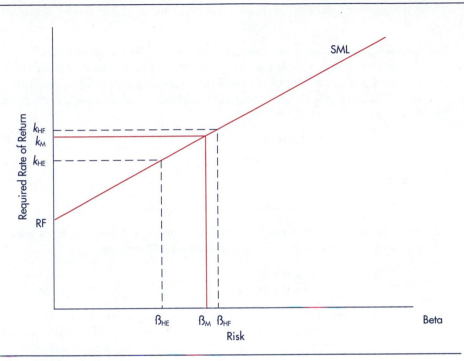

■ *Figure 14–3*
Using the CAPM to
Determine the Required
Rate of Return on Equity

Note: RF = the risk-free rate
HF = Hershey Foods, HE = Hawaiian Electric, M = market index
SML = security market line

Evaluating the Two Approaches

Regardless of the approach used, estimating k_e is difficult. Using the dividend valuation model assumes that dividends will grow at a constant rate for an indefinite period. Furthermore, it is difficult to estimate g. Regardless of what g has been in the past, what matters is the g expected by investors in the future. Obviously, g can only be estimated—it cannot be determined conclusively.

The CAPM approach also has its problems. A primary issue is the accurate determination of beta. Research suggests that individual-stock betas are nonstable over time. Betas are typically estimated using historical data, but the model calls for the beta expected to prevail in the future. Other problems with the CAPM approach include the estimation of k_M and k_{RF}.

It is extremely important to remember that the estimation of k_e will always be an art and not a science. We are dealing with the uncertain future, and estimates will be subject to error. Every approach is subject to error because of the estimates required. It is a mistake to criticize one methodology as being subject to error without pointing out that all methodologies are subject to error. Although a decision maker may have good reason to use a particular approach, he or she can never state categorically that this is the correct approach to use and that the parameters chosen are the correct ones.

Cost of Equity, k_E

Although common stock and retained earnings have the same investors' required rate of return, they do not have the same cost of capital. In studying this issue, we use the constant-growth version of the dividend discount model, Equation 14–6.

1. *Common stock.* When new common stock is issued, the firm incurs flotation costs that reduce the cash proceeds the firm receives. Since the dividend payments are not tax deductible, there is no tax adjustment to make. Therefore, a flotation cost adjustment to Equation 14–6 is made as follows:

$$\text{Cost of new common stock} = k_{CS} = \frac{D_1}{(1 - f)P_0} + g \quad\quad \textbf{(14–9)}$$

where:

$$f = \text{flotation costs as a percentage of } P_0$$

2. *Retained earnings.* When the firm retains earnings, no flotation costs are involved. Nor are there any tax adjustments. Therefore:

$$\text{Cost of retained earnings} = k_{RE} = \frac{D_1}{P_0} + g = k_e \quad\quad \textbf{(14–10)}$$

Because there are no flotation costs when earnings are retained, retentions have a lower cost of capital than common stock. That's one of the reasons that firms retain earnings: going to the market (to sell new common shares) incurs flotation costs. Notice that because there are no flotation costs, $k_{RE} = k_e$, the investors' required rate of return on equity.

- **Example**

Consider the following financial data that are relevant to new equity capital raised by the Timberlake Shoe Company:

Next year's expected earnings: $10.
Next year's expected dividend: $5.
Current common stock price: $50.
Expected dividend growth: 8 percent per year.
Flotation cost for new stock: 6 percent of current stock price.

Therefore:

$$\text{Cost of new common stock} = k_{CS} = \frac{\$5}{(0.94)(\$50)} + 0.08 = 0.186 = 18.6\%$$

$$\text{Cost of retained earnings} = k_{RE} = \frac{\$5}{\$50} + 0.08 = 0.180 = 18.0\%$$

Since retained earnings incur no flotation costs, $k_{RE} < k_{CS}$. ▪

The Relative Size of Costs of Capital

A final point about the cost of equity is its relative size compared to the previously calculated cost of debt and cost of preferred. Any specific cost of capital reflects the market's required rate of return on that capital source as well as its tax-deduction characteristics. Since equity is the riskiest of these three financial claims, equity has the highest cost of capital. For any company $k_E > k_P > k_D$.

DETERMINING THE CAPITAL STRUCTURE WEIGHTS

We have examined several sources of long-term capital and shown how to estimate the explicit cost of each. We now need to consider the next step, determining the weights to go along with the costs of capital. An explanation of the weighting scheme requires a brief explanation of capital structure.

Capital Structure

The picture of what kinds of long-term capital a firm has used to finance its long-term investments is revealed by looking at the firm's balance sheet. As noted, the proportionate use of these long-term sources of capital is called the *capital structure* of the firm.

■ *Example*

Consider the capital structure, or long-term financing, for Utilicorp at the end of one recent year. The firm used long-term debt, preferred stock, and common equity to finance its operations. The following amounts carried on the balance sheet represent the historical book-value capital structure as of that point in time.

$$
\begin{aligned}
\text{Long-term debt} &= \$317{,}697{,}000 \\
\text{Preferred stock} &= \$\ 25{,}000{,}000 \\
\text{Common equity} &= \$264{,}448{,}000 \\
\text{Total capitalization} &= \$607{,}145{,}000
\end{aligned}
$$
■

In Chapter 15, we will discuss the concept of an *optimal target capital structure,* which each firm is presumed to have. For example, according to the annual report, UtiliCorp's capital structure was very close to the industry average for similar utility companies, and "the firm's goal is to maintain debt-to-equity at about industry levels."

In this discussion, we assume that the firm is currently operating with a desired, or target, capital structure that will remain constant. However, even with a target capital structure and target (versus historic or current) weights, the weights used in the weighted average cost of capital could be, and are, calculated in two different ways: from book values and from market values.

■ *Example*

To illustrate the calculations of both weighting schemes, we again use data for Timberlake Shoes. Table 14–1 shows the relevant data and the calculations for book value weights and market value weights.

- *Book value weights* are determined by dividing the book value of each capital source by the sum of the book values of all the long-term capital sources. As we can see from Table 14–1, the book value weights are debt, 40 percent; preferred, 20 percent; and common equity, 40 percent.
- *Market value weights* are determined by dividing the market value of each capital source by the sum of the market values of all the sources. The

■ **Table 14–1**
Calculation of
Book-Value and
Market-Value Weights
for Timberlake Shoes

Timberlake Shoe Company
Summary of Long-Term Financing
(from Balance Sheet)

Mortgage bonds ($1,000 par)	$20,000,000
Preferred stock ($100 par)	10,000,000
Common stock ($40 par)	20,000,000
Total long-term financing	$50,000,000

The book value weights would be calculated as:

Source	Book Value	Weights
Debt	$20,000,000	0.40
Preferred stock	10,000,000	0.20
Common stock	20,000,000	0.40
Total long-term financing	$50,000,000	1.00

Number of mortgage bonds = $20,000,000/$1,000 = 20,000
Number of preferred shares = $10,000,000/$100 = 100,000
Number of common shares = $20,000,000/$40 = 500,000

Current price of mortgage bonds = $900 per bond
Current price of preferred stock = $80 per share
Current price of common stock = $60 per share

The market value weight would be calculated as:

Source	Number of Securities	Price per Security	Market Value	Weight
Debt	20,000	$900	$18,000,000	0.321
Preferred stock	100,000	80	8,000,000	0.143
Common stock	500,000	60	30,000,000	0.536
			$56,000,000	1.000

market value of any capital source is the number of securities outstanding times the price per security. ■

If the market and book values of the various sources are considerably different, as in the example, the weights calculated under the two methods can be considerably different. Which is the correct weighting system?

From the standpoint of theory, there is little debate among finance scholars. The theoretical development of the weighted-average cost of capital uses market weights; that is a compelling reason for preferring market values. Also, note that our emphasis on valuation throughout this text leads to the conclusion that the use of book-value weights with market-determined costs of financing is logically inconsistent.

There are also some arguments in favor of using book weights. Because market weights are determined by market prices, which may fluctuate quite widely, market weights are subject to much more variation than book weights. Also, it may be difficult to determine market values of some kinds of financial instruments. Book-value information is certainly much easier to get.

In practice, firms may calculate both measures. Hershey Foods, for example, calculates the cost of capital "based on current book weights" as well as on market values.[11]

CALCULATING THE WEIGHTED AVERAGE COST OF CAPITAL (WACC)

Once the various costs of capital and their weights have been determined, the overall (composite) cost of capital, referred to as the **weighted average cost of capital (WACC),** can be calculated:

weighted average cost of capital (WACC)
a firm's composite cost of capital

$$\text{The weighted average cost of capital} = k_{WACC} = \Sigma \left(\begin{array}{c} \text{Capital structure} \\ \text{weights (\%)} \end{array} \times \begin{array}{c} \text{Cost of each} \\ \text{capital source} \end{array} \right)$$

Writing this definition more compactly:

$$k_{WACC} = w_1 k_1 + w_2 k_2 + \ldots + w_N k_N = \sum_{J=1}^{N} w_J k_J \qquad \textbf{(14-11)}$$

where:

$$k_{WACC} = \text{the weighted average cost of capital}$$
$$k_J = \text{cost of capital of the } j\text{th source}$$
$$w_J = \text{percentage of capital supplied by the } j\text{th source}$$
$$N = \text{number of long-term capital sources in firm's capital structure}$$

Once again, the rationale for this equation is that, over time, the firm will use several sources of capital in combination. The stockholders will supply part of the financing, the bondholders will supply part of the financing, preferred stockholders may supply part of the financing, and so forth. Since each of these sources of capital has a different cost, it is appropriate to think of the composite, or weighted average, of these separate costs of funds to reflect the proportions of the total that each source constitutes.

▪ *Example*

Timberlake Shoe Company has three sources of capital: debt, preferred stock and common equity. In this case, the weighted average cost of capital is written:

$$k_{WACC} = w_D k_D + w_P k_P + w_E k_E$$

For Timberlake Shoe, using the market weights and capital costs computed earlier, and assuming equity capital comes solely from retained earnings:

Source	Market Weights, w	Cost of Capital, k	wk
Debt	0.321	0.067	0.022
Preferred stock	0.143	0.126	0.018
Common equity	0.536	0.180	0.096
Total	1.000		k = 0.136 = 13.6%

---

[11]See Panel Discussion/Cost of Capital, "Divisional Hurdle Rates and the Cost of Capital," *Financial Management,* Spring 1989, p. 23.

Given the above market weights, k represents what it would cost Timberlake Shoe Company today to raise one dollar of capital composed of 32.1 percent debt, 14.3 percent preferred, and 53.6 percent common equity.

Many firms use more than three sources of capital in financing their investments, but this poses no real problem. We use Equation 14–11 regardless of the number of capital sources.

USING THE WEIGHTED AVERAGE COST OF CAPITAL (WACC)

The WACC applies to the cash flows generated by a firm's current investments; that is, the WACC is based on the firm's current risk level, which in turn is determined by its assets and capital structure. In effect, a firm must earn its weighted average cost of capital on its current investments if the market value of its stock is to be maintained. Looking at the same concept from the standpoint of the suppliers of capital, the weighted average cost of capital can be thought of as the required rate of return that the suppliers of capital demand for their funds, adjusted for the firm's taxes and flotation costs.

We have continually represented k as the firm's cost of capital. It's important to point out the qualifications of this representation, however, as stated at the beginning of the chapter. As we have calculated it in this chapter, k is the firm's overall cost of capital, provided:

1. The firm intends to finance future projects with new long-term capital that is raised in approximately the same proportions as its present capital structure.
2. Projects under consideration have approximately the same amount of risk as the firm has currently.

The first condition means that the firm will keep the same capital structure in the future as it currently has.[12] The second condition means that the firm's asset structure—its composition of assets—will not change. If the firm makes major changes in the riskiness of its asset structure, k will change.

The weighted average cost of capital is an important concept. Firms should invest in projects where the expected return is greater than WACC. However, it is important to recognize that the firm's cost of capital, and therefore its investment decisions, is affected by the amount of financing that the firm does.

As the amount of a firm's financing changes, the WACC also changes. Specifically, if the amount of financing increases, the costs of the capital structure components eventually will rise, as will the WACC. This is because the required rates of return demanded by the suppliers of capital will increase to compensate for the greater risk involved with the additional financing. For example, debt is risky to the firm because interest and principal payments must be paid when due. As a firm sells more and more debt, it increases the risk that at some point it will be unable to meet these obligations.

The changing cost of the WACC is easiest to see in the case of common equity. If a firm must sell new common stock rather than use retained earnings for the common equity proportion of the cost-of-capital calculation, the cost of equity

---

[12]We will estimate k under changing capital structures in Chapter 15.

will be higher. Thus, once retained earnings are exhausted, the firm must sell new—and more expensive—common stock. The question sometimes arises, then, What do we mean when we say *the* cost of common equity?

As with any other specific cost of capital, the cost of common equity should properly be thought of as a *marginal-cost* concept. The cost of common equity should therefore reflect what it costs the firm to raise an additional dollar of equity financing. If the firm were planning to raise equity only by retaining earnings, for example, the firm's cost of common equity should equal its cost of retained earnings. Conversely, if the firm were planning to raise equity only through the sale of new stock, the cost of common equity should equal its cost of new common stock. In theory, the firm should know whether the next additional dollar of equity is coming from a stock sale or from retentions. Therefore:

$$\text{Cost of common equity} = k_E = k_{CS} \text{ if new common stock is used}$$
$$= k_{RE} \text{ if retentions are used}$$

Often it is convenient to think of the firm's cost of common equity as being the cost of a mixture of the two equity sources. This approach ignores the theoretical point that the cost of common equity, at any time, should equal k_{RE} or k_{CS}, depending on the source of the additional dollar of equity financing.

MARGINAL COST OF CAPITAL (MCC)

We noted above, and elsewhere in the text, that the correct measure of a capital component's cost, as well as the cost of capital itself, is a marginal measure. In this analysis, *marginal* refers to the last dollar raised. We saw in the discussion above that the volume of financing can affect a firm's WACC. This is attributable to the fact that as more and more financing is raised, the WACC increases as more expensive sources must be used.

Given this situation, we need to consider the **marginal cost of capital (MCC),** which reflects *the weighted average cost of the last dollar raised by the firm.* The MCC increases as more and more capital is raised during a period. The MCC is always equal to, or greater than, the WACC.

marginal cost of capital (MCC)
weighted average cost of the last dollar of capital raised, reflecting higher marginal costs

A graph relating the WACC to the volume of financing during a given period is referred to as the *marginal cost of capital schedule.* In working with the MCC schedule, it is convenient to think of *break points.* These points reflect the level of total financing at which the cost of a component of the overall cost of capital rises. These break points can be found by dividing the amount of funds available for a particular capital component at a stated cost by its capital structure weight, or:

$$BP_J = FA_J/W_J \tag{14-12}$$

where:

BP = the break point for capital component J
FA = the amount of funds available for capital component J
W = the capital structure weight for component J

■ *Example*

Timberlake Shoes has expected earnings of $5,000,000 and an expected dividend of $5 per share. Thus, retained earnings are $2,500,000 (there are 500,000 shares outstanding as previously calculated). Therefore, the break point for Timberlake for retained earnings is calculated by dividing the amount of retained earnings by the capital structure weight for common equity.

$$BP_{RE} = \$2,500,000/.536$$
$$= \$4,664,179$$

Timberlake can raise up to $4,664,179 next year in total long-term financing without changing its weighted average cost of capital of 13.6 percent. Once it goes beyond this point, its marginal cost of capital must be calculated using the higher cost of new common stock financing. This will raise the new weighted average cost of capital to:

Source	Market Weights, w	Cost of Capital, k	wk
Debt	0.321	0.067	0.022
Preferred stock	0.143	0.126	0.018
Common equity	0.536	0.186	0.100
Total	1.000		$k = 0.140 = 14.0\%$

This $4,664,179 level represents a break point in the MCC schedule. This is illustrated in Part A of Figure 14–4. Up to $4,664,179, the marginal cost of capital will be equal to the average cost of capital, 13.6 percent. Beyond this level of financing, $4,664,180 or more, each new dollar of common equity will cost 18.6 percent and each dollar of financing will cost 14.0 percent. That is, the cost of capital rises from 13.6 percent to 14.0 percent.

Thus, the cost of capital is properly viewed as a *marginal weighted cost of capital*. Up to the first break point, the MCC is equal to the WACC. Thereafter, new MCCs must be calculated as the cost of any of the capital components changes.

Although the use of new common stock financing in place of retained earnings is perhaps the easiest to visualize, it is not the only capital component whose cost will change as more and more financing is raised. At some point, a firm's cost of debt may rise above the cost projected if the firm sells a substantial amount of new debt. The reason for this is that bond investors will demand higher rates of return as the firm issues more debt because the firm becomes more risky as a result of the increased debt payments it is obligating itself to pay. For example, from a risk standpoint, given the highly competitive auto market that now exists, Chrysler with 60 percent debt in its capital structure is not the same firm as Chrysler with only 30 percent debt in its capital structure. The result of the rising cost of debt is a new break point in the MCC schedule at the amount of debt that can be sold before the required rate of return on the debt rises.

■ *Example*

Assume that Timberlake Shoe can sell up to $2,000,000 of bonds at the 10 percent before-tax rate used in the previous examples. Any new debt beyond $2,000,000 will carry a required rate of return of 11.5 percent (and an after-tax, after-flotation cost of 7.7 percent). The second break point for Timberlake would be:

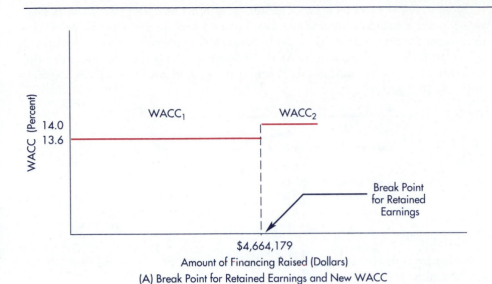

■ *Figure 14–4*
Marginal Cost of
Capital Schedule for
Timberlake Shoes

(A) Break Point for Retained Earnings and New WACC

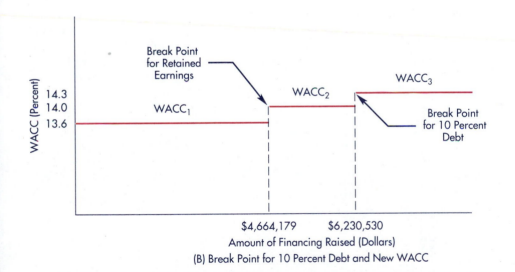

(B) Break Point for 10 Percent Debt and New WACC

$$BP_{Bonds} = \text{Amount of 10\% bonds/Debt percentage}$$
$$= \$2,000,000/.321$$
$$= \$6,230,530$$

In this example, if the firm raises more than $6,230,530, the cost of the debt financing will rise, as will the MCC.

Figure 14–4B shows an MCC schedule for Timberlake with two break points, one for the exhaustion of retained earnings and one for the exhaustion of the amount of 10 percent debt that could be raised before the rate of return demanded by investors for new debt rises. As the following calculations demonstrate, the new MCC for every dollar raised beyond the second break point, $6,230,530, will cost 14.3 percent.

Source	Market Weights, w	Cost of Capital, k	wk
Debt	0.321	0.077	0.025
Preferred stock	0.143	0.126	0.018
Common equity	0.536	0.186	0.100
Total	1.000		$k = 0.143 = 14.3\%$

Other break points are possible. In fact, there will be $n + 1$ different MCCs for n break points.

It is convenient to envision a smooth MCC schedule, representing the incorporation of all break points. Such a schedule is shown in Figure 14–5.

THE MCC SCHEDULE AND CAPITAL BUDGETING

The MCC schedule can be used in conjunction with the firm's *investment opportunity schedule* (IOS) to determine the appropriate discount rate to be used in capital budgeting. To do this, we need an IOS, which is a graph of the firm's investment opportunities ranked in descending order of expected rate of return for projects.

 Figure 14–5
Continuous
MCC Schedule

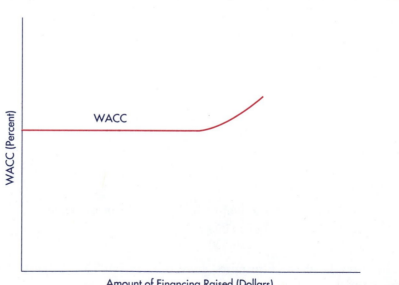

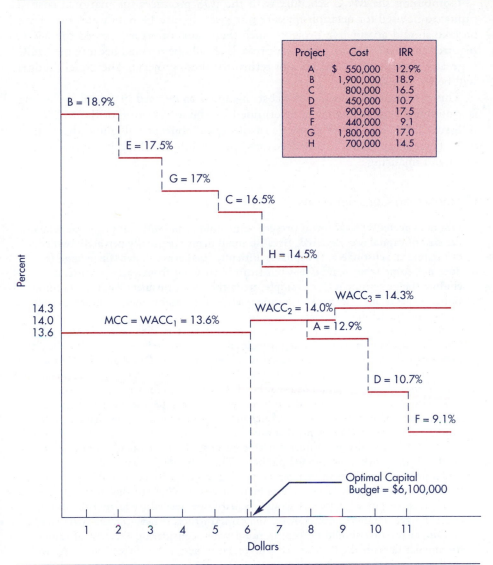

Project	Cost	IRR
A	$ 550,000	12.9%
B	1,900,000	18.9
C	800,000	16.5
D	450,000	10.7
E	900,000	17.5
F	440,000	9.1
G	1,800,000	17.0
H	700,000	14.5

That is, the project with the highest expected return is plotted first, followed by the project with the second-highest expected return, and so forth. In effect, the IOS schedule shows the amount of funds that can be invested at different rates of return.

A hypothetical IOS schedule for Timberlake Shoe is shown in Figure 14–6. Details for eight projects, A through H, are shown at the top of the figure. Projects have been ranked in the graph in descending order of return by IRR (or, equivalently, the discount rate at which their NPV = 0). The vertical bar representing each project shows the cost of the project.[13]

---

[13]For ease of discussion, we assume that all projects are independent and are equally risky; their risk is comparable to that of the firm's average projects.

Combining the MCC schedule with the IOS produces the marginal cost of capital to be used for decision-making purposes. Figure 14–6 indicates that Timberlake should accept five projects since their rates of return exceed the MCC required to finance them. The other projects should be rejected because the MCC is greater than the expected rates of return for these projects. The capital budget will be $6,100,000.

This discussion shows that the cost of capital to be used in capital budgeting is a marginal cost of capital as determined by the intersection of the MCC and IOS schedules. Use of the correct cost-of-capital concept will allow the firm to make correct capital budgeting decisions and reach optimal levels of both investment and financing.

Small-Firm Considerations

Not unexpectedly, small firms present some unique and difficult problems when the cost of capital is considered. Because small firms are usually privately owned, estimating the cost of equity capital is difficult. Furthermore, debt financing often does not come from bond issues but from borrowing from various sources, including the government (for example, from the Small Business Administration). Other sources include banks, commercial finance companies, venture capital firms, and the leasing of assets.

As always, calculating the cost of equity capital is the most difficult job. Calculating the cost of equity is difficult, if not impossible, using the methods previously discussed—the constant-growth version of the DDM and the CAPM. First, most small firms do not pay dividends, nor plan to in the foreseeable future, and the model simply cannot be used. Furthermore, even for small firms that may pay a dividend, or plan to in the future, the growth rate of expected dividends often would be high and expected to change at some point. A constant-growth model cannot be used in such situations.

The CAPM is also not directly usable because the firm's beta cannot be calculated if the stock is not traded publicly. The only possibility in this case is to find a publicly traded firm that can be viewed as generally comparable, estimate its beta, and use that as a proxy for the unobservable beta of the small firm. In doing this, certain adjustments would probably be needed, reflecting the differences in size, stability, market share, and capital structure between the two firms.

One factor that should be kept in mind when considering the cost of capital for smaller firms is the flotation cost involved in new issues of securities. As we shall see in Chapter 18, flotation costs, as a percentage of the funds raised, are inversely related to the size of the issue. The smaller the dollar amount of the issue, the larger the flotation costs as a percentage of the funds raised. Since smaller firms generally raise relatively small amounts of capital at any given time, the flotation costs will hit these firms the hardest. For example, a new issue of stock amounting to several hundred thousand dollars would have average flotation costs of 20 percent or more, a prohibitive cost by any standard. As a point of reference, the flotation costs on a large issue of common stock, for example, $100 million, would average 4 percent or less.

Even if flotation costs are ignored, the chance to sell new common stock is very limited for small firms. First, the owners usually do not want to sell stock and risk losing voting control of the firm. Second, there is no effective market for the stocks of most small firms. Investors are often scarce because of the risk involved in a small venture and because of the limited liquidity. If an investor decides to sell, who is going to buy the stock?

Finally, computing the cost of equity for a small firm is a difficult task that must, of necessity, involve subjective judgment. Perhaps the most common approach is to estimate the cost of equity for large, publicly traded companies in the same line of business and then add a risk premium to reflect the additional risk involved with the small firm.

FOCUS ON BUSINESS PRACTICE

In actual practice, most large firms use required rates of return in the capital budgeting process. According to an analysis by Scott and Petty, the range of respondents from different surveys computing a weighted average cost of capital was 30 to 61 percent.[14] Little evidence was available on the type of capital structure weighting schemes used.

According to a 1980 survey of the largest firms on the NYSE, the most commonly used method of calculating the cost of equity was the dividend valuation model, with some 20 percent of the response. The CAPM model by itself was used by 2 percent, and the two together by 14 percent.[15]

We know from the above discussion that equity capital is the most expensive source of financing. Thus, a finding from a second survey of nonfinancial corporations in 1984 that "equity financing was mentioned most frequently (57%) as the financing source whose cost is excessive in comparison to the costs of other types of financing" is not surprising.[16]

SUMMARY

- The weighted average cost of capital (WACC), designated k, is the percentage cost to the firm of raising capital in the same proportions that the firm has been raising capital historically.
- To calculate k we calculate costs for all relevant long-term sources of capital and their percentage weights.
- To estimate specific costs of capital, we first estimate investors' required rates of return from these investments and then adjust for company tax effects and flotation costs where appropriate.

- Cost of debt $= k_D = \dfrac{(1 - T)}{(1 - f)} k_d$

- Cost of preferred stock $= k_P = \dfrac{d}{(1 - f)P}$

- Cost of equity $= k_E =$

$$\text{Cost of common stock} = k_{CS} = \frac{D_1}{(1 - f)P_0} + g$$

$$\text{Cost of retained earnings} = k_{RE} = \frac{D_1}{P_0} + g$$

[14]See David F. Scott, Jr., and J. William Petty II, "Capital Budgeting Practices in Large American Firms: A Retrospective Analysis and Synthesis," *The Financial Review,* March 1984, p. 116.

[15]See Marshall Blume, Irwin Friend, and Randolph Westerfield, *Impediments to Capital Formation* (Philadelphia: Rodney L. White Center for Financial Research, the Wharton School, December 1980).

[16]See Marshall Blume, Irwin Friend, and Randolph Westerfield, *Factors Affecting Capital Formation: Summary Report on a Second Survey of Non-Financial Corporations* (Philadelphia: Rodney L. White Center for Financial Research, the Wharton School, December 1984).

- Both the dividend valuation model and the CAPM may be used to estimate k_e, investors' required rate of return on equity.

- Weighted average cost of capital $= k_{WACC} = \sum_{J=1}^{N} w_J k_J$

- The weights should reflect target capital structure proportions and can be based on either book or market value. Market weights are theoretically better, but it is often easier to use book weights.
- The weighted average cost of capital, WACC, is the required rate of return that the suppliers of capital demand for their funds, adjusted for taxes and flotation costs.
- The marginal cost of capital, MCC, measures the weighted average cost of the last dollar raised by the firm and reflects the increases in WACC as more expensive sources of financing are used.
- The investment opportunity schedule and the MCC schedule can be combined to determine the appropriate discount rate to be used in capital budgeting and the optimal capital budget for a particular period.

KEY TERMS

capital structure, p. 419
cost of capital, p. 418
marginal cost of capital (MCC), p. 435

weighted average cost of capital
  (WACC), p. 433

QUESTIONS

14–1. If the firm's marginal cost of capital increases, how will that affect the amount of new investment the firm undertakes, other things being equal?

14–2. Explain these statements:
   a. Debt is usually considered the cheapest source of financing available to the firm.
   b. The cost of internal equity (retentions) is less than the cost of external equity (common stock).
   c. The cost of retentions is not zero.

14–3. The calculation of any specific cost of capital requires the firm's financial staff to estimate both the net proceeds the firm will receive from the capital source and the expected future payments the firm will make to the investors. Despite the similarity of estimation problems, it is well recognized that the cost of equity is the most difficult cost to estimate. Briefly explain why.

14–4. The cost of capital may be computed using book or market weights. What are the advantages and disadvantages of using book weights rather than market weights in calculating the firm's weighted average cost of capital?

14–5. Other things being equal, explain how the following events would affect the firm's cost of capital:
   a. The corporate income tax rate is increased.
   b. The firm begins to make substantial new investment in assets less risky than those presently owned.
   c. Flotation costs of issuing new securities increase.
   d. Moody's bond rating service lowers its rating of the firm's bonds because, in Moody's opinion, these bonds are now riskier.

14–6. Describe what effects the following events might have on companies' preferences for raising new capital by issuing common stock.
   a. Congress allows tax deduction of common dividends.

     b. The price of the company's common stock is low because of a depressed stock market.

     c. Flotation costs associated with new common stock increase significantly because the stock market is going through a period of substantial fluctuations.

     d. The firm's investment bankers informally advise the firm's financial officers that certain influential New York investment analysts feel that the firm's debt level is getting excessively high in comparison to the firm's industry competitors.

14–7. Financial journalists often equate the coupon rate on a new bond issue with the cost of capital for that bond issue. List the assumptions necessary to make this equation valid.

14–8. Briefly explain in what sense a company's marginal cost of capital may be thought of as a weighted average cost of capital.

14–9. Explain the two methods discussed in the text for calculating the required rate of return on equity.

14–10. Evaluate the following statement: Internally generated funds are freely available to a firm.

14–11. Discuss the advantages and disadvantages of using market value weights versus book value weights to calculate the weighted cost capital.

14–12. Which capital components are affected by flotation costs? How?

14–13. Why is the required rate of return on equity an opportunity cost?

14–14. What is the relationship between the required rate of return on externally provided equity and internally provided equity?

14–15. What is the relationship between the price of a preferred stock and the required rate of return on a preferred stock? What is the required rate of return on preferred stock?

14–16. What would be the likely effect on the required rate of return on equity if investors became less risk-averse? If the expected return on the market increased?

14–17. Under what conditions can k legitimately be referred to as the firm's cost of capital?

DEMONSTRATION PROBLEMS

14–1. Assuming that the Okleshen Financial Company can sell new common stock at $75 per share, find the company's costs of internal and external equity for the following situations:

     a. Stockholders expect that the next dividend will be $9 and that dividends will grow at 10 percent per year. Flotation costs are 6 percent of sale price.

     b. Stockholders expect the next dividend will be $6 per share and that dividends will not grow. Flotation costs are $5 per share.

14–2. Ferris Tax Services has obtained the following information about the cost of new long-term financing:

Source	Net Proceeds to Firm
Bonds, $1,000 par (7%)	$980 per bond
Common stock, $20 par	$20 per share

The firm expects earnings to be $3 per share for the foreseeable future, and all earnings are paid out as dividends. The firm's tax rate is 40 percent. The firm's most recent balance sheet (in millions of dollars) is:

Assets		Claims	
Current assets	$200	Current liabilities	$100
Net fixed assets	400	Long-term debt	300
		Common equity	200
Total assets	$600	Total claims	$600

Assuming that Ferris will finance its future long–term investments in about the same capital proportions as it has in the past, calculate the firm's cost of capital:

a. Using book weights.

b. Using market weights, assuming that $P_0 = \$25$ and that the current bond price is 5 percent above par value. Also, par values on Ferris' old securities are the same as on their new securities.

Solutions to Demonstration Problems

14–1.

Internal	*External*

$$k_{RE} = \frac{D_1}{P_0} + g \qquad\qquad k_{CS} = \frac{D_1}{(1 - f)P_0} + g$$

a.

$$\frac{9}{75} + .10 = .220 \qquad\qquad \frac{9}{(.94)(75)} + .10 = .228$$

b.

$$\frac{6}{75} + 0 = .080 \qquad\qquad \frac{6}{\left(1 - \dfrac{5}{75}\right)(75)} + 0 = .086$$

14–2.

$$k_D = \frac{(.6)(70)}{980} = .043$$

$$k_{CS} = \frac{3}{20} = .15$$

a.

Source	Book Value (Millions $)	w	k	wk
Long-term debt	300	.6	.043	.026
Common equity	200	.4	.15	.060
	500	1.0		k_{AVG} = .086

b.

Source	Market Value (Millions $)		w	k	wk
Long-term debt	(1.05)(300)	= 315	.558	.043	.024
Common equity	(25/20)(200)	= 250	.442	.15	.066
		565	1.000		k_{AVG} = .090

PROBLEMS

14–1. Calculate the cost of debt for each of the following situations where the company issues $1,000 face value bonds with maturity of 30 years. The bonds are sold for $1,000 each.
   a. The bonds pay 9 percent interest annually, flotation costs are 2 percent, and the marginal tax rate is 40 percent.
   b. The bonds pay 8 percent interest annually, flotation costs are 3 percent, and the marginal tax rate is 40 percent.
   c. The bonds pay $100 interest annually, flotation costs are 2 percent, and the marginal tax rate is 40 percent.

14–2. The company issues $1,000 face value bonds with maturity of 40 years. Flotation costs are negligible, and the tax rate is 40 percent. Find k_D when the bonds pay x percent interest annually and are sold for y, where:
   a. $x = 7$ percent, $y = \$900$ per bond.
   b. $x = 6$ percent, $y = \$1,100$ per bond.
   c. $x = 10$ percent, $y = \$800$ per bond.

14–3. If the Bingman Sportswear Company can issue $100 par preferred stock at $80 per share, find the cost of preferred stock in each of the following situations:
   a. The stock pays an annual dividend of $4 per share, and flotation costs are 4 percent of sale price.
   b. The stock pays an annual dividend of $6 per share, and flotation costs are 3 percent of sale price.
   c. The stock pays an 8 percent dividend, and flotation costs are 4 percent of the sale price.

14–4. Finch Inc. wants to determine its cost of capital assuming that the firm maintains its same capital structure. A portion of the firm's present balance sheet is shown below:

Long-term debt ($1,000 par)	$ 8,000,000
Common stock ($10 par)	10,000,000

New long-term bonds would carry a 7 percent coupon rate and would net Finch 95 cents for each dollar of bond issued. Next period's expected common stock dividend is $2 a share, and the anticipated dividend growth rate is 6 percent. Each share of common sold would net the firm $25. Current stock price is $30 a share; the present long-term debt has a market value of $1,100 per bond. The tax rate is 40 percent. Find the company's weighted cost of capital using market weights.

14–5. Dlabay Corporation analysts are attempting to determine the company's cost of equity. They have estimated that the required rate of return on a market index is about 25 percent, while the risk-free interest rate is 15 percent. If Dlabay Corporation stock is judged to be about 20 percent riskier than the market index, what is Dlabay's cost of equity (ignoring flotation costs)?

14–6. Determine the weighted marginal cost of capital for the following firm using constant book weights.

Balance Sheet
($ Millions)

Assets		Claims	
Current assets	$200	Current liabilities	$100
Net fixed assets	400	Long-term debt	200
		Preferred stock	100
		Common equity	200
Total assets	$600	Total claims	$600

Sources of Capital

30-year bonds: sale price = $1,000 (face value), 8% coupon, 2% flotation costs

Preferred stock: sale price = $30/share, $3/share annual dividend, 4% flotation costs

Common stock: sale price = $10/share, 6% flotation costs

The firm's marginal tax rate is 40 percent. Next year's dividend is expected to be 75 cents per share, and the anticipated growth rate in these dividends is 6 percent per year.

14–7. As a financial analyst for the D. Vetter Supply Company, you have been given the assignment of determining the company's cost of capital. Toward that end, the following financial information has been collected.

Present Capital Structure

Source of Capital	Par ($)	Total Book Value ($ Millions)	Market Value
Debt	1,000	4	$1,317 per bond
Preferred stock	100	1	120 per share
Common stock	10	5	22 per share
		10	

Anticipated External Financing Opportunities

Source of Capital	Par ($)	Maturity	Stated Coupon/ Dividend Rate	Flotation Costs (%)	Sale Price
Debt	1,000	30 yr.	7% coupon	4	$1,000 per bond
Preferred stock	100	—	8% dividend	5	100 per share
Common stock	10	—	—	10	22 per share

Next year's expected common dividend is $1.05 per share, the anticipated growth rate in dividends is 8 percent per year, and the firm pays out all of its earnings in dividends. The company's marginal tax rate is 40 percent.

a. Determine the weighted average cost of capital using book-value weights.

b. Determine the weighted average cost of capital using market-value weights.

c. Briefly explain why the k calculated in (b) is greater than the k calculated in (a).

14–8. Given the following information, calculate the required rate of return on equity:

$$k_{RF} = 8 \text{ percent}$$
$$\text{Beta} = 1.5$$
$$\text{Expected market return} = 14 \text{ percent}$$

a. How would your answer change if the expected market return declined to 11 percent?

b. Assume that the risk-free rate is 7 percent, beta = 1.2, and the market risk premium is 6 percent.

14–9. Using the dividend growth model, calculate the required rate of return on equity for a company whose current dividend is $2.00, the current stock price is $40, and the expected growth rate of dividends is 6 percent.

14–10. Assume that White Corporation is expected to have dividend and earnings growth of 6 percent a year for the next 12 years. The current dividend being paid is $1.00, and the current market price of the stock is $25. What is the required rate of return on equity for White?

14–11. Calculate the required rate of return on equity for a stock expected to pay $2.00-per-share dividends every year for the foreseeable future.

14–12. Agrawa Products is currently selling at $50 per share. Dividends have grown at a 12 percent rate for the last 15 years, reaching a current level of $2.00 per share. Analysts are estimating that future dividends will grow at only 8 percent per year. Calculate the required rate of return for Agrawa Products.

14–13. The detailed Statement of Capitalization for Utilicorp is shown below for 1987.
   a. Verify the capital structure dollar amounts reported in the chapter for Utilicorp for debt, preferred, and common.
   b. Calculate the capital structure weights for Utilicorp.

Consolidated Statement of Capitalization
(thousands of dollars) 1987

Common shareholders' equity	
Common stock, par value $1 per share, authorized 50,000,000 shares, outstanding 17,556,481 shares (9,614,062 at December 31, 1986)	$ 17,556
Premium on capital stock	189,085
Retained earnings	56,896
Translation adjustment	911
Preferred and preference stock	
Preference stock, without par value, authorized 10,000,000 shares, outstanding:	
$2.4375 series, 600,000 shares	15,000
$2.6125 series, 400,000 shares	10,000
Long-term debt	
First mortgage bonds	203,092
Pollution control bonds	7,300
Secured debentures	34,050
Subordinated debentures	61,527
Notes and other obligations	14,170
	320,139
Less current maturities	
First mortgage bonds	1,868
Notes and other obligations	574
Total current maturities	$ 2,442

SELECTED REFERENCES

A discussion of the yields on various financial assets can be found in:

Bey, Roger P., and J. Markham Collins. "The Relationship Between Before- and After-Tax Yields on Financial Assets." *Financial Review,* August 1988, pp. 313–31.

A discussion of calculating cost of capital numbers based on historical data can be found in:

Ibbotson, Roger G., and Rex A. Sinquefield. *Stocks, Bonds, Bills, and Inflation* (SBBI), 1982. Updated in *SBBI 1990 Yearbook.* Chicago, Ibbotson Associates: 1990, pp. 31 and 86.

15

Leverage and Capital Structure

The Use of Debt Financing

Santa Fe Southern Pacific Company discovered in 1987 that other companies were acquiring its stock with the possible intention of a takeover in order to have access to its many assets.[1] Forced to sell the Southern Pacific Railroad, Santa Fe also decided to sell almost $1 billion in other assets.

As part of its corporate restructuring, Santa Fe borrowed heavily and used the proceeds to pay shareholders a special dividend of $30 a share.[2] Not only were some of the assets that had made the company appealing gone, liquidity was also reduced. In 1987, the company had some $1,700 million in long-term debt and $5,260 million in net worth. By 1988, the figures for long-term debt were $3,400 million and net worth of less than $500 million. For the railroad industry as a whole the ratio of long-term debt to net worth was approximately two-thirds.

One interesting result of this recapitalization of Santa Fe was that while the company earned 5.8 percent on total capital and 6.6 percent on net worth in 1987, the 1988 figures were 9.5 percent on capital and 30 percent on net worth. In other words, although net profits in 1988 were only $147 million, compared to $346 million in 1987, the reduced equity base (compared to 1987) produced a 30 percent return on net worth. The ultimate question about these capital structure changes, however, was what happened to the stock price. At the time it remained basically unchanged, dropping to about $20 per share from about $50 per share to reflect the one-time dividend of $30 per share. It then stayed in the same range through the middle of 1990.

---

[1] See James Cook, "And Still They Howl," *Forbes*, May 16, 1988, pp. 63–64.
[2] These numbers, as well as others, were taken from *The Value Line Investment Survey*, September 30, 1988, p. 299.

capital structure
long-term sources of
financing for a firm

We studied cost of capital in Chapter 14, discussing its meaning and how it is calculated. However, our investigation was made under the assumption that the firm's **capital structure**—the composition of the long-term financing—did not change. Unfortunately, although it is very difficult to determine capital costs when the capital structure is relatively stable, it is even more difficult when the capital structure is changing. There is, in fact, considerable controversy about estimating the cost of capital when capital structure changes.

Our concern from a valuation perspective is the effect that financing decisions have on stock price. That is, will a particular mix of financing sources maximize the share price? In the case of Santa Fe just discussed, by mid-1989 the price was still around $20 per share despite a strong stock market, suggesting that investors were concerned about the risk aspects of the capital structure changes made by Santa Fe.

Primary *chapter learning objectives* are:

1. To understand the concept of leverage and recognize its importance in financial management.
2. To investigate the relationship between stock price and capital structure. The main question of interest is whether the firm can increase the price of its stock by choosing one particular capital structure.

THE CONCEPT OF LEVERAGE

Leverage refers to the fulcrum principle. A mechanic applies a wrench to a nut to gain mechanical leverage. In finance, it is profit that is leveraged. This result is not magical; it depends on the fact that businesses have fixed costs, both operating and financial, that will be incurred regardless of the firm's success.

- When sales rise within a certain sales range, fixed costs remain constant, leaving more of the sales dollar as operating profit.
- When operating profit goes up, creditors will still be paid the same fixed dollar amounts for the financing they provided, leaving more money for the stockholders.

Thus, there are two kinds of leverage in finance—operating and financial. We are mainly concerned with financial leverage, but it will help to study operating leverage first.

Operating Leverage

**earnings before
interest and taxes
(EBIT)**
sales minus total costs
operating leverage
magnification of
operating earnings
as a result of a change
in sales

An important finance concept is **earnings before interest and taxes (EBIT).** It is defined as sales minus total costs. **Operating leverage** refers to the magnification of gains and losses in EBIT by changes that occur in sales. This magnification occurs because in employing assets, the firm incurs different types of costs.

In the short run, operating costs can be divided into variable costs and fixed costs.

- *Variable costs* are related to the sales level, and they include such items as materials costs, direct labor costs, and repair and maintenance expenses. As sales change, variable costs change proportionately.[3]
- *Fixed costs* are independent of the sales level in the short run and over the relevant sales range. Fixed costs include items such as depreciation, indirect labor costs, and overhead expenses like office rental, light and heating bills, and executive and staff salaries. In the long run, all costs are variable.[4]

The higher the percentage of a firm's fixed costs to total costs, the higher the firm's degree of operating leverage.[5] Other things being equal, a high (low) degree of operating leverage implies that a relatively small change in sales will produce a large (small) change in EBIT.

- **Example**

To illustrate the concept of operating leverage, assume that two companies, X and Y, face the same sales schedule (sales can range from 10,000 units to 70,000 units) and have the same price per unit for their sales, $3 per unit. Company X has a fixed cost of $25,000 and a variable cost per unit of $2.00, and Company Y has a fixed cost of $50,000 and a variable cost per unit of $1.50. Thus, other things being equal, Company X has less operating leverage than Company Y because it has lower fixed costs although it has higher variable costs.

The relationship between sales, revenue, costs, and EBIT for these two companies is shown in Table 15–1 (notice that unit volume, and therefore sales revenue, is the same for both X and Y). As we can see, because of the higher operating leverage Company Y has greater losses at lower sales levels but greater EBIT at higher sales levels. Y's higher operating leverage magnifies the EBIT in both directions. This illustrates an important point about leverage—it magnifies results whether positive or negative.

■ *Table 15–1*
Example of Operating Leverage for Two Hypothetical Companies

Volume	Company X Sales	Costs	EBIT	Company Y Sales	Costs	EBIT
10,000	$ 30,000	$ 45,000	−$15,000	$ 30,000	$ 65,000	−$35,000
20,000	60,000	65,000	− 5,000	60,000	80,000	− 20,000
30,000	90,000	85,000	5,000	90,000	95,000	− 5,000
40,000	120,000	105,000	15,000	120,000	110,000	10,000
50,000	150,000	125,000	25,000	150,000	125,000	25,000
60,000	180,000	145,000	35,000	180,000	140,000	40,000
70,000	210,000	165,000	45,000	210,000	155,000	55,000

Fixed costs: For X, $25,000; for Y, $50,000
Per-unit variable costs: For X, $2.00; for Y, $1.50

[3]This means the variable cost ratio (ratio of variable costs to sales) is constant, at least over some relevant range of sales.
[4]Actually, even in the short run, the firm can change some of its fixed costs, such as salaries, in response to temporary sales fluctuations. These are called *semivariable costs*.
[5]A firm with only variable costs would, by definition, have no operating leverage.

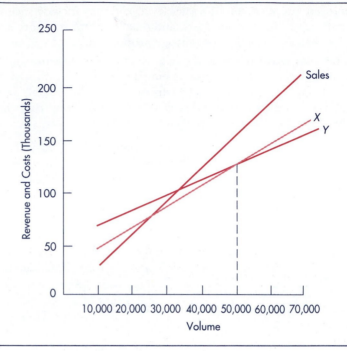

Company Y's break-even point is higher than company X's, a point that can be confirmed by inspection of Figure 15–1, which illustrates the operating leverage concept for these two companies. The steepest upward-sloping line in Figure 15–1 is the sales revenue line, which is the same for both companies. The line labeled *X* in the diagram is the total-cost line for Company X, and the line labeled *Y* is the total-cost line for Company Y. As can be seen, X crosses the sales revenue line, or has a lower break-even point, sooner than does Y. Company X has a lower level of operating leverage, and less magnification of the EBIT level for a given change in sales (in either direction), than does Y. ■

Operating leverage can be described algebraically by the *degree of operating lever-age* (DOL). The DOL shows the percentage change in EBIT that will occur for a 1 percent change in sales. The larger the DOL, the higher the fixed costs relative to variable costs, and the more operating leverage the firm has. The larger the DOL, the greater the magnification of sales changes into EBIT changes.

The degree of operating leverage can be calculated as:

$$\text{Degree of operating leverage} = \text{DOL} = \frac{\text{Percent change in EBIT}}{\text{Percent change in sales}} \qquad \textbf{(15–1)}$$

where:

$$\text{EBIT} = \text{earnings before interest and taxes}$$

Another expression for DOL can be derived from Equation 15–1:

$$\text{DOL} = 1 + \frac{F}{\text{EBIT}}$$

where:

$$F = \text{fixed operating costs}$$

■ *Example*

The meaning of a 3.0 DOL result is that from the current base sales level, for every 1 percent change in sales *within the relevant range,* there will be a 3 percent change in EBIT in the same direction as the sales change. If sales increase (decrease) by 10 percent, EBIT will increase (decrease) by 30 (10 × 3) percent. ■

Operating leverage is often analyzed in conjunction with *break-even analysis.* An efficient method to algebraically solve for the break-even sales level is presented in Appendix 15–A.

Operating Leverage and Business Risk

Operating leverage is related to the firm's **business risk**, which refers to the risk inherent in the firm's investments—the uncertainty surrounding sales and costs. Let:

business risk
risk inherent in the firm's assets or investments

$$R = \frac{\text{The rate of return on assets}}{\text{(before interest and taxes)}} = \frac{\text{EBIT}}{\text{Total assets}}$$

Then business risk may be defined as:

$$\text{Business risk} = \text{Cov}_{RM} = \text{Corr}_{RM}\sigma_R\sigma_M \qquad (15\text{–}2)$$

where:

Cov_{RM} = covariance between R and the market index rate of return
Corr_{RM} = correlation between R and the market index rate of return
σ_R = standard deviation of R
σ_M = standard deviation of the market index rate of return

Consistent with our earlier work on risk (Chapter 5), business risk is covariant with the market index. The higher this covariance, the larger the business risk. It is associated with how the rate of return on the firm's income stream prior to interest charges and taxes covaries with the market.

Business risk is determined by the type of investments the firm makes and is reflected in the type of business operated by the firm. Utility companies, for example, own assets whose returns covary less with the market, year in and year out, than those of mobile home companies; therefore, utilities have less business risk than mobile home companies. Business risk can be associated with the asset side of the firm's balance sheet.

The firm's operating leverage is related to σ_R in Equation 15–2. Other things being equal, the greater the firm's operating leverage, the greater σ_R, and the greater the firm's business risk. It must be noted, however, that although one company may have a higher σ_R than another company, the first company does not necessarily have more business risk. The company with the higher Cov_{RM} has the higher business risk.

■ *Example*

Consider the following two companies:

	AB	CD
σ_R	2	4
Corr_{RM}	0.9	0.3

Then from Equation 15–2:

$$AB \text{ business risk} = (0.9)(2)\,\sigma_M = 1.8\,\sigma_M$$
$$CD \text{ business risk} = (0.3)(4)\,\sigma_M = 1.2\,\sigma_M$$

Because the value of σ_M is always positive, AB has more business risk, even though the σ_R term is smaller for AB. ∎

Financial Leverage

financial risk
risk caused by the use of fixed-cost financing

In the previous section we considered business risk. Another source of risk to the firm is **financial risk,** which refers to the risk of the firm's long-term financing decisions. Financial risk refers specifically to the increased variability in EPS and the increased probability of bankruptcy that stockholders assume because of the use of fixed-cost financing by the firm. Financial risk is associated with the right side of the balance sheet.

financial leverage
use of fixed-cost financing to finance a portion of the firm's assets to try to magnify the EPS

Whereas operating leverage is created by investing in assets that have fixed costs, **financial leverage** is created by sources of financing that have fixed costs, primarily debt (requiring interest payments), preferred stock (which obligates the company to make preferred dividend payments), and leases (which require specified lease payments). These financing fixed costs affect the firm's earnings per share (EPS) in the same way that operating fixed costs affect EBIT. The more fixed-charge financing the firm uses, the more financial leverage it will have.

The *degree of financial leverage* (DFL) is sometimes calculated as a measure of the leverage in the firm that is due solely to the firm's financing policy. It shows the percentage change in EPS that will result from a 1 percent change in EBIT.

■ *Example*

A DFL of 2.0 indicates that a 1 percent change in a firm's EBIT will result in a 2 percent change in its EPS in the same direction.[6] ■

The degree of financial leverage is calculated as:

$$\text{Degree of financial leverage} = \text{DFL} = \frac{\text{Percent change in EPS}}{\text{Percent change in EBIT}} \qquad (15\text{–}3)$$

$$= \frac{\blacktriangle \text{EPS}/\text{EPS}}{\blacktriangle \text{EBIT}/\text{EBIT}}$$

where:

$$EPS = \text{earnings per share}$$
$$EBIT = \text{earnings before interest and taxes}$$
$$\blacktriangle = \text{change in}$$

Another formula for calculating the degree of financial leverage may be derived from Equation 15–3:

$$\text{DFL} = \frac{\text{EBIT}}{\text{EBIT} - I - L - d/(1 - T)} \qquad (15\text{–}4)$$

---

[6]A DFL of 1.0 means that a 1 percent change in a firm's EBIT will result in a 1 percent change in its EPS in the same direction (there is no magnification of EPS in this case because there is no financial leverage).

where:

$$I = \text{interest payments}$$
$$L = \text{lease payments}$$
$$d = \text{preferred dividend payments}$$
$$T = \text{tax rate}$$

Unlike interest and lease payments, preferred dividends are not tax deductible. Therefore, a dollar paid in preferred dividends is more costly to the firm than a dollar paid in interest or lease payments. Dividing any preferred dividend paid by $(1 - T)$ accounts for this and puts interest, lease, and preferred dividend payments on an equivalent basis.

The degree of financial leverage reflects the leverage in the firm that is due solely to the firm's financing policy. The effect of financial leverage is to magnify changes in EBIT into larger changes in EPS. Thus, in effect, financial leverage is *second stage* leverage, taking up where operating leverage, which affects EBIT, leaves off.

■ Example

Suppose that two companies, The Conserta Company and Ballard, Inc., are alike in all respects except that Conserta is an all-equity company (it has no long-term debt) and Ballard has a long-term debt-to-equity ratio of 1:1. Financial data for the two companies are shown in Table 15–2. Notice that both companies have

■ **Table 15–2**
Calculating the Degree of Financial Leverage

Current Financial Data

Conserta Company		Ballard, Inc.	
Total assets	$12,000,000	Total assets	$12,000,000
Current liabilities	2,000,000	Current liabilities	2,000,000
Common (1,000,000 shares)	10,000,000	Long-term debt (8%)	5,000,000
		Common (500,000 shares)	5,000,000
EBIT	$ 1,500,000	EBIT	$ 1,500,000
Interest	0	Interest	400,000
EBT	$ 1,500,000	EBT	$ 1,100,000
Tax ($T = 0.4$)	600,000	Tax ($T = 0.4$)	440,000
Net income	$ 900,000	Net income	$ 660,000
EPS	$0.90	EPS	$1.32

Degree of Financial Leverage

Conserta Company		Ballard, Inc.	
EBIT	$1,500,000	EBIT	$1,500,000
I	0	I	400,000
L	0	L	0
$d/(1-T)$	0	$d/(1-T)$	0

$$\text{DFL} = \frac{\$1,500,000}{\$1,500,000 - 0}$$

$$= 1.00$$

$$\text{DFL} = \frac{\$1,500,000}{\$1,500,000 - \$400,000}$$

$$= 1.36$$

■ *Table 15–3*
The Concept of Total
(Combined) Leverage

Total (combined) leverage is the end result of:
1. Operating leverage:
   Revenues
       − Cost of goods sold
       = Gross profit
       − Operating expenses
       = EBIT
2. Financial leverage:
   EBIT
       − Interest expense
       = Income before tax
       − Taxes
       = Net income after tax
       − Preferred stock dividends
       = Earnings after tax, which is divided by shares outstanding
       = Earnings per share or EPS

the same levels of total assets and current liabilities and the same EBIT. However, the presence of debt (and therefore the smaller number of common shares outstanding) in Ballard gives it higher EPS.

Ballard has a larger DFL because it has debt in its capital structure. Applying Equation 15–4 to the two companies, as shown in Table 15–2, indicates that the DFL for Conserta is 1.0, which means that a 1 percent change in the company's EBIT will result in a 1 percent change in its EPS in the same direction. There is no magnification of the EPS in this case.[7]

In contrast, Ballard's DFL is 1.36, which means that for every 1 percent change in EBIT, EPS will change 1.36 percent. This magnification of EPS is due solely to the use of fixed-charge financing and illustrates what is meant by financial leverage: changes in EBIT are levered (magnified) into larger changes in EPS. Note, however, that leverage is a two-way street. If both companies had decreases in EBIT, Ballard would suffer a greater percentage decrease in EPS. ■

Combined Leverage

combined leverage
total leverage, consisting
of operating leverage
and financial leverage

Combined leverage, or total leverage, consists of operating leverage and financial leverage. Operating leverage links revenues to EBIT, while financial leverage links EBIT to earnings after tax. The concept of combined leverage as it relates to both operating leverage and financial leverage is illustrated in Table 15–3.

The *degree of combined leverage* (DCL) is calculated as:

$$\text{Degree of combined leverage} = \text{DCL} = \frac{\text{Percent change in EPS}}{\text{Percent change in sales}}$$

---

[7]Firms that do not use fixed-charge financing will have no financial leverage, and their DFL will equal 1.

The DCL is simply the product of DOL times DFL.[8] That is:

$$DCL = (DOL)(DFL)$$ **(15–5)**

- *Example*

If a firm has a DOL of 1.25 and a DFL of 1.15, the DCL will be 1.25 times 1.15 = 1.44. This means that for every 1 percent change in sales, EPS will change 1.44 percent in the same direction. This magnification is the result of both operating and financial leverage.[9] ■

The DCL can also be used in assessing the approximate effects of new investment and financing plans on EPS. For example, if the firm begins to invest heavily in riskier assets than usual, operating leverage will increase. If the firm's financing policy remains relatively constant (that is, if the firm finances the new investments with approximately the same proportions of debt, leasing, preferred, and equity capital as used in the past), financial leverage will remain fairly constant. The effect of increased operating leverage and unchanged financial leverage will result in increased combined leverage because DCL = (DOL)(DFL).

Alternatively, the firm may consciously choose instead to finance the new investments with more equity than it has used in the past. This would decrease financial leverage and compensate for the increased operating leverage.

EFFECTS OF FINANCIAL LEVERAGE—THE GOOD, THE BAD, AND THE FATAL

We are primarily concerned in this chapter with understanding financial leverage and analyzing the effect of capital structure on the price of the stock.[10] In this section, we consider these points:

1. The effects of financial leverage on the firm's EPS.
2. The effects of financial leverage on the firm's financial risk.
3. The extreme risk of financial leverage.

After our analysis of these points, we will consider in detail the important relationship between capital structure and stockholder wealth.

---

[8]This expression for the DCL is consistent with its definition because:

$$DCL = (DOL)(DFL)$$
$$= \frac{\text{Percent change in EBIT}}{\text{Percent change in sales}} \times \frac{\text{Percent change in EPS}}{\text{Percent change in EBIT}}$$
$$= \frac{\text{Percent change in EPS}}{\text{Percent change in sales}}$$

[9]The firm's DCL approximately describes the effect that sales changes will have on EPS. However, we must be careful to realize the approximate nature of this calculation. If the anticipated sales change is beyond the relevant range of sales described earlier, the variable-cost ratio may change, and if the time period is too long, fixed costs may change. In such cases, the DCL estimates may not be very accurate.

[10]Although all forms of fixed-charge financing are important, we emphasize the role of debt financing.

Effect of Financial Leverage on EPS: The Good

Suppose a new firm, Tyro Company, is currently incorporating and is considering financing plans. The firm needs $100,000 of long-term capital to begin operations and has narrowed the choice to two financing plans:

1. Sell 1,000 shares of common stock at $100 per share.
2. Sell 500 shares of common stock at $100 per share and borrow $50,000 from the bank at 5 percent interest.

Plan 1 is an all-equity plan. The company's long-term debt-to-equity ratio would be 0. Plan 2 involves the sale of equal amounts of debt and equity, and the firm's ratio of long-term debt to equity would be 1.0.

What effect would these plans have on Tyro's EPS? It depends on the relationship between the before-tax cost of debt and the rate of return on assets before interest and taxes (EBIT/total assets, or EBIT/TA).

Most companies' EBIT will be influenced by general economic conditions. If the economy is strong, EBIT will be favorable, and if the economy is weak, EBIT will be unfavorable. Tyro estimates that EBIT will be $4,000 if the economy is weak, $6,000 if the economy is about average, and $8,000 if the economy is strong. These estimates imply that Tyro's EBIT/TA will be 4 percent ($4,000/$100,000) in a weak economy, 6 percent in an average economy, and 8 percent in a strong economy. In comparison, Tyro's before-tax cost of debt is 5 percent.

We may now look at what Tyro's EPS would be next year with each of the two financing plans and for the estimated market conditions. Table 15–4 shows these results. In a weak economy, EPS is higher under the all-equity plan. But in

■ *Table 15–4*
Effect of Financial Leverage on EPS for the Tyro Company

	Economic Conditions ($)		
	Weak	Average	Strong
Plan I: All Equity (LT Debt/Equity = 0)			
EBIT	$4,000	$6,000	$8,000
Interest	0	0	0
EBT	4,000	6,000	8,000
Tax (T = 0.5)	2,000	3,000	4,000
Net income	2,000	3,000	4,000
No. shares common	1,000	1,000	1,000
EPS	2.00	3.00	4.00
Plan 2: 50% Equity and 50% Debt (LT Debt/Equity = 1)			
EBIT	4,000	6,000	8,000
Interest*	2,500	2,500	2,500
EBT	1,500	3,500	5,500
Tax (T = 0.5)	750	1,750	2,750
Net income	750	1,750	2,750
No. shares common	500	500	500
EPS	1.50	3.50	5.50

*Interest = (0.05)($50,000) = $2,500.

either an average or a strong economy, EPS of Plan 2 are higher. Actually, Plan 2 will result in higher EPS so long as EBIT/TA is greater than the before-tax cost of debt of 5 percent. As a general proposition, if EBIT/TA is greater than the before-tax cost of debt, the effect of financial leverage on EPS is favorable.

Indifference Point EBIT-EPS Analysis

We can see the effect of financial leverage on EPS more clearly by preparing an EBIT-EPS chart, which is constructed by plotting EPS against EBIT for the two plans. Figure 15–2 shows these plots, which are straight-line relationships between EPS and EBIT for each plan. The EBIT-EPS chart shows two things. First, the straight line shows what EPS would result for either plan from a given EBIT. Under Plan 1, for example, if EBIT equals $2,000, the Plan 1 line indicates that EPS will be $1 per share.

Second, Figure 15–2 shows that, above some critical level of EBIT, Plan 2 always results in higher EPS than Plan 1. The reverse is true below this critical level of EBIT. This critical level of EBIT occurs at the intersection of the two straight lines, called the *EBIT-EPS break-even point,* because at that EBIT level, EPS of the two plans are equal. From the graph, at this break-even point, EBIT is $5,000 and EPS is $2.50.[11]

Notice when EBIT = $5,000, EBIT/TA = $5,000/$100,000 = 5 percent. Also, recall that Tyro's before-tax cost of debt is 5 percent. Therefore, for all levels of EBIT where EBIT/TA exceeds 5 percent, Plan 2 results in higher EPS. That is what was meant in an earlier statement that *the effect of financial leverage on EPS depends on the relationship between the before-tax cost of debt and the EBIT rate of return on assets.*

Effect of Financial Leverage on Financial Risk: The Bad

Let us pick up the Tyro example again. Assume that estimated EBIT outcomes of $4,000, $6,000, and $8,000 are equally likely; that is, the probability of each is one third. The probability functions for the two financing plans would be:

---

[11]We can also solve algebraically for EBIT at the break-even point. By definition:

$$\text{EPS} = \frac{(\text{EBIT} - I - L)(1 - T) - d}{N}$$

where:

N = number of shares of common stock
I = interest payments
L = lease payments
d = preferred dividend payments

Expressions for Tyro's EPS under Plans 1 and 2 are:

$$\text{Plan 1. EPS} = \frac{(\text{EBIT} - 0)(0.5) - 0}{1,000} = 0.0005 \text{ EBIT}.$$

$$\text{Plan 2. EPS} = \frac{(\text{EBIT} - \$2,500)(0.5) - 0}{500} = 0.001 \text{ EBIT} - \$2.50.$$

The break-even point is where the two EPSs are equal. Equating the two EPS expressions and letting EBIT* be break-even point EBIT:

$$0.0005 \text{ EBIT*} = 0.001 \text{ EBIT*} - \$2.50$$
$$\text{EBIT*} = \$5,000$$

■ *Figure 15–2*
EBIT-EPS Chart

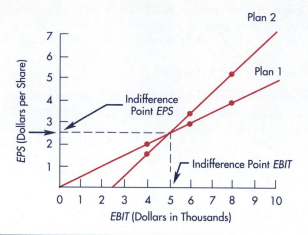

EBIT ($)	Probability	EPS ($ per share)	
		Plan 1	Plan 2
4,000	1/3	2.00	1.50
6,000	1/3	3.00	3.50
8,000	1/3	4.00	5.50

We now calculate expected EPS, $\overline{EPS}$, and standard deviation of EPS, σ_{EPS}, for each plan using concepts developed in Chapter 5.

For Plan 1, the all-equity plan:

$$\overline{EPS} = 1/3(\$2) + 1/3(\$3) + 1/3(\$4) = \$3 \text{ per share}$$
$$\sigma_{EPS} = [1/3(\$2 - \$3)^2 + 1/3(\$3 - \$3)^2 + 1/3(\$4 - \$3)^2]^{1/2}$$
$$= \$0.82 \text{ per share}$$

For Plan 2, the sale of equal amounts of debt and equity:

$$\overline{EPS} = 1/3(\$1.50) + 1/3(\$3.50) + 1/3(\$5.50) = \$3.50 \text{ per share}$$
$$\sigma_{EPS} = [1/3(\$1.50 - \$3.50)^2 + 1/3(\$3.50 - \$3.50)^2 +$$
$$1/3(\$5.50 - \$3.50)^2]^{1/2}$$
$$= \$1.63 \text{ per share}$$

In reexamining the two plans, note that there are two effects of financing with debt; that is, *there are two effects of financial leverage:*

1. Expected earnings per share increase.[12]
2. The standard deviation of earnings per share increases.

---

[12]It is possible for earnings to be lower under the debt-financing plan. This would occur when the cost of borrowing is greater than the expected EBIT rate of return on assets.

The reason that debt financing causes EPS to be larger is that debt is a safer investment—from an investor's standpoint—than common stock. As a result, the required rate of return on debt is lower than on stock, and therefore the cost of debt is lower than alternative sources of financing, such as equity. This difference causes EPS (and hence expected dividends) to be greater under debt financing.

Increases in EPS are desirable, *other things being equal,* but notice that other things are not equal in this example. The standard deviation of earnings per share also increases as financial leverage increases. This, in turn, will cause the standard deviation of rate of return on the stock to increase. Why? The stock will respond to EPS results as they are announced periodically by the firm. A greater standard deviation of EPS means bigger information shocks, which will cause more variability (standard deviation) in the stock price and in the rate of return stockholders receive.

The risk associated with the firm's stock equals the covariance between the rate of return on the firm's stock and the rate of return on the market index. But one of the determinants of this covariance is the standard deviation of rate of return on the firm's stock:

$$\text{Cov}_{rM} = \text{corr}_{rM}\, \sigma_r\, \sigma_M \qquad (15\text{--}6)$$

where

σ_r = standard deviation of rate of return on the firm's stock
σ_M = standard deviation of rate of return on a market index of wealth
Corr_{rM} = correlation of stock and market index rates of return

As Equation 15–6 shows, the greater the σ_r, the greater the covariance, and the greater the risk associated with the common stock. Therefore, the progression goes like this:

Increased financial leverage $\rightarrow$ Increased σ_{EPS} $\rightarrow$ Increased σ_r $\rightarrow$ Increased Cov_{rM} $\rightarrow$ Increased stock riskiness

In the Tyro example, the standard deviation of EPS under Plan 2, where debt is used, is greater than under Plan 1, where debt is not used, and therefore more risk is involved in Plan 2. This additional risk introduced into the firm is solely due to financial leverage, and we conclude that financial leverage increases stockholders' risk.

Adverse Effects of Financial Leverage: The Fatal

The use of debt financing can have very adverse effects, which ultimately can result in bankruptcy. As we saw earlier, below some critical level of EBIT, the use of leverage may lower EPS relative to what it would have been with only equity financing. Moreover, the heavy use of leverage can result in even greater difficulties, as the following examples show.

▪ *Example*

In 1987, Southland, which operates the 7–Eleven convenience store chain, went private in a leveraged buy-out. Within a couple of years the company was trying to stay afloat by borrowing even more money and selling some assets. Cash flow was inadequate to pay the interest, much less principal repayments which were coming due. According to *The Wall Street Journal,* "The Southland saga shows that leverage can hurt even so-called ideal LBO candidates."[13] ∎

▪ *Example*

Integrated Resources, strapped for cash to pay its creditors, reduced its assets to raise funds. When this was insufficient, it proposed a debt restructuring (outside of bankruptcy proceedings) that would pay senior creditors in part and the common stockholders nothing. Given the failure of this last-ditch restructuring attempt to break up the company and liquidate much of the business to pay creditors, all that was left was bankruptcy proceedings.[14] ∎

▪ *Example*

Finally, consider the ultimate result of too much debt. In late 1987, an investor group took control of Dart Drug Stores, Inc., a discount retailer.[15] The group inherited a substantial debt burden. An effort was made to revitalize the stores. By June 1989, however, Dart opted to delay payment of the interest on some junk bonds for the full 30-day grace period, and in July it did the same with interest on additional debt. In August 1989, Dart filed for bankruptcy under Chapter 11 of the federal Bankruptcy Code.[16] The chairman of the company stated that it "simply could not afford to continue to make payments" on its debt. ∎

CAPITAL STRUCTURE AND STOCKHOLDER WEALTH

We have now established that financial leverage can increase both expected EPS and the standard deviation of EPS. However, the ultimate question of interest about leverage and capital structure, as it should be about other financial decisions, is, How will this decision affect the price of the common stock and, therefore, contribute to maximizing the stockholders' wealth? In this case, we want to know if there is an optimal capital structure, which means optimal proportions of the different types of long-term financing, at which the price of the stock will be maximized.

The question of optimal capital structure has relevance in decisions about financing new investments and about recapitalizing the firm. Unless the firm finances new investments over the long run in the same approximate proportions as it has financed its old assets, the capital structure will change. How should the firm deal with this?

- If the firm currently has an optimal capital structure, it should finance new investments by a financing mix approximately like the current mix.
- If the current capital structure is not optimal, the firm should finance new assets so that the capital structure will be moved toward the optimal position.

---

[13]See Linda Sandler, "Southland's Junk Bonds Face Trouble," *The Wall Street Journal,* September 7, 1989, p. C1.
[14]See Linda Sandler, "Integrated Resources Offers Plan on Debt, Slashing Creditor Payout," *The Wall Street Journal,* August 16, 1989, p. C1.
[15]See Vinder P. Goel, "Dart Drug Makes Chapter 11 Filing, Plans to Pay Secured Creditors in Full," *The Wall Street Journal,* August 9, 1989, p. A4.
[16]Under Chapter 11, a company is protected from its creditors while it devises a plan to repay its debt.

- If the present capital structure is significantly suboptimal, the firm should give consideration to recapitalizing, perhaps exchanging debt for equity or equity for debt so that an optimal position is attained.

Of course, this discussion assumes that an optimal capital structure for each firm does in fact exist, an issue we consider in detail below.

In choosing among capital structures, the firm encounters the all-pervasive trade-off between risk and expected return that dominates financial decision making. If the firm tries to increase expected earnings per share (and hence stockholders' wealth) by using financial leverage, the stock's risk also increases. Do expected return and risk increase at the same rate? If using debt financing causes expected return to increase more than risk increases, then stock price will increase. However, if the increase in risk is viewed more unfavorably by investors than the expected increase in return is viewed favorably, the stock price will decline.

To answer these questions, we need to investigate the nature of the risk-return trade-off caused by debt financing. To do this, we use the dividend discount model developed in Chapter 6 and repeated here as Equation 15–7:

$$P_0 = \sum_{t=1}^{\infty} \frac{D_t}{(1 + k_e)^t} \tag{15–7}$$

where:

D_t is the expected dividend per share in period t

k_e is the required rate of return on equity

The dividend discount model expresses the current price of the stock, P_0, as a function of future expected dividends and the required rate of return on equity. We can use this model to investigate the debt-financing risk/return trade-off and, ultimately, to assess the effect of capital structure on stock price.

For simplicity, assume that the expected dividend stream is constant ($D_t = D$) for a very long time ($n \to \infty$). Recall from Chapter 6 that these assumptions reduce Equation 15–7 to a simpler expression:

$$P_0 = \frac{D}{k_e} \tag{15–8}$$

Assume further that the firm has a 100 percent dividend payout: the firm pays out all earnings as dividends. This means the constant expected dividends per share equals expected earnings per share.

We are now prepared to address the issue—Is there a particular capital structure that will maximize the stock price? A great controversy has occurred about the effect of capital structure on stock price. To understand fully and highlight this controversy, it will be useful to separate the analysis into two parts. First, we ignore taxes. Under this obviously unrealistic assumption, some finance theorists argue, there is no such thing as an optimal capital structure. Second, we introduce taxes into the analysis and reexamine the controversy.

Optimal Capital Structure: No Taxes

Suppose that the Bradley Manufacturing Company is an all-equity firm (no long-term debt). As Table 15–5 shows, as an all equity firm Bradley has expected dividends per share of $1. Using Equation 15–8, stock price is $1/.10 = $10.

■ *Table 15–5*
Calculating Stock
Price before and after
the Use of Debt for
Bradley Manufacturing

Number of shares of common stock: 1,000,000
Expected EBIT: $1,000,000 per year (for a very long time)
All earnings are paid out as dividends
Required rate of return on equity: $k_e = 0.10$

As an all equity firm
   Expected net income: $1,000,000
   Expected EPS: $1,000,000/1,000,000 shares = $1 per share
   Expected dividends per share = Expected EPS = $1 per share

*Using $5 million of 8 percent debt to buy back 500,000 shares
at $10 per share*

Common stock	500,000 shares
Long-term debt (8%)	$5,000,000
Expected EBIT	$1,000,000
Interest	$400,000
Expected net income	$600,000
Expected EPS	$1.20
Expected dividend per share	$1.20

Now assume Bradley borrows $5 million at 8 percent and uses this money to buy back half of its stock at $10 per share. Exactly as in the Tyro example, the use of debt increases expected EPS and the expected dividend per share. In Bradley's case, the expected dividend increases by 20 percent (from $1.00 to $1.20). Equation 15–8 shows that the greater D is, other things being equal, the greater P_0 will be:

Before Recapitalization   *After Recapitalization*

$$P_0 = \frac{\$1.00}{0.10} = \$10 \text{ per share} \qquad P_0 = \frac{\$1.20}{k_e} = ?$$

What will P_0 be after recapitalization? That depends on how k_e is affected by the recapitalization, which creates financial leverage and financial risk. We know that k_e is a function of financial risk, and the greater the financial risk, the greater k_e. However, if k_e does not increase as much as the expected dividend does, P_0 will increase.

Two principal theories explain how k_e and P_0 are affected by financial leverage in a taxless environment: the traditional theory and the M&M theory.[17]

Traditional Theory

The traditional theory asserts that within the range of prudent financial leverage positions and up to some particular point, the expected dividend will increase proportionately more than k_e as debt financing increases. That is, up to some point:

Percentage change in D > Percentage change in k_e

---

[17] A third theory, called the *net income theory*, has been refuted by financial research. This theory argues that k_e does not increase with increasing financial leverage.

There is no exact assertion in the traditional theory about what the precise percentage increases in k_e will be—only that it will be less than the percentage increase in D.

▪ *Example*

Assume for Bradley that $5 million of debt financing is within the prudent range of financial leverage positions. Then the traditional theory argues that k_e will increase by less than the 20 percent increase in D. Suppose the percentage increase in k_e is 15 percent, raising k_e to 0.115. Then:

$$P_0 = \frac{\$1.20}{0.115} = \$10.43$$

That is, k_e increases as investors observe increased financial risk, but up to some point this increase in k_e is not as large as the percentage increase in D. Consequently, P_0 increases.

To continue this theory, when the firm reaches financial leverage positions that are too risky, k_e will increase proportionately more than D does, and the stock price will start to decline. That is, beyond a certain financial leverage position, P_0 will start to drop as:

Percentage change in k_e > Percentage change in D

Why does k_e start to increase more rapidly at some point than expected dividends? Because the firm is viewed by investors as being overextended, and excessive debt raises the specter of bankruptcy.

These arguments imply that there is some optimal capital structure at which P_0 will be maximized. Stockholders' wealth is thus a function of the firm's capital structure, and to maximize stockholders' wealth the firm should seek out the capital structure that will give it optimum financial leverage. The relationship between stock price, P_0, and financial leverage under the traditional theory is shown in Figure 15–3(A).[18] Up to the optimal capital structure, P_0 increases as the percentage change in dividends exceeds the percentage change in k_e. Beyond the optimal capital structure, P_0 decreases as the percentage change in k_e exceeds the percentage change in dividends.

In summary, according to the traditional approach, there is an optimal capital structure. Up to the optimal debt–equity ratio, the firm can and should employ debt. Beyond the optimal capital structure, the firm has employed too much debt.

M&M Theory

In a classic article in the finance literature, Modigliani and Miller (hereafter, M&M) demonstrated a formal model that showed why—*in a taxless world*—there would be no preference for debt financing by the firm and, therefore, no optimal capital structure.[19] Their analysis was built on a set of assumptions, including no corporate taxes, perfect capital markets, homogeneous expectations by investors,

[18]Leverage is usually portrayed as a ratio of long-term debt to equity or some variant (such as long-term debt to total capital).
[19]See Franco Modigliani and Merton Miller, "The Cost of Capital, Corporation Finance, and the Theory of Investment," *American Economic Review*, June 1958.

■ *Figure 15–3*
Stock Price versus
Financial Leverage:
No Taxes

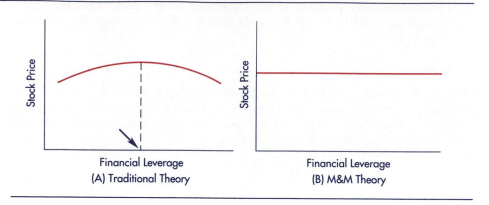

and the ability to categorize firms into "equivalent return" classes within which all firms have the same degree of business risk.

Because stocks in the same risk class were perfect substitutes for one another, investors would perform *arbitrage* operations (buying and selling stocks that were perfect substitutes for one another) whenever firms with the same business risk, but different capital structures, had different values. This market activity would soon equalize the prices of the stocks in question.[20]

In a taxless world, according to the M&M theory, there is no advantage to debt financing; stock price is independent of financial leverage. According to this argument, as the firm adds debt, k_e increases at exactly the same rate as the expected dividend increases:

$$\text{Percentage change in } k_e = \text{Percentage change in } D$$

■ *Example*

Using the Bradley example, if D increases 20 percent from \$1.00 per share to \$1.20 per share, k_e will also increase 20 percent from 0.10 to 0.12. So P_0 after recapitalization will equal (\$1.20/0.12 = \$10), the same value as before recapitalization (\$1.00/0.10 = \$10). ■

Investors are assumed to fully understand that increases in expected dividends caused by the firm's increased use of debt also result in increased financial risk. The response of investors is to raise their required rate of return exactly the same amount as the expected dividend increase; therefore, the gains that accrue to the stockholders because of increased expected dividends are exactly offset by the increased required rate of return on the common stock.

The relationship between stock price and financial leverage under the M&M theory is shown in Figure 15–3(B). There is no such thing as an optimal capital structure. In other words, value is value—rearranging the financing of the firm does not change that value.

The main implication of the M&M theory is that—in a taxless world—it is a matter of indifference how the firm finances its investments in the long run. Short-

---

[20]This theory is also called the *net operating income* (NOI) theory.

run circumstances may lead the firm to issue new debt (the stock market may be temporarily depressed) or new equity (the bond market may be temporarily saturated), but in the long run, there is no reason for the firm to prefer debt financing over equity financing. The firm need not borrow on the investors' behalf when investors can borrow themselves, if they so choose. Since investors can substitute personal leverage for corporate leverage and replicate a firm's capital structure, the firm's financing decision is an unimportant long-run decision, according to the M&M theory.

Optimal Capital Structure: With Taxes

When taxes are introduced into the analysis, the traditional and M&M theories begin to look a lot alike. They both have been interpreted as implying optimal capital structures.[21]

Why would taxes have an important impact on the debate over optimal capital structure? Consider how the firm's EBIT is split up. Assuming for simplicity that the firm has only two long-term financing sources, debt and equity, EBIT has three groups of claimants:

1. Stockholders.
2. Debtholders.
3. Taxes (government).

The size of the EBIT is determined by the firm's investments; that is, EBIT is not influenced by the firm's capital structure. What the capital structure does do is determine how the EBIT is divided among the three groups of claimants identified above.

▪ *Example*

Suppose a company's tax rate is 40 percent and its EBIT is $10,000 per year for the foreseeable future. Consider what the lower half of the firm's income statement would look like under two different capital structures: Plan A—no debt, Plan B—an amount of debt such that annual interest payments are $2,000 per year.

	Plan A	Plan B
EBIT	$10,000	$10,000
Interest	0	2,000
EBT	10,000	8,000
Tax (0.4)	4,000	3,200
Net income	$ 6,000	$ 4,800

---

[21]Another theory has been proposed that revives a long-standing finance argument that capital structure may not be important, even when taxes are considered. Professor Merton Miller has argued that when personal tax considerations are introduced into the capital structure problem, there is generally no longer any optimal capital structure for individual firms, although there may be for all firms in aggregate. This argument concerns the effects on interest rates and corporate borrowing of the corporate tax rate and of differential personal tax rates for investors (capital gains versus ordinary). It concludes that there is no fundamental advantage to a firm in issuing debt. See "Debt and Taxes," *Journal of Finance*, May 1977, pp. 261–75.

Thus, these alternative plans divide the $10,000 EBIT among the three claimant groups as follows:

	Plan A		Plan B	
Stockholders	$ 6,000 ⎫		$ 4,800 ⎫	
Debtholders	0 ⎭	$6,000	2,000 ⎭	$6,800
Taxes	4,000		3,200	
	$10,000		$10,000	

We see that the stockholders' total receipts have gone down in Plan B. However, there are also fewer shares because of the debt financing. The important point is that taxes have been reduced in B by $800. Consequently, the combined stockholders' and debtholders' claims have increased in B by $800. This causes the value of the firm to increase. ■

In the M&M theory, the value of the firm increases by the present value of this tax subsidy caused by the tax deductibility of interest.

$$V = V_U + \text{Present value of interest tax shield}^{[22]} \tag{15–9}$$

where:

$$V = \text{market value of the firm}$$
$$V_U = \text{market value of the firm if it were all equity}$$

Equation 15–9 indicates that in the presence of taxes, the value of the firm (and stock price) will increase as the capital structure is more heavily weighted with debt. However, according to the M&M theory, the only advantage of debt financing is the tax deductibility of the interest payments on the firm's debt. But the fact remains that the M&M theory acknowledges that tax-deductible debt is a more desirable form of financing according to Equation 15–9. Does this mean the optimal capital structure is 99.9 percent debt? This question reintroduces the *bankruptcy problem*.

When bankruptcy possibilities are considered in conjunction with the tax deductibility of interest payments, the financial structure optimal to M&M looks much like the optimal structure under traditional theory. As financial leverage is increased, this increases the value of the firm and stock price. At some point, however, as financial leverage is increased further, expected bankruptcy costs exceed the interest tax effect, causing firm value and stock price to fall. As a result of the countervailing forces of the tax deductibility of interest and expected bankruptcy costs, there is an optimal capital structure.[23] We could also add agency costs in with bankruptcy costs, which would further offset the present value of the tax shield.

---

[22]If the debt that creates the interest tax shield is presumed to be very long-lived, the present value of the interest tax shield can be approximated by the product of the firm's tax rate and the market value of the debt:

Present value of interest tax shield = (Company tax rate)(Market value of debt)

[23]Although M&M themselves have never proclaimed that expected bankruptcy costs played an important role in their model, the popularized version of their model does include an expected-bankruptcy term.

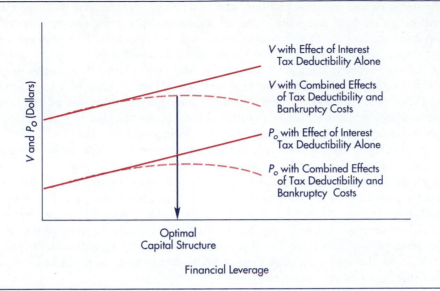

■ *Figure 15–4*
Firm Value (*V*) and Stock
Price (*P*) versus Financial
Leverage with Taxes and
Bankruptcy Costs

Building on Equation 15–9:

$$V = V_U + \left[\left(\begin{array}{c} \text{Present value of} \\ \text{interest tax shield} \end{array} \right) - \left(\begin{array}{c} \text{Present value of} \\ \text{expected bankruptcy costs} \end{array} \right) \right] \quad \textbf{(15–10)}$$

As leverage increases, the present value of the interest tax shield increases, but the present value of expected bankruptcy costs decline.[24] At some point, firm value and stock price are maximized. Figure 15–4 illustrates this idea.

The substance of the traditional theory is largely unchanged by the addition of taxes and bankruptcy. The arguments used previously to describe the traditional theory would still apply here. The traditional theory supports the concept of an optimal capital structure in the presence of taxes.

Some Conclusions on Capital Structure

Arguments about whether an optimal capital structure exists have been going on for several decades. Along with these arguments a number of empirical tests have been done in hope of resolving the controversy or at least providing suggestive evidence to support a position.

It is extremely difficult to perform a decisive test of the competing capital structure theories because of data problems, statistical model-building problems, and because the concepts in the theories deal with expectations of the future, which are not measurable with accuracy today. Thus, every test of capital structure

---

[24]Equations 15–9 and 15–10 represent a subtle orientation change. Rather than emphasize the market value of the firm's *stock,* as we have done throughout the book, Equations 15–9 and 15–10 emphasize the market value of the *firm,* which is the combined market value of stock plus debt. In most cases, maximizing the market value of the firm is consistent with maximizing the market value of the stock. The presumption underlying that coincidence of goals is that any extra net present value generated by the firm enhances the stock's market value while the market value of the bonds is unaffected. At times that presumption is not true, but we will not delve into that more advanced topic here. We presume instead that maximizing the value of the firm is generally consistent with maximizing stockholder wealth.

theory is flawed in some fashion, and what we have today in finance is two collections of empirical work. One set seems to support the theory that capital structure matters and that there is an optimal capital structure. The other set seems to support the argument that there is no optimal capital structure.

Newer theories, such as *agency theory,* offer some insights into the matter. Recall that agency theory is concerned with the inherent conflict of interest among stockholders, bondholders, and the firm's managers. Proponents of this theory argue that viewing the capital structure problem as one of balancing off the interest tax benefits and bankruptcy costs of debt is an incomplete view.

According to agency theorists, the capital structure issue also involves analyzing agency costs inherent in the problem. One important agency cost is the cost of establishing mutually acceptable contracts among the various parties (like covenants on debt securities and performance bonuses for managers). Bondholders will seek to protect themselves from the incentive that stockholders have to engage in riskier projects that will benefit the stockholders at the expense of the bondholders, whose claims are fixed in amount. Bondholders will seek to protect themselves through such devices as restrictive covenants in the debt contracts, and this increases agency costs.

Monitoring cost is another important agency cost. It is concerned with expenditures incurred by the principal to measure, observe, and control the agent's behavior. According to agency theory, the practice of issuing accounting statements is an instance of monitoring costs.

Agency theory thus approaches the capital structure problem from an entirely different direction. The end result of the theory is that an optimal capital structure does exist, although the analysis to arrive at the optimal structure is much different from the "capital structure matters" theory we saw earlier. Perhaps the best way to think about agency costs relative to capital structure arguments is to incorporate them into the analysis depicted in Figure 15–4. Agency costs are another factor, similar to the potential bankruptcy costs, that causes the curve depicting the firm's market value to turn down. In other words, taking this factor into account, along with others, means that there is an optimal capital structure.

Other new ideas in financial management may also help in understanding the capital structure issue. The concept of *asymmetric information,* which continues to be developed, starts out with the idea that the firm's managers possess information that investors do not. Managers can *signal* information to investors in an attempt to cause a favorable change in the value of the firm. For example, dividends could be used to signal investors about future prospects. As for capital structure, the signaling approach suggests that there is no single optimal debt-equity ratio because managers, who have more information than investors, use their flow of information to change how the firm will raise funds. Thus, debt may be used this time, equity next time, and so on.

Final conclusions about leverage and capital structure are difficult. Nevertheless, it's probably safe to say that majority opinion favors the view that capital structure does matter. What has emerged is a position that capital structure is "determined out of a static trade-off between the tax advantage of debt and the risk of bankruptcy."[25] Unfortunately, the empirical research is not only incon-

---

[25]Jonathan Baskin, "An Empirical Investigation of the Pecking Order Hypothesis," *Financial Management,* Spring 1989, p. 26.

clusive but it offers very little support for the "static trade-off theory." However, an old hypothesis, which is receiving increasing attention and which could represent the emerging new view on capital structure, may explain the behavior of firms regarding capital structure. Therefore, we can finish our discussion by examining this view.

The Pecking Order Hypothesis

The pecking order hypothesis (POH) represents empirical observations in search of a theory.[26] For some years observers of corporate financial practices thought that the POH described what firms actually did, but there was no accepted theoretical justification. Now, according to Baskin, incorporating new ideas like asymmetric information and signaling equilibrium makes possible a rationale for this hypothesis; furthermore, he argues, a large body of accumulated evidence supports this theory.[27]

Briefly, the **pecking order hypothesis (POH)** states that firms avoid new equity issues and borrow to finance new investment only after exhausting retained earnings (and drawing down its marketable securities). Thus, managers have a pecking order or preference order for financing:

1. Internal equity.
2. Debt.
3. External equity.

In effect, according to the POH, asymmetric information restricts equity financing because such issues are interpreted as signs that the stock is overpriced, motivating managers to sell stock during this time, which in turn leads to a sharp drop in stock price.[28] Furthermore, since dividends are needed as a signaling mechanism, asymmetric information creates an imperfectly elastic supply of equity funding by restricting access to retained earnings. Taxes and transaction costs also motivate the firm to prefer internally generated funds to external equity, and to prefer debt to equity. Although bankruptcy costs do restrict borrowing, the supply of debt remains more elastic than that of equity. When firms need external funds to finance their investment projects, they issue debt if possible, and new common stock only as a last resort.

The bottom line from the POH is that in practice, *capital structure is passively determined* as firms try to fund investment projects with an imperfectly elastic supply of retained earnings. After adjusting for the firm's activities in the past, the use of debt financing appears to be residual in nature. There is little evidence that firms adjust toward a static optimal capital structure.

Where does this leave us? The pecking order hypothesis is consistent with the idea of a **target capital structure**, which suggests that firms seek to be somewhere within a range of capital structures that are all approximately equally good

> **pecking order hypothesis (POH)**
> firms seek to raise funds in the following order: retained earnings, new debt, and new equity

> **target capital structure**
> range of capital structures that are approximately equally good

---

[26]For a very readable discussion, see Stewart Myers, "The Capital Structure Puzzle," *Journal of Finance,* July 1984, pp. 575–92. The original hypothesis is based on Gordon Donaldson's work. See Gordon Donaldson, *Corporate Debt Capacity: A Study of Corporate Debt Policy and the Determination of Corporate Debt Capacity* (Boston: Harvard Graduate School of Business Administration, 1961).

[27]See Baskin, "An Empirical Investigation," pp. 26–27.

[28]M&M theory holds that all investors have homogeneous expectations. Asymmetric information means that different groups of market participants have different information. The typical assumption is that management's information is different from that of stockholders. A new issue is often taken to mean that management believes the stock is overvalued.

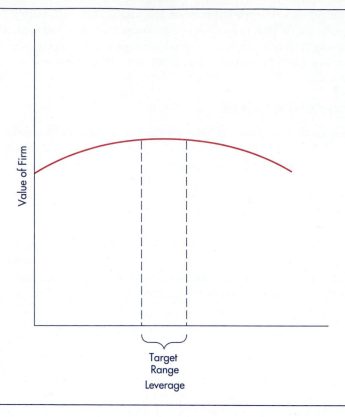

and that are thought to be appropriate for the firm in question. In other words, there is no single optimal capital structure, but an optimal range exists, and within this range the value of the firm is maximized. This is illustrated in Figure 15–5, which shows a relatively flat portion of the value curve within the target range.

The POH is consistent with the target capital structure idea. It does not specify a designated debt-equity ratio because of the discontinuous nature of the equity used—retained earnings followed by debt and then by new common stock issues. Therefore, the firm's debt-equity ratio will fluctuate over time, depending on the firm's investment opportunities, dividend policy, and overall profitability. In a sense, this is a more flexible view than traditional capital structure theory, and one that may be more consistent with observed business practice.

SUMMARY

■ Operating leverage, a result of the firm's use of assets with fixed costs, magnifies changes in the firm's sales into larger changes in EBIT.

■ The degree of operating leverage (DOL) measures the firm's operating leverage position and is defined as the percentage change in EBIT divided by the percentage change in sales.

■ The greater the firm's operating leverage, the greater its business risk, or risk associated with the firm's investments.

- A second form of leverage, financial leverage, results from the use of fixed-charge financing. The major sources of long-term fixed-charge financing are debt, preferred stock, and leasing.
- The degree of financial leverage (DFL) measures the firm's financial leverage position and is defined as the percentage change in EPS divided by the percentage change in EBIT.
- Financial leverage is also reflected by the firm's ratio of long-term debt to equity or some variant such as the ratio of long-term debt to total assets.
- The greater the firm's use of fixed-charge financing, the greater its financial leverage and financial risk.
- The greater the financial leverage, the riskier the stock, and the riskier the expected earnings per share. Financial leverage thus leads to both greater expected earnings per share (and therefore greater expected dividends) and increased financial risk.
- The increased financial risk caused by increased financial leverage manifests itself in a higher required rate of return on equity, k_e, partially offsetting the gains to the stockholders caused by increased EPS.
- In a world where interest payments are tax deductible, this offsetting is not complete up to some particular leverage position. It is advantageous to have the firm finance with debt up to some point, but beyond this point it is disadvantageous for the firm to finance with debt because of bankruptcy possibilities.
- The preceding item implies the existence of an optimal capital structure that will optimize stockholder wealth. Both the traditional and M&M theories of capital structure agree that an optimal capital structure exists for the firm if taxes are considered.
- Guides for finding the optimal position are not well spelled out in the finance literature. The task entails balancing out the gains due to the tax deductibility of debt financing and the expected costs of bankruptcy.
- Capital structure remains a controversial issue.
- It may be necessary to analyze agency costs when evaluating capital structure considerations.
- The pecking order hypothesis appears to offer some progress in resolving this issue.

KEY TERMS

business risk, p. 453

capital structure, p. 450

combined leverage, p. 456

earnings before interest and taxes
  (EBIT), p. 450

operating leverage, p. 450

financial leverage, p. 454

financial risk, p. 454

pecking order hypothesis, p. 471

target capital structure, p. 471

QUESTIONS

15–1. Compare and contrast operating leverage with financial leverage.

15–2. Why is financial leverage sometimes referred to as *second-stage leverage?*

15–3. What is meant by combined leverage?

15–4. Explain the concept of total leverage by using the components of an income statement to show the two leverage stages.

15–5. An analyst is comparing the operating leverage of two similar firms. If all operating data for the two companies were identical except for the differences listed on the next page, which company would have the greater amount of operating leverage in each instance?

    a. Company A has a higher EBIT level than Company B.

    b. Company A has higher fixed costs than Company B.

15–6. Company X has a lower DOL than Company Y. Which company has the greater amount of business risk? Explain your answer.

15–7. What is the purpose of an EBIT–EPS chart?

15–8. In comparing the financial leverage of two companies, A and B, with the same amount of assets and EBIT, we notice that A has less debt (and lower interest charges) than B.

    a. Other things being equal, which company would have the greater amount of financial risk? Why?

    b. Suppose that even though B has more debt financing, higher interest charges, and the same amount of assets and EBIT as A, A still has a larger calculated degree of financial leverage. Explain whether this is possible or not.

15–9. Financial leverage has two effects on earnings per share. Identify these two effects and explain why they occur.

15–10. In the simplified world of no taxes, two competing theories describe how stock prices are related to capital structure.

    a. Identify these two theories.

    b. Briefly describe them.

    c. What main impact does including taxes have on the debate?

15–11. In a sales-EBIT analysis, it is common to talk about a relevant range of sales within which the analysis is valid. Discuss what is meant by the *relevant range,* and indicate why this concept is important.

15–12. Most financial theorists and analysts would agree that in the presence of taxes, there is an optimal capital structure, and that it is established by a trade-off involving two things. Discuss this trade-off and show graphically what it looks like, being careful to label relevant parts of the trade-off graph.

15–13. What is the main implication of the M&M theory in a taxless world?

15–14. What is the rationale of the "capital structure matters" theory?

15–15. What are the implications of considering agency theory for the capital structure controversy?

15–16. What are the major sources of long-term fixed charge financing?

15–17. Summarize the empirical evidence concerning the existence of an optimal capital structure.

15–18. A new analyst with the Western Mexico Import-Export Company has completed preparing a break-even EBIT chart for the company. The analyst is preparing to present this chart to the boss and wants to make a good impression. There is some question in the analyst's own mind about how accurately and realistically the chart reflects what the firm's EBIT would be for particular sales levels. What could you tell the analyst about the validity of the break-even chart?

DEMONSTRATION PROBLEM

15–1. Wylie Products is considering some changes in the amount of leverage employed by the firm. Two proposals, A and B, have been suggested to alter the current situation. The following information has been compiled.

	Current	Proposal A	Proposal B
Operating data			
Sales	$4,000,000	No change	$4,000,000
Variable costs/sales	.4	from current	.25
Fixed costs	$1,500,000	↓	$2,000,000
Financial data			
Interest payments	$ 75,000	$100,000	No change
Lease payments	85,000	30,000	from current
Preferred dividends	50,000	48,000	↓
Number of common shares	500,000	600,000	

The firm's tax rate is 40%.

a. For the current situation, Proposal A, and Proposal B, determine the following:
   (1) Degree of operating leverage.
   (2) Degree of financial leverage.
   (3) Degree of combined leverage.

b. Assuming everything else constant, rank the three plans from most risky to least risky in these terms:
   (1) Business risk.
   (2) Financial risk.
   (3) Overall risk.

Solution to Demonstration Problem

15–1. First, we calculate EBIT for each alternative using the basic formula:

$$\text{EBIT} = \text{Sales} - \text{Variable costs} - \text{Fixed costs}$$

Current EBIT $= \$4,000,000 - (.4)(\$4,000,000) - \$1,500,000 = \$ 900,000$
Plan A EBIT $= \$4,000,000 - (.4)(\$4,000,000) - \$1,500,000 = \$ 900,000$
Plan B EBIT $= \$4,000,000 - (.25)(\$4,000,000) - \$2,000,000 = \$1,000,000$

a. (1) DOL $= 1 + F/\text{EBIT}$:

$$\text{Current DOL} = 1 + \$1,500,000/\$900,000 = 2.67$$
$$\text{Proposal A DOL} = 1 + \$1,500,000/\$900,000 = 2.67$$
$$\text{Proposal B DOL} = 1 + \$2,000,000/\$1,000,000 = 3.0$$

  (2) DFL $= \text{EBIT}/[\text{EBIT} - I - L - d/(1 - T)]$:

$$\text{Current DFL} = \$900,000 / \left[\$900,000 - \$75,000 - \$85,000 - \frac{\$50,000}{.6} \right] = \frac{\$900,000}{\$656,667} = 1.37$$

$$\text{Proposal A DFL} = \$900,000 / \left[\$900,000 - \$100,000 - \$30,0000 - \frac{\$48,000}{.6} \right] = \frac{\$900,000}{\$690,000} = 1.30$$

$$\text{Proposal B DFL} = \$1,000,000/(\$1,000,000 - \$243,333) = \frac{\$1,000,000}{\$756,667} = 1.32$$

  (3) DCL $= (\text{DOL})(\text{DFL})$:

$$\text{Current DCL} = (2.67)(1.37) = 3.66$$
$$\text{Proposal A DCL} = (2.67)(1.30) = 3.47$$
$$\text{Proposal B DCL} = (3)(1.32) = 3.96$$

b. (1) B > A = current.
  (2) Current > B > A.
  (3) B > current > A.

PROBLEMS

15–1. Current selected financial data for the Tuttle Power Company are as follows:

Sales	$2,000,000
Variable cost ratio	0.4
Fixed costs	700,000
Interest payments	75,000
Lease payments	125,000
Preferred dividends	100,000
Tax rate	0.50
Number of common shares	50,000

Determine:
a. DOL.
b. DFL.
c. DCL.
d. The percent change in EPS if EBIT increases by 5 percent.
e. The percent change in EPS if sales increase by 8 percent.
f. The percent change in EBIT if sales decrease by 5 percent.

15–2. Consider the following operating information about companies H and I:

	H ($ Millions)	I ($ Millions)
Sales	$10,000,000	$12,000,000
Fixed costs	3,000,000	6,000,000
Variable costs	5,000,000	3,000,000

Find the degree of operating leverage for each company.

15–3. Given the following information about the present situation of a company, determine what percent change in earnings per share the company would experience if its sales decreased by 2 percent.

Annual EBIT	$2,800,000
Annual operating fixed costs	$4,480,000
Annual lease payments	0
Annual interest payments	$2,000,000
Preferred stock	none

15–4. Sullivan, Inc., has $1 billion face value of long-term debt outstanding with a 10 percent coupon rate. Sullivan also has 20 million shares of common stock outstanding. EBIT is currently $500 million per year and is expected to stay at that level indefinitely. Sullivan's tax rate is 0.5, and the required rate of return on equity is 20 percent. All earnings are paid out as dividends. If Sullivan were to buy back half of its stock at the current market price and pay for this purchase with new long-term debt, the company estimates its required rate of return on equity would become 30 percent and the coupon rate on the new bonds would still be 10 percent. Would you recommend that this change in capital structure be made?

15–5. The financial staff for Dunkleburg, Inc., has been doing some capital structure planning. A team of analysts has estimated Dunkleburg's costs of equity and cost of debt for several ratios of debt to total financing. This information is shown below. Assuming that the company only has debt and equity in its capital structure, determine—within some range—what Dunkleburg's best capital structure is.

Ratio of Debt to Total Financing	k_E	k_D
0	0.100	.030
0.10	0.105	.030
0.20	0.111	.032
0.30	0.118	.035
0.40	0.130	.038
0.50	0.145	.044
0.60	0.163	.050

15–6. Anderson Electronics is currently making substantial new investments in semiconductors. Anderson plans to finance this investment with either a new stock issue (100,000 shares) of new 8 percent debt. Total financing required is $500,000. The firm's preexpansion income statement is as follows:

Sales	$2,000,000
Operating costs	1,500,000
EBIT	500,000
Interest	100,000
EBT	400,000
Tax ($T = 0.5$)	200,000
Net income	200,000
EPS (200,000 shares)	$1/share

Anderson estimates that EBIT after the new investment will be $500,000, or $600,000, or $800,000, with associated probabilities of 0.3, 0.5, and 0.2.
  a. Determine the EPS for both plans under each EBIT possibility.
  b. Calculate expected EPS and the standard deviation of EPS for each plan.
  c. If the correlation between Anderson stock and market index rates of return is essentially the same under the two plans, which plan has more financial risk? Explain your answer.

15–7. Wolfe Company is considered to be a no-growth company by the market. Annual dividends are $1.40 per share, and the required rate of return on Wolfe's equity is 20 percent. The company is considering changing its capital structure in a way that would allow greater annual dividends of $1.60 per share, which would be expected to be the new permanent dividend level from then on. Because Wolfe would be riskier after the capital structure change, Wolfe's required rate of return on equity would change to 25 percent. Would you recommend that Wolfe make the proposed change?

15–8. Financial analysts for Hill Company have been doing some capital structure planning. The numbers below show expected costs associated with bankruptcy at various levels of debt. The amount-of-debt row does not exceed $3 million because investment bankers have said that there is virtually no likelihood that Hill can acquire more debt than that. The tax rate for Hill is 40 percent.

Amount of debt ($ millions)	1.0	1.5	2.0	2.5	3.0
Expected bankruptcy costs ($000)	100	200	300	500	1,000

Determine the optimal amount of debt for Hill.

15–9. Taylor Windows has no long-term debt outstanding. The company has 500,000 shares of common stock selling at $10 per share. Current EPS is a dollar a share, and the company's policy is (and will be) to pay out all earnings as dividends. Taylor needs to raise $5 million for new investment purposes and is considering two alternative financing plans (ignoring flotation costs):

    A: Sell 500,000 shares of stock at $10 per share.

    B: Sell $2 million in 5 percent bonds and 300,000 shares of stock at $10 per share.

    a. If after the expansion Taylor anticipates earning $2.5 million before interest and taxes (EBIT) for the foreseeable future, calculate EPS and dividends per share under each plan. The tax rate is 40 percent.

    b. Assume the conditions given in (*a*) and that, furthermore, the cost of equity is estimated to be 10 percent if Plan A is adopted and 11 percent if Plan B is adopted. Estimate the market price of the stock under both plans.

    c. Assume that you and another financial analyst on Taylor's corporate planning staff are presenting your results to several of Taylor's top executives.

      (1) How would you explain the anticipated increase in stock price over the current $10 price if Plan A is adopted?

      (2) How would you explain the further anticipated increase in stock price (over that of Plan A) if Plan B is adopted?

      (3) One of the executives asks how a third alternative financing plan, namely, issuing $5 million in debt, would compare with the other plans. Your colleague responds that that plan was considered. However, it was estimated that the coupon rate on the debt would go up to 6 percent, and that the estimated stock price would be $11 per share. As your colleague talks, you are signaled to calculate the EPS result for this case. Do this and also determine what cost of equity is implied in the calculation of the $11 stock price.

      (4) How would you justify using different costs of equity capital for the three different plans?

      (5) Based on all these calculations, which plan do you recommend? Why?

SELECTED REFERENCES

A good discussion of the current status of testing capital structure theories can be found in:

Baskin, Jonathan. "An Empirical Investigation of the Pecking Order Hypothesis." *Financial Management.* Spring 1989, pp. 26–35.

The effect of taxes on debt management is discussed in:

Maur, David C., and Wilbur G. Lewellen. "Debt Management under Corporate and Personal Taxation." *The Journal of Finance,* December 1987, pp. 1275–92.

A general discussion of the capital structure issue can be found in:

Myers, Stewart C. "The Capital Structure Puzzle." *Journal of Finance*, July 1984, pp. 575–92.

Operating and financial leverage are discussed in:

Prezas, Alexandros P. "Effects of Debt on the Degree of Operating and Financial Leverage." *Financial Management*, Summer 1987, pp. 329–44.

APPENDIX 15–A   BREAK-EVEN CONCEPTS FOR OPERATING LEVERAGE

Break-Even Analysis with Operating Leverage

Operating leverage is often analyzed in conjunction with *break-even analysis,* the purpose of which is to determine how EBIT changes with the level of production. The sales level that corresponds with a zero EBIT level is called the *break-even sales level.*

There are several ways to determine the break-even sales level. An efficient approach is to solve for break-even sales algebraically. Let:

$$S^* = \text{Break-even sales}$$
$$F = \text{Fixed costs}$$
$$v = \text{Variable cost ratio} = \text{Variable costs/Sales}$$

Now:

$$EBIT = \text{Sales} - \text{Variable costs} - \text{Fixed costs}^{29}$$
$$= S - (v)(S) - F$$
$$= S(1 - v) - F$$

But at break-even: EBIT $= 0$ and $S = S^*$; therefore, at break-even:

$$0 = S^*(1 - v) - F$$

and

$$S^* = \frac{F}{1 - v} \qquad\qquad \text{(15–A1)}$$

▪ *Example*

Suppose that $F = \$30,000$ and $v = 0.7$. Then:

$$S^* = \frac{\$30,000}{1 - 0.7} = \$100,000$$

Sales would have to drop below $100,000 before the firm would have a negative EBIT level. ▪

---

[29] Total costs = variable costs + fixed costs.

Break-Even Analysis Limitations

Although break-even analysis is a useful technique for examining the operating leverage of the firm or a project, we must be careful to note some important limitations. There is a narrow range of sales over which we might reasonably expect fixed costs to be actually fixed, and where there might be stable linear relationships among variable costs, EBIT, and sales. However, the relationships are more likely to be nonlinear, which means we must regard the linear break-even sales calculation from Equation 15–A1 with some skepticism. A nonlinear analysis is more complex, and it eliminates the advantage of break-even analysis—its simplicity.

Another difficulty with break-even analysis is the categorization of costs into fixed and variable components. It is extremely difficult to classify some costs into these categories because many costs appear to be *semivariable* (partly fixed and partly variable). Thus break-even analysis is not readily applied to complex cost structures. Finally, there is the problem of the long run versus the short run. In the long run, all costs are variable. This means that a break-even chart may not be a very reliable representation of the relationships among sales, costs, and EBIT because they are inherently unstable over time. Furthermore, in its simple form break-even analysis disregards the time value of money, one of the key concepts of finance.

QUESTIONS

1. Other things being equal, what happens to the break-even sales level if:
   a. Costs unrelated to sales volume decrease?
   b. The variable cost ratio increases?
   c. Prices on all the firm's products are lowered with no increase in sales volume?

16

Dividend Policy

The Effects of Dividend Policy

In the 1980s, a well-known corporate raider attempted to take over CPC International, a food processor.[1] The company decided to buy back 20 percent of its outstanding shares, and paid some $350 million for several million shares at a price per share of about $44, the then-current market price. To finance both the stock buy-back and some acquisitions, CPC increased its outstanding debt sharply, coming close to its net worth for a short period.

CPC stockholders did not suffer from the stock buy-back. Earnings were up significantly. After the repurchase, the company split the stock 2-for-1 and the dividend increased each year thereafter. The price following the takeover attempt was higher than when the raider sold out.

Did the attempted takeover and/or stock buy-back raise the price of the stock? What role did the stock split and the increased dividend play in raising the price?

---

[1]See James Cook, "Back to Business," *Forbes*, October 5, 1987, pp. 40–41. Figures are based on *The Value Line Investment Survey*, various issues.

Should a firm pay dividends to its stockholders, and if so, how much? This may seem a strange question to ask, but the truth is that dividend policy remains one of the most controversial topics in financial management. Fischer Black, a well-known financial expert, sums it up well: "The harder we look at the dividend picture, the more it seems like a puzzle, with pieces that just don't fit together."[2]

Many different opinions have been advanced over the years concerning dividend payments, but this issue remains an unsettled topic. Part of the problem is that what firms actually do about dividends seems to diverge in significant detail from the theory of what firms should do about dividends. In effect, what is puzzling about dividends is why firms pay the cash dividends they do when they have alternative methods of distributing cash to equity holders. Even after the Tax Reform Act of 1986 and the modifications in 1990, most individual shareowners are in the 28 percent or higher marginal tax bracket, and the marginal tax rate for corporations is 34 percent, not counting state tax rates. Dividends are taxed twice, once at the corporate level and then at the individual level. It appears, therefore, that equity is the most heavily taxed capital market security.

Since dividends allow the stockholder to receive value directly from the firm, or "cash out," their potential importance to stockholders is obvious. And as always, our emphasis is on maximizing the stockholders' wealth. Financial managers should seek the optimal dividend policy that will maximize the price of the stock.

Primary *chapter learning objectives* are:

1. To examine the concept of cash distributions to shareholders.
2. To consider both the theory and practice of dividend policy.

CASH DISTRIBUTIONS TO SHAREHOLDERS

What exactly is a *dividend*? The term refers to any direct payment by the firm to its stockholders, whether in cash or in property of any kind. The most important type of dividend, and what is typically being referred to when the term *dividend* is used, is the regular **cash dividend** paid four times a year. For example, in 1989 Phelps Dodge Corporation paid a quarterly dividend of 75 cents per share of common stock.

A firm sometimes pays its regular cash dividend plus an *extra dividend* that depends on how well the firm fared during the year.

cash dividend
cash payment made by the firm to its stockholders, usually quarterly

▪ *Example*

In September 1989, Phelps Dodge declared a special dividend of $10 per share (a total cost of $350 million) in addition to its regular quarterly dividend of 75 cents a share. Although subject to the cyclical swing in metal prices, this copper producer had recently reported record earnings for the first half of the year and decided to make a special distribution. ▪

Cash dividend payments are only part of the broader concept of *cash distributions to equity holders,* which can take one of three primary forms:

---

[2]Fischer Black, "The Dividend Puzzle," *Journal of Portfolio Management*, Winter 1976, p. 5.

Cash Distributions to Shareholders   ■ *Figure 16–1*

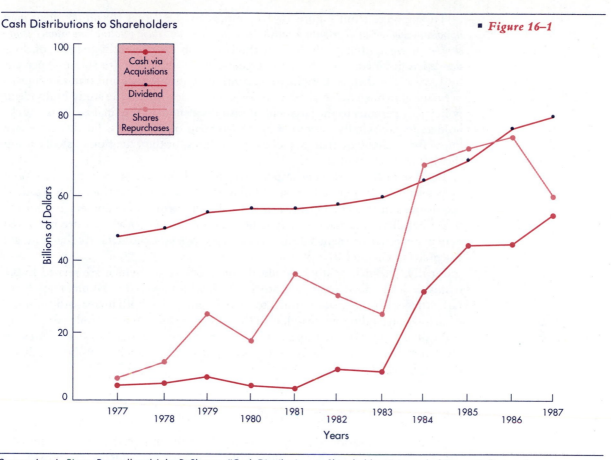

Source: Laurie Simon Bagwell and John B. Shoven, "Cash Distributions to Shareholders," *Journal of Economic Perspectives,* Summer 1989, p. 131.

■ Direct cash payments in the form of regular cash dividends.
■ Stock repurchase programs.
■ Cash-financed mergers and acquisitions.

It is essential to recognize all three forms because the latter two methods of cash distributions to equity holders have increased dramatically in importance, as Figure 16–1 shows.

Figure 16–1 graphs some data that illustrate the importance of nondividend cash payments. The data cover nearly 2,500 companies, representing the largest and most significant firms from the major stock exchanges, for the period 1977 to 1987. The numbers are in millions of 1986 constant dollars in order to remove any effects of inflation.[3]

As Figure 16–1 shows, real (inflation-adjusted) dividends grew smoothly over the period, increasing by a total of about 60 percent. Cash via acquisitions and stock repurchases grew explosively by 900 percent and 825 percent, respectively. Both approximately tripled in one year alone, between 1983 and 1984.

[3]See Laurie Simon Bagwell and John B. Shoven, "Cash Distributions to Shareholders," *Journal of Economic Perspectives,* Summer 1989, pp. 129–40.

The message from Figure 16–1 is important. *Dividends remain the single most important method of distributing cash to shareholders, but their relative importance is declining.* If we aggregate all three methods of cash distributions, the role of dividends has declined from about 80 percent of the total in 1977 to about 40 percent by 1986. Nevertheless, because of its continuing importance and traditional place in financial management, most of this chapter is devoted to the study of dividend policy as it pertains to the payment of cash dividends. In the final analysis, stockholders remain vitally interested in the payment of dividends. Furthermore, we know from Chapter 6 that dividends are the basis for the valuation of stocks using the dividend discount model.

Because of their growing importance, we will analyze stock repurchases as a means of distributing cash to stockholders. We will not consider cash-financed acquisitions in this chapter because typically the firm's stockholders are not the direct beneficiary of the cash payments paid in the merger and we are interested here in how management's decisions affect its own stockholders. Acquisitions are discussed in Chapter 21.

Finally, we analyze stock dividends and stock splits, which are related to the firm's cash dividend policy. A stock dividend involves the payment of shares rather than cash and is very similar to a stock split in that both increase the number of shares outstanding while reducing the value per share. For example, a 5 percent stock dividend means that a shareholder receives one new share of stock for every 20 shares owned, while a 2-for-1 stock split means that the number of shares outstanding is doubled.

THE CONTROVERSY OVER DIVIDEND POLICY

There has been considerable recent debate about the importance of dividend policy. Some have argued that dividend policy has a strong influence on stock price, while others have held that dividend policy has no influence on stock price. *The controversy concerns how dividend policy affects value,* which in turn dictates the level of dividends the firm should pay. That is, Is it advantageous to have a particular dividend policy? In order to consider this issue, we first must define dividend policy.

What Is Meant by Dividend Policy?

The cash flow in any year for a firm is approximately equal to its earnings plus depreciation. If depreciation charges are used as intended—to replace worn-out fixed assets—the firm's primary financial management decision regarding internal financing concerns how much of its earnings to keep and how much to pay out as dividends to common stockholders. This is the *dividend decision.* In turn, **dividend policy** refers to the policies and practices that a firm employs to implement the dividend decision. Dividend policy actually refers to two separate aspects of the cash payments made:

dividend policy
policies and practices
used to implement a
firm's dividend decisions

1. The *level* of dividends.
2. The *stability* of dividends paid.

Dividend levels are indicated by the dollar-per-share amount being paid. For example, if DFL, Inc., pays a dividend this year of $3 per share, that is a clear statement of DFL's current dividend level in absolute terms. In relative terms, dividend levels are indicated by the **dividend payout ratio**, or the ratio of dividends to earnings, which is calculated as:

$$\text{Dividend payout ratio} = \frac{\text{Dividends per share}}{\text{Earnings per share}} \qquad (16\text{--}1)$$

dividend payout ratio
the ratio of dividends to earnings

Because different firms have different earnings levels, it is very difficult to compare dividend policies among companies by comparing dollar-per-share dividend levels. The dividend payout ratio facilitates comparison by describing how much of each dollar's worth of earnings is returned to stockholders as dividends. As a percentage, the payout ratio ranges from zero to 100 percent.

■ *Example*

Suppose that Abbott Company is paying an annual dividend of 20 cents per share and that DFL Inc. is paying $3.00 per share. It is not possible to compare dividend policies of these two firms solely on the basis of this information about dividends per share. If Abbott earns 40 cents per share and DFL $6.00 per share, both companies have 50 percent payout ratios and have the same relative level of dividend payments. Both companies are paying out half their earnings to common stockholders. ■

Dividend stability refers to the steadiness, or lack of variability, of the stream of dividends. There is no universally accepted measure of dividend stability, but what is usually meant is a nondecreasing pattern of dividends per share. In Figure 16–2, the A and B patterns are examples of stable dividend streams; the C pattern is not. We will see below that most firms strive for stable dividend patterns that increase over time, like Pattern A.

It is very important to note that we are talking about dividend policy, not the dividend payments themselves. *The dollar amount of cash dividends paid is relevant.*

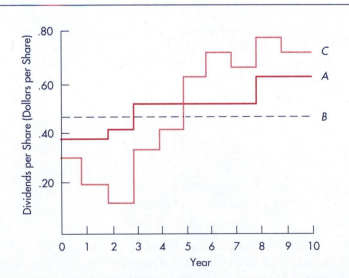

■ *Figure 16–2*
Dividend Patterns

Clearly, investors always prefer higher dividends to lower dividends, other things being equal (i.e., the dividend level is held constant at all other points in time). If investors suddenly expect the dividend payments to decrease, the price of the stock will probably adjust to reflect this change in expectations.

■ *Example*

In late 1990, in talking with the investment community, Manufacturer's Hanover Corporation, a major New York bank, suggested the possibility of a cut in the dividend being paid. Many investors saw the possibility of a dividend cut at the next scheduled quarterly payment. The shares of Manufacturer's Hanover fell sharply immediately. Given the dividend at that time of $3.28 per year, the dividend yield (dividend divided by stock price) was in the range of 15 percent at the time of announcement. ■

Thus, dividend policy determines when dividends will be paid; if more is paid now, less will be paid later. In effect, dividend policy establishes the trade-off between dividends at different dates. The question to be answered is, Is a company's dividend policy relevant or irrelevant?

Is Dividend Policy Irrelevant?

A very strong theoretical argument can be made that dividend policy is irrelevant: a change in dividend policy does not affect the value of the stock. The *dividend irrelevance argument* asserts that, given the firm's investment policy (that is, given the firm's decision to make certain investments), investors are indifferent to the firm's dividend policy:

- If the firm's payout ratio is too low for some investors, they can sell a portion of their stock to increase current income.
- If the firm's payout ratio is too high for some investors (they would prefer that the firm invest more on their behalf), they can always reinvest the dividend proceeds themselves by purchasing more stock.

In either case investors can arrange their own dividend stream with the result that the choice of a dividend policy does not affect the stock price.

It may at first seem paradoxical to argue that dividend policy has no effect on stock price. This is because the basic dividend valuation model we developed clearly shows that a stock's current price is a function of future dividend payments. Recall that the basic dividend valuation model developed is:

$$P_0 = \sum_{t=1}^{\infty} \frac{D_t}{(1 + k)^t} \qquad (16\text{–}2)$$

where:

$$P_0 = \text{current price}$$
$$D_t = \text{dividend per share in period } t$$
$$k = \text{required rate of return}$$

Obviously, more dividends are preferred to fewer according to Equation 16–2. But what would cause the dividend stream to increase? The answer is successful investments. Dividend irrelevance proponents argue that *given the firm's investment policy,* dividend policy only rearranges the stream of dividends without affecting P_0. We can illustrate this point with an example.

■ *Example*

Isotex Corporation is an all-equity company (no long-term debt) with 100,000 shares of common outstanding. The company expects to earn about $100,000 per year on its present set of assets and normally pays out all earnings as dividends. Therefore, its expected dividend from present operations is about $1 per share each year. The firm's stock is selling at $10 per share, and k is 10 percent.

Assume Isotex needs $100,000 next year for new investments that will return $10,000 per year for an indefinitely long period of time. The firm has decided to finance the investment with equity because it does not wish to issue any debt.

Two completely different financing plans are available:[4]

Plan 1. Maintain the $1-per-share dividend and issue $100,000 worth of new stock to finance the investments.

Plan 2. Omit next year's dividends and finance the investments with next year's earnings of $100,000, which will become retained earnings.

Notice that, under either plan, the investment takes place at the end of Year 1, and annual earnings beginning in Year 2 will be $110,000 per year. ■

The analysis in Table 16–1 shows that the theoretical current price of Isotex's stock is $10 per share under either of these two extreme plans. All the firm has accomplished in choosing one dividend plan over the other is to rearrange the dividend stream. In particular, there is no enhancement of current stock price by choosing a high dividend payment ratio (as was done in Plan 1) in Year 1.

The dividend irrelevance argument is based on a classic article by Miller and Modigliani (M&M), the same two financial economists we encountered in Chapter 15 in connection with the question of capital structure relevancy.[5] The basis of the dividend irrelevance theory is that capital markets are perfect and investors are rational. Perfect capital markets have no *friction costs*. Examples of friction costs are transaction costs that investors pay to buy and sell securities, flotation costs that firms pay to issue new securities, and tax differentials arising from the treatment of dividend income versus capital gains income. The assumption that investors are rational means that investors are indifferent to whether they receive dividend income or income obtained from sale of their stock.

These assumptions lead to the conclusion that dividend policy is irrelevant. If investors can buy and sell stock without friction costs and if there are no tax differentials between dividend income and income obtained from the sale of stock, investors should be indifferent between dividend income and capital gains income because they can create their own dividend streams at no cost. And there should be no such thing as a best dividend policy that firms should follow.

In today's finance world this M&M proposition is generally accepted as correct *given the assumptions under which it was derived*. However, other theorists have

---

[4]Other financing plans are possible, such as paying $50,000 in dividends in the coming year and issuing $50,000 of new stock. However, the two extremes represented by Plans 1 and 2 illustrate the point.

[5]See Merton H. Miller and Franco Modigliani. "Dividend Policy, Growth and the Valuation of Shares." *Journal of Business,* October 1961, pp. 411–33.

■ *Table 16–1*
An Illustration of
Dividend Irrelevancy

*Plan 1. Sell new common stock—100 percent payout;
sale price of new stock issued = $10 per share[a]*

$$\text{Number of new shares issued} = \frac{\$100,000}{\$10 \text{ per share}} = 10,000 \text{ shares}$$

$$D_1 = \$1 \text{ per share}$$

$$\text{Subsequent dividends per share } (D_2 \ldots D_\infty) = \$110,000/110,000 \text{ shares}$$

$$= \$1 \text{ per share}[b]$$

Therefore, from Equation 16–2:

$$P_0 = \sum_{t=1}^{\infty} \frac{\$1}{(1.10)^t} = (\$1)(\text{PVIFA}_{.10,\infty}) = (\$1)(10)$$

$$P_0 = \$10 \text{ per share}$$

Plan 2. Retain all earnings—0 percent payout

$$D_1 = 0$$

$$\text{Subsequent dividends per share } (D_2 \ldots D_\infty) = \$110,000/100,000 \text{ shares}$$

$$= \$1.10 \text{ per share}$$

Therefore:

$$P_0 = 0 + \sum_{t=1}^{\infty} \frac{\$1.10}{(1.10)^t} = (\$1.10)(\text{PVIFA}_{.10,\infty})(\text{PVIF}_{.10,1})$$

$$P_0 = (\$1.10)(10)(0.909) = \$10 \text{ per share}$$

[a]This calculation ignores any flotation costs associated with the issue.
[b]This calculation assumes Isotex will maintain its policy of paying out all earnings in subsequent years. The 110,000 shares in Years 2 and onward are the sum of the original 100,000 shares plus the additional 10,000 shares issued in Year 1.

argued that the real-world conditions that were assumed away by M&M negate the dividend irrelevance argument and lead to the conclusion that dividend policy is relevant.

The Case for Dividend Policy Relevancy

Given the real-world factors that can potentially affect stockholders and firms, and therefore the dividend decision, it is not surprising that many observers believe that dividend policy is relevant. We will now consider why.

In doing so, we first will analyze two real-world factors, uncertainty and transaction costs, that have led some to argue that high dividend payouts are preferable. We then consider two real-world factors, differential taxation and flotation costs, that have led others to suggest that low dividend payouts are preferable.

The Case for High Dividend Payouts

**dividend
preference theory**
a theory asserting that
investors prefer high
dividend payout ratios

One major component of the dividends-are-relevant school is the Gordon–Lintner dividend preference theory. The **dividend preference theory** asserts that investors prefer high dividend payout ratios, and other things being equal, firms with relatively high payout ratios will have relatively high stock prices. Conversely, firms that have relatively low payout ratios will have relatively low stock prices. This theory questions two key assumptions of the dividend irrelevance position:

(1) that future dividends are no more risky than current dividends, and (2) that transactions costs paid by investors who arrange their own dividend stream are negligible.

The basic tenet of the dividend preference theory is that the dominant feature of the investment environment is uncertainty. Moreover, uncertainty usually increases with time. If the firm makes an investment, it is usually more certain what cash flows will result in the early years of the investment than in later years. Since the firm ultimately looks to its cash flows to pay dividends, this increasing uncertainty over time implies that the more distant in the future an expected dividend is, the more uncertain it is. Therefore, since investors are risk averse, they prefer receipt of certain, current dividends to the expected receipt of increased but riskier future dividends. Investors prefer a bird in the hand to two in the bush.

- ▪ *Example*

Using the Isotex example, we can compare the expected dividend stream of Plans 1 and 2 from a slightly different perspective. It is very informative to net the expected dividend streams from the competing plans:

Expected Dividend Payments (Dollars per Share)				
	D_1	D_2	D_3	. . . D_∞
Plan 2	0	1.10	1.10	1.10
Plan 1	1.00	1.00	1.00	1.00
Plan 2 − Plan 1	−1.00	0.10	0.10	0.10

The difference between the two plans is clearly illustrated here. A decision to finance the new investments with retained earnings means giving up a dollar-per-share dividend in Year 1 but also results in increasing expected future dividends by 10 cents per share. The dividend preference theory contends, however, that these future increases in dividends will be riskier because they are deferred to the future; that is, it asserts that k will be larger under Plan 2 than under Plan 1 to reflect the increased riskiness of the Plan 2 dividend stream. Suppose, for example, that k remains at 10 percent if Isotex opts for dividend Plan 1, but increases to 12 percent if Plan 2 is chosen. These assumptions imply the following current stock prices:

Plan 1:

$$P_0 = \sum_{t=1}^{\infty} \frac{\$1}{(1.10)^t} = \$10$$

Plan 2:

$$P_0 = 0 + \sum_{t=1}^{\infty} \frac{\$1.10}{(1.12)^t} = (\$1.10)(\text{PVIFA}_{.12,\infty})(\text{PVIF}_{.12,1}) = \$8.19$$

The higher k under Plan 2 causes stock price to decline. The principal point argued here by the dividend preference theory is that low payout ratios cause risk to increase, and this causes k to increase; therefore, k and payout are inversely related. Thus, firms that have high payouts will have low k values, which will enhance stock price. Firms with low payout ratios will have high k values, which will depress stock price. The dividend irrelevance theory denies the inverse relationship between k and payout, asserting instead that there is no relationship between k and payout. ∎

It is important to note that we are not talking about the time value of investors' money preferences here. We already know that any rational investor would prefer a guaranteed dollar of dividends today rather than a guaranteed dollar of dividends at some time in the future. By retaining a dollar rather than paying it out as current dividends, the firm expects to pay larger future dividends. This is because the dollar should earn a rate of return in the interim. The question here, then, is whether investors prefer the *certain* current dollar of dividends to the *expectation* of increased future dividends.

Dividend preference theory also criticizes the irrelevance theory for ignoring transactions costs. According to the dividend irrelevance theory, an investor who didn't consider this dividend to be high enough could always sell a portion of the stock and thus create his or her own dividend. Similarly, an investor who felt the dividends were too high could always reinvest a portion of them. Dividend preference theorists argue that this would be true if no transaction costs were involved. However, since investors have to pay brokerage fees, they lose a portion of their capital by buying and selling securities to arrange their own dividend stream.

In summary, dividend preference theory argues that investors prefer current dividends to future dividends. This conclusion has a strong dividend policy implication: firms should maintain high payout ratios. According to dividend preference theory, firms that pay out relatively large proportions of their earnings will be following a dividend policy that will maximize their stock price.

The Case for Low Dividend Payouts

Two other real-world factors support the case for dividend policy relevancy, but in the opposite direction from the previous discussion. Specifically, acknowledgment of different tax rates on dividend income and capital gains and the presence of flotation costs could create a preference for lower dividend payout policies. *Traditionally,* dividends and capital gains have been taxed differently for most investors, with tax rates on dividends higher than those on capital gains. Consequently, some have argued that investors on balance would prefer to receive low dividend payments and have the firm retain earnings. In theory, this should cause stock price to rise, and if and when the investor sells the stock, the gain would be taxed at the more favorable capital gains tax rate.

The Tax Reform Act of 1986 eliminated the differential treatment between dividends and capital gains, although the 1990 legislation restored a maximum capital gains rate of 28 percent, leaving a slight differential in taxation between ordinary income and capital gains income. Furthermore, even if the differential is entirely eliminated, the timing issue remains—investors who have no need or desire to sell the stock in the immediate future can defer taxes on capital gains, but dividends are taxable in the year received. This can create differences in the *effective* tax rate on the two components.[6]

---

[6]The recent growth in tax-deferred investment opportunities, such as IRAs, Keogh plans, and 401-B and 403-K plans, has helped to neutralize differences in tax rates. It is also possible to neutralize tax rate differences through personal portfolio operations. For example, investors can borrow and offset their interest payments against their dividend income. Furthermore, institutional investors, such as pension funds, are exempt from taxes on dividend payouts.

The dividend irrelevance theory also assumes zero flotation costs (the costs incurred by the firm when it issues new securities). As we know from Chapter 14, because of flotation costs, the cost of retained earnings is less than the cost of common stock. Therefore, the use of new common stock raises the firm's cost of capital, which, other things being equal, reduces the value of the firm. Small issues of new stock are particularly expensive.

Resolving the Dividend Policy Controversy

Which position is correct? Because the dividend policies that follow from them vary greatly, the resolution of the conflict is important.

The debate on dividend policy ultimately revolves around the realism of the assumptions of the dividend irrelevance theory. Proponents of this theory agree that their assumptions are not perfectly realistic, but they maintain that the realism of the assumptions of a theory is not an adequate test of the validity of the theory. Any theory is an abstraction from reality, so it will never be perfectly descriptive of reality; moreover, the appropriate test of the theory is not its realism, but whether its predictions are consistent with observed behavior in the real world. Furthermore, for every criticism made by the dividends-are-relevant proponents, the irrelevance theory has a rebuttal.

For example, consider the resolution of the uncertainty issue. A relevant question here is, What will investors do with their increased dividends? If investors do not consume all the increase, the remainder will be reinvested. But reinvested monies are exposed to the same uncertain future as the firm's reinvested earnings are. The fact that the future is uncertain doesn't really change the investor's attitudes regarding required rates of return.

A second way to resolve the controversy would be with empirical testing. Unfortunately, although many tests have been conducted, the results are conflicting. We are unable to state with conviction either that investors prefer dividends to retained earnings and capital gains, or that they prefer the opposite.

As an example of the empirical side, one well-known study indicated that stocks with high dividend yields exhibited higher total returns than stocks with low dividend yields.[7] Thus, as dividend yield increased, required return increased, implying that firms would have lower costs of capital with higher retained earnings. However, other studies do not support these findings or find the opposite results.

Who is right and who is wrong in the dividend policy debate? There is no real agreement, and the controversy has continued for several years. Each side has its strong supporters. Thus, we cannot conclude this section with a definitive answer to the question, What dividend policy should a firm follow? We can conclude, however, by considering an additional position that combines the irrelevancy of dividends with real-world market imperfections.

Clientele Effect

The **clientele theory** acknowledges that investors have reasons for preferring particular payout ratios. Some will prefer high payout ratios. This group would

clientele theory
asserts that investors have reasons for preferring particular payout ratios

---

[7]See Robert H. Litzenberger and Krishna Ramaswamy, "The Effect of Personal Taxes and Dividends on Capital Asset Prices," *Journal of Financial Economics*, June 1979, pp. 162–96.

include institutional investors as well as individual investors who receive dividend income tax free in their retirement accounts. It would also include investors (like retired people) who need the current income for living expenses and who do not wish to sell even a small portion of their stock, either because of the transactions costs involved or because they disapprove of "living off capital." Others will prefer low dividend payouts, including those who hold stocks for the long run and want the firm to reinvest earnings in order to grow more quickly. This group would also include investors who do not wish the firm to issue more stock because it is cheaper for the firm to retain earnings rather than issue stock.

The reasons for investors' different preferences are unimportant. What matters, according to the clientele theory, is that some individuals will be attracted to high-payout firms and some individuals to low-payout firms—there are different clienteles. Therefore, neither payout ratio will command a stock price premium. The value of the firm is the same either way; only the clientele of shareholders has changed.

If a firm could change its dividend policy and increase its market value, this would indicate that an unsatisfied clientele existed. But such opportunities should not exist in relatively efficient markets, even with imperfections. Only if there were some fundamental change in the underlying preferences of investors in the aggregate would dividend policy influence stock price.

M&M suggested that a clientele effect might exist, and this theory is consistent with the dividend irrelevance theory. However, it is also dependent on the existence of real-world factors. The firm chooses whatever dividend policy it wishes, and it accumulates an ownership clientele that approves of that policy. Once the firm has selected a target dividend policy, it may be harmful (to stock price) to deviate from it radically. If the firm has a relatively low payout, for example, switching to a high payout may cause the old clientele to sell their stock and seek out relatively low-dividend payers. Although a new clientele would be attracted, the transaction costs involved in this change of ownership would be expected to have an adverse effect on stock price.

CHOOSING A DIVIDEND POLICY

We have now examined the major theories concerning dividend policy. Each suggests a different approach, ranging from favoring high payouts to saying that the payout policy will not matter. Finally, the clientele theory argues that groups of investors will be attracted to firms on the basis of their payout policies.

The question remains—What dividend policy is appropriate for a firm? Because this topic remains controversial, we cannot find an answer that is widely accepted. But we can (1) analyze the factors that influence dividend policy, (2) consider the alternatives a firm has, and (3) examine the actual practices of dividend-paying firms. This information, combined with the decision maker's beliefs about the importance of the real-world factors considered earlier, will aid in actually establishing a dividend policy.

Factors Influencing Dividend Policy

A firm's dividend policy is a function of many factors. We have already discussed some, including the possible existence of an optimal payout ratio. Other factors that influence dividend policy can be broadly categorized as pertaining to legal constraints, control issues, investment and financing considerations, and other issues.

Legal Constraints

Management does not have complete discretion regarding how large a dividend it may pay. For example, statutes have been enacted in most states that limit the amount of cash dividends the firm may pay. In most states, cash dividends paid may not exceed current net income plus cumulative retained earnings. That is, the firm may not impair the common stock capital account by paying a regular dividend that would reduce the dollar amount of the common stock capital account. The intention of this kind of law is to protect the claims of preferred stockholders and creditors. Without the protection of the capital-impairment rule, preferred stockholders and creditors could have their preference positions eroded by common dividends that are, in effect, liquidation payments.[8]

Bond indentures often contain provisions (covenants) that restrict the amount of dividends the firm may pay. This protects the bondholders.

Since dividends *traditionally* were taxed at investors' ordinary income tax rates, which *was* higher than their capital gains rate, there was some incentive for firms not to pay cash dividends. To prevent firms from restricting dividends solely to allow stockholder avoidance of ordinary income tax rates, the Internal Revenue Service (IRS) prohibits unwarranted retention of earnings. The IRS is empowered to force the firm to pay dividends when unwarranted earnings retention can be proved.

Control Issues

Dividend policy may be influenced by stockholder or managerial control motives. If a controlling (majority ownership) interest does not wish new shares to be sold, the firm's only source of new equity will be retentions. This may impel the firm to maintain a low payout ratio to ensure an adequate supply of new equity money. Dividend policy may also be dictated by the income tax status of its controlling owners. If they have high tax rates, they may prefer that earnings be plowed back into the firm rather than paid (and taxed) as dividends.

Firms with low payouts have occasionally been the target of takeover bids by companies that promise a higher dividend to stockholders if the takeover is successful. This kind of situation may cause the incumbent management to raise the payout immediately to deprive the acquiring company of a psychological weapon.

Investment and Financing Considerations

Other factors that can influence dividend policy relate to the firm's investment needs and financing opportunities.

Firms that have abundant investment opportunities often prefer to retain a large fraction of their earnings, which causes the payout to be relatively low. Analysts frequently describe such firms as growth companies. Likewise, firms with fewer

---

[8]A firm is insolvent in the bankruptcy sense when its liabilities exceed its assets. A firm is technically insolvent when it is unable to pay its bills. If the firm is insolvent in either sense, it is prohibited from paying dividends, and it may not pay a dividend that would cause insolvency.

investment opportunities often have relatively high payout ratios. A related factor is the extent to which the firm has access to the capital markets. If a firm is not big enough to be able to issue bonds to investors, it can still lease assets and borrow through term loans at banks. Thus, most firms have access to the debt segment of the capital market. However, only the largest few thousand U.S. companies have access to the public equity segment of the capital market. Companies without such access can obtain new equity capital financing only from retained earnings and therefore tend to have lower dividend payout ratios.

Other Issues

Stability of the earnings stream also affects dividend policy. In general, the more stable the company's income stream, the higher its payout ratio. This effect is linked to the fact that firms are reluctant to reduce dividends and tend to set dividend levels they can be reasonably sure of meeting. Firms with relatively stable earnings are more confident that a high dividend payment level can be safely maintained and are more likely to choose a relatively high payout ratio. Public utility companies are good examples of firms with stable earnings patterns and relatively high payout ratios.

A different point pertains to the decision to pay a minimum dividend. Many financial institutions are prohibited by their state charter from buying stock in companies that pay no dividends. Since these institutions play a major role in today's capital markets, some firms that would otherwise choose to pay no dividends pay a minimum dividend to qualify for the list of securities that financial institutions may purchase.

Alternative Dividend Policies

A dividend policy implies some sort of long-range plan for distributing dividends to common stockholders. An imaginative financial manager could establish many such plans, but most fall into one of three categories.

Residual Dividend Policy

residual theory of dividends
a theory asserting that any dividends paid be viewed as a residual, after investment needs are met

The firm could treat dividends as a residual decision, subservient to the investment decision. The **residual theory of dividends** suggests that any dividends paid be viewed as a residual, meaning that the firm would pay out dividends whenever it had more earnings than were needed for financing new investments, and would pay no dividends when it needed all of its earnings for investment purposes.

To implement the *residual dividend policy,* a firm would do as follows:

1. Determine the optimal capital budget.
2. Determine the capital required by this budget.
3. Use retained earnings for the equity component of the financing to the extent possible.
4. Pay cash dividends only if earnings remain after all financing requirements.

Under this approach, growth companies with large financing needs would be expected to pay small or no dividends, and mature companies with few attractive investment opportunities would be expected to pay large dividends. If a firm follows this policy, it will have no particular target payout ratio, and its dollar-dividend and dividend payout ratios will fluctuate as its earnings and investment plans fluctuate.

Stable Dollar-Dividend Policy

Traditionally, many firms seem to follow the dividend policy of maintaining a relatively stable per-share dividend payment. This policy results in a dividend stream that is fairly constant, with dividend increases when earnings have increased substantially and dividend decreases only when the firm can no longer support the present level of dividends. In effect, dividends follow earnings, but with a lag. Significantly, the annual dividend will not be cut unless absolutely necessary.

Under this policy the *dividend payout* will fluctuate as earnings fluctuate. Selection of a stable dividend-per-share policy may be coupled with a long-range target payout ratio. As earnings per share grow over time, the firm will raise dividends per share in accordance with this target ratio. The range of possible target payout ratios is from 1.0, where all earnings are paid out, to 0, where all earnings are retained. Relatively high target payout ratios may require the firm to seek outside capital frequently, whereas relatively low target payout ratios will provide a greater amount of internal financing.

The firm may also pay a dividend when a loss is incurred. The firm often will continue to pay the dividend until it is obvious that it can no longer be sustained.

■ Example

To illustrate both the gradual increase in dividends as earnings are growing and the reluctance to cut a dividend level once it is established, consider the case of Tenneco, Inc., a holding company whose subsidiaries engage in several businesses. Earnings per share and dividends per share for the years 1978–1987 were as follows:

	1978	1979	1980	1981	1982	1983	1984	1985	1986	1987
EPS	$4.53	5.30	5.95	6.01	5.18	4.75	4.01	2.52	.50	−.20
DPS	$2.05	2.25	2.45	2.60	2.63	2.74	2.83	2.95	3.04	3.04

Notice that in the years 1978 to 1981 EPS continued to grow, and DPS did likewise. In 1982, EPS declined from the previous year, and DPS remained roughly constant. EPS continued to decline from 1983 through 1987, and DPS continued to grow through 1986, remaining constant for 1987. Although the company made only 50 cents per share in 1986 and lost money in 1987, the DPS remained constant at $3.04.

Figure 16–3 illustrates the Tenneco EPS and DPS patterns. The stable nature of the dividend stream as opposed to the sharp changes in the earnings stream is immediately apparent. ■

Constant-Payout-Ratio Policy

An alternative policy is to pay out a fixed percentage of each year's earnings. That is, the firm attempts to keep a constant payout ratio. Therefore, dividends per

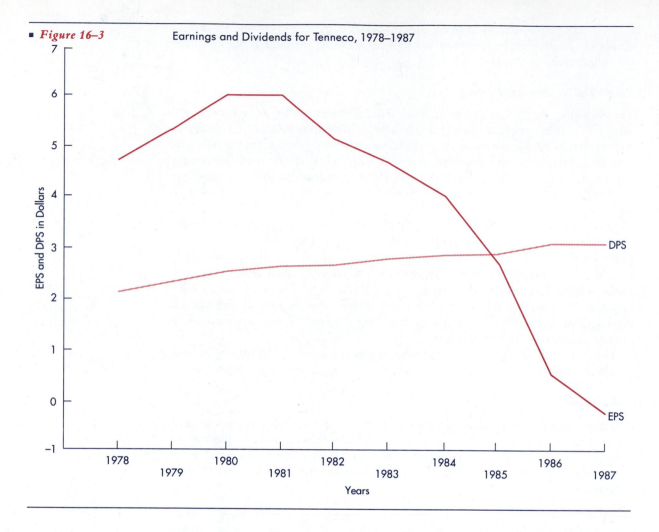

▪ Figure 16–3   Earnings and Dividends for Tenneco, 1978–1987

share will fluctuate with earnings per share. Very few U.S. companies appear to have adopted this kind of dividend policy.

Some companies have relatively low payout ratios and pay an annual extra dividend at the end of the year. The size of this extra dividend usually depends on how well the firm fared during the year. However, regular extra dividends are probably considered by investors to be part of the firm's normal annual total.

OBSERVED DIVIDEND PRACTICES

Level of Dividends

Most major U.S. corporations regularly pay cash dividends. Even in the depression year of 1930, almost 70 percent of the firms on the New York Stock Exchange (NYSE) paid cash dividends. In 1950, there were 1,039 stocks listed on the NYSE, and 930 of them, or 90 percent, paid a cash dividend. In 1960, 1,126 companies were listed, and 981, or 87 percent, paid cash dividends. Corresponding figures for 1970 were 1,330 firms and 1,120 (84 percent) paying dividends, and for 1980,

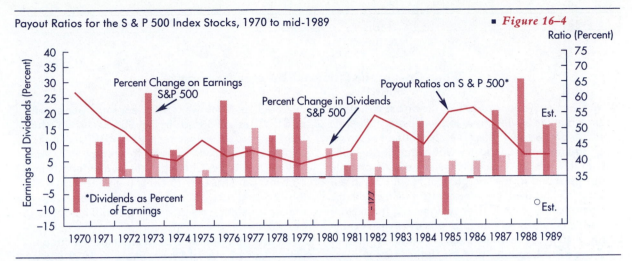

Payout Ratios for the S & P 500 Index Stocks, 1970 to mid-1989   ■ *Figure 16–4*

Source: *The Outlook*, August 30, 1989, p. 612. Reprinted by permission of Standard & Poor's Corporation.

1,540 firms and 1,361 (88 percent) paying dividends.[9] Clearly, most of the largest and best known U.S. corporations pay cash dividends.

What percentage of earnings are paid out as dividends? The payout ratio varies from year to year, but it almost always is above 40 percent and it ranges as high as 55 percent in some years. Figure 16–4 shows the payout ratio on the Standard & Poor's 500 Composite Index for the years 1970 to mid-1989. Note that the payout ratio (right scale) ranged from a high of slightly over 60 percent in 1970 to a low of slightly less than 40 percent in 1979.

Stability of Dividends

As illustrated earlier with the Tenneco data, a common dividend practice of large firms is the observance of a fairly stable dividend-per-share policy. Most firms seem to favor a policy of establishing a nondecreasing stream of dividends per share over time. The firm will raise its dividend per share as earnings per share increase over time, but the firm is careful not to raise dividends above a level that can be sustained safely in the future. This cautious creep up of dividends per share results in a flat dividend pattern during periods when earnings per share trends are flat or declining, and one that rises stepwise during periods when earnings per share are rising.

Researchers surveyed managers of the 100 largest NYSE companies to determine which factors are considered important in determining the level of dividends.[10] They used three categories—very important, moderately important, and not important—to express their opinions on the degree of importance. Ninety percent rated "continuity of dividends" as very important, and "level of current and prospective profitability" was rated very important by 77 percent and moderately important by 23 percent.

---

[9]Figures calculated from *Fact Book 1987*, New York Stock Exchange, Inc., New York, 1987, p. 76.

[10]See Marshall E. Blume, Irwin Friend, and Randolph Westerfield, "Impediments to Capital Formation: Summary Report of a Survey of Nonfinancial Corporations," Working Paper, Wharton School, University of Pennsylvania, 1980, p. 6.

- - -

FINANCIAL MANAGEMENT INSIGHTS

When Cuts in the Dividend Become Necessary

Virtually eveyone is aware of the disaster that occurred in the savings and loan industry in the late 1980s and early 1990s. The cost to the taxpayers of bailing out the industry was a staggering sum, with the final bill not yet determined. As a result of this scandal, the increase in regulatory pressures spilled over to the banking industry, with the Comptroller of the Currency tightening loan standards. Numerous other changes were also occurring, such as higher equity standards, higher charges to banks to pay for the insurance fund, and increased accounting standards.

Even ignoring these changes for banks, the recessionary environment of 1990–91 had a negative impact on bank earnings. A slowdown in business activity tends to lower the creditworthiness of borrowers, which increases the problems for banks. Adding to the problems for banks is a reduction in fee income that can be earned. In addition, during this period the severe slump in the real estate market compounded the problems for banks, and loans to lesser developed countries remained a problem for the large banks who engaged in such loans. Some of the large banks, in turn, were forced to make painful adjustments. Three money center banks stand out in particular in this analysis.

Chemical Bank went from earnings per share of $12.02 in 1988 to a loss of $8.29 in 1989. The bank increased its loss reserve by $120 million in one quarter of 1990. In order to strengthen its equity capital base, Chemical cut its dividend from 68 cents per share to 25 cents per share. Even at this reduced rate, the common and preferred dividends together were absorbing about half of expected earnings in 1991.

Chase Manhattan was in a similar situation, with a loss of almost $8 per share in 1989 and a loss of some magnitude assured for 1990. After undergoing staff reductions and asset reallocations, Chase also cut its dividend, reducing it from 62 cents per share to 30 cents per share.

Citicorp is yet a third large New York money center bank. During 1989–90, it faced problem loans and foreclosed real estate. Unlike Chemical Bank and Chase Manhattan, Citicorp's earnings were positive in 1989 and 1990, $1.16 and an estimated $2.20, respectively. Nevertheless, given the problem loans and depressed real estate market faced by Citicorp, the dividend of $1.59 in 1989 represented a very large percentage of the earnings. By early 1991, the dividend had been cut to 25 cents per share.

How Dividends Are Paid

Cash dividends are paid quarterly, with amounts based on the firm's dividend policy. The first step in this procedure is for the board of directors, on the *declaration date,* to declare a specified dollar dividend amount to be paid on a specified *payment date.* It also announces a *record date* approximately two to eight weeks in the future. Dividends are to be payable to shareholders of record on the record date. A shareholder of record for a record date is an owner of shares who is so recorded on the company's books as of the close of business for that date. Because of the lag from day of sale of a stock to the time the firm is able to record the transaction on its books, the brokerage industry has established a standard *ex-dividend date* for stocks. After this date, the stock trades without the dividend. A dividend remains with a stock until four business days before the record date.

■ *Example*

Suppose that on March 1 A. C. ("Big Al") Boyette is thinking about buying 100 shares of Syntex stock and wants to be sure he receives the dividend about to be

---

Time Diagram Illustrating Important Dates in the Payment of Dividends   ■ *Figure 16–5*

Announcement Date	Ex-dividend Date	Record Date	Payment Date
February 10	March 11	March 15	April 1

---

paid. The board of directors of Syntex met on February 10 and declared a 25 cent-a-share regular quarterly dividend payable to stockholders of record on Friday, March 15. Payment is to be made on April 1.

The company closes its stock transfer books on the holder-of-record date, March 15, and prepares a list of stockholders as of the close of business on that date. The ex-dividend date is four days before March 15, or Monday March 11. If Big Al plans to receive this dividend payment, he must purchase the stock by the close of brokerage business the preceding business day, Friday, March 8. The dividend checks will be mailed on the payment date, April 1. This process is illustrated by the time diagram in Figure 16–5. ■

A number of firms have recently instituted *dividend reinvestment plans* whereby shareholders can have cash dividends automatically reinvested in additional shares of stock. Such plans can save the participants some brokerage fees because a trustee pools the money available, purchases shares on the open market, and allocates them accordingly. In some plans the cash dividends are used to purchase newly issued shares of stock, often at a discount from the market price and free of brokerage costs.

STOCK REPURCHASES

Stock repurchases refer to the firm buying its own stock. Repurchased stock is called **treasury stock.** From time to time, repurchase activity among U.S. corporations has been intense. For example, in the late 1960s and early 1970s, treasury stock was acquired at a rapid rate. Following the market crash of October 1987, some 300 companies announced new or expanded stock repurchase programs.

treasury stock
a firm's own repurchased stock

Methods of Stock Repurchasing

There are two principal methods of stock repurchase:

1. In a *tender offer,* the company advertises that it stands ready to buy a stated number of shares at a stipulated price that is set above the current market price (to entice stockholders to tender their shares). Sometimes the tender will be oversubscribed (more shares are tendered than the firm agreed to take). The firm may then either prorate its purchases or agree to take all the shares.

   ■ *Example*

   Teledyne once made a tender offer for 1 million shares, and shareholders tendered 8.9 million shares, more than a quarter of the company's total shares. Teledyne bought all 8.9 million shares. ■

2. A second method of acquiring treasury stock is by buying it in the stock market, or an *open market purchase,* exactly as any investor would purchase stock. A large number of firms have repurchased stock through a program of regular stock market purchases in recent years.

   ■ *Example*

   Phelps Dodge, cited earlier in connection with a special dividend of $10 per share, announced at the same time that it planned to buy back from time to time up to 2 million of its shares. This plan replaced an earlier one whereby the company had repurchased some 2.3 million shares. ■

Reasons for Repurchasing Stock

Traditionally, many buy-back programs were initiated to meet the needs of executive stock options programs (or employee profit sharing plans) or to obtain treasury shares for future acquisitions. Most companies have stock option plans for their executives and employee stock purchase plans that are a part of the company's retirement program. Implementation of these programs motivates many companies to regularly purchase their stock. It might be better, however, for the firm to use authorized but unissued shares for this purpose, assuming all such shares have not been issued.

Many companies use treasury stock to finance their merger and acquisition activities (see Chapter 21). This may require that the firm actively buy back its own stock to assure that it has sufficient equity to pursue all the profitable expansion plans it intends. However, some fairly rigid accounting standards must be met with respect to using buy-back shares in mergers.

Much of the recent buy-back activity is probably attributable to corporate restructuring activities. Many firms have generated excess cash that is not needed at the time for reinvestment in the business. Rather than pay out the cash to stockholders, who then become immediately liable for taxes on the dividends, the firms repurchase shares of stock. Such repurchases typically involve relatively small amounts of stock purchased over a period of time on the open market.[11] Of course, some firms with excess cash choose not to buy back shares and thus return the money to stockholders in this manner, as the following example illustrates.

■ *Example*

Pinnacle West, parent of Arizona Public Service, has been diversifying from the regulated utility business. Not needing to build new generating capacity for a while, it generated excess funds. In a relatively short time, Pinnacle purchased Arizona's biggest thrift, a vacation resort and undeveloped real estate, large stocks of processed uranium plus uranium mines, and it committed considerable sums to venture capital. Management was asked why it did not return excess cash to shareholders in stock buy-backs, as some other utilities were doing. The response

---

[11]If the firm has reached a point where its investment needs are outstripped by its current cash-generating capacity, the firm may repurchase its stock as a partial liquidation dividend. This motive is economically valid but is rarely practiced because most managements are reluctant to reduce the size of their firm voluntarily.

was basically that the company's shareholders had confidence in management's ability to invest in other projects.[12] ▪

A frequently heard reason for stock repurchase is that it represents a good investment opportunity. Many firms have publicly announced that they were repurchasing stock because it was undervalued. However, this motive presents two problems. First, as we will see in Chapter 17, finance markets are considered to be highly efficient in that stock prices fully reflect all publicly available information about the stocks. For a company to believe that repurchase of its stock represents a good investment means either that the company does not believe in market efficiency or that the company has better information than the market.

Second, it may be considered unethical for the firm to buy back its stock on the basis of insider information. Unless there is full disclosure by the company of all information pertinent to the repurchase, the repurchase may also be viewed as illegal.[13]

Accounting Treatment of Stock Repurchases

It is worthwhile to consider the accounting treatment of stock repurchases, particularly given the buy-back purpose mentioned above, that the stock is a good investment. Under a 1938 securities rule, repurchased shares of stock must be held as treasury stock or retired (this was intended to prevent firms from speculating in their own shares).[14] Thus, proper accounting for the repurchase requires that the firm's assets be reduced or its debt load be increased to reflect the cash (or borrowed funds) used to finance the repurchase. Either way, equity is reduced and the shares disappear. However, the company's annual report will not reflect the buyout transaction in the major financial statements—for example, if the shares repurchased subsequently decline in value, this will not be reported to shareholders as losses. In contrast, if a firm buys stock in another company, the typical accounting procedure is to treat such an investment as long-term assets. If the price of this investment declines, the assets must be marked to market at the reporting period. Furthermore, significant losses on such a transaction may require a disclosure of the loss by the firm, often in a footnote.

▪ *Example*

In September 1987 Hospital Corporation of America (HCA), having obtained cash from the sale of some assets, repurchased 12 million of its shares at $47 per share, a transaction worth some $564 million.[15] By December 31, 1987, the price of these shares was only $31.125, a "loss" of some $191 million dollars in only a few months. According to current accounting principles, HCA did not lose a cent on the buy-back, and its annual report reflected that fact. In contrast, in 1986 the

---

[12]See John Heins, "Overload," *Forbes,* December 14, 1987, p. 124.

[13]The firm must be mindful of the legal and moral issues involved. One of the most obvious is the question of conflict of interest. There have been instances in which much of the tendered stock was from the firm's executives. If the stock price should subsequently fall, nontendering stockholders may be properly suspicious that the executives possessed inside knowledge and "got out while the getting was good." This is a special case of the more general issue of how to perform the stock repurchase so that all investors have similar access to information regarding the future prospects of the firm and also have equal opportunity to participate in the buy-back plan.

[14]See Penelope Wang, "Losses? What Losses?", *Forbes,* February 8, 1988, p. 118.

[15]Ibid., and *The Value Line Investment Survey,* various issues.

Williams Companies lost some $240 million because of a write-down of its long-term investments, and this was reported to shareholders. ▪

Effects on Stockholder Wealth

In principle, there should be no effect on stockholder wealth in a fair stock repurchase arrangement. *Fair* refers here to the assumption that management is not acting on information that would cause the value of the stock to be revalued upward if it were publicly known. In fact, a fair stock repurchase arrangement may be logically equated to a cash dividend, a point which can be illustrated by an example.

▪ *Example*

Drum, Inc., has the following financial data:

Number of shares outstanding	2,000,000 shares
Net income per year (assumed constant)	$5,000,000 per year
Dividend payout ratio	1.0
Required rate of return on equity k	0.10

Since the payout ratio is 1.0, or 100 percent, Drum's annual dividend is:

$$\frac{\text{Dividends}}{\text{per share}} = \frac{\text{Earnings}}{\text{per share}} = \frac{\$5,000,000}{2,000,000 \text{ shares}} = \$2.50 \text{ per share}$$

Assuming the next dividend is a full year away:

$$P_0 = \sum_{t=1}^{\infty} \frac{\$2.50}{(1.10)^t} = (\$2.50)(\text{PVIFA}_{.10,\infty}) = (\$2.50)(10) = \$25$$

Suppose that in lieu of paying the $5 million earnings as dividends, Drum buys back $5 million of its stock via a tender offer at $27.50 a share. What effect would this have on stockholder wealth?

$$\frac{\text{Number of shares}}{\text{repurchased}} = \frac{\$5,000,000}{\$27.50 \text{ per share}} = 181,818 \text{ shares}$$

$$\frac{\text{Number of shares}}{\text{remaining}} = 2,000,000 - 181,818 = 1,818,182 \text{ shares}$$

$$\frac{\text{Future dividends}}{\text{per share}} = \frac{\$5,000,000}{1,818,182 \text{ shares}} = \$2.75 \text{ per share}$$

Assuming k remains at 10 percent:

$$P_0 = \sum_{t=2}^{\infty} \frac{\$2.75}{(1.10)^t} = (\$2.75)(\text{PVIFA}_{.10,\infty})(\text{PVIF}_{.10,1}) = (\$2.75)(10)(0.909) = \$25$$

There is no effect on P_0 of omitting the dividend and substituting an equivalent stock repurchase plan. Why? Under the dividend alternative, earnings and dividend per share stay at $2.50, and the next dividend is one year in the future. Under the repurchasing alternative, the next year's dividend is omitted, but future dividends and earnings per share will increase to $2.75, which means the stock price at the end of Year 1 is expected to be $27.50. The repurchase plan thus substitutes a $2.50 stock price gain for the $2.50 dividend omitted. ▪

The previous analysis assumes that:

- k does not change.
- There are no preferences for a particular form of income (dividend versus capital gains income).
- The firm uses only the amount of the usual dividend to repurchase stock (the firm does not pay a premium to repurchase stock).

Under these conditions, repurchasing stock has no effect on stockholder wealth because it is merely an alternate way of distributing profits. If these conditions do not fairly approximate real-world conditions, repurchase plans will have some effect on P_0.

Companies sometimes buy back their shares to improve earnings per share. Repurchased stock that is carried as treasury stock reduces the number of common shares outstanding. With fewer shares outstanding, there must by definition be a positive effect on earnings per share and on return on equity. But to believe that this automatically would improve stockholder wealth implies that the market is easily fooled by the repurchasing company, which is inconsistent with the evidence that the market is efficient. This is not a valid economic reason for repurchase of stock.

STOCK DIVIDENDS AND STOCK SPLITS

In addition to or in lieu of paying cash dividends, firms may pay **stock dividends,** which are *pro rata* dividend payments of shares of stock to current owners. **Stock splits** are distributions of new shares to current owners and exist for other than dividend purposes; nevertheless, their impact is similar to that of stock dividends. Stock dividends and splits are treated differently for accounting purposes, and the motives for using them can be different. However, there is no real financial difference between the two, and the two terms are often used interchangeably or simultaneously in the announcement of such actions, as illustrated by the following statement from Ameritech, the parent of five midwestern Bell companies and seven information industry subsidiaries.

stock dividend
a dividend payment in the form of shares of stock

stock split
a distribution of new shares of stock to current owners

- *Example*

"On December 17, 1986, the board of directors authorized a three-for-two stock split of Ameritech's common stock, effected in the form of a stock dividend. The additional shares were distributed in January 1987 to shareowners of record on December 31, 1986. As a result of the split, 48,809,000 additional shares were issued and $48.8 (million) was transferred from proceeds in excess of par to common stock."[16] ▪

---

[16] *Annual Report 1987,* American Information Technologies Corporation (Ameritech), Chicago, Illinois, 1988, p. 36.

■ *Table 16–2*
Stock Dividends and
Splits, 1980–1989

	Less than 25%	25% to 49%	50% to 99%	2 for 1 to 2½ for 1	3 for 1 to 3½ for 1	4 for 1	Over 4 for 1	Total
1989	28	9	34	66	2	2	1	142
1988	34	11	29	25	4	1	—	104
1987	36	18	59	118	10	1	2	244
1986	43	22	78	118	9	1	1	272
1985	40	17	43	60	6	—	—	166
1984	57	12	50	51	6	1	1	178
1983	54	21	80	131	12	—	2	300
1982	61	21	36	28	—	—	—	146
1981	63	23	67	98	6	2	1	260
1980	65	25	55	98	5	1	—	249

Note: Includes common and preferred issues. Data based on effective dates.
Source: *Fact Book 1989*, New York Stock Exchange, Inc., New York, 1989, p. 41. Reprinted by permission.

For NYSE stocks, there were a total of 142 stock dividends and stock splits in 1989, and in the 10-year period from 1980 to 1989, in any one year there were no fewer than 104 such distributions, nor more than 300. The overwhelming majority of stock splits for NYSE stocks in any year consisted of two-for-one splits, and four-for-one or more are exceedingly rare. In 1989, Philip Morris had a four-for-one stock split, and Honda Motor Company had a five-for-one stock split. Table 16–2 shows the complete distribution of stock dividends and stock splits for NYSE stocks for the years 1980–1989.

Reasons for Stock Dividends and Splits

Stock dividends are often paid by companies that believe it is important to have a track record of dividends, but they need the cash generated from operations for investment projects and do not wish to raise external capital to pay cash dividends. Some growth companies pay small (2 to 5 percent), regular stock dividends. Companies sometimes pay stock dividends in lieu of cash dividends because they are experiencing cash flow difficulties yet wish to maintain a dividend record.

Stock splits are typically undertaken to keep the stock price in a popular trading range. Many financial executives seem to believe in an optimum price range for trading in their stock (some propose a range from about $10 to $50 per share). Stocks that sell in this range supposedly attract a broader array of investors because of favorable brokerage fee schedules and because more investors can afford to buy round lots (100-share increments) of the stock. If stock price gets to be, say, $90, the firm can split the stock three for one (issuing three new shares for each old share), and the price will be about $30 per share.

A firm can execute a *reverse stock split,* which decreases the number of shares outstanding. Such maneuvers are sometimes used to bring a low-priced stock up to the popular trading range. Obviously, such paper shuffling cannot really change the true nature of a firm.

Effects on Stockholder Wealth

A stock split or stock dividend is itself valueless to the shareholder or investor. If there are no changes in the firm's earning power or risk characteristics, there should be no change in total stockholder wealth. All that has occurred is a change in the number of pieces of paper evidencing ownership of the firm, not in the firm's ability to generate cash or realize earnings. This is shown in the accounting treatment for stock dividends and stock splits, which is discussed in Appendix 16-A.

Stock dividends clearly have no real value in themselves, although some financial market observers feel that stockholders sometimes perceive stock dividends as giving them something they did not have before. As for stock splits, in today's world where institutional investors dominate trading on the NYSE and own substantial amounts of many common stocks outstanding, it is difficult to believe that lowering the price of the stock will enhance trading activity. In the end, stock dividends and stock splits are of no value to shareholders.

■ *Example*

Suppose the stock price is $50 per share, there are 1 million shares outstanding, and the stock is split two for one. Total stockholders' wealth before the split is $50 million. After the split, if there is no change in the firm's profitability or risk, each of the 2 million shares of stock should be worth about $25 per share, which results in total stockholders' wealth of $50 million. ■

If the firm's profitability and/or risk changes or is perceived to change, the total market value of the firm's shares will change. One of the most closely watched variables at the time of a stock split is the dividend rate. If, in the above example, the presplit cash dividend had been $2 per share and was raised to $1.10 per share at the time of the split, the stock price would probably be more than $25 after the split.[17] In general, if the firm increases total cash dividends (the number of shares times the cash dividend per share), the total market value of the shares will usually increase. Similarly, if the firm reduces total cash dividends, total market value of the shares will usually decrease.

According to some financial market observers, dividends can be used to *signal* new information to stockholders about current and expected earnings beyond existing information. It is important to note that changes in the market value of the stock following a split or dividend are caused by the *information content* in the cash dividend change and not the stock split or stock dividend itself. Stock splits and stock dividends themselves are valueless to investors and appear to be so recognized.

SUMMARY

■ A dividend is a direct payment by the firm to its stockholders, typically the payment of a quarterly cash dividend.

---

[17]The change from a $2 per share to $1.10 per share is an *increase* in dividends. An investor who owns 10 shares before the split would receive $20 in dividends. The investor would receive $22 (20 × $1.10) in dividends after the split.

- Dividend payments are only one of the cash distribution methods used by firms. Stock repurchases and cash-financed acquisitions have experienced explosive growth in the last few years.
- Another type of dividend payment is the stock dividend, involving payment in shares rather than in cash.
- Dividend policy is usually described in terms of the level and stability of the stream of dividends paid by the firm. The level of dividends refers to the dollar-per-share amount in the absolute sense and to the dividend payout ratio in the relative sense; dividend stability refers to the lack of variability in the stream of dividends.
- An important aspect of dividend policy is the debate about an optimal payout level. Does an optimal payout—one that will maximize share price—exist?
- The dividend irrelevance theory argues that rational investors are indifferent to whether their income is from dividends or capital gains income and so will not prefer either high or low payout ratios. This implies there is no optimal payout ratio that will maximize stock price.
- The dividend relevancy school argues that real-world imperfections make dividend policy relevant.
- The dividend preference theory argues that since investors are risk averse and since risk increases with time, investors will prefer relatively high dividend payout ratios. Investors are presumed to prefer a certain dividend now to an uncertain increase in future dividends and stock price, implying that an optimal corporate dividend policy would be to establish as high a payout ratio as the firm can maintain.
- The clientele theory states that some investors have compelling reasons to prefer low payout ratios and others to prefer high ones. If investors acquire stocks of companies whose dividend policies match these preferences, there is no such thing as an optimal payout ratio. However, once a firm selects a target payout ratio, it should not depart radically from the policy because of the costs of replacing one clientele with another.
- Most firms are observed to pay some cash dividend and to prefer a nondecreasing, stable dividend-per-share pattern over time. These practices reflect management's perception of investor preferences.
- Other factors that influence dividend policy are legal constraints, control issues, investment and financing considerations, and miscellaneous factors.
- Although a stock repurchase plan is logically equivalent to a cash dividend, it is undertaken for other reasons. Firms engage in stock buy-backs for many reasons, but there are few compelling economic reasons.
- Stock dividends and splits are valueless in themselves and have no real economic impact on stockholder wealth. However, stock splits are often accompanied by cash dividend changes that do affect stockholder wealth because of their information content concerning the future profitability of the firm.

KEY TERMS

cash dividend, p. 482
clientele theory, p. 491
dividend payout ratio, p. 485
dividend policy, p. 484
dividend preference theory, p. 488

residual theory of dividends, p. 494
stock dividends, p. 503
stock split, p. 503
treasury stock, p. 499

QUESTIONS

16–1. All firms do not have equal access to capital markets. How does that fact affect dividend policy?

16–2. Identify the legal constraints that may influence a company's dividend policy.

16–3. Most U.S. business firms are observed to be reluctant to reduce dividends per share. What would this reluctance imply about the pattern of the firm's dividends-per-share and dividend payout ratio over time?

16–4. With respect to the dividend irrelevance theory:
   a. Briefly describe the theory, including its main assumptions.
   b. What optimal dividend policy is implied by this theory?
   c. Identify and discuss the weak points of this theory according to the dividend preference theory.

16–5. With respect to the dividend preference theory:
   a. Briefly describe the theory, including its main assumption.
   b. What optimal dividend policy is implied by this theory?

16–6. Explain the clientele theory and how it fits into the dividend policy controversy.

16–7. Explain the three alternative dividend policies.

16–8. How prevalent is the payment of cash dividends by NYSE firms?

16–9. What are the major reasons for stock repurchase programs?

16–10. How has the Tax Reform Act of 1986 affected the controversy about dividend policy?

16–11. What effect would the following conditions be expected to have on the firm's dividend policy? Explain your answer.
   a. The company has recently borrowed heavily. The loan agreement carries a very restrictive dividend covenant.
   b. The firm is declared legally insolvent.
   c. A new group of stockholders has gained controlling interest in the firm by steadily buying stock over time. Their tax rates are so high they are averse to receipt of ordinary income.
   d. The company has recently gone private by buying back all stock held by minority stockholders. There are now only three stockholders in the firm. Plans are to remain privately held.
   e. The firm has had several loss years but has continued to pay a small dividend. Cumulative retained earnings are now zero.
   f. The company has identified several exciting new investment opportunities that will require large amounts of new capital.

16–12. What probable effects would the following situations have on dividend payout ratios *in general?*
   a. Interest rates decrease.
   b. There is a gradual reduction in new investment opportunities.
   c. A reduction in ordinary income tax rates and an increase in capital gains tax rates occur.
   d. A widely publicized finding by the National Bureau of Economic Research reveals that most blue-chip (very high quality) stocks have a payout ratio of about 0.5.

16–13. Explain the main difference between a stock split and a stock dividend from:
   a. An accounting standpoint.
   b. An economic standpoint.

16–14. Given the following dividend-per-share information, other things being equal, which company's stock price do you think would have performed best during this period? Why? Which stock price do you think would have performed worst? Why?

	Year					
Company	1	2	3	4	5	6
A	$2.00	2.00	3.00	3.00	4.00	4.00
B	6.00	6.00	6.25	6.25	6.50	6.50
C	1.00	4.00	1.75	1.00	2.50	2.00

16–15. How is the concept of *signaling* related to the issue of dividend policy?

16–16. Explain the accounting treatment for stock repurchases. How does this treatment differ from an investment by the firm in the securities of another firm?

DEMONSTRATION PROBLEM

16–1. Alpha and Beta, two companies in the space technology industry, are close competitors, and their asset composition, capital structure, and profitability records have been very similar for several years. The primary difference between the companies from a financial management perspective is their dividend policy. Beta tries to maintain a nondecreasing dividend-per-share series, while Alpha maintains a constant dividend-payout ratio equal to 1/6. Their recent earnings per share, dividend per share, and stock price history are as follows:

	Beta			Alpha		
Year	EPS	DPS	Stock Price Range	EPS	DPS	Stock Price Range
19+7	$3.79	$0.50	$31–43	$4.00	$0.67	$26–39
19+6	3.20	0.50	30–40	3.40	0.57	28–36
19+5	4.00	0.50	27–42	4.05	0.68	22–45
19+4	2.55	0.45	21–27	2.45	0.41	16–24
19+3	2.01	0.40	14–22	2.05	0.34	7–16
19+2	1.48	0.40	11–16	1.40	0.23	5–13
19+1	1.86	0.40	15–18	1.90	0.32	12–16

In all calculations below that require a stock price, use the average of the two prices given in the stock price range.

 a. Determine the dividend payout ratio and price-earnings (P/E) ratio for both companies for all years.

 b. Determine the average payout ratio and P/E for both companies over the period 19+1 through 19+7.

 c. The management of Alpha is puzzled about why its stock has not performed as well historically as Beta's, even though the Alpha profitability record is slightly better. The past three years are particularly puzzling. How would you explain this?

Solution to Demonstration Problem

16–1. *a.*

				Year			
	+1	+2	+3	+4	+5	+6	+7
Payout Ratio							
Beta	.215	.270	.199	.176	.125	.156	.132
Alpha	.167	.167	.167	.167	.167	.167	.167
Stock Price							
Beta	$16.50	$13.50	$18.00	$24.00	$34.50	$35.00	$37.00
Alpha	14.00	9.00	11.50	20.00	33.50	32.00	32.50
P/E							
Beta	8.9	9.1	9.0	9.4	8.6	10.9	9.8
Alpha	7.4	6.4	5.6	8.2	8.3	9.4	8.1

b. Beta

$$\text{Average payout ratio} = 1.273/7 = .182$$
$$\text{Average P/E} = 65.7/7 = 9.4$$

Alpha

$$\text{Average payout ratio} = .167$$
$$\text{Average P/E} = 53.4/7 = 7.6$$

c. Notice first that over the entire seven-year period, Beta has a greater dividend payout. However, if the dividend irrelevance theory is true, this higher payout should make little difference. Also, in the last three years Alpha has paid a better dividend. The probable reason is that the stock market is responding adversely to Alpha's fluctuating dividend per share history in comparison to Beta's nondecreasing dividend per share. Another explanation for the most recent three years is that the market views the future more favorably for Beta.

PROBLEMS

16–1. H&R Ford, Inc., has 5 million shares of common stock outstanding. Current share price is $30 per share. If Ford's annual net income is $25 million and Ford retains $15 million, find the following:
a. Dividend payout ratio.
b. Dividend yield.
c. Price-earnings ratio.

16–2. Assume the market expects Abbott Company's dividend stream to be $31.25 per share each year for the next five years (first payment one year from now) and then $20 per share each year thereafter, indefinitely. Abbott stock is currently priced at $110 per share. Assuming the dividend irrelevance theory to be true, determine what infinite-life constant-dividend level would be fully equivalent to the current plan.

16–3. A firm is considering two alternative dividend and financing policies, and the expected future dividend payments resulting from these two plans are as follows:

	Year					
	1	2	3	4	...	x
Plan A	1.45	1.45	1.45	1.45	...	1.45
Plan B	1.00	1.54	1.54	1.54	...	1.54

The firm believes that if it adopts B, k will be 25 percent, and if it adopts A, k will be 20 percent.
a. Determine P_0 for each plan.
b. With respect to the dividend policy controversy, what dividend theory does the firm believe in?

16–4. Consider the following information about Weinraub Industries:

Future Years	Net Income (Dollars)	Capital Expenditure Budget (Dollars)
1	1,000,000	500,000
2	800,000	600,000
3	1,200,000	1,200,000
4	1,300,000	500,000
5	1,300,000	-0-
6	500,000	100,000

In year zero, the company earned $1 million and paid dividends of $1 per share on the 500,000 shares outstanding.
a. Determine the company's dividend per share for each year (1) using a residual dividend policy, assuming that the capital budget will be financed using internal equity; (2) using a constant payout ratio of 0.6.
b. Which policy would result in the higher average dividend over the six-year period?

16–5. Zivney Canning Products is in the midst of some dividend policy planning. The company's net income last year was $12 million, and the board of directors paid a 40-cent dividend on 15 million shares. The president would like to increase dividends if possible, but there are two complicating factors. First, Zivney is vigorously expanding its canning capacity and has decided to use internally generated funds to accomplish this goal. The company's board has considered and rejected any external financing plans for this purpose. The expansion is expected to take about five years. This veto on externally financed expansion strongly affects the dividend policy question, particularly when considered in light of the second complicating factor. Zivney's board is proud of its long record of non-decreasing dividend-per-share payments. The firm has not had a dividend reduction since 1939, and the board will veto any proposed dividend increase so large that it couldn't be sustained.

Given this background information, Zivney's finance staff has prepared an estimate of the firm's net income for the next few years along with a schedule of estimated amounts of retained earnings needed to implement the coming expansion. As shown below, the firm's net income is rising, and the need for retained earnings peaks out in four years.

Year	Net Income ($ Millions)	Needed Retained Earnings ($ Millions)
1	13	5
2	14	6
3	17	8
4	18	12
5	25	5

a. Assuming the firm can always profitably use any extra retained earnings beyond the coming expansion needs, and being mindful of the board's desires, determine how much of a dividend-per-share increase, if any, the company could make at present.

b. When would a (possibly further) increase in dividends appear feasible?

16–6. Zeitlow's Buckeye Imports has the following current financial data, taken from the firm's balance sheet:

Common stock ($5 par)	$ 500,000
Additional paid-in capital	200,000
Retained earnings	450,000
Equity	$1,150,000

a. Determine what the equity accounts would look like if Zeitlow's stock is selling for $20 per share and the company pays a 10 percent stock dividend.

b. Repeat part (*a*) to show the results if the company splits the stock two for one.

c. Determine what Zeitlow's new stock price should be for both (*a*) and (*b*), other things being equal.

d. What do we mean by "other things being equal" in (*c*)?

16–7. Clayton Corporation has the following current financial data taken from the firm's balance sheet:

Common stock ($5 par)	$ 200,000
Additional paid-in capital	800,000
Retained earnings	750,000
	$1,750,000

Determine what the equity accounts would look like if Clayton splits its stock five for one.

SELECTED REFERENCES

Actual management views on dividend policy are discussed in:

Baker, H. Kent; Gail E. Farrelly; and Richard B. Edelman. "A Survey of Management Views on Dividend Policy." *Financial Management,* Autumn 1985, pp. 78–84.

Dividends as a signaling mechanism is discussed in:

> Asquith, Paul, and David W. Mullins, Jr. "Signaling with Dividends, Stock Purchases, and Equity Issues." *Financial Management,* Autumn 1986, pp. 27–44.

Stock dividends and stock splits are discussed in:

> Grinblatt, Mark S.; Ronald W. Masulis; and Sheridan Titman. "The Valuation Effects of Stock Splits and Stock Dividends." *Journal of Financial Economics,* December 1984, pp. 461–90.

APPENDIX 16–A   ACCOUNTING TREATMENT OF STOCK DIVIDENDS AND STOCK SPLITS

Current accounting practices treat stock splits and stock dividends quite differently. A stock dividend involves a transfer from the retained earnings account to the common stock and paid-in capital accounts. The net effect of a stock dividend is to simply rearrange funds among the firm's capital accounts. Total stockholders' equity remains unchanged, as does each stockholder's proportionate claim.

With a stock split, on the other hand, the per-share par value of the stock is decreased while the number of shares of stock outstanding is increased (except in the case of a reverse split). The firm's capital accounts do not change in dollar amount, only the designation of number of shares and per-share par value.

We can illustrate the accounting treatment for both a stock dividend and a stock split with the same data. Assume the following data for Rodin Company.

Common stock ($10 par, 1,000,000 shares)	$10,000,000
Additional paid-in capital[18]	10,000,000
Retained earnings	30,000,000
Total equity	$50,000,000

Current stock price = $100 per share

Stock Dividend

Suppose Rodin pays a 2 percent stock dividend. This will result in an equity rearrangement as follows:

Number of new shares issued	$= (0.02)(1,000,000 \text{ shares}) = 20,000 \text{ shares}$
Market value of stock dividend	$= (20,000 \text{ shares})(\$100 \text{ per share}) = \$2,000,000$
Increase in common stock account	$= (20,000 \text{ shares})(\$10 \text{ per share}) = \$200,000$
Increase in additional paid-in capital account	$= \$2,000,000 - \$200,000 = \$1,800,000$
Decrease in retained earnings	$= \dfrac{\text{Market value of}}{\text{stock dividend}} = \$2,000,000$

---

[18]This is the excess over par that a company may receive for a new issue of common stock. A share of $10 par value stock that a company sells for $30 will increase additional paid-in capital by $20.

The new equity position is therefore:

Common stock ($10 par, 1,020,000 shares)	$10,200,000
Additional paid-in capital	11,800,000
Retained earnings	28,000,000
Equity	$50,000,000

Because the stock dividend transaction illustrated for Rodin Company is considered a dividend payment, the dividend's market value, $2 million, is deducted from retained earnings and allocated between common stock and additional paid-in capital. Therefore, each amount in the original capital accounts as shown on the balance sheet is changed, as is the number of shares outstanding—only the par value per share remains unchanged. Nevertheless, this is only a rearrangement of the equity accounts because total equity is still $50 million.

Stock Split

Referring back to the original Rodin equity position, suppose the stock is split four for one. Par value of each share is one fourth of original value, and now there are four times as many shares. Individual account values do not change. The resulting values would be:

Common stock ($2.50 par, 4,000,000 shares)	$10,000,000
Additional paid-in capital	10,000,000
Retained earnings	30,000,000
Equity	$50,000,000

Long–Term Financing Decisions:

Needs and Sources

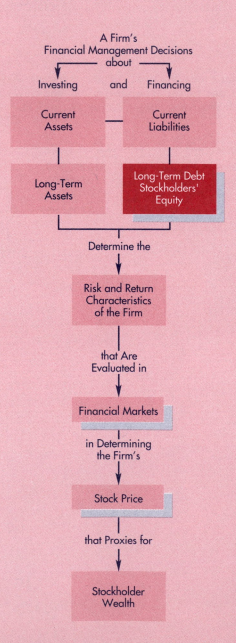

A Firm's
Financial Management Decisions
about

Investing   and   Financing

Current
Assets

Current
Liabilities

Long-Term
Assets

Long-Term Debt
Stockholders'
Equity

Determine the

Risk and Return
Characteristics
of the Firm

that Are
Evaluated in

Financial Markets

in Determining
the Firm's

Stock Price

that Proxies for

Stockholder
Wealth

In Part V we learned how to calculate the cost of capital and analyzed related issues such as capital structure. Now we need to consider the details of long-term financing, involving the need for, and the sources of, long-term external capital. Virtually all firms need to raise external long-term funds in order to finance their assets. The purpose of Part VI is to consider when, and how, this is done.

The first step in the process of obtaining long-term financing involves planning and analyzing. Chapter 17 describes the financial planning process from the standpoint of estimating how much long-term external financing a firm needs. The emphasis in this analysis is on a basic approach called the constant-percent-of-sales method. Having determined the total need for funds and the funds available from internal sources, external financing needs can be estimated. Chapter 17 also reconsiders (from Chapter 2) the important topic of capital markets where external funds are raised.

Chapter 18 describes the two equity securities, common stock and preferred stock. The emphasis is on understanding these securities, and the advantages and disadvantages of each in raising external capital. Common stock is of particular importance because it represents the ownership of the corporation. As we know, the objective of financial management is to maximize the stockholders' wealth. Chapter 18 also explains how new securities are issued, which involves the important concept of investment bankers. The two primary types of public offerings are considered.

Chapter 19 is a logical continuation of our study of sources of external long-term financing, focusing on debt as a source of capital. Bonds, a creditor's claim on the firm, are a standard and important source of capital. The numerous characteristics of bonds are considered in detail because it is important for the financial manager to understand the advantages and disadvantages of debt financing. Chapter 19 also considers convertible securities, primarily convertible bonds, as a natural extension of the discussion. At times some firms choose to issue bonds that are convertible into shares of common stock. Another security that can be converted into common stock, warrants, is discussed in Appendix 19–B.

Chapter 20 concludes our analysis of the sources of external long-term financing by considering lease financing and term loans. Lease financing is an alternative to borrowing funds in order to purchase assets and provides the financial manager additional flexibility in financing the assets of the firm. It is a popular source of financing for many firms, and it has its own unique characteristics that must be understood. Finally, term loans also are an alternative source of financing, typically offering a firm the chance to raise funds from an institutional lender for an intermediate period of time.

17

Financial Planning and Capital Markets

The Need for External Financing

Upper Peninsula Power Company provides electric power to Michigan's Upper Peninsula. Earnings per share in one recent year from continuing operations were $2.94, compared to $2.29 for the previous year. Assets at year-end were about $100 million.

According to the annual report for that year, the company estimated plant expenditures of $9.3 million for the next year, some 71 percent of cash requirements. The remainder of the next year's cash needs was to be for debt and preferred stock retire- ment. About 56 percent of the estimated cash requirements was expected to be generated from operations. A small percentage of the total need was expected to be met by the issuance of common stock through stock plans. The rest was expected to come from short-term borrowings, which Upper Peninsula expected to be converted into long-term debt during the year. The company also planned to issue additional long-term debt during the coming year.[1]

---

[1] Information about Upper Peninsula Power Company was taken from its 1987 *Annual Report*.

When the firm increases its assets, it must decide how to finance the increase. The firm may look either internally or externally for financing:

- Internal financing refers to cash flow generated by the firm's normal operating activities.
- External financing refers to capital provided by parties external to the firm.

External financing consists of short-term and long-term sources. We define *long-term* as a period of time longer than one year; any lesser period is *short-term*.[2] We studied short-term financing sources in Chapter 10. We will concentrate on long-term financing sources in these chapters.

Specific *chapter learning objectives* are:

1. To study financial planning from the perspective of estimating how much long-term external financing the firm must acquire.[3]
2. To reconsider the topic of capital markets, first introduced in Chapter 2. As a part of this discussion, we will also refer to the theory of efficient markets, introduced in Chapter 6, because it has important implications for the firm's financing operations.

ESTIMATING FINANCING NEEDS

Estimating how much financing the firm will need is an important planning problem. For one thing, it takes time, often months, to arrange external financing. Also, accurate estimation can lower flotation costs by reducing the number of trips made to the external financing market.

Procedures for estimating future financing requirements are varied, and some are very sophisticated. Our analysis here focuses on a simple approach called the *constant-percent-of-sales* method. It assumes that as sales increase, most asset levels will increase proportionately. This assumption is then used to forecast what asset levels are required to support the new (projected) sales level.

It is important to recognize the simplifying nature of the assumption being made with the percent-of-sales method, and the simplicity of the method itself. Firms may need to do more analysis, and in some cases this method may not be appropriate. Nevertheless, for our purposes the percent-of-sales method is adequate.

Pro Forma Sources and Uses of Funds

In estimating a firm's financing requirements, we use the sources-and-uses-of-funds concepts. Throughout the text we have considered the firm's investment activity, involving the use of funds, and the firm's financing activity, involving sources of funds. However, our emphasis here is on estimating future results rather than simply recording what went on in the past. The projection of future financial statement numbers is called *pro forma* analysis.

---

[2]Some financial analysts use *intermediate-term* for financing whose life is greater than 1 year but shorter than 5 to 10 years.

[3]Chapters 11, 12, and 13 are germane to part of this task because they lead the firm through the difficult questions of how much long-term investment and associated working capital will be required.

The following are broad sources-and-uses-of-funds categories:[4]

Uses	Sources
Investment in assets	Cash flow from operations
Repayment of financing	Sale of assets
Cash dividend payments	New financing

Determining the firm's future financing requirements can be accomplished by systematically determining the firm's *uses* for funds in the upcoming planning period and then planning for *sources* to meet those uses or financing needs.

As the uses list above shows, there are three major uses of funds:

1. First and foremost are the firm's investment activities. Firms continually buy new assets and replace old ones.
2. Repayment of financing refers to retiring of existing financing either as it matures or prematurely. In either case, the firm needs funds to buy back the financing from investors.
3. Cash dividends is the other major use-of-funds category. We know from Chapter 16 the importance of paying a stable dividend, which generates a continuing cash outflow.

Once the estimation of uses is complete, we turn to the sources list. We first focus on funds generated internally via cash flow from operations. If any asset sales are planned, those are accounted for, which leaves only new financing. As we will see below, we will further divide new financing into two parts, one of which will show how much external financing is necessary to satisfy our financing needs.

Finally, note that the analysis begins with a sales forecast, which is then related to asset levels. In summary, the process looks like this:

1. Estimate the change in sales.
2. Estimate total uses for:
   a. Investment in assets.
   b. Repayment of financing.
   c. Cash dividends.
3. Estimate total sources available from:
   a. Cash flow from operations.
   b. Sale of assets.
   c. *New financing.*

Notice that (3c), *new financing,* is highlighted. It is an end product of the analysis. As managers and analysts, we're trying here to estimate how much new financing we need to accommodate all the uses (i.e., needs) for funds we have, less the sum of cash flow from operations and decreases in assets. That is:

$$\text{New financing} = \begin{matrix}\text{Total uses}\\\text{of funds}\end{matrix} - \left(\begin{matrix}\text{Cash flow}\\\text{from operations}\end{matrix} + \begin{matrix}\text{Sale of}\\\text{assets}\end{matrix}\right) \quad \textbf{(17–1)}$$

---

[4]Note that a decrease in a noncash asset such as depreciation is a source of funds while an increase is a use.

The logic behind Equation 17–1 is that we're trying to determine how much new financing we need to satisfy our total needs (uses). As Equation 17–1 shows, we need new financing to cover only that portion of total uses that cannot be covered by cash flow from operations plus asset sales. If, for example, cash flow from operations were large enough to cover all uses, the firm would need no new financing.

There is one last step. The increases in financing are composed of spontaneous financing and arranged financing. Recall from Chapter 10 that spontaneous financing refers to those financing sources the firm receives automatically as the firm's sales increase. The most common examples are (1) accounts payable and (2) wage and tax accruals. Since spontaneous financing is provided automatically as sales rise, we should account for that fact in our analysis:

$$\text{New financing} = \text{Spontaneous financing} + \text{Arranged financing} \qquad \textbf{(17–2)}$$

In the context of our analysis, arranged financing represents the amount of external financing we need to accomplish our sales goal. It is a kind of residual in that it is what's left after all other financing sources have been used. Therefore, turning Equation 17–2 around to solve for arranged financing and renaming it *external financing needed:*

$$\text{External financing needed} = \text{New financing} - \text{Spontaneous financing} \qquad \textbf{(17–3)}$$

Combining Equations 17–1 and 17–3:

$$\text{External financing needed}$$
$$= \text{Total uses of funds} - \left(\begin{array}{c} \text{Cash flow from} \\ \text{operations} \end{array} + \begin{array}{c} \text{Sales of} \\ \text{assets} \end{array} + \begin{array}{c} \text{Spontaneous} \\ \text{financing} \end{array} \right) \qquad \textbf{(17–4)}$$

This is the final equation. It shows that the amount of external financing the firm needs to arrange equals the total uses that are planned less all other sources of funds. As a practical matter, external financing includes short-term loans and notes, as well as long-term debt, leases, common stock, and more exotic securities like convertible securities.

A Financing Needs Example

At this point, an example will help solidify these ideas. Table 17–1 shows a current balance sheet and income statement for Hambright Company that we will use to study how to calculate a firm's external financing needs. Hambright analysts are preparing to estimate how much external financing the company needs to facilitate its sales expansion plans.

In addition to the information shown in Table 17–1, analysts at Hambright have made two timing assumptions.

1. The planning horizon is one year (next year).
2. Any revenues received from new investments made will not be received during the planning year.

Assumption 1 establishes the time frame of the problem, one year in the Hambright example. The second assumption reflects the analysts' opinion that the lag between new-project initiation and completion is sufficiently long to eliminate

Current Balance Sheet

Cash*	$ 1,200,000	Accounts payable*	$ 5,100,000
Accounts receivable*	15,400,000	Accruals*	3,600,000
Inventory*	16,600,000	Notes payable	7,700,000
Total current assets	$33,200,000	Total current liabilities	$16,400,000
Net fixed assets*	$21,600,000	Bonds	$ 6,100,000
		Common stock	$12,000,000
		Retained earnings	20,300,000
Total assets	$54,800,000	Total claims	$54,800,000

Current Income Statement

Net sales	$81,800,000
Less	
Cost of goods sold	$54,400,000
Selling and administrative†	17,000,000
Interest	6,200,000
Taxes	1,700,000
Net income	$ 2,500,000
Dividends	$ 500,000

*These items normally change with sales changes.
†Included in selling and administrative expenses are $2 million of depreciation charges.

from consideration—during the planning period—any cash flows from the newly completed projects. That is, their cash flows will be deferred until after the planning period. We are now ready for some calculations.

The Sales Forecast

Most analyses of financing needs revolve around a sales forecast, which is then used to estimate increases in assets and spontaneous financing by working through various ratios related to sales. The different ways to forecast sales form an important topic in their own right, but for illustration purposes, assume the analysts have predicted that:

$$\text{Projected increase in sales} = \$20,000,000$$

An expansion of fixed assets will be necessary to enable the firm to produce this increased output. Current asset accounts must also be expanded to support the new production level. Some of this increase in current assets will be financed by increases in current liabilities. Table 17–1 shows what asset and financing items will be normally affected by increases (and decreases) in sales. All of the short-term assets will be affected. Changes in net fixed assets are primary *causes* of sales changes. On the claims side, accounts payable and accruals will change in the same direction as sales. The other claims items will not automatically change with sales changes. They are *discretionary or external* financing sources. One of the aims of this analysis is to determine how much external financing the firm needs to facilitate its investment plans.

Investment in Assets

Sales expansions typically require investment in new fixed assets, unless the company is not operating at capacity prior to the sales expansion. A straightforward way to estimate the change in fixed assets is to find the ratio of fixed assets to sales *before* the sales expansion, from Table 17–1, and relate this ratio to the projected increase in sales.

$$\text{Projected sales expansion} = \$20,000,000$$
$$\text{Fixed assets/sales} = \$21,600,000/\$81,800,000 = 0.264$$

Therefore:

$$\text{Expansion of fixed assets} = (0.264)(\$20,000,000) = \$5,280,000$$

The rationale for this calculation is that it will take almost $5.3 million of new long-term assets to keep up with the sales increase if the present ratio of fixed assets to sales of 0.264 is maintained.

Generally, we should not stop our fixed-asset estimation work here. The problem is that the $5.3 million figure we have estimated ignores any replacement investments Hambright must make to keep its sales up to the current level.

How much replacement investment will be required? That's not an easy question to answer without having more information, but as an approximation, suppose we assume that the annual depreciation charge equals the replacement investment (the bottom of Table 17–1 shows that this amount is $2 million). Combining the expansion and replacement estimates:

$$\begin{matrix}\text{Fixed-asset} \\ \text{investment}\end{matrix} = \begin{matrix}\text{Expansion of} \\ \text{fixed assets}\end{matrix} + \begin{matrix}\text{Replacement} \\ \text{investments}\end{matrix} \qquad \textbf{(17–5)}$$

$$= \$5,280,000 + \$2,000,000$$
$$= \$7,280,000$$

Next we estimate the increases in current assets that will accompany the anticipated sales increase. We do this by dividing these accounts by current sales:

Current Assets/Sales	
Cash	1.5%
Accounts receivable	18.8
Inventory	20.3
Total	40.6%

These calculations show that, on average, every dollar's worth of sales requires 1.5 cents worth of cash, 18.8 cents worth of accounts receivable, and 20.3 cents worth of inventory. In total, every dollar of sales requires about 40.6 cents of current-asset support. Now, if sales increase by a dollar, the firm will need to invest 40.6 cents in current assets to support this increase.[5] Therefore:

$$\text{Increase in current assets} = .406 \times \text{Projected sales expansion}$$
$$= (.406)(\$20,000,000) = \$8,120,000$$

---

[5] This is true if total current assets as a percent of sales remains constant as sales figures change. The constant ratio assumption is the heart of the constant percent-of-sales method we're using here.

The economic meaning of this calculation is that Hambright must commit an extra $8.12 million to current assets to support the projected $20 million sales expansion. Notice that this is a larger investment commitment than that to fixed assets.

The total investment-in-assets estimate equals the investment in fixed assets plus the increase in current assets:

$$\begin{array}{ll} \text{Investment} \\ \text{in assets} \end{array} = \begin{array}{ll} \text{Fixed-asset} \\ \text{investment} \end{array} + \begin{array}{ll} \text{Increase in} \\ \text{current assets} \end{array} \qquad \textbf{(17–6)}$$

$$= \$7,280,000 + \$8,120,000$$

$$= \$15,400,000$$

In total, if Hambright wants to expand sales by $20 million per year, it appears the company must commit about $15.4 million to investment in assets.

Repayment of Financing

Repayment of financing refers to the retirement of existing financing. It occurs either because the existing financing is about to expire or because management decides that now is an advantageous time to retire the existing financing. By definition, short-term financing is continually expiring. For the Hambright case, all of the notes payable must be retired, a total of $7.7 million. Assume that no new long-term retirement appears desirable to Hambright. So:

$$\text{Repayment of financing} = \$7,700,000$$

Cash Dividend Payments

The last use of funds to consider is cash dividends, both common and preferred. Hambright has no preferred stock (see Table 17–1). Assuming that Hambright's common dividends will be continued at the $500,000 level for the coming year:

$$\begin{array}{ll} \text{Cash dividend} \\ \text{payments} \end{array} = \begin{array}{ll} \text{Common} \\ \text{dividends} \end{array} + \begin{array}{ll} \text{Preferred} \\ \text{dividends} \end{array} \qquad \textbf{(17–7)}$$

$$= \$500,000 + 0 = \$500,000$$

Total Uses of Funds Equals Total Financing Need

Bringing all the parts together on the uses-of-funds side, we can now estimate Hambright's total uses:

$$\begin{array}{ll} \text{Total uses} \\ \text{of funds} \end{array} = \begin{array}{ll} \text{Investment} \\ \text{in assets} \end{array} + \begin{array}{ll} \text{Repayment} \\ \text{of financing} \end{array} + \begin{array}{ll} \text{Cash dividend} \\ \text{payments} \end{array} \qquad \textbf{(17–8)}$$

$$= \$15,400,000 + \$7,700,000 + \$500,000$$

$$= \$23,600,000$$

We turn next to where the needed $23.6 million will come from. That's the *sources* side of the picture. Recall that there are three main categories: (1) cash flow from operations, (2) sales of assets, and (3) new financing.

Cash Flow from Operations

Hambright's analysts assumed that the new investments made during the upcoming planning year would produce no cash flow during that year (see above). The cash flow from these new investments would come later. Therefore, cash flow from operations during this upcoming year can only come from the firm's investments already in place. An approximate measure of cash flow from operations is the sum of net income plus noncash charges that were deducted as expenses to calculate net income.[6] The principal component of noncash charges from most companies is depreciation. Therefore, as a first approximation:

(17–9)

$$\text{Cash flow from operations} = \text{New income} + \text{Depreciation}$$

If we further assume that this year's cash flow will be approximately the same as last year's, we can use the data shown in Table 17–1 to estimate cash flow.

$$\text{Cash flow from operations} = \$2,500,000 + \$2,000,000$$
$$= \$4,500,000$$

During the coming year, Hambright expects to generate about $4.5 million from internal operations that can be used to finance its new investments. It takes a full year to produce this $4.5 million, and therefore this money will not be available at the first of the year. However, as we noted earlier, the firm will not need the entire $23.6 million of financing at Time 0. The investment in plant will come first, followed by the buildup in current assets. This gives the firm some time to generate internal funds. For simplicity, we assume that the firm will be able to use all $4.5 million of internal financing generated during the year.

Sale of Assets

If the company disposes of assets, that too is a source of funds. This has recently become a more important source of funds for many companies. Assets—from single pieces of equipment to product lines to entire subsidiary companies—are sold for numerous reasons. They may not be productive enough for the seller, or they may not be a good fit with the selling firm's other assets. Some assets are satisfactory in all regards, but the selling firm needs money and feels it has limited alternatives elsewhere. Pan American Airlines, in 1991, sold off profitable international routes during a severe period of financial distress. Selling assets primarily to raise capital is called *left-hand-side financing,* which refers to financing from the asset (left-hand side) of the balance sheet.

Whatever the motive of an asset sale, the sale does provide a source of funds to the selling company. In the Hambright example, their analysts have not projected the sale of any assets, so:

$$\text{Proceeds from sale of assets} = \$0$$

This total of $23.6 million represents Hambright's financing need for the coming year. It includes all of Hambright's investment plans, financing retirement needs, and cash dividend requirements. Some of these needs—namely, the investment plans—are directly related to Hambright's sales expansion target. The other fi-

---

[6]It cannot be overemphasized that this is *only* an approximation. What the definition attempts to do is undo the income statement by adding back those items that were not cash expenses. See Chapter 3, especially Equations 3–20 and 3–21.

nancing needs in this example—the financing repayment and dividends—are not directly related to the sales target. But taken all together, the company's financing needs total almost $24 million.

Investment in plant and equipment usually precedes (in time) the buildup in current assets. Also, the dividends are spread out over the year. This causes the financing requirements to have important timing elements that should be considered. In our analysis, we assume that all of the $23.6 million is needed within the coming year, and we do not attempt to account for timing differences. We will briefly discuss this problem at the end of the analysis.

Spontaneous Financing

Spontaneous financing, which was introduced above, refers to sources of financing that tend to fluctuate directly and automatically with the sales level. As the firm's sales level rises (falls), this source of new financing rises (falls) also. There are two main types of spontaneous financing:

1. Accounts payable.
2. Accruals.

As sales increase, the firm's suppliers will automatically grant the firm more trade credit, provided the firm has a good credit rating. This automatic increase in payables is a source of funds. If it were not available, the firm would be forced to seek funds elsewhere. Likewise, as sales increase, it is likely that the firm's accrued wages and accrued taxes will go up. These, too, are automatic sources of financing.

Making use of the constant-percent-of-sales concept again by assuming that the ratio of spontaneous financing to sales will remain constant, we find the following relationships from Table 17–1:

	Spontaneous Financing/Sales
Accounts payable	6.2%
Accruals	4.4
Total	10.6%

Every dollar increase in sales will, on average, cause current liabilities to increase by about 10.6 cents. This automatic rise in current liabilities reduces the need for financing elsewhere. Therefore, the spontaneous financing that will be generated by the $20 million sales increase is:

$$\text{Increase in spontaneous financing} = .106 \times \text{projected sales expansion}$$
$$= (.106)(\$20,000,000) = \$2,120,000$$

External Financing Needed

Recall from Equation 17–4 that the amount of external financing needed is:

$$\frac{\text{External}}{\text{financing needed}} = \frac{\text{Total uses}}{\text{of funds}} - \left(\frac{\text{Cash flow from}}{\text{operations}} + \frac{\text{Sales of}}{\text{assets}} + \frac{\text{Spontaneous}}{\text{financing}} \right)$$

We now have estimated all the right-hand-side variables. Plugging these estimates into their appropriate places, we get:

$$\text{External financing needed} = \$23,600,000 - (\$4,500,000 + 0 + \$2,120,000)$$
$$= \$23,600,000 - \$6,620,000 = \$16,980,000$$

What we have done to this point is illustrate how the firm might go about forecasting its external financing needs. In this example, Hambright needs to raise about $17 million externally.

In a couple of instances in the Hambright example, we have referred to timing problems. The buildup of investment in long-term assets prior to the buildup in working capital is one example. The time it takes to generate the internal financing is another. Although we did not deal directly with these timing issues, they are important problems.

The next step in the analysis would be to attempt to accurately time the cash inflows and outflows associated with the planning period. This would first entail estimating the timing and amounts of the proposed long-term investments and associated buildup in working capital. Once this schedule was prepared, the next task would be to tailor a financing schedule that provides full coverage of the financing requirements, including their timing.

CAPITAL MARKETS

capital markets
a set of markets where funds are exchanged for long-term securities

Markets are places where things are bought and sold, and **capital markets** are merely a set of markets where suppliers of capital offer cash to those who need long-term capital (demanders) in return for pieces of paper (securities) that obligate the demanders of capital to make future payments to the suppliers. Many different groups or economic agents supply capital to the firm. First, there are individual investors. Additionally, individuals indirectly provide capital to corporations through *financial institutions*. There are several types of such financial intermediaries:

1. Deposit institutions (commercial banks, mutual savings banks, and savings and loan associations).
2. Investment companies (mutual funds).
3. Contractual institutions (insurance companies and pension funds).

Deposit institutions make term loans and lease equipment to corporations through their commercial lending operations, and they purchase common stock and debt from corporations through their trust departments. Investment companies collect capital from individuals by selling shares and then investing this capital in marketable securities. Some companies invest primarily in government securities, but the vast majority of investment companies invest in stocks and bonds of corporations. Mutual funds are particularly important economic agents in the secondary securities markets described below. Insurance companies collect insurance premiums from individuals and reinvest a portion of the premiums. Insurance companies have been one of the more active groups in buying corporate securities—mainly debt—via private placements (which are explained below).

Capital markets include both *impersonal* and *customer* markets:

- In impersonal or open markets, capital suppliers and capital demanders do not directly negotiate; rather, intermediaries arrange for the sale of securities. When the firm sells common or preferred stock or bonds, it usually operates in the impersonal capital market.

- In the customer capital market, there is direct negotiation between borrower and lender. When the firm arranges a term loan at a bank or leases an asset or places debt privately with an insurance company, it is operating in the customer capital market.

It is important to emphasize that capital markets deal with long-term funds, whereas *money markets* deal with short-term funds. In the block of chapters we are now beginning, we deal only with capital markets.

METHODS OF ACQUIRING EXTERNAL CAPITAL

Having done its financial planning—and our Hambright analysis is but one example of doing this—the firm must decide how to obtain the long-term external capital that it needs. What kinds of long-term external financing should the firm use? Equity securities? Bonds? Negotiated financing? To answer this question, we must consider the sources of external long-term capital available to the firm.[7]

We will divide our discussion of sources of external long-term capital into two broad categories based on how the firm can go about raising funds:

1. The firm may sell securities, primarily debt securities and equity securities. There are two primary methods of selling securities:
   a. A *public offering*.
   b. A *private placement* with a financial institution.
2. The firm can negotiate directly for financing. For our purposes, this involves term loans and leasing.

These methods of acquiring external capital are outlined below, and explained in detail in subsequent chapters.

Public Offerings

Public offerings involve the sale of new securities to the general public. There are two primary types of public offerings:

1. A general cash offer, made to all investors and typically involving the use of intermediaries who assist in the sale.
2. A privileged subscription, or rights offering, made to the firm's current stockholders.

These are discussed in detail in Chapter 18. Regardless of the type of offering, however, the role of securities markets is important in the acquisition of capital.

Role of Securities Markets

Securities markets may be characterized in different ways, but from the firm's standpoint there is a particularly important distinction between *primary* and *sec-*

---

[7]We do not consider short-term financing sources here. These sources were considered in Chapter 10.

ondary markets (as discussed in Chapter 2 and reviewed here). When the firm sells securities, it does so in the primary market, which is also called the *new issues* market because the firm issues its new securities through this market. The primary market consists of (*a*) firms that wish to issue securities and (*b*) individual and institutional investors who will buy the newly issued securities. As we will see, it is usually necessary to have middlemen (investment bankers and brokers) to bring the buyers and sellers together.

Once the firm sells the securities, they may then be traded among investors. Original buyers of newly issued General Electric stock, for example, may decide after holding the stock for a few years that they need the money for other purposes or that the stock no longer suits their investment goals. Since the firm will only buy back securities under stipulated conditions that rarely match most individuals' selling decisions, the investor must find another investor to purchase the stock. When one investor sells a security to another, it is through the *secondary* market. The only effect on the firm is that ownership of a previously issued financial instrument is changed. Stock ownership files of the firm will be changed, and future dividend checks and other stockholder mailings will be sent to the new owners.

Our interest in the firm's acquisition of *new* capital dictates a focus on *primary* markets. However, the secondary markets are essential to the operation of the primary markets. Without some means of bringing unacquainted sellers and buyers together, there would obviously be a very limited secondary market. Each market participant would have to personally find a buyer or seller to negotiate with. In most instances, this would involve a costly and time-consuming search. The probable result of such an arrangement would be less investment in corporate securities than now exists. As a result, companies would have more difficulty issuing securities in the primary market.

The obvious conclusion of this simplified discussion is that well-developed secondary markets are crucial to the success of the primary market where the firm operates. Anyone who possesses the necessary capital may purchase securities in secondary markets.

Private Placements

private placement
the sale of an issue of securities to a financial institution, bypassing the public markets

As an alternative to selling securities to the public or through privileged subscriptions, the firm may consider a **private placement** (sometimes referred to as a direct placement) with financial institutions, such as life insurance companies or pension funds. Many different kinds of securities are placed privately, but the most common private placement involves debt. Some $115 billion in bonds and $26 billion in stocks were privately placed in 1989. Although smaller than public offerings, private placements are important—in 1989, the $115 billion of privately placed bonds constituted about 36 percent of the total dollar value of all bond issues that year. The private placements for stocks in 1989 constituted some 44 percent of the dollar value of all stock issues that year.

Many firms do not use investment bankers in arranging private placements but work directly with the lending institutions. Dealing directly with the lender saves the firm the investment banking fees. However, other firms prefer to use investment bankers in arranging private placements, for at least two reasons. First, the investment bankers have a much wider range of contacts among financial institutions than the borrowing firms do. Consequently, investment bankers have better knowledge of when financial institutions have money available, which institutions are ready to lend, and what kind of securities would most interest them.

Second, since the investment bankers are also intimately aware of conditions in the public issues market, they can provide comparative information the firm may use in evaluating terms offered by the financial institutions. If the offer is out of line with the public market, the bankers will advise the firm that it might do better elsewhere. Also, the banker can suggest ways to resolve differences blocking agreement between the two negotiating sides.

There are two primary advantages of private placements in comparison to public offerings:

1. Speed of transaction.
2. Reduced flotation costs.

The speed advantage refers to the specified timetable required for public offerings. A proposed public issue must be registered with the proper authorities, and if it is a federal registration, there is a minimum 20-day wait before marketing. Frequently the waiting period is much longer (from 40 to 60 days), and during this period market conditions may change and impair the issue's success. However, direct placements are exempt from registration, so there is no comparable waiting time. This speed advantage eliminates some of the uncertainty regarding the timing of the issue. However, the advantage of private over public placements has been reduced by the *shelf rule,* which went into effect in 1982. Under the shelf rule, a company can file a short-form registration, place the securities "on the shelf," and sell them over time by auctioning pieces to the lowest-cost bidder. This saves the issuer money, and provides it with flexibility.

Direct placements have lower flotation costs than public placements, mainly because of the lack of underwriting expenses; there are also savings on registration fees. If the investment banking firm is not used, there is also the saving of its fees for launching a public issue.

The major disadvantage of private placements is the higher interest cost required (or dividend cost, if stock is involved). Financial institutions charge higher interest rates than a comparable publicly issued security would yield, and they also frequently demand an equity "kicker" or "sweetener," such as warrants. This gives the lender some chance to share in any capital appreciation on the stock, should it do well.

Private placements accounted for about one fourth of the domestic securities market in the first half of 1990, down from about 40 percent in 1989. On the other hand, they figured in approximately half of all large takeovers in 1990.

A significant development occurred in 1990 with regard to private placements. Under Rule 144A implemented by the Securities and Exchange Commission, institutions with portfolios of at least $100 million can buy any privately placed security. Issuers can avoid some of the disclosure paperwork that was previously required. This means that it is now cheaper to invest in U.S. companies, the private placement market is more liquid, and the costs of doing a transaction such as this have been reduced—by some estimates, a cut of two thirds has occurred. Such a deregulation of paperwork for sophisticated investors makes the capital markets more liquid and healthy.

Negotiated Financing

Term loans and leasing are also methods of raising *long-term* capital without going to the public. They are forms of long-term direct placements; the firm negotiates directly with the lender or lessor.

- Term loans originate primarily with commercial banks and are arranged directly by the firm with the bank without the help of an intermediary. This is a very important source of capital to all firms, but particularly for small firms, which may be unable to raise capital elsewhere. We investigate term loans in Chapter 20.

- In a lease arrangement the firm does not actually purchase an asset it has decided to acquire but rather obtains the use of the asset by leasing (renting) it from its owner (the lessor). There are two kinds of leases, distinguished mainly by the ease with which the lease can be canceled. A wide variety of capital equipment that U.S. corporations used to purchase is now being leased. Airlines, for example, used to purchase all their airplanes but now lease many of them. We study lease financing in Chapter 20.

FINANCING ACTIVITIES AND EFFICIENT MARKETS

We first looked at the concept of efficient markets in Chapter 6. The theory of efficient markets should be kept in mind because of its implications for financing activities. Although the theory remains somewhat controversial and although numerous financial market participants do not agree with some (or all) of its implications, the evidence supporting this theory is substantial enough that it cannot be ignored. The prudent course of action is to be at least aware of this theory and its implications because it may help us to understand what we actually observe in the marketplace.

We restate the theory below and draw the main inferences from the theory that relate to financial policy. It also may be advantageous for you to review the material on this topic in Chapter 6.

The Meaning of Efficiency

In an efficient market, all information relevant to pricing an asset is quickly incorporated into the price in an unbiased fashion. Therefore, in an efficient market an asset's price reflects all available and useful information. Furthermore, new useful information is, on average, *quickly* and *accurately* incorporated into the stock price. Loosely stated, if you envision the market as a very smart, very well informed investor who gets new information promptly and uses it wisely and quickly, that is approximately what is meant by an efficient market. Investors who have access only to publicly available information, the same as other investors, will find it virtually impossible to outperform the market. In even looser terms, it is difficult to beat the market when the market is highly efficient except by luck, by superior ability, or by using private information.[8]

---

[8]Using private or inside information is illegal.

Main Implications of Market Efficiency

There are several ramifications of market efficiency, both for investors and business firms. In general, most investors will not be able to beat an efficient market; that is, they should not earn abnormally large risk-adjusted returns. Our concern here, however, is with implications for the firm. Among the several implications for the firm, one stands out preeminently: *It is more difficult to add value to the firm through financing activities than through investment activities.*[9]

To a typical company treasurer, this statement would be startling. The treasury function is to raise money for the company, and the financial staff gives considerable effort to the best ways to raise money. They are convinced their skills and expertise result in advantageous financing plans that do indeed make the firm more valuable and, hence, the stockholders wealthier. However, there is a case to be made that financing activities do not *consistently* add value to the extent that treasury personnel usually believe. To see this, we will consider some specific implications of the efficient market theory for the firm's financing activities. The most important ones are these:

1. Market prices are fair.
2. Investors have other alternatives.
3. Financing timing is difficult.
4. Firms cannot regularly deceive the market.

We'll look at each of these in turn.

Market Prices Are Fair

This is simply a different way to say that an efficient market correctly prices assets. The important implication here, however, is that differences among financing alternatives—from a *price* standpoint—are more apparent than real.

Suppose, for example, the firm plans to raise money by issuing bonds and can either add a sinking fund provision to the bonds or not.[10] In a market where prices are set fairly, it should be a matter of indifference to the firm whether the sinking fund provision is added. The difference in prices—and, therefore, proceeds to the firm—between the alternative bond plans should exactly reflect the cash flow consequences of the company having to make sinking fund payments prior to maturity on one set of bonds. The end result of the market setting fair prices is that the financing alternatives the firm faces—like what kind of bonds to issue—are not important from the price or value perspective because the market will adjust for the differences. There may, of course, be nonprice considerations that are perceived to be important by managers.

Investors Have Other Alternatives

When the firm's financial alternatives are being considered, the firm should remember that investors have their own set of alternatives. Consequently, investors

---

[9]Sometimes, an even more extreme statement is made: financing activities will not add *any* value to the firm. This more extreme position seems unwarranted because we will see some instances later where financing activities do appear to add value to the firm.

[10]Issuing debt and all its attendant provisions—like sinking funds—are discussed at length in Chapter 19.

will not pay premiums for financial securities that merely offer them something they could arrange themselves without the benefit of the firm.

This issue of investors having their own set of alternatives entered into the theoretical debate in Chapter 15 when we studied whether firms could further stockholder wealth maximization through debt financing rather than through equity financing. One point in the argument is, Can't stockholders themselves borrow rather than have firms do it for them?

The second place we saw this implication of efficiency is in the dividend policy debate, in Chapter 16. The question there is whether stockholders prefer generous dividend payouts or lower payouts with more reinvestment in the firm. A point in that debate is, Can't stockholders arrange their own preferred dividend payments by judiciously selling and buying shares?

Regardless of the specific finance question at hand, the implication here of the efficient-market hypothesis is that investors will not reward the firm for things they can do as easily as the firm can.

Financing Timing Is Difficult

In an efficient financial market, the best estimate of tomorrow's market price is today's price. Said another way, you cannot consistently predict with a high degree of accuracy the direction market prices will take in an efficient market. Therefore, when the firm is trying to decide when to issue securities, its attempts to predict the best time to issue often will be frustrated. Suppose, for example, interest rates are high and the firm wants to delay issuing new bonds because it doesn't want to be committed to high interest rates. The efficient-market theory implies that it will be difficult to predict when interest rates will fall. If the firm waits, interest rates may go even higher.

Similarly, many companies don't like to issue new common shares when their stock prices are depressed from what are considered normal levels. In such instances, many firms will postpone issuing new equity, waiting for stock prices to rise. But the efficient-market theory implies that you can't consistently predict accurately when or whether the firm's stock price will rise. Stock price could, in fact, decline further.

The end result is that attempts by firms to time financing activities often may be unsuccessful. The firm may plan on issuing lower-coupon debt in six months only to find interest rates have risen. Or shares that could have been sold today at $20 may, instead, be sold a year later at $15, even though the firm had hoped for a $30 price. The message is, Who knows what tomorrow will look like? In an efficient market, the best guess of what tomorrow looks like is to observe what today looks like.

Firms Can't Regularly Deceive the Market

A corollary of the notion that market prices are fair is that firms can't deceive the market. If the market prices assets fairly, the market is not being fooled. That is, the relevant information is being used by the market, and the irrelevant is not. What this means to firms is that attempts to make financing instruments appear to be something other than what they truly are will not work. The market will not be fooled and the debt or stock (or whatever) will be priced correctly.[11]

As an example, stock dividends—covered in Chapter 16—are not valuable in and of themselves because they do not convey any extra *cash* to stockholders. So, when management says, as they occasionally do, "We're giving our stockholders a stock dividend as a financial reward," the market sees it for what it is actually worth. The dividend of real importance to stockholders is a cash-related dividend.

In the same spirit, attempts to increase *accounting* earnings where there are no *economic* (i.e., cash) earnings increases will be discovered by the market. Attempts to disguise how much debt the firm uses by not including lease obligations in the financial statements will meet with the same fate. In a completely efficient market, firms can't deceive the market. In a generally efficient market, they cannot expect to do so regularly.

Real versus Financial Markets

Given all that's been said above, it's important to identify which markets are relatively efficient and which are not. Most theorists and researchers think that *financial markets* are efficient, at least to a working approximation. By financial markets, recall that we mean all the markets dealing in pieces of paper (financial assets) that command legal claims on real or physical assets. Financial markets include both short-term (money markets) and long-term (capital markets) financial assets.

In contrast, *real-asset markets* are not considered fully efficient. Whether it be lack of sufficient competition or information or whatever, few people seriously believe that real-asset markets are efficient, even to a working approximation. The main implication of imperfect real-asset markets is that managers will add more value to the firm through their capital investment (real-asset) activities than they will by their financing operations. And that leads us back to the central point of this section on the implications of efficient markets for the firm's financing activities. It was said earlier and it's worth repeating: *It is more difficult to add value to the firm through financing activities than through investment activities.*

It's also worth noting that most officers and staff charged with procuring capital for the firms and most investment bankers would tend to disagree with this statement. And there are times when differences in financing alternatives can add value to the firm. For example, if the firm can borrow from a government source at an artificially low rate—a rate below the going market rate—that source of debt will be very valuable to the firm. Companies have used industrial revenue bonds (IRBs) extensively in recent years to finance projects at artificially low rates. These have been very advantageous.

Firms will also experience cases where 1st State Bank will offer better loan terms than 1st National Bank. Shopping around for a loan can indeed pay off. But the main message is still true more often than not: because of the relative

---

[11]This does not mean successful frauds cannot and do not occur. They don't occur very often in the United States. But when clever people commit fraud, and no one—leaders, other managers, auditors, etc.—catches them, the market can be fooled, at least temporarily. A more precise statement would be this: absent fraud, firms can't fool the market.

differences in market efficiency, it is certainly harder to add value through financing activities than through investment activities.

⟋International Perspective

It is important to recognize the increasing globalization of the capital markets. U.S. firms continue to raise most of their external long-term capital domestically, but numerous firms raise capital in the international markets. This is true particularly of debt. In 1987, for example, some $23 billion worth of bonds was sold abroad.

When we add the international dimension to capital markets, we introduce new considerations. On the positive side, borrowing costs may be cheaper abroad. On the negative side, firms raising capital abroad face exchange rate risk—the risk that U.S. currency will move unfavorably relative to the foreign currency. We will consider this issue in detail in Chapter 22.

A distinguished feature of international capital markets is the large role played by banks in foreign countries. Whereas U.S. banks historically have not been allowed to operate as investment bankers, commercial banks in many other countries are able to do so. These banks combine several activities together and often act in concert with the government of the country.

One aspect of the global nature of capital markets that U.S. firms may not appreciate is the competition from foreign firms within this country for scarce capital. A good example of this occurred in 1990 when Sumitomo Bank of Japan raised $500 million in the United States by selling 10-year notes. This means that Japanese banks are competing with, among others, large U.S. banks that have been directed to expand their own capital base. The additional capital can be used by the foreign firms to expand their U.S. operations. Also, as a result of Rule 144A, discussed earlier, foreign issuers will find it easier to make private placements in the United States because of the decrease in the stringent registration and disclosure requirements that have traditionally existed.

SUMMARY

■ The decision to invest in fixed and/or current assets creates long-term financing needs for the firm.

■ One procedure for estimating the firm's external financing requirements, called the *constant-percent-of-sales* method, assumes that as sales increase, most asset levels will increase proportionately. It is predicated on the firm's sales forecast, which is the beginning point in any analysis of this type.

■ The sources-and-uses-of-funds concept is used to estimate the firm's external financing need. This pro forma analysis involves systematically determining the firm's uses for funds in the upcoming planning period and then planning for sources to meet those uses or financing needs.

■ Uses include investment in assets, repayment of financing, and cash dividend payments. Sources of funds include cash flow from operations, sale of assets, and new financing.

■ The total uses of funds is equal to the total financing need. The external financing needed can be calculated by subtracting from total uses the sum of cash flow from operations, sale of assets, and spontaneous financing.

■ Capital markets are where firms satisfy their requirements for long-term external financing.

- External long-term financing sources include the sale of securities through public offerings and private placements, and negotiated financing sources such as term loans and leases.
- The efficient-market theory has certain implications for the firm's financing activities. In an efficient capital market, financial assets are priced accurately, and new information relevant to the assets is quickly and without bias incorporated into prices.
- The main implication of this theory is that it will be hard to add value to the stock through the firm's financing activities.

KEY TERMS

capital markets, p. 526   private placement, p. 528

QUESTIONS

17–1. Suppose a firm's investment plans for the next two or three years have been fairly well decided; the firm knows about how much its capital investment will be over that period. Other things being equal, how would the following factors affect how much external financing the firm would need to implement its investment plans? Briefly explain your answer.
  a. The firm's cash flow from operations increases.
  b. The firm's board of directors decides to increase dividends.
  c. The firm's inventory turnover ratio increases because of better inventory control.
  d. The company's collection period increases because of a decision to sell merchandise on credit to customers who are slower paying than was previously acceptable.
  e. Flotation costs increase because of increased market uncertainty.

17–2. Briefly explain the difference between internal financing and external financing.

17–3. Consider the following discussion between two analysts regarding estimating total financing requirements for their company for the upcoming year.

  Analyst A: Look, here are the numbers. We need $60 million for new plant and equipment investment. Also, we need $10 million for replacing some of our older equipment. The $10 million is, of course, a netted number that reflects any salvage of older equipment that may be possible. Altogether, our total financing requirement is $70 million.

  Analyst B: I think there are a couple of other things we ought to consider before we can decide what our total financing requirement is.

  Analyst A: What?

  Analyst B: Well, we should consider . . . .

  Finish B's answer.

17–4. What is meant by *spontaneous financing?* What are the two main types of spontaneous financing?

17–5. How is the external financing need calculated?

17–6. How are dividends handled in calculating the external financing need? Is there any difference in preferred and common dividends in this regard?

17–7. What is meant by an efficient market?

17–8. What are the primary implications of market efficiency for investors? firms?

17–9. What is the meaning of the statement "Market prices are fair?"

17–10. Contrast the efficiency of financial markets with that of real markets.

17–11. What is meant by the expression "Investors also have alternatives" when discussing the implications of the efficient market theory for the firm's financing activities?

17–12. Under what condition might a sales expansion not require an expansion in a firm's fixed assets?

PROBLEMS

17–1. Tallman Industries has just published its balance sheet as shown:

Tallman Industries
Balance Sheet
($ Millions)

Assets		Claims	
Cash and securities	$ 4.2	Accounts payable	$ 6.1
Accounts receivable	7.5	Accruals	3.6
Inventory	10.3	Notes payable	1.5
Property and equipment	20.5	Long-term financing	31.3
Total assets	$42.5	Total claims	$42.5

Tallman's present ratio of fixed assets to sales is 0.4. The company begins a major expansion of its plant facilities this year to accommodate a projected sales increase of $20 million.

a. Find Tallman's current sales level.

b. Find Tallman's new fixed-assets level after the expansion, assuming the company's ratio of fixed assets to sales remains at 0.4.

c. Estimate the amount of extra net working capital needed because of the expansion assuming a constant ratio of working capital to sales.

17–2. The Lee Company has the following income statement relating to the year just completed:

Income Statement
($ Millions)

Sales	$60
Expenses	
Operating costs	40 (includes $20 million depreciation)
Interest	4
Taxes	8
Net income	$ 8
Dividends	$ 2

Lee is planning to spend $20 million on plant expansion this coming year and another $20 million on renovating and replacing present plant and equipment. These investments in fixed assets will also require an investment of about $6 million in net working capital.

Estimate Lee's external financing requirement for the coming year, assuming that the cash flow and the dividends during the coming year will be approximately equal to those of the year just completed, and that refinancing needs equal $5 million.

17–3. Use the data shown below to estimate the external financing requirement.

	($ Millions)
Increase in accounts payable	2
Increase in current assets	10
Retirement of bonds	20
Net income	40
Investment in plant and equipment	50
Increase in retained earnings	30
Increase in accruals	3
Cash flow from operations	60

17–4. Lamoureux, Inc., is planning to make a $10 million investment in fixed assets and is attempting to estimate how much net working capital will be needed to support this expansion. The fixed–asset turnover ratio on the new investment is estimated to be about 2. From past experience Lamoureux estimates that its total assets turnover is about 1. Also, for every dollar increase in current assets the firm experiences, about half of the increase can be financed through increased accounts payable and accruals.

Determine the increase in net working capital that should accompany the anticipated increase in fixed assets.

17–5. Dyl and Company is planning on doubling its annual sales by the end of the next year from the current level of $300,000. Dyl estimates that all assets except cash will be affected by the sales expansion. All affected asset accounts will increase by amounts that will keep ratios of assets to sales at about the same levels as they are now. Dyl also plans to keep the same ratio of short-term debt to sales; this plan applies to all forms of short-term debt. Finally, Dyl does not plan to increase equity financing above the present level of $100,000. Given the present balance sheet data shown below and the plans described above, fill out the new (pro forma) balance sheet Dyl would be expected to have next year.

Balance Sheets
($000)

	Present	Next Year (Pro Forma)
Assets		
Cash	50	
Accounts receivable	50	
Inventory	100	
Fixed assets	300	
Total assets	500	
Liabilities		
Accounts payable	75	
Notes payable	75	
Long-term debt	250	
Equity	100	
Total claims	500	

17–6. The Southern Service Company is trying to estimate how much financing it will need during the next five years. Southern's balance sheet for last year is shown below. Sales were $2.5 million last year.

Balance Sheet
($000)

Assets		*Claims*	
Cash	$ 158	Accounts payable	$ 188
Accounts receivable	201	Notes payable	20
Inventory	250	Accruals	107
Total current assets	609	Total current liabilities	315
Net fixed assets	873	Bonds	100
		Common stock	800
		Retained earnings	267
Total assets	$1,482	Total claims	$1,482

Estimate Southern's total financing requirement in the coming five years assuming that sales will increase by 10 percent per year and that *all* assets and the relevant claims accounts keep their present relationship to sales. No refinancing is planned, and annual replacement of investments is budgeted at $100,000 per year.

17–7. Pearce International is in the process of increasing fixed assets by $12 million during the coming year. Another $5 million will be spent on fixed-asset replacement, and $3 million refinancing is scheduled. Also, current assets must be increased by $5 million. Pearce analysts believe that for every dollar current assets increase, current liabilities will automatically increase by 40 cents.

Determine Pearce's total financing requirement for the coming year.

SELECTED REFERENCES

Actual financing practices are discussed in:

Scott, David F., Jr., and Dana J. Johnson. "Financing Policies and Practices in Large Corporations." *Financial Management,* Summer 1982, pp. 51–59.

Seitz, Neil. "Shareholder Goals, Firm Goals and Firm Financing Decisions." *Financial Management,* Fall 1982, pp. 20–26.

18

Common Stock, Preferred Stock, and the Issuance of Securities

Too Much Equity?

Navistar International Corporation, a truck maker, grew out of the old, well-known but financially troubled International Harvester Company.[1] The company suffered from a number of problems, losing several billion dollars in the early 1980s. In 1986, Navistar, with the aid of investment bankers, planned an equity offering of 110 million shares, worth about $600 million. The proceeds were to be used to pay down long-term debt, saving millions annually in interest expense. The new offering would bring Navistar's equity capitalization to more than 200 million shares, or more than the shares outstanding of many companies with several times the revenue. In addition to the number of common shares outstanding, Navistar had other securities outstanding which were convertible into common stock. By the time of the announcement of this proposed transaction, the stock price had declined to a little over $5 per share, a decline of more than 50 percent during the year.

---

[1]See Barry Stavro, "A Surfeit of Equity," *Forbes*, December 28, 1986, pp. 62–64, *The Value Line Investment Survey*, various issues, and company annual reports.

A firm has two basic sources of long-term funds for financing its assets:

1. Internally generated funds, primarily retained earnings and depreciation.
2. Externally raised funds, including the sale of securities and funds obtained from creditors.

Internally generated funds are the most important source of funds for firms, accounting for roughly 70 percent of total funds in most years. Nevertheless, as the Navistar example shows, the externally generated funds are important, and it is to this subject that we now turn our attention.

Specific *chapter learning objectives* are:

1. To understand common stock, the one security that every corporation, whether publicly traded or privately held, must issue.
2. To analyze the pros and cons of preferred stock, the other equity security.
3. To consider how new securities are issued, with special emphasis on common stock.

COMMON STOCK

Common stock is the primary source of funds for most firms. The common shareholders must put up initial equity money to start the business. Thus, the common stock represents the ownership of the corporation and it is a perpetual security. It will exist as long as the firm exists, even if no other security is in existence. Over time, total equity funds come from the initial sale of shares to start the business, subsequent sales of additional shares as authorized by the board of directors, and retained earnings.

A firm's charter specifies the *authorized* number of shares of common stock that the firm can issue. The *issued* number of shares is the total shares that are sold to investors, while the *outstanding* number of shares refers to the total actually held by investors. *Treasury stock* is the difference between the number issued and the number outstanding, or the shares repurchased by the firm.

As with any other security, common stock has certain basic features that must be recognized in understanding common stock and considering it as a source of financing. These features are summarized in Table 18–1 and are discussed below.

PREROGATIVES OF COMMON STOCKHOLDERS

Common owners basically have two sets of prerogatives:

1. Claim prerogatives.
2. Control prerogatives.

Claim Prerogatives

The common stockholder is a *residual claimant*. This residual ownership claim has two distinct aspects:

1.	Type of security		Equity security denoting full ownership except in unusual circumstances
2.	Prerogatives		
	a.	Claims	(1) Residual claim on income—no guarantees of payment
			(2) Residual claim on assets—in case of bankruptcy
	b.	Control	(1) Voting rights on corporate charter and board of directors
			(2) Preserve proportionate ownership by preemptive right
3.	Retirement provisions		No formal provisions—has no maturity date
4.	Advantages to issuer		a. Not required to pay dividends
			b. No maturity date—no obligation to redeem
			c. Enhances equity base
5.	Disadvantages to issuer		a. Potential dilution of control
			b. Potential dilution of earnings per share
			c. Highest flotation costs
			d. Highest explicit cost of capital

■ *Table 18–1*
Basic Features of
Common Stock

- The *income* claim in normal times when the firm is viewed as a going concern.
- The *asset* claim when the firm is contemplating dissolution.

Income Claims

The common stockholder's income claim is through the dividend paid by the firm. The residual status of this claim is clear. The firm must first pay its operating expenses, followed by its interest expenses and tax liabilities. If the firm has preferred stock outstanding, it must also pay preferred dividends. The resultant residual, the firm's *earnings available for common,* is available for distribution to the common stockholders. Thus, the common owners are at the end of a long line of claimants. Moreover, the firm is not obligated to pay out earnings as dividends. It may decide to retain either all or a portion of earnings for investment purposes.

Just as common stockholders are the residual claimants on a firm's income stream, so, too, their liability is limited to the amount of their investment. This limited-liability feature has always been a key reason why firms incorporate rather than operate under some other format.

Asset Claims

Dissolution can occur because of failure, business combination, or termination of business. Common stockholders are also residual claimants here. In a failure situation, the residual status of the common position usually means that common owners receive little or nothing.

Control Prerogatives

Corporate control has different meanings. One definition is having the power to determine the broad policies of the firm. Control of the routine operations of the firm naturally rests with management, but major decisions, like issuing new common stock or debt or making a major investment, are approved by the board of directors. Consequently, control may be more narrowly defined as the power to elect a majority of the directors. This power is legally vested in the common stockholders. If management ignores their interests, they can always vote management out of office. Although such happenings are rare, prolonged periods of poor profitability can and do lead to replacement of management, if not by the board itself, then by irate stockholders.

Common stockholders have two primary control prerogatives:

- Common stockholders have the major voting rights for the firm.
- Common stockholders have the right to preserve proportionate ownership.[2]

Voting Rights

Two kinds of proposals must be voted on by common owners. First, any change in the corporation's charter must be voted on. An example would be to increase the number of shares authorized. Authorized shares represent the maximum number of shares the firm may have outstanding. Similarly, any business combination proposal that would change the charter, such as a merger, requires stockholder approval. Second, the election of the board of directors requires a stockholder vote.

Directors are elected at the annual meeting; however, in large corporations, relatively few stockholders attend the meeting. To ensure that all stockholders may vote, proxies are used. A **proxy** is a written authorization that empowers another to vote for the signer. Prior to the annual meeting, management will solicit proxies from the stockholders for director candidates that management has nominated. In normal times, when things are proceeding smoothly for the company, the stockholders will return their signed proxies, and the nominated candidates will be elected.

In other times, a group of stockholders may wish to elect directors who have not been nominated by the firm. This situation may arise because the firm's profitability has declined and some stockholders think that the candidates proposed by management will do little to improve conditions. Alternatively, there may be a takeover bid by outsiders who wish to gain control. Or some stockholders may wish to place a member of their group on the board of directors to champion their interests. These situations lead to battles for votes called *proxy fights*. Accordingly, it may be important for stockholders to examine the nature of the election procedures.

The key point to remember in director elections is that stockholders receive one vote per share of stock for each board vacancy. If, for example, a firm is electing four new board members, and you own 100 shares of common, you will have 400 (100 × 4) votes in the election. Two types of voting plans are used in electing directors: *majority* and *cumulative* voting. Majority voting limits the number of ballots an investor may cast for any one candidate to the number of *shares* owned, making it very difficult for a minority group to elect any directors. Cumulative voting allows stockholders to cast all their *votes* for one candidate and makes it easier for minority groups to elect directors.

proxy
a written authorization permitting someone to vote a stockowner's shares in corporate matters

---

[2]In addition, the common owners have the right to examine the firm's books and to secure names and addresses of fellow stockholders. These rights are very important when battles for control are waged.

Preserving Proportionate Ownership

A *preemptive right* is a provision in the company's charter that grants the stockholders the right to purchase new common stock in the same proportion as their current ownership. Thus, a stockholder who owns 10 percent of the firm's common has a preemptive right to buy 10 percent of new common issued. The stockholder may, of course, decline to exercise this right. Since rights are options to buy shares of common at a specified price (the subscription price) during a specified period of time, usually two to four weeks, recipients of the rights (the firm's current stockholders) have alternatives:

1. They can exercise the rights and buy new stock.
2. They can sell the rights.
3. They can do nothing.

The first alternative permits them to maintain proportionate ownership, which is the main purpose of the rights offering. Alternative 2 permits them to sell their rights should they not wish to maintain their ownership percentage. We will consider these rights when we discuss the issuance of securities.

ADVANTAGES AND DISADVANTAGES OF COMMON STOCK FINANCING

Advantages

One advantage of issuing new common is that the firm is not required to pay common dividends. This is most crucial when cash flow levels are low. A skipped interest payment may lead to bankruptcy, but a skipped dividend payment will not. To be sure, stockholders will be unhappy with an omitted or reduced dividend, and stock price will suffer, but the decline in stock price is not as severe when a dividend is cut as when an interest payment is not met. The fact that dividend payments are not legal obligations gives the firm some flexibility, which is particularly important in difficult times.

In the same context, because common stock has no maturity date, there is no obligation to redeem it. Firms occasionally do repurchase stock, but they do so when they have the cash available, at a time of their own choosing. Debt, on the other hand, does have a maturity date, and the firm must have cash for redemption on that date. If the firm cannot meet its redemption obligation, it may be forced into bankruptcy.

Last, addition of common to the firm's capital structure enhances the future borrowing capacity of the firm. Creditors prefer to lend to firms with a substantial equity base, and new common increases this base. Future financing needs may occur when stock prices are depressed to such low levels that management does not wish to sell stock. Debt financing may be difficult to obtain if the firm has too much debt relative to its equity base. At such times the firm may wish it had financed earlier with equity.

Disadvantages

Most new common issues, even when accomplished through rights, bring in new owners. The old owners may feel this control dilution is a disadvantage, although as long as their right to proportionate ownership is protected, this would not seem an important criticism.[3] Another frequent stockholder complaint is that earnings per share will be lower because more shares are now outstanding, and stock price will decline. But this view is short-sighted. The funds received from the stock sale are invested, and these investments presumably have positive expected net value. By definition, such investments should increase stock price. Of course, if the investments turn out badly, the stock price will suffer, but not because new stock was issued. Then, stock price suffers because the investments do not pay off.

It is true, however, that it is relatively expensive to issue stock. The flotation costs associated with common stock are high because of the risk involved. Also, we saw in Chapter 14 that equity has the highest cost of capital.

WHO OWNS THE EQUITY SECURITIES?

It is interesting to analyze the levels of, as well as trends in, ownership of corporate equities among the various sectors of the economy. In 1988, households—broadly defined to include individuals, banks, savings institutions, and mutual funds—owned about 60 percent of the total equities outstanding, which had a value of about $3,118 billion. Individuals accounted for about 90 percent of the holdings in this category, and the three institutions together only about 10 percent. This 60 percent figure has declined over the years, from about 80 percent in 1970 to about 69 percent in 1980 and about 60 percent by 1988.

Tax-exempt institutions accounted for about 30 percent of the equity ownership in 1988. This represented a doubling from 1970. Thus, these institutions have steadily increased their ownership while individual ownership has decreased. Pension funds were by far the largest owner of equities among the tax-exempt institutions, with more than twice the amount of the next largest group, the state and local government retirement funds.

Foreigners owned some 6 percent of U.S. equities by 1988, a doubling since 1970. The remainder was held by insurance companies, whose 3 percent ownership has remained steady over time.

PREFERRED STOCK

Preferred stock is an equity security because it has no maturity date and because it represents ownership (although usually with limited voting rights). Nevertheless, preferreds are called *fixed-income securities* because they offer an expected constant (fixed) income to investors. An investor who buys preferred expects to receive the dividend each year until either the stock is sold to another investor or the company redeems (buys back) the stock. There is no guarantee the company will actually pay the preferred dividend each period it is due, but barring difficulty, the firm will honor its commitment.

Because preferred stock has some features of stock and some of debt, it is called a *hybrid* or *quasi-debt security*.

---

[3]An exception might be where original owners cannot raise the money to maintain their desired percentage of ownership.

- *From the common stockholder's viewpoint,* preferred looks almost like debt. Its fixed payment schedule creates financial leverage (see Chapter 15), which magnifies the earnings per share that result from increases and decreases in operating profits. Preferred is not exactly the same as debt, however, because preferred stockholders cannot force the firm into bankruptcy as the result of a missed dividend.

- *From a creditor's perspective,* preferred looks like equity. Creditors have a prior claim to both income and assets. Thus, preferred serves as an equity cushion should the firm fail, and it increases the chances that creditors will recover their full investment.

FEATURES OF PREFERRED STOCK

Several features characterize preferred stock. Some major features apply to virtually all preferred stocks; others are somewhat rare. These features are summarized in Table 18–2; the major features are discussed below.

Priority Status

Preferred is distinguished from common stock by its relative seniority position. Preferred stockholders have a prior claim on the firm's income, in that the firm must pay the preferred dividends first. They also have a prior claim on the firm's assets in the event the firm is dissolved. However, the preferred claim is behind

---

1.	Type of security	A hybrid security—technically an equity security, but has features of debt securities
2.	Prerogatives	
	a. Claims	(1) Priority status
		(a) Paid before common stockholders but after debt holders
		(b) In case of bankruptcy, comes ahead of common but behind debt
		(2) Fixed-income status—fixed dividends stated in dollar terms or as a percent of par
		(3) Cumulative feature—all arrearages must be paid before common dividends can be paid
		(4) Participation feature, although rare, allows preferred owners to share in unusual profits of firm
	b. Control	Contingent voting rights—vest only when firm is in arrears on preferred dividends by a specified amount
3.	Retirement provisions	Has no maturity date, but can be retired by:
		a. A conversion into common stock if the preferred is convertible
		b. The call provision
		c. A sinking fund
4.	Advantages to issuer	a. Leverage with no default risk
		b. Cash flow flexibility—dividends can be omitted
		c. Preservation of stockholder control
5.	Disadvantages to issuer	a. Dividends are not tax deductible
		b. More expensive than debt financing

■ *Table 18–2*
Basic Features of Preferred Stock

the firm's creditors' (e.g., bondholders) claims. Preferred stock's priority position makes it a safer investment than common stock. In return for this prior claim status, preferred stockholders give up their voting rights as owners and their right to share in any exceptionally good profits the firm may realize. Essentially, preferred holders trade away higher returns for greater safety.

Fixed-Income Status

Preferred stockholders receive dividends that are contractually stipulated. They are stated either as a percentage of par value or in dollar terms. Par value represents the face amount of each preferred share. When the preferred dividend is stated as a percentage of par, the dollar amount of the dividend is determined by multiplying par value times the percentage.

■ *Example*

Grolier preferred stock has a 5 percent dividend, and par value is $50 per share. The annual Grolier preferred dividend is therefore $2.50 per share. Like common stock, preferred usually pays a quarterly dividend. In the Grolier case this would amount to 62.5 cents per share each quarter. ■

Many preferred stocks have either no par value or a nominal value, usually $1 per share. For these, and even for many preferreds with par values, dividends are stated simply in dollar terms.

■ *Example*

Merck and Company's no-par preferred has a stated $3.50 dividend, and B. F. Goodrich's $1 par preferred has a $7.85 dividend. ■

Cumulative Dividends

The cumulative dividend feature is a protective device for preferred stockholders. When the firm fails to pay a scheduled preferred dividend, an *arrearage* is created. A cumulative dividend feature requires that all arrearages must be paid before any common dividends are paid. Preferred stockholders can neither force the firm to pay scheduled preferred dividends nor force the firm into bankruptcy because of omitted dividends, but the cumulative dividend feature does allow the preferred holders to block the payment of common dividends.

■ *Example*

If Rath Industries preferred stock is supposed to pay an annual dividend of $3 per share but nothing has been paid for four years, there is a $12-per-share arrearage, and common dividends on Rath may not be paid until this arrearage is paid off. ■

As an alternative to paying off the arrearage, the firm might try to negotiate a settlement with its preferred stockholders.

Retirement Provisions

Preferred stock has no fixed maturity date, but several provisions may be included in the preferred agreement to provide for retirement of an outstanding issue.

Convertibility

A convertibility feature permits preferred stockholders to convert their preferred into shares of common. Preferred stocks that permit this are called *convertible preferred*. We will discuss convertible securities in Chapter 19.

Call Feature

The call feature allows the firm to buy back the preferred at a *call price* stipulated when the preferred is first sold. The call price is set above the initial sale price of the preferred, creating a *call premium,* which is the difference between call price and face value. Usually the firm agrees not to call the preferred for at least two or three years after issue. The firm will exercise its call option only when the market price of the preferred stock is above the call price, for if the preferred market price is below call price, the firm can purchase preferred in the open market, or it can make a *tender offer,* where it publicly advertises to buy preferred stock at a stipulated price (set above the current market price).

Sinking Fund

A sinking fund provision requires the firm to set aside money to retire the issue sequentially. The money is used either to purchase preferred stock in the open market (if the preferred's market price is below call price) or to call the preferred (if market price is above call price). In either situation, the amount of preferred outstanding is decreased. Sinking funds on preferreds are quite rare.

Advantages of Issuing Preferred Stock

By advantages we mean advantages to the firm and, ultimately, the common stockholders.

Leverage with No Default Risk

Preferred dividends are a fixed obligation and thus create financial leverage, but if the firm omits a dividend, the preferred stockholders cannot force the firm into bankruptcy. Firms make every effort to meet their preferred obligations on schedule, and failure to meet them will affect the common stock price adversely, but the consequences are not as severe as when the firm misses scheduled debt charges.

Cash Flow Flexibility

Preferred gives the firm some cash flow flexibility because its dividends can legally be omitted if necessary and because, unlike debt, it has no maturity date. On the other hand, the firm can choose to retire preferred when it has sufficient financial resources.

Preservation of Stockholder Control

Frequently the financing choice is between common or preferred because the firm believes it cannot safely service more debt. Issuing preferred increases the equity base but, because preferred carries no normal voting rights, does not dilute the control position of current common owners.

Tax Advantage in Mergers and Acquisitions

Many firms have recently used convertible preferred stock in their merger and acquisition activities because of the structure of U.S. tax laws. If the common stockholders of a company being acquired sell their stock for cash or exchange it for bonds of the acquiring company, they will incur an immediate capital gains tax on the difference between the price received on their stock and their original cost basis. However, if the acquiring firm issues to them convertible preferred stock, the transaction is exempt from the capital gains tax. The tax is deferred until the preferred is sold.

Disadvantages of Issuing Preferred Stock

Although preferred stock is perceived by common stockholders as being like debt, it does not have the tax advantage of debt. Unlike debt interest payments, preferred dividends are not tax deductible to the firm. At today's 34 percent tax rate, $1 of interest expense costs the firm only $0.66 after tax, while $1 of preferred dividends costs $1 after tax. The cost of debt is thus less than the cost of preferred (recall the cost-of-capital discussion in Chapter 14). Because preferred is like debt in its fixed payment feature but lacks debt's tax deductibility, many firms consider preferred to be one of the worst kinds of financing available.

THE ISSUANCE OF NEW SECURITIES

Which Security Should Be Sold?

Existing firms needing long-term external financing from the sale of securities must first decide which capital market security to sell. The basic choice is between equity financing and debt financing. Although the equity category technically includes both common stock and preferred stock, it is generally necessary to sell common stock when equity financing is needed. Within the debt category is a very wide choice, ranging from secured bonds to subordinated unsecured bonds to bonds convertible into shares of common stock.

The choice of which security to sell at a particular time is contingent on a number of issues we have considered previously. One key issue is the firm's capital structure. If it is currently optimal, the firm may try to keep the revised structure close to the optimum by selling a combination of securities over a period of time. It would normally be too expensive to sell a combination of securities at any one time. Alternatively, the firm may decide to sell one type of security now and another the next time external financing is needed in order to maintain the optimal capital structure over the longer-term horizon.

A second important consideration is current market conditions. If interest rates are viewed by the firm as being unusually low or high, the firm may seek to use debt financing, or avoid it, because of the unusual conditions. Obviously, for

Type of Issue or Issuer, or Use	1987	1988	1989
1 All issues*	392,674	410,811	376,488
2 Bonds	326,166	353,010	318,617
Type of Offering			
3 Public, domestic	209,790	202,132	181,230
4 Private placement, domestic	92,070	127,700	114,629
5 Sold abroad	24,306	23,178	22,758
Industry Group			
6 Manufacturing	60,657	70,574	76,345
7 Commercial and miscellaneous	49,773	62,104	49,307
8 Transportation	11,974	10,075	10,050
9 Public utility	23,004	19,318	17,056
10 Communication	7,340	5,952	8,503
11 Real estate and financial	173,418	184,990	157,355
12 Stocks	66,508	57,802	57,870
Type			
13 Preferred	10,123	6,544	6,194
14 Common	43,225	35,911	26,030
15 Private placement	13,157	15,346	25,647
Industry Group			
16 Manufacturing	13,880	7,608	9,308
17 Commercial and miscellaneous	12,888	8,449	7,446
18 Transportation	2,439	1,535	1,929
19 Public utility	4,322	1,898	3,090
20 Communication	1,458	515	1,904
21 Real estate and financial	31,521	37,798	34,028

■ *Table 18–3*
New Security Issues,
U.S. Corporations
(Millions of Dollars)

*Figures that represent gross proceeds of issues maturing in more than one year are principal amount or number of units multiplied by offering price. Excludes secondary offerings, employee stock plans, investment companies other than closed-end, intracorporate transactions, equities sold abroad, and Yankee bonds. Stock data include ownership securities issued by limited partnerships.

Source: Adapted from *Federal Reserve Bulletin*, November 1990, p. A34.

either equities or debt, judging interest rates and prices to be high and low is, at least in part, a subjective judgment.

Other issues should also be considered. Examples include the effect of taxes, the risk to the firm of excessive levels of debt, agency costs, and the likely impact of the security's issuance on existing stockholders. Stock prices tend to react negatively to the announcement of new securities offerings, particularly common stock. According to Clifford W. Smith, the average abnormal (risk-adjusted) stock return for industrials in the two days surrounding the announcement of new security offerings is −3.14 percent for common stock, −0.19 percent for preferred stock, and −0.26 percent for straight bonds.[4]

Table 18–3 provides a perspective on the size of the new issues market in the United States in recent years. For 1989, the total amount raised from all issues was $376 billion. Of this total, some $319 billion was in the form of debt; the

---

[4]See Clifford W. Smith, Jr., "Investment Banking and the Capital Acquisition Process," *Journal of Financial Economics*, January/February 1986, p. 5.

remainder, $58 billion, was from stocks. Notice that the total of new issues for 1989 was less than that for 1988 because fewer bonds were sold. Also notice that new issues of preferred stock were a relatively small item.

HOW SECURITIES ARE SOLD THROUGH PUBLIC OFFERINGS

Having decided which security to sell, as well as when and in what amount, the firm must decide how it wants to sell the security. We will concentrate in this discussion only on public offerings.[5] The two primary types of public offerings are (1) the general cash offer made to all investors and typically involving the use of investment bankers and (2) a privileged subscription, or rights offering, made to the firm's current stockholders. We will consider each of these in turn.

General Cash Offers

general cash offers
public issues offered to any investors

initial public offering (IPO)
a firm's first equity issue to the general public

General cash offers involve the sale of securities to all interested investors; that is, they are public issues offered to any investor. A public issue, unless very small, must be registered with the SEC. An **initial public offering (IPO)** is the first public-equity issue made by a firm as it goes from private ownership to public ownership. These issues are referred to as *unseasoned new issues* because no previous publicly owned common stock existed.

Virtually all public offerings of debt are cash offers, whereas equity is sold by a combination of cash offers and rights offerings. Cash offers typically involve investment bankers.

Investment Bankers

investment bankers
financial specialists involved in the issuance of new securities and other corporate financial matters

Unlike investment decisions, which the firm makes continually, decisions about long-term external financing are made only periodically by most firms. When they do seek long-term capital, most firms turn to financing experts called **investment bankers,** who are specialists in being intermediaries between firms and investors. U.S. firms use investment bankers extensively when issuing new securities.

In bringing firms and investors together, the investment banker performs three functions: the advisory function, the underwriting function, and the market function. We discuss each of these in turn.

1. Advisory Function   Because investment bankers are experts in selling securities, an important part of their service to client firms is providing advice during the planning stage, before any securities are issued. This advice typically covers all aspects of the issue:

1. Which securities to sell (bonds, stocks, or various other possibilities).
2. The price of the new security.
3. The nonprice features (for example, on a bond issue, the maturity, coupon interest rate, provision for sinking fund, and so on).
4. The issuing date.

---

[5]Private placements are discussed in chapter 17.

Arrangements between investment bankers and issuing firms are of two types. Most firms can choose either procedure, but the negotiated offering is the most prevalent form.[6]

The *negotiated offering* is an arrangement in which the firm selects an investment banker or group of investment bankers at the beginning of the planning stage and negotiates and works with the banker to decide on all details of the planned issue. In such an arrangement, the investment banker provides advice and counsel.

The other type of arrangement is called *competitive bids*. The firm decides before approaching any investment bankers the kind of securities it will issue and other associated details, and then asks investment bankers to bid on the issue. The firm then takes the best offer. In competitive bids, the firm does not use the investment banker as an advisor.[7] Many regulated companies are required by law to secure competitive bids.

The theory behind requiring competitive bids is that they result in lower costs to the issuing firm. However, this advantage is offset by the fact that the firm loses the expert advice of the investment banker. A securities sale planned without the help of an investment banker may turn out to be relatively unattractive to investors, and what the firm saves on advisory expenses may be more than offset by losses because of lower net proceeds that result from a relatively unattractive securities issue. What matters ultimately is the net proceeds to the company, and these seem comparable between the two alternative methods. However, firms that are not required to seek competitive bids seem to prefer the negotiated arrangement.

2. Underwriting Function   Once the details of the issue have been worked out, the firm has two basic choices:

1. Sell the issue to investment bankers.
2. Have the issue sold on a best-efforts basis.

A firm generally sells the issue to the investment banker, who then resells the securities to investors. The sequential nature of this process means that the investment banker will own the securities until they can be resold. Many issues are sold out the very day they are first offered to the public, but some may take several weeks. If their price declines between the time the investment banker buys them and finishes reselling them, the investment banker can suffer a loss. Because the investment bankers are very competent at selling securities, most issues are successful. But errors in judgment—and losses—do occur, and some of these losses are large.

This process is known as *underwriting* the issue. Because the investment banker bears the risk of price declines of the securities while they are being issued, the underwriting function is an insurance function. Investment bankers, of course, attempt to protect themselves. They very carefully analyze any proposed securities issue. Basically, they are trying to predict what investor response will be at the time of issue. When issues fail to receive a good investor response, the reason is

---

[6]Some public utilities are required by law to use competitive bidding.
[7]Some companies will use an investment banking firm for advisory purposes and then preclude that firm from bidding on the issue.

■ *Figure 18–1*
The Investment
Banking Process

usually that either the firm or the capital market is unhealthy, although sometimes the type of security being issued is unattractive to investors. If the investment community is jittery about the future and unreceptive to new securities, investment bankers may hesitate to underwrite any but the very strongest companies' securities.[8] Frequently firms postpone new issues until market conditions become more favorable.

Investment bankers protect themselves by forming *syndicates,* that is, a group of investment bankers that handles a new issue of securities. This spreads the risk of failure over several investment bankers. Underwriting syndicates are, in fact, a good example of the advantages of diversification. One (sometimes more) of the investment banking firms oversees the underwriting syndicate and is called the underwriting manager. Figure 18–1 illustrates the investment banking process.

The alternative arrangement is for investment bankers to sell the issue on a *best-efforts* basis, whereby the investment bankers do not actually buy the new securities, but only agree to sell as many as they can at the agreed price. The risk

---

[8]Contracts between investment bankers and firms may contain *out clauses* that permit the cancellation of the banker's agreement to arrange the sale if market conditions turn bad. This protects the investment bankers from unexpected adverse market conditions.

of not selling all the securities is borne by the issuer, not by the investment bankers. No underwriting function is performed in such situations. Most frequently, best-efforts arrangements involve securities of small, riskier firms that the investment banking community would not otherwise agree to handle. Occasionally particularly strong firms will issue securities through a best-efforts offering if they are very confident the new issue will be well received by the market. This arrangement spares them the underwriting expense.

3. Marketing Function   Securities are usually sold through a *selling group* established by the investment banking syndicate expressly for the purpose of marketing the securities to investors. This group comprises the sales organization of the underwriters, as well as dealers who are specialists in marketing new issues. Sales achieved through the underwriters will receive a full commission, and large investment banking firms have well-developed sales organizations that are a regular part of the selling team. The dealers receive only a sales commission for their efforts. This commission is less than the underwriting commission because the dealers are not exposed to underwriting risk.

In a negotiated offering, the underwriting syndicate assembles the selling group even before the Securities and Exchange Commission has approved the sale. A preliminary *prospectus* outlining the features of the new issue is sent to investors. Because the issue has not yet been approved, no offering date or price is shown on the prospectus. In addition, a prominently displayed statement, printed in red ink, clearly indicates the prospectus is only an information circular and not an offer to sell securities to investors. The red-ink statement has led investors to call the prospectus a *red herring*.

Once the issue has been approved, the selling group begins marketing the securities. If the group has done its homework properly and the market and the new issue under consideration are healthy, the issue will be fully subscribed (completely sold) quickly. However, if something goes wrong, the issue could be very hard to sell.

The difference between what the investment bankers purchase an issue of securities for and what they offer these securities for to the public is referred to as the *spread*. In effect, it is the underwriter's compensation. The spread, in turn, is part of the flotation costs of issuing new securities, a topic we will consider next.

Flotation Costs

Flotation costs have two components:

1. Underwriter's spread.
2. Issue expenses.

The spread includes all compensation for investment banking services: advising, underwriting, and selling.

$$\text{Underwriter's spread} = \frac{\left(\begin{array}{c}\text{Gross sales} \\ \text{proceeds}\end{array} - \text{Net sales}\right)}{\begin{array}{c}\text{Gross sales} \\ \text{proceeds}\end{array}} \qquad \text{(18–1)}$$

■ *Example*

Eli Lilly and Company issued 950,000 shares of new common stock through an underwriting team managed by Morgan Stanley and Company. The underwriters paid Lilly $74,908,153 and sold the securities for $77,187,500.

$$\text{Underwriter's spread} = \frac{\$77,187,500 - \$74,908,153}{\$77,187,500}$$
$$= 0.02953 = 2.953\%$$ ■

The underwriting spread is the larger of the two components of flotation costs. Issue expenses include legal fees, printing costs, registration fees, and taxes.

For all three securities forms, the flotation cost decreases as size of issue increases. It is important to note that flotation cost is expressed as a percentage of gross proceeds, so it is *percentage cost* that decreases as size of issue increases. It would cost the firm more total dollars to market $50 million worth of securities than $30 million worth of securities, but the percentage cost would be reduced. This is partly because of the fixed component of flotation costs, which, when expressed as a percentage of gross proceeds, will naturally fall as issue size increases. A second reason is that larger firms tend to sell securities in larger blocks, and these companies are thought to be safer. Consequently, they are charged less by the investment bankers for underwriting and selling the issue.

Common stocks often have higher flotation costs than preferred stocks, which in turn have higher flotation costs than debt. This reflects the relative riskiness of the different security forms. From an investor's standpoint, debt is the safest security to own, and common stock the riskiest. This means the underwriter is exposed to the most risk in marketing common stocks and the least risk in marketing debt. The underwriter prices these relative risks to the firm in the form of relative flotation costs: highest for common, lowest for debt.

Other factors also influence flotation costs. If firms try to sell securities in periods of market uncertainty, they will face higher flotation costs because underwriter risk increases in such periods.

New Trends in Investment Banking

A significant development in recent years in the primary markets is the *shelf rule,* formally known as Securities and Commission Rule 415. Under this rule, large public companies are able to file a master registration statement with the SEC and then sell securities over a period of two years by filing a short-form statement immediately prior to each sale. During the two-year period, the firm can issue the securities registered at any time and in any amounts up to the total amount specified. The term **shelf registration** comes from the concept of the firm placing its securities, once registered, on the shelf and then selling them when it judges the conditions to be favorable. Many shelf registrations result in securities being privately placed.

shelf registration
SEC regulation allowing firms to register an issue of securities and sell them over time as conditions warrant

The advantages of shelf registration are the reduction in issue expenses that arise from multiple separate sales and a reduction in the time required to issue securities (once the shelf regulation is in place, a sale can occur within a few days). Furthermore, the firm can more readily take advantage of favorable market conditions, which are subject to frequent and large changes.

Another important development is the *unsyndicated stock offering,* which uses the underwriting process without the selling syndicate. The entire securities issue

- - -

FINANCIAL MANAGEMENT INSIGHTS

The Joys of Investment Banking[9]

Burlington Industries, at the time the largest domestic textile company, was taken over in 1987 by Morgan Stanley & Company, a large investment banker. In the 1980s, several such banking firms purchased industrial companies. Morgan had to put up less than $50 million of the total purchase price of $2.2 billion. Junk bonds and bank loans provided more than 90 percent of the total financing in this leveraged buyout! In effect, Morgan got the stock of Burlington, and Burlington got the debt—a lot of debt on which interest had to be paid.

Within a few weeks of taking over Burlington, Morgan collected $87 million in fees, including a $29 million fee for advising Burlington on how to be taken over by Morgan Stanley. Thus, in a short time Morgan had recovered far more than what it had put up in cash to purchase Burlington.

In 1988, Morgan collected another $22 million in advisory fees for advising Burlington on divestitures. In 1989, Morgan collected several million in underwriting fees for a junk bond issue. It also collected a fee of $2.5 million from Burlington for advising the company on a recapitalization. As part of the recapitalization, Burlington was forced to pay a dividend of $175 million, a large part of which ($56 million) went to Morgan. Finally, Morgan collected another $1 million fee in 1990 for retiring junk bonds.

As for Burlington, it shrank in size because of the divestitures and seemed to be performing better by 1989. Although it had an operating profit of over $200 million, it suffered a loss because of its interest costs. By 1990, however, the company had a record loss and its situation deteriorated as the economy weakened. As for Morgan, it sold all of its shares back to Burlington in late 1990. Burlington paid for its purchase with some nonvoting stock plus a new preferred stock whose yield was payable in more preferred stock.

[9]See George Anders, "Morgan Stanley Found a Gold Mine of Fees by Buying Burlington," *The Wall Street Journal*, December 14, 1990, pp. A1, A10. Reprinted by permission of *The Wall Street Journal*, © 1990 Dow Jones & Company, Inc. All rights reserved worldwide.

is sold directly to institutional investors. The underwriting fee is smaller for the issuer. The use of unsyndicated stock offerings increased significantly during the mid-1980s.

Privileged Subscriptions

Instead of selling new securities to the general public, the firm may offer them to its current stockholders with a right-of-first-refusal. The majority of these involve new common stock.[10] Many corporations have discretion over whether a new stock issue will be sold to the general public or to existing common stockholders, but in most companies the common stockholders legally have the right of first refusal (called the *preemptive right*) to buy any newly issued common stock. New common issues offered first to existing shareholders are called *privileged subscriptions* or *preemptive right issues*.

Firms rely less heavily on investment bankers when issuing new securities via a rights offering. When firms do use investment bankers to underwrite the issue,

[10]To a lesser extent, new securities that are convertible into common (such as convertible preferred stock and convertible bonds and warrants, all discussed in Chapter 20) are sometimes offered to current common owners on a privileged basis.

it is usually on a standby basis, where the underwriting syndicate agrees to buy all unsold shares at a stipulated price.

Setting the Subscription Price

One of the decisions management must make in a rights issue is what the subscription price should be. The subscription price should be set below the current market price of the common; otherwise, if market prices should dip, investors would prefer to buy the less expensive old stock on the secondary market rather than new stock via the rights issue. The new stock would never be sold, and the firm would have failed to raise new capital. So the subscription price is always set below the current stock price. How much below? If the subscription price is too close to the current stock price, even a small drop in stock price could cause the issue to fail.

The safe course of action is to set the subscription price well below current stock price. Some find this a questionable practice because a low subscription price means that more new shares must be sold to raise the required capital. This high number of new shares dilutes the firm's earnings per share. But the more important goal is to ensure that the rights issue is fully subscribed, and sales of this new stock are heavily influenced by the size of the spread between market price and subscription price: the lower the subscription price, the greater is the probability that all rights will be exercised.

Effect of Rights Issue on Stockholder Wealth

Remember that the firm's goal is stockholder wealth maximization. Since a rights issue causes stock price to decline on the ex rights date—the date after which rights are not attached to the stock—it may seem at first that the issue has a detrimental effect on stockholder wealth. Actually, stockholders should not be harmed unless they are negligent and let the rights expire. A stockholder has three options with regards to rights: (1) exercise them and buy new stock, (2) sell them, or (3) do nothing and let them expire. Only in the last case will the stockholder be harmed.

Advantages and Disadvantages of Rights Issues   There are two primary advantages to issuing common stock through a rights issue:

1. The stockholders' control position is protected, as they can maintain their proportionate ownership if they wish. This has most meaning in firms where there is a struggle for control. In such times the rights privilege protects proportionate ownership positions.
2. A second advantage to selling stock through a rights issue is the lower flotation cost (relative to a straight public issue) because there is usually no underwriting fee.[11]

The primary disadvantage of a rights issue is that it creates losses to forgetful stockholders. Some firms overcome this disadvantage by selling the rights of these

---

[11]Many rights issues do have standby underwriting arrangements, in which investment bankers pledge to buy all unsubscribed shares. The less sure management is that most of the rights will be exercised, the more likely is such an arrangement which increases flotation costs because of underwriting fees.

negligent shareholders at the end of the sale period and remitting the proceeds to them.

SUMMARY

- Common stock is an equity ownership instrument providing the owners with a residual position with regard to both income and asset claims.
- The primary control prerogatives of common owners are their right to elect the board of directors and their right to maintain proportionate ownership.
- The main advantages of issuing new common are cash flow flexibility and the enhancement of future borrowing capacity. The major disadvantage of common stock financing is its higher cost of capital.
- Preferred stock has a priority status over common with respect to claims on both income and assets and is therefore a safer security.
- While preferred has no maturity date, the firm can provide for retirement of preferred stock in future years (a) by issuing the stock as convertible preferred, (b) by calling the stock at its call price, or (c) by creating a sinking fund arrangement.
- The advantages of preferred stock are that it offers leverage with no default risk, it provides cash flow flexibility, it does not dilute stockholder control, and it affords tax advantages in business-combination activities.
- The disadvantages are that common stockholders view preferred as being equivalent to debt, but preferred dividends, unlike interest charges, are not tax deductible. Preferred looks like debt but costs more.
- New securities may be issued by a public sale through an investment banker or via a preemptive rights issue.
- Firms rely heavily on investment bankers to market new securities. Investment bankers provide advice and counsel, underwrite securities issues, and distribute (sell to the public) the new securities.
- The fee they receive for these services is the spread between what they pay for the securities and what they sell them for.
- In lieu of marketing new securities to the general public, the firm may sell them to current securities holders. The most common form of such a sale is the privileged subscription or preemptive rights issue.
- Flotation costs are composed of the underwriter's spread and issue expenses, and are higher (on a percentage basis) for small issues than for large ones. Also, flotation costs are highest for common stock and lowest for debt.

KEY TERMS

general cash offers, p. 550
initial public offering (IPO), p. 550
investment bankers, p. 550

proxy, p. 542
shelf registration, p. 554

QUESTIONS

18–1. Explain the claim prerogatives of common stockholders.

18–2. Explain the control prerogatives of common stockholders.

18–3. Many states have laws that require all companies incorporated therein to have preemptive rights in their charter. You have been asked to testify as an expert witness at a state congressional hearing about the advantages of maintaining such a provision. Briefly explain what the major advantages are.

18–4. At the annual stockholders meeting, an irate investor complains that the recent sale of stock via a rights issue depressed the company's stock price. He asks the treasurer to explain why the subscription price was set so low. How would you answer him?

18–5. A firm incorporated in a state where there is no requirement to use preemptive rights is preparing to issue new common. Management is considering the good and bad features of a rights offering, as opposed to a public offering of stock. How would the following circumstances influence the firm's choice? Explain your answer.

a. Two opposing groups of shareholders, who have entirely different views of how the firm should be managed, each own substantial amounts of stock. Either group would probably sue management if it thought that there were an inequitable distribution of shares.

b. It would be advantageous to broaden the ownership of the stock by having more investors owning shares.

c. The president of the firm would insist on a relatively high subscription price if a rights issue were employed.

18–6. A dissident minority stockholder group is meeting to discuss its chances for placing a candidate on the firm's board of directors at the upcoming election. The firm's charter requires a cumulative voting procedure, but a quick calculation indicates the dissident group does not own a large enough percentage of the total shares outstanding to assure a successful election. Several members of the group point out, however, that they may still be in good shape.

a. What voting phenomenon are they counting on in making this assessment?

b. If the group is unwilling to be content with its chances of winning despite the phenomenon noted in (a), what action could it take to absolutely assure success?

18–7. Preferred stock is frequently called a *hybrid security*. Explain what this means.

18–8. Many view preferred stock as an inferior financing alternative to debt.

a. Explain their reasons for this conclusion.

b. Discuss rebuttals to their position.

18–9. Nine months ago Zeigler Products missed its regularly scheduled $2-per-share preferred quarterly dividend payment because of severe cash flow problems. Three months later Zeigler missed another payment. Three months ago Zeigler was able to pay the regularly scheduled preferred dividend but was still in arrears two quarterly payments. Today, Zeigler not only paid its scheduled $2-per-share preferred quarterly dividend but made up the arrearage by paying an additional $4 per share to preferred stockholders.

In announcing the extra payment, Zeigler's president noted that its preferred stockholders have been "made whole again. Their loss is completely recouped." As a Zeigler preferred stockholder, do you agree with this statement? Explain your answer.

18–10. Summarize the advantages and disadvantages of preferred stock financing.

18–11. Preferred has no fixed maturity date and yet it often disappears from a firm's balance sheet. How can this occur?

18–12. What is meant by the *contingent* voting rights of preferred stock?

18–13. With regard to the issuance of new securities:

a. Indicate the methods by which new securities can be issued.

b. What is the difference between a general cash offer and a privileged subscription?

c. Briefly explain the underwriting function of the investment banker.

d. Occasionally a legislator will criticize the common practice of forming underwriting syndicates and selling groups to handle new securities issues.

If you were a securities industry representative, what economic justifications would you cite to defend these practices?

18–14. For years many public utilities have been required to issue new securities through competitive bid arrangements. Recently, however, it has been proposed that utilities be permitted to issue new securities through a negotiated offering. Given that the regulatory agencies are concerned with holding down flotation costs when the utilities issue new securities, why do you suppose this proposal was made?

18–15. Many planned issues of new securities are canceled or postponed before the sale actually takes place. Sometimes this withdrawal occurs at the last minute, even though considerable effort and expense have already been incurred. List some factors that could cause withdrawal of new securities issues.

18–16. Whenever possible, many firms prefer to place new securities, particularly debt, with private lenders rather than engaging in a public sale. What advantages and disadvantages do private placements offer in comparison to public sales?

18–17. Ball Company is preparing to issue some new long-term bonds. Two investment banking companies, X and Y, have been in contact with Ball about handling the issue. The underwriter's spread is 2.6 percent for X and 2.4 percent for Y. Regardless of which underwriter is chosen, Ball expects the issue to be fully subscribed. Suppose Ball chooses X and justifies that choice by arguing that it's economically more attractive. Comment on whether that justification is possible or not.

18–18. What is the *shelf rule?* What impact has it had on investment banking?

18–19. What is meant by the term *privileged subscription?*

18–20. How is the subscription price set in a privileged subscription?

18–21. What is the difference between a competitive offering and a negotiated offering?

18–22. When would an investment banker opt for a *standby arrangement?*

PROBLEMS

18–1. Vetter Batteries issued some $100-par preferred stock five years ago. The stock has a call price of $104 per share. Vetter is now interested in retiring the stock. Indicate whether the company should attempt to buy back the stock in the open market or exercise the call feature if the current market price of the preferred is the following:
   a. $110.
   b. $102.
   c. $104.
   d. $85.

18–2. Determine the underwriter's spread in each of the following situations:
   a. Gross sales proceeds are $40 million. Net sales proceeds are $39 million.
   b. Common stock is sold to investors at $10 per share. The firm nets $8.50 per share.
   c. Common stock is sold to investors at $20 per share. The underwriter takes $2.50 per share.
   d. Two million shares of common are sold. Net sales proceeds are $25 million. Sale price to investors is $15 per share.

18–3. Gupta Dental Supply is preparing to issue new bonds through its investment banker. Gupta needs to net $40 million from the sale to finance its investment plans.

a. Determine how much total debt (in dollars) Gupta must issue if the underwriter's spread is 2.60 percent and issue expenses are $100,000. (Round *up* the answer to the nearest $10,000.)

b. How many $1,000 bonds will be issued if the bonds are priced as follows (1) $1,100 each, (2) $900 each, (3) $1,000 each.

18–4. Brandi Automotive Parts is preparing to issue some new stock. The firm's investment banker proposes two alternatives to Brandi:

> Plan I: The investment banker will guarantee the sale of 500,000 shares at a price of $3 per share below the market price of Brandi's present stock on the last day of registration.

> Plan II: The investment banker will sell stock on a best-efforts basis for a fixed fee of $300,000. The sale price will be fixed at a price of $2 per share below the prevailing Brandi stock price on the last day of registration. Brandi assumes that 90 percent of the shares would be sold, with probabilities of 50 percent each that the price will be $29 or $33 on the last day.

a. Find the expected stock price on the last day of registration.
b. For each plan determine:
   (1) The expected net proceeds to Brandi.
   (2) The expected percentage underwriting spread.
   (3) The maximum net proceeds to Brandi.
c. Which plan is better if the firm wants to minimize its expected percentage underwriting spread?
d. Which plan is better if the firm wants to maximize the probability of raising at least $14 million?

18–5. Branch Labs, Inc., has common stock selling for $20 per share. The company currently has 5 million shares outstanding and plans to issue 4 million new shares through a rights issue.
a. How many rights must be presented to buy one share of stock during the rights issue?
b. What is the cost of a new share if the subscription price is set at $18 per share?

18–6. Zivney Company plans to sell 2 million new shares of common stock through a rights offering. The subscription price will be $16 per share. Zivney has 6 million shares of common stock prior to the offering. If the price of stock is $20 per share, rights on, find:
a. The ex rights price of the stock.
b. The value of a right.

18–7. Taylor and Flint, Inc., is issuing $10 million of the new common through a rights issue. The cost of a new share is $10 plus five rights. How many total shares of common will be outstanding after the rights issue?

18–8. Nelson Copper and Zinc (NLCZ) is preparing to raise $30 million through a rights issue. The firm needs the funds to finance new mineral deposit purchases. After public announcement of the deposit purchases, NLCZ's stock price bounced around some, but has now steadied at about $35 per share. There are 10 million shares outstanding. NLCZ's financial staff is currently attempting to set the subscription price on the new stock. Two plans have been proposed. Plan A's subscription price is $30; plan B's price is $15.
a. Assuming that both plans would be successful (in that all new shares were sold), determine the number of new shares issued under each plan.
b. How many rights will be issued under each plan? And how many rights will be required to purchase a new share of stock?
c. What should be the ex rights price of the stock in each plan?
d. What should be the value of a right in each plan?

e. Which plan is preferable from the standpoint of maximizing stockholder wealth? Why?

f. Which plan is preferable with an eye to ensuring that the issue will be fully subscribed? Why?

g. Which plan would you recommend to NLCZ? Why?

SELECTED REFERENCES

Issuing costs in public offerings are examined in:

Bhagat, Sanjai, and Peter A. Forts. "Issuing Cost to Existing Shareholders in Competitive and Negotiated Underwritten Public Utility Equity Offerings." *Journal of Financial Economics,* January–February 1986, pp. 233–59.

The decision to issue additional common stock is discussed in:

Bhagat, Sanjai; James A. Brickley; and Ronald C. Lease. "The Authorization of Additional Common Stock: An Empirical Investigation." *Financial Management,* Autumn 1986, pp. 45–53.

Booth, James R., and Richard L. Smith II. "Capital Raising, Underwriting and the Certification Hypothesis." *Journal of Financial Economics,* January–February 1986, pp. 261–81.

An interesting discussion of common stock voting rights can be found in:

Levy, Haim. "Economic Valuation of Voting Power of Common Stock." *Journal of Finance,* March 1983, pp. 79–93.

Marsh, P. "The Choice between Equity and Debt: An Empirical Study." *Journal of Finance,* March 1982, pp. 121–44.

The underpricing of new issues is discussed in:

Rock, Kevin. "Why New Issues Are Underpriced." *Journal of Financial Economics,* January–February 1986, pp. 187–212.

Investment banking and its role in external financing is discussed in:

Smith, Clifford W. "Investment Banking and the Capital Acquisition Process." *Journal of Financial Economics,* January–February 1986, pp. 3–29.

APPENDIX 18–A   A RIGHTS OFFERING

One of the key features in a rights offering is that each share of current stock receives one right. If 4 million shares of Andar Corporation common are outstanding and if the company has a rights offering, 4 million rights will be issued. A stockholder who owns 40,000 shares of Andar common will receive 40,000 rights.

The *subscription price* is the price at which the new stock is sold. It is set below the current market price to ensure that the new shares will be sold. If the stock's market price ever fell below the subscription price, investors would buy stock on the secondary market rather than buy the new stock. The subscription price determines how many shares of new common will be issued.

■ *Example*

The Andar Corporation has 4 million shares of common outstanding, with a market price of $60 per share. It needs to raise $20 million for investment purposes and has decided to sell new common through a rights issue. Andar's management has set the subscription price at $40 per share. We can readily determine several things.

$$\text{Number of new shares issued} = \frac{\text{New funds raised}}{\text{Subscription price}} \qquad \text{(18A–1)}$$
$$= \frac{\$20,000,000}{\$40 \text{ per share}}$$
$$= 500,000 \text{ shares}$$

Andar is raising $20 million by selling stock at $40 per share. This requires the firm to issue 500,000 new shares. After the rights issue is closed, there will be 4,500,000 shares outstanding.

How will the rights to buy the 500,000 shares of new stock be distributed among the holders of the 4 million shares of existing stock?

$$\text{Number of rights per new share} = \frac{\text{Number of rights issued}}{\text{Number of new shares}} \qquad \text{(18A–2)}$$
$$= \frac{4,000,000 \text{ rights}}{500,000 \text{ shares}}$$
$$= 8 \text{ rights per new share}$$

Since 4 million rights are issued, and a half million new shares will be sold, it will take eight rights to claim a new share of stock. Recall the investor who owns 40,000 shares of Andar stock, which is 1 percent of the company's original 4 million shares. That investor will receive 40,000 rights. These rights entitle the investor to buy 5,000 (40,000/8) shares of new stock, which is 1 percent of the 500,000 new shares.

$$\text{Cost of a new share} = \frac{\text{Subscription}}{\text{price}} + \frac{\text{Number of rights}}{\text{per new share}} \qquad \text{(18A–3)}$$
$$= \$40 + 8 \text{ rights}$$

The total cost of a new share of stock is the subscription price plus the number of rights per new share required. A stockholder who wishes to exercise the rights will remit this total cost to the firm. In the Andar case, this is $40 plus eight rights per new share. In the example, the investor who owns 40,000 shares of Andar has the opportunity to buy 5,000 new shares at $40 per share. To exercise all these rights, the investor must remit $200,000 plus 40,000 rights to Andar.

Table 18A–1 illustrates what happens to an investor who owns eight shares of Andar stock, worth $480 before the rights issue. That owner receives eight rights, just enough to buy one new share. If the investor exercises the rights, the value of the original wealth remains at $480, although the total investment in Andar has now increased to $520. Selling the rights likewise protects the value of the original wealth, but the investor has decreased investment in Andar to $462.24. Only the investor who does nothing has lost money, and the expected loss would be the value of the rights, $17.76. In almost every rights issue some stockholders, because of negligence, neither exercise nor sell their rights.

Alternative 1

Exercise the Rights: Tender Eight Rights + $40 for One New Share

Owns nine shares at $57.78 per share*	=	$520.00
Less $40 investment cost	=	−40.00
Current value of original wealth	=	$480.00

Alternative 2

Sell the Rights

Sell eight rights at $2.22 per right**	=	$ 17.76
Owns eight shares at $57.78 per share	=	462.24
Current value of original wealth	=	$480.00

Alternative 3

Do Nothing

Owns eight shares at $57.78 per share	=	$462.24
Current value of original wealth	=	$462.24

Assumptions

An Investor Has Eight Shares of Andar Stock
    Original wealth of the investor = eight shares at $60
    per share = $480.

*The new price of $57.78 is a weighted average of eight shares at $60 and one share at $40.00.

**The rights price of $2.22 is one eighth of the difference between $57.78 and $40.00.

19

Bonds and Convertible Securities

The Limits of Debt Financing?

In one of the most dramatic takeover battles in U.S. corporate history, Kohlberg Kravis Roberts & Company (KKR), a major investment banking firm, emerged as the winning bidder for RJR Nabisco, Inc. The leveraged buyout, in which companies are purchased primarily with debt securities, carried a price tag of some $25 billion. KKR put up only $1.5 billion in equity to fund its purchase. The major portion of its financing plan consisted of $14 billion in new bank debt, $4 billion in existing RJR debt, $5 billion in new junk bonds (high-yield, low-quality bonds, explained later in the chapter), and $6.0 billion in new convertible bonds and preferred stock.[1]

The total of $15 billion, in new and existing bonds and high-yield preferred stock, amounted to a significant percentage of the total $175 billion worth of junk bonds in existence, three times as much as any other company had outstanding in the junk bond market. The $5 billion worth of junk bonds includes $3 billion in interest-paying bonds and another $2 billion in zero coupon bonds, which pay no coupon but are sold at a discount from face value. The $4 billion worth of preferred stock (like the convertible bonds, these were noncash-paying securities; they pay dividends initially in more preferred stock) was much larger than the entire existing market for such payment-in-kind preferred stock.

KKR's winning bid was $109 per share for the 227 million RJR shares. However, payment was to consist of $81 in cash, $18 in preferred stock, and $10 in converting debentures. Overall, three of the new securities being used required no cash outlays for interest or dividend payments: the zero coupon bonds, the preferred stock, and the convertible bonds.

---

[1]See Randall Smith and John Helyar, "KKR Gets to Work Lining Up Money for RJR Nabisco," *The Wall Street Journal*, December 5, 1988, pp. A3 and A5, and *The Value Line Investment Survey*, various issues.

Bonds, a form of debt representing a creditor claim on the issuer, are a standard long-term source of capital. As the financing plans for RJR show, bonds have played a prominent role in many large corporate takeovers. As we learned from Table 18–3, bonds are the major source of long-term external financing for corporations, constituting by far the largest portion of all new issues each year. Finally, we saw, in Chapter 14, that debt is the cheapest source of financing for corporations, but we also learned, in Chapter 15, that it is the riskiest source of financing and that a firm's capital structure plays a prominent role in the valuation of the firm.

The two primary types of equity-derivative instruments are convertible securities and warrants; they entitle investors to acquire common stock at some future time. These securities are unique because of their claim on the underlying common stock. They are referred to as *contingent-claim* forms of financing. Because most convertibles are bonds, we will study convertibles, with primary emphasis on convertible bonds, following our discussion of bonds in general. Warrants are often attached to bond issues, and understanding convertibles aids in understanding warrants. Warrants are analyzed in Appendix 19–B.

Primary *chapter learning objectives* are:

1. To understand the mechanics of bonds as a source of financing for firms.
2. To analyze convertible bonds, a special form of bond financing.

BONDS

bonds
long-term, fixed-income, creditor financial instruments

Bonds are long-term, fixed-income, creditor financial instruments. They are, in effect, legal claims on the firm. The firm promises to pay bond principal and interest on specified dates in the future.

Bondholders have a prior claim on the firm's assets relative to owners of preferred and common stock. More important, however, from the firm's standpoint, bondholders' claims must be satisfied when due or the firm can be declared in default, which can lead to bankruptcy. The bond's priority status depends on its classification, which we will discuss below. Some bonds look to the assets pledged to them, although most bonds are secured only by the viability of the firm itself. We will consider these major differences in the claims that bonds have on the issuing firm at the outset of our discussion by using the bond's priority status to categorize the types of long-term debt.

As we saw in Chapters 17 and 18, there are two methods of issuing securities, private issues and public issues, and these conditions apply likewise to bonds. Private issues are placed directly with a lending institution—therefore, they are *private placements*. According to Table 18–3, a significant percentage of all new bond issues are private placements. Public issues are sold to investors in the capital markets, often with the aid of investment bankers. The investment banking process explained in Chapter 18 applies to bonds as well as stocks.

■ *Example*

As an example of a public issue, consider the hypothetical sale of new bonds by Centrex Telephone Company of North Carolina, as reported in the daily financial press (see Figure 19–1). Malmon Brothers handled this new issue, which carries an 8.15 percent coupon and matures in 2021. This 30-year maturity is about the

Typical Announcement of a New Bond Issue in the Financial Press   ■ *Figure 19–1*

This announcement is neither an offer to sell nor a solicitation of an offer to buy these securities.
The offer is made only by the Prospectus and the related Prospectus Supplement

July 12, 1991

$150,000,000

Centrex Telephone Company of North Carolina

Thirty Year 8.15% Debentures, due July 15, 2021

Price 100%

Copies of the Prospectus and the related Prospectus Supplement may be obtained in any State
in which this announcement is circulated where the undersigned
may legally offer these securities in such State.

Malmon Brothers

maximum length of a bond issue, although some bonds have maturities of as much as 40 years. The 8.15 percent rate reflects what investors were demanding at that time for a bond with the degree of riskiness and maturity date of Centrex Telephone and having this bond's particular characteristics. ▪

Types of Long-Term Debt

There are many kinds of bonds and alternative ways to classify them. One useful classification scheme uses a bond's security feature. Bonds are either secured or unsecured.

Secured Bonds

A *secured bond* has specific assets pledged as collateral. Should the firm default on scheduled payments, an appointed trustee can seize the collateral on behalf of the bondholders. Secured debt includes mortgage bonds, equipment trust certificates, and collateral trust bonds:

mortgage bonds
bonds secured by
mortgages on the firm's
fixed assets

- *Mortgage bonds.* While any assets may be pledged as collateral, long-term lenders prefer fixed assets. **Mortgage bonds** are (most commonly) bonds with mortgages on the firm's fixed assets. The firm may support two bond issues with the same property. If one issue has a favored position, it is called the *first-mortgage* bonds, and the less favored bonds are *second-mortgage* bonds. First-mortgage bonds have priority should default occur, and second-mortgage holders cannot receive payment until all first-mortgage claims are satisfied.

  - *Example*

    A $75,000,000 issue of mortgage bonds by Utilicorp United Inc., referred to as a *Series 1,* were issued in 1988. These bonds were scheduled to mature in 1998 and carried a coupon rate of 9⅞ percent.[2] ▪

- *Equipment trust certificates.* Equipment trusts are not actually bonds, but loans secured by equipment. The firm orders equipment from a manufacturer and sells equipment trust certificates to investors to pay for the equipment. A trustee is established who, on behalf of the investors, holds title to the equipment that secures the certificates. The firm makes periodic lease payments to the investors through the trustee. When the certificates mature, they are redeemed by the firm, and the trustee passes title to the equipment to the firm. Should the firm fail to meet its lease payment obligations, the trustee can seize the equipment on behalf of the investors. Equipment trust certificates have been used extensively in financing the purchase of buses, trucks, railroad cars, and aircraft.

- *Collateral trust bonds.* Many firms own stocks and bonds of other corporations, including their own subsidiaries. These may be used to secure bonds of the issuing firm and are called collateral trust bonds, whose quality depends on the quality of the pledged stocks and bonds.

---

[2] *The Wall Street Journal,* October 28, 1988, p. C18.

Unsecured Bonds

Unsecured bonds have no specific assets pledged as collateral, and holders of these bonds are general creditors. If the firm should default, unsecured bondholders would look to those assets of the firm that are not pledged elsewhere to satisfy their claims. Unsecured debt includes debentures, subordinated debentures, and income bonds:

- *Debentures.* Unsecured long-term bonds are called **debentures.**[3] The firm's earning power mainly determines the attractiveness of its bonds because few investors would buy bonds with a high probability of default. Consequently, many debentures enjoy high investment ratings and compare favorably with secured bonds. From the firm's standpoint, an advantage of issuing debentures is that no specific assets are pledged as security. Since other general creditors will not have the priority of their claim status on the firm's assets impaired, they may be more willing to extend credit.

debentures
unsecured long-term bonds

- *Example*

As Figure 19–1 indicates, the Centrex Telephone bonds are debentures. They are debentures because no specific real assets are being used as collateral and the issue is not called *mortgage bonds* or *equipment trust certificates*. ▪

- *Subordinated debentures.* These debentures are inferior to some specified senior debt, including bank loans, and in some cases are subordinate to all other debt of the firm. In the event of failure, the subordinated debenture holders' claims will not be honored until the specified senior debt claims have been completely satisfied. Some subordinated debentures may be junior to other subordinated debentures.

- *Example*

In November 1988, financial sources carried an announcement of new debt financing totalling $1,082,887,000 by Federated Department Stores, Inc., divided into two parts. $500,000,000 of this total consisted of 16 percent senior subordinated debentures, due in the year 2000, and $582,887,000 consisted of $17\frac{3}{4}$ percent subordinated discount debentures, due in the year 2004.[4] Thus, the latter subordinates were junior to the senior subordinates. ▪

Subordinated debentures are risky relative to other kinds of bonds, and only companies with substantial earning power could hope to persuade investors to buy them. The main advantage of issuing this type of debt is that it preserves the firm's borrowing capacity with respect to other lenders.

Virtually all publicly issued industrial and finance company bonds are debentures. Thus, whenever we refer to a typical bond for a

---

[3]The word *note* is typically used for bond issues with maturities of 10 years or less.
[4]*The Wall Street Journal,* November 7, 1988, p. C20.

• • •

FINANCIAL MANAGEMENT INSIGHTS

The Use of Long–Term Debt by Major Corporations

IBM is one of the largest and most financially successful corporations in the history of American business. Its financial integrity is unquestioned, and it has access to a wide variety of funds when raising capital. How does long-term debt fit into IBM's financing activities?

In 1988, IBM had revenues of $60 billion and total assets of $73 billion. Long-term debt in that year amounted to approximately $8.5 billion, an increase in the company's worldwide long-term debt of some $1.4 billion over the previous year. This increase included a U.S. public debt offering of $500,000,000 and several non-U.S. borrowings directly related to the financing of customers' long-term leases in its non-U.S. operations.

An examination of IBM's financial statements for 1988 indicates that the company identified 21 different sources of long-term debt denominated

in U.S. dollars. Nineteen of these issues were shown with the coupon and specified maturity date. The coupons ranged from 6¾ percent to 12¼ percent, and the maturity dates ranged from 1988 to the year 2004. The different forms of debt included notes, extendable notes, debentures, and convertible subordinated debentures. Annual maturity and sinking fund requirements were stated to total over $1 billion for the next five years, and over $3 billion thereafter.

In addition to the U.S. debt, IBM listed other long-term debt payable in French francs, Australian dollars, Japanese yen, Canadian dollars, Swiss francs, and other currencies. Maturities on this debt ranged from the following year all the way out to the year 2018, and interest rates on the debt ranged from 4.875 percent to 13.4 percent.

manufacturing or finance company, we are talking about a debenture. On the other hand, most railroad bonds, as well as many utility bonds, are bonds secured by the real assets of the issuing company.

■ *Income bonds.* The other bonds we have discussed have mandatory interest schedules, but *income bonds* yield interest only when the firm has sufficient earnings to pay it. Although the firm could be forced into bankruptcy by failure to pay a scheduled interest payment on the normal kind of bond, interest payments can be skipped with income bonds. These bonds are somewhat rare and are typically issued to creditors when a firm is reorganized under bankruptcy proceedings. The firm is trying to get back on its feet, and income bonds permit some breathing room.[5]

Important Bond Features

Investors must consider a number of features of any bond issue, such as its coupon, maturity, collateral, retirement provisions, and so on. Table 19–1 summarizes the important features of a typical bond. These will be explained below, following a discussion of the agreement governing a bond issue.

Indenture Agreement

The *indenture agreement,* known as the *trust* or *bond indenture,* is a lengthy contract that establishes the terms of the loan and specifies relationships among (1) the

---

[5]There is usually a *cumulative clause* that permits holders of these bonds to recover omitted interest payments.

■ *Table 19–1*
Important Features
of a Bond

Feature	Explanation
Amount of issue	Total dollar amount of a particular bond issued
Face value	Principal amount of bond, typically $1,000
Coupon	Annual dollar amount of interest paid, equal to the product of the coupon rate and the face value
Maturity date	Date at which bonds will mature and be paid off if still outstanding
Security	Either secured (e.g., mortgage bonds) or, more typically, unsecured (debentures)
Rating	Relative probability of default as determined by rating agency
Call provision	Allows issuer to call in the bonds and pay them off
Sinking fund	Provides for the systematic retirement of the bond issue
Convertibility	The bond may be convertible, at the holder's option, into a stated number of shares of common stock

borrowing firm, (2) bondholders, and (3) the indenture trustee. The trustee is a disinterested third party, usually a trust company or bank, appointed to represent the interests of the bondholders. Because ownership of publicly held bonds of large corporations is diffuse, the trustee can efficiently perform certain necessary functions. The major duties of the trustee are these:

- To ensure that all legal requirements related to the bond issue have been satisfied by the issuing firm.
- To ensure that the firm meets all scheduled interest and principal payments and all other agreements in the trust indenture.
- To take appropriate action to protect the interests of the bondholders if the firm fails to comply with the trust indenture articles.

In effect, the trustee acts as legal representative, watchdog, and conservator for the bondholders.

Most of the important bond features we need to consider are spelled out in the indenture agreement.

Protective Covenants   Statements contained in the indenture agreement limiting the actions of a firm during the term to maturity of the bond issue are called **protective covenants.** Negative covenants prohibit, or limit, certain actions the company might undertake, such as paying out too much in dividends, merging with another firm, or selling off its assets. Positive covenants specify certain actions that the company agrees to undertake, such as furnishing financial statements on a timely basis to the lender.

Most bond indenture agreements include protective covenants. The obvious reasons are to protect the bondholder and to enhance the value of the bonds. The most common provision on publicly issued debt is restrictions on the issuance of additional debt.

protective covenants
indenture agreement statements limiting a firm's actions during the life of a bond issue

Principal

The face amount of each bond, as stated on the bond certificate, is the **principal** of the bond. The total principal value of a particular bond issue is the product of

principal
face amount of a bond, typically $1,000

the face amount and the number of bonds issued. The face value of most bonds is $1,000, and the par value (or initial accounting value) of most bonds is also $1,000.

Bonds are priced as a percentage of face value.

■ *Example*

A price of 100 indicates a market price of $1,000, while a price of 89 indicates a price of $890, or 89 percent of face value. ■

As we know from Chapter 6, the actions of buyers and sellers in the market determine the actual market prices of assets traded in the market. Because bond prices depend heavily on the general level of interest rates, the market price for bonds that are outstanding will typically differ from the face value of $1,000. However, new bonds are typically sold at prices close to 100 percent, or $1,000 per bond.[6]

Coupon

coupon
annual dollar interest
payment on a bond

The dollar **coupon** on a bond issue is always known at the time the bond is issued. The *coupon rate* is normally fixed and equals market interest rates (going rates) on comparable bonds at the time the bond is issued. The dollar coupon is simply the coupon rate multiplied by the face value of the bond, which as we know is $1,000 for the typical bond (we will always use $1,000 as the face value of a bond). Bond interest is paid semiannually.

■ *Example*

The Centrex Telephone Company bonds carry a coupon of 8.15 percent. This is equivalent to $81.50 per year because the face value or par value of the bonds is $1,000. Interest is actually paid semiannually on bonds, so the coupon payments for Centrex Telephone would be $40.75 every six months. ■

There are important exceptions to the fixed coupon on most bond issues. Through the 1970s, coupon rates on bonds were almost always fixed rates. That is, the coupon rate was established at the time the bonds were first issued, and that rate was maintained throughout the life of the bond. But in the mid-1970s, inflation pushed up interest rates to record levels, reducing the prices of fixed-rate bonds that had been issued in previous years. Rising interest rates and falling bond prices made bondholders (i.e., lenders) reluctant to buy new long-term bonds with fixed interest rates. This made it more difficult for firms to obtain long-term debt capital.

In response to these pressures, some firms, especially major banks, began issuing *floating-rate* notes, where the coupon rate is changed periodically as market interest rates change.

---

[6]It is also necessary to add any accrued interest to the price of the bonds when they are sold. The bond buyer must pay the bond seller for any interest earned from the date of the last interest payment to the date of sale. Since bond interest is paid semiannually, accrued interest can amount to a maximum of one coupon payment.

- *Example*

Citicorp, a major New York City bank, sold $650 million worth of 15-year floating-rate notes. The coupon rate on these notes was 9.7 percent for the first 10 months, and the rate was adjusted semiannually thereafter to be 1 percent above that of the three-month U.S. Treasury bill note. ∎

In 1981, companies began issuing **zero coupon bonds,** which pay no interest directly to the bondholders but instead are sold at significant discounts from face value. The bonds have face values (par) at which the issuing company will buy them back at maturity. Because the bonds do not pay periodic interest, their price at any point in time equals the present value of the par value upon redemption.

zero coupon bond
bond paying no interest that is sold at a significant discount and redeemed for face value

- *Example*

Suppose Celonese issues $1,000-par-value zeros with a 15-year maturity during a period when annual interest rates on equally risky bonds are 12 percent. The market value of the bond is the present value of the $1,000 to be received at redemption in 15 years:

$$B_0 = \$1,000 \text{ PVIF}_{.12,15} = \$183$$

As maturity approaches, the market value of the bonds will increase in accordance with present-value mathematics.[7] ∎

Zero coupon bonds are an extreme version of what are called *original-issue deep-discount* bonds. *Deep-discount* refers to the situation where a bond's coupon rate is well below the bond's yield to maturity (the rate of return required by the market); thus, the bond's market price is well below its par value. Historically, when bonds are sold, the coupon rate is set at approximately the current required rate of return. In the early 1980s, some issuers began to set the coupon rate well below the rate of return required by the market, forcing the bonds to sell at a deep discount at the time of original issue.

- *Example*

Martin Marietta issued $175 million worth of original-issue deep-discount 30-year bonds at a 7 percent coupon rate when the market required that comparable bonds pay about 13.25 percent. These bonds were sold originally for a little less than 54 percent of their par value. ∎

Maturity

Unlike preferred and common stock, bonds have a specified maturity date. This date is contained in the indenture, and therefore is known precisely when the bonds are issued. On the maturity date the firm pays the bondholders the principal of the bonds plus any remaining interest due, thus redeeming the bonds.

---

[7]If you need a short review, Chapter 6 covers the present-value mathematics of bond valuation.

■ *Example*

The Centrex Telephone Company bonds have a maturity date of 2021. Unless other arrangements are made to provide for the retirement of these bonds, the company will need to pay off the bondholders at a total cost of $150,000,000 in the year 2021. ■

In many instances the bonds do not remain outstanding until the maturity date but instead are redeemed.

Redemption

Most early redemptions are accomplished by the use of either a call provision or a sinking fund:

call provision
provision allowing an issuer to buy back an issue of debt and retire it

- *Call provision*. The **call provision** enables the firm to prematurely retire debt by buying it back at a stipulated *call price* above the bond's face value, the difference being the *call premium*. The call premium typically amounts to one year's interest. An 8 percent bond, for example, would have a call price of about $1,080.

  If interest rates have fallen, the firm can call the outstanding debt and reissue new debt at a lower interest rate, thereby reducing its interest expense in future years. This operation is called a *refunding* and is discussed below. Because interest rates have fallen, investors who hold the called bonds can invest their proceeds from the refunding only in bonds having lower interest rates than those called. The call premium is intended to compensate them for this loss. To protect the bondholders further, some indenture agreements stipulate that the bonds cannot be called for a specific number of years (often, five years).

sinking fund
provision for the systematic retirement of a bond issue

- *Sinking fund*. A **sinking fund** is a cash reserve set up to provide early retirement of the bonds. The fund is under the control of the indenture trustee. Periodic payments are made by the firm to the sinking fund, which can be used to retire some of the bonds.

  The firm is usually permitted to use the fund to retire bonds in the cheapest manner, either buying back bonds in the market or using the call provision. If interest rates have risen since the time of issue, the market price of bonds will be below their face value, and the firm will prefer to buy bonds in the market. If interest rates have fallen substantially since the time of issue, the market price of bonds will be well above their face value, and the firm will prefer to call the bonds, paying a premium over face value (this call premium is discussed below). Bonds chosen for early call are selected by lottery. Some sinking funds invest the payments in other securities, like government bonds, and use the accumulated investment proceeds to retire the firm's bonds at maturity.

  A primary reason for requiring a sinking fund provision is that it compels the firm to regularly set aside a portion of the principal repayment for the retirement of the debt. If no such payment were set aside, the firm would be required to pay off the entire principal at maturity. A large maturity date payment is called a *balloon payment*. If the maturity date came during bad economic times for the company, the firm could possibly have difficulty in making payment.

AAA	Indicates the highest rating and the strongest capacity to pay interest and repay principal.	
AA	Indicates a very strong capacity to pay interest and repay principal.	
A	Indicates a strong capacity to pay interest and repay principal.	
BBB	Indicates an adequate capacity to pay interest and repay principal.	
BB	Indicates that adverse circumstances could lead to inadequate capacity to repay.	
B	Currently has capacity to pay interest and repay principal in accordance with the terms of the obligation but greater vulnerability.	
CCC	CCC indicates debt with currently identifiable uncertainties or major risk exposures to adverse conditions.	
CC, C	These ratings are reserved for debt subordinated to CCC-rated debt.	
D	Indicates the debt is in default.	
NR	Indicates no rating has been requested or insufficient information for a rating.	
Plus (+) or minus (−)	Some ratings may be modified by a plus or minus sign to show relative standing within a category.	

Convertibility

A convertible feature permits bondholders to convert their bonds into common shares, giving them an option on the common if the common price rises. Whether, and when, to convert is at the option of the holder. Convertibles are examined later in the chapter.

Bond Ratings

Although not a part of the indenture agreement, **bond ratings** are an important feature of bonds. Firms pay to have their debt rated, and several financial services companies provide ratings on debt. Standard & Poor's and Moody's are the best known of the rating companies.

bond ratings
grade assigned to a
bond issue expressing its
relative probability of
default

Table 19–2 shows Standard & Poor's rating categories and definitions. The top category is AAA and the bottom is D. Grades AAA down to BBB are referred to as *investment grade*. Lower-rated bonds are often called *junk bonds* and are discussed later in the chapter.

Notice that the phrase "capacity to pay interest and repay principal" dominates the category descriptions in Table 19–2. The categories are, in fact, meant to describe the relative riskiness of debt, with AAA debt being the safest.

It is important to recognize that bond ratings measure only the relative risk of default and say nothing directly about the absolute risk of default. Consistent with the key finance idea that risk and return are virtually inseparable, it should seem reasonable that the riskier the bonds, the greater their yield (required rate of return). And, in fact, comparison of the yields on AAA and BBB debt supports the financial risk/return concept: BBB debt yields exceed AAA debt yields.

BOND REFUNDINGS

As noted above, a particular bond issue may be terminated before its original maturity date as a result of a refunding operation. *Bond refunding* refers to calling in outstanding bonds and issuing new ones. There are several reasons to refund.

The foremost is that interest rates have fallen, and the new bonds will have a lower rate, resulting in smaller interest payments. A second reason is that the outstanding bonds have restrictive covenants that inhibit the firm's financial operations. Such bonds may have been issued when the firm was experiencing difficulties. The indenture agreement may restrict the firm from issuing new debt, for example. If the firm now needs new debt financing and feels strong enough to issue it, the old bonds may be refunded to clear the way for new debt.

Refunding is a capital budgeting problem. An initial outlay of funds is required to call the old bonds, and there are cash inflows in later periods because of interest savings. Because refunding is a capital budgeting problem, we need to know the usual capital budgeting data: (1) all after-cash flows associated with the investment and (2) the appropriate required rate of return.

The refunding mechanics are straightforward: the firm issues new bonds, takes these proceeds plus cash, and retires the old bonds. A complete example of a bond refunding is shown in Appendix 19–A.

JUNK BONDS

One of the major financial events of the last few years is the emergence of the so-called junk bond market. This revolutionary development has had a significant impact on corporate finance and investors alike. As we saw in the RJR example, it plays a major role in corporate takeovers. Because of its importance both currently and prospectively, we will examine this issue in some detail.[8]

What Are Junk Bonds?

junk bonds
high-yield, noninvestment grade bonds

The term **junk bonds** generally refers to publicly traded debt obligations rated below investment grade (that is, below the S&P rating of BBB or the Moody's rating of Baa3). Alternative names for junk bonds are *high-yield, speculative grade, low-rated,* or *noninvestment grade bonds.* The term *junk* originated in the mid-1970s as a description of securities that lost their investment grade rating due to a significant deterioration, or fall, in their financial condition. These securities were referred to as *fallen angels,* and they included both industrials and utilities whose probability of default on debt had reached a level high enough to warrant dropping them from the investment grade list.

The composition of the junk market has changed from the mid-1970s to include securities other than fallen angels. Today, the immense junk bond market includes at least the following type of bonds:[9]

- Fallen angels—for example, Bethlehem Steel.
- Emerging growth companies, or companies that are too young or small to rate an investment grade rating—for example, Continental Cablevision.
- Companies undergoing a restructuring, typically a leveraged buyout (a transaction that takes a company private by a restructuring primarily

---

[8]This discussion is indebted to Edward I. Altman and Scott A. Nammacher, *Investing in Junk Bonds* (New York: John Wiley & Sons, 1987).
[9]See Alexandra Peers, "How to Take a 'Junk' Bond Plunge . . . ," *The Wall Street Journal,* November 15, 1988, p. C1.

involving debt)—for example, Metromedia, Inc. Such bonds are often paid off by cash generated by the sale of assets rather than from the company's cash flow.

At the end of the 1980s, the third category constituted the bulk of the junk bond market.

The Junk Bond Market

The participants in the junk bond market include:

- The issuers.
- The investors.
- The underwriters (investment bankers).
- Rating agencies.

As we saw above, the issuers of junk bonds have increased and involve a range of companies. The emergence of the junk bond market really occurred because financial institutions began to buy such securities. Attracted by the higher yields and the rapid expansion in supply (thereby increasing liquidity and diversification possibilities), these institutional investors began to buy the lower-rated bonds.

The major investment banker in the junk bond market in the 1980s was Drexel Burnham Lambert. This company played the prominent role in the development of this market, which in turn allowed it to become one of the major investment banking firms. However, intense competition emerged among underwriters to market junk bonds. The reason was that the fees for doing so average 3 percent of the issue size and can amount to 4 to 5 percent, significantly above the fees from investment grade issues.

The two principal rating agencies, Standard & Poor's and Moody's, continue to develop their resources to serve the junk bond market. Given the number of issues in this market, such attention is necessary.

The growth, as well as size, of the junk bond market is impressive. In 1976, the total junk bond market amounted only to about $8 billion. By the mid-1980s, it was a $100 billion market in rated, nonconvertible debt securities. This was some 20 percent of total newly issued debt. Junk bonds accounted for some 23 percent of bonds outstanding by the end of 1987 compared to 6 percent in 1980. Junk bond issues continued to increase as the 1980s approached an end, primarily because of the large number of corporate mergers and restructurings. However, this market underwent a major crash at the end of 1989 and into 1990. The leading firm in junk bonds went bankrupt, the leading proponent of junk bonds was convicted of wrongdoing, and the junk bond market fell into despair. By fall of 1990, many junk bonds were offering record yields because of their riskiness, and the junk bond market was, in many respects, decimated.

The Role of Junk Bonds

As we have seen, fallen angels now constitute less of the junk bond market as other types of companies use these financial instruments. This category was only 15 percent of the high-yield issuers by the mid-1980s.

Junk bonds have played a prominent role in the merger and acquisitions wave that swept the United States in the last years of the 1980s. The size and number of such deals have been staggering and have captured widespread attention and generated considerable concern. Debt ratios of firms involved rose to high levels relative to traditional norms. Junk bonds in particular were focused upon.

Leveraged buyouts have increasingly dominated the news in this area, reaching a fevered pitch by the end of 1988. In a **leveraged buyout (LBO),** a company is taken private in a deal involving the use of debt supported by the firm's own earnings. Assets are often sold off to reduce the debt burden. The high debt ratio resulting from the transaction often causes the ratings to fall below investment grade and into speculative grades.

leveraged buyout
taking a company private through the heavy use of debt

The many corporate restructurings that have caused a downgrading in the bonds have created a shift in wealth among debtholders. This has led to new demands by bond investors for protection, and new attempts by issuers to meet such demands. Some new approaches include:

- Coupon rates that can change in the event of a major restructuring.
- "Poison puts," whereby bondholders are to get back their initial investment in the event of a takeover, merger, or recapitalization. Two companies filed to sell bonds with this form of protection in late 1988. The underwriters claimed that the borrowing costs would be reduced significantly as the result of this investor protection, said to be the strongest safeguard to that time.

Whatever the true role of junk bonds in the broad merger and acquisitions area, the controversy surrounding their use as a financing mechanism has been enormous. Perhaps no single event caused such a reaction, and had such an impact on the corporate bond market, as the announcement by RJR Nabisco's management of the initial attempt at an LBO in October 1988. Investors began to fear that a widespread increase in such LBOs would cause the leverage ratio for many companies to be excessively high. RJR's bonds went from A-rated to high-yield, high-risk junk bonds. Some RJR bonds lost 20 percent of face value within a month of the announcement. In turn, the entire corporate bond market was negatively affected. This was one more piece of evidence of the impact junk bonds have had on corporate finance in the United States.

ADVANTAGES AND DISADVANTAGES OF FINANCING WITH DEBT

The advantages and disadvantages of financing with debt are as follows:

- The primary advantage: because interest charges are tax deductible and the required rate of return demanded by bondholders is less because of their senior position relative to other claims, financing with debt is cheaper than any other capital source.
- The major disadvantage of debt financing is its increased risk. Financing with debt adds financial leverage to the firm. Recall that financial leverage causes the required rate of return on equity, k_e, to increase. A different aspect of increased risk caused by the addition of debt is the increased probability of bankruptcy.

Corporate Financing through Debt Instruments   ■ *Figure 19–2*

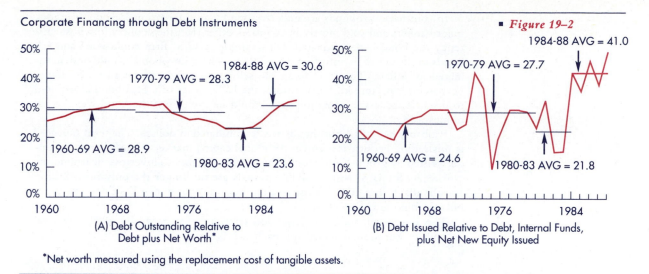

(A) Debt Outstanding Relative to
Debt plus Net Worth*

(B) Debt Issued Relative to Debt, Internal Funds,
plus Net New Equity Issued

*Net worth measured using the replacement cost of tangible assets.

Source: Yolanda K. Henderson, "Is Leverage a Tax Dodge—or Not?", *New England Economic Review*, Federal Reserve Bank of Boston, March/April 1990, p. 13.

TRENDS IN THE USE OF DEBT FINANCING

The use of debt financing in the United States has been increasing in recent years. The percentage of assets financed by debt in the 1980s exceeded that for any other period in the last 45 years. In terms of Chapter 15, financial leverage increased for domestic corporations.

Figure 19–2 shows this increase in debt financing by focusing on the amount of debt outstanding. Part A shows the leverage ratio, defined as credit market debt relative to the sum of debt and net worth. After rising through 1970 to about 31 percent, this ratio declined to about 24 percent in the period from 1980 to 1983. By 1988, however, this ratio stood at 34 percent. The recent trend was clearly upward, with the final level higher than in the previous two decades.

Part B of Figure 19–2 shows how firms raised their funds during the same period. In the 1960s and 1970s, about 25 percent of funds were raised through debt instruments, while 75 percent came from equity financing. Since 1984, however, more than 40 percent of the funds came from the issuance of debt.[10]

☑ International Perspective

Firms raise significant amounts of debt capital in the international markets. International bond issues are those sold outside the issuer's own country. Additional technical distinctions must be made. Foreign bonds are underwritten and sold in one foreign country by an issuer in another country. For example, a Canadian company could sell a foreign bond in the United States, and this bond would be underwritten by a U.S. firm and denominated in dollars.

---

[10]In this analysis, debt includes bonds, mortgages, commercial paper, and bank loans. Equity consists of both retained earnings and new share issues.

In contrast, Eurobonds are underwritten by an international group of investment bankers and sold mostly in countries other than the country in whose currency the bond is denominated. For example, a U.S. firm could issue and sell bonds in Europe to investors holding dollars. These Eurobonds would be denominated in dollars. The firm doing the selling would do so because of a lower borrowing cost abroad. Furthermore, the U.S. issuer of a Eurobond is required to disclose far less information than would be the case if the bond were issued domestically.

Probably half of all Eurobonds are denominated in dollars. The term *Eurobond* is misleading because it involves the global capital markets. These bonds are underwritten by groups from around the world, and sold to investors all around the world. As for U.S. issuers, multinationals are no longer the only firms selling Eurobonds. Other firms are also issuing them, although their basic operations are only within the United States.

The Eurobond market is large and continues to grow. By 1987, the total amount of Eurodollars issued approached $150 billion.

CONVERTIBLE SECURITIES

convertible securities
bonds or preferred stocks that can be converted into shares of common stock of the same company

Convertible securities are bonds or preferred stocks that may be converted into shares of common stock of the same company. A convertible is simply a senior security with an option to convert into a specified number of common shares. Almost all convertible bonds are subordinated debentures, and virtually all of them are callable. Because convertible bonds are used more often than convertible preferred as a source of financing, we will concentrate primarily on the bonds; however, the ensuing discussion is applicable to either, and with small modifications it would be completely applicable to convertible preferreds.

Conversion Terms

A convertible security has clearly designated *conversion terms* that establish how many shares of common will be exchanged for the convertible and the effective price that will be paid for the common stock. Conversion terms may be stated in either of two ways:

conversion ratio
number of shares of common stock received per convertible security

1. **Conversion ratio:** The number of shares of common stock received per convertible security.

conversion price
effective price paid for the common stock upon conversion

2. **Conversion price:** The effective price paid for the common stock upon conversion.

Knowledge of either one of these two quantities permits us to calculate the other because they are related:

$$\text{Conversion ratio} = \frac{\text{Par value of conversion security}}{\text{Conversion price}} \qquad (19\text{--}1)$$

■ *Example*

AVX Corporation, the largest U.S. manufacturer of multilayer ceramic capacitors, issued a convertible debenture in May 1987. This issue matures in 2012 and carries a coupon of 8.25 percent. It is convertible into 45.455 shares of common stock, which is its conversion ratio. The conversion price is $1,000/45.455 = $22 per share. [11] ■

Mechanics of Issuing Convertibles

A company issuing convertibles receives the proceeds of the sale, less flotation costs. This one-time receipt of proceeds is the cash inflow from the capital source. In return, the firm pays preferred dividends (if the convertible is a preferred stock issue) or interest payments (if the convertible is a bond issue) until conversion or termination of the issue. When investors convert, no cash changes hands. They exchange one form of security (debt or preferred stock) for another (common stock). They no longer receive preferred dividends or interest payments but instead receive common dividends. Their position becomes the same as that of any other common stockholder.

Valuation of Convertibles

The key to understanding and valuing convertibles is to realize that they are designed to limit the holder's downside risk while allowing an upside potential if the common stock does well. Therefore, convertibles have more than one value that must be considered in the valuation process. Because of the possibility of conversion, there are three values to consider: investment value, conversion value, and market value.

Investment Value

The **investment value** is what the senior security should be worth without its conversion privilege. That is, the investment value of the convertible equals the value of the straight (nonconvertible) senior security, or what the senior security should be worth without its conversion privilege. It is the present value of future interest payments and principal redemption at a required rate of return for equally risky senior securities that do not have the conversion option. Determination of this investment value is no more than an application of the valuation principle from Chapter 6.

investment value
what the senior security should be worth without its conversion privileges

■ *Example*

At the time of observation of the AVX bond, the required rate of return for comparable nonconvertible bonds of similar quality and maturity (24 years) was 10 percent. Therefore, the investment value of these bonds would be:

$$\text{Investment value} = \sum_{t=1}^{24} \frac{\$82.50}{(1.10)^t} + \frac{\$1,000}{(1.10)^{24}}$$
$$= \$82.50 \text{ PVIFA}_{.10,24} + \$1,000 \text{ PVIF}_{.10,24}$$
$$= \$741.26 + \$102.00 = \$843.26 \qquad ■$$

As interest rates change, required rates of return and investment values change.

---

[11] This information is taken from *The Value Line Convertible Survey*, August 15, 1988, p. 142. This is an excellent source of information on convertible securities, warrants, and options.

Conversion Value

conversion value
amount of money the convertible would be worth if it were converted into common now

The product of the conversion ratio and the common's current market price determines the convertible's **conversion value,** or the amount of money the convertible would be worth if it were converted into common now.

$$\text{Conversion value} = \frac{\text{Conversion}}{\text{ratio}} \times \frac{\text{Common}}{\text{stock price}} \qquad \text{(19–2)}$$

■ *Example*

In the AVX example, the conversion ratio is 45.455 to 1. At the time of observation of the bond data, the common stock price was $19.125. Therefore, the conversion value is:

Conversion value of AVX bonds = $45.455 \times \$19.125 = \$869.33$ ■

Market Value

Until all the convertible securities are either converted or called back (retired), they may be bought and sold in the market by investors. The market value is the current market price at which the convertible is selling.

■ *Example*

At the time of observation of the AVX data, the convertible bond was priced at 108 (or $1,080) in the market. ■

Conversion Premium

conversion premium
difference between the convertible's market value and its conversion value

The **conversion premium** is the difference between the convertible's market value and its conversion value. Premiums are frequently expressed as percentages.

$$\begin{array}{c}\text{Percentage}\\\text{conversion}\\\text{premium}\end{array} = \frac{\text{Market value} - \text{Conversion value}}{\text{Conversion value}} \times 100 \qquad \text{(19–3)}$$

■ *Example*

For the AVX convertible bond, given the above data:

$$\begin{array}{c}\text{Percentage}\\\text{conversion}\\\text{premium}\end{array} = \frac{\$1,080 - \$869.33}{\$869.33} = 24\%$$ ■

Relationships among Values

A convertible's market value is closely related to its investment value and its conversion value. A convertible's market value should not fall below either its investment value or its conversion value.

First, consider why market value should never fall below conversion value. If market value were ever less than conversion value, there would be arbitrage possibilities for investors. *Arbitrage* means to buy and sell the same securities in different markets to take advantage of unequal prices. Thus, the conversion value provides a "price floor" for the convertible security.

▪ *Example*

Suppose that when the AVX stock price was $22 (and therefore conversion value = $1,000), the convertible's market value was $980. Ignoring transactions costs (brokerage fees and taxes), investors could buy the convertible for $980, convert into 45.455 shares of stock, and sell the stock for $1,000 (45.455 × $22 per share), yielding an instantaneous $20 profit. Competition to buy the convertible and sell the stock would create an upward pressure on the market value of the convertible and a downward pressure on stock price, eventually causing the convertible's market value to be at least as large as its conversion value. More precisely, market value should never fall below conversion value by an amount greater than the transactions costs necessary to arbitrage. ▪

Market value should also not fall below investment value. Why? Because by definition investment value represents the price investors would pay for the convertible security even if it were not convertible. The investment value provides a second price floor below which the price of the convertible would not be expected to go.

Figure 19–3 illustrates the major points concerning the valuation of convertibles. Other things being equal, a convertible's investment value is unrelated to the common stock price because, by definition, investment value is the value of the senior security without the conversion privilege. So the investment value line in Figure 19–3 is horizontal. Equation 19–2, however, shows that conversion value is related directly to the common stock price, so the conversion value line looks as shown in Figure 19–3. Since we have just shown that a convertible's market value must not be lower than its conversion value or its investment value, the market value line in Figure 19–3 should not be below either the conversion value line or the investment value line. As Figure 19–3 shows, however, the market value line is typically above both the conversion and investment value

▪ *Figure 19–3*
Valuation of
Convertible Securities

lines. That is, we normally observe premiums on the convertible. Premiums exist because as long as there is some chance the stock price may advance above the conversion price, the conversion option has value.

What happens if the stock price does rise above the conversion price? Some investors, of course, will cash in on the conversion feature of their securities by exchanging them for common stock or selling them in the market. Others, however, will hold on to their convertible securities for a while, hoping the price of the common will increase even more. As the stock price increases, the convertible's market value increases by an amount approximately equal to the conversion ratio times the dollar increase in the stock price. However, when stock price decreases, the convertible will also decrease by an amount approximately equal to the conversion ratio times the dollar decrease in the stock price.

At lower stock prices, the convertible's price does not fluctuate so much. As the convertible's price rises, however, its covariance with the market is greater, and therefore it is a riskier investment. This riskiness works to lower the convertible's price. As a result, the conversion premium, *as a percentage of stock price,* is less than when the stock price was lower, as Figure 19–3 shows.

Thus, we see that the conversion price is a benchmark for explaining the market value fluctuations of convertibles. When a convertible is first issued, the conversion price is typically set between 10 and 20 percent above the current common stock price. If the common price is substantially below the conversion price, there will be little interest in conversion. The conversion privilege will be worth little, and the convertible's market value will be roughly equal to its investment value. As the common stock price approaches the conversion price, however, conversion becomes increasingly possible, and the market value of the convertible security becomes more and more dependent on the value of the common stock. In effect, the common stock pulls the convertible with it.

Reasons for Issuing Convertibles

Delayed Equity Financing

The most commonly stated reason for issuing convertibles is that the firm really wants to issue equity capital but feels the time is not right because its stock price is too low. In comparison with the number of shares that would be issued if the price were not depressed, more shares must be issued to get the same amount of capital. Conversion prices are usually set from 10 to 20 percent higher than the common stock price prevailing at the time the convertibles are issued. This means that when investors exchange their convertible for common, there will be fewer shares of common outstanding than if the capital had been raised by an issue of common to begin with.

▪ *Example*

A firm can issue common at $20 per share currently, but can issue a convertible security that will convert at $25 per share. The firm will ultimately have 25 percent fewer new shares outstanding if it chooses the convertible route. Essentially, the firm has made a deferred equity sale at the higher $25 per share price. ▪

Marketability Reasons

If the firm has already decided to issue a senior security, attaching the conversion privilege facilitates the sale. Underwriters may even insist that the issue be convertible. The convertibility feature broadens the range of possible buyers for the issue because investors who are primarily attracted to equity securities may now be interested. Also, convertible securities traditionally have paid lower dividend and interest rates than straight senior securities of similar quality because of the value of the conversion privilege. Therefore, by offering an *equity sweetener,* the issuer can obtain a lower cost on its new debt or preferred issue.

One potential problem to consider in deciding whether to issue a convertible is the prospect of an *overhanging issue*. If the convertibles were issued as a delayed equity financing scheme, but the price of the common fails to increase enough to permit conversion, the issue is said to be overhanging. Having an overhanging issue is detrimental to attempts to obtain any kind of external long-term capital. If the firm is highly levered and counting on conversion to create more debt capacity, it may be hard to sell any form of senior securities. And common stock will be unattractive because of its depressed price.

A second consideration is the potentially adverse reaction of the common stock. This has two aspects. At time of issue, the convertible, being a senior security, imposes a fixed charge in front of the earnings stream, making the common stock riskier. Also, the convertible will be converted some day, which ultimately means a dilution of earnings per share.

When Conversion Occurs

While investors have the conversion option, conversion may occur voluntarily or the firm may force conversion. In either case the security holder converts because there is an economic advantage to converting.

Voluntary Conversions

If the firm is doing well, the common dividends will probably be steadily increased, and there will be a spread between common dividends and the fixed convertible dividends or interest payments. Even allowing for the extra risk on the common, this spread could induce investors to convert. Also, if the common price is increasing, the convertible price will also increase, reducing the downside protection of the convertible.[12]

Forced Conversions

The firm can force conversion by exercising the *call provision,* which permits the firm to retire a security by buying it back from investors at the *call price*. Unlike calls on ordinary senior securities, however, very few convertibles are actually

[12]Voluntary conversion also occurs when the conversion privilege is about to expire and the common stock is selling above its conversion price. Some convertibles have a scheduled expiration of the conversion privilege, and on that date the convertible will be worth less because of the loss of its conversion value. This induces conversion. Last, if a struggle for control occurs, opposing parties may buy the convertibles and convert to increase their voting strength.

bought back by the firm. Instead, the call forces conversion into common. If the purpose of the call is to force conversion, the firm will issue the call only when conversion value is safely above the call price.[13] When the call is announced, the convertible investor must choose between:

1. Converting into common.
2. Selling the convertible at its market value (to someone who will convert into common).
3. Allowing the firm to buy back the convertible at the call price.

Rather than accept the lower call price, investors will opt for (1) or (2), depending on whether they wish to hold the firm's common or not.[14]

▪ *Example*

In December 1990, Medco Containment Services Inc. called for redemption all of its 7½ percent convertible subordinated debentures. These bonds were due to mature in the year 2000. Medco called the bonds at a redemption price of $1,053.57, which with the accrued interest from the last interest payment to the redemption date of $30.83 made a total redemption payment per $1,000 bond of $1,084.40. Bondholders were given two weeks to convert, and no interest accrued after that period. Their only recourse at that point would be to turn the bonds in and receive the redemption price plus accrued interest. However, each bond was convertible into 50 shares of common stock, and at the time of the call notice, the stock was trading for approximately $32 per share, resulting in a total market value of approximately $1,600 per bond. Clearly, Medco bond holders should have sold the bonds in the market at a price that should reflect the conversion value or convert into the common stock. ▪

SUMMARY

▪ Bonds are the main source of long-term, fixed-charge financing. The firm is committed to future fixed charges when it uses bonds.

▪ Fixed-charge financing is less expensive than equity financing but also involves more risk.

▪ Bond refunding—exchanging one bond issue for another—most often occurs during periods of falling interest rates when the firm may wish to issue new debt with a lower coupon rate than its current bonds. This possibility is analyzed as a long-term investment problem. The firm incurs an initial investment cost to effect the refunding and compares this cost with the present value of future after-tax interest savings.

▪ Convertible securities are bonds or preferred stocks that may be converted into shares of common.

---

[13]Conversion policy refers to the way firms influence conversion once conversion value exceeds the call price. One common policy is to force conversion whenever conversion value is approximately 20 percent greater than the call price. There is usually a 30-day period or so from the time the call is announced to the exercising of the call, and the 20 percent cushion ensures that, should the firm's stock price decline in this 30-day period, it would have to be a severe drop before conversion would become unprofitable. Should the stock drop below the call price, investors would sell convertibles back to the firm at the call price rather than convert, and the firm would have to find the cash to buy these securities back. The purpose of the call would have been defeated.

[14]Another way to force conversion is with an *acceleration clause,* which provides that on designated dates the conversion price increases (accelerates). When the conversion price increases, the conversion ratio and conversion value decrease. Since the conversion value provides a floor for the convertible's market value, the market value will decrease also. Rather than suffer this drop in market value, investors will convert.

- The terms of conversion specify the conversion ratio (how many shares of common each convertible may be exchanged for), the conversion price (the effective price paid for the common on conversion), and the period during which conversion may take place.
- On conversion no cash changes hands; the holder merely returns the convertible to the firm and receives common stock.
- The relationship between conversion value (what the convertible is worth if conversion is made) and the convertible's market value typically involves a premium because convertible securities offer investors the advantage of holding a senior security plus the possibility of leverage should the common stock prosper.
- The advantages of issuing convertibles are that they provide delayed equity financing, enhance the marketability of the underlying senior security, and are frequently useful in financing mergers and acquisitions.
- The main disadvantages are the effect on future financing of an overhanging issue and the potentially adverse reaction of the common.

KEY TERMS

bonds, p. 566
bond ratings, p. 575
call provision, p. 574
conversion premium, p. 582
conversion price, p. 580
conversion ratio, p. 580
conversion value, p. 582
convertible securities, p. 580
coupon, p. 572

debentures, p. 569
investment value, p. 581
junk bonds, p. 576
leveraged buyout (LBO), p. 578
mortgage bonds, p. 568
principal, p. 571
protective covenants, p. 571
sinking fund, p. 574
zero coupon bond, p. 573

QUESTIONS

19–1. Why is debt financing more risky to the firm than equity financing? Why is it less risky to investors?

19–2. What is meant by an indenture agreement? What are restrictive covenants?

19–3. From the firm's standpoint, why is a particular bond rating from Standard & Poor's important?

19–4. Firms often choose to redeem bonds before their maturity date. Identify ways in which this may be accomplished.

19–5. Far West Trucking has some 6 percent coupon bonds outstanding that mature in about 20 years. Current interest rates are 8 percent, and Far West is talking about refunding. What motives can you identify for refunding at this time? Discuss them.

19–6. Double Eagle Manufacturing is preparing to issue new bonds. In a preliminary discussion, Sherr and Johnson, the firm's Chicago investment bankers, and the firm talk about the need for and the desirability of arranging a call feature and a sinking fund provision for the bond.
   a. Explain which of these two features would be considered desirable from the firm's standpoint and why. From bond investors' standpoint and why.
   b. How would the omission of the call feature affect the bonds' desirability from investors' viewpoint? What effect would its omission have on the bonds' yield, other things being equal?
   c. Repeat (b), but from the standpoint of omitting the sinking fund provision.

19–7. How should the following expectations on the firm's part affect its willingness to include a sinking fund provision and its insistence on including a call feature on a new bond issue?
   a. Interest rates are expected to fall.
   b. Serious cash flow problems are expected for the next 10 years.
   c. Interest rates are expected to rise.

19–8. Explain precisely the meaning of the term *junk bond*. What are some alternative names?

19–9. Discuss the participants in the junk bond market.

19–10. Explain how junk bonds have impacted corporate finance.

19–11. Distinguish between a zero coupon bond and an original-issue deep-discount bond.

19–12. Describe what is meant by the investment value of a convertible security. Explain why the investment value acts as a floor to the convertible's market value.

19–13. Explain in what sense the conversion price of a convertible preferred stock is an effective common stock price.

19–14. The right to convert a convertible security rests ultimately with the investor. However, the firm can include provisions when a convertible security is first issued that will effectively cause conversion. Explain these provisions.

19–15. Basic Products has an issue of $100 par convertible preferred stock with a five-to-one conversion ratio. What effect should the following circumstances have on the number of shares of Basic's preferred outstanding if the common stock is selling for about $25 per share?
   a. The conversion ratio is scheduled to decrease soon due to the acceleration clause.
   b. The conversion privilege is about to expire.
   c. A dividend increase on the common is declared.
   Repeat (*a*) through (*c*) for common selling at $17.

19–16. A firm is preparing to float a new bond issue. The firm's investment banker says that current bond market conditions are such that either the bond will have to be convertible or five-year warrants will have to be attached. Which of these alternatives would be more compatible with the following situations?
   a. There is a strong possibility that the firm will need external financing in about five years.
   b. The firm's long-range plans anticipate a major financing push in about seven to eight years, and this could be jeopardized by any overhanging issues.

PROBLEMS

19–1. A firm issues $100,000,000 of bonds priced at 99 percent and carrying a coupon of 12 percent. Calculate:
   a. The number of bonds actually issued.
   b. The price paid by the investors for each bond.
   c. The dollar coupon to be paid on the bonds.

19–2. A firm issues a $1,000 zero coupon bond with a 20 year maturity when bonds of similar risk are carrying interest rates of 10 percent. Calculate the price of these bonds.

19–3. Phillips Inc. issued some 30-year, $500 par value, 8 percent coupon convertible debentures 15 years ago. Interest is paid annually, and the next interest payment is one year from now. The conversion price is $5.

    a. Find the conversion value today of these debentures if the stock price is currently $8 a share.

    b. Determine the investment value today of these debentures if the interest rate on comparable nonconvertible debentures is 10 percent per year.

    c. If the present conversion premium is $60, what is the present percentage conversion premium?

19–4. Sartoris and Company has an issue of $100 par value convertible preferred outstanding. Determine the conversion price, conversion value, and percentage conversion premium for this issue under the following conditions:

	Conversion Ratio	Common Stock Price	Preferred Stock Price
A	10/1	$20	$225
B	10/1	5	51
C	4/1	30	140
D	1/1	85	87

19–5. A 5 percent, $1,000 convertible bond has 20 years of life remaining. Determine the market value of the bond assuming that the conversion privilege has no value and that the required rate of return on equally risky, nonconvertible bonds with similar maturities is 7 percent. Assume annual interest payments are made.

19–6. The conversion price of a $100 par convertible preferred stock is $25. If this convertible has a conversion value of $64 per share, what is the common stock price?

19–7. Kamath Industries wants to retire its convertible bonds. These $1,000–par–value bonds have a call price of $1,050 and a 10-to-1 conversion ratio. Assuming zero premium, would it be better for Kamath to buy the bonds back in the open market or exercise the call option if the price of common stock is as follows?

    a. $100.

    b. $90.

    c. $120.

    d. $105.

19–8. The Nelson Corporation currently has an EBIT level of $20 million. The firm has 10 million shares of common stock outstanding and no interest-bearing debt. The firm's tax rate is 50 percent, and Nelson's common stock price-earnings (P/E) ratio is 10. To finance new investments, the company plans to issue $5 million worth of $1,000 par value, 8 percent convertible bonds. The conversion price on the bonds will be set at 25 percent above current stock price.

    a. Determine the conversion ratio.

    b. Calculate how many shares of new stock will be issued if all the bonds are converted.

    c. If Nelson's EBIT increases by $1 million next year because of the new investments, determine the firm's earnings per share for next year with conversion (and therefore no interest charges) and without conversion.

    d. Assuming the firm's P/E ratio increases to 12, and assuming no conversions had occurred, what would the stock price be in (*c*)?

19–9. Clayton Seeds is preparing to issue $3 million of bonds. Clayton is either going to make the bonds convertible or attach warrants. If the bonds are made convertible, they will carry a 7 percent interest rate; if warrants are attached, the bond will carry a 9 percent interest rate. Clayton has $10 million in assets.

    a. Clayton anticipates earning 10 percent on its assets before interest and taxes, the company's tax rate is 40 percent, there are no interest charges on current liabilities, and there are currently 200,000 shares of common stock outstanding. Determine earnings per share under each plan prior to either converting any bonds or exercising any warrants.

 b. Repeat (*a*) for each plan assuming that EBIT will be 20 percent of assets.

 c. If the P/E ratio on the common is 20, determine the *expected* common price for both plans if there is a 50 percent chance that EBIT will be $1 million and a 50 percent chance that EBIT will be $2 million. Which plan is better? Why?

 d. Repeat (*c*) assuming that the expected P/E ratio under the convertible plan is 20 and the expected P/E ratio under the warrant plan is 22.

SELECTED REFERENCES

A discussion of bond ratings can be found in:

Ederington, Louis H. "Why Split Ratings Occur." *Financial Management,* Spring 1986, pp. 37–47.

The valuation of convertible bonds is discussed in:

Billingsley, Randall S.; Robert E. Lamy; and G. Rodney Thompson. "Valuation of Primary Issue Convertible Bonds." *Journal of Financial Research* 39 (Fall 1986), pp. 251–60.

The pricing of convertible bonds is discussed in:

Marr, Wayne M., and G. Rodney Thompson. "The Pricing of New Convertible Bond Issues." *Financial Management* 13 (Summer 1984), pp. 38–40.

Agency costs in connection with debt are discussed in:

Thatcher, Janet S. "The Choice of Call Provision Terms: Evidence of the Existence of Agency Costs of Debt." *Journal of Finance,* June 1985, pp. 549–61.

APPENDIX 19–A   EXAMPLE OF A BOND REFUNDING

Newton Tire Company is considering refunding its old bonds. Interest rates have dropped since Newton issued the bonds 10 years ago, and the company is trying to determine if it is economically advantageous to refund now. Pertinent data are as follows:

Old Bonds	
Par value	$100,000,000
Remaining life	20 years
Coupon rate	10%
Call price	$1,070 per bond
Unamortized flotation costs	$1,500,000
New Bonds	
Par value	$100,000,000
Life	20 years
Coupon rate	8%
Flotation costs	$2,000,000
Other Data	
Tax rate	40%

Proceeds from the sale of new bonds are used to pay for the redemption of the old bonds. If the firm planned to issue new bonds simultaneously with the redemption of its old bonds, but bond market conditions were bad and the new issue was delayed—as occasionally happens—the firm might have trouble paying off its old bonds. To protect themselves from this possibility, firms usually issue the new bonds at least a month or so prior to the redemption of the old bonds. This creates a temporary overlap interest rate payment situation. The premature proceeds are typically invested in U.S. government securities until needed for the retirement of the old bonds, which tends to eliminate the need to include the overlap effect in the analysis.[15]

Should the firm refund? To answer this question we must first determine the cash flows associated with the refunding. Refunding is actually a capital budgeting replacement problem: the firm is trying to decide whether to replace one set of bonds with another. As in any capital budgeting problem, the issue involves the present value of the outflows matched against the present value of the inflows. The cash flows are changes in cash flow incurred by replacing the old bonds with new ones.

Initial Investment

We first calculate the initial investment before tax consequences are incorporated in the analysis:

Before-Tax Calculations	
Repay old bond principal	$100,000,000
Pay call premium (7% of principal)	7,000,000
	$107,000,000
Less: net proceeds of new bonds*	−98,000,000
Before-tax initial investment	$ 9,000,000

*Net proceeds of new bonds equal sale price minus flotation costs: $100,000,000 − $2,000,000 = $98,000,000

We turn now to tax considerations. First, the firm expenses the call premium for tax purposes. Also, flotation costs incurred with issuing bonds are amortized over the life of the bonds, and the firm gets a tax deduction against ordinary income each year equal to the amount of the amortized cost. When bonds are retired early, the unamortized flotation costs on the old bonds are expensed at time of refunding. For Newton Tire:

Tax Deductible Expenses	
Call premium on old bonds	$7,000,000
Unamortized flotation costs on old bonds	1,500,000
Total tax-deductible expenses	$8,500,000

Tax Savings

Tax savings = (Tax rate)(Total tax-deductible expenses)
= (0.40)($8,500,000) = $3,400,000

After-Tax Calculations	
Before-tax initial investment	$9,000,000
Less: tax savings	−3,400,000
After-tax initial investment	$5,600,000

---

[15]This is strictly true only if the proceeds of the new issues are reinvested during the overlap period at the same after-tax rate as that which applies to the new issue. Also, it is necessary to discount all cash flows to the same point in time. Most textbooks discount the cash flows from the new issue to the issue date and discount the cash flows from the old issue to the date of retirement. If there is an overlap period, this approach is incorrect.

Because the unamortized flotation costs and call premium are tax deductible ($8.5 million in the example), a tax savings ($3.4 million) is created. The resultant after-tax initial investment is the money the firm must pay to effect the refunding.

Annual Interest Savings

There are alternative ways to determine the annual interest savings. Our approach is to calculate separately the after-tax annual costs of servicing the old and new bonds and then net these figures. This difference represents the annual after-tax interest savings attained by issuing the new bonds. Each separate calculation has two parts, the before-tax interest cost and the tax considerations. Both the annual interest payments and the amortization of flotation costs are tax deductible.

Old Bonds

Before-tax annual interest (0.10)($100,000,000)		$10,000,000 per year
Tax deduction		
Interest	$10,000,000	
Amortized flotation costs*	75,000	
Total tax-deductible expenses	$10,075,000	
Tax savings (0.4)($10,075,000)		−4,030,000 per year
Annual after-tax interest payments		$ 5,970,000 per year

New Bonds

Before-tax annual interest (0.08)($100,000,000)		$ 8,000,000 per year
Tax deduction		
Interest	$ 8,000,000	
Amortized flotation costs**	100,000	
Total tax-deductible expenses	$ 8,100,000	
Tax savings (0.4)($8,100,000)		−3,240,000 per year
Annual after-tax interest payments		$ 4,760,000 per year

$$\begin{array}{l}\text{Annual after-tax}\\\text{interest savings}\end{array} = \begin{array}{l}\text{Annual after-tax}\\\text{interest payments}\\\text{on old bonds}\end{array} - \begin{array}{l}\text{Annual after-tax}\\\text{interest payments}\\\text{on new bonds}\end{array}$$
$$= \$5,970,000 - \$4,760,000 = \$1,210,000 \text{ per year}$$

*Amortized flotation costs = $1,500,000/20 = $75,000 per year.
**Amortized flotation costs = $2,000,000/20 = $100,000 per year.

By refunding, the firm will save itself $1,210,000 per year for 20 years. This is the direct result of a lower interest rate on the new bonds.

Net Present Value of Refunding

Recall that the firm must pay an initial investment of $5,600,000 to achieve the interest saving of $1,210,000 per year for 20 years. Therefore:

$$NPV = -\$5,600,000 + \sum_{t=1}^{20} \frac{\$1,210,000}{(1+k)^t}$$
$$= -\$5,600,000 + \$1,210,000\ PVIFA_{k,20}$$

The next question is, What should we designate as k, the required rate of return? In Chapter 13 we developed the idea that it should reflect the risk inherent in that project.

For projects where cash flows have low covariance with the market index, the project's risk will be relatively low, and the required rate of return will therefore be low. Bond refunding is a good example of this. Unlike most projects the firm undertakes, the cash flows associated with the bond refunding are known with a large degree of certainty because they represent interest savings that are certain, barring failure of the firm. Therefore, covariance risk is low, and the required rate of return used to compute the refunding NPV should be low, certainly lower than the firm's average cost of capital.

We will use the after-tax interest rate (the coupon rate times 1-T, assuming the bonds are sold at face value) on the new bonds used in the refunding, 4.8 percent. This rate reflects the after-tax required rate of return demanded by the market.[16]

For $k = 0.048$:

$$PVIFA_{.048,20} = 12.676$$

so:

$$NPV = \$-5,600,000 + (\$1,210,000)(12.676) = \$9,737,960$$

As with any capital budgeting decision, if net present value is positive, the firm should accept the project, and if negative, the firm should reject the project. In this example, the decision should be to refund. Of course, another alternative is to wait to refund. If interest rates fall further, the firm would achieve even more interest savings by deferring refunding. However, predicting future interest rates is a difficult task, and many financial managers would prefer to refund before a favorable opportunity disappears.

PROBLEMS

19A–1. The Scott Company currently has a $30 million issue of 6 percent bonds outstanding whose call price is $1,050. Remaining life of the bonds is 20 years. The company is contemplating refunding with a new $30 million issue of 5 percent, 20-year bonds. Sale price of the new bonds is expected to be $980 per bond, and issue costs are $100,000. The effective tax rate for Scott is 0 percent. Should the Scott Company refund the old issue?

19A–2. Zumwalt Electronics currently has 1,000 bonds outstanding with $1,000 par value, a 9 percent coupon rate, and a remaining life of five years. Interest rates have declined in recent months, and Zumwalt figures it could replace these bonds with five-year, 5 percent notes. A financial analyst for Zumwalt has been assigned the task of determining if it would be advantageous to refund. The analyst has gathered the following pertinent financial data:

Flotation costs on new notes	$50,000
Sale price of new notes	$1,000 each
Unamortized flotation costs of old bonds	$10,000
Call premium on old bonds	8%
Tax rate	40%

Determine if a refunding should be made.

---

[16]Agreement on the choice of the appropriate discount rate is by no means widespread. According to the major competing theory about *k*, one should not make a tax deductibility adjustment. Thus, *k* would be the same as the before-tax interest rate. In our example, this would cause *k* to equal 8 percent.

APPENDIX 19–B   WARRANTS

A *warrant* is a long-term option to buy a specified number of shares of common stock at some specific price during a designated time period. Warrants are usually attached to a debt issue as a *sweetener,* enabling the issuer to obtain a lower interest cost on the debt issue. Warrants are almost always *detachable,* meaning they can be separated from the bond and sold.

A warrant is, like a convertible security, a contingent claim. However, unlike a convertible security, its entire value depends on the value of the underlying common stock on which it is a claim.

Warrant Terms

Exercise Price

The firm is obligated to sell common stock to its warrant holders at the warrant's *exercise price,* regardless of the current market price of the stock. The exercise price is thus a guaranteed price at which warrant holders may opt to buy stock.[17] The exercise price typically is some 10 to 30 percent above the price of the common stock at time of issuance.

Exercise Ratio

Similar to the conversion ratio of convertible securities, a warrant's exercise ratio specifies how many shares may be purchased per warrant (at the option price). The exercise ratio is frequently 1 to 1: one share of stock per warrant. However, every warrant issued is unique because the company sets the terms at issuance, and different ratios may be specified. When a warrant is exercised, the investor surrenders the warrant to the firm along with a cash payment equal to the option price times the exercise ratio.

Expiration Date

Almost all warrants have expiration dates, generally from about 5 to 10 years, after which they can no longer be used to purchase common stock. The expiration date is occasionally extended.[18] At the expiration date, if the common stock is selling above the option price, any remaining warrants will be exercised. If the common is selling below the option price, the remaining warrants are worthless and will not be exercised.

Warrant Valuation

Warrants have no value independent of the common stock; a warrant is merely an option to buy common stock. There are two valuation terms to define, formula value and market value.

Formula Value

A warrant is an option to buy a specified number of shares (determined by the exercise ratio) at some specified price (the option price). Therefore, the warrant's formula value—what the warrant should be worth—is determined by the common stock price, the option price, and the exercise ratio. Because a warrant cannot be valued below zero:

---

[17]The exercise price normally remains constant over the warrant's life.

[18]Some warrants have no expiration date and are called *perpetual warrants*.

- If stock price ≥ option price:

$$\begin{matrix} \text{Formula} \\ \text{value} \end{matrix} = \begin{matrix} \text{Exercise} \\ \text{ratio} \end{matrix} \times \left(\begin{matrix} \text{Stock} \\ \text{price} \end{matrix} - \begin{matrix} \text{Option} \\ \text{price} \end{matrix} \right) \qquad \textbf{(19B–1)}$$

- If stock price < option price:

$$\text{Formula value} = 0$$

■ *Example*

If the exercise ratio on Bell Industries warrants is four to one, the option price is $30, and the common is selling for $50, the formula value is 4 × ($50 − $30) = $80. ■

This is no more than a commonsense solution to evaluating the warrant. Suppose an investor wanted to buy four shares of Bell stock. Forgetting the transactions costs involved, it would cost $200 (4 × $50) to buy the stock. However, an alternative way to acquire the stock would be to buy one warrant, which controls four shares, and exercise it. Now, what would the investor pay for the warrant, again forgetting the transactions costs? Once the warrant is purchased, the investor must present the warrant plus $120 (4 × $30). But this is $80 less than the cost of buying stock directly. So the warrant should be worth (have a formula value equal to) what an investor can buy stock for without the warrant minus the cost of the stock with the warrant. In our example, the formula value is $80.

When the stock price is less than the option price, applying Equation 19B–1 would give a negative formula value. Because this is a nonsense answer, we define formula value to be zero when stock price is less than the option price.

Market Value

The market value of a warrant is the price the warrant trades for in the market.

Premiums

Warrants, like convertibles, typically sell above their formula value. The difference between the price of the warrant and its formula value is called the *premium,* which may be stated in either dollars or percentages. For comparison purposes they are best stated as percentages:

$$\begin{matrix} \text{Percentage} \\ \text{premium} \end{matrix} = \frac{\text{Market value} - \text{Formula value}}{\text{Formula value}} \times 100 \qquad \textbf{(19B–2)}$$

Figure 19B–1 shows the typical relationships that exist between stock price and the warrant's formula and market values. Notice that market value is always greater than formula value, so there are premiums. Why do premiums exist? Because of leverage possibilities.

■ *Example*

Recall the Bell Industries warrants, whose exercise ratio is four to one and option price is $30. If Bell common stock is currently selling at $50 per share, the formula value of the option would be $80 [4 × ($50 − $30)]. Suppose Bell's stock price went up to $60. The stock investor would have made a 20 percent rate of return. But the formula value of the warrant would now be $120 [4 × ($60 − $30)], which would have provided option investors a 50 percent rate of return. ■

■ *Figure 19B–1*
Market and Theoretical
Values of a Warrant

Because this leverage is appealing to many investors, they are willing to pay a premium to own the warrants. The percentage premium is greatest when stock price is near option price. Why? At low stock prices, there is only a small chance of imminent exercising; at high stock prices, the leverage creates huge downside risk. So percentage premiums are least when stock prices are very low or high relative to the option price.

Arbitrage opportunities should prevent a warrant's market values from falling below its formula value. As we have seen, if the exercise ratio were four to one, the option price were $30, and the stock were selling for $50, the formula value of the warrant would be $80. If the warrant's market value were less than $80, say $75, arbitragers would buy the warrant (for $75), exercise it (pay the firm 4 × $30 = $120), and then sell the stock (for 4 × $50 = $200). An arbitrager would have made an instantaneous $5 profit by buying stock for $195 ($75 + $120) and selling immediately for $200. Competition for this profit would bid up the warrant market value to the point where it equaled formula value.

Why Warrants Are Issued

The most commonly stated reason for issuing warrants is that the warrant serves to sweeten the senior instrument, once the firm has decided to issue bonds or preferred stock. This need to add an equity sweetener may arise for two reasons:

1. The firm may feel that the interest rate (on bonds) or the dividend yield (on preferred) is unacceptably high on the straight senior security, so warrants are attached to induce investors to accept a lower return.

2. The underwriters may believe that the issue will not be fully subscribed unless warrants are included in the financing package.

An alternative to issuing warrants is to make the bonds or preferred stock convertible, which is another form of equity sweetening. Like convertibles, warrants provide for delayed equity financing. By setting the option price above the stock price prevailing when the warrants are issued, a delayed sale of equity at the option price is set up. This presumes, however, that the warrants will eventually be exercised, which occasionally does not occur. Note that an inflow of capital to the firm occurs when warrants are exercised, unlike the conversion of convertible securities, because the warrant holder exchanges the warrant plus cash for the new common. Furthermore, the company is able to sell stock without incurring underwriting costs.

In considering the issuance of warrants, it is worthwhile to remember that warrants do not have call provisions. Thus, exercising them is entirely at the investors' discretion.

20

Lease Financing and Term Loans

Leasing as a Way of Life

Emery Air Freight is a worldwide carrier and cargo air service with 1987 revenues of $1.2 billion and assets of $811 million.[1] According to its 1987 balance sheet, Property and Equipment (net of depreciation) amounted to $216 million, of which $116 million was accounted for by Facilities Held under Capital Leases. Under the Liabilities section of the balance sheet, Emery reported some $102 million of Obligations under Capital Leases (less current portion), an amount larger than its long-term debt of $85 million and approaching its reported Stockholders' Equity of $143 million. This obligation of $101 million covered only the firm's long-term leases. Its various short-term leases cost it another $88 million in 1987 and represented a total future commitment of $639 million.

According to the footnotes accompanying the financial statements, the company leases aircraft facilities and ground transportation vehicles and equipment under various lease agreements expiring in the current year as well as various years out to 2009. Approximately 54 percent of all of Emery's leases are for aircraft, 40 percent are for facilities, and 6 percent for ground transportation vehicles and equipment. Emery's primary long-term lease, representing a 30-year rental term, is for its "Superhub" sorting facility in Dayton, Ohio.

[1]See the *1987 Annual Report*, Emery Air Freight.

Once attractive investments are identified, the firm considers alternative methods of financing them. The firm can sell new securities to finance its investment opportunities. We have discussed equity and debt financing in the preceding chapters. Such financing allows the firm to purchase the assets it needs.

Alternatively, the firm need not own the asset; it may lease (rent) the services of an asset rather than buying it. Firms can lease almost any asset on a short-term and/or long-term basis. Our emphasis here, however, is on long-term leasing as an alternative source of long-term financing. Leasing, like the sale of stock or bonds, is a form of financing.

One major alternative to selling securities to purchase assets is to obtain a term loan, or intermediate-term credit. This negotiated source of financing is less permanent than long-term bonds. We consider term loans in the last part of the chapter.

Both of these sources of external financing represent negotiated sources of financing, involving direct negotiations. This is quite different from the impersonal sale of securities in the market.

Primary *chapter learning objectives* are:

1. To analyze lease financing as an alternative to borrowing funds to use when purchasing assets.
2. To consider term loans as an alternative method of financing for the firm.

LEASING

Terminology

A *lease* is a contractual agreement between two parties establishing an arrangement for the use of an asset in return for periodic payments by the user. In a lease arrangement:

- The *lessor* is the asset owner, who receives the periodic payments.
- The *lessee* makes the payments to the lessor in return for using the asset.

The lessee views leasing as an alternative to buying the asset using borrowed funds. The lessee is concerned primarily with the use of the asset, not who holds title to the asset. In the following discussion the firm is the lessee.

Types of Leases

Although leasing arrangements vary widely, all leases can be categorized broadly as either operating or financial leases. In turn, financial leases can be categorized into specific types. We will discuss the various types of leases below, organized by the major categories of operating leases and financial leases. Figure 20–1 summarizes the differences between these two major categories from the standpoint of both the lessor and the lessee.

Operating Leases

operating lease
a short-term, cancelable lease

An **operating lease** (also called a service lease) is a short-term, cancelable lease. A simple example of an operating or service lease is a lease for telephone service. For business firms, computers and copiers are often obtained by operating leases,

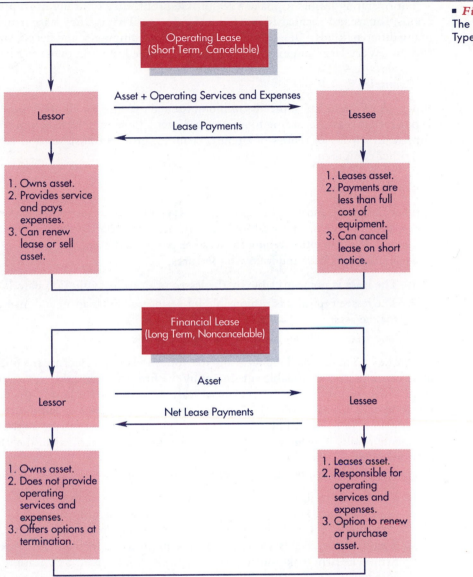

■ *Figure 20–1*
The Two Major
Types of Leases

as are automobiles. An operating lease is usually characterized by the following features:

1. The lease is cancelable by the lessee prior to its expiration.[2]
2. The lessor provides service, maintenance, and insurance.
3. The sum of all the lease payments by the lessee does not necessarily fully provide for the recovery of the asset's cost.[3]

[2]Operating leases typically have options that permit the lessee to renew the lease.
[3]That is, the asset is not fully amortized over the lease life. The lessor looks to leasing the same asset to subsequent lessees or to its sale to fully recover the investment.

For operating lessors to make a reasonable profit, they typically must provide goods that are not peculiar to one kind of industry. That is, they lease items that many different kinds of lessees can use, like offices, computers, and fleets of trucks and cars. Very large and expensive items also can be leased on operating leases.

▪ *Example*

Emery Air Freight had some $88 million of rental expense for all operating leases in one recent year. According to its *Annual Report,* "operating lease commitments consist principally of rentals of aircraft, facilities, ground transportation vehicles and other equipment." ▪

Financial Leases

financial lease
a long-term, noncancelable lease

A **financial lease** (also called a capital lease) is typically a long-term, noncancelable lease—the opposite of an operating lease. At the termination of the lease contract, the lessee often can either renew the lease or purchase the asset.
Financial leases have the following features:

1. The lease is not cancelable by the lessee prior to its expiration date.[4]
2. The lessee typically is responsible for service, maintenance, and insurance for the asset.[5]
3. The asset is fully amortized over the life of the lease.

The key points are the long term and the noncancelability. Because the financial lease involves a noncancelable agreement by the firm to acquire the services of an asset, a decision to enter into a financial lease is an important commitment and merits special attention. Financial leases are a form of financing, similar to purchasing an item by obtaining a secured loan. That is, failure to make all the lease payments results in default and can lead to bankruptcy, exactly as in the case of debt financing.
Financial leases can be divided into two basic forms:

1. *Direct lease.* In this straightforward arrangement, the firm leases an asset it did not previously own. The firm simultaneously signs the lease agreement with the lessor and orders the equipment from the manufacturer. The lessor pays for the equipment, which is sent to the firm. The firm makes lease payments to the lessor based on a lease agreement worked out by the two parties. If the direct lease is from the manufacturer, then the manufacturer and lessor are one and the same.
2. *Sale and leaseback.* In this arrangement the firm sells an asset it currently owns and then leases the same asset back from the buyer. Lease payments are set to return the full purchase price plus a rate of return deemed reasonable. The advantages to the lessee are that it allows the firm to continue using the asset while providing cash that can be used elsewhere.

leveraged lease
a lease involving a third party that lends the lessor part of the funds necessary to purchase the asset to be leased

A special form of financial lease is the **leveraged lease,** a new form of leasing that has come into widespread use. Here, a third-party lender is involved, in

---

[4]The lessee usually has the right to renew the lease on expiration.
[5]In these cases, the lease payments are net of these costs, and such leases are referred to as *net leases.*

addition to the lessee and lessor, because of the large capital outlays involved. In this situation, the lessor borrows part of the funds from the lender to pay for the asset being leased, and the loan (plus interest) is repaid with lease payment revenue.[6] Except for this, the arrangement is the same as in a direct lease; in particular, from the lessee's standpoint, there is no difference at all between a leveraged lease and any other type of lease.

Sources of Lease Financing

Three kinds of companies provide lease financing. The largest group of lessors are equipment manufacturers. Durable-goods manufacturers often establish subsidiary (called *captive*) leasing or credit companies. One of the main reasons that manufacturing companies provide lease financing is to encourage the use of their product. A second source of lease financing is financial institutions: banks, bank holding companies, and life insurance companies. These institutions are heavily involved in longer-term financial leases. From their standpoint, leases are merely a form of secured lending. A third source of lease financing is independent leasing companies, which provide much of the direct leasing.

THE EFFECTS OF LEASING ON THE FIRM

The Financing Effects

A key point to remember about a financial lease is that it is a form of borrowing. The contractual agreement on the lease payments is noncancelable. Therefore, as with other types of debt, failure to make the lease payments can result in bankruptcy. Both lessors and lessees generally, and correctly, view a financial lease as a form of borrowing, and they treat it with the careful attention that all debt obligations receive.

　　Because leasing is similar to debt, it has an impact on the amount of borrowing a firm can do. Generally, the more a firm leases, the less it can borrow. This *debt displacement* is an implicit cost of leasing. It is important to note that while leasing is similar to debt, it is not identical. Lessors have less strong claims in case of bankruptcy, for example, and the restrictive covenants in the respective contracts are different.

The Tax Effects

For tax purposes, the lessee is entitled to a full deduction of all qualified lease payments. Therefore, like other forms of borrowing, the government subsidizes the cost of leasing.

　　A lease agreement must be recognized by the IRS as a genuine lease agreement if the full tax benefits are to be received. The purpose of these rules is to ensure that lease agreements do not simply become tax avoidance schemes. Tax avoidance is accomplished by making the lease payments similar to accelerated depreciation benefits for the lessee, thereby speeding up the tax deductions for the lessee.

---

[6]The lender uses a *nonrecourse loan*, which is a loan with no recourse to the lessee in case of default.

■ *Example*

A firm needs a piece of manufacturing equipment that has a seven-year class life. The machinery costs $9,000,000. Under straight-line depreciation, the depreciation deduction would be $1,285,714 per year. Assume, however, the firm could lease the equipment for three years at an annual lease payment of $3,000,000 per year, and purchase it at the end of the lease contract for a nominal amount. The present value of the benefits from the lease would exceed the present value of the depreciation deduction. In effect, the lessee would be substituting lease payments for depreciation expenses and distorting the intended treatment under the tax laws. ■

The Reporting Effects

Leasing used to be referred to as *off-balance sheet* financing. Under prior accounting practices, because the firm did not own the asset, neither the asset nor the companion lease liability had to appear in the body of the balance sheet. A footnote reference, often a very terse one, was sufficient. The superficial effect was to understate the firm's indebtedness position.

After much consideration and preparation, the Financial Accounting Standards Board (FASB) issued in 1976 its Statement of Financial Accounting Standards No. 13, "Accounting for Leases" (FASB #13). This statement establishes the criteria for reporting by both lessees and lessors. It is a complex and lengthy statement, so much so that seven additional statements and six interpretations were required between 1976 and 1979.[7]

FASB #13 is founded on the basic concept that when substantially all the benefits and risks of asset ownership are transferred in a lease, the financial reporting by the lessee and lessor should reflect that transfer. A company should not be able to make a major obligation in the form of a lease contract without disclosing its effects on the balance sheet.

Lessee Reporting

From the lessee's standpoint, leases are classified as either *capital leases* or *operating leases*. If the lease meets *any* of the four following criteria, it should be classified as a capital lease:

1. The lease transfers ownership of the asset to the lessee by the end of the lease.
2. The lease contains a bargain purchase option for the benefit of the lessee.
3. The lease term is 75 percent or more of the asset's estimated economic life.
4. The present value of the minimum lease payments is 90 percent or more of the original market value of the asset.

The capitalized value of capital leases and their companion liabilities are put in the body of the lessee's balance sheet. These capitalized values are present values of the lease payments. Thus, the present value of the lease payments appears on

---

[7]All of this material was combined into FASB's *Accounting for Leases*, May 1980.

the right-hand side of the balance sheet as a liability and on the left-hand side as an asset.

- *Example*

Emery Air Freight reported some $116 million of facilities held under leases as assets and some $102 million of obligations under capital leases as obligations. ▪

THE LEASE DECISION

We turn now to analyzing the desirability of leasing. Lease analysis has been a controversial topic in recent years, largely as a result of an unusual characteristic of leasing. When the firm decides to lease an asset, it simultaneously makes an investment decision (accept the project) and a financing decision (lease the project). In previous chapters, we have separated long-term investment and financing decisions. The joint decision involved in leasing analysis has led to a considerable amount of disagreement in the finance literature. Nevertheless, we can illustrate the analysis involved in deciding whether to lease or buy, while recognizing that disagreements exist in doing these calculations.

The leasing decision has also been controversial because of the advantages and/ or disadvantages that a lease supposedly carries with it. Therefore, in making the lease decision, it is important to consider these advantages and to determine how real they actually are.

In the following discussion, we will first consider the question of whether firms should lease. We will then analyze the purported advantages of leasing. Finally, if a firm has decided that leasing is a viable alternative, it should evaluate the lease decision according to economic analysis. Thus, we conclude this section with a consideration of the factors involved in making such an analysis.

Should Firms Lease?

If capital markets are perfect, the lessee would be indifferent between leasing and borrowing. Debt obligations and lease obligations would be identically valued by both lessors and lessees. In effect, leasing would not matter because it would have no value. Although this may seem a startling conclusion, it is the only reasonable conclusion in a perfect market.

A perfect market has certain characteristics, including no transaction costs, no bankruptcy costs, equivalent tax rates for all parties, and information that is free and widely available to everyone. In such a market, neither lessor nor lessee will be able to gain an advantage in a lease contract. In effect, this situation would be analogous to the capital budgeting situation where the NPV is zero. Both parties would be indifferent to the lease. The present value of the cash inflows will be equal to the present value of the cash outflows. Regardless of whether the lessee leases an asset or incurs debt to purchase the asset, the cost will be the same.

Given this analysis, the case for leasing must rest on market imperfections. And, in fact, such market imperfections must exist or we would not experience such a massive amount of leasing as actually occurs. Advocates of leasing claim several advantages for it, only some of which are valid. We will consider these claims below.

Why Do Firms Lease?

As noted, there has been a substantial increase in the volume of leasing in recent years. The logical conclusion from this observation is that leasing must be perceived as offering advantages over alternative sources of financing. However, any investigation of the factors that influence the choice in a lease-or-buy decision must be careful to distinguish between perceived and actual advantages of leasing.

The Perceived Advantages of Leasing

Among the perceived advantages, the most prominent are shifting obsolescence risk, conserving working capital, eliminating equipment disposal problems, and preserving credit capacity. We consider each of these major claims that have been advanced to justify leasing as opposed to purchase.

Shifting Obsolescence Risk   If equipment purchased becomes obsolete because of the development of better equipment, its market value will be impaired. Leasing supposedly shifts this risk from the lessee to the lessor. This would be true if the lessor did not pass on the expected costs of obsolescence to the lessee by charging higher lease payments. But if we presume (as seems likely) that lessors are as smart as lessees, then there is little merit to the contention that a lease arrangement shifts the risk of obsolescence to the lessor.

Conserving Working Capital   The firm may be able to arrange 100 percent lease financing so that no cash is needed to acquire the asset. By comparison, borrowing frequently requires a down payment. For large companies in normal times, however, other forms of outside capital are available, and the firm could arrange 100 percent financing from these sources. Also, many lease arrangements require a down payment. Thus, this point seems valid only for small firms that have limited access to other sources of financing and would otherwise have to finance internally. It may also be a valid reason for lease preference in times of tight money. Not surprisingly, there is increased demand for leasing in such times.

Eliminating Equipment Disposal Problems   This is a convenience advantage, not an economic one. There is little reason to think the lessee will salvage the asset for less than the lessor. Even if the equipment has negative market value (nuisance value) at disposal time, the lessor may be counted on to pass this expected cost on to the lessee.

Preservation of Credit Capacity   Leasing is equivalent to borrowing in that it commits a firm to a schedule of fixed payments. However, some companies think that creditors do not perceive leasing as equivalent to debt; thus, by leasing, rather than buying, assets, they believe that they can preserve their future borrowing capacity.

   The success of off-balance sheet financing depends on finding lenders who are naive or who do not view debt and leasing equivalently—either condition is highly unlikely. The new accounting standards appear to significantly limit off-balance sheet financing possibilities for public firms.

The Actual Advantages of Leasing

If the perceived advantages of leasing do not hold up to close scrutiny, what is the justification for leasing? The most important reason for leasing remains the tax reason. This advantage exists because firms are in different tax brackets, allowing a firm that cannot take full tax advantage of a potential tax shield to shift such a shield to another firm. If the lease payments are set at the proper rate, the firm that does the transferring can benefit, as can the lessor. Although someone has to lose, that someone will be the IRS. Absent corporate taxes, long-term corporate leasing would be severely limited or quite possibly would cease to exist.

Low-tax-bracket firms tend to be the lessees, and high-tax-bracket firms the lessors. The low-tax-bracket firm is unable to use, or fully use, the interest from the debt and the depreciation from an asset that could be purchased via secured financing.

Moreover, there is also some evidence that transaction costs are reduced in operating leases compared to available alternatives. In fact, this may be the principal reason for the existence of short-term leases.

The Economic Analysis

We have recently recognized that some approaches that look somewhat different are actually equivalent. The approach that we take here is straightforward; it employs net present value (NPV) and is relatively simple to follow. Three steps are involved:

1. Compute the NPV of the buy alternative.
2. Compute the incremental NPV impact of the lease alternative.
3. Take the alternative that leads to the higher positive NPV. If neither alternative leads to a positive NPV, do not acquire the asset.

■ *Example*

Wingler Products is considering acquisition of an asset whose characteristics are shown in Table 20–1. Given these data, we can proceed through the three-step

■ *Table 20–1*
Example Data for Lease-Buy Analysis

Annual revenue	$4,000
Expected useful life	4 years
Tax rate	40%
Increase in net working capital	0

If the Asset Is Bought	If the Asset Is Leased
Purchase price = $6,000	Annual lease payment = $2,800 per year
Class life = 3 years	(first payment due at end of Year 1) for
Estimated salvage = 0	4 years
Straight-line depreciation with 3-year recovery period and half-year convention	Annual operating costs = $1,000
Annual operating costs = $1,000	
CFBT = $4,000 − $1,000 = $3,000	

sequence outlined above. This is a simplified example for ease of exposition. Straight-line depreciation is used, although the MACRS method, discussed in Chapter 11, is often applicable and will typically be the preferred choice. The estimated salvage value is assumed to be zero. Furthermore, lease payments are typically required to be made at the beginning of the year, but we use year-end payments to correspond to our previous discussion in Chapter 11 and for simplicity.

Step 1—Buy Alternative   This analysis is identical to that developed in the capital budgeting chapters. We estimate the entire series of expected cash flows after tax (CFAT) associated with the purchase, based on cash flows before tax of $3,000 per year. We discount the CFATs at an appropriate required rate of return (k) to obtain the expected NPV of the buy alternative. Table 20–2 summarizes these calculations, assuming $k = 12$ percent. The format of Table 20–2 parallels almost exactly that used in the capital budgeting chapters. Starting with cash flow before tax (revenues minus operating costs), subtract depreciation to obtain taxable income. Subtracting out taxes leaves cash flow after tax, for which a net present value is obtained using 12 percent as the discount rate, or required rate of return.

The required rate of return of 12 percent would be determined by procedures, developed in Chapter 14, involving the cost of capital. If this new asset had equal risk with the firm's other assets and was financed similarly, the average cost of capital would be the appropriate required rate of return. If these assumptions were not approximately met, we could estimate an appropriate risk-adjusted discount rate (as discussed in Chapter 13). One way of estimating k might be to look at required rates of return of firms owning assets similar to the asset under consideration.

Step 2—Lease Alternative   Several direct *incremental* effects occur if the asset is leased rather than bought. Recall that we are looking at this problem from the lessee's perspective:

- The lessee does not have to pay the purchase price of the asset.
- The lessee loses the depreciation tax shields created by the annual depreciation deductions.

■ **Table 20–2**
Calculations for
Buy Alternative

Year	CFBT[a]	Depreciation[b]	Taxable Income[c]	Tax[d]	CFAT[e]	PV$_{.12}$
0	—	—	—	—	−$6,000	−$6,000
1	$3,000	$1,000	$2,000	$800	2,200	1,965
2	3,000	2,000	1,000	400	2,600	2,072
3	3,000	2,000	1,000	400	2,600	1,851
4	3,000	1,000	2,000	800	2,200	1,399
					NPV =	$1,287

[a]CFBT = Revenue − Operating costs.
[b]Full year's depreciation = $6,000/3 = $2,000.
[c]Taxable income = CFBT − Depreciation.
[d]Tax = (0.4)(Taxable income).
[e]CFAT = CFBT − Tax.
CFAT$_0$ = −$6,000.

Year	Initial Investment Saved	Lost Depreciation Tax Shield[a]	Lease Payments[b]	Total	$PV_{.06}$[c]
0	+$6,000	—		+$6,000	+$6,000
1	—	−$400	−$1,680	− 2,080	− 1,962
2	—	− 800	− 1,680	− 2,480	− 2,207
3	—	− 800	− 1,680	− 2,480	− 2,082
4	—	− 400	− 1,680	− 2,080	− 1,648
				NPV =	−$1,899

[a](Depreciation)(0.40).
[b]($2,800)(1 − 0.40) = $1,680.
[c]Assumes a 10 percent required rate of return on borrowing, so $k = (1 − 0.40)(0.10) = 0.06$.

- Buying and leasing may have different operating costs and different salvage effects.
- The lessee must make annual lease payments.

It's important to properly handle the tax details associated with the various parts of this problem. That is, all incremental benefits and costs created by leasing should be after-tax benefits and costs. With regard to the four points raised immediately above:

Initial investment saved (after tax)	=	Initial investment
Lost depreciation tax shield (after tax)	=	Depreciation × (Tax rate)
Operating cost savings or loss (after tax)	=	Change in operating cost × (1 − Tax rate)
Lease payment (after tax)	=	Lease payment × (1 − Tax rate)

We will use these formulas for our example problem begun in Table 20–1.[8] The appropriate calculations are shown in Table 20–3. In the case of leasing, the initial investment is saved by leasing and represents an inflow in Year 0. The tax shield from depreciation, on the other hand, is lost as a result of leasing and is shown with negative signs. The lease payments, of course, are an expense and are shown as negatives. Once again, a cash flow stream exists for which an NPV can be calculated. Notice that the operating cash flows do not appear in Table 20–3. Since they are unaffected by the decision to lease or buy, they are not incremental effects and therefore are not part of the analysis in Table 20–3.

It is important to note that the appropriate discount rate, *k,* is:

$$k = (1 − T) × \text{Required rate of return on borrowing}$$

In the example, if the required rate of return on borrowing is 10 percent:

$$k = (1 − 0.40)(0.10) = 0.06$$

---

[8]Please note these considerations regarding the example problem data shown in Table 20–1 and the solution shown in Tables 20–2 and 20–3. First, there are no operating cost differences to consider. Second, there is no salvage value. If there were a salvage value to consider, its tax effects would also need to be considered. We would use the procedures developed in Chapter 11.

The leasing discount rate is basically the firm's after-tax cost of debt. This is considered appropriate because the leasing cash flows have very little risk and therefore require a relatively low discount rate. It is often argued that, when there is a salvage value to consider, the salvage cash flows, being riskier, should be discounted at a commensurately greater discount rate.

Finally, by using the after-tax cost of debt as the discount rate for the incremental leasing cash flows, we are automatically taking account of a major indirect effect of leasing, the reduction in the firm's debt capacity. Debt and leasing are near substitutes. As more leasing is used, less borrowing capacity is available. Financial research has demonstrated that using an after-tax cost of debt for the incremental leasing cash flows takes care of this issue.

Step 3—Comparing the Alternatives   Other things being equal, the firm should take the alternative that leads to the larger positive NPV. In our example, the NPV of the buy alternative is positive, but the NPV of the incremental effects of the leasing alternative is negative. Therefore, the firm should buy the asset.

The complete set of NPV outcomes is as follows:

NPV of Buy Alternative	NPV of Incremental Lease Effects	Decision
Positive	Positive	Lease
Positive	Negative	Buy
Negative	Negative	Don't use the asset
Negative	Positive	Lease the asset if the sum of the two calculated NPVs is positive; otherwise don't use the asset

Since the lease NPV calculations consider only the additional (incremental) effects of leasing compared to buying, the last case above—where the NPV of the buy alternative is negative but the lease NPV is positive—is a bit tricky. Only if the additional effects of the lease are attractive enough to overcome the negative NPV of the buy alternative would the asset be leased. ▪

TERM LOANS

Terms loans are loans with a maturity of more than one year. They are obtained by private placement rather than public subscription. Commercial banks are the primary term lenders. Because banks receive much of their loanable funds from demand deposits (checking accounts) that can be drawn down quickly by depositors, banks prefer to make term loans for relatively short periods of time, usually no longer than three to five years. Insurance companies and pension funds provide the majority of the longer-term loans because the liabilities of these institutions are longer lived than banks' demand deposits. For many marginal companies with either poor or nonexistent records of success, commercial finance companies are an important, although expensive, source of term lending.[9]

Features of Term Loans

The basic features of term loans are (1) maturity, (2) the direct negotiation with the lender, (3) collateral, (4) restrictive provisions, and (5) the repayment schedule.

Maturity

Term loan maturities vary from about 1 to 15 years. Banks, the major term lenders, have historically been active in supplying three- to five-year term loans, and in recent years have made term loans greater than five years. Longer-lived term loans are usually made by insurance companies. A bank and an insurance company may make a cooperative loan, the bank making the shorter maturity portion of the loan and the insurance company making the longer portion.

Direct Negotiations

Unlike a public sale of bonds, a term loan is a private placement. Since the firm and lender negotiate directly, there is no need for an investment banker; however, firms sometimes use investment bankers to locate potential term lenders.

Collateral

The lender's attitude toward collateral is directly related to the perceived safety of the loan. Other things being equal, the lender is more apt to require collateral from a small firm than from a large one. Lenders are also more likely to be able to negotiate a collateral provision if money is relatively tight. Firms with a relatively large amount of debt outstanding, or relatively low cash flow projections for the future, will be required to pledge assets to the loan. The riskier the projected cash flow stream, the more likely it is that collateral will be required.

Restrictive Provisions

To protect itself further, the lender may attempt to add restrictive provisions to the loan. If the firm's position is relatively weak, it may find it can only acquire the loan under very stringent terms. In addition to the commonplace requirement that the firm provide financial statements, the following provisions are most commonly found in term loans.

Asset Control Provisions   Even if a loan is secured, the lender is interested in the firm's maintaining its asset base. Should the firm default and the collateral not be sufficient to pay off the loan, the lender will become a general creditor and will look to the firm's other assets for satisfaction. There are two main asset control provisions. First, the firm may be required to maintain some specified minimum

---

[9]State and federal agencies that specialize in providing loans to small businesses serve as a last possible source of borrowing for many marginal firms. A well-known federal lending agency is the Small Business Administration (SBA). The SBA prefers to lend jointly with private lending institutions but on smaller loans may be the sole lender.

net working capital position (current assets minus current liabilities), stated in terms of either the minimum dollars of net working capital or a minimum current or quick ratio. Second, the firm may be prohibited from selling fixed assets in excess of some specified dollar amount without the lender's approval.

Liability Control Provisions   The lender may attempt to restrict the amount of new debt issued. Almost always the lender will demand a negative pledge clause in which the firm agrees not to pledge to others the assets purchased by the loan. Also, the lender will usually attempt to restrict the number of leasing agreements the firm can undertake. Sale and leaseback arrangements are usually prohibited.

Cash Flow Control Provisions   Lenders may attempt to restrain the firm's cash outflow by restricting cash dividends, salaries, bonuses to officers, and major fixed-asset purchases.

Management Control Restrictions   The lender provides the loan on the expectation that the firm's management will be at least as competent in the future as it is at the time of the loan. To assure this, the lender may insist on insurance on the firm's top executives. At the extreme, the lender may require that named key executives maintain their association with the firm during the life of the loan.

Repayment Schedule

The repayment schedule specifies when interest payments and principal repayments are due. A common plan is to amortize the loan by making periodic payments to reduce the loan balance. It avoids the necessity of having a large end-of-loan repayment, called a *balloon payment.* The amortization schedule includes both interest and principal payments, and it is usually set up to make equal amortization payments.

▪ *Example*

Suppose the Baddour Company negotiates a $30,000, six-year term loan that charges 10 percent on the unpaid balance. The loan will be amortized over the life of the loan through six equal year-end payments, the last coming at the maturity date. What is the repayment schedule?

The answer to this question is based on concepts discussed in Chapter 4.

$$C = \frac{V_0}{\text{PVIFA}_{k,n}} \tag{20–1}$$

where:

$$C = \text{periodic equal payment}$$
$$V_0 = \text{current sum of money}$$
$$\text{PVIFA}_{k,n} = \text{annuity discount factor for } k \text{ percent for } n \text{ periods}$$

Therefore:

$$C = \frac{\$30,000}{\text{PVIFA}_{.10,6}} = \frac{\$30,000}{4.355} = \$6,889$$

■ *Table 20–4*
Example Loan
Amortization Schedule

Year	(1) Loan Balance at Beginning of Year	(2) Total Loan Payment	(3) Interest Payment [0.10 × (1)]	(4) Principal Payment [(2) − (3)]	(5) Loan Balance at End of Year [(1) − (4)]
1	$30,000	$ 6,889	$ 3,000	$ 3,889	$26,111
2	26,111	6,889	2,611	4,278	21,833
3	21,833	6,889	2,183	4,706	17,127
4	17,127	6,889	1,713	5,176	11,951
5	11,951	6,889	1,195	5,694	6,257
6	6,257	6,883*	626	6,257	0
		$41,328	$11,328	$30,000	

*The last loan payment is slightly different from the equal payments made in the earlier years. This is to compensate for rounding errors by making the last principal payment exactly pay off the last year's loan balance.

If Baddour pays $6,889 to the lender at the end of each year for six years, the lender will recover the investment plus 10 percent interest over the loan period.[10] A portion of this annual payment is interest, and a portion is principal recovery. Since the periodic payment is constant, the interest portion declines as the loan balance declines. We can determine what portions of the annual payment are interest and principal repayment because we know the interest rate, initial loan balance, and annual amortization payment. Because interest is tax deductible but principal repayment is not, this separation into interest and principal payment is important for income tax purposes. These calculations are shown in Table 20–4. ■

Cost of Term Loans

The firm figures the cost of term loans the same way it determines the cost of capital for any source of financing. Interest charges are tax deductible, and we use the same concepts developed previously.

Sometimes the term loan interest rate is tied to the Federal Reserve discount rate, which is the rate that the Federal Reserve system charges member commercial banks on short-term loans. Term loan rates may be fixed or variable. A fixed rate commits the firm to one interest rate over the life of the loan. A variable rate permits the interest rate to be changed at designated points in time as money market conditions change.

In addition to interest charges, the firm must pay for the preparation of the loan documents and the commitment fee from the bank. These flotation costs are small compared to underwriting expenses. Assume in the example in Table 20–4 that these costs are $150. The cost of this term loan is found by equating the net proceeds received from the loan with the present value of the after-tax

---

[10]In this example, *C* actually equals $6,888.63, but we have rounded to the nearest whole dollar. This practice causes a slight rounding error in the work presented in Table 20–4.

payments made to the lender. The most complete calculation of the cost of borrowing would solve the following equation for k:[11]

$$B_0(1 - f) = \sum_{t=1}^{n} \frac{B_t + (1 - T)I_t}{(1 + k)^t} \tag{20-2}$$

where:

$$
\begin{aligned}
B_0 &= \text{loan amount} \\
f &= \text{flotation costs as a percent of the loan amount} \\
B_t &= \text{principal repayment in year } t \\
T &= \text{tax rate} \\
I_t &= \text{interest payment in year } t
\end{aligned}
$$

However, we can get a reasonably good approximation of k by using a shortcut equation:

$$k = \frac{(1 - T)}{(1 - f)} \text{ (Interest rate)} \tag{20-3}$$

where the interest rate is the stated loan rate.

- ### Example

Using our previous data, $f = \$150/\$30{,}000 = 0.005$, the interest rate is 10 percent, and we assume that $T = 40$ percent. Therefore:

$$k = \frac{(0.6)(0.10)}{0.995} = 0.0603 \qquad \blacksquare$$

An additional factor is the bank's requirement that the firm keep compensating balances. This raises the cost of term loans. Any other covenants placed on the firm by the lender would also effectively increase the cost of the loan.

Advantages of Term Loans

Term loans, like other debt, have tax-deductible interest payments. But these loans have certain advantages over bonds as a source of funds.

- Term loans usually can be placed faster than bond issues, which protects the firm from the possible deterioration of interest conditions in the market.
- Term loan flotation costs are less.
- Because of the personal nature of the relationship between borrower and lender, it should be able to negotiate more readily with the lender if the firm encounters financial problems. Term lenders are mostly financial institutions with significant financial expertise. Although they will vigorously protect their investment, the personal nature of the

---

[11]Flotation costs are tax deductible and could be incorporated into Equation 20–2 on either the left-hand side, if the flotation costs can be written off immediately, or on the right-hand side, if these costs must be amortized over a number of periods. Under either scenario, a tax shield of flotation costs would be incorporated into this equation.

• • •

FINANCIAL MANAGEMENT INSIGHTS

Term Loans Are an Important Source of Financing for Smaller Companies

California Microwave is an information technology company. It manufactures electronic systems that obtain, process, and deliver information. Its largest operation is its Satellite Transmission Systems, Inc., that services both the U.S. government and export markets. Sales are about evenly split between commercial sales and government sales.

In 1989 California Microwave had sales of $125 million, up substantially from the $97 million in 1988. Total assets increased during that period from $63 million to $85 million. California Microwave has paid no dividends, and has no plans to do so.

The company's performance was strong in 1989, with some $146 million in bookings, an amount larger than its sales for the year. Net income was up over 60 percent. By all accounts, this 20-year-old company was doing well, with sales, bookings, and backlog all at record levels.

Along with this success, however, came some liquidity problems. The company's cash position declined by $24 million during 1989 because of working capital requirements for its satellite earth station business. Thus, the record level of bookings and sales lead to a need for substantially more working capital, with inventory and receivables increasing more than proportionally to the growth in sales and backlog. Management had to face the problem of how to handle this increased need for working capital in the face of its success.

Management noted in the annual report that the company increased borrowings in order to finance the higher operating levels and to accomplish other objectives. California Microwave already had outstanding some $2.2 million in industrial development bonds bearing a floating rate based on market conditions. However, these bonds were scheduled to be repaid in 15 annual installments, although they could be repaid at any time without penalty. These bonds also were backed by a letter of credit and the entire obligation secured by a mortgage on the property. Such restrictions do not normally apply to a regular bond issue, but apparently for a company the size of California Microwave the sale of debentures in the capital markets was not a viable alternative.

To finance its rapid growth, the company negotiated an increase in its bank credit line to $15 million and obtained a $4 million three-year term loan. This term loan carried an interest rate of 11.24 percent and required repayment in three installments: $1 million in September 1990, $2 million in September 1991, and $1 million in March 1992. During 1989, the maximum amount of interest-bearing debt was about $19 million, and the average amount borrowed was about $8 million. Therefore, the term loan constituted a significant percentage of California Microwave's interest-bearing debt that year. It constituted two thirds of the total long-term debt of $6.2 million carried on the balance sheet, with the remainder the industrial development bonds.

relationship provides the firm greater access to the lender and more opportunity to negotiate around the difficulty.

- Most firms prefer to match up the maturities of assets and financing. If the firm buys an asset with an expected life of five years, it will normally seek financing that will last about five years. If the firm decides to borrow to buy the asset, it can readily tailor a five-year term loan. Therefore, term loans facilitate the investment-financing match up.

- Term borrowing provides long-term debt capital for small firms that find it difficult or impossible to raise money through the market because of their size. As an example, see the Financial Management Insights.

Disadvantages of Term Loans

- In comparison with equity, term loans have the usual disadvantage of debt: more risk.
- Like other debt, term loans carry the risk of bankruptcy. If the firm cannot service the debt, it will fail.
- Term loans usually have fairly stringent restrictions, and in periods of tight money, term lenders frequently demand "equity sweeteners" (some stock) as part of the loan agreement.

SUMMARY

- Leasing is a form of long-term, fixed-charge financing. The firm is committed to future fixed charges when it leases, similar to incurring debt.
- Similar to other fixed-charge financing, leasing is less expensive than equity financing but also involves more risk.
- An operating lease is a short-term, cancelable lease. A financial or capital lease is a long-term, noncancelable lease in either of two forms: a direct lease or a sale and leaseback.
- Most financial leases are leveraged leases involving a third party to lend funds to the lessor.
- The leasing decision refers to the question of whether it is more profitable to lease than to purchase an asset. The economic analysis involves computing the NPV of the purchase alternative, computing the incremental NPV impact of the lease alternative, and choosing the alternative leading to the higher positive NPV.
- Term loans are a negotiated source of financing obtained from major term loan suppliers like commercial banks, insurance companies, and commercial finance companies.
- Maturities vary from one year to several years, collateral is directly related to the perceived safety of the loan, and restrictive provisions may be attached to the loan.
- The repayment schedule typically calls for equal amortization payments that include both principal and interest. Term loans, like other debt, have tax-deductible interest payments.

KEY TERMS

financial lease, p. 600   operating lease, p. 598
leveraged lease, p. 600

QUESTIONS

20–1. Distinguish between three parties involved in at least some leases: the lessor, the lessee, and a lender.

20–2. Briefly distinguish between a sale and leaseback arrangement, a financial lease, and a service lease.

20–3. What kinds of companies provide lease financing?

20–4. List the features of a financial lease.

20–5. It is frequently argued that one of the advantages of leasing (in comparison to buying) is that it preserves working capital. Explain what this statement means and then describe under what conditions the purported advantage really exists.

20–6. What would the NPV of a lease be in perfect markets? Why?

20–7. What is the biggest single reason for leasing?

20–8. Outline the steps involved in the economic analysis of the lease decision.

20–9. What is the leasing discount rate used? Why?

20–10. List the perceived advantages of leasing and explain the problems with these perceived advantages.

20–11. How did FASB #13 change the leasing requirement for firms?

20–12. What are the accounting criteria to be met in order to classify a lease as a financial lease?

20–13. Term loans frequently carry restrictive provisions intended to protect the lender. Identify the four main such provisions and *briefly* describe the purpose of each.

20–14. What are the primary differences between financing with bonds and term loans? What advantages does term borrowing have over issuing bonds?

PROBLEMS

20–1. Prepare a loan amortization schedule for a $20,000, four-year term loan, assuming the bank charges 18 percent interest annually on the declining balance of the loan and annual amortization payments are equal amounts.

20–2. A merchant borrows $10,000 for remodeling. He amortizes the debt, including 8 percent interest, by making equal end-of-year payments for 10 years. In computing his income tax in later years, he will need to know how much interest he paid. Determine how much interest was paid in each of the first five years.

20–3. Yang and Company has just had an application for a $1,000, three-year term loan approved by a local bank. At the end of each year, Yang will pay an agreed-upon amount of principal plus 7 percent interest on the loan balance that was outstanding at the beginning of the year. The bank has offered Yang three alternative amortization schedules:

> Plan A. The loan is amortized by equal annual payments.
>
> Plan B. At the end of the first year $600 principal is paid, $300 principal is paid at the end of the second year, and the remainder of the loan is retired at the end of year three.
>
> Plan C. No principal payment is made at the end of the first year, while principal payments of $500 are made at the end of each of the second and third years.

    a. Prepare a loan amortization schedule showing yearly interest, principal, and total payments for each plan. Note that an interest payment must be paid each year under each plan.

    b. Determine the total amount of undiscounted dollars paid in interest under each plan.

    c. Use Equation 20–3 to determine the cost of term borrowing for each plan, assuming that flotation costs are negligible and that Yang's tax rate is 34 percent.

    d. Rank-order the plans from economically most to least desirable. Explain your rankings.

    e. What cash flow circumstances at the company level could cause Yang to prefer one plan over the other two?

20–4. In each situation shown below, make a lease-buy recommendation:

	NPV of Buy Alternative	NPV of Incremental Lease Effects
A	$1,000	−$ 500
B	2,000	500
C	− 4,000	4,500
D	− 3,000	2,000
E	1,000	1,000

20–5. D. Scott and Company is making a lease-buy decision. The buy alternative has been analyzed to have NPV = $5,000. Given the information shown below, complete the analysis for Scott and make a recommendation. Depreciation schedule if bought:

Year	Depreciation
1	$ 5,000
2	10,000
3	10,000
4	5,000

Initial investment saved by leasing	$28,200
Lease payments	$8,000 at end of each year for four years
Operating costs	Equal under lease and buy plans
Tax rate	40%
Required rate of return on borrowing	0.10

20–6. Work Problem 20–5 with the buy alternative NPV = − $5,000.

20–7. Richter Builders, Inc., is considering the use of some equipment for four years. The manufacturer of the equipment has offered to either lease or sell the equipment to Richter. Lease payments would be $90,000 per year, due at the end of each year. If purchased, the equipment would cost $300,000 and Richter would use straight-line depreciation with a three-year class life and recovery period. Estimated salvage is zero. The tax rate is 50 percent. Annual CFBT under the buy plan is $150,000. Annual operating costs are the same for both plans. Finally, the discount rate is 10 percent for the buy plan and the required rate of return on borrowing is 8 percent. Determine whether the asset should be leased or bought. Under either alternative, old equipment worth $18,000 will be sold.

SELECTED REFERENCES

Leasing as a form of financing is discussed in:

Bower, Richard S., and George S. Oldfield, Jr. "Of Lessees, Lessors and Discount Rates and Whether Pigs Have Wings." *Journal of Business Research,* March 1981, pp. 29–38.

Discussions about the terms of leasing can be found in:

Crawford, Peggy J.; Charles P. Harper; and John J. McConnell. "Further Evidence on the Terms of Financial Leases." *Financial Management,* Autumn 1981, pp. 7–14.

Grimland, Richard A., and Robert Capettini. "A Note on the Evaluation of Leveraged Leases and Other Investments." *Financial Management,* Summer 1982, pp. 68–72.

An overall discussion of leasing policy is contained in:

Smith, Clifford W., and L. McDonald Wakeman. "Determinants of Corporate Leasing Policy." *Journal of Finance,* July 1985, pp. 895–908.

Special Topics

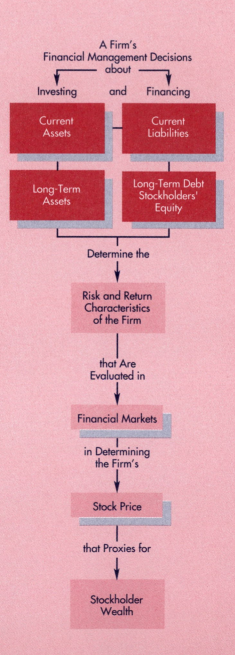

A Firm's
Financial Management Decisions
about

Investing   and   Financing

Current Assets	Current Liabilities
Long-Term Assets	Long-Term Debt Stockholders' Equity

Determine the

Risk and Return
Characteristics
of the Firm

that Are
Evaluated in

Financial Markets

in Determining
the Firm's

Stock Price

that Proxies for

Stockholder
Wealth

Chapter 21
Mergers and Corporate Restructurings
Chapter 22
International Financial Management

We conclude our study of financial management with an analysis of topics that can be important issues for the firm. Because of the necessity of covering the main principles of financial management in a logical and coherent order, these topics have been saved until the end of the text.

Chapter 21 considers mergers and corporate restructurings, which can include acquiring companies or divisions, disposing of companies or divisions, spinoffs, major changes in capital structure, and leveraged buyouts. While many firms will never engage in these activities, a significant number will, and the dollar amounts involved, as well as the impact on affected parties, will be large. The 1980s was a decade of headline-grabbing mergers, acquisitions, and other corporate restructurings. While the 1990s probably will not see that much activity in this area, the potential is always there and the issues must be considered.

Chapter 21 considers the firm's external growth. As always, the firm's objective is to maximize the stockholders' wealth. Although corporate restructurings are considered in general, the primary emphasis is on mergers and acquisitions. Merger decisions are understood as a variant of the capital budgeting process. Leveraged buyouts, considered in an earlier chapter, receive further analysis in this chapter. Appendix 21–B considers the firm's failure in some detail, outlining the alternatives available to the firm if it fails.

Chapter 22 discusses the important issue of international financial management. The reader will recall that in earlier chapters, sections have been included entitled "International Perspective." This was done to emphasize international issues where appropriate without resorting to an in-depth discussion of international finance that would make the analysis of the topic at hand even more difficult. As the world economy continues to become more integrated, international financial management becomes even more important. This chapter allows us to focus specifically on the issues involved when a firm operates with an international perspective, as many of the largest U.S. corporations do. Particular attention is paid to currency or exchange rate risk.

21

Mergers and Corporate Restructurings

To Merge or Not to Merge—That Is the Question

In 1988, Kodak paid over $5 billion for Sterling Drug, Inc., a pharmaceutical company probably best known as the maker of Bayer aspirin. The price represented a multiple of about 35 times the earnings of Sterling, which is high by most standards.

Kodak sought to cut costs and increase funds available for Sterling's research. Given the long lead times necessary to develop new drugs, Kodak's argument was that fixing Sterling's problems was quicker than developing a new pharmaceutical operation.

Sterling's money-makers, such as Bayer aspirin, faced declining revenues, and its biggest pharmaceutical product faced increased competition. Sterling continued to face well-known distribution problems—getting its drug products into the offices of doctors.

Thus, Kodak, which was working on its fourth restructuring in five years, left investors with grave doubts about the virtues of this acquisition. Total earnings (including Sterling) for Kodak were expected to drop in 1989, and, in fact, did decline sharply for that year. No wonder, then, that when Kodak made the acquisition, according to *Business Week*, "All it received from investors was a resounding Bronx cheer."[1] At the beginning of 1991, when quarterly earnings were again disappointing, the jury was still out—was this a good acquisition or not?

---

[1] See "Kodak May Wish It Never Went to the Drugstore," Business Week, December 4, 1989, pp. 72 and 76, and *The Value Line Investment Survey*, various issues.

Thus far, we have considered *internal growth,* which is brought about by investment in projects the firm develops itself through its capital budgeting process. *External growth* takes place when the firm purchases already existing assets, as when Company A buys Company B. Our focus here is specifically on external growth through mergers and acquisitions.

As always in our study of managerial finance, the firm's objective is to maximize the stockholder's wealth. Thus, a firm should undertake a merger only if it contributes to this goal. In effect, merger decisions are investment decisions, involving an initial outflow and a series of inflows. The financial manager must determine how much to pay to acquire the expected stream of benefits. Therefore, merger decisions are a variant of the capital budgeting process. A firm must decide—as in Kodak's case—if the proposed acquisition is a good one, and if so, how much should be paid for the company.

Primary *chapter learning objectives* are:

1. To understand corporate restructurings in general.
2. To understand and analyze mergers/acquisitions in particular.

A PERSPECTIVE ON CORPORATE RESTRUCTURINGS

As noted, external growth involves the expansion of one firm as a result of acquiring all or part of another firm. Firms may also dispose of large segments of their business, by selling off plants or divisions, or spinning off entire subsidiaries to their stockholders. Furthermore, the capital structure can be radically changed, as in the case of the leveraged buyout of RJR, referred to earlier. In all of these cases, what is involved is *corporate restructuring,* or a rearrangement of the corporate entity.

Corporate restructurings constitute the deals on Wall Street that were so popular in the 1980s and received so much attention in the popular press—the acquisitions, leveraged buyouts, stock buybacks, and public offerings. Closely related to these activities was the continuing issuance of junk bonds (discussed in Chapter 19) because many of these deals would not have occurred without the use of junk bond financing.

Table 21–1 shows the 10 largest deals in 1990, including the value of the transaction and how it was made. As we can readily see, the numbers are enormous, and the transactions in some cases quite complex. Given that a major interest in this chapter is mergers and acquisitions, note that most of the transactions shown in Table 21–1 were acquisitions, either for cash or cash and stock. In fact, most of the major deals in recent years involved mergers and acquisitions, and we are thus justified in devoting much of the chapter to the study of mergers.

In a sense, what we are talking about is corporate control. The battle for corporate control has had, and will continue to have, a significant impact on corporate behavior and, therefore, on the financial manager. In theory, corporate takeovers offer society an effective private-market method of replacing ineffective management, thereby better utilizing resources. This should serve the stockholders' interests—if management is doing a poor job, it can be replaced, and the stockholders' position will be enhanced.

In practice, however, the battle for corporate control is controversial. Americans worry about a few large firms gaining control in an industry—for example, airlines—and reducing competition, leading to higher prices, less service, and so

	Rank	Value (000)	Transaction
1.	*Matsushita Electric Industrial* acquires 97 percent of *MCA* (entertainment company).	$6,273,600	Cash tender offer, December 29, as part of a $6.46 billion acquisition due to close in early 1991.
2.	*Philip Morris* (consumer goods) acquires *Jacobs Suchard* (Swiss coffee and confectionery company).	$4,183,368	Acquisition for cash, September 18.
3.	*McCaw Cellular Communications* acquires 42 percent of *Lin Broadcasting*, increasing its ownership to 52 percent.	$3,800,000	Acquisition for cash and stock, March 27.
4.	*Georgia-Pacific* (building products, paper and pulp) acquires *Great Northern Nekoosa* (paper and pulp).	$3,640,564	Acquisition for cash, June 26.
5.	*Rhone-Poulenc* (French chemical company) acquires 68 percent of *Rorer Group* (pharmaceuticals).	$3,486,000	Cash tender offer and merger of Rorer Group and Rhone-Poulenc's human pharmaceuticals to form Rhone-Poulenic Rorer, July 31.
6.	*Ameritech* and *Bell Atlantic* (telecommunications) acquire *Telecom* from New Zealand government.	$2,460,000	Acquisition for cash, September 12.
7.	*Roche Holding* (Swiss health care company) acquires 60 percent of *Genentech* (pharmaceuticals).	$2,120,544	Acquisition for cash and stock, September 7.
8.	*Lin Broadcasting* acquires 46 percent of the New York non-wireline cellular franchise from *Metromedia*, increasing its ownership to 93 percent.	$1,900,000	Acquisition for cash and stock, August 10.
9.	*Cie de Saint-Gobain* (French glass manufacturer) acquires *Norton* (abrasives).	$1,853,000	Acquisition for cash, September 18.
10.	*FLGI Acquisition* acquires *General Instrument* (electronics).	$1,527,645	Leveraged buyout for cash, August 22.

Source: Jaclyn Fierman, "Deals of the Year," *Fortune,* © 1991 The Time Inc. Magazine Company. All rights reserved.

on. Even more at issue in today's world is the takeover of American firms by foreign companies, and the resulting "threat" to U.S. interests. Besides the obvious takeovers by Japanese firms, countries not normally thought of as acquirers are now active—for example, France made $3 billion worth of acquisitions in 1988. Furthermore, takeovers are costly, in both time and resources. Many managements are heavily occupied by the threat of a potential takeover, and they concentrate on possible defenses that may be detrimental to the stockholders.

The scope of this issue is enormous, affecting many firms at one time or another in major ways. For example, in the past 10 years General Electric spent almost $20 billion on acquisitions. The decade of the 1980s was an era of merger activity, and controversial merger activity at that, involving junk bonds, merger deals, and so on.

As with other major financial decisions, the stakes involved in external growth are large. The cost of failure can be high, but the rewards from a successful acquisition can be large.

■ *Example*

Ron Perelman controlled MacAndrews and Forbes Group.[2] In 1983, this company paid $125 million for Technicolor, with $2 million in cash and the remainder borrowed. Four months after the transaction was completed, Perelman took MacAndrews and Forbes private. He then sold the company in 1988 for $780 million, in cash. Any way you calculate it, this is not a bad rate of return on a $2 million equity investment. ■

FORMS OF BUSINESS COMBINATIONS

There is some disagreement on the precise definition of terms relating to external growth because some have narrow legal meanings and others do not. In addition, some terms are commonly used interchangeably, even when there are legal distinctions between them.

Mergers/Acquisitions

merger
combination of two (or more) companies such that only the surviving company continues to operate under its own name

consolidation
combining two or more companies into a new firm

acquisition
acquiring another company by acquiring either its stock or its assets

Technically, a **merger** is a combination of two (or more) companies such that only the surviving company continues to operate under its own name. A **consolidation,** on the other hand, means to combine two or more companies into a new firm. None of the consolidating firms legally survives (as will be reflected by the name of the new organization), so there is no designation of buyer and seller; all consolidating companies are dissolved, and a new one appears.[3] Finally, the term **acquisition** refers to acquiring another company by acquiring either its stock or its assets. A common feature of mergers and consolidations is that the surviving company buys the stock of the other companies involved using either cash or securities—as explained below, the form of payment is important in determining the tax status of the transaction. In some situations, a company may wish to purchase only assets, either all or part of another company, with the buyer not assuming the liabilities of the seller.[4]

Regulatory agencies that are charged with preventing a significant decline in competition because of business combinations are not concerned so much with what kind of business combination is proposed, but rather with the effect the resultant combination would have on competition. Because of this interest in the end result rather than in the legal name of the combination, the terms *merger,*

[2]See Ralph King, Jr., "Ron Perelman's $640 Million Unsure Thing," *Forbes,* October 30, 1989, p. 42.
[3]Consolidations are typical among companies of roughly the same size, whereas companies that differ significantly in size usually merge.
[4]If a firm sells all of its assets for cash, leaving it simply a "corporate shell," it may choose to liquidate by paying off its creditors and distributing the residual funds to the stockholders (a "liquidating dividend"). Alternatively, it may reinvest the proceeds in new assets, or if it received payment in stock, it may simply hold this stock.

consolidation, and *acquisition* tend to be used interchangeably, and we will simply use the term *merger* to refer to any absorption of one or more existing firms by another firm.

- **Example**

There are, of course, many examples of mergers. See Table 21–1 for examples of major mergers that have occurred recently. ▪

Economic Distinctions

From an economic viewpoint there are three kinds of business combinations: (1) horizontal, (2) vertical, and (3) conglomerate.

- *Horizontal.* When two firms in the same type of business combine, a horizontal merger occurs. The firms are competitors. Horizontal mergers are obvious targets of concern by the government because of the implications for competition.

  - **Example**

  Chevron's acquisition of Gulf Oil was a horizontal merger. ▪

- *Vertical.* A vertical combination is formed when a company combines with either a supplier or a customer. In effect, a buyer-seller relationship exists between the companies; that is, one company's output is the other company's input. Merger of a canned goods food processor and a can manufacturer would be a vertical merger. Vertical mergers have decreased in relative importance.

  - **Example**

  The merger of Du Pont and Conoco Oil was classified as a vertical merger. Du Pont is a heavy user of petroleum in its production activities. ▪

- *Conglomerate.* A conglomerate merger involves two firms in unrelated business activities. These firms are not competitors with each other. This has been the predominant form of merger activity since World War II.

  - **Example**

  The acquisition of Montgomery Ward by Mobil Oil was a conglomerate merger. ▪

Joint Ventures

Rather than combine the resources of two firms together in a formal manner, firms may choose to join together to pursue a common objective while maintaining their independence. The joint venture is directed by the management of both of the firms involved.

■ *Figure 21–1*
Holding Company
Arrangement

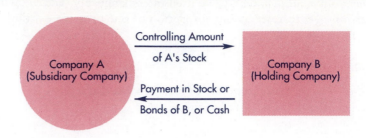

- *Example*

In 1989, Merck & Company, a pharmaceutical firm, entered into an agreement with The Du Pont Company to develop a new class of therapeutic agents for high blood pressure and heart disease. ■

Holding Company

A holding company is a firm that owns (holds) common stock of other companies. By owning enough stock, the holding company (frequently called the *parent* company) controls the *subsidiary* companies. If the parent company owns all of the subsidiary's stock, the controlled company is called a *wholly owned subsidiary*.

Figure 21–1 shows the transactions that occur when a holding company arrangement is set up. Company B, the holding company, buys a controlling interest in A, which then becomes a subsidiary of B. In theory, B would need over 50 percent of A's common to ensure control. In reality, effective control can be maintained with a much lower percentage of A's common, sometimes as low as 10 to 20 percent. This is, in fact, one of the allures of the holding company arrangement.

- *Example*

UtiliCorp United Inc., discussed in earlier chapters, has three wholly owned domestic subsidiaries and one wholly owned foreign subsidiary. ■

MERGER MECHANICS

Payment Methods

Financing packages are extremely varied. Buyers may use common, preferred, convertible securities, cash, straight debt, warrants, or some combination of these. Rightly or wrongly, one of the main considerations in determining the financing package has been its effect on current earnings per share.

Cash

In a *cash-for-common* exchange, the selling company's stockholders receive cash for their common stock, which results in a taxable transaction (explained below). It may also result in a favorable EPS because the buying firm is acquiring new earnings without increasing its shares outstanding. This presumes that the buyer has cash to make the acquisition. If it does not, it must determine how to raise the cash, and one way is to issue stock. In that case, the buying firm is effectively engaging in a stock-for-stock swap, but is incurring transactions costs in selling stock to the stock market rather than exchanging stock with the seller's stockholders.

Many of the top transactions in recent years involved an acquisition for cash.

- *Example*

As we saw in Table 21–1, Matsushita paid over $6 billion in cash for MCA. ▪

Common Stock

In a *common-for-common* swap, the selling company's stockholders give up their stock in return for common in the buying company. The most obvious advantage of this method of financing is that it is consistent with a tax-free exchange (explained below). A perceived disadvantage is that the issuance of stock increases the number of the buyers' shares outstanding, which can dilute its earnings per share.

- *Example*

Dun & Bradstreet acquired IMS International, an information services firm, for common stock in a transaction valued at over $1.5 billion. ▪

Convertible Securities

Convertible debentures and convertible preferred stock were used frequently to finance conglomerate acquisitions during the 1960s because of their favorable effect on EPS. Under accounting practices then permitted, convertibles were not counted as owner's equity financial instruments, even though they would eventually be converted into common. The number of shares the convertibles would eventually be converted into were not included in determining the number of shares the firm had outstanding. This resulted in artificially high earnings-per-share figures.[5]

Tax Considerations

A crucial consideration in a merger is its tax status. Mergers are classified either *taxable* or *tax free* transactions for purposes of determining the immediate federal income tax liability of the seller and its stockholders.

- *Taxable*. If a merger is determined (by the Internal Revenue Service) to be taxable, the tax basis of the assets acquired will change to reflect the price paid by the buyer; that is, the buyer writes up the value of the assets acquired to reflect the excess of market value over book value. The buyer

---

[5]In the late 1960s the Accounting Principles Board issued an opinion that required calculation of EPS on a fully diluted basis. This means that the number of shares controlled by the convertibles would be used in determining the number of common shares outstanding and EPS. These requirements led to a distinction between earnings per share and *fully diluted* earnings per share. The new requirements also led to a marked decrease in the use of convertible securities in mergers.

will be able to show a higher depreciation charge, thereby lowering taxes and cash flow after taxes. With a taxable merger, the seller (if assets are sold) or its stockholders (if stock is sold) must pay federal income tax in the current year on any gains made from the transaction.

- *Tax-free.* Mergers ruled to be tax-free require no current-year tax payment on such gains. The selling company can defer paying capital gains tax on the sale of assets until the stock received in the transaction is sold. Any tax for the stockholders of the selling company is deferred until the *new* securities received in the merger are sold by the stockholder. Therefore, other things being equal, sellers prefer a tax-free transaction.

To qualify for tax-free status, the sellers' stockholders must receive voting equity securities, either common stock or voting preferred stock.[6] Conversely, if the acquired company's stockholders receive cash or nonvoting securities (such as debt securities) in exchange for their common shares, gains are taxable in the year of merger. Acquisitions are considered taxable unless they have been declared tax-free.

Under the Tax Reform Act of 1986, mergers are less profitable than they were in the past. If the buying company writes up the assets for tax purposes to reflect a price in excess of book value, the selling company must pay taxes (capital gains) in the year of the merger. Furthermore, the capital gains rate rose from the maximum 20 percent that existed before the 1986 Act, resulting in higher taxes for the sellers.

Accounting Policies: Purchase versus Pooling of Interests

There are two accounting methods for handling mergers, the purchase method and the pooling-of-interest method, and they have considerably different impacts on the buying firm. Because of merger premiums, the price of the seller's assets exceeds its book value.

purchase method
price of the seller's assets is allocated between tangible assets and goodwill accounts

1. Under the **purchase method,** the price of the seller's assets is allocated between *tangible assets* and *goodwill* accounts. The tangible-asset account will include that portion of the purchase price deemed to be the *fair market value* of the assets. This amount is depreciable both for reporting to stockholders *and* for tax purposes. The remainder of the purchase price is assigned to goodwill, which is depreciable for reporting, but *not* for tax purposes; it must be deducted from net income after taxes.

   - *Example*

   Forest Laboratories, Inc., a drug manufacturer, acquired all of the capital stock of the Tosara Group. The acquisition was accounted for as a purchase, and the purchase price was assigned to the net assets based on the fair value at date of acquisition. The excess of cost over the net assets acquired is being amortized on a straight-line basis over 40 years.[7] ∎

---

[6]Also, the acquisition must have a business purpose and not be merely for tax purposes.
[7]This information is based on the *Annual Report,* 1989, of Forest Laboratories, Inc.

2. Under **pooling of interests,** the seller's assets are brought into the merged company's books at their book value. No premium over book is recognized. The book value brought into the merger company is depreciable both for reporting and for tax purposes.

This difference in treatment of the premium over book creates an advantage and a disadvantage between the two accounting methods. One of these is *economic;* the other is a *perceived* or *cosmetic* advantage.

It is economically advantageous to have increased depreciation for tax purposes. Since the seller's assets are brought into the merged tangible asset accounts at their market value, which is generally higher than their book value, tax-deductible depreciation will increase more under the purchase method, causing the merged company to have greater cash flow after tax. However, since the higher market value must also be depreciated for stockholder reporting purposes, this means lower *reported* earnings. Moreover, the goodwill incurred must also be depreciated, which also lowers reported earnings, and there is no commensurate depreciation tax shield for the goodwill. Because there is no premium under pooling of interest, depreciation for both tax and reporting increases by a lower amount.

In summary:

- Reported earnings will be higher under the pooling method because depreciation will not increase and because goodwill will not have to be amortized on the buyer's income statement.
- Cash flow will be higher under the purchase method.

Empirical research in accounting generally has shown that the market can accurately distinguish between economic and cosmetic effects. This implies that the purchase method, which has an economic advantage (higher cash flow after tax) and a cosmetic disadvantage (lower reported EPS) in comparison to pooling of interest, should be a preferred accounting technique. However, in the past, the cosmetic effect led to widespread preference for the pooling method along with widespread abuses of the method. The accounting profession has attempted to eliminate the artificial advantages of the pooling method by eliminating some of the obvious enticements and by making it more difficult to qualify for pooling of interest. Several tests must be met today to qualify for this treatment.

REASONS FOR BUSINESS COMBINATIONS

Any proposed merger should be consistent with the firm's goal of stockholder wealth maximization. We will see that some of the stated motives for forming business combinations are not necessarily related to this goal. It is particularly important that mergers be carefully compared against comparable investments aimed at internal growth. We should note at the outset that waves of merger activity occur from time to time for reasons not fully understood even today.

We will divide the reasons for business combinations into two categories: those with some justification and those having questionable validity.

Justifiable Reasons	*Questionable Reasons*
Synergistic operating economies	Diversification
Growth in size	Earnings growth
Tax reasons	

Justifiable Reasons

Synergistic Operating Economies

One of the most common reasons given for merging is that there are potential synergistic operating economies to be gained: *Synergy,* meaning working together, is often described as $2 + 2 = 5$, that is, one combined company is more efficient than two separate companies. As a result, savings should occur in operating costs, operations should become more profitable, and the worth of the combined companies should be greater than the sum of the worths of the separate companies.

Synergistic operating gains would seem most likely in horizontal mergers having many opportunities for eliminating duplicate facilities. At the other extreme, conglomerate mergers would appear to offer the least opportunity to achieve operating economies.

Growth in Size

A second reason advanced to justify a merger is that it typically offers the fastest and most convenient way to grow. The alternative to mergers is to grow internally through the capital budgeting process. This is a time-consuming process, however—plants must be built, equipment installed, and employees trained. In some cases, growth may be blocked by legal obstacles such as patents held by other companies, or exclusive franchising arrangements granted to one or a few companies.

Although growth through acquisition can be advantageous, the problem is to identify growth that will provide the acquiring firm with a net gain when all benefits and costs are included. Growth for growth's sake is not an intelligent strategy. Furthermore, the ultimate concern of shareholders is not growth in sales, assets, or total earnings—it is growth in stockholder wealth. A key concern regarding acquisitions is growth in earnings per share (EPS), which adjusts for any additional shares of common that may be issued in acquisitions. EPS is one half the valuation equation that states that the value of a share is equal to earnings per share multiplied by the price-earnings ratio.

Tax Reasons

Some mergers and acquisitions take place because one of the partners has a tax loss, which shields the income of the merging partner from taxation. Tax losses can be carried back and then forward to offset the tax liability in a particular year. If the losses are large enough, they may not be used up and the benefits could be lost if a merger does not occur.

Questionable Reasons

Diversification

Diversification is one of the most frequently cited reasons for conglomerate merger activity, which has been at a high level in recent years. The diversification principle says, Don't put all your eggs in one basket. In other words, the firm should invest in many different kinds of assets whose cash flows are not perfectly correlated.

Conglomerate mergers provide one way to acquire an entirely different class of assets. Recall from the portfolio theory work in Chapter 5 that the standard deviation of a portfolio may be reduced by adding assets whose returns are not perfectly correlated with the portfolio's. As applied to mergers, the case for diversification goes like this: the addition of another company will reduce the variability of the firm's earnings if, as is almost always the case, the correlation between the buyer's earnings and the seller's earnings is less than $+1.0$ Since the firm is now less risky, a lower required rate of return on equity should be imposed by the market. Under this argument, there is no requirement that the combination lead to operating economies.

There is strong opposition to this argument, however, which goes like this: investors already hold diversified portfolios of stocks; that is, they perform their own diversification and do not need to have the firm perform this diversification function for them. If, for example, investors owned shares of both Company A and Company B and these two companies merged, investors would not realize any diversification advantages from the combination. They already enjoyed diversification from holding the individual stocks. The majority opinion supports this counterargument that it is not valid to merge solely to reduce the required rate of return (and hence raise the value of the stock) on the basis of risk reduction.

Another aspect of diversification is related to the firm's debt capacity. Recall from Chapter 15 that, up to a point, there is an advantage to debt financing because of the tax deductibility of interest. And this point of debt usage is set, in part, by the amount of debt lenders believe is safe. Given this advantage of debt financing, if the firm can establish that it can safely support more debt, then doing so will increase stockholders' wealth. It has been argued that business combinations permit increased debt capacity because of the increased stability of cash flows from the portfolio effect of combining companies. This increased stability means the combination of two or more firms can safely support a debt level greater than the firms could carry separately.

Earnings Growth

In past years, many firms established attractive earnings growth rates through their merger activities—that is, they achieved an immediate increase in reported earnings per share. A large part of this growth was caused by lenient accounting practices permissible in business combinations. Earnings growth often was illusory, and accounting standards have been changed to eliminate potentially deceptive earnings-per-share calculation procedures. This is discussed more fully below. Also, as noted above, growth in stockholder wealth is what really matters, and earnings growth is only one component of this.

EVALUATING PROPOSED BUSINESS COMBINATIONS

Given the firm's goal, a merger proposal should be evaluated in terms of its potential effect on stockholder wealth. In other words, mergers should be analyzed as valuation issues. We will analyze this evaluation from the perspectives of both buyer and seller.

With all the glamour associated with mergers, it is easy to lose sight of some of their disadvantages. Many mergers simply do not work out. For example, estimates of costs and benefits associated with the acquisition may have been too optimistic. Also, there may be turmoil associated with integrating the firms and friction between the two managements. And there may be problems with dissenting minority stockholders of the acquired firm about the value they received for their stock, as well as vocal dissension about the prudence of the acquisition from some stockholders of the acquiring firm.

Merger proposals also should be compared to the alternative of *internal investment,* that is, investing directly in an industry rather than buying into it through acquisition. Under present antitrust laws, which are designed to discourage reductions in competition, direct investment is easier and safer. For example, the proposed acquisition may be blocked or delayed so long that it becomes unprofitable. Moreover, initial approval of a merger provides no guarantee that the combination is permanent. A divestiture may be enforced later.

Evaluation by the Seller

Essentially, the seller is offered an exchange opportunity. It gives up its stock or assets (depending on the nature of the acquisition) and receives in return a package of financial assets from the buyer. This package may be cash, common stock, preferred stock, bonds, warrants, or some combination of these. From the seller's standpoint, the question is whether the value of this received package is greater than the value of the stock or assets being given up. No rational management would accept an acquisition offer less than its current market value; consequently, the seller's premerger market value acts as a floor for acquisition offers. Once again, we can see how valuation underlies managerial finance.

A *premium* is the difference between the offered value and the seller's market value before the offer. Even if offered a premium, firms receiving acquisition offers frequently resist, claiming the market doesn't fully appreciate the value of the firm, and the premium is therefore deceiving. To be consistent with the goal of stockholder wealth maximization, the potential acquired firm should evaluate acquisition and merger proposals on the basis of whether the value received is greater than the value surrendered.

Evaluation by the Buyer

From the buyer's standpoint, the proposed business combination can be evaluated as an investment decision. The buyer makes an initial investment (the cost of the acquisition) and expects to receive future cash flows in return. To evaluate this investment, the buyer needs to be able to estimate cash flows associated with the proposal and an appropriate discount rate. Therefore, the steps are these:

- *Estimate the cash flows.* As we learned in Chapter 11, the estimated cash flows should be *incremental* and should reflect (1) any cost savings arising from the acquisition or merger and (2) any changes in revenues related to the proposal.

- *Estimate an appropriate discount rate*. There is some disagreement over what this discount rate is, but one approach is that it should be the required rate of return of the acquired firm. This rate reflects the market's opinion of the risk inherent in that firm and is thus the appropriate discount rate for the buyer to use in evaluating the seller.

- *Do the present-value calculation*. Once the present value of the seller has been determined, the buyer can decide if it wishes to pursue the acquisition further.

- ### Example

The Fireside Company, in considering the purchase of Artificial Log, Inc., is attempting to determine the incremental cash flows associated with the acquisition. Fireside estimates that Artificial's current after-tax cash flows amount to $4,000,000 per year if Artificial's current management stays in control. If Fireside acquires Artificial, many of Artificial's personnel would be released, and Artificial's manufacturing operation would be moved into the Fireside plant. Together these two actions should result in after-tax cost savings of $1,000,000 per year. At the same time, Fireside would discontinue its gas log product and increase the sales effort in Artificial's gas log product line. The discontinuance of the Fireside gas log will cause its cash flows after tax to decrease by $1,500,000 per year. However, Fireside estimates that the additional sales effort put into Artificial's gas log would increase cash flows after tax by $1,700,000 per year.

If all of these estimated cash flows are expected to occur for an indefinitely long time period, and the appropriate required rate of return is 10 percent, is the acquisition worthwhile from Fireside's perspective? The following analysis is directed toward answering that question:

	CFAT per Year
Artificial's current CFAT	$4,000,000
Incremental CFAT caused by merger:	
Operating cost savings	+ 1,000,000
Discontinue Fireside product line	− 1,500,000
Enhance Artificial product line	+ 1,700,000
Total	$5,200,000

$$\text{NPV} = \$5,200,000 \; \text{PVIFA}_{10,\infty} = (\$5,200,000)(10)$$
$$= \$52,000,000$$

Fireside should pay no more than about $52 million to acquire Artificial. At any lower price, Artificial is an attractive buy for Fireside. ∎

TERMS OF EXCHANGE

Naturally, both firms in the proposed merger will seek the best terms possible for their respective stockholders. If negotiations are successful, the combination will be formed, provided it is legally sanctioned. Often, however, negotiations

⋯

FINANCIAL MANAGEMENT INSIGHTS

The Impact of Acquiring Another Company

Philip Morris is a successful company, combining tobacco, beer, food, and financial services into a potent combination.[8] Operating revenues increased from approximately $10 billion in 1980 to approximately $45 billion in 1989. The 1989 increase in operating revenues alone was about 50 percent. Total assets almost doubled between 1986 and 1988, while long-term debt almost tripled. In 1984 earnings per share was 91 cents, and in 1989 it was $3.18.

What would make its financial numbers such as those cited above change so dramatically even though Philip Morris is a good company? Acquisitions have played a major role in this company's recent history. General Foods was acquired in 1985, and Kraft, Inc., was acquired in late 1988. Consolidated results for Philip Morris include the operating results of these companies since their acquisition. Such acquisitions can have significant impact on the financial performance of acquiring companies.

The total price of Kraft (including retirement of stock options, etc.) was approximately $13 billion, which was accounted for as a purchase. The purchase price exceeded the fair value of the net assets acquired by more than $12 billion, which is being amortized over 40 years.

It often takes time for acquisitions to be absorbed and start paying off. In 1988 the company provided for restructuring costs of 23 cents per share for General Foods, and in 1987 restructuring cost the company 2 cents in earnings per share. Philip Morris estimates that if the acquisition of Kraft had occurred at the beginning of 1988 or 1987, earnings per share would have been $1.63 as compared to the $2.22 actually reported for 1988 and $1.21 as compared to the $1.94 actually reported for 1987. In 1988 Kraft was combined with General Foods to form Kraft General Foods, Inc. Philip Morris charged $180 million pretax income to accomplish this.

Operating revenues for 1989 for Philip Morris increased $13 billion and operating profit increased $2.5 billion, and Kraft accounted for 90 percent and 37 percent respectively of these increases. On the other hand, total net earnings after tax increased only 26 percent as interest and other debt expense almost tripled from 1988. Philip Morris showed strong earnings growth in 1990, and expected still more growth for 1991, although this growth was not due solely to the food division.

[8]See *1989 Annual Report*, Philip Morris, and *The Value Line Investment Survey*, various issues.

are unsuccessful, and the proposed combination is called off. The aim of the negotiations is to agree on the *terms of exchange*, which are ratios that indicate what each party receives and gives up by entering into the combination.

Market Value Exchange Ratio

Because the firm's goal is to maximize stockholder wealth, the critical consideration is the *market value exchange ratio*, which is the market value of the financial assets offered to the stockholders of the seller divided by the market value of the seller's stock:

$$\text{Market value} \atop \text{exchange ratio} = \frac{\text{Market value of cash and securities offered to seller's stockholders}}{\text{Market value of seller's stock}} \qquad \text{(21–1)}$$

This ratio directly measures the increase in wealth of the stockholders of the acquired company as a result of entering the merger.

- ### *Example*

Suppose the Alderon Company, whose common stock sells for $28 per share, has made a merger offer to Telrate, whose stock sells for $10 per share. What is the market value exchange ratio under the following plans?

1. Alderon offers 0.5 shares of common for each share of Telrate.
2. Alderon offers $15 cash for each share of Telrate.
3. Alderon offers 1 share of convertible preferred stock worth $95 per share and 1 share of common for each 10 shares of Telrate.

Using Equation 21–1, according to Plan 1:

$$\text{Market value exchange ratio} = \frac{(0.5)(\$28)}{\$10} = 1.4$$

According to Plan 2:

$$\text{Market value exchange ratio} = \frac{(\$15)}{\$10} = 1.5$$

According to Plan 3:

$$\text{Market value exchange ratio} = \frac{\$95 + \$28}{(10 \text{ shares})(\$10 \text{ per share})}$$

$$= \frac{\$123}{\$100} = 1.23$$

In each case the market value exchange ratio measures the wealth the Telrate stockholders will receive per dollar of wealth they now have in Telrate stock. Plan 1 is called a *common-for-common* exchange, 2 is a *cash-for-common* exchange, and 3 is a *combination* plan. ▪

Market value exchange ratios greater than 1.0 reflect *premiums* paid to the seller, and the greater the premium, the more attractive the merger will appear to the seller's stockholders. Premiums are commonplace and typically average about 20 percent or so.[9] Theoretically, the buyer can afford to offer premiums because of the cost savings it expects to achieve. It is questionable, however, whether extremely large premiums are justified. Buyers are often so eager to make the acquisition that they pay exorbitant premiums, with the consequence that the investment turns out badly. All the buyer did was enrich the seller's stockholders.

Negotiation Limits

If the intended seller is interested in negotiating, it will seek to arrange the largest premium possible. The only market value exchange ratio limit the seller sees is the lower limit of 1.0, but the bigger the ratio the better. From the buyer's perspective, the lower the ratio the better, and the upper limit should be set by the investment evaluation developed earlier in this chapter.

---

[9]There would be no normal incentive for a company to let itself be acquired at a discount (market value exchange ratio less than 1.0).

- *Example*

Suppose Simkowitz Sailboats has just evaluated Hettenhouse Outboard Motors as a possible acquisition. Simkowitz estimates that Hettenhouse's assets are worth $2 million. It arrived at this number by determining the present value of Hettenhouse's cash flows after accounting for some cost savings Simkowitz thinks it can effect. Hettenhouse has 200,000 shares of stock outstanding that are trading at about $7 per share. What is the upper limit of the market value exchange ratio from Simkowitz's point of view under two alternative scenarios?

1. Hettenhouse is an all-equity company.
2. Hettenhouse has $300,000 in debt outstanding.

Under (1):

$$\begin{aligned}
\text{Market value of Hettenhouse's common} &= (200{,}000 \text{ shares})(\$7 \text{ per share}). \\
&= \$1{,}400{,}000 \\
\text{Simkowitz's upper limit of market value exchange ratio} &= \frac{\$2{,}000{,}000}{\$1{,}400{,}000} = 1.43
\end{aligned}$$

Under (2):

$$\begin{aligned}
\text{Market value of Hettenhouse's common} &= \$1{,}400{,}000 \\
\text{Market value of Simkowitz's offer for Hettenhouse's common} &= \$2{,}000{,}000 - \$300{,}000 \\
&= \$1{,}700{,}000 \\
\text{Simkowitz's upper limit of market value exchange ratio} &= \frac{\$1{,}700{,}000}{\$1{,}400{,}000} = 1.21
\end{aligned}$$

If Simkowitz buys Hettenhouse for $2 million, the net present value of the project will be zero, and Simkowitz will not have changed the value of its own common stock. If Simkowitz can negotiate the acquisition for less than $2 million, its stockholders' wealth should be increased. ∎

P/E Ratios

Rightly or wrongly, P/E (price/earnings) ratios often play a key role in merger evaluations. The P/E exchange ratio is the P/E ratio of the buyer divided by the P/E ratio of the seller:

$$\text{P/E exchange ratio} = \frac{\text{Buyer's P/E}}{\text{Seller's P/E}} \qquad\qquad \textbf{(21–2)}$$

Buyers are concerned with this ratio because of its effect on earnings per share (EPS) *after* the merger. When the buyer's P/E exceeds the seller's P/E, the P/E exchange ratio will be greater than 1.0. Many merger-oriented companies will not consider acquisitions unless the P/E exchange ratio is greater than 1.0. This is because the EPS of the *combined* company will be less than the EPS of the buyer whenever the P/E exchange ratio is less than 1.0.

■ *Example*

Samsong Electronics is considering buying two companies, Baker Transistors and Cowden Manufacturing. Financial data for the three companies are as follows:

	Samsong	Baker	Cowden
Earnings	$ 1,000,000	$ 200,000	$ 200,000
Number of shares	500,000	200,000	100,000
EPS	$2.00	$1.00	$2.00
Market value of stock:			
Per share	$40.00	$25.00	$30.00
Total	$20,000,000	$5,000,000	$3,000,000
P/E	20	25	15

Let us determine the EPS of Samsong *after* acquisition of Baker and compare this result to what Samsong's EPS would be *after* acquisition of Cowden, assuming the companies are bought for their premerger market value (i.e., the market value exchange ratio is 1.0)[10] and they are acquired with common stock. The analysis is as follows:

	Acquisition of	
	Baker	Cowden
Cost	$5,000,000	$3,000,000
No. of Samsong shares required	$\frac{\$5,000,000}{\$40 \text{ per share}} = 125,000$	$\frac{\$3,000,000}{\$40 \text{ per share}} = 75,000$
Postacquisition Samsong data		
Earnings	$1,200,000	$1,200,000
No. shares	625,000	575,000
EPS	$1.92	$2.08

The effect of buying Baker, which has a higher P/E than Samsong, is to dilute Samsong's EPS from $2.00 to $1.92. The opposite effect occurs when Samsong buys Cowden, which has a lower P/E. ■

Many buyers will not enter mergers that would result in dilution of current EPS because of the presumed bad effect of this dilution on stock price and stockholder wealth. However, the dilution of current EPS caused by an acquisition may be more than offset by other factors. The acquisition may, for example, lead to increased earnings growth expectations, and as a result, the stock price may increase. Figure 21–2 illustrates this point with the Samsong purchase of Baker. Current and projected future EPS for Samsong with and without the Baker

---

[10]It is, of course, unrealistic to assume that either Baker or Cowden would sell at premerger market values; they would require a premium to induce them to sell. This unrealistic assumption is made only to keep the example simple. It does not distort the results or implications of the example.

■ *Figure 21–2*
Effect of Merger on *EPS*
when *P/E* Exchange Ratio
Is Less Than 1.0

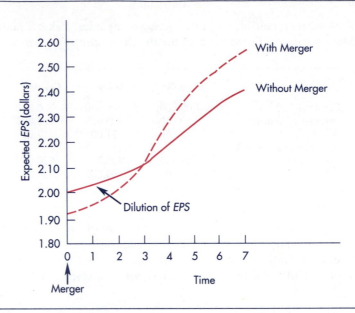

■ *Figure 21–2*
Effect of Merger on *EPS* when *P/E* Exchange Ratio Is Less Than 1.0

merger are plotted across time. Dilution occurs at the time of merger and for a short time in the future, but the growth of EPS caused by the merger is greater than EPS growth without the merger.

A reverse situation to that shown in Figure 21–2 can occur for cases where there is an initial EPS *gain* from acquisition (as when Samsong buys Cowden). The initial gain may be wiped out by adverse future earnings growth.

The main point, then, is that an initial EPS dilution or gain may be offset by growth, and it is a mistake to think that a merger looks good or bad from the buyer's standpoint solely because its P/E is higher or lower than the seller's. The real test of whether a proposed acquisition is a good one from the buyer's view is a present value investment analysis such as the one developed earlier.

ARE MERGERS PROFITABLE?

Much merger research has been performed in recent years. A particularly important question addressed in this literature is whether mergers are profitable from either the buyer's or seller's standpoint. Some of the earlier studies were concerned with accounting definitions of profit, like return on equity (net income/net worth) and the ratio of EBIT to total assets. Later studies have properly focused on stockholders' wealth, as measured by the rate of return on the market value of the stock.

Profitability to Sellers

As we would expect, in selling firms, stockholders do well because of the premiums offered to induce acceptance of the merger. There is ample evidence to support the argument that the selling companies' stockholders earn significantly larger than normal rates of return, after adjusting for risk, because of the premiums paid by the buyers. Premiums average roughly 30 percent, and often go substantially higher.

We would expect the market price of the seller to rise as soon as information of a possible takeover becomes available. Even rumors of a potential takeover can make the stock price spurt. What is interesting to note is that the price of the stock typically begins to rise before the announcement, often by a few weeks before.

Profitability to Buyers

Results for stockholders in buying companies are less clear, and there is considerable debate about their interpretation. The issue is clear: A premium is paid for a successful takeover. Are the benefits to be received real? And do they exceed the premium paid? Is there enough synergy, improvement in operations, or cost savings?

A few studies have found positive returns for buyers' stockholders. Others claim proof of abnormally low returns, and still others find virtually no effect. Most observers would agree that some takeovers are beneficial. Many appear questionable, however, and it may take years to determine if a merger is successful. Before turning to the empirical evidence, we can consider an argument that acquirers tend to pay too much.

The Winner's Curse

Do acquirers tend to overpay in a takeover? According to research by Varaiya and Ferris, there is a high probability of successfully completing the merger when the value of the target company is overestimated—the winning bidder is the one that perceives the largest value in the target company.[11] This phenomenon is sometimes referred to as the *winner's curse*.

The winner's curse predicts that the winning bid premium, on average, overstates the takeover gain. The implication is that the winner will earn an unsatisfactory rate of return, that is, one less than its required rate of return.

Empirical results presented by Varaiya and Ferris indicate that the average level of overpayment by winning bidders is both positive and significant. This is consistent with the winner's curse—the winning bidder, on average, pays a premium that overstates the expected takeover gain. Winners are paying too high a price.

Empirical Evidence

Some new research suggests that takeover premiums have risen, and may support the winner's curse hypothesis indirectly. According to Nathan and O'Keefe, the premiums for takeovers doubled between the period 1963 to 1973 and 1974 to 1985.[12] Average premiums, calculated using the price per share in excess of the previous trading price, rose from 41 percent to 75 percent for cash tender takeovers, from 29 percent to 70 percent for cash mergers, and from 32 percent to 67 percent for stock mergers. The authors speculate that a structural shift occurred

---

[11]See Nikhil P. Varaiya and Kenneth R. Ferris, "Overpaying in Corporate Takeovers: The Winner's Curse," *Financial Analysts Journal*, May–June 1987, pp. 64–70.

[12]See Kevin S. Nathan and Terrence B. O'Keefe, "The Rise in Takeover Premiums: An Exploratory Study," *Journal of Financial Economics*, June 1989, pp. 101–18.

in 1973–1974 that caused premiums to rise, but a satisfactory explanation remains unclear.

A comprehensive study of the synergistic gains from corporate acquisitions has been done by Bradley, Desai, and Kim.[13] They estimate the amount of any synergistic gains on the basis of the combined wealth of target-firm and acquiring-firm shareholders for a large sample of successful tender offers between 1963 and 1984. The average synergistic gain created was 7.4 percent for the combined wealth of the stockholders of the target and acquiring firms—clearly indicating that such mergers do create synergy. However, the *target* stockholders captured most of the gains from tender offers. Acquiring firms had a significant positive gain only during the period 1963 to 1968 and suffered a significant loss during the most recent subperiod, 1981 to 1984. Interestingly, the total percentage gains from synergy were notably constant over time.

Figure 21–3 shows the cumulative abnormal (risk-adjusted) returns to each group of stockholders. Part (A) shows the returns to the target firms, and part (B) shows the returns to the acquiring firms. As we would expect, returns to the targets firms are highest when multiple bidders are involved.

CORPORATE TAKEOVER FIGHTS

Negotiations concerning a possible merger may be friendly or hostile. In a friendly negotiation, a dialogue takes place between executives of the companies involved, and if no agreement can be reached on the terms of exchange, the merger proposal is terminated.

Sometimes, however, the buying firm decides to pursue the merger unilaterally against the will of the management of the target company. The buyer attempts a *takeover* of the target company by making a *tender offer,* which is an offer made by the buying firm directly to the stockholders of the target firm to sell (tender) their shares of stock, usually for cash. In effect, the tender offer bypasses the target company's management. If the buyer can induce enough target company shareholders to tender their stock, the buyer can gain control of the target company and force the merger on the reluctant target company management.

The inducement for stockholders tendering their shares comes from setting the tender price well above the current market price of the target's stock. The tender offer has an expiration date, usually a few weeks after the offer's effective date, and the stock must be tendered before then. The tender offer typically is made in financial newspapers such as *The Wall Street Journal*.

Target Companies

Historically, certain kinds of companies have been likely takeover candidates. Cash-rich companies, for example, attract tender offers because a buying company can readily use the cash. Companies that underutilize debt (have low debt-to-equity ratios) are also likely targets. Given the tax advantage of debt, a buying

---

[13]See Michael Bradley, Anand Desai, and E. Han Kim, "Synergistic Gains from Corporate Acquisitions and Their Division between the Stockholders of Target and Acquiring Firms," *Journal of Financial Economics,* March 1988, pp. 2–40.

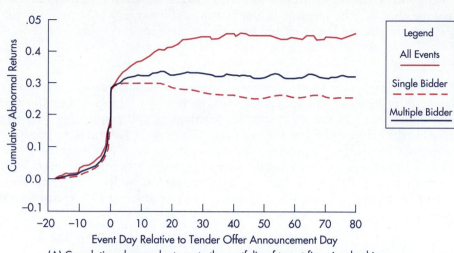

(A) Cumulative abnormal returns to the portfolio of target firms involved in
236 contests,163 single-bidder contests, and 73 multiple-bidder contests,
1963–1984. Event day relative to tender offer announcement day.

■ *Figure 21–3*
Cumulative Abnormal
Returns to Target and
Acquiring Firms

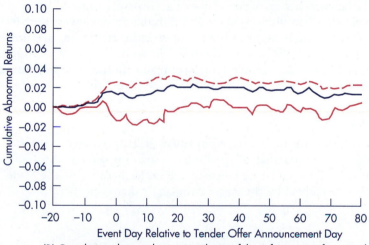

(B) Cumulative abnormal returns to the portfolios of acquiring firms involved in
236 contests, 163 single-bidder contests, and 73 multiple-bidder contests,
1963–1984. Event day relative to tender offer announcement day.

Source: Michael Bradley, Anand Desai, and E. Han Kim, "Synergistic Gains from Corporate Acquisitions
and their Division between the Stockholders of Target and Acquiring Firms," *Journal of Financial
Economics*, March 1988, pp. 24, 26. Reprinted by permission.

company can increase its debt capacity by acquiring a firm having low leverage.
A third financial indicator that appears to be shared by many takeover targets is
a low P/E ratio. As we saw earlier in this chapter, there is a presumed magic in
buying firms with lower P/E ratios because of immediate EPS gains by the buying
company.

In addition to these factors, companies can become potential takeover targets
for a variety of reasons. If the company produces a good product but has suffered

disappointing earnings performance, it may attract the interest of companies that assume that an improvement in short-term performance would produce good gains in the price of the stock and the value of the firm.

■ *Example*

Cummins Engine Company, widely regarded as a manufacturer of high-quality heavy-duty diesel engines, suffered setbacks in the 1980s.[14] Despite the difficulties, it continued its well-known charitable contributions and emphasized long-term goals at the expense of short-term earnings. This caused Cummins to be viewed negatively by many on Wall Street, and it attracted the interest of other companies. First, a British conglomerate known for its aggressive acquisitions bought an 8.8 percent stake in Cummins, but was later bought off by local interests. Next, Industrial Equity, a Hong Kong investor, bought almost a 15 percent interest, posing a sizable threat to Cummins. ■

Defensive Tactics

When a takeover bid is made, the target company's management must decide whether to oppose the takeover. If the decision is to fight the raider (buying company), several approaches are open. However, managements of firms acquired by takeovers are often discharged, and in fighting the takeover, they frequently appear to be protecting their jobs rather than acting to maximize stockholder wealth. These kinds of inconsistencies do occur, and in evaluating a proposed takeover, stockholders of the target company should precisely assess whose interests are being served by management's opposition to the merger.

Publicity Campaign

The first defensive tactic by the target company is usually to initiate its own publicity campaign to counter that of the raider. This campaign will typically question the advisability of tendering stock to the raider because of the "true" value of the stock as perceived by the target company's management.

■ *Example*

In late 1990, AT&T made an offer for NCR. The management of NCR conducted a public campaign to argue against the proposed merger on the basis that NCR was worth more than AT&T was offering. ■

Stock Purchases

Another alternative open to the target company is to purchase its own stock on the open market, which soaks up stock available for tendering. Since the tender offer pulls the stock price up close to the tender price, the target company can expect to pay a high price for any repurchases. A similar approach is to purchase

---

[14]See Robert Johnson, "With Its Spirit Shaken but Unbent, Cummins Shows Decade's Scars," *The Wall Street Journal,* December 13, 1989, p. A1.

stock of the raiding company (the so-called *Pacman defense*); this tactic will be most effective if the target company is considerably larger than the raider. Alternatively, the target company may opt to buy its own shares back from the corporate raider. If these shares are bought back at a premium, the excess of purchase price over market value is often referred to as *greenmail*.

Legal Tactics

Target companies use several legal avenues to impede takeovers. The most obvious is to build a case against the merger on grounds of infringement of antitrust laws. A second tactic is to encourage stockholders of either the target or raiding company to seek a stockholder's injunction against the takeover because of misrepresentation of value in the tender offer. Last, while the target is obligated to provide stockholder lists to the raider, it can delay doing so as long as possible, giving itself more time to fight the takeover.

Defensive Mergers

As a last resort, some target companies actively seek out a merger with a friendlier company, known as a *white knight*. However, defensive mergers give the impression that management is more concerned with its own survival than with shareholder wealth maximization, particularly when the offer made by the friendly company is no greater than the raider's.

LEVERAGED BUYOUTS

No discussion of corporate restructurings in the United States would be complete without a review of **leveraged buyouts (LBOs),** whereby an investment group uses a substantial amount of borrowed money, along with some equity money, to purchase the stock of a company and take it private. Typically, the managers of the company are heavily involved, and the previously publicly held stock ends up under the control of the managers of the firm.

Leveraged buyouts dominated much of the news of corporate restructurings in the late 1980s despite being a relatively small percentage of the total deals transacted. For example, of the top 10 deals in 1990 as compiled by *Fortune* (Table 21–1), only 1 was an LBO. However, the size of these transactions, and the implications to the capital markets, employees, suppliers, and so forth, guarantee that they will capture a disproportionate amount of media attention. The $25 billion RJR Nabisco leveraged buyout by Kohlberg Kravis & Roberts (KKR) generated tremendous attention and controversy.

An LBO usually occurs when the firm's managers wish to take over the company by taking it private. The managers, together with institutional investors, put up some equity money and borrow the rest by selling junk bonds with the help of an investment banking firm. The group then offers to purchase the publicly owned shares through a tender offer (or buys a division of a company). Alternatively, a firm specializing in such transactions as LBOs, in particular KKR, initiates the transaction by selecting a likely candidate and approaching the management of the firm with a proposal to execute an LBO. In effect, the arranger, such as KKR, puts up the equity funds and arranges junk bond financing as before.

leveraged buyouts (LBOs) investors use a substantial amount of borrowed money, along with some equity money, to purchase the stock of a company and take it private

▪ *Example*

In 1986, Union Carbide restructured itself and put its subsidiary, First Brands, a manufacturer of consumer products such as trash bags and car wax, on the auction block.[15] Managers put up $9.5 million to buy 12 percent of the deal, and another group—including First Boston, Manufacturing Hanover Venture Capital, and Metropolitan Life Insurance—put together some $70 million. The company sold junk bonds and borrowed from banks for an additional $760 million. Debt was almost nine times equity. ▪

Certain characteristics of LBOs stand out:

- ▪ The company is heavily leveraged—as in the case of First Brands. Junk bonds typically are issued to raise capital.
- ▪ Asset shuffling typically occurs as the new firm sells off certain assets to try to repay the mountain of debt incurred.
- ▪ If it works out, the managers (as well as other equity partners) stand to make a large return on their investment. In 1989, First Brands was considering selling some 30 percent of the company to the public at $20.50 per share, about five times what the stock cost some three years earlier.

What are the benefits to the acquiring group of an LBO? The company is now owned by a relatively small group of investors who presumably are more so-phisticated than investors in general. The management in particular should know the most about the firm itself, and given that management typically has an equity interest, it should be dedicated to doing a first-rate job. Furthermore, dividend payments are, in effect, converted into tax-deductible interest payments.

The benefits to the public stockholders are the same as those discussed above. Their shares will be purchased at a premium for cash, thereby providing them with more for their shares than they might otherwise realize.

In evaluating a possible LBO candidate, the buyers must believe that the stock market has failed to correctly value the company. It is widely believed in the United States that companies are managed for short-term profits rather than for long-term returns. A company may have great long-term potential but be penalized in the short run because of an inability to produce satisfactory earnings.

In actually deciding to do an LBO, earnings do not matter to the acquiring group so much as cash flow, particularly the amount of interest coverage. To a large extent, the key variable in determining the price to pay for an LBO is the amount of cash that can be generated to service debt. Thus, private value analysis is, in effect, cash flow analysis.

▪ *Example*

R. H. Macy went private in 1986 in the largest management-led LBO to date—a transaction of almost $4 billion, most of it borrowed.[16] By the end of the 1980s, Macy had to pay $500 million annually in interest, about 10 cents on the sales

---

[15]See "First Brands: Anatomy of an LBO That Worked," *Business Week,* December 4, 1989, p. 104, and *The Value Line Investment Survey.*

[16]See Subrata N. Chakravarty, "The Benefits of Leverage," *Forbes,* May 1, 1989, p. 42.

dollar. However, in 1988 Macy had a cash flow from operations of almost $300 million, after paying out the $500 million in interest charges. In 1989, operating cash flow approached $1 billion, significantly more than the interest charges, which had risen to $600 million. In 1989, Macy was worth roughly $8 billion, or $3 billion more than the long-term debt. ■

INVESTMENT BANKERS AND CORPORATE RESTRUCTURINGS

As we saw in the KKR example, specialized firms play a big role in LBOs. Managers typically cannot supply all of the equity funds needed, and junk bonds must be sold to raise the debt capital required.

Investment bankers are essential to mergers and acquisitions in general. They help to arrange most mergers, they help unwilling targets fight off a merger, and they provide expertise to the acquiring firm in attempting to value the target company. They also arrange much of the financing involved in these deals.

The scope of operations for the large investment banking firms involved in mergers and acquisitions is impressive. For example, Shearson Lehman Hutton completed more mergers than any other firm during the 1980s—some 1,250 transactions, with a value of almost $325 billion. In 1989, Shearson was involved in such major mergers as the $12.5 billion of Bristol-Myers Co. and Squibb. Salomon Brothers, another major player in this area, completed over 160 transactions in 1989 on five continents. It had a staff exceeding 225 people involved directly in mergers and acquisitions. Merrill Lynch's merger-and-acquisition group worked with more than 140 clients in 1989, with a total value of transactions in excess of $85 billion. And so on!

The fees earned on the 1990 top deals are large—over $45,000,000 in the case of Philip Morris, some $80,000,000 in the case of Campeau. Advisory fees in 1988 alone are estimated at roughly $700 million (not counting related financing and not counting the RJR deal). No wonder investment bankers love, and promote, mergers, LBOs, and other corporate restructurings.

SUMMARY

■ In a merger, only the buying company retains its corporate identity, while in a consolidation, none of the original firms survive—a new entity appears.

■ Vertical combinations are supplier-customer combinations; horizontal combinations take place within a single industry; conglomerate combinations involve firms in unrelated industries.

■ Holding companies and joint ventures are other forms of business combinations.

■ Merger financing is strongly influenced by the tax status of the combination. Convertible preferred and common stock have been used advantageously in recent years to preserve the *tax-free* status of a combination.

■ Although the *purchase* method of accounting offers an economic incentive of increased cash flow after tax through increased depreciation tax shields, many firms prefer the *pooling-of-interest* method. A *common-for-common* swap is virtually required today to qualify for pooling of interest.

■ The most common motives for the active formation of business combinations are synergistic operating economies, diversification gains, taxation advantages, and earnings growth potential.

■ The evaluation of a merger from the seller's standpoint involves comparison of the current market value of its stock against the market value of the proposed package being offered.

■ From the buyer's perspective, the evaluation procedure entails computing the present value of the relevant cash flows associated with purchase of the seller. This present value represents the theoretical maximum price the buyer would offer the seller.

■ The market value exchange ratio shows the premium the seller's stockholders receive.

■ While selling companies' stockholders have financially benefited from mergers, there is little evidence that buying companies' stockholders have gained.

■ Leveraged buyouts (LBOs) involve a group of investors, typically with management, borrowing large amounts of money through junk bonds and other means and buying out the public stockholders. The company, heavily burdened with debt, is taken private.

■ Emphasis in evaluating LBOs is on cash flow.

■ Investment bankers play a prominent role in corporate restructurings, advising the various firms involved, arranging financing, and even suggesting the deals to be made.

KEY TERMS

acquisition, p. 624

consolidation, p. 624

leveraged buyouts (LBOs), p. 643

merger, p. 624

pooling of interest, p. 629

purchase method, p. 628

QUESTIONS

21–1. Many executives cite mergers as an effective way to attain corporate diversification. Discuss the pros and cons of this idea.

21–2. Firms that engage in acquisitions direct their employees and officers who are involved in the analysis and negotiations not to buy stock of the target company. One reason for this warning is that the law prohibits insiders from benefiting from privy information. However, even if there were no such laws, the buying company would have another motive for the prohibition on target company stock purchases by employees and officers. What is this other motive?

21–3. Woolf, Inc., is an aggressive, rapidly growing conglomerate firm that has just made a tender offer to Glitter Company stockholders. If Glitter's management is against the acquisition, indicate and briefly discuss what actions could be taken to try and block the proposed acquisition.

21–4. "Many U.S. businesspeople feel that federal regulators are against bigness and will block any proposed business combination that leads to or furthers bigness." Comment on this statement.

21–5. *a.* What are the main differences among vertical, horizontal, and conglomerate business combinations?

b. Other things being equal, which of the three combinations in (*a*) is most likely to be blocked for antitrust reasons? Which is least likely? Explain your answers.

21–6. What is usually the dominant consideration when arranging a financing package for a proposed business combination?

21–7. Identify and discuss the relative advantages and disadvantages of the following business combination financing plans:

a. Common for common.

b. Convertibles for common.

c. Cash for common.

21–8. What is the evidence on the gains from mergers to the acquirers' stockholders? The sellers?

21–9. What provides the gains to stockholders in a merger? What is the magnitude of this item?

21–10. What are the essential differences between purchase and pooling methods of accounting for mergers?

21–11. As noted in the chapter, Conoco Oil was acquired by Du Pont. However, other suitors were involved. Classify the type of merger that would have occurred if the following companies had been successful in their attempt to purchase Conoco.
  a. Mobil Oil.
  b. Seagram Distillers.

21–12. It has been said that General Motors purchased EDS, the world's largest data processing company, for synergistic benefits. Explain how these might occur.

21–13. Explain what an LBO is. Why do you think LBOs generate so much media attention?

21–14. It has been said that some of the biggest takeover attempts were thwarted by using leverage. What does this mean?

21–15. What is meant by a hostile tender offer?

21–16. A conglomerate firm can diversify its portfolio of assets by buying unrelated businesses. Is this of value to its stockholders?

21–17. What is the important consideration in evaluating an LBO? Why is this variable of utmost importance?

PROBLEMS

21–1. Determine the P/E exchange ratio in each of the following situations:

	Buyer's P/E	Seller's P/E
A	10.0	5.0
B	5.0	2.0
C	2.0	3.0

21–2. Telrate Company is about to buy the Bronx Company. Given the information shown below, determine the P/E exchange ratio.

	Bronx	Telrate
Total earnings	$ 400,000	$10,000,000
Total market value of stock	$4,000,000	$80,000,000

21–3. American Television is preparing to make Target Soaps a merger offer. American's stock is selling for $30 per share and Target's stock is selling for $50. Determine the market value exchange ratio for each of the following proposed terms of exchange.
  a. American offers 1.6 shares of common plus $5 cash for each share of Target.
  b. American offers nine shares of common for each five shares of Target stock.
  c. American offers a $1,000 face value convertible bond whose estimated market value is $900 per bond for each 16 shares of Target stock.

d. Ignoring taxes and other possible reasons for preference for a particular kind of payments package, which of the three plans is most favorable to Target stockholders? Why?

21–4. Young Company is being merged into Atom Industries. Combined earnings for the merged companies are expected to be $14 million this year. The market value exchange ratio is 1.2. Atom currently has 4 million shares of common, and Young has 2 million shares. Current stock prices: Atom is $8 per share and Young is $10 per share. Atom's P/E ratio after the merger is expected to be 6.0. Determine Atom's expected postmerger stock price assuming Atom would finance the merger by exchanging common stock with Young stockholders.

21–5. Mammoth Manufacturing is considering the acquisition of the Conway Foundry. Analysts for Mammoth estimate that Conway's cash flow after taxes will be $1 million next year and will remain constant for the foreseeable future, with no changes in current operations. If the acquisition is made, Mammoth will be able to close its present warehouse operation at an annual after-tax savings of $300,000 per year. Mammoth expects to lose $175,000 per year after tax on the sales of a line of wrenches that will be discontinued if the tool company is purchased, but expects to add a new line of metric tools contributing $75,000 per year in after-tax cash flows. These changes are forecast to persist for the indefinite future. What is the maximum price that Mammoth would be willing to pay for Conway if the appropriate discount rate is 12 percent?

21–6. Meeker Bankshares, Inc., has just made a merger offer to Fidelity Savings. The market value exchange ratio is 1.3. Fidelity's stock price is $5 per share. Meeker offered Fidelity's stockholders $2 cash plus one share of Meeker stock for each share of Fidelity stock. Find the value of the Meeker stock at the time of the merger offer.

21–7. The Mid-West Marble Company is considering three potential merger opportunities for which the financial data are presented below.

	Mid-West Marble Company	A	B	C
Net present value	—	$475,000	$4,125,000	$5,800,000
Shares common	500,000	100,000	400,000	300,000
Stock price	$ 10.00	$ 3.00	$ 6.00	$ 12.00
Debt	$2,000,000	$150,000	$1,000,000	$1,400,000
Expected earnings	$ 500,000	$ 90,000	$ 500,000	$ 350,000
Stock exchange terms*	—	1 for 3	3 for 4	4.25 for 3

*The number of shares of Mid-West stock for merged company stock proposed by the target company.

a. Determine the upper limit for the market value exchange ratio for each potential merger.
b. Compare the calculations made in a market with exchange ratios implied by the proposed offer to Mid-West to determine which mergers appear feasible.
c. Determine the postcombination EPS of the *feasible mergers*.
d. Which company is the best merger candidate for Mid-West? Explain your answer.

21–8. Simon Diversified, Inc., is studying the possibility of adding a costume jewelry manufacturing division to the company. After considerable research, Simon has identified three possible means of accomplishing this addition. Two of the possibilities would entail acquiring existing costume jewelry manufacturing companies. The two target companies are Magnifico, Inc., and Quality Jewelry. A

Simon analyst estimates that Simon would realize about $400,000 per year in after-tax cash flows if Magnifico were acquired. Similarly, after-tax cash flows of about $200,000 per year would result from the acquisition of Quality Jewelry. The third alternative is for Simon to start its own jewelry lines. The analyst estimates this would create after-tax cash flows of about $100,000 per year. In all three instances, the anticipated life of the venture is 20 years. The analyst anticipates no termination (salvage) cash flows for any of the three alternatives. Furthermore, the estimated costs of capital are Magnifico, 16 percent, and Quality, 12 percent. The discount rate for the internally developed jewelry lines is estimated to be 15 percent.

Both Magnifico and Quality stocks are only infrequently traded, and most of each stock is owned by the management. Most recent quotes on the stocks are $10 per share for Magnifico (150,000 shares outstanding) and $1 per share for Quality (500,000 shares outstanding). However, discussions with managements of the two companies indicate they would settle for quite different market premiums. Magnifico would require a 40 percent premium over the stock's current market price, but Quality Jewelry would require a 100 percent premium. The after-tax initial cost of Simon's developing jewelry lines on its own is estimated to be $400,000. Evaluate the three mutually exclusive alternatives and recommend to Simon which investment action should be taken.

SELECTED REFERENCES

For a book covering a wide range of topics on mergers:

Auerbach, Alan J. ed. *Corporate Takeovers: Causes and Consequences*. Chicago: University of Chicago Press, 1988.

For a thorough discussion of corporate restructuring motives, see:

Stewart, G. Bernett and David M. Glassman. "The Motives and Methods of Corporate Restructurings, Parts I and II." *Journal of Applied Corporate Finance,* Spring 1988, pp. 85–99 and Summer 1988, pp. 79–88.

APPENDIX 21–A   ANTITRUST CONSIDERATIONS

Actions by the various regulatory agencies to block mergers are called *antitrust* actions. State agencies regulate *intrastate* commerce and are less important to large companies with *interstate* business activities. At the federal level, many agencies have antitrust responsibilities. The Antitrust Division of the Department of Justice has the broadest responsibility of the federal agencies. It is charged with enforcing federal antitrust laws like the Sherman Antitrust Act, the Clayton Act, and so on.

Firms considering mergers should assess the likelihood of approval *before* a commitment is made to participate in the proposed combination. The cost of pursuing a merger that is blocked or significantly delayed by an antitrust lawsuit can be considerable. Moreover, there is no statute of limitations in many antitrust laws, and long-standing combinations can, under certain circumstances, be dissolved. Many firms seek from antitrust agencies an informal advance opinion of the possibilities of legal action before seeking stockholder approval.

Basic Antitrust Issues

Antitrust laws exist to ensure that markets for goods and services are competitive. So the basic antitrust issue in mergers is, Will competition be reduced because of the merger? The antitrust intent is sometimes interpreted to be "antibigness" since antitrust actions occur most often in cases where one or all firms are large. Actually, antitrust actions are not instigated because of the absolute size of the principals, but rather because of the relative size and number of companies in the industry after the combination. Two basic tenets of competition are (1) many competitors, with (2) none being so large that its actions dominate the market. The real intent of merger antitrust law is to facilitate these conditions.

Assessing the likelihood of antitrust actions is difficult because many proposed combinations have such unique features that it is hard to generalize why one is approved and another not. Also, laws become more or less restrictive as time passes. In addition there are frequent personnel changes in regulatory agencies; some regulatory personnel are trustbusters and antimerger, and others are more sympathetic to business combinations. But there are some broad guidelines that firms can use to assess the likelihood of regulatory approval.

Reduction of Competition within an Industry

Mergers will generally be held illegal if *substantial actual or potential* competition exists between the principals. Unfortunately, no precise standards exist for measuring what *substantially* means, in terms of either market share (percentage of total market sales) or dollar volume of business. Elimination of *actual* competition is most obvious in horizontal mergers. However, not all horizontal mergers are blocked. If many competitors are in the field, if the market shares of the principals are relatively small, if no substantial barriers to entry in the field are found, and if the number of competitors is not generally declining, there is much less danger of antitrust action. In addition, if a firm is in financial distress, a horizontal combination may receive approval. But horizontal mergers are generally viewed with suspicion and are closely analyzed.

Elimination of *potential* competition is a more difficult interpretive issue and cuts across all types of combinations. The basic guideline is a judgment by the regulatory agency concerning the ability of the buyer to enter the seller's industry as a competitor. Procter & Gamble's proposed merger with Clorox was denied because Procter & Gamble was considered to be a *potential* competitor in the bleach market.

Reduction of Competition between Industries

Antitrust actions are also likely when vertical combinations lessen competition between companies in industries that have a buyer-seller relationship. Antitrust theory's foremost concern is the effect of foreclosing competitors from competitive access to supply or customer markets. For example, if a shoe manufacturer merged with a large leather-processing company, competing shoe manufacturers might be disadvantaged in the supply (of leather) market. If the same shoe manufacturer merged with a retail shoe store, competing shoe manufacturers might be disadvantaged in their customer market.

Antitrust law also specifically prohibits combinations in which potential *reciprocal dealing* exists. Suppose a textile fabricator (Company A) buys processed cotton from a cotton mill (Company B) that buys chemicals from a chemical company (Company C) to process raw cotton. If Companies A and C were to combine into Company AC, a potential reciprocal dealing opportunity exists. Company AC would insist that Company B purchase chemicals from it, or AC would no longer buy B's cotton. If AC represented a substantial part of B's market, the pressure to agree to this reciprocal deal would be great. But such deals reduce competition between buyers in one industry and sellers in another, and antitrust law prohibits business combinations that create such opportunities.

APPENDIX 21–B   FAILURE OF THE FIRM

Alternatives in Failure

When the firm is economically failing, there are two ways to resolve the problem:

- Make an *out-of-court* settlement among claimants.
- File for bankruptcy and proceed through an *in-court* resolution.

Figure 21B–1 illustrates the two routes that may be taken. The various branches of this diagram are discussed below.

Out-of-Court Settlements

Out-of-court settlements are simple agreements among principals involved that are reached without going to court. There are three kinds of such settlements: extensions, compositions, and assignments.

Extensions   When the firm is unable to pay its creditors on schedule, it will usually approach them and ask for more time. If the creditors agree, they grant the firm an *extension*, which extends the due date and provides for a repayment schedule. Because an extension is somewhat risky—things could get worse instead of better—creditors are hesitant to grant it unless they feel the firm (1) is trustworthy and (2) has a good chance of recovering from its current difficulties.

In negotiating for an extension, the firm will stress that any other form of settlement will give the creditors a worse chance of recovering the full amount owed them within a reasonable length of time. Other settlements may provide for only fractional repayment of the debt and/or involve a considerable delay in time. If some creditors involved do not agree to the extension and if their claims are relatively small, the consenting creditors may permit them to be paid in full to avoid the possibility of a bankruptcy proceeding. If the dissenting creditors' total claims are too large, however, there is little hope of reaching an acceptable extension agreement—the consenting creditors would be afraid of being left on a sinking ship while others are getting off. The extension

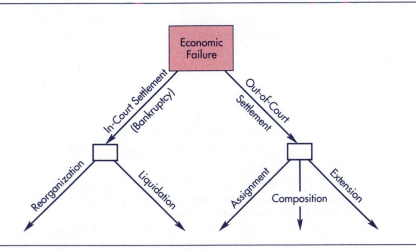

■ *Figure 21B–1*
Alternate Ways to Handle Failure

agreement usually includes some legal safeguards for the consenting creditors. These vary from assignment of assets as collateral, to required approval of some of the operations of the firm, to countersigning disbursement checks.

Compositions   In a composition the creditors agree to receive fractional settlement of their claims. Rather than accept a composition, the creditors may force the firm into bankruptcy, but this substantially prolongs the payment date, and the costs involved in bankruptcy proceedings may further reduce the amount of payment the creditors eventually receive. Creditors will often be better off if they accept a composition. The fraction of payment is negotiated and must be agreed to by all creditors. As in extensions, dissenting creditors may be paid off in full if their total claims are not too large. If no agreement can be reached with dissenting creditors, they can force the firm into bankruptcy proceedings.

Assignments   There are technical differences among various kinds of assignments, but the main features of an assignment are (1) liquidation (2) without recourse to courts. If all claimants (creditors and stockholders) can agree that the assignment is fair, considerable costs can be saved and passed on to the claimants by avoiding bankruptcy proceedings. However, if the claimants cannot agree, then the firm will be pushed into bankruptcy.

In-Court Settlements: Bankruptcy

In lieu of an out-of-court settlement the courts may be called upon to supervise the liquidation or reorganization of the failed firm. These in-court settlements are called bankruptcy proceedings. Although there are both state and federal bankruptcy laws and procedures, our discussion will address federal procedures.

Procedure   The basis for federal bankruptcy proceedings is the Bankruptcy Reform Act of 1978. A petition for bankruptcy proceedings may be filed *voluntarily* by the firm, or it may be filed by creditors to bring the firm *involuntarily* into bankruptcy. A petition for involuntary bankruptcy proceedings must establish either that the debtor firm is not paying its debts as they come due or that a creditor or another party has taken control of the debtor's assets. In general, a substantial fraction of the creditors or claims must support the petition.

A trustee, whose duty is to operate the firm during the bankruptcy period, may be elected by the creditors, or the creditors may allow the firm to continue the managerial operations. Less frequently, the court may appoint a trustee. A reorganization or liquidation plan must be brought forward and approved by the court. Reorganizations are undertaken under Chapter 11 of the Bankruptcy Act, while liquidations are arranged under Chapter 7.

Legal Rights of Claimants

Upon failure, the distribution of the remaining value of the firm, in either a liquidation or a reorganization, will follow a schedule based on the priority of claims. This priority schedule is as follows:

1. *Secured claims.* Secured creditors receive the value of the secured assets backing up their claims. If such value is insufficient to fully satisfy their claims, the unsatisfied remainder reverts to general-creditor status.
2. *Bankruptcy administration expenses.* This category includes all the legal, accounting, and trustee expenses associated with the bankruptcy.

3. *Postbankruptcy unsecured expenses*. This category refers to claims created *after* the commencement of the case.

4. *Unsecured wages, salaries, and commissions*. These claims are limited to $2,000 per person and must have been incurred within 90 days of the bankruptcy petition.

5. *Unsecured employee benefit claims*. These have the same limitations as unsecured wages, above.

6. *Unsecured customer deposit claims*. These are limited to $900 each.

7. *Tax claims*. These claims refer to unpaid tax obligations.

8. *General creditor claims*. Anyone who has made a loan to the firm without specified collateral is a general creditor. Normally, such loans include mainly debentures and accounts payable. In addition, secured creditors whose claims are not completely satisfied by the assets pledged to them have general creditors' rights on the unsatisfied portion of their claims.

9. *Preferred stockholders*. These claims have preference over only those of the common stockholders. Frequently, however, after the creditors have settled, no assets are remaining, and the preferred holders receive nothing.

10. *Common stockholders*. The common stockholders are last in line; they are the residual claimants. They often receive nothing.

Relative Priority

In principle, bankruptcy plans follow the *absolute priority* doctrine, which says creditor claims should be honored in strict adherence to the priority schedule. Junior claims cannot be paid until senior claims are fully satisfied. In practice, however, courts appear to include an element of *relative priority* in making distributions. In a relative-priority settlement, junior claimant classes receive partial distributions even though all senior claims are not fully satisfied.

Evaluation of Bankruptcies

One of the first tasks of a bankruptcy trustee is to decide whether the bankrupt firm should be liquidated or reorganized. The basis for this decision is a comparative evaluation of (1) the firm's liquidation value and (2) the value of a reorganized firm. Because these evaluations are subjective, whatever the decision, criticism is almost certain by some parties who feel they received less than they deserve.

To guide us through the comparative evaluation, we use an extended illustration. Table 21B–1 is a balance sheet for Spitzer Novelties, a firm recently adjudged bankrupt, and the trustee assigned to the case is facing the problem of deciding what to do with the firm. We use this illustration to work through the alternatives noted above.

Liquidation

The first step in an evaluation for liquidation is to estimate the sale value of the firm's assets. The balance sheet indicates these assets are worth $6.4 million. But balance sheet values are book values, and these may have no close relationship with realizable liquidation values. Liquidations are often distress sales. Companies in industries with highly specialized inventories and equipment will have particular difficulties because of a limited number of prospective buyers.

After considerable time and effort the trustee has prepared the following schedule of projected liquidation values for the firm's assets:

■ *Table 21B–1*
Balance Sheet for
Spitzer Novelties, Inc.

Spitzer Novelties, Inc.
Balance Sheet
Assets

Current assets	$1,400,000	
Net long-term assets	5,000,000	
Total assets		$6,400,000

Liabilities

Accounts payable	$ 600,000	
Notes payable	1,000,000	
Accrued taxes and wages	200,000	
Mortgage bonds*	2,000,000	
Debentures	1,000,000	
Preferred stock	600,000	
Common stock	1,000,000	
Total liabilities		$6,400,000

*Mortgage bonds are secured by all the firm's plant and equipment.

Estimated Liquidation Proceeds	
Cash and securities	$ 100,000
Collection of accounts receivable	100,000
Sale of inventory	700,000
Sale of plant and equipment	1,200,000
Sale of land	2,000,000
Total liquidation value	$4,100,000

Notice first the tremendous shrinkage of the value of the assets from what the balance sheet shows. Some of the accounts receivable have been judged uncollectible, some of the inventory is obsolete, and part of the plant and equipment is old.

The next step is to decide how to distribute the $4.1 million to the claimants if the firm is liquidated. In determining the allocation, the trustee will be guided by the *rule of absolute priority*, which says that there is a legally recognized priority of claims beginning with priority creditors and ending with common stockholders.

Applying the rule to this illustration, the trustee will first earmark the $1.2 million proceeds from the sale of plant and equipment for the mortgage bond holders. The plant and equipment secures their bonds, so they are entitled to those proceeds up to the amount of their claim. If the proceeds from the sale of collateral exceeded the secured claim, the surplus would be returned to the trustee to parcel out to other creditors. If, as in our example, the proceeds from the collateral sale are insufficient to satisfy the secured claim, the unsatisfied portion of that claim becomes a general creditor claim. The secured mortgage bonds have claims of $2 million and the $1.2 million from the sale of the assets securing the bonds (all the plant and equipment) are dedicated to the mortgage bonds. The remaining portion of the mortgage bond claims ($800,000) will go into general creditors' claims. Next, the trustee would satisfy creditors whose status precedes that of general creditors. Assume their claims are as follows:

	Claims	Distribution
Bankruptcy costs	$ 800,000	$ 800,000
Accrued wages	60,000	60,000
Accrued taxes	140,000	140,000
	$1,000,000	$1,000,000

After the legal claims of these and the secured creditors are satisfied, $1.9 million remains ($4,100,000 − $2,200,000) for all other claimants. The trustee will now consider general creditors, who will receive their pro rata share of the remaining $1.9 million.

General Creditors	Claims	Pro Rata (Percent)	Pro Rata Distribution
Accounts payable	$ 600,000	17.6	$ 334,000
Notes payable	1,000,000	29.4	559,000
Mortgage bonds	800,000	23.6	448,000
Debentures	1,000,000	29.4	559,000
	$3,400,000	100.0	$1,900,000

Total general creditor claims amount to $3.4 million, but only $1.9 million is available for distribution, so two things are immediately clear: (1) the general creditors' claims will not be fully honored, and (2) preferred and common stockholders will receive *nothing*. There simply is not enough to go around, and the big losers under this liquidation plan will be the preferred and common stockholders. In summary, the liquidation plan, including distribution of proceeds and percent recovery of each claimant's claim, is as follows:

Claimant	Claim	Proceeds Received	Percent Claim Received
Accounts payable	$ 600,000	$ 334,000	56
Notes payable	1,000,000	559,000	56
Accrued taxes and wages	200,000	200,000	100
Mortgage bonds	2,000,000	1,648,000	82
Debentures	1,000,000	559,000	56
Preferred stock	600,000	0	0
Common stock	1,000,000	0	0
Bankruptcy costs	800,000	800,000	100
Total	$7,200,000	$4,100,000	

Several interesting points are revealed in this liquidation plan. First, the only claimants made whole (receiving 100 percent of their claim) are the high-priority creditors: the bankruptcy administrators and those owed accrued taxes and wages. All other creditors lose part of their principal, with the mortgage bond holders in the best position because of the extra protection of their secured claim. We emphasize once again that the preferred and common stockholders receive nothing.

The large bankruptcy costs are also worth noting. Not a great deal is known today about the size of bankruptcy costs. A recent study on railroad bankruptcies estimated that certain *direct* costs of bankruptcy were only about 2 to 10 percent of the market value of the firm at the time of filing a bankruptcy petition. Some earlier studies have estimated higher costs. Going through the bankruptcy proceedings in the example cost the creditors about $800,000. If they could have reached an out-of-court liquidation agreement (an assignment), they could have saved most of this $800,000. However, it may have been impossible for them to have reached such an agreement.

Subordinated Debt   In Chapter 19, we saw that debentures are often *subordinated* to some specific senior debt, which means that the claims of the subordinated debenture holders will not be honored until the specified senior debt claims have been fully satisfied. To see the impact this has on the distribution of liquidation proceeds, assume that the Spitzer Novelties debentures are subordinated to the mortgage bonds.

The subordination feature changes the distribution of the $1.9 million available to general creditors. But it changes the distribution between *only* subordinated and specified senior debt. The *other* general creditors are not affected. The subordinated feature diverts proceeds from the subordinated to the specified senior debt.

In the Spitzer Novelties example, the mortgage bonds were not fully paid by the proceeds of liquidating the property. The unpaid balance, $800,000, became a general creditor claim. Recall that *without* subordination, only $448,000 of this $800,000 claim was satisfied. The debentures, meanwhile, received $559,000. Their *combined* proceeds were ($448,000 + $559,000) = $1,007,000. *With* subordination, the mortgage bonds would have first chance at this combined-proceeds total. Their full $800,000 general creditor claim would be satisfied, leaving the debentures only $207,000 ($1,007,000 − $800,000). The other general creditors, however, would not be affected by this reallocation between subordinated and senior debt.

Reorganization

In addition to estimating how much the firm is worth "dead" (liquidated), the trustee will also estimate how much the firm is worth "alive" via a reorganization. This evaluation requires the trustee to consider both *external* and *internal* reorganization possibilities. In an external reorganization, the trustee would seek out a merger partner for the bankrupt firm; an internal reorganization would be a recapitalization of the bankrupt firm, reducing its debt position to a manageable level.

A reorganization plan, whether internal or external, must satisfy both *fairness* and *feasibility* standards. The fairness doctrine primarily requires that the reorganization be consistent with the rule of absolute priority. But it also requires the value received by the claimants to be satisfactory in terms of risk and return, compared with alternative reorganization plans and also with possible liquidation. This doctrine can create some difficulty because the financial claims given to various claimants under a reorganization will frequently not be the same kind of claims they currently have. If, for example, the reorganization is arranged so that debenture holders receive preferred or common stock, clearly they are not receiving financial claims equivalent to their previous holdings. The crucial test, however, is what alternatives are available. If the only other alternative is liquidation, and the debenture holders will receive less under liquidation than under the reorganization, then the reorganization satisfies the fairness standard.

In some cases, the Securities and Exchange Commission (SEC) will make an independent appraisal of the reorganization and will inform the court of its opinion on the fairness of the plan. The SEC's role is purely advisory, and the court is not obligated to accept the SEC's conclusion that the plan is unfair; however, the SEC has often had a major impact on the valuation process that leads to a proposed plan.

The feasibility doctrine requires that the proposed reorganization results in a firm that would not face the same difficulties as the bankrupt firm. There should be no substantial chance of a repetition of failure. This requires two basic assurances. First, all operating difficulties (like incompetent management personnel, poor inventory management, and so on) have been identified and can reasonably be expected to be corrected. This ensures that the earning power of the reorganized firm will be sufficient to justify its continued existence. Second, the capital structure must be arranged so that the firm will not fail because it is top-heavy with debt. If both of these conditions can be reasonably assured, then the reorganization is said to be feasible.

Internal Reorganization   An internal reorganization requires the trustee to evaluate the firm as an ongoing enterprise. This means the trustee must estimate the market value of the reorganized firm. The evaluation process has several steps:

1. Determine if the reorganization is infeasible because of management problems.
2. Estimate the cash flows the firm will generate after the reorganization.
3. Estimate the cost of capital for the reorganized firm.
4. Establish a market value for the firm by discounting the expected cash flows at the estimated cost of capital.
5. Establish a feasible capital structure for the reorganized firm.
6. Determine the distribution of new financial claims.

None of these steps is easy, but Steps 2, 3, and 4 are particularly difficult because they are so subjective. The question of the feasibility of the reorganization is explicitly considered in Steps 1 and 5. Step 1 directly addresses this question from the managerial side. If the management looks incompetent or is uninterested in reconstructing the firm, there is little hope of a successful reorganization. Consequently, there would be no reason to proceed with a detailed evaluation. Capital structure feasibility is directly considered in Step 5. The trustee must take special care that the proposed structure is not so debt-heavy that the reorganized firm will have difficulty meeting its interest obligations.

In further analyzing the internal reorganization procedure, let us continue the Spitzer example. After conferring with Spitzer managers, discussing their managerial ability with outside parties, and giving the entire matter careful consideration, the trustee decides the current management team is both willing and able to carry out a reorganization successfully. The trustee is also satisfied that all past operating problems can be resolved. The trustee is then prepared to begin the evaluation, which is shown in Table 21B–2.

	Forecast		
	Unfavorable	*Middle*	*Favorable*
Estimate of Probability	0.30	0.50	0.20
Sales per year	$3,000,000	$4,000,000	$4,500,000
Cost of goods sold per year	2,600,000	3,500,000	3,800,000
Gross margin per year	400,000	500,000	700,000
Operating expenses per year	200,000	250,000	300,000
Net operating income per year	$ 200,000	$ 250,000	$ 400,000

Expected net operating income $= \overline{NOI} = 0.3(200{,}000) + 0.5(250{,}000) + 0.2(400{,}000)$

$= \$265{,}000$ per year

Estimated average cost of capital $= k_{AVG} = 10\%$

Estimated value of reorganized firm $= \dfrac{\overline{NOI}}{k_{AVG}} = \dfrac{\$265{,}000}{0.10} = \$2{,}650{,}000$

■ *Table 21B–2*
Internal Reorganization Valuation Worksheet for Spitzer

As the worksheet indicates, the trustee thinks that sales will be either $3 million, $4 million, or $4.5 million. The trustee has also listed relevant projections about the probabilities associated with these sales and the resultant net operating incomes. The expected net operating income is $265,000 per year, and the estimated average cost of capital is 10 percent, which leads to an estimated valuation of the reorganized firm of $2,650,000. This figure is considerably lower than the $4,100,000 liquidation value the trustee estimated for the firm, which means that creditors would rather have the firm liquidated than reorganized *internally*. However, there is still the possibility that external reorganization will be more attractive.

External Reorganization   In seeking a merger partner for the bankrupt firm, the trustee keeps two things in mind. First, merger will be recommended over liquidation or internal reorganization only when the value offered to the bankrupt firm from the merger is the largest of the three alternatives. This is in accordance with the fairness doctrine. Second, the trustee must evaluate the feasibility of the proposed merger. If the company formed by the combination would be financially shaky, the trustee should reject the merger proposal because the claimants would be in a position where they may be facing a new bankruptcy situation soon. This would not be consistent with the feasibility standard. In Spitzer's case, only one merger offer was made, for $3.5 million. This is better than the internal reorganization valuation, but is still not as good as the liquidation route. Consequently, the trustee would recommend liquidation.

Out-of-Court versus In-Court Settlements

From the stockholders' standpoint it is very advantageous to arrange an out-of-court settlement. Once the firm goes into bankruptcy, the stockholders usually have little chance of participating to any great extent in either a subsequent liquidation or a reorganization. The firm's goal is to maximize stockholder wealth, but the bankruptcy court's goal is to protect the value of the claimants' assets in order of seniority. Because stockholders are last in line in either a reorganization or a liquidation, they usually receive little in either case.

If the settlement is fair, creditors should also prefer an out-of-court settlement. The costs associated with court-supervised settlements will reduce the proceeds the claimants eventually receive. Moreover, bankruptcy proceedings are much lengthier than out-of-court settlements. Creditors will usually receive their payment more promptly in an out-of-court settlement.

There are, however, obvious advantages to creditors associated with in-court settlements. Most important, they are more likely to receive seniority treatment in court-administered proceedings because the courts usually use the rule of absolute priority, at least to some degree.

22

International Financial Management

Doing Business Internationally

Merck & Company, the largest pharmaceutical company in the United States, is a very strong and successful company, with 1988 sales of almost $6 billion and net income of $1.2 billion.[1] For the three years ended 1988, Merck's stock provided a total return of 165 percent.

Merck manufactures pharmaceuticals in 24 plants worldwide. Outside the United States, its operations are conducted mostly through subsidiaries, which accounted for about 50 percent of its sales for the last few years. This means that Merck is subject to currency fluctuations, both good and bad, in the countries in which it does business. For example, total sales in 1988 grew about 17 percent from the previous year—of this amount, "price and the exchange effect of the strengthening of foreign currencies against the U.S. dollar each added 3 percentage points to growth." In 1987 the strengthening of foreign currencies had added 6 percentage points to growth.

On the other hand, while exchange rate changes had a favorable effect on year-to-year sales growth in 1986, 1987, and 1988, this was not true in the past. The values of foreign currencies in countries that affect Merck, measured in U.S. dollars, had not yet returned to their historic levels. If 1988 foreign sales had been made at the exchange rates in existence from 1978 to 1980, according to Merck, sales would have been some $200 million higher.

---

[1]Adapted from Merck's 1988 *Annual Report*.

International finance is becoming increasingly important to us today. American consumers use thousands of foreign products, American businesses do an increasing amount of export-import trade, and several thousand American firms have foreign subsidiaries. One result of this is the growing awareness of the need to understand the special financial management problems that arise from international business transactions.

It is important to recognize that the principles of managerial finance that we have studied thus far are equally applicable to international firms. In particular, the valuation principle that serves as the unifying theme of our study of finance is as applicable to firms with international operations as to domestic firms. Like domestic firms, international firms should seek to maximize their stockholders' wealth. The same concepts of net present value, leverage, and cost of capital apply. The only difference is that the international dimension adds some additional problems for financial managers.

Firms engaged in international business transactions are exposed to several kinds of problems that do not occur in domestic transactions. First, and most important, is the problem of payments or receipts in a foreign currency. The company must know something about exchange rates, which are relationships between the prices of currencies. A second problem may be broadly described as international differences in legal and tax structures and in business practices and customs. Restrictions and problems imposed by these differences may be substantial. These risks and problems are not to be ignored, but neither are the opportunities involved in international operations.

■ *Example*

The following statement from Merck & Company illustrates nicely the risks and opportunities in international finance:

> The Company's worldwide business is subject to risks of currency fluctuations, governmental actions, including nationalization and expropriation, and other governmental proceedings abroad. The Company does not regard these risks as a deterrent to further expansion of its operations abroad.[2] ■

The purpose of this chapter is to provide an introduction to some of the major topics in international financial management. Because the subject is so broad and complex, we deal only with selected topics here.

Primary *chapter learning objectives* are:

1. To consider managerial finance from an international objective.
2. To analyze some of the special issues in international finance, such as exchange rate risk.

THE IMPORTANCE OF INTERNATIONAL FINANCE

Virtually everyone today understands that we are living in a global economy. World trade has increased dramatically, with enormous impacts on countries, firms, and people. All U.S. consumers, and most workers, are aware of the tre-

---

[2]See Merck & Company, Inc., 1988 *Annual Report*, p. 38.

mendous advantages and disadvantages of Japan's emergence as an economic superpower. Indeed, in a 1989 Japanese poll, a majority of the respondents indicated that they expect Japan to replace the United States as the world's leading economic (and political) power.

Japan has been a major factor in the rise of *foreign direct investment* (FDI) in the United States. FDI, which can be defined as development of a new business or acquisition of at least a 10 percent interest in a domestic company or tangible asset, constituted about one fourth of total foreign investment in the United States in 1988.[3] By 1988, FDI had reached some $330 billion in the United States, an annual growth rate of about 19 percent a year from 1983.[4] It should be noted, relative to our discussion of mergers in Chapter 19, that in the 1980s the percentage of all new FDI accomplished through mergers and acquisitions increased sharply.[5]

From a societal standpoint, competing internationally could not be more important for U.S. firms. In 1985, for the first time since the early years of the 20th century, the United States owed more to other countries than they owed to it. The United States became a large debtor in 1985, with a net international investment position of −$111 billion. By 1989, this figure exceeded $600 billion.

International financial conditions constantly affect firms from a financial standpoint. In the previous chapter, we considered the issue of mergers and acquisitions and noted the increased foreign acquisition activity that has been occurring. The year 1988 is a good example of the international aspects involved. Because the dollar was cheaper, foreign companies had an extra incentive to seek American companies. Japanese raiders became more aggressive, and more successful. Bridgestone, a Japanese firm, beat out Italy's Pirelli to take control of Firestone Tire & Rubber, a long-standing American tradition in tire manufacturing. Sony, the Japanese electronics giant, bought CBS Records. Campeau (Canadian) bought Federated Department Stores and BAT Industries (British) bought Farmers Group, an insurance company.

U.S. firms obviously compete in an international arena, and they must be prepared to do more. They must sometimes compete against firms that are heavily subsidized by foreign governments. For example, Airbus Industries is a government-financed aircraft consortium with record demand for its planes—orders for over 750 aircraft worth almost $50 billion. Airbus, however, is subsidized by West Germany, Britain, France, and Spain. U.S. manufacturers argue that Airbus enjoys unfair advantages both in the U.S. market and around the world. From its formation in 1969 through the end of the 1980s, these subsidies amounted to some $16 billion.

Multinational corporations (MNCs), which perform a substantial part of their operations outside their own national borders, now play an especially important role in business. The majority of major corporations today are multinational corporations, and they often have subsidiary companies in foreign countries. By definition, MNCs must worry about international finance problems, but

multinational corporations (MNCs)
corporations with a substantial part of their operations outside their own national borders

---

[3]The other form of foreign investment in the United States is portfolio investment, such as the purchase of stocks and bonds.

[4]This information is based on the *Economic Report of the President,* February 1990. This annual document is a very useful source of information on the state of the U.S. economy.

[5]Foreign-owned firms operating in the United States come under the "national" treatment, meaning they are treated as domestically owned firms with regard to antitrust regulations, environmental considerations, and so forth. They are liable for U.S. taxes as affected by international tax treaties.

as we will see, any firm that has international dealings needs to have some minimum amount of expertise in international financial management.

▪ *Example*

The Coca-Cola Company is truly a multinational company, selling in more than 160 countries.[6] It sells almost half of the soft drinks consumed in the world, and in 1989 some 80 percent of its operating earnings came from abroad, up from 50 percent four years earlier. While we often think of Coca-Cola as an American institution, Coke now earns more in Japan than in the United States. ▪

INTERNATIONAL FINANCIAL MANAGEMENT

The basic elements of international financial management are identical to those we have discussed throughout the book. Firms seek to maximize stockholder wealth, as represented by the price of the stock, by focusing on the expected returns and risks involved in the financial decisions that are made. This is as true for Coca-Cola, with extensive worldwide interests, as it is for Duke Power, which sells all of the electricity it generates in a limited geographical area of the United States. Firms may sell more exotic financing instruments when they enter international capital markets, but their basic objectives are the same—to minimize the cost of capital, to maintain an appropriate capital structure, to have financial ratios in line with creditor and investor expectations, and so forth. Similarly, when making investment decisions, they are guided by investing in projects with the largest positive net present values.

International financial management is unique primarily because the firm must deal in more than its own currency. International transactions are conducted in more than one currency, and international financial management must be concerned with multiple currencies. **Currency (exchange rate) risk** is the risk that the currency of a country in which a firm is doing business will drop in value relative to its own currency. Companies doing business on an international basis have an exchange-risk exposure, and must deal with it if satisfactory financial decisions are to be made.

currency (exchange rate) risk
risk of adverse fluctuations in the currency of a country in which a foreign firm is doing business

▪ *Example*

Perrier, the famous seller of bottled water, suffered problems because of a drop in the value of the dollar.[7] Its U.S. subsidiary represented about 20 percent of its bottled water sales, and a larger percentage of profits. From 1985 to 1986, the dollar lost over one third of its value relative to the franc. Perrier received fewer francs for the goods it sold in the United States. Profits were hit even harder because most of its costs are incurred in francs. ▪

In order to understand and learn to deal with this risk, we must understand foreign exchange markets and exchange rates. Because the determinants of ex-

---

[6]See Michael J. McCarthy, "As a Global Marketer, Coke Excels by Being Tough and Consistent," *The Wall Street Journal,* December 19, 1989, p. A1.
[7]See Tatiana Pouschine, "Perrier, Your Bubbles Are Too Big," *Forbes,* May 1, 1989, p. 106.

change rates are not constant, we need to analyze the impact of exchange risk on cash flows. Finally, we will consider how to manage foreign exchange risk.

FOREIGN EXCHANGE MARKETS AND EXCHANGE RATES

Foreign Exchange Markets

International business transactions are conducted in many different currencies. Suppose a German exporter sells merchandise to an American importer. The German company expects to be paid in deutsche marks (marks or DM), and the American company will want to pay in dollars. The *foreign exchange market* allows both buyer and seller to deal separately in its preferred currency.

Foreign exchange markets are marketplaces for currencies. The main participants are several dozen large commercial banks that transact business on behalf of customers such as the German exporter and American importer described above. The other major participants are brokers, several large international money center banks, and central banks of the various countries, like the United States Federal Reserve Bank. The foreign exchange market is the world's largest market, with average daily trading of over $500 billion by the end of the 1980s. London is the largest single market, with the United States second and Japan third.

Exchange Rates

The **foreign exchange rate** between two currencies is simply the price of one currency in terms of the other. It can be expressed two ways. The exchange rate between U.S. dollars ($) and German marks (DM), for example, may be expressed from the U.S. point of view as dollars per mark ($/DM), the "direct" quotation, or marks per dollar (DM/$), the "indirect" quotation.[8]

foreign exchange rate price of one currency in terms of the other

■ *Example*

Assume that the exchange rate between these two currencies is approximately $0.50/DM. That is, each mark is worth about 50 cents. This exchange rate represents the dollar price of the mark. In the U.S. financial news media, foreign currencies are usually quoted in terms of their dollar price: the amount of U.S. dollars required to purchase one unit of foreign currency. The reciprocal of the above dollar price of the mark is DM2/$, which is the mark price of the dollar; it describes how many deutsche marks are required to buy one U.S. dollar. ■

The two versions of the exchange rate are simply different ways to say the same thing: they translate amounts of money from one currency into the other. In the German exporter–American importer example above, if the sale were for DM 2,000 worth of merchandise, at the example exchange rate of $0.50/DM this would be:

$$(\text{DM } 2,000)(\$0.50/\text{DM}) = \$1,000$$

---

[8]Actually, several countries use the "dollar" as their currency numeraire. To be precise, we should use the symbol $US for the American dollar. However, we will use the traditional symbol $ by itself for the U.S. dollar. Other examples are the Australian dollar, $A, and the Canadian dollar, $C.

■ *Table 22–1*
Example Exchange Rates
as of the End of 1990
(U.S. Dollar Value of
One Unit of Foreign
Currency)

		Forward Rates	
	Spot Rate	*Three Months*	*Six Months*
British pound (£)	1.9299	1.9026	1.8799
Canadian dollar ($C)	0.8634	0.8550	0.8477
French franc (FR)	0.19760	0.19632	0.19489
German (deutsche) mark (DM)	0.6720	0.6692	0.6660
Japanese yen (YN)	0.007506	0.007506	0.007504
Swiss franc (SF)	0.7853	0.7829	0.7807

Spot Rates

Exchange rates that apply as of today's date are called *spot rates*. They pertain to currencies bought and sold for immediate delivery. Some realistic examples of spot rates are shown in Table 22–1. The exchange rates shown are quoted in terms of the dollar price of the foreign currencies.[9] The spot exchange rates are merely conversion factors for changing from one currency to another today.

■ *Example*

If an American company receives a check for 450,000 yen (YN) and sells the yen to buy dollars (that is, if the Japanese money is exchanged for U.S. money), according to Table 22–1 the company will receive:

$$(\text{YN } 450,000)(\$0.007506/\text{YN}) = \$3,377.70$$ ■

And, as noted earlier, exchange rates translate both ways. Suppose a Swiss company must make a payment of $3,000 U.S. How many Swiss francs must it sell to buy the $3,000 needed?

$$(\$3,000) \, \frac{1}{0.7853 \, \$/\text{SF}} = \text{SF } \$3,820.20$$

Forward Rates

An exchange rate for currency to be delivered at a future date is called a *forward rate*. That is, forward rates are agreements to exchange currencies in the future at a ratio established today. Typical forward contracts are for 30, 90, and 180 days, but longer ones can be obtained. The mechanics of using forward rates are the same as those with spot rates.

■ *Example*

Assuming that the forward rates shown in Table 22–1 hold, if a company sells 1,000 French francs (FR) three months forward (receiving dollars for francs), the company will receive (in 90 days):

$$(\text{FR } 1,000)(\$0.19632/\text{FR}) = \$196.32$$ ■

---

[9]Actually, dealers in foreign exchange work with two spot rates, the *bid* price and the *ask* price. Dealers will buy currencies at the bid price and sell currencies at the (higher) ask price. They make their profit on the spread (difference) between the two.

It is important in studying exchange contracts to remember that each participant both buys and sells something. In the dollar-franc example above, the company that sells 1,000 francs forward is simultaneously buying $196.32 forward. On the other side of the transaction, the participant is buying francs and selling dollars forward.

As we will see below, forward contracts, which are agreements to exchange currency in the future at an agreed-upon rate, are convenient ways to eliminate exchange rate risk, which, as previously noted, occurs whenever a future receipt or payment is not denominated in the domestic currency. Because exchange rates vary over time, the future receipts or payments in terms of the domestic currency can fluctuate.

Forward rates can be thought of as expectations of the market about *future* spot rates. Strong currencies that are expected to appreciate relative to weak ones will display forward rates that have a *premium* over the current spot rate. Alternatively stated, weak currencies (currencies that are expected to depreciate) will have forward rates that have a *discount* against the current spot rate. For any particular currency, such as the dollar, a strong currency will have forward rates greater than the spot rate: there will be a premium in the dollar price of these currencies. Currencies that are weak relative to the U.S. dollar will have forward rates less than the spot rate: there will be a discount in their dollar price.

Currency Futures

Beginning in 1972, the International Monetary Market (IMM) of the Chicago Mercantile Exchange began offering *currency futures* contracts on selected foreign currencies. Currency futures and forward contracts have strong similarities. Both are agreements to exchange currencies at a future date at a price established today. But there are also important differences. The futures market is regulated by the Commodity Futures Trading Commission, but the forward market is self-regulating. Also, forward contracts may be tailored regarding amount and time, but futures contracts, which tend to be smaller than forward contracts, are standardized. Another important difference is that there are daily limits on price fluctuations of futures contracts, whereas the forward market has no such restrictions. Finally, since the futures market deals in major currencies, it is impossible to make futures contracts in many currencies.

Currencies in which there is a futures market have tended to dominate the forward market. That is, agents who need to enter into forward rate contracts appear to prefer to operate in the currency futures market when possible. However, since traders also need to transact in currencies not represented among currency futures, the forward market is still important.

FOREIGN EXCHANGE RISK

Until relatively recently, the world monetary system was based on *fixed* exchange rates, where currency values were pegged to gold, and later to world currencies like the British pound and the U.S. dollar. Central banks attempted to keep their exchange rates within "gliding bands." Extreme currency problems led to *devaluations,* and very strong currency positions led to *revaluations*. In the early 1970s, the prolonged weakness in the major world currency, the U.S. dollar, led to initiation of a *floating* exchange rate system, in which exchange rates are allowed to fluctuate freely. Although it is a floating system, central banks still intervene, which means the current system is actually a managed, or "dirty," floating system.

Since the initiation of the floating exchange rate system, the nominal values of many major currencies have fluctuated greatly—some would say wildly. During the 1970s, the dollar declined approximately 30 percent against 10 major currencies, while the German mark was up almost 80 percent. In the first half of the 1980s, on the other hand, the dollar rose some 85 percent in value; however, it then declined back to its 1981 value. These sharp swings in the value of currencies demonstrate the need for companies to be concerned with currency risk.

If exchange rates were constant, there would be no foreign exchange risk. Foreign exchange risk occurs whenever the firm's profitability, either current or future, can be adversely affected by changes in exchange rates. It is convenient to divide foreign exchange risks into economic (cash flow) risk and translations (accounting) risk.

Economic (Cash Flow) Risk

Movements in exchange rates can have important impacts on cash flows. A normal sales–purchase transaction between two firms that do not have the same home currency will necessarily involve exchange risk to one of the parties.

■ *Example*

If an American exporter sells shoes to a German importer, the sales contract will specify payment in either dollars or marks. If payment is in dollars, the exchange risk will be borne by the German company because an appreciation of the dollar can make the purchase more expensive than originally planned. Suppose the invoice is for $50,000, the spot rate at time of sale is $0.50/DM, and the German firm receives trade credit for three months. At time of purchase the German company has an obligation of DM 100,000 ($50,000 ÷ $0.50/DM) due in three months. But if, at the end of the three months, the spot rate has changed to $0.46/DM (the dollar has appreciated relative to the mark), the German importer will have an obligation of DM 108,695 ($50,000 ÷ $0.46/DM), about a 9 percent increase in the obligation in terms of its home currency. This unfavorable increase in the cost of goods sold may significantly impact the company's profit margin. If the contract were written for payment in marks, the exchange risk (that the mark may appreciate) would be shifted to the U.S. firm. As long as the two parties do not have the same home currency, someone will bear an exchange risk. ■

Exchange risk also affects longer term investment and financing activities. If an American firm invests overseas by, say, starting a subsidiary company, and if the currency of the foreign country where the subsidiary is located depreciates relative to the U.S. dollar, profits brought back to the United States will be lower. On the financing side, if a firm borrows in foreign currencies that appreciate relative to the home currency, their debt obligations will be more expensive than originally planned in terms of the home currency. In the past, many U.S. firms prepaid large amounts of mark-denominated debt because the mark was rapidly

. . .

appreciating relative to the U.S. dollar. They financed the prepayments with dollar-denominated debt issues.

The inevitable conclusion is that exchange risk can have serious economic consequences for cash flows. It is therefore quite important to give careful consideration to how to manage exchange risk. Exchange risk can be reduced, but this involves certain costs. We study various ways to manage exchange risk below.

Translations (Accounting) Risk

Accounting exposure refers to the impact that exchange-rate changes have on financial statements. When a firm or its subsidiary has assets and liabilities denominated in foreign currencies, all of the income statement and balance sheet accounts must be translated to the home currency. The form of this translation—which is for reporting, not tax, purposes—can have a major impact on the company's income statement and balance sheet.

Companies are quite concerned with how they must report their financial results (like quarterly and annual statements). U.S. companies are now required to report foreign currency transactions and financial results according to the *Statement of Financial Accounting Standards (SFAS) No. 52*, "Foreign Currency Translation." This statement, issued in December 1981, replaced the controversial Financial Accounting Standards Board (FASB) *Statement No. 8*, which created great turmoil in accounting circles because of its tendency to spotlight unrealized (noncash) gains and losses from foreign operations. The main feature of *SFAS #52* is that all asset and liability accounts are translated at *current* exchange rates. This approach is called the *current-rate method*.[10]

MANAGING TRANSACTIONS RISK

Given the existence of foreign exchange risk, the question is how to manage it. The ultimate objective of a program of managing foreign exchange should be consistent with the goal of stockholder wealth maximization. The practical aim is to permit the firm to make as much profit as it would if there were no currency problems.

At the outset, we should define two important terms: *covering* and *hedging*. Technically, the two terms have different meanings. Covering means to protect the value of a specific, identifiable cash flow transaction (like a DM 10,000 receivable due in 90 days). Hedging refers to protecting asset and financing positions the firm has in foreign countries. Hedging thus refers to actions aimed at protecting anticipated future cash flows earned by these assets or finances. Although the two terms are different technically, we will use them interchangeably to refer to actions taken to avoid exchange risk.

In managing foreign exchange risk, we consider a wide range of actions open to the firm. Specifically, the firm can do the following:

1. Do nothing.
2. Attempt always to transact in the home currency.
3. Use foreign exchange markets.
4. Use currency swaps.
5. Maintain monetary balance.
6. Attempt funds flow adjustments.

The Do-Nothing Strategy

To begin with, a firm may make no attempt to hedge. At first glance, this appears to be a purely passive or unmanaged policy. Many times it is. Some companies never hedge, usually on the grounds that foreign exchange markets are efficient (in the sense described earlier), reflecting unbiased expectations about future exchange rates. Companies that adopt this policy are presumably willing to play the long-run averages, gaining on some transactions in some years, losing on others.

The do-nothing policy is not necessarily passive, however. If a company has a net positive exposure (monetary assets exceed monetary liabilities) in a strong currency, there is an *expected* gain. A decision to leave the exposure can be the result of a conscious choice to benefit from the expected foreign exchange gain.

Transacting in the Home Currency

If firms always could make and receive payments in their home currency, they could eliminate the exchange risk associated with current cash flows. Under floating exchange rates, there are generally intense negotiations to determine the cur-

---

[10]*FASB #8*, in contrast, translated inventories, long-term assets, and equity at *historical* exchange rates, which is called the *temporal method*.

rency used to bill a transaction. The weakness of the dollar in the 1970s led many foreign exporters to press U.S. importers to pay in the exporters' currencies. As the choice of billing currency is negotiable, other factors also will affect it. The importance of the two transacting companies to each other's operations and any relative weaknesses in their respective markets are important factors. In a few cases, buyers and sellers share the risk by billing fractionally in *both* currencies.

Using Foreign Exchange Markets

Operating in the foreign exchange market is one of the traditional ways to manage exchange risk. Both the forward and spot markets can be used. To illustrate how these markets are used, consider the following example.

- ### *Example*

Imfoods, Inc., an American foodstuffs importer, has just placed an order with a British meat-processing firm for meat pies. The billing is for 200,000 pounds due in three months. The spot and forward exchange rates and prevailing three-month interest rates (annualized) available in the market place are as follows:

Foreign Exchange Market		Three-Month Interest Rates (%)	
Spot rate	$1.84/£	United States	12
Three-month forward rate	$1.86/£	United Kingdom	8

*Annualized rates.

Since the billing is in pounds, the American importer, Imfoods, is bearing the exchange risk in this transaction. ■

Covering in the Forward Market

If Imfoods were to adopt a do-nothing policy with regard to this transaction, the amount of dollars required to pay the £200,000 bill would not be known until the due date three months from now. Whatever the prevailing spot rate was then would determine the dollar price of the merchandise. However, Imfoods can eliminate this uncertainty by buying pounds (selling dollars) for delivery in three months. That is, Imfoods would enter into a forward contract to receive £200,000 in exchange for $372,000 (£200,000 × $1.86/£). The sequence of events of these transactions is summarized as follows.
   Today:

1. Imfoods orders £200,000 of meat pies from the British firm; payment is due in three months.
2. Imfoods buys a £200,000 three-month forward contract. (No money exchanges hands today.)

Three months later:

1. Imfoods exchanges $372,000 for £200,000, as agreed upon in the forward contract.
2. Imfoods pays £200,000 to the British firm.

Imfoods has eliminated the uncertainty with regard to how many dollars it must pay, but at a cost. A part of this cost is the *cost of cover:*

$$\text{Cost of cover} = \frac{X_1 - X_0}{X_0} \times \frac{12}{N} \tag{22-1}$$

where:

$$X_1 = \text{forward exchange rate}$$
$$X_0 = \text{spot exchange rate}$$
$$N = \text{length of forward contract}$$

For Imfoods:

$$\text{Cost of cover} = \frac{1.860 - 1.840}{1.840} \times \frac{12}{3} = 0.0435$$

On an annualized basis, Imfoods is paying a 4.35 percent cost of cover. This represents the cost to Imfoods of locking itself into a forward contract where the foreign currency is selling at a premium to the home currency. The other part of the cost is the commission the dealer will charge to arrange the forward contract. Notice also that the cost of cover can be negative, if the foreign currency is selling at a forward discount.

Covering in the Spot and Money Markets

One implication of the interest rate parity theorem (IRPT) discussed in Appendix 22–A is that the interest rate differential between two countries is approximately equal to the cost of cover. Notice that this is true for the Imfoods example. The cost of cover is 4.35 percent, and the interest rate differential between the United States and the United Kingdom is 4 percent. This means that an alternative way to cover exchange risk is to operate in the spot and money markets.[11]

To cover in the spot and money markets in the example we have been working with, Imfoods would perform the following operations.
Today:

1. Imfoods orders £200,000 of meat pies from the British firm; payment is due in three months.
2. Imfoods buys £196,078 with $360,784 (£196,078 × $1.84/£) in the spot market.
3. Imfoods invests the £196,078 for three months in Britain at the prevailing interest rate of 8 percent per year (2 percent per three months).

Three months later:

1. Imfoods receives £200,000 (£196,078 × 1.02) from the three-month British money market security that matures.
2. Imfoods pays £200,000 to the British firm.

---

[11]The IRPT guarantees that the results of this alternative covering procedure will be approximately equivalent to covering in the forward market.

In this arrangement, Imfoods uses the spot market to get pounds immediately, and then invests those pounds in the British money market (short-term interest market). Imfoods purchases just enough pounds today (£196,078) to compound up to £200,000 three months later (using the British interest rate).

The cost of cover in this arrangement is the difference between the U.S. and British interest rates. By investing in the money market in Britain, which has a lower interest rate, Imfoods forgoes an extra 4 percent per year, which is 1 percent per quarter. Imfoods also incurs a commission cost to transact in the exchange market.

If the IRPT is valid, it is a matter of indifference whether covering is done in the forward or the spot and money markets. In some situations, however, it is difficult to secure forward contracts. This is true, for example, if a currency is weakening to the extent that a large devaluation is expected.[12]

Currency Swaps

Currency swaps are temporary exchanges of monies between two parties that do not go through the foreign exchange market. In *official* swaps, the two parties are central banks. *Private* swaps, between central banks and business firms, started after World War II because of shortages of convertible currencies and lack of forward markets for some countries.

- *Example*

Suppose a U.S. firm wants to inject capital into its Nigerian subsidiary. The U.S. company signs a swap contract with the central Nigerian bank, then deposits dollars at the bank. The bank then makes a loan in Nigerian currency to the subsidiary firm. At the end of the loan period, the subsidiary pays off the loan to the bank, which returns the original dollar deposit to the U.S. company. The central bank usually does not pay interest on the foreign currency deposit it receives but does charge interest on the loan it makes. Therefore, the cost of the swap includes *two* interest components: the interest on the loan and the forgone interest on the deposit. ■

In recent years, companies have made *direct* swaps with each other.

Monetary Balance

Monetary balance refers to minimizing accounting exposure. If a company had net *positive* exposure (more monetary assets than liabilities), it could use more financing from foreign monetary sources to balance out the two sides. Companies with assets and liabilities in more than one foreign currency can try to reduce risk by balancing off exposure in the different countries. The monetary balance is often practiced across several countries simultaneously.

---

[12]Although empirical evidence tends to support the IRPT, many money managers and market specialists doubt that the IRPT is valid. They therefore believe that an astute manager will usually not be indifferent to which covering operation should be selected. They advocate comparing the costs of covering of the two alternatives and taking the one with lower cost.

Funds Flow Adjustments

Another way to avoid exchange losses is by shifting funds between countries. Such funds flow adjustments may be made through the firm's dealings with *third parties* or through *intercompany operations*.

Third-Party Dealings

Transactions with creditors and customers are known as third-party dealings. The basic idea is to reduce liabilities in strong currencies and to convert assets from weak to strong currencies. That is, borrow in weak-currency countries, and invest in strong-currency countries. These activities are limiting ones. They should not disrupt the basic production function of the firm.

In weak-currency countries, the firm may attempt to stretch its payables and offer substantial cash discounts to customers to encourage prompt payment of receivables. Inventory may be factored. In strong-currency countries, the firm should attempt to pay payables promptly and may offer relatively lavish credit terms to customers.

Intercompany Operations

Multinationals shift funds between the parent company and its subsidiaries or between subsidiaries. The idea behind these shifts of funds is the same as before: limit asset exposure and encourage liability exposure in weak currencies, and encourage asset exposure and limit liability exposure in strong currencies.

Several methods have been used to shift funds:

- Directing the subsidiary to buy stock of the parent company.
- Buying government securities in strong-currency countries.
- Directing the subsidiary to make a "technological payment"—pay the parent firm for its industrial know how.
- Billing the subsidiary at inordinately high prices when a subsidiary in a weak-currency country imports parts and/or materials from other subsidiaries or the parent. This has apparently been done extensively with U.S. subsidiaries in Latin America, which has caused the governments of Latin American countries to try to curb the practice.

INTERNATIONAL INVESTMENT DECISIONS

One indication of the importance of international investment decision is international earnings flows. Figure 22–1 shows earnings by the United States on foreign assets and by foreigners on assets in the United States during the 1980s. As we can see, payments by the United States to foreigners have been trending upward over the years. In 1987, U.S. receipts from assets abroad exceeded U.S. payments on assets by some $20 billion; however, payments exceeded receipts by the second quarter of 1988.

In principle, foreign investment projects should be analyzed with the same procedures used in domestic projects. Estimates of incremental cash flows and an appropriate cost of capital are needed. To maximize stockholder wealth, projects

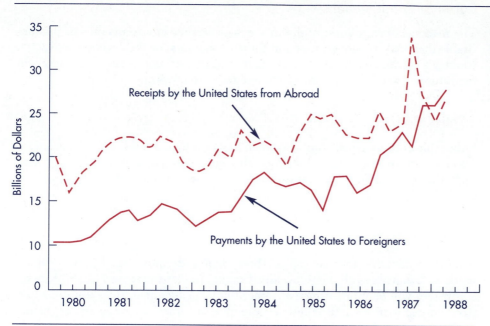

Source: *Economic Report of the President*, January 1989, p. 134.

■ *Figure 22–1*
Earnings by the United States on Foreign Assets and by Foreigners on Assets in the United States, 1980–1988 (Billions of Dollars, Seasonally Adjusted)

with positive net present values should be undertaken. Foreign investment projects are more complicated, however, in that more variables can affect the cash flows and required rate of return.

■ *Example*

Three air carriers, American, United, and Delta, now control about 50 percent of the U.S. market. To expand further, they must grow by seeking international routes, which they have been doing. United, for example, is planning to fly to Europe for the first time. American is expanding in the Pacific and in Central and South America. In each of these cases, these companies should make these decisions using the same principles they would to evaluate expansion of routes in the domestic market. ■

A key point is that the relevant cash flows from foreign projects are those that ultimately are available to the firm's shareholders—since they are earned in a foreign currency, they must be converted to the currency of the firm's country, and this involves currency risk.

We will not make a detailed study here of how to incorporate the various relevant factors into the capital budgeting framework, but we will consider briefly the primary issues that are likely to arise in foreign investments that are not present in domestic ones. It is important to remember in this discussion that the larger risks come from any future *changes* that may occur in the various factors. If the several economic and political elements were stable, it would be much easier to analyze foreign investment climates.

Currency Considerations

The firm can operate successfully in a weak-currency environment, but it is desirable that well-developed spot and forward markets for the currency exist. If a country's economic outlook is so bleak that substantial depreciations are likely in the future, it will be very hard to arrange forward covering and hedging.

Inflation Prospects

Other things being equal, countries with higher inflation rates will be less attractive for investment. Higher inflation rates mean higher local interest rates and higher costs of capital for local capital sources, which may also mean a weaker currency.

Capital Market Access

It is often desirable to raise capital, both debt and equity, in the local capital market. Countries with well-developed capital markets that are open to foreign companies will be more attractive, other things being equal, than countries that have limited markets and/or restrict foreign companies' access to any segments of the capital market.

Political Stability

Political stability refers to the long-run continuity of the government and the institutions of government. Political instability tends to discourage foreign investment.

Capital and Exchange Controls

Capital controls refer to prohibitions on moving funds into or out of the country. More frequently, the latter form of movement is restricted, as in a profit repatriation restriction.

Government Aid Programs

Government aid can include low-interest loans, advance payment of receivables, and elimination of foreign exchange risk. Tariff and import quota protection also may be offered. *Tariffs* are taxes on imported goods, and *quotas* are limitations on the amount of imports allowed.

Expropriation Possibilities

Expropriation by a foreign government can be accomplished by a forced sale of assets or equity, frequently at very low prices, or an outright takeover, which is usually unreimbursed. Many U.S. companies now include in their analysis the cash flow consequences of projected nationalizations of investments at different points in the future.

INTERNATIONAL FINANCING DECISIONS

The principles governing the financing of international operations are basically the same as for domestic financing, but there are more sources and methods to consider, and there are additional complicating factors.

International firms can finance foreign operations by borrowing in the foreign country in which the operations are located. Alternatively, they can raise funds in their own domestic market and use the funds in the foreign country. A third alternative is to borrow in the market where costs are lowest.

International money (short-term) and capital (long-term) markets are simply more complicated versions of national money and capital markets. The markets include a wide array of short- and long-term financing methods and sources. We will emphasize several of the most important parts of these markets.

Short-Term and Medium-Term Financing

Eurocurrencies are monies deposited in and lent from banks outside the country of their origin; therefore, the **Eurocurrency market** consists of any currency on deposit in another country. As an example, British pounds deposited in a French bank are part of the Eurocurrency market. Eurocurrencies are the heart of today's international money market.[13]

Eurocurrency market market for currencies on deposit in other countries

The Eurocurrency market is a pool of funds available for lending to qualified borrowers, primarily international business firms and governments. This market has expanded rapidly since the early 1960s, and Eurodollars have played a dominant role in the Eurocurrency market mainly due to the U.S. dollar's designated role as an international currency exchange standard and the U.S. balance of payments deficit that has accumulated dollars overseas.

The mechanics of obtaining a Eurodollar loan are varied, but in their simplest form they parallel the procedures in getting a U.S. bank loan. U.S. firms can apply directly for a straight bank loan in Eurodollars from a bank outside the United States for a fixed term. Maturities vary from overnight (one day) to about five years. Short-term loans are normally issued from one day to six months. There are also Eurodollar certificates of deposit (CDs).

Interest rates on Eurodollar loans are quoted on the basis of the **London Interbank Offered Rate (LIBOR),** which is used in place of the prime rate in the case of Eurodollar loans. The spread between the rate quoted for a particular company and the LIBOR will depend on the perceived risk of the borrower. These rates often are *floating rates*. Differences between Eurodollar and U.S. interest rates can lead a company to prefer using the Eurodollar market for financing, or vice versa.

London Interbank Offered Rate (LIBOR) interest rate on Eurodollar loans

International Bond Markets

Numerous firms raise large amounts of debt capital in international markets. The main feature that distinguishes the international bond market from the many

---

[13]Originally, the Eurocurrency market was called the *Eurodollar* market, since it was mainly a market for U.S. dollars located in European banks. Eurodollars are still a major factor in the Eurocurrency market today. Lately, *Asiadollars,* located mainly in Singapore and Hong Kong, have become important elements in the Eurocurrency market.

domestic bond markets is that international bonds are always sold outside the country of the company issuing them. A further distinction is usually made between foreign bonds and Eurobonds.

foreign bonds
bonds issued in a country's bond market by a foreign company

   Foreign bonds are issued by a foreign company in a particular country's domestic bond market. They are denominated in that country's domestic currency and pay interest and principal in that country's currency. Foreign bonds are underwritten by a syndicate of the country's underwriters and are subject to the laws of that country. In effect, these bonds would be identical to bonds issued by comparable firms in that country, with the only difference being that the issuer is a foreign borrower.

▪ *Example*

A German company issues bonds in Great Britain, denominated in British pounds. ▪

Eurobonds
bonds issued simultaneously in countries other than the country whose currency denominates the bonds

   Eurobonds are bonds issued simultaneously in countries other than the country of the currency in which the bond is denominated.[14] The majority of these bonds are bearer bonds arranged by international syndicates. The issuers face fewer required disclosures than if the bonds were issued in domestic markets, and a less strict set of government regulations. Investors often prefer the bearer bond form that Eurobonds have, whether for privacy reasons or tax avoidance.

▪ *Example*

A Germany company sells mark-denominated bonds in the United States and Great Britain. ▪

   Eurobonds issued in more than one currency are called *multiple-currency* bonds. These bonds will specify alternative currencies, usually two, that the bondholder may choose from in receiving interest and principal payments. In both straight Eurobonds and multiple-currency bonds, the currency denomination is usually U.S. dollars and/or a strong currency like German marks.
   The emergence of the international bond market in recent years as a competing source of long-term debt capital has enabled many companies to reduce their costs of borrowing.

▪ *Example*

Beatrice Foods issued $100 million in Eurobonds to help finance its acquisition of Tropicana Products. By issuing Eurobonds, rather than bonds in the U.S. market, Beatrice was able to reduce the coupon rate to 7.75 percent from the 8.05 percent rate projected in the U.S. bond market. This difference of 30 basis points (0.30 percent) on a $100 million dollar issue amounts to a pre-tax interest savings of $300,000 per year. An added attraction was the speed at which the Eurobonds were issued. It took only six weeks, compared to the three months it usually takes in the United States. The reduced time was because there was no registration

---

[14]The prefix *Euro* indicates that the bonds are issued in countries other than those in whose currencies they are denominated.

process to go through in the Eurobond market. In the U.S. market, the Securities and Exchange Commission must approve the issue. ▪

Other Financing Sources

Besides commercial bank loans and open-market financial instruments, firms can use several international lending agencies and government-sponsored programs.

International Lending Agencies

Foremost in this group of agencies is the World Bank and its associated agency, the International Finance Corporation. Both are global in scope. Other international lending agencies are regional in scope, like the European Investment Bank and the Asian Development Bank. Finally, there are national development banks that support the export-import activities of firms in their country, like the Export-Import Bank (Eximbank) in the United States.

Government Export Incentives

Many countries' governments will assist firms in financing export trade since that will have a favorable impact on their balance of trade and domestic employment. Most countries provide loans at interest rates below the market rate to beef up exports. Firms can also occasionally take advantage of situations where export-hungry countries go even further to assist financing.

Financing Trade Credit

Arrangements made to finance international trade credit are very much like the intracountry arrangements, but they also involve the extra complications of the international environment. The major trade credit instruments are these:

1. *Letter of credit*—a written statement made by a bank that it will pay a specified amount of money when certain trade conditions have been satisfied.
2. *Draft*—an order to pay someone (it is like a check).
3. *Banker's acceptance*—a draft that has been accepted by a bank.

▪ *Example*

A Kansas company, House of Joy, wants to import $75,000 worth of Japanese radio components. The House of Joy first gets the Japanese company to grant it 60 days' credit from the shipment date. Then the Kansas company arranges a *letter of credit* through its Kansas bank, which is sent to the Japanese company. The Japanese company ships the equipment and presents a 60-day *draft* on the Kansas bank to its Japanese bank. Then the Japanese bank pays the Japanese company. The draft is then forwarded to the Kansas bank and, if all paperwork is in order, becomes a *banker's acceptance,* which is a $75,000 debt that the Kansas bank owes the Japanese bank. At the end of 60 days, the House of Joy pays the Kansas bank, which in turn pays the acceptance. In the interim, the Japanese bank could sell the acceptance on the open market. The final owner of the banker's acceptance would then present it to the Kansas bank for payment. ▪

Notice that at least four parties are involved in the example: an importer, an exporter, and their respective banks. Often other banks are involved, too. In addition, the whole process has several detailed features and options associated with it that we have not discussed. Finance companies and factors are also involved in financing trade credit.

SUMMARY

- Most large U.S. firms are multinational corporations and must compete in a global marketplace.

- Understanding how foreign exchange markets work is essential to understanding international finance. An *exchange rate* is the relative prices of two currencies; it is the ratio at which two parties agree to exchange the two currencies.

- The *spot rate* is today's exchange rate; the *forward rate* is a future exchange rate whose terms are agreed upon today. Weak currencies are expected to depreciate in value relative to strong ones.

- Changes in exchange rates create *exchange risk,* which has two aspects. The more important one is probably the impact of changing exchange rates on cash flows. The other aspect is *accounting exposure.*

- Several techniques are available for managing exchange risk; *covering* and *hedging* activities through the foreign exchange markets play prominent roles.

- Foreign investment analysis is similar to the standard domestic capital budgeting analysis, but the international setting presents new and complicating features.

- The main additional factors to consider are (1) currency considerations, (2) foreign inflation prospects, (3) capital market access, (4) political stability prospects, (5) capital and exchange controls, (6) government aid programs, and (7) expropriation possibilities.

- In financing international operations, international money and capital markets, which are more exotic counterparts of domestic money and capital markets, are important.

KEY TERMS

currency (exchange rate) risk, p. 662
Eurocurrency market, p. 675
Eurobonds, p. 676
foreign bonds, p. 676

foreign exchange rate, p. 663
London Interbank Offered
 Rate (LIBOR), p. 675
multinational corporations (MNCs), p. 661

QUESTIONS

22–1. Other things being equal, what effect would the following situations have on the U.S. balance of payments?
  a. French exports to the United States decrease.
  b. The number of foreign tourists to the United States increases.
  c. The United States reduces the level of its worldwide military aid programs.
  d. Purchase of U.S. stocks and bonds by foreigners decreases.

22–2. From a financial-management viewpoint, the study of international finance is very similar to the study of the merger and restructuring issue. Agree or disagree with this statement and explain your reasoning.

22–3. What is the major risk of foreign operations? Why does it matter?

22–4. The Coca-Cola Company does a lot of business in Japan. Assume that the value of the yen weakens significantly relative to the dollar. What effect would this have on the Japanese operations of Coca-Cola, and on the company as a whole?

22–5. What is the difference between Eurodollars and Eurocurrencies?

22–6. Other things being equal, what kind of exchange rate movements do you think Merck would like to see in a given year?

22–7. Assume that spot and forward rates for the British pound and U.S. dollar are quoted in terms of the dollar price of the pound. Which country should have the higher level of interest rates if the pound is selling at a discount in the forward market?

22–8. Identify what impact the following inflation situations would have on U.S.-Japanese exchange rates that are expected in the future, assuming that current exchange rates are not affected by the situations:
   a. Expected inflation rate in Japan exceeds that in the United States.
   b. Expected inflation rates in Japan and the United States are equal.
   c. Japan expects inflation, but the United States expects deflation.

22–9. Explain the difference between a bank draft and a banker's acceptance.

22–10. What is the difference between a foreign bond and a Eurobond?

22–11. Suppose that Ranger Oil Limited, a Canadian oil and gas exploration firm, needs U.S. funds to finance exploration activities in the United States. Explain the advantages and disadvantages to Ranger of selling an issue of foreign bonds in the United States.

22–12. What is currency risk? When is it adverse for a U.S. firm?

22–13. What is the exact meaning of the term *exchange rate?*

22–14. What are the alternatives for managing foreign exchange risk?

22–15. What is a currency future? A currency swap?

22–16. Assume that Coca-Cola borrows a large amount in Japan to finance its operations. The yen appreciates relative to the dollar. How is the company affected by this?

PROBLEMS

22–1. Use Table 22–1 to convert $10,000 in American money to all six foreign currencies, rounding to the nearest whole unit of currency and using:
   a. Spot rates.
   b. Three-month forward rates.

22–2. Use Table 22–1 to convert the following amounts of foreign currency to U.S. dollars at the spot rate (round to the nearest dollar):
   a. 100,000 French francs.
   b. 200,000 pounds.
   c. 2,000,000 yen.
   d. 60,000 Swiss francs.

22–3. Compute the spot exchange rate between U.S. dollars and Japanese yen under the following conditions:

Forward rate	$0.0040/YN
U.S. interest rate	10%
Japanese interest rate	15%

22–4. Compute the expected U.S. inflation rate during the coming period under the following conditions:

U.S.-German spot exchange rate	$0.35/DM
U.S.-German forward exchange rate	$0.30/DM
Expected German inflation rate	20%

22–5. Find the U.S. interest rate consistent with the following conditions:
    a. Spot exchange rate ($/YN) = 0.95 times the forward exchange rate ($/YN), and the Japanese interest rate = 10 percent.
    b. Spot exchange rate ($/YN) = forward exchange rate ($/YN) and the Japanese interest rate = 6 percent.

22–6. Compute the forward U.S. dollar-French franc exchange rate for the following situations:

	Spot Rate ($/FR)	Inflation/Deflation Rate (%) United States	France
A	0.25	20	10
B	0.25	−10	10
C	0.20	20	−10
D	0.20	−10	−20

22–7. An American importer has ordered merchandise from a German supplier. The bill of lading is in marks, and payment is due in one month. Assume that annualized one-month interest rates are 12 percent in the United States and 6 percent in Germany. The spot rate is $0.500/DM and the one-month forward rate is $0.503/DM.
    a. Determine the cost of cover in the forward market.
    b. Determine the cost of cover in the spot and money markets.
    c. Which of these two alternatives should be more attractive to the American company?

22–8. An American firm has a payable due, in yen, in one year. Spot and forward exchange rates are $0.00460/YN and $0.00465/YN, respectively. If the one-year U.S. interest rate is 10 percent, what must the Japanese one-year interest rate be to make the American firm indifferent to covering in forward versus spot and money markets?

22–9. A U.S. company owes 2 million Swiss francs to a supplier in two months. How many U.S. dollars will be required to satisfy this payable, ignoring transactions costs, if:
    a. The U.S. company buys a forward contract today at X_1 = $0.52/SF.
    b. The U.S. company buys francs in the spot market today at X_0 = $0.51/SF and invests these francs at the Swiss interest rate of 12 percent per year.

SELECTED REFERENCES

Numerous texts are available on this subject, such as:

Modena, Jeff. *International Financial Management,* 2nd ed. St. Paul, Minn.: West Publishing Company, 1987.

A basic discussion of corporate exchange exposure can be found in:

Block, Stanley B., and T. J. Gallogher. "Managing Corporate Exchange and Interest Rate Exposure." *Financial Management,* Autumn 1986, pp. 64–73.

APPENDIX 22–A   DETERMINANTS OF EXCHANGE RATES

Exchange rates are merely prices of the currencies that are traded in foreign exchange markets. Like the price of any other commodity, the price of a currency is established by supply and demand conditions. Both supply and demand for foreign currencies arise from *transactions requirements, speculation,* and *government operations.*

Transactions requirements cover a wide variety of activities, including tourists who exchange their home currency for foreign currencies, firms that deal in export and/or import trade, firms that have operations in more than one country, and investors who buy foreign stocks, bonds, and real estate. Speculation refers to purchases of currencies investors think will appreciate and sales of currencies they think will depreciate. Government operations include actions by central banks to maintain their exchange rates within certain limits or to finance foreign aid programs.

In addition to these broad supply and demand reasons, there are several specific economic determinants of exchange rates: (1) balance of payments, (2) interest rates, (3) inflation/deflation, and (4) government considerations.

Balance of Payments

A country's balance of payments summarizes the economic transactions between it and the rest of the world. Essentially, any transaction that brings external purchasing power (very loosely this means money) *into* a country represents a *source* of funds to that country. Any transaction that takes external purchasing power *from* a country represents a *use* of funds by that country. The principal sources are exports, receipts for interest and dividends from foreigners, receipts from foreign tourists, gifts and grants from abroad, foreign direct investment in domestic companies, and foreign purchases of domestic securities. The main uses are imports, payments of interest and dividends to foreigners, tourism expenses of domestic citizens abroad, gifts and grants to foreigners, direct investment in foreign companies, and purchases of foreign securities by domestic citizens.

We will use the United States as an example. If the total of U.S. sources of funds exceeds total uses of funds as defined above, the country will have a balance-of-payments *surplus*. This surplus of external purchasing power must eventually be paid (financed) by foreigners in U.S. dollars. The surplus will cause foreigners to buy U.S. dollars, exerting an upward pressure on the price of the dollar making it a relatively strong currency, other things being equal. Exactly the opposite happens if the U.S. has a balance-of-payments *deficit,* where uses exceed sources.

Interest Rates

Interest rates have an important influence on exchange rates. If Country B has a higher interest rate than Country A, investors from A may be enticed to invest in Country B's bonds, provided such other factors as inflation differences and government restrictions are not too unfavorable.

There is, in fact, an important economic relationship between any two countries' spot rates, forward rates, and interest rates. This relationship is called the *interest rate parity theorem* (IRPT). It is applicable to any two countries, but let us illustrate it in terms of the United States and any foreign country. The IRPT says that the ratio of the forward and spot rates is directly related to the two interest rates:

$$\frac{X_1}{X_0} = \frac{1 + i_{US}}{1 + i_F} \qquad\qquad \textbf{(22A–1)}$$

where:

$$X_0 = \text{spot exchange rates (\$/foreign currency)}$$
$$X_1 = \text{forward exchange rate (\$/foreign currency)}$$
$$i_{US} = \text{U.S. interest rate}$$
$$i_F = \text{foreign interest rate}$$

The IRPT is frequently used to illustrate forward premiums or discounts. Assume the following data concerning French and U.S. currency:

$$X_0 = \$0.200/FR$$
$$X_1 = \$0.210/FR$$
$$i_F = 10\%$$

Then:

$$\frac{0.210}{0.200} = \frac{1 + i_{US}}{1.10}$$

So:

$$i_{US} = 0.155 = 15.5\%$$

Notice that the forward franc is selling at a premium and that U.S. interest rates are higher than French interest rates. One of the implications of the IRPT is that countries with relatively low interest rates (France, in the example above) will have relatively low spot rates and relatively high forward rates. That is, relatively low interest rates lead to forward premiums in the foreign exchange markets.

Equation 22A–1 can also be used to illustrate what happens to foreign exchange and international money markets when interest rates within a country change. In the French–U.S. example above, suppose the U.S. interest rate began to climb from its current level of 15.5 percent. The rising U.S. interest rate would attract investors holding French securities into the U.S. money market. These investors would sell their French money market securities (putting downward pressure on these French security prices, and thus upward pressure on French interest rates) and convert francs to dollars in the spot market (putting downward pressure on the franc spot rate, X_0). These dollars would be invested in U.S. marketable securities (putting some downward pressure on U.S. interest rates). Thus, forward markets, besides protecting investors, tend to even out interest rates among countries, other things being equal. For investors who wish to convert back to francs eventually, there is some risk involved in adverse exchange rate movements during the time the monies are invested in U.S. securities. To eliminate this risk, many investors will *cover* their exchange risk by buying francs (selling dollars) in the forward market (thereby putting upward pressure on the franc forward rate, X_1).

None of these international currency movements would take place if it were not for dealers looking to make a profit from discrepancies in currency prices and interest rates. Their activities are known as *arbitrage*. In general, arbitrage refers to the simultaneous purchase and sale of the same asset or similar assets in order to take advantage of price discrepancies. This activity forces any discrepancies to shrink almost to the vanishing point. It also assures that IRPT will be a reasonably accurate representation of the relationship between exchange rates and interest rates.

Several studies have recently attempted to verify whether the IRPT is in fact a reasonably good approximation of market relationships. In general, it does appear to describe well the relationships between forward and spot rates and interest rates, although some discrepancies have been noted. These discrepancies are usually explained by transactions costs, governmental exchange controls, or inaccuracies in the data used to test the IRPT.

Inflation/Deflation

Inflation and deflation, which are changes in price levels, also affect future exchange rates. For example, if inflation is greater in one country than in another, purchasing power is eroding faster in the first country. Several months down the road, that country's currency will be worth less of the second country's money than it is today. The mathematical relationship that links changes in exchange rates and changes in price levels is called the *purchasing power parity theorem* (PPPT). Using the United States and any foreign country as an example:

$$\frac{X_1}{X_0} = \frac{1 + I_{US}}{1 + I_F} \qquad (22A-2)$$

where:

X_1 = next-period exchange rate ($/foreign currency)
X_0 = current exchange rate ($/foreign currency)
I_{US} = U.S. inflation/deflation rate
I_F = foreign inflation/deflation rate

The left-hand side of Equation 22A–2 is the relative change in exchange rates, and the right-hand side is the relative change in inflation/deflation rates. If there is inflation, I will be a positive fraction; if there is deflation, I will be a negative fraction.

We also can consider the effects of inflation and deflation on expectations. We use X_1 to designate the forward rate, which many believe to be an unbiased estimator of the future spot rate.

■ *Example*

Assume the following data on currency relationships between the United States and France:

Expected U.S. inflation rate = 5%
Expected French inflation rate = 10%
X_0 = $0.220/FR

Then:

$$\frac{X_1}{0.220} = \frac{1.05}{1.10}$$
$$X_1 = \$0.210/FR$$

If France has the higher inflation rate, then the purchasing power of the franc is declining faster than that of the dollar. This will lead to a forward discount on the franc relative to the dollar, which the example illustrates. ■

Government Considerations

Governments, through their central banks, are important participants in foreign exchange markets. Governments intervene in the market, buying or selling their own currency to keep their exchange rates at what they feel are appropriate levels. Governments can have even more impact by imposing foreign exchange controls, which prohibit some or all transactions in the exchange market. Countries with weak currencies are more likely to impose exchange controls, which may include prohibiting domestic citizens and firms from transacting in the forward market, limiting transactions in the spot market, and the like. At the extreme, the Communist countries do not tie their currencies to the international market. The government sets the rates. In the past France has had one of the tightest sets of exchange controls in Western Europe. Governments may also impose capital controls and other restrictions, as well as tariffs and quotas, all of which affect exchange rates.

Mathematical Tables

■ *Table A–1*   Future Value of $1 at the End of t periods = $(1 + r)^t$

Period	1%	2%	3%	4%	5%	6%	7%	8%	9%
1	1.0100	1.0200	1.0300	1.0400	1.0500	1.0600	1.0700	1.0800	1.0900
2	1.0201	1.0404	1.0609	1.0816	1.1025	1.1236	1.1449	1.1664	1.1881
3	1.0303	1.0612	1.0927	1.1249	1.1576	1.1910	1.2250	1.2597	1.2950
4	1.0406	1.0824	1.1255	1.1699	1.2155	1.2625	1.3108	1.3605	1.4116
5	1.0510	1.1041	1.1593	1.2167	1.2763	1.3382	1.4026	1.4693	1.5386
6	1.0615	1.1262	1.1941	1.2653	1.3401	1.4185	1.5007	1.5869	1.6771
7	1.0721	1.1487	1.2299	1.3159	1.4071	1.5036	1.6058	1.7138	1.8280
8	1.0829	1.1717	1.2668	1.3686	1.4775	1.5938	1.7182	1.8509	1.9926
9	1.0937	1.1951	1.3048	1.4233	1.5513	1.6895	1.8385	1.9990	2.1719
10	1.1046	1.2190	1.3439	1.4802	1.6289	1.7908	1.9672	2.1589	2.3674
11	1.1157	1.2434	1.3842	1.5395	1.7103	1.8983	2.1049	2.3316	2.5804
12	1.1268	1.2682	1.4258	1.6010	1.7959	2.0122	2.2522	2.5182	2.8127
13	1.1381	1.2936	1.4685	1.6651	1.8856	2.1329	2.4098	2.7196	3.0658
14	1.1495	1.3195	1.5126	1.7317	1.9799	2.2609	2.5785	2.9372	3.3417
15	1.1610	1.3459	1.5580	1.8009	2.0789	2.3966	2.7590	3.1722	3.6425
16	1.1726	1.3728	1.6047	1.8730	2.1829	2.5404	2.9522	3.4259	3.9703
17	1.1843	1.4002	1.6528	1.9479	2.2920	2.6928	3.1588	3.7000	4.3276
18	1.1961	1.4282	1.7024	2.0258	2.4066	2.8543	3.3799	3.9960	4.7171
19	1.2081	1.4568	1.7535	2.1068	2.5270	3.0256	3.6165	4.3157	5.1417
20	1.2202	1.4859	1.8061	2.1911	2.6533	3.2071	3.8697	4.6610	5.6044
21	1.2324	1.5157	1.8603	2.2788	2.7860	3.3996	4.1406	5.0338	6.1088
22	1.2447	1.5460	1.9161	2.3699	2.9253	3.6035	4.4304	5.4365	6.6586
23	1.2572	1.5769	1.9736	2.4647	3.0715	3.8197	4.7405	5.8715	7.2579
24	1.2697	1.6084	2.0328	2.5633	3.2251	4.0489	5.0724	6.3412	7.9111
25	1.2824	1.6406	2.0938	2.6658	3.3864	4.2919	5.4274	6.8485	8.6231
30	1.3478	1.8114	2.4273	3.2434	4.3219	5.7435	7.6123	10.063	13.268
40	1.4889	2.2080	3.2620	4.8010	7.0400	10.286	14.974	21.725	31.409
50	1.6446	2.6916	4.3839	7.1067	11.467	18.420	29.457	46.902	74.358
60	1.8167	3.2810	5.8916	10.520	18.679	32.988	57.946	101.26	176.03

■ *Table A–1*   (concluded)

Interest Rate

10%	12%	14%	15%	16%	18%	20%	24%	28%	32%	36%
1.1000	1.1200	1.1400	1.1500	1.1600	1.1800	1.2000	1.2400	1.2800	1.3200	1.3600
1.2100	1.2544	1.2996	1.3225	1.3456	1.3924	1.4400	1.5376	1.6384	1.7424	1.8496
1.3310	1.4049	1.4815	1.5209	1.5609	1.6430	1.7280	1.9066	2.0972	2.3000	2.5155
1.4641	1.5735	1.6890	1.7490	1.8106	1.9388	2.0736	2.3642	2.6844	3.0360	3.4210
1.6105	1.7623	1.9254	2.0114	2.1003	2.2878	2.4883	2.9316	3.4360	4.0075	4.6526
1.7716	1.9738	2.1950	2.3131	2.4364	2.6996	2.9860	3.6352	4.3980	5.2899	6.3275
1.9487	2.2107	2.5023	2.6600	2.8262	3.1855	3.5832	4.5077	5.6295	6.9826	8.6054
2.1436	2.4760	2.8526	3.0590	3.2784	3.7589	4.2998	5.5895	7.2058	9.2170	11.703
2.3579	2.7731	3.2519	3.5179	3.8030	4.4355	5.1598	6.9310	9.2234	12.166	15.917
2.5937	3.1058	3.7072	4.0456	4.4114	5.2338	6.1917	8.5944	11.806	16.060	21.647
2.8531	3.4785	4.2262	4.6524	5.1173	6.1759	7.4301	10.657	15.112	21.199	29.439
3.1384	3.8960	4.8179	5.3503	5.9360	7.2876	8.9161	13.215	19.343	27.983	40.037
3.4523	4.3635	5.4924	6.1528	6.8858	8.5994	10.699	16.386	24.759	36.937	54.451
3.7975	4.8871	6.2613	7.0757	7.9875	10.147	12.839	20.319	31.691	48.757	74.053
4.1772	5.4736	7.1379	8.1371	9.2655	11.974	15.407	25.196	40.565	64.359	100.71
4.5950	6.1304	8.1372	9.3576	10.748	14.129	18.488	31.243	51.923	84.954	136.97
5.0545	6.8660	9.2765	10.761	12.468	16.672	22.186	38.741	66.461	112.14	186.28
5.5599	7.6900	10.575	12.375	14.463	19.673	26.623	48.039	85.071	148.02	253.34
6.1159	8.6128	12.056	14.232	16.777	23.214	31.948	59.568	108.89	195.39	344.54
6.7275	9.6463	13.743	16.367	19.461	27.393	38.338	73.864	139.38	257.92	468.57
7.4002	10.804	15.668	18.822	22.574	32.324	46.005	91.592	178.41	340.45	637.26
8.1403	12.100	17.861	21.645	26.186	38.142	55.206	113.57	228.36	449.39	866.67
8.9543	13.552	20.362	24.891	30.376	45.008	66.247	140.83	292.30	593.20	1178.7
9.8497	15.179	23.212	28.625	35.236	53.109	79.497	174.63	374.14	783.02	1603.0
10.835	17.000	26.462	32.919	40.874	62.669	95.396	216.54	478.90	1033.6	2180.1
17.449	29.960	50.950	66.212	85.850	143.37	237.38	634.82	1645.5	4142.1	10143.
45.259	93.051	188.88	267.86	378.72	750.38	1469.8	5455.9	19427.	66521.	*
117.39	289.00	700.23	1083.7	1670.7	3927.4	9100.4	46890.	*	*	*
304.48	897.60	2595.9	4384.0	7370.2	20555.	56348.	*	*	*	*

*FVIF > 99,999.

■ *Table A–2*   Present Value of $1 to Be Received after t Periods $= 1/(1 + r)^t$

Interest Rate

Period	1%	2%	3%	4%	5%	6%	7%	8%	9%
1	0.9901	0.9804	0.9709	0.9615	0.9524	0.9434	0.9346	0.9259	0.9174
2	0.9803	0.9612	0.9426	0.9246	0.9070	0.8900	0.8734	0.8573	0.8417
3	0.9706	0.9423	0.9151	0.8890	0.8638	0.8396	0.8163	0.7938	0.7722
4	0.9610	0.9238	0.8885	0.8548	0.8227	0.7921	0.7629	0.7350	0.7084
5	0.9515	0.9057	0.8626	0.8219	0.7835	0.7473	0.7130	0.6806	0.6499
6	0.9420	0.8880	0.8375	0.7903	0.7462	0.7050	0.6663	0.6302	0.5963
7	0.9327	0.8706	0.8131	0.7599	0.7107	0.6651	0.6227	0.5835	0.5470
8	0.9235	0.8535	0.7894	0.7307	0.6768	0.6274	0.5820	0.5403	0.5019
9	0.9143	0.8368	0.7664	0.7026	0.6446	0.5919	0.5439	0.5002	0.4604
10	0.9053	0.8203	.07441	0.6756	0.6139	0.5584	0.5083	0.4632	0.4224
11	8.8963	0.8043	0.7224	0.6496	0.5847	0.5268	0.4751	0.4289	0.3875
12	0.8874	0.7885	0.7014	0.6246	0.5568	0.4970	0.4440	0.3971	0.3555
13	0.8787	0.7730	0.6810	0.6006	0.5303	0.4688	0.4150	0.3677	0.3262
14	0.8700	0.7579	0.6611	0.5775	0.5051	0.4423	0.3878	0.3405	0.2992
15	0.8613	0.7430	0.6419	0.5553	0.4810	0.4173	0.3624	0.3152	0.2745
16	0.8528	0.7284	0.6232	0.5339	0.4581	0.3936	0.3387	0.2919	0.2519
17	0.8444	0.7142	0.6050	0.5134	0.4363	0.3714	0.3166	0.2703	0.2311
18	0.8360	0.7002	0.5874	0.4936	0.4155	0.3503	0.2959	0.2502	0.2120
19	0.8277	0.6864	0.5703	0.4746	0.3957	0.3305	0.2765	0.2317	0.1945
20	0.8195	0.6730	0.5537	0.4564	0.3769	0.3118	0.2584	0.2145	0.1784
21	0.8114	0.6598	0.5375	0.4388	0.3589	0.2942	0.2415	0.1987	0.1637
22	0.8034	0.6468	0.5219	0.4220	0.3418	0.2775	0.2257	0.1839	0.1502
23	0.7954	0.6342	0.5067	0.4057	0.3256	0.2618	0.2109	0.1703	0.1378
24	0.7876	0.6217	0.4919	0.3901	0.3101	0.2470	0.1971	0.1577	0.1264
25	0.7798	0.6095	0.4776	0.3751	0.2953	0.2330	0.1842	0.1460	0.1160
30	0.7419	0.5521	0.4120	0.3083	0.2314	0.1741	0.1314	0.0994	0.0754
40	0.6717	0.4529	0.3066	0.2083	0.1420	0.0972	0.0668	0.0460	0.0318
50	0.6080	0.3715	0.2281	0.1407	0.0872	0.0543	0.0339	0.0213	0.0134

■ *Table A–2*   (concluded)

Interest Rate

10%	12%	14%	15%	16%	18%	20%	24%	28%	32%	36%
0.9091	0.8929	0.8772	0.8696	0.8621	0.8475	0.8333	0.8065	0.7813	0.7576	0.7353
0.8264	0.7972	0.7695	0.7561	0.7432	0.7182	0.6944	0.6504	0.6104	0.5739	0.5407
0.7513	0.7118	0.6750	0.6575	0.6407	0.6086	0.5787	0.5245	0.4768	0.4348	0.3975
0.6830	0.6355	0.5921	0.5718	0.5523	0.5158	0.4823	0.4230	0.3725	0.3294	0.2923
0.6209	0.5674	0.5194	0.4972	0.4761	0.4371	0.4019	0.3411	0.2910	0.2495	0.2149
0.5645	0.5066	0.4556	0.4323	0.4104	0.3704	0.3349	0.2751	0.2274	0.1890	0.1580
0.5132	0.4523	0.3996	0.3759	0.3538	0.3139	0.2791	0.2218	0.1776	0.1432	0.1162
0.4665	0.4039	0.3506	0.3269	0.3050	0.2660	0.2326	0.1789	0.1388	0.1085	0.0854
0.4241	0.3606	0.3075	0.2843	0.2630	0.2255	0.1938	0.1443	0.1084	0.0822	0.0628
0.3855	0.3220	0.2697	0.2472	0.2267	0.1911	0.1615	0.1164	0.0847	0.0623	0.0462
0.3505	0.2875	0.2366	0.2149	0.1954	0.1619	0.1346	0.0938	0.0662	0.0472	0.0340
0.3186	0.2567	0.2076	0.1869	0.1685	0.1372	0.1122	0.0757	0.0517	0.0357	0.0250
0.2897	0.2292	0.1821	0.1625	0.1452	0.1163	0.0935	0.0610	0.0404	0.0271	0.0184
0.2633	0.2046	0.1597	0.1413	0.1252	0.0985	0.0779	0.0492	0.0316	0.0205	0.0135
0.2394	0.1827	0.1401	0.1229	0.1079	0.0835	0.0649	0.0397	0.0247	0.0155	0.0099
0.2176	0.1631	0.1229	0.1069	0.0930	0.0708	0.0541	0.0320	0.0193	0.0118	0.0073
0.1978	0.1456	0.1078	0.0929	0.0802	0.0600	0.0451	0.0258	0.0150	0.0089	0.0054
0.1799	0.1300	0.0946	0.0808	0.0691	0.0508	0.0376	0.0208	0.0118	0.0068	0.0039
0.1635	0.1161	0.0829	0.0703	0.0596	0.0431	0.0313	0.0168	0.0092	0.0051	0.0029
0.1486	0.1037	0.0728	0.0611	0.0514	0.0365	0.0261	0.0135	0.0072	0.0039	0.0021
0.1351	0.0926	0.0638	0.0531	0.0443	0.0309	0.0217	0.0109	0.0056	0.0029	0.0016
0.1228	0.0826	0.0560	0.0462	0.0382	0.0262	0.0181	0.0088	0.0044	0.0022	0.0012
0.1117	0.0738	0.0491	0.0402	0.0329	0.0222	0.0151	0.0071	0.0034	0.0017	0.0008
0.1015	0.0659	0.0431	0.0349	0.0284	0.0188	0.0126	0.0057	0.0027	0.0013	0.0006
0.0923	0.0588	0.0378	0.0304	0.0245	0.0160	0.0105	0.0046	0.0021	0.0010	0.0005
0.0573	0.0334	0.0196	0.0151	0.0116	0.0070	0.0042	0.0016	0.0006	0.0002	0.0001
0.0221	0.0107	0.0053	0.0037	0.0026	0.0013	0.0007	0.0002	0.0001	*	*
0.0085	0.0035	0.0014	0.0009	0.0006	0.0003	0.0001	*	*	*	*

*The factor is zero to four decimal places.

■ *Table A–3*   Present Value of an Annuity of $1 per Period for *t* Periods = $[1 - 1/(1 + r)^t]/r$

Number of Periods	Interest Rate								
	1%	2%	3%	4%	5%	6%	7%	8%	9%
1	0.9901	0.9804	0.9709	0.9615	0.9524	0.9434	0.9346	0.9259	0.9174
2	1.9704	1.9416	1.9135	1.8861	1.8594	1.8334	1.8080	1.7833	1.7591
3	2.9410	2.8839	2.8286	2.7751	2.7232	2.6730	2.6243	2.5771	2.5313
4	3.9020	3.8077	3.7171	3.6299	3.5460	3.4651	3.3872	3.3121	3.2397
5	4.8534	4.7135	4.5797	4.4518	4.3295	4.2124	4.1002	3.9927	3.8897
6	5.7955	5.6014	5.4172	5.2421	5.0757	4.9173	4.7665	4.6229	4.4859
7	6.7282	6.4720	6.2303	6.0021	5.7864	5.5824	5.3893	5.2064	5.0330
8	7.6517	7.3255	7.0197	6.7327	6.4632	6.2098	5.9713	5.7466	5.5348
9	8.5660	8.1622	7.7861	7.4353	7.1078	6.8017	6.5152	6.2469	5.9952
10	9.4713	8.9826	8.5302	8.1109	7.7217	7.3601	7.0236	6.7101	6.4177
11	10.3676	9.7868	9.2526	8.7605	8.3064	7.8869	7.4987	7.1390	6.8052
12	11.2551	10.5753	9.9540	9.3851	8.8633	8.3838	7.9427	7.5361	7.1607
13	12.1337	11.3484	10.6350	9.9856	9.3936	8.8527	8.3577	7.9038	7.4869
14	13.0037	12.1062	11.2961	10.5631	9.8986	9.2950	8.7455	8.2442	7.7862
15	13.8651	12.8493	11.9379	11.1184	10.3797	9.7122	9.1079	8.5595	8.0607
16	14.7179	13.5777	12.5611	11.6523	10.8378	10.1059	9.4466	8.8514	8.3126
17	15.5623	14.2919	13.1661	12.1657	11.2741	10.4773	9.7632	9.1216	8.5436
18	16.3983	14.9920	13.7535	12.6593	11.6896	10.8276	10.0591	9.3719	8.7556
19	17.2260	15.6785	14.3238	13.1339	12.0853	11.1581	10.3356	9.6036	8.9501
20	18.0456	16.3514	14.8775	13.5903	12.4622	11.4699	10.594u	9.8181	9.1285
21	18.8570	17.0112	15.4150	14.0292	12.8212	11.7641	10.8355	10.0168	9.2922
22	19.6604	17.6580	15.9369	14.4511	13.1630	12.0416	11.0612	10.2007	9.4424
23	20.4558	18.2922	16.4436	14.8568	13.4886	12.3034	11.2722	10.3741	9.5802
24	21.2434	18.9139	16.9355	15.2470	13.7986	12.5504	11.4593	10.5288	9.7066
25	22.0232	19.5235	17.4131	15.6221	14.0939	12.7834	11.6536	10.6748	9.8226
30	25.8077	22.3965	19.6004	17.2920	15.3725	13.7648	12.4090	11.2578	10.2737
40	32.8347	27.3555	23.1148	19.7928	17.1591	15.0463	13.3317	11.9246	10.7574
50	39.1961	31.4236	25.7298	21.4822	18.2559	15.7619	13.8007	12.2335	10.9617

■ *Table A–3*   (concluded)

Interest Rate

10%	12%	14%	15%	16%	18%	20%	24%	28%	32%
0.9091	0.8929	0.8772	0.8696	0.8621	0.8475	0.8333	0.8065	0.7813	0.7576
1.7355	1.6901	1.6467	1.6257	1.6052	1.5656	1.5278	1.4568	1.3916	1.3315
2.4869	2.4018	2.3216	2.2832	2.2459	2.1743	2.1065	1.9813	1.8684	1.7663
3.1669	3.0373	2.9137	2.8550	2.7982	2.6901	2.5887	2.4043	2.2410	2.0957
3.7908	3.6048	3.4331	3.3522	3.2743	3.1272	2.9906	2.7454	2.5320	2.3452
4.3553	4.1114	3.8887	3.7845	3.6847	3.4976	3.3255	3.0205	2.7594	2.5342
4.8684	4.5638	4.2883	4.1604	4.0386	3.8115	3.6046	3.2423	2.9370	2.6775
5.3349	4.9676	4.6389	4.4873	4.3436	4.0776	3.8372	3.4212	3.0758	2.7860
5.7590	5.3282	4.9464	4.7716	4.6065	4.3030	4.0310	3.5655	3.1842	2.8681
6.1446	5.6502	5.2161	5.0188	4.8332	4.4941	4.1925	3.6819	3.2689	2.9304
6.4951	5.9377	5.4527	5.2337	5.0286	4.6560	4.3271	3.7757	3.3351	2.9776
6.8137	6.1944	5.6603	5.4206	5.1971	4.7932	4.4392	3.8514	3.3868	3.0133
7.1034	6.4235	5.8424	5.5831	5.3423	4.9095	4.5327	3.9124	3.4272	3.0404
7.3667	6.6282	6.0021	5.7245	5.4675	5.0081	4.6106	3.9616	3.4587	3.0609
7.6061	6.8109	6.1422	5.8474	5.5755	5.0916	4.6755	4.0013	3.4834	3.0764
7.8237	6.9740	6.2651	5.9542	5.6685	5.1624	4.7296	4.0333	3.5026	3.0882
8.0216	7.1196	6.3729	6.0472	5.7487	5.2223	4.7746	4.0591	3.5177	3.0971
8.2014	7.2497	6.4674	6.1280	5.8178	5.2732	4.8122	4.0799	3.5294	3.1039
8.3649	7.3658	6.5504	6.1982	5.8775	5.3162	4.8435	4.0967	3.5386	3.1090
8.5136	7.4694	6.6231	6.2593	5.9288	5.3527	4.8696	4.1103	3.5458	3.1129
8.6487	7.5620	6.6870	6.3125	5.9731	5.3837	4.8913	4.1212	3.5514	3.1158
8.7715	7.6446	6.7429	6.3587	6.0113	5.4099	4.9094	4.1300	3.5558	3.1180
8.8832	7.7184	6.7921	6.3988	6.0442	5.4321	4.9245	4.1371	3.5592	3.1197
8.9847	7.7843	6.8351	6.4338	6.0726	5.4509	4.9371	4.1428	3.5619	3.1210
9.0770	7.8431	6.8729	6.4641	6.0971	5.4669	4.9476	4.1474	3.5640	3.1220
9.4269	8.0552	7.0027	6.5660	6.1772	5.5168	4.9789	4.1601	3.5693	3.1242
9.7791	8.2438	7.1050	6.6418	6.2335	5.5482	4.9966	4.1659	3.5712	3.1250
9.9148	8.3045	7.1327	6.6605	6.2463	5.5541	4.9995	4.1666	3.5714	3.1250

■ *Table A–4*   Future Value of an Annuity of $1 per Period for t Periods $= [(1 + r)^t - 1]/r$

Number of Periods	Interest Rate								
	1%	2%	3%	4%	5%	6%	7%	8%	9%
1	1.0000	1.0000	1.0000	1.0000	1.0000	1.0000	1.0000	1.0000	1.0000
2	2.0100	2.0200	2.0300	2.0400	2.0500	2.0600	2.0700	2.0800	2.0900
3	3.0301	3.0604	3.0909	3.1216	3.1525	3.1836	3.2149	3.2464	3.2781
4	4.0604	4.1216	4.1836	4.2465	4.3101	4.3746	4.4399	4.5061	4.5731
5	5.1010	5.2040	5.3091	5.4163	5.5256	5.6371	5.7507	5.8666	5.9847
6	6.1520	6.3081	6.4684	6.6330	6.8019	6.9753	7.1533	7.3359	7.5233
7	7.2135	7.4343	7.6625	7.8983	8.1420	8.3938	8.6540	8.9228	9.2004
8	8.2857	8.5830	8.8932	9.2142	9.5491	9.8975	10.260	10.637	11.028
9	9.3685	9.7546	10.159	10.583	11.027	11.491	11.978	12.488	13.021
10	10.462	10.950	11.464	12.006	12.578	13.181	13.816	14.487	15.193
11	11.567	12.169	12.808	13.486	14.207	14.972	15.784	16.645	17.560
12	12.683	13.412	14.192	15.026	15.917	16.870	17.888	18.977	20.141
13	13.809	14.680	15.618	16.627	17.713	18.882	20.141	21.495	22.953
14	14.947	15.974	17.086	18.292	19.599	21.015	22.550	24.215	26.019
15	16.097	17.293	18.599	20.024	21.579	23.276	25.129	27.152	29.361
16	17.258	18.639	20.157	21.825	23.657	25.673	27.888	30.324	33.003
17	18.430	20.012	21.762	23.698	25.840	28.213	30.840	33.750	36.974
18	19.615	21.412	23.414	25.645	28.132	30.906	33.999	37.450	41.301
19	20.811	22.841	25.117	27.671	30.539	33.760	37.379	41.446	46.018
20	22.019	24.297	26.870	29.778	33.066	36.786	40.995	45.762	51.160
21	23.239	25.783	28.676	31.969	35.719	39.993	44.865	50.423	56.765
22	24.472	27.299	30.537	34.248	38.505	43.392	49.006	55.457	62.873
23	25.716	28.845	32.453	36.618	41.430	46.996	53.436	60.893	69.532
24	26.973	30.422	34.426	39.083	44.502	50.816	58.177	66.765	76.790
25	28.243	32.030	36.459	41.646	47.727	54.865	63.249	73.106	84.701
30	34.785	40.568	47.575	56.085	66.439	79.058	94.461	113.28	136.31
40	48.886	60.402	75.401	95.026	120.80	154.76	199.64	259.06	337.88
50	64.463	84.579	112.80	152.67	209.35	290.34	406.53	573.77	815.08
60	81.670	114.05	163.05	237.99	353.58	533.13	813.52	1253.2	1944.8

■ *Table A–4*   (concluded)

Interest Rate

10%	12%	14%	15%	16%	18%	20%	24%	28%	32%	36%
1.0000	1.0000	1.0000	1.0000	1.0000	1.0000	1.0000	1.0000	1.0000	1.0000	1.0000
2.1000	2.1200	2.1400	2.1500	2.1600	2.1800	2.2000	2.2400	2.2800	2.3200	2.3600
3.3100	3.3744	3.4396	3.4725	3.5056	3.5724	3.6400	3.7776	3.9184	4.0624	4.2096
4.6410	4.7793	4.9211	4.9934	5.0665	5.2154	5.3680	5.6842	6.0156	6.3624	6.7251
6.1051	6.3528	6.6101	6.7424	6.8771	7.1542	7.4416	8.0484	8.6999	9.3983	10.146
7.7156	8.1152	8.5355	8.7537	8.9775	9.4420	9.9299	10.980	12.136	13.406	14.799
9.4872	10.089	10.730	11.067	11.414	12.142	12.916	14.615	16.534	18.696	21.126
11.436	12.300	13.233	13.727	14.240	15.327	16.499	19.123	22.163	25.678	29.732
13.579	14.776	16.085	16.786	17.519	19.086	20.799	24.712	29.369	34.895	41.435
15.937	17.549	19.337	20.304	21.321	23.521	25.959	31.643	38.593	47.062	57.352
18.531	20.655	23.045	24.349	25.733	28.755	32.150	40.238	50.398	63.122	78.998
21.384	24.133	27.271	29.002	30.850	34.931	39.581	50.895	65.510	84.320	108.44
24.523	28.029	32.089	34.352	36.786	42.219	48.497	64.110	84.853	112.30	148.47
27.975	32.393	37.581	40.505	43.672	50.818	59.196	80.496	109.61	149.24	202.93
31.772	37.280	43.842	47.580	51.660	60.965	72.035	100.82	141.30	198.00	276.98
35.950	42.753	50.980	55.717	60.925	72.939	87.442	126.01	181.87	262.36	377.69
40.545	48.884	59.118	65.075	71.673	87.068	105.93	157.25	233.79	347.31	514.66
45.599	55.750	69.394	75.836	84.141	103.74	128.12	195.99	300.25	459.45	700.94
51.159	63.440	78.969	88.212	98.603	123.41	154.74	244.03	385.32	607.47	954.28
57.275	72.052	91.025	102.44	115.38	146.63	186.69	303.60	494.21	802.86	1298.8
64.002	81.699	104.77	118.81	134.84	174.02	225.03	377.46	633.59	1060.8	1767.4
71.403	92.503	120.44	137.63	157.41	206.34	271.03	469.06	812.00	1401.2	2404.7
79.543	104.60	138.30	159.28	183.60	244.49	326.24	582.63	1040.4	1850.6	3271.3
88.497	118.16	158.66	184.17	213.98	289.49	392.48	723.46	1332.7	2443.8	4450.0
98.347	133.33	181.87	212.79	249.21	342.60	471.98	898.09	1706.8	3226.8	6053.0
164.49	241.33	356.79	434.75	530.31	790.95	1181.9	2640.9	5873.2	12941.	28172.3
442.59	767.09	1342.0	1779.1	2360.8	4163.2	7343.9	22729.	69377.	*	*
1163.9	2400.0	4994.5	7217.7	10436.	21813.	45497.	*	*	*	*
3034.8	7471.6	18535.	29220.	46058.	*	*	*	*	*	*

*FVIFA > 99,999.